INTERNATIONAL HANDBOOK OF EDUCATION FOR
SPIRITUALITY, CARE AND WELLBEING

International Handbooks of Religion and Education

VOLUME 3

Aims & Scope

The *International Handbooks of Religion and Education* series aims to provide easily accessible, practical, yet scholarly, sources of information about a broad range of topics and issues in religion and education. Each Handbook presents the research and professional practice of scholars who are daily engaged in the consideration of these religious dimensions in education. The accessible style and the consistent illumination of theory by practice make the series very valuable to a broad spectrum of users. Its scale and scope bring a substantive contribution to our understanding of the discipline and, in so doing, provide an agenda for the future.

For further volumes:
http://www.springer.com/series/7477

International Handbook of Education for Spirituality, Care and Wellbeing

Part One

Edited by

Marian de Souza
Australian Catholic University, Ballarat, Australia

Leslie J. Francis
University of Warwick, UK

James O'Higgins-Norman
Dublin City University, Ireland

and

Daniel G. Scott
University of Victoria, Canada

Editors

Dr. Marian de Souza
Australian Catholic University
National School of Religious
  Education
1200 Mair St
Ballarat VIC 3350
Ballarat Campus
Australia
m.desouza@acu.edu.au

Dr. James O'Higgins-Norman
Dublin City University
School of Education Studies
Glasnevin, Dublin
Ireland
james.norman@dcu.ie

Prof. Leslie J. Francis
University of Warwick
Warwick Inst. Education
Coventry
United Kingdom CV4 7AL
leslie.francis@warwick.ac.uk

Dr. Daniel G. Scott
University of Victoria
School of Child & Youth Care
Victoria BC V8W 2Y2
Canada
dgscott@uvic.ca

ISSN 1874-0049   e-ISSN 1874-0057
ISBN 978-1-4020-9017-2   e-ISBN 978-1-4020-9018-9
DOI 10.1007/978-1-4020-9018-9
Springer Dordrecht Heidelberg London New York

Library of Congress Control Number: 2009926828

© Springer Science+Business Media B.V. 2009
No part of this work may be reproduced, stored in a retrieval system, or transmitted in any form or by any means, electronic, mechanical, photocopying, microfilming, recording or otherwise, without written permission from the Publisher, with the exception of any material supplied specifically for the purpose of being entered and executed on a computer system, for exclusive use by the purchaser of the work.

Printed on acid-free paper

Springer is part of Springer Science+Business Media (www.springer.com)

Contents

Author Biographies xiii

General Introduction 1
    Marian de Souza, Leslie J. Francis, James O'Higgins-Norman,
    and Daniel Scott

**I The Psychology of Religion and Spirituality: Implications for
Education and Wellbeing – An Introduction** 7
    Leslie J. Francis

1 Ways of Studying the Psychology of Religion and Spirituality 15
    Ralph W. Hood, Jr.

**2 Measuring Religiousness and Spirituality: Issues, Existing
Measures, and the Implications for Education and Wellbeing** 33
    Peter C. Hill and Lauren E. Maltby

**3 Examining Religious and Spiritual Development During Childhood
and Adolescence** 51
    Chris J. Boyatzis

4 Understanding and Assessing Spiritual Health 69
    John W. Fisher

**5 The Contribution of Religiousness and Spirituality to Subjective
Wellbeing and Satisfaction with Life** 89
    Ralph L. Piedmont

6 Culture, Religion and Spirituality in Relation to Psychiatric Illness   107
    Kate M. Loewenthal

7	**Psychological Type Theory and Religious and Spiritual Experiences** .... Leslie J. Francis	125
8	**Understanding the Attitudinal Dimensions of Religion and Spirituality** .... Leslie J. Francis	147
9	**Social, Religious and Spiritual Capitals: A Psychological Perspective** .... Chris Baker	169
10	**Mystical, Religious, and Spiritual Experiences** .... Ralph W. Hood, Jr.	189
11	**The Spiritual Dimension of Coping: Theoretical and Practical Considerations** .... Kenneth I. Pargament	209
12	**The Psychology of Faith Development** .... Jeff Astley	231
13	**The Psychology of Prayer: A Review of Empirical Research** ...... Tania ap Siôn and Leslie J. Francis	247
II	**The Role of Spirituality in Human Development and Identity: An Introduction** .... Daniel G. Scott	269
14	**Spirituality and Mental Health: The Mystery of Healing** .... David Tacey	275
15	**The Dynamics of Spiritual Development** .... C. Glenn Cupit	291
16	**Does Positive Psychology Have a Soul for Adolescence?** .... Paul King	311
17	**Voices of Global Youth on Spirituality and Spiritual Development: Preliminary Findings from a Grounded Theory Study** .... Elisabeth M. Kimball, Marc Mannes, and Angela Hackel	329
18	**Moment to Moment Spirituality in Early Childhood Education** ... Mindy Upton	349

19	**Children's Spiritual Intelligence** Mollie Painton	365
20	**In Search of the Spiritual: Adolescent Transitions as Portals to the Spirit Self** Peter J. Perkins	381
21	**Reflection for Spiritual Development in Adolescents** Charlene Tan	397
22	**Developing Contemplative Capacities in Childhood and Adolescence: A Rationale and Overview** Aostre N. Johnson	415
23	**The Contribution of Spirituality to "Becoming a Self" in Child and Youth Services** Douglas Magnuson	433
24	**Coming of Age as a Spiritual Task in Adolescence** Daniel G. Scott	453
25	**Youthful Peak Experiences in Cross-Cultural Perspective: Implications for Educators and Counselors** Edward Hoffman and Fernando A. Ortiz	469
26	**Peak Experiences Explored Through Literature** Ann M. Trousdale	491
27	**Developing Spiritual Identity: Retrospective Accounts From Muslim, Jewish, and Christian Exemplars** Kevin S. Reimer, Alvin C. Dueck, Lauren V. Adelchanow, and Joseph D. Muto	507
III	**The Spiritual Dimension in Educational Programs and Environments to Promote Holistic Learning and Wellbeing: An Introduction** Marian de Souza	525
28	**Educating for Evolving Consciousness: Voicing the Emergency for Love, Life and Wisdom** Jennifer M. Gidley	533

29	**A Quest for the Realm of Spirituality** .... Zehavit Gross	563
30	**Education and Eros** .... John P. Miller	581
31	**Awareness and Compassion for the Education of Enlightenment** .... Yoshiharu Nakagawa	593
32	**Towards a Reclaimed Framework of "Knowing" in Spirituality and Education for the Promotion of Holistic Learning and Wellbeing – Kataphatic and Apophatic Ways of Knowing** .... Peter Mudge	611
33	**Whence Wisdom? Human Development as a Mythic Search for Meaning** .... Inna Semetsky	631
34	**Reconnecting with Earth: Ecospirituality as the Missing Dimension in Spirituality and Sustainability Education** .... Caroline Smith	653
35	**Promoting Wholeness and Wellbeing in Education: Exploring Aspects of the Spiritual Dimension** .... Marian de Souza	677
36	**How Then Shall We Teach?** .... Joyce Bellous	693
37	**Cultivation of Mindfulness: Promoting Holistic Learning and Wellbeing in Education** .... Ngar-sze Lau	715
38	**The Importance of Happiness to Children's Education and Wellbeing** .... Jane Erricker	739
39	**Holistic Education and Teacher Training** .... Peter Schreiner	753
40	**Metaphors for Wellbeing: Enhancing Students' Learning and Teaching Perceptions Within a Pre-service Education Course** ..... Mary Nuttall	771

41	**Relating to the Spiritual in the Classroom** Roz Sunley	793
42	**Seeking the Spiritual: The Complexities of Spiritual Development in the Classroom** Kate Adams	809
43	**Responding to Difference: Spiritual Development and the Search for Truth** Jacqueline Watson	821
44	**Reaching Out: The Subversive Nature of Touch in the Kindergarten Schoolroom** Sheri Leafgren	839
45	**Spiritually Intelligent Kids: Children Using SQ to Enhance Holistic Learning and Wellbeing** Brendan Hyde	855
46	**Narratives of Everyday Spirituality: Pedagogical Perspectives from Three Early Childhood Settings in Aotearoa New Zealand** Jane Bone	873
47	**Grappling with Spirituality in the Classroom** Anne Kennedy and Judith Duncan	891
48	**Spiritual Confidence and Its Contribution to Wellbeing: Implications for Education** Philip Hughes	907
49	**Youth Work, Informal Education, and Spirituality** Sally Nash	921
IV	**Integrating Spirituality, Care and Wellbeing in Educational Settings** James O'Higgins-Norman	937
50	**Ethical Leadership in an Age of Evaluation: Implications for Whole School Wellbeing** Gerry McNamara and Joe O'Hara	943
51	**Wounding the Body in the Hope of Healing the Spirit: Responding to Adolescents Who Self-Injure** Amelio A. D'Onofrio and Julie Balzano	961

| 52 | Spirituality, Meaning and Counselling Young People 977
Ciarán G. Dalton |

| 53 | Facing Up to Workplace Bullying in the Context of Schools and
Teaching 991
Jacinta M. Kitt |

| 54 | Social and Emotional Aspects of Learning
in Secondary Schools: The Use of Circle Time 1011
Marilyn Tew |

| 55 | The Effect of Background Music on Learning 1029
Dr. Anne Savan |

| 56 | The Aspiration to Care and Its Frustration: A Literary Exploration 1041
Kevin Williams |

| 57 | Children in Kenya: The Role of Play
Therapy in Recovery from Abuse 1057
Kathryn Hunt |

| 58 | Healthy Development for Healthy Spirituality:
Social Transformations Among Chilean
Youth in the New Millennium 1075
Klaus Püschel and Gabriela Cassigoli |

| 59 | The Development of a School-Based Curriculum to Enhance
Wellbeing Among Somali Immigrant Children in the United States 1087
Sorie Koroma and John C. Carey |

| 60 | Violence and Conflict in Schools: Negotiating Pathways to Wellbeing 1101
James O'Higgins-Norman and Edward J. Hall |

| 61 | Teaching a Theology of Suffering Through Story 1115
Caroline Renehan |

| 62 | Encountering Different Spiritual Traditions in the Classroom:
The Contribution of ICT 1127
Fiona Williams |

| 63 | Building Trust with Gay and Lesbian Students in Universities 1141
Michael J. Maher |

64 Educating for Spirituality and Wellbeing Through Learning Sacred Texts in the Jewish Primary School 1157
Deena Sigel

65 Liberation Through Story: Children's Literature and the Spirit of the Child 1173
Robert Hurley

66 Enhancing Children's Wellbeing: The Role of Sex and Relationships Education—A Case Study from Greece 1189
Margarita Gerouki

Author Index 1207

Subject Index 1217

Author Biographies

Kate Adams is a senior lecturer in Education Studies at Bishop Grosseteste University College Lincoln, UK. Her research interests lie in children's understanding of their spiritual experiences and she maintains an interest in children's spirituality in schools which do not have a faith based tradition. Kate's research has specialised in children's dreams and the impact that some make on their spiritual lives. Kate serves on the Board of Directors of the International Association for the Study of Dreams and is co-author of The Spiritual Dimension of Childhood (2008), published by Jessica Kingsley.

Lauren V. Adelchanow is currently working toward her doctorate in clinical psychology at Azusa Pacific University (APU). She holds a Bachelor of Arts in Psychology from UCLA and a Master of Arts in Clinical Psychology from APU. Her research interests include such topics as the moral personality, prosocial behavior, attachment security, and mood disorders. Her future goals include serving as a university psychologist and establishing her own private practice.

Tania ap Siôn is a Senior Research Fellow within the Warwick Religions and Education Research Unit, Institute of Education, University of Warwick, UK and Executive Director of the St Mary's Centre at St Deiniol's Library, Hawarden, UK. Her recent publications include 'Looking for signs of the presence of God in Northern Ireland: religious experience among Catholic and Protestant sixth-form pupils', *Archiv für Religionspsychologie* (2006), 'Listening to prayers: an analysis of prayers left in a country church in rural England', *Archiv für Religionspsychologie* (2007) and 'Distinguishing between intention, reference, and objective in an analysis of prayer requests for health and wellbeing: eavesdropping from the rural vestry', *Mental Health, Religion, and Culture* (2008).

Jeff Astley is Director of the North of England Institute for Christian Education, and Honorary Professorial Fellow in Practical Theology and Christian Education in the University of Durham, UK. He is the author or editor of over thirty books on Christian education, practical theology or religious faith, including *The Philosophy of Christian Religious Education*; *Theological Perspectives on Christian Formation*; *Learning in the Way: Research and Reflection on Adult Christian Education*; and *Ordinary Theology: Looking, Listening and Learning in Theology*. He was the editor and principal author of the Church of England Report, *How Faith Grows: Faith Development and Christian Education*.

Christopher Baker is Director of Research at the William Temple Foundation and part-time lecturer in Urban Theology at the University of Manchester. He researches and writes extensively on the role of faith-based engagement in UK civil society and urban regeneration, and the postsecular city. A second edition of his book *The Hybrid Church in the City – Third Space Thinking* (SCM Press) was published in 2009. Other co-edited volumes include *Entering the New Theological Space – Blurred Encounters of Faith, Politics and Community* (Ashgate, 2009) and *Remoralising Britain – Political, Ethical and Theological Perspectives on New Labour* (Continuum, 2009).

Julie Balzano is a doctoral student in the Counseling Psychology program in the Graduate School of Education at Fordham University. She received her undergraduate psychology degree from Georgetown University. Julie's research and clinical interests are in the areas of chronic illness, stress and coping, adolescent development, and multicultural considerations in teaching and clinical practice.

Joyce Bellous is associate professor of Lay Empowerment and Discipleship at McMaster Divinity College, McMaster University in Hamilton, Ontario, where she has taught since 1993. She researches and teaches in the areas of spirituality, ethics, post-modernism and multiculturalism. She is a consultant, speaker and writer for church congregations, seminaries and denominational leaders on the subjects of leadership and ministry education. Her special interest is children and spirituality and she also does research in the areas of culture, education, ethics and leadership studies.

Two of her recent books are *Educating Faith* (Clements, 2006), an approach to spiritual formation, and *Conversations That Change Us* (Clements, 2007).

Jane Bone has been involved in early childhood education for a number of years in Aotearoa New Zealand. Currently she lectures at Monash University, Australia. Her interests include ethical issues in research with young children and different pedagogical approaches to early childhood education. She completed doctoral research about spirituality in three early childhood educational contexts in 2007 and since that time has written extensively about spirituality as part of a holistic approach to education, development and wellbeing. In her research, as in life, she enjoys crossing borders and exploring the spiritual possibilities always present in everyday life.

Chris J. Boyatzis is Professor of Psychology at Bucknell University, Lewisburg PA, USA. He studies religious and spiritual development from childhood throughout the lifespan with a main interest in parent-child communication about religious and spiritual issues. He has organized four special issues or sections of journals devoted to religious and spiritual development and has organized since 2001 a small biennial conference on religious and spiritual development. He is on the editorial board of many journals, including *The International Journal for the Psychology of Religion*.

Over the last 46 years, **John Fisher** has taught in schools (Principal for 14 years) and teacher education and has researched in chemistry, science education, psychology and health education. John's main research interest for the last 15 years has been in spiritual wellbeing in schools, universities, healthcare settings, churches and the wider community (PhD, University of Melbourne 1998 and recently completed EdD at the University of Ballarat).

Professor John C. Carey is the Director of the National Center for School Counseling Outcome Research and a Professor of School Counseling at the University of Massachusetts, Amherst. His research interests focus on the development and evaluation of effective school-based interventions to promote personal–social and career development. He is the author of *Evidence-based school counseling: Making a difference with data-driven practice* and the coeditor of *Multicultural counseling in schools: A practical handbook*.

Gabriela Cassigoli has taught English in a number of well-known colleges in Chile, the UK, and the USA. These include the Universitario Inglés School and Universidad Metropolitana de Ciencias de La Educación in Chile, and Cedar River Montessori School and Wedgwood Montessori School in Washington, USA. She is currently a teacher of English at St. George's College, Chile. She has wide experience working with adolescents at Catholic schools, where she has participated in rural and urban missions, San Ignacio spiritual exercises and in programs for the development of young people's wellbeing.

C. Glenn Cupit is a senior lecturer in Child Development in the deLissa Institute of Early Childhood and Family Studies at the University of South Australia where he coordinates undergraduate research training and the Honours strand of the Bachelor of Early Childhood Education. His doctorate was titled *Spiritual development and the public educative care of children*. Glenn has published four books, *Kids and the scary world of video*, *The child audience*, *Socialising the superheroes* and *Perspectives on children and spirituality*. In between professional life and raising children and grandchildren he has been a folk and jazz musician and amateur actor.

Professor Amelio A. D'Onofrio is Clinical Professor and Director of the Psychological Services Institute in the Graduate School of Education at Fordham University where he has been a member of faculty since 1994. He also works as an independent clinical practitioner in adolescent and adult psychotherapy in New York City where he is a licensed psychologist. Amelio teaches and provides clinical supervision to students in the Doctoral Program in Counseling Psychology. His teaching and clinical interests include developmental psychopathology, interpersonal and existential approaches to psychotherapy, the neuropsychobiology of affect regulation, and clinical supervision.

Ciarán G. Dalton is manager of the Village Counselling Service in Tallaght, Dublin, Ireland. He holds a Masters Degree in Educational Guidance and

Counselling from Trinity College, Dublin and worked from 2003 to 2008 as healthcare chaplain in Connolly Hospital, Dublin. Today, Ciarán contributes to professional programmes in counselling at the Institute of Integrative Counselling and Psychotherapy in Dublin and at the School of Education Studies in Dublin City University.

Marian de Souza is a Senior Lecturer and Student Adviser at Australian Catholic University, Ballarat Campus and is the Editor of the *Journal of Religious Education*. Marian has published extensively, nationally and internationally on her research which has investigated spirituality as pertaining to the relational dimension of the human person. She has developed an approach to learning that encourages imaginative, creative and intuitive thinking and which addresses the spiritual dimension. Marian is also interested in how small ethnic communities hand on their religious and spiritual cultures to the next generation in the secular and pluralist context of contemporary Australia. Her most recent work has examined the role of non-conscious learning to promote and impede relationality, an important consideration in a society where problems related to religious diversity are becoming apparent.

Al Dueck is Frank and Evelyn Freed professor of psychology at the Graduate School of Psychology, Fuller Theological Seminary. He is author of *From Jerusalem to Athens* (1995) and *A Peaceable Psychology* (2009).

Judith Duncan is an Associate Professor in Education, School of Maori, Social and Cultural Studies at the University of Canterbury College of Education, Christchurch, New Zealand. When this study was carried out Judith was employed at the University of Otago, New Zealand. Judith is an established researcher with over 15 years of research experience, predominantly using qualitative research methods in a range of education settings.

Jane Erricker is an associate dean in the Faculty of Education, University of Winchester. She has taught science and citizenship and researches children's spirituality with Clive Erricker and Cathy Ota. Together they founded the Children and Worldviews Project and the International Journal of Children's Spirituality and initiated the annual international conferences on Children's Spirituality. Most recently she has been concerned with quality and learning and teaching in the Faculty, and has been researching aspects of students' happiness with their university education.

Leslie J. Francis is Professor of Religions and Education, Institute of Education, University of Warwick, UK. He also holds honorary research appointments in York St John University, UK, and Boston University, USA. His recent books include *The naked parish priest* (2003), *Faith and psychology* (2005), *Fragmented faith* (2005), *Urban hope and spiritual health* (2005), *British Methodism* (2006), *Gone for good?* (2007) and *Preaching with all our souls* (2008). Currently he serves as editor of *Rural Theology*, associate editor of *Journal of Beliefs and Values* and review editor of *Archive for the Psychology of Religion*.

Margarita Gerouki is a researcher at the Department of Applied Sciences of Education in the University of Helsinki, Finland. Prior to her current work she worked for a number of years as a teacher in a primary school in Greece and as a language teacher in both Greece and Finland. Her current research on sexuality and relationships education is funded by the Greek Ministry of Education.

Jennifer Gidley is a psychologist, educator and futures researcher. Her transdisciplinary career spans three decades and all educational levels. She founded and directed an innovative private school inspired by Steiner pedagogy in Australia (1984–1994). She co-designed and lectured in the online Masters in Strategic Foresight at Swinburne University, Melbourne (2003–2006). Jennifer has published widely in educational and youth futures, and global socio-cultural change, including two books: The University in Transformation and Youth Futures. She is an Executive Board member of the World Futures Studies Federation (WFSF). Currently a research fellow, Global Cities Research Institute, RMIT University, Melbourne, she wrote this chapter during Ph.D. candidature, Southern Cross University, Lismore.

Zehavit Gross is a senior lecturer and the head of graduate program of social education in the School of Education, Bar-Ilan University, Israel. Her main area of specialization is socialization processes (religious, secular, feminine and civic) among adolescents. Currently she is actively participating in four international projects: An international study in Jewish day schools in Brussels, Paris, and Geneva. A research study on Jewish day schools in Sydney and Melbourne, Australia. A research on Femininsm among modern orthodox women in Montrael and Toronto, Canada and a comparative research in Europe among ten countries on Religiosity Worldviews and Values of Adolescents.

Angela Hackel is a research assistant for the Center for Spirituality in Childhood and Adolescence at Search Institute. Her research interests include examining what factors hinder and assist in the spiritual development of youth in the international context.

Edward J. Hall CP is a member of the Passionist Community and resides at the Calvary Centre for Spirituality in Shrewsbury, Massachusettes, USA. He is a former director of religious education at the University of Connecticut and has lectured at Dublin City University. He has studied mediation and negotiation at the Harvard School of Law and in recent years he has turned his research towards wellbeing and emotionally disturbed youth and has worked as a mediator in community conflict.

Peter C. Hill is professor at Rosemead School of Psychology, Biola University, in La Mirada, California (USA). In 2006, he was a Visiting Senior Research Scholar on the Faculty of Divinity at Cambridge University, England. Dr. Hill has published over 60 articles in peer-reviewed journals and has co-authored (with Ralph Hood and W. Paul Williamson) *The Psychology of Religious Fundamentalism* (2005) co-edited (with Ralph Hood) *Measures of Religiosity* (1999), and co-edited (with David Benner) The *Baker Encyclopedia of Psychology* (1999). He is a past president of Division 36 (Psychology of Religion) of the American Psychology Association (APA) and was elected Fellow of the APA in 1998.

Edward Hoffman—Dr. Hoffman is an adjunct associate professor at Yeshiva University and director of its undergraduate psychology internship program. For the past 20 years, he has been a New York State licensed psychologist specializing in children. Dr. Hoffman has authored several books in psychology including major biographies of Alfred Adler and Abraham Maslow and works on psychological assessment. He is on the editorial board of the *Journal of Humanistic Psychology*. He has also written books on Jewish philosophy and spirituality, including *The Way of Splendor*, *Opening the Inner Gates*, and most recently *The Wisdom of Maimonides*. With a strong cross-cultural focus, his research interests encompass childhood spiritual experience, conscious parenting, and creative education.

Ralph W. Hood Jr. is Professor of Psychology at the University of Tennessee at Chattanooga. He is a former president of the Division of the Psychology of Religion of the American Psychological Association and a recipient of its William James Award as well as its Distinguished Service and Mentor Awards. He is a former editor of the *Journal for the Scientific Study of Religion*; a former co-editor of *The International Journal for the Psychology of Religion*. He is a current co-editor of the *Archive for the Psychology of Religion*.

Philip Hughes has been a senior research officer with the Christian Research Association since its foundation in 1985. He has postgraduate degrees in philosophy, theology and education, has undertaken many empirical studies in the areas of religion, values and personal and communal wellbeing. Philip Hughes is also an honorary research fellow at Edith Cowan University and a minister in the Uniting Church of Australia.

Over the past 5 years, the major foci of his research have been the spirituality of young Australians and spirituality and wellbeing. Recent publications include a book on youth spirituality, *Putting Life Together: Findings from Australian Youth Spirituality Research* and *Building Stronger Communities*, both of which were published in 2007.

Kathryn Hunt has worked in primary schools as a teacher and a manager. She has also worked as a local education adviser for early years' education and has 17 years experience working as a counsellor educator in higher education. Since 2003, she has worked in Kenya, East Africa, training counsellors in play therapy and recently has moved into lecturing in therapeutic childcare in North Wales at Glyndwr University.

Robert Hurley is professor of New Testament Studies and Childhood Catechetics at the Faculté de théologie et de sciences religieuses at Université Laval, Quebec City. Using reader-response criticism and narratology to interpret biblical texts and children's literature, he is particularly interested in explaining the effects of spiritual transcendence which these texts sometimes produce in their readers.

Brendan Hyde is a senior lecturer in the National School of Religious Education at Australian Catholic University, and a member of the Australian College of Educators. His research interests include children's spirituality and Godly play as an approach for engaging children in the religious and spiritual dimensions. He has many published journal articles and book chapters, and is the author of *Children and Spirituality: Searching for Meaning and Connectedness*, and co author of *The Spiritual Dimension of Childhood*, both published through Jessica Kingsley Publishers in London.

Aostre N. Johnson is currently professor of education at Saint Michael's College in Colchester, Vermont. She teaches courses in integrated curriculum theory and practice and in spirituality, ethics and education, and she directs a master's program in curriculum. She has written many articles related to aesthetics, ethics, spirituality, religion, human development, and education, and is a coauthor of *Nurturing Child and Adolescent Spirituality: Perspectives from the World's Religious Traditions*. Previously, she cofounded and directed schools for children in Massachusetts, New York and North Carolina. She received her B.A. and M. Ed. from Harvard University and her doctorate from the University of North Carolina, Greensboro.

Anne Kennedy is an experienced primary teacher and former Catholic school principal who works presently as a consultant to Catholic schools in New Zealand. She is the editor of the current New Zealand Religious Education programme. Her area of interest is teachers and children's spirituality.

Elisabeth M. Kimball is a lecturer in the Youth Studies program, School of Social Work, University of Minnesota, and a research associate with the Center for Spiritual Development in Childhood and Adolescence at Search Institute. Her research and teaching focus on the role of spirituality in youth and community development across secular and religious contexts.

Paul King is a lecturer in the School of Education Studies, Dublin City University, Ireland, where he is also the program director for MSc in Guidance and Counselling. He is also actively involved in second-level teacher training education teaching on the Graduate Diploma in Education program, the only part-time second-level teacher training program in Ireland. He has worked as a counsellor, school chaplain and teacher in a number of schools both in Northern Ireland and in the Republic of Ireland. His area of research interests includes positive psychology and well being, mental health and adolescents, mindfulness and the role of the guidance counsellor. He is also an appointee of the Irish National Mental Health Commission as a panel member for the Mental Health Tribunals which are convened on a regular basis to adjudicate on the lawful admission of patients with mental illness to psychiatric hospitals.

Jacinta M. Kitt is an independent lecturer and researcher based in Dublin, Ireland. She also works as an organisational advisor on workplace environment and bullying awareness and prevention. Jacinta holds a Masters Degree in Educational

Management from Trinity College, Dublin. She has been a guest lecturer in several universities in Ireland and abroad. Through her work and research, Jacinta has greatly contributed to an increased awareness of bullying in the workplace. She has been a key note speaker at a number of professional and academic conferences and was instrumental in establishing the first bullying in the workplace conference in Ireland.

Sorie Koroma is a Graduate Assistant in the National Center for School Counseling Outcome Research and a doctoral candidate in Child and Family Studies at the University of Massachusetts Amherst. Prior to entering graduate studies he was a high school teacher in Sierra Leone and witnessed how the mass trauma associated with the civil war affected his students and family.

Sheri Leafgren serves as an assistant professor in the Department of Teacher Education at Miami University in Oxford, Ohio, USA. She had once been a kindergarten teacher at an African-centered elementary school where she enjoyed the beneficent wisdom of the very young and old in daily interactions with the children and the elders with whom she shared the school. She continues to learn and live in a different space, revisiting her own naivety as a teacher via interactions with pre-service early childhood teachers in her role as a faculty member. She is particularly interested in the spiritual and moral wisdom of young children and how children find space to live out their moral and spiritual selves in the classroom.

Kate M. Loewenthal graduated in Psychology at University College London, and gained her PhD there. She has held academic posts in the University of Wales Bangor, the City University, and Bedford College London University, now Royal Holloway, University of London. Her research has examined the impact of a range of religious and cultural factors on mental health, and she has many publications in this field. She also helps with service provision, particularly in improving culturally and religiously-sensitive care. She currently teaches Abnormal Psychology at New York University in London, and is Professor Emerita of Psychology at Royal Holloway University of London.

Doug Magnuson is associate professor, School of Child & Youth Care, University of Victoria, Canada. He has published on residential education, youth development, youth work, evaluation, and spirituality, moral development, and he is coeditor of the book, *Work with Youth in Divided and Contested Societies*, and is the editor of *Child & Youth Services*.

Michael J. Maher has been a Chaplain at Loyola University Chicago, USA since 1996. During this time, he has also lectured at that university's School of Education where he has conducted research on aspects of youth and Catholic education. He has published a number of highly regarded works on sexuality, education, and the Catholic Church.

Lauren E. Maltby is pursuing her Ph.D. in clinical psychology at Rosemead School of Psychology, Biola University, in La Mirada, California (USA). She has previously published with Peter Hill (2008) on the intersection between comparative psychology and positive psychology. Her research focuses on ambivalent sexism and the psychology of women, with a special emphasis on the impact of religious beliefs on attitudes toward women.

Marc Mannes has held leadership positions in the non-profit sector, government, and the academy for nearly three decades. His career has focused on the intersections of applied research, policy formulation and implementation, program and product development, organizational and community change, and training. Marc currently serves as the Director of Applied Research for Search Institute located in Minneapolis, Minnesota.

Professor Gerry McNamara is an associate professor and researcher at the School of Education Studies in Dublin City University, Ireland. Gerry worked for many years as a teacher of civic, social and personal education in a second-level school before moving into higher education. He is the author of many works on action research and educational evaluation. He has led evaluations at home and abroad and is the founder of the Centre for Educational Evaluation at DCU. Gerry's current research is in the area of school and teacher evaluation.

Professor John (Jack) Miller has been working in the field of holistic education for over 30 years. He is author/editor of more than a dozen books on holistic learning and contemplative practices in education which include *Education and the Soul, The Holistic Curriculum*, and *Educating for Wisdom and Compassion*. His writing has been translated into seven languages. Jack has worked extensively with holistic educators in Japan and Korea for the past decade and has been visiting professor at two universities in Japan. Jack was one of 25 scholars invited to a UNESCO conference on cultural diversity and transversal values held in Kyoto and Tokyo. He was also a keynote speaker at the Soul-in-Education conferences held in Findhorn Scotland, Hawaii, Australia, and South Africa. He teaches courses on holistic education and spirituality in education at the Ontario Institute for Studies in Education at the University of Toronto where he is Professor.

Peter Mudge is a team leader, Administrator of Mission in the diocese of Wilcannia-Forbes, far western NSW, Australia. His areas of interest and research include religious education, spirituality, sacred space, connected knowing, transformative pedagogies and the role of the arts in religious education and spirituality. He has received formal training in drawing and painting which he pursues in his art studio. A selection of his copyright-free religious art images can be found at: www.flickr.com/photos/ceoreals/sets He can be contacted at: pjpmudge@bigpond.net.au

Joseph D. Muto is a second year doctoral student in the clinical psychology program at Azusa Pacific University (APU). He received a Bachelor of Science degree in Psychobiology from UCLA and a Master of Arts degree in Psychology from APU. Upon graduation, he plans to work in forensic assessment.

Yoshiharu Nakagawa is a professor of education at Ritsumeikan University in Kyoto, Japan. He earned his Ph.D. from the Ontario Institute for the Studies in Education of the University of Toronto. His current interests include holistic and integral education, spirituality, and Eastern philosophy. He is the author of *Education for*

Awakening: An Eastern Approach to Holistic Education (Foundation for Educational Renewal, 2000) and the co-editor of *Nurturing Our Wholeness: Perspectives on Spirituality in Education* (Foundation for Educational Renewal, 2002). His contribution also appeared in *Nurturing Child and Adolescent Spirituality: Perspectives from the World's Religious Traditions* (Rowman and Littlefield, 2006).

Sally Nash is director of the Midlands Centre for Youth Ministry, a partnership between St John's Theological College, Nottingham, England and Youth for Christ. She lectures in the fields of youth work, practical theology, and leadership. Research interests include spiritual and ministerial formation of youth workers, Christian youth work, place, reflective practice, and the spirituality of young people. Publications include Sustaining Your Spirituality, A Theology for Urban Youth Work and Skills for Collaborative Ministry (with Jo Pimlott and Paul Nash).

Mary Nuttall rsm began her career as a primary school teacher. She is a lecturer in the School of Education at Australian Catholic University and works in the fields of teaching, learning and classroom management, teaching children with special needs and curriculum development. Mary's research interests are in the area of life-long learning with a specific focus on holistic learning and development of personal wellbeing, curriculum development and community involvement in schools.

Joe O'Hara is a senior lecturer and researcher at the School of Education Studies in Dublin City University, Ireland where he has been central to the development of several teacher education programmes. He has authored a number of works on student behaviour and teacher professionalism. Joe is a member of the Council of the European Educational Research Association and Vice President of the Irish Educational Studies Association. Joe's current research is in the area of school and teacher evaluation.

James O'Higgins-Norman is a lecturer and researcher at the School of Education Studies in Dublin City University where he is also Chair of Graduate Teacher Education. For over 10 years, his research has been concerned with aspects of equality and wellbeing in schools, and his work on homophobic bullying is considered to be seminal in the field of Irish education. He regularly contributes to more than one journal including *Pastoral Care*, *Sexuality and Culture* and *Sex Education* and has authored a number of books and reports on aspects of equality and wellbeing in schools. He is co-founder of the Spirituality and Wellbeing in Education Research Group (SWERG) at Dublin City University.

Fernando A. Ortiz—Dr. Ortiz is an assistant professor at Alliant International University, California School of Professional Psychology, San Diego Campus, where he specializes in personality assessment, multicultural competencies, and clinical skills. He received his Ph.D. in counseling psychology at Washington State University specializing in cross-cultural research and Mexican ethnopsychology. He completed a postdoctoral internship at the University of California, Santa Barbara Counseling Center with a specialization in multicultural clinical training. His research interests include minority personality assessment and cross-cultural issues, Mexican ethnopsychology, and indigenous healing modalities. He has worked extensively with ethnic minorities in the California mental health system.

Mollie Painton a nationally recognized lecturer on play therapy and children's spirituality, lives in Fort Collins, Colorado, where she is a licensed psychologist since 1994; and in private practice since 1989 specializing in work with children and families. Dr. Painton founded and directs both The Interplay Center and the Spirit-Play Institute. An APT Registered Play Therapist/Supervisor and EMDR Level II trauma therapist, she taught play therapy to doctoral students at the University of Northern Colorado. Dr. Painton has discovered the world of spirit in children. She is the author of the innovative book, *Encouraging Your Child's Spiritual Intelligence*, inspired by the children in play therapy with her. These boys and girls range from developmentally disabled, ADD/ADHD, the intellectually gifted, children traumatized by events among which are the death of a parent or a divorce, and others who need help making troublesome adjustments to difficult situations, such as a move or birth of a sibling.

Kenneth I. Pargament is Professor of clinical psychology at Bowling Green State University. He is author of *The Psychology of Religion and Coping: Theory, Research, Practice* and *Spiritually Integrated Psychotherapy: Understanding and Addressing the Sacred*. He is editor-in-chief of the forthcoming two-volume *APA Handbook of Psychology, Religion, and Spirituality*. Dr. Pargament's awards include the Virginia Staudt Sexton Mentoring Award and William James Award for excellence in research in the psychology of religion from Division 36 of APA, and most recently the Oskar Pfister Award from the American Psychiatric Association for empirical and applied contributions to psychiatry and religion.

Peter Perkins is senior associate and owning partner of Global Learning Partners, Inc. and has been a practitioner of Dialogue Education (DE) since 1985, applying this progressive approach to teaching and learning to government, non-profits, NGOs, community-based organizations, and corporations. Peter is also the principal learning consultant, coach and teacher with *Five Dimensions* of Calais, Vermont, focusing on the facilitation of adolescent learning, and holistic adolescent development emphasizing spiritual growth. He started the first Prevention and Community Development Program in the United States as its founding Chair at *Woodbury College* of Montpelier, Vermont and designed two nationally recognized substance abuse prevention programs for youth. Education includes an M.A. in Human Organizational Development from Fielding Institute, Santa Barbara, California and B.A. in Sociology from Lakeland College, Sheboygan, Wisconsin. He has authored, co-authored, or contributed to works on Dialogue Education, Adolescent Spirituality, and Youth Substance Abuse Intervention and Prevention.

Ralph L. Piedmont received his Ph.D. in Personality Psychology from Boston University and completed a postdoctoral fellowship at the National Institute of Aging. His current research interests focus on the measurement of Spiritual Transcendence.

Dr. Piedmont is extensively published in the scientific literature and serves on several editorial boards. He is currently editor of *Research in the Social Scientific Study of Religion* and is founding editor for *Psychology of Religion and Spirituality*. Dr. Piedmont is a full professor in the Department of Pastoral Counseling at Loyola College, and serves as the Director of Research.

Professor Klaus Püschel is Chair of the Department of Family and Community Medicine in the School of Medicine at the Pontificia Universidad Católica de Chile. He has had extensive experience working in primary health care in underserved urban areas in Santiago, Chile. His experience working with community groups and people in cultural and social inequality has shaped his clinical and academic career.

Kevin S. Reimer is professor of psychology at Azusa Pacific University and research faculty in the Graduate School of Psychology at Fuller Theological Seminary. Educated in the United States and Canada, he holds degrees in developmental psychology, biological sciences, theology, and literature. His postdoctoral fellowships were completed at the University of British Columbia and the University of Oxford. Reimer's grant-funded research program explores the interface of virtue and religion in positive psychology. Program funding awards include the US Department of Justice, John Templeton Foundation, Fetzer Institute, Institute for Research on Unlimited Love, Azusa Pacific University, Center for Theology and the Natural Sciences, and Council for Christian Colleges and Universities. Reimer is widely published in academic journals and volumes of collected works. His book projects include *The Reciprocating Self* (InterVarsity, 2005), *Can We Talk?* (Brazos, 2009), and *Living L'Arche* (Continuum, 2009). Reimer is ordained to ministry of Word & Sacrament in the Presbyterian Church (USA).

Caroline Renehan is a lecturer in education and theology at the Mater Dei Institute of Education, Dublin City University, Ireland. She holds a Ph.D. in Divinity from the University of Edinburgh and a Ph.D. in Education from the University of London. Caroline taught history and religious education at second level before becoming a Diocesan Advisor for Religious Education and subsequently the first National Catechetical Director to the Irish Catholic Bishop's Conference. In addition to her work as a lecturer, she also co-ordinates the practice of teaching and learning for undergraduate student teachers and is engaged in research on aspects of gender, education and feminist theology.

Anne Savan is a teacher at Aberdare Boys' School, in the Cynon Valley, South Wales. Her qualifications include a Ph.D. from the University of Reading. Her research work on the effect of background music on the learning process has been published in a number of journals on the psychology and education and her work has also featured on several television programmes, including *Watchdog Healthcheck*, BBC2 *Newsnight*, BBC *Wales Today*, *Newsround* and *Breakfast TV*.

Peter Schreiner is currently a senior researcher at Comenius-Institut in Muenster, Germany, a Protestant Centre for Educational Research and Development. He is president of the Intereuropean Commission on Church and School (ICCS), a non-governmental organisation with participatory status at the Council of Europe and an associated member organisation of the Conference of European Churches (CEC). He is also moderator of the Coordinating Group for Religious Education in Europe (CoGREE), a network of six organisations active in the field of religion and education in Europe. His interests include comparative religious education in Europe, intercultural and interreligious learning, alternative approaches to education philosophy and ecumenical learning. He is currently engaged in a research project on, "Religion in the Context of a Europeanization of Education."

Daniel G. Scott is an associate professor and currently director of the School of Child and Youth Care, University of Victoria, Victoria, Canada. His background includes careers in theatre, a decade as a diocesan youth program coordinator, and stints in journalism and retail business. He serves on the board of the ChildSpirit Institute in Georgia and the editorial board of the *International Journal of Children's Spirituality*.

Inna Semetsky earned her PhD at Columbia University and is currently a research academic at the Institute of Advanced Study for Humanity, University of Newcastle, Australia. Email: inna.semetsky@newcastle.edu.au; Personal website www.innasense.org Her books "Deleuze, Education and Becoming" (2006) and "Nomadic Education: Variations on a Theme by Deleuze and Guattari" (Ed.; 2008) are published by Sense Publishers, Rotterdam. She contributed five entries "Noddings," "Dewey," "Jung," "Semiotics," and "Tarot," to the *Encyclopedia of Religious and Spiritual Development* (SAGE, 2006). Among her latest articles are "Simplifying Complexity: Know Thyself... and others," in *COMPLICITY: An International Journal of Complexity and Education*, Vol. 5, No 1; and "The transversal communication, or: reconciling science and magic," in *Cybernetics and Human Knowing*. Vol. 15, No. 2.

Deena Sigel is a bible teacher and researcher based in Israel. She holds a doctorate in education from the Institute of Education, London. Over the past 25 years, Deena has worked on bible education in Israel, the United Kingdom and the United States and during this time she has designed educational programmes for children and adults.

Caroline Smith is senior lecturer in science and sustainable futures education in the Faculty of Education Australian Catholic University. Her main teaching areas are in Science and Futures Education, through which she introduces an ecospiritual dimension to her students. She is also active in teacher professional learning. Her current research interests include education for sustainability for preservice primary teachers and the development of ecological literacy. She is also an organic farmer and permaculturalist, and is active in her local community promoting sustainability through the development of local food production systems. She is currently co-editing a book describing the experiences of prominent Australian permaculturalists.

Roz Sunley is a senior lecturer in Education at the University of Winchester in England, leading an innovative teacher training programme for secondary teachers in Religious Education. She is currently undertaking 2 years of funded research into professional values and the secondary classroom teacher; following doctoral studies at the University of Bristol where she explored teachers' perceptions of the spiritual dimension in secondary education. Her other main research interests include the integrity of professionalism; learning through dialogue and consultancy-enhanced teaching. Spending several years as a secondary teacher, her earlier career also spanned sales, politics and involvement in local community work.

Ngar-sze Lau is a teaching fellow of the Centre for Religious and Spirituality Education at the Hong Kong Institute of Education. Her research interest is on mindfulness, spiritual education, and meditation in different religious traditions and religious ethics. She has been practising mindfulness meditation and Zen meditation, and joining retreats in Hong Kong, Myanmar, Sabah, China, Taiwan, France, Germany, and England for over 15 years. Besides writing articles for magazines, she has been a translator, instructor, and organizer for meditation talks and retreats in Hong Kong. In the institute, she serves in-service teachers, children, and adolescents by offering meditation workshops in schools and communities.

David Tacey is associate professor in the School of Critical Enquiry, La Trobe University, Melbourne. He teaches courses on spirituality and rites of passage, analytical psychology and literary studies. He is the author of nine books, including 'The Spirituality Revolution: The Emergence of Contemporary Spirituality', London: Routledge, 2004; and 'ReEnchantment: The New Australian Spirituality', Sydney: Harper Collins, 2000. His most recent books are 'How to Read Jung', London: Granta, 2006, and 'The Idea of the Numinous', London: Routledge, 2006. His main research topic is the recovery of meaning in the contemporary world.

Charlene Tan is an assistant professor in Policy and Leadership Studies, National Institute of Education, Nanyang Technological University, Singapore. An editorial board member of *Reflective Practice*, she has published papers on religious and spiritual education in *Journal of Philosophy of Education*, *British Journal of Religious Education*, and *International Review of Education*. Her research interests include philosophical issues in education, religious and religious education, Islamic education and comparative education in Asia.

Marilyn Tew is development director with Antidote, a non-governmental organisation based in London, England, which develops emotionally literate approaches to learning and wellbeing. Prior to her work with Antidote, Marilyn worked as a teacher and consultant in second-level education. She holds a Ph.D. from the University of Bristol where she has been involved in research into emotional literacy and young people. She is a co-author of *Quality Circle Time: A Practitioner's Handbook* and *Circles: PSHE and Citizenship*. Her latest book was published in 2007 and is entitled *School Effectiveness: Supporting Student Success Through Emotional literacy*.

Ann M. Trousdale is an associate professor at Louisiana State University, where she teaches courses in children's literature and storytelling. Her current scholarship is in the area of using literature to support children's spiritual lives. Ann is an ordained deacon of the United Methodist Church.

Mindy Upton has been teaching for 30 years. She is the owner and lead teacher for Blue Sky Kindergarten in Boulder Colorado. She has been part of the adjunct faculty of Naropa University since 1982 and is on the board of advisors for the National Institute for Play. She is the mother of Sam and Mia. She is devoted to nurturing the magic of early childhood every day in her classroom, and the basic goodness inherent in all children.

Jacqueline Watson is a visiting Fellow at the University of East Anglia and an Associate of the Keswick Hall Centre for Religious Education. Her research interests include the notion of spiritual development in the context of state schooling in England, religious education, citizenship education and pupil voice. She was a Religious Education teacher in secondary schools in England for 12 years.

Kevin Williams is senior lecturer in Mater Dei Institute, Dublin City University, and a former president of the Educational Studies Association of Ireland. Widely recognised as a philosopher of education, his most recent publications include *Faith and the Nation: Religion, Culture, Schooling in Ireland* (Dominican Publications, 2005) *Education and the Voice of Michael Oakeshott* (Imprint Academic, 2007) and *Religion and Citizenship Education in Europe* (2008), written as part of the Children's Identity and Citizenship Education in Europe (CiCe) project funded by the European Commission.

Fiona Williams is a teacher at Holy Faith Secondary School in Killester, Dublin and a part-time lecture at the School of Education Studies, Dublin City University. She has designed several websites in the area of religious and civic education on behalf of the national Department of Education and Science. These are available on Teachnet and are widely used in Irish schools.

General Introduction

Marian de Souza, Leslie J. Francis, James O'Higgins-Norman, and Daniel Scott

In this handbook we will examine the relationship between the concepts of wellbeing, care and spirituality in educational settings and the relationship to the provision of holistic education for young people. We will argue that there are serious consequences for not recognizing the importance of spirituality as a core dimension to a person's development. Spirituality, here, is conceived as relational, the connectedness that an individual feels to everything that is other than self. Vygotsky recognized the importance of the relational character of teaching when he argued that the first stage in the construction of knowledge and meaning by an individual arises out of an "*interpsychological*" relationship with others (1978, p. 57). In other words, we come to learn about our world, society, various subjects and issues and most importantly we learn about ourselves through interaction with others. Totterdell (2000) further expounds this view when he argues that there is a connection between what we *understand* and how we *behave*:

> Acknowledging the primacy of relationships as fundamental to human flourishing leads us to advocate an ethic based on a clear-eyed estimate of the consequences of behaviour on human well-being... (p. 133).

Both these arguments point to the ethic of care which has become a central motif in the discourse surrounding teaching and compulsory schooling in Western societies. They are especially relevant today, given the social, political and cultural influences that have shaped the contexts within which individuals attempt to understand and make meaning of their life experiences and within which education systems are endeavouring to find approaches that will address the whole student.

The first decade of the twenty-first century has been a particularly eventful time in human history in terms of scientific and technological advances. The rapid pace of change and communication, while it may be exciting and stimulating for many, also generates an underlying level of anxiety as people barely have time to get used to one innovation before the next one is on the horizon. The ability to "dip" into

M. de Souza (✉)
National School of Religious Education, Australian Catholic University, Ballarat, VIC 3350, Australia
e-mail: m.desouza@acu.edu.au

and out of a variety of human experiences, whether it relates to a relationship, job, living accommodation or country tends to bring a certain level of superficiality. For many young people who know no other way of being, the skills and ability to ground themselves in a particular worldview that offers them meaning and purpose seems to be ever elusive.

It is not surprising, then, that statistics and anecdotal evidence reflect the fact that many young people appear to experience disillusionment and a sense of hopelessness and disconnection and that they contribute to the rising statistics of mental health problems in many Western countries. Further statistics from these countries regularly indicate the growing indifference of a large number of young people to traditional institutions, such as religion, that in previous years may have offered some hope, meaning and purpose. Instead, many declare themselves to be spiritual and not religious, and their search for meaning takes place in spaces without boundaries which can be unsatisfying and, sometimes, detrimental to their wellbeing.

Without doubt, the perceived differences between spirituality and religion have continued to attract attention with resultant discussions trying to arrive at a common understanding of contemporary spirituality, its links to religion and its role in care and wellbeing. Certainly, the fact that contemporary spirituality has been perceived as relational—a "relational consciousness" (Hay & Nye, 1998) has significant implications for the wellbeing of an individual. As well, Tacey's (2003) notion that spirituality is a search for the sacred in the everyday where "such encounters change lives and expose young people to the mystery and presence of the sacred within themselves, even as they are moved by the sacred in nature" (p. 181) has relevance.

In particular, new insights from brain research into the biological nature of spirituality have prompted the articulation of various theories of spiritual intelligence which cannot be overlooked in any discussion on education for care and wellbeing. Potentially, the individual's sense of connectedness to Self and to Other in the community, the world and to a Transcendent Other should provide him/her with a sense of meaning and purpose thereby enhancing a sense of wellbeing. It is not surprising, then, that the links between spirituality, care and wellbeing have continued to generate research, conferences, forums and debates in education, health and other related fields.

Another feature of the contemporary world that has pertinence to education for care and wellbeing is that for a variety of reasons such as large-scale disasters—floods, earthquakes, drought, famine and war, and other human reasons such as seeking employment and improved lifestyles in a world made more accessible by improved travelling opportunities, an unprecedented number of people have continued to shift and resettle across the globe. This has created tensions, overt and concealed, as hosts and new arrivals negotiate and develop new relationships often with little understanding of the cultural beliefs and practices held by the other. More particularly, on the part of the host countries, there is little real understanding of the horror and trauma that are inherent elements of the broken and uprooted lives of so many people who arrive on their shores. In particular, 9/11 marked a distinct point in the contemporary world when the act of terrorism inserted itself into the world's consciousness and subsequently shaped global politics. One outcome has been the levels of religious divisiveness that have become features of some societies and it has successfully impeded the path that could lead from tolerance to empathy and compassion.

These are elements for concern, particularly when we consider a new generation that has grown up against this backdrop of anxiety and hostility. New and traditional avenues need to be examined to find strategies that will provide some resolutions. One way forward is to re-look at education programs. It is time to recognize that the educational frameworks that were born out of a twentieth century scientific, positivistic and reductionistic framework are not an adequate response to the world today. Instead, what is needed is an approach to education that reflects a change in consciousness and which is more appropriate to the context of the contemporary world, one that is grounded in the totality of human experience. The collection of writings in this handbook is one attempt to do this. It considers the dynamic relationship between education, spirituality, care and wellbeing. It examines the theory underpinning the practice of education in different societies where spirituality and care are believed to be at the heart of all educational experiences. As well, it recognizes that, regardless of the context or type of educational experience, education is a caring activity in which the development of the whole person—body, mind and spirit is a central aim for teachers and educators in both formal and informal learning.

The chapters also acknowledge that different understandings of spirituality have created tensions for some scholars in the Western world, particularly in the fields of religion and theology. Traditionally, spirituality was firmly placed within the framework of religion, so that often the term was used interchangeably with religion and religiosity. Hanegraaff argues that:

> "Spiritualities" and "religions" might be roughly characterized as the individual and institutional poles within the general domain of "religion". A religion without spiritualities is impossible to imagine. But. . . the reverse—a spirituality without religion—is quite possible in principle. Spiritualities can emerge on the basis of an existing religion, but they can very well do without. New Age is the example par excellence of this latter possibility: a complex of spiritualities which emerges on the foundation of a pluralistic secular society. (1999, p. 151)

The concept of spirituality that inspires the writings contained in this handbook assumes that spirituality is an innate element of the human person and an integral aspect of human development. Its nature is relational: the expressions of connectedness that an individual experiences to Self (as in inner Self) and everything that is other than self. Spirituality complements, integrates and balances the rational and emotional aspects of the human person. Accordingly, the chapters in this handbook will present and discuss topics that focus on spirituality as an integral part of human experience which is, consequently, essential to educational programs which aim to address personal and communal identity; foster resilience, empathy and compassion; and promote meaning and connectedness. Ultimately, these elements should make possible the care and wellbeing of all students.

The structure of this book is divided into two volumes with two parts in each volume. The first part will focus more on the theoretical aspects of education for spirituality, care and wellbeing. The second part will examine the application of theory for professional practice in the respective areas of education, spirituality, care and wellbeing.

The first part is edited by Professor Leslie J. Francis and has as its theme: The psychology of religion and spirituality with attention being given to the implications for education, care and wellbeing. Francis notes that religion and spirituality used to be important factors in the field of psychology but this had somewhat diminished through the mid-twentieth century, only to resurface at the end of the century and become an important topic for consideration and study. He clearly explains why the focus of the chapters in this part is drawn from quantitative research studies where the findings and conclusions that are presented have been generally tested and established by statistical procedures. This part, then, provides a foundation for the ideas and essays that follow through the rest of the handbook.

Dr Daniel Scott is the editor of the second part which focuses on human development and identity for children and young people. He refers to the potential problems that arise when spirituality is divorced from these areas of research and highlights the need to identify and describe the nature of spiritual development. The chapters provide an extensive examination of relevant literature and draw on practice-based experience and observations to propose theories pertaining to spiritual development which may inform the practice of those in the caring professions and assist them to understand spirituality as it is experienced and expressed. The answers to questions such as: What role does spirituality play in human maturation? What are some possible ways in which spirituality may be studied? and so on, become the focus of the discussions and deliberations of the writers in this part. In the end, it becomes clear that integrating spirituality into practice can contribute to the wellbeing of child and youth.

The third and fourth parts make up the second volume. The third part is edited by Dr de Souza and concentrates on the pedagogical aspects of education for spirituality, care and wellbeing. The chapters, here, identify the concerns shared by many scholars and practitioners that many educational programs and curricula on offer today do not cater for all students and there is much evidence that, as we have entered the new millennium, there are several indications that a growing number of children and adolescents are afflicted by social and health problems and that mental illness, most commonly depression, is on the rise amongst them. These scholars highlight the fact that most education systems are failing to adequately cater for all their students since they do not have a holistic approach and, instead, continue to focus on cognitive learning. The writings provide a thorough examination of related literature and discuss various pedagogical approaches that will enable practitioners to enhance and nurture the spirituality and wellbeing of the students in their care.

Dr James O'Higgins-Norman edits the fourth and final part of the handbook. The chapters, here, draw together many of the concepts that have been investigated in the earlier parts. The focus here is on the application of the theories of spirituality, care and wellbeing to different educational settings and involving different professionals. As O'Higgins-Norman notes in his introduction, no one profession should be allowed custody of the human spirit. In particular, there is a clear understanding that is indicated through these chapters that the care and wellbeing of a student is intrinsically bound up with the spirituality of their being. Accordingly, the central theme that underlies the writings in this part is that education is a process that is inseparable from human fulfilment.

The chapters in this handbook reflect the breadth of interest in the discipline of education for spirituality, care and wellbeing. The authors have developed excellence and expertise in their various fields: psychology, sociology, theology, education, counselling and chaplaincy, and they provide perspectives from a range of countries across the globe. Their writings are indicative of the concern and passion they have for the education and wellbeing of young people in the contemporary world. Ultimately, the writings in this handbook provide illuminating insights to inform and enhance future directions and policies in education and, indeed, in other caring professions so that they will be able to identify strategies and approaches in education that will nurture spirituality and attend to the care and wellbeing of future generations.

References

Hanegraaff, W. J. (1999). New Age spiritualities as secular religion: A historian's perspective. *Social Compass, 46*(2), 145–160.

Hay, D., & Nye, R. (1998). *The spirit of the child*. London: Fount Paperbacks.

Tacey, D. (2003). *The spirituality revolution*. Pymble, NSW: HarperCollins Publisher.

Totterdell, M. (2000). The moralisation of teaching: A relational approach as an ethical framework in the professional preparation and formation of teachers. In R. Gardner, J. Cairns, & D. Lawton (Eds.), *Education for values: Morals, ethics and citizenship in contemporary teaching*. London: Kogan Page.

Vygotsky, L. S. (1978). *Mind and society: The development of higher mental processes*. Cambridge, MA: Harvard University Press.

Part I
The Psychology of Religion and Spirituality: Implications for Education and Wellbeing – An Introduction

Leslie J. Francis

According to its etymology, the discipline of psychology is concerned with the study of the mind, with the study of the soul, with the study of the human *psyche*. This broad definition, however, is far from unproblematic. What is meant by the human mind, the human soul, the human psyche? And what tools are available to study such phenomena anyway? The broad history of the development of psychology as an academic discipline in its own right is the story of how these two problems have been addressed: the problem of substance (what is being studied) and the problem of method (how is the study being conducted). Right from the early days of the developing discipline of psychology, religion and spirituality have been seen as a matter of central concern (see, for example, William James, 1902). Although this central concern with religion and spirituality seemed to disappear from the radar of psychology for a number of years, the topic is now firmly back on the agenda as evidenced by the foundation of the *International Journal for the Psychology of Religion* in 1980, the revitalisation of the *Archive for the Psychology of Religion* in the 1990s and the development of a new journal from the American Psychological Association in 2009 dedicated to the psychology of religion and spirituality. The aim of this chapter is to provide a general introduction to and overview of the perspective on the psychology of religion and spirituality taken by and shaped within this handbook concerned with education, care and wellbeing. This perspective has been informed by three considerations.

The first consideration concerns the range of people on whom the perspective is focused. Different branches of psychology are properly concerned with different populations: the mentally ill (say, clinical psychology), the criminal and the deviant (say, forensic psychology) or the general population of people who have been diagnosed as neither "mad" nor "bad" (say, "normal" psychology). This part of the handbook is concerned with the normal population broadly conceived.

The second consideration concerns the subject matter (the data) under consideration. Different branches of psychology are properly concerned with different approaches to their subject. Some approaches are concerned with examining the functioning of the human brain (say, neuroscience) and this concern has proved to be fruitful within the broad field of the psychology of religion and spirituality. Other approaches are concerned with ways of accessing human experience and interpreting the meaning and significance of human responses. This part of the handbook is concerned with the latter of these two approaches.

The third consideration concerns the ways in which human experiences and human responses can be accessed and studied (the methodology). Broadly within the social sciences the main methodological division occurs between qualitative and quantitative approaches. The qualitative approach (say, using interviews) has the strength of providing rich and deep description, often allowing the voices of individuals to be heard with clarity. The quantitative approach (say, using questionnaire surveys) has the strength of providing access to a large number of people and of allowing more secure generalisations to be made. This part of the handbook is concerned primarily with the quantitative approach, although it is fully recognised that the two approaches are complementary and properly inform and enrich one another. Good use is made of the qualitative approach as and when appropriate.

Within the quantitative tradition there are certain key assumptions that shape what is taken seriously and how the methodology proceeds. The first key assumption concerns the notion of measurement. It is assumed that central psychological constructs can be accessed and calibrated in ways that mimic the measurement of physical constructs. Such a notion is far from being unproblematic. It may be relatively straightforward to measure the length of an individual's arm or the circumference of an individual's head, but it is much more problematic to measure intelligence, extraversion or spirituality. In a sense, all these psychological notions (unlike the physical notions of arms and heads) are abstractions. They are ways of talking about elusive aspects of the human psyche rather than being objective "things" in their own right. In order to measure such abstractions, it is necessary to be very clear about the way in which terms are to be used (the issue of definition) and about the way in which accepted definitions are to be translated into measures (the issue of operationalisation).

Many of the notions with which the quantitative approach to psychology deals are highly contested within other spheres of debate (say other disciplines). There is, for example, no one accepted definition of constructs like intelligence, extraversion, religion or spirituality. It is for this reason that definitions adopted by psychologists as a basis for developing measuring instruments themselves remain contested. There are, for example, a number of generally accepted measures of the notion of extraversion, but it cannot be assumed that these instruments all measure the same "thing". The view generally taken within this part of the handbook is that it is sensible and proper to work with the precise definitions offered by the instruments used and to take care not to generalise research findings beyond these definitions to the wider area of concern. For example, if an instrument sets out to access and operationalise one definition of spirituality, it is a fundamental mistake to assume that the findings can be generalised to embrace a wide diverse range of definitions.

The operationalisation of carefully argued definitions remains problematic in its own right. Those who develop and deploy psychological measures need to demonstrate that these measures are in fact measuring what they claim to be measuring. Technically this problem involves issues of reliability and validity. A reliable instrument is one that can be trusted to produce consistent findings. If I measure the circumference of an individual's head today and measure it again tomorrow, I would expect consistent findings. If I measure an individual's level of intelligence today and measure it again tomorrow, I would expect similar if not identical findings. A test that is not reliable cannot be valid. A valid instrument is one that can be trusted to measure the construct under review. If I measure an individual's right arm, I cannot validly claim to have measured the outstretched span of both arms. I could extrapolate from my findings and make an informed prediction, but I still need to be honest about what has been measured and about what has not been measured. There is a variety of ways in which psychologists deal with this issue.

The second key assumption within the quantitative tradition is that measurement enables precise hypotheses to be tested and the significance of associations between variables to be established by statistical procedures. The main findings from research and the main conclusions presented in this part of the handbook have been generally tested and established by these kinds of statistical procedures. The implications of findings established in this way can be illuminated and illustrated by data generated within the qualitative tradition.

Against the background of this broad theoretical perspective, the intention of the rest of this chapter is to introduce and to contextualise the 13 focused contributions. In Chapter 1, Ralph W. Hood Jr. discusses the ways of studying the psychology of religion and spirituality. Rather than applaud and promote a single method, Hood explores the range of methods available to psychologists who study religion and spirituality. He alerts us to the proper limitations associated with different methods, but is clear in his rejection of the position argued by some recent commentators claiming the primacy of experimental approaches. Hood's chapter is especially important because it helps to establish the value and the importance of the wider range of methods on which the authors of subsequent chapters draw.

In Chapter 2, Peter C. Hill and Lauren E. Maltby go to the heart of the individual differences approach that shapes this part of the handbook in order to discuss issues concerned with measuring religiousness and spirituality. After discussing general issues related to measurement, they provide a very useful introduction to and a critique of a range of existing measures in the field. This review builds on the earlier influential and authoritative volume that Peter C. Hill co-edited with Ralph W. Hood Jr. under the title, *Measures of Religiosity* (Hill & Hood, 1999).

In Chapter 3, Chris J. Boyatzis focuses attention on what is known from research about religion and spiritual development during childhood and adolescence. He tackles key questions including the following. What does spirituality look like in a child? Does religion make a genuine difference in the lives of children and youth? How do we measure spiritual and religious development in children and adolescents? How can we characterise religious and spiritual development in its processes, sequences and stages? After a long period during which empirical research in the field was conspicuous by its neglect, Boyatzis identifies the signs of new developments and growth in this field.

In Chapter 4, John W. Fisher introduces the notion of spiritual health and rehearses his well-established model of characterising good spiritual health as involving four domains of life. For Fisher the individual who experiences good spiritual health has developed good relationships with the self, good relationships with other people, good relationships with the environment and good relationships with the transcendent, however this is conceived. This model of spiritual health is attractive because it is well defined, coherent and open to operationalisation. Fisher proceeds to describe the instruments that he has developed to assess spiritual health across the four domains: The Spiritual Health in Four Domains Index, Spiritual Health and Life-Orientation Measure, Feeling Good Living Life and Quality of Influences Survey. He illustrates the application of these instruments among school pupils, university students and other adults in Australia and the United Kingdom.

In Chapter 5, Ralph L. Piedmont examines the research evidence concerning the contribution of religion and spirituality to subjective wellbeing and satisfaction with life. Building on one of his own major contributions to the research literature, Piedmont examines the numinous constructs of religiosity and spirituality relative to one another and to the five-factor model of personality. The strength of this approach is that it highlights the ways in which spirituality and religion have an unmediated impact on levels of life satisfaction. Piedmont develops two main conclusions from this finding. First, spirituality and religiosity represent universal human motives that are additional to the areas generally covered by models of human personality. In other words, models of human functioning need to be expanded to embrace spirituality and religiosity if they are to be comprehensive. Second, because spirituality and religiosity are capable of impacting subjective wellbeing and satisfaction with life, they suggest the potential for identifying a new class of intervention techniques that can promote durable psychological change.

In Chapter 6, Kate M. Loewenthal examines the interactions between culture, religion and spirituality in relation to psychiatric illness. Given that most of the extant research in this area has been conducted in Western Christian cultures, Loewenthal focuses on the research evidence from other religions and cultures. She asks whether such evidence generates new perspectives on the problems and conclusions. She illustrates her case by discussing four well-developed areas: somatisation, schizophrenia, obsessive compulsive disorder and depression. Loewenthal's analysis clearly demonstrates that religion and spirituality are neither "a universal destroyer of wellbeing, nor a universal panacea". The effects of religion and spirituality on wellbeing are many and varied, and can definitely be modulated by culture.

Personality theories provide one of the main frameworks within which the individual differences approach to religion and spirituality operates. In Chapter 7, Leslie J. Francis provides an introduction to one personality theory that has been particularly influential in recent years in shaping an awareness of the association between personality and ways of expressing religiosity and spirituality. This is the notion of psychological type as proposed by Carl Jung and modified and developed by assessment tools like the Myers Briggs Type Indicator and the Kiersey Temperament Sorter. This model distinguishes between two orientations (introversion and extraversion), two perceiving functions (sensing and intuition), two judging functions (thinking and feeling) and two attitudes towards the outer world (judging and perceiving). In this chapter, Leslie J. Francis draws on recent, empirical research concerned with profiling religious professionals, with profiling religious adherents and with examining the association between type preferences and preferred modes of spirituality.

Research concerned with establishing the correlates of individual differences in levels of religiosity and spirituality has to confront the problem of the way in which these constructs are multidimensional. In Chapter 8, Leslie J. Francis distinguishes between distinct dimensions of religion and spirituality defined as self-assigned affiliation (the groups with which individuals identify), self-reported practices (the things that individuals do), beliefs (the cognitive aspect of religion and spirituality) and attitudes (the affective aspect of religion and spirituality. Then Francis proceeds to argue for the primacy of the attitudinal dimension in accessing the core of an individual's religion and spirituality. The chapter concludes by summarising a wide field of research concerned with establishing the correlates, antecedents and consequences of individual differences in the attitudinal dimension of religion and spirituality.

In Chapter 9, Chris Baker offers a psychological perspective on the growing literature concerned with the notions of social, religious and spiritual capital. These notions have their roots in thinkers like Coleman and Bourdieu and were brought to wider public attention by Putnam's now classic study, *Bowling alone* (Putnam, 2000). Using the ideas of capitals, these notions trace the contributions made to individual lives and to society by social networks, by religious organisations and by the realm of spirituality. Drawing on original data generated by his association with the William Temple Foundation, Chris Baker profiles the considerable benefits to individuals and to society associated with religious and spiritual capitals.

From the early and original work of William James (1902) in his classic study, *The varieties of religious experience*, researchers have been concerned with the experiential aspects of religion and spirituality. In Chapter 10, Ralph W. Hood Jr. discusses the variety of ways in which the terms religious and spiritual experience are employed in current discussion and how they are distinguished one from the other. Then Hood examines the implications for education and wellbeing of five recent research traditions concerned with deconversion, conversion, glossolalia, different forms of prayer and meditation, and mysticism. In this last part, Hood draws on his own pioneering research, begun in the 1970s with the development of the Hood Mysticism Scale as a means of accessing and measuring responses to religious experience (Hood, 1975).

Kenneth I Pargament is well-known within the fields of the psychology of religion and spirituality for his original and pioneering research linking religion and coping strategies, as displayed in his book, *The psychology of religion and coping: Theory, research and practice* (Pargament, 1997). In Chapter 11, Pargament suggests that religion is designed first and foremost to facilitate spirituality and to help people achieve spiritual goals. Building on this premise, he maintains that attempts to understand religion in purely biological, psychological or social terms can provide, at best, an incomplete picture and, at worst, a distorted view of religious life. Demonstrating this point, Pargament presents a model for understanding spirituality as a normal and natural part of life. Then he examines the spiritual dimension of coping with life stressors within the context of that larger model of spirituality.

The notion of the psychology of faith development is now closely linked with the pioneering empirical research and theory construction undertaken by James Fowler. In Chapter 12, Jeff Astley provides an overview of Fowler's theory. He argues that, although the theoretical framework and the research support for it have both been vigorously critiqued, many educators, pastors and counsellors have found their own thinking illuminated by Fowler's claims. Fowler uses the term "faith" in a wide, generic sense. According to Fowler, religious faith is only one species of human faith; it is faith directed to religious things, in particular to a transcendent God or gods. According to Fowler, everyone has his/her "gods" in the wider sense of realities and ideas that they value highly and to which they are committed including their health, wealth, security, family, ideologies and their own pleasure. In this chapter, Astley identifies the theological and psychological roots of Fowler's theory, its empirical support and the critical literature that it has attracted. Then Astley traces the relevance of Fowler's account of faith for those concerned with pastoral care, with spiritual counselling and with wider educational contexts.

A number of early researchers concerned with the psychology of religion and spirituality identified prayer as being the core expression of what it means to be religious or spiritual (see Francis & Astley, 2001). Empirical research in these areas, however, was largely eclipsed until a renaissance in the 1990s. In Chapter 13, Tania ap Siôn and Leslie J. Francis present and evaluate three strands of the research that have re-established prayer as of central importance in understanding the role of religion and spirituality in human development and human functioning. The first strand of research is concerned with the subjective effects of prayer, looking at the correlates of prayer among those who engage in that activity. The second strand of research is concerned with the objective effects of prayer, giving particular attention to clinical trials of "prayer treatment", examining the medical outcomes of patients who do not know that they are being prayed for. The third strand of research is concerned with the content of prayer as a window through which to view the religion and spirituality of ordinary people.

The 13 chapters in this part of the handbook have all been written by acknowledged authorities in the particular aspect of the psychology of religion and spirituality on which they have contributed. The editorial process has deliberately allowed the distinctive voices and perspectives of these authors to stand on their own terms. Contradictions of interpretation and discrepancies of evaluation simply serve to remind us that the psychology of religion and spirituality is an ongoing and developing field of enquiry stimulated by debate, controversy and disagreement. Enough secure evidence has, however, been marshalled to make the irrefutable case that religion and spirituality matter a great deal in the fields of education, pastoral care and wellbeing. Practitioners within these applied fields are already able to draw valuable insights from the research literature. At the same time, the case has been clearly made for the value of investing further in the promotion of ongoing empirical research, informed by the insights of psychology, into the correlates, antecedents and consequences of individual differences in religiosity and in spirituality.

References

Francis, L.J., & Astley, J. (Eds.). (2001). *Psychological perspectives on prayer: A reader.* Leominster: Gracewing.
Hill, P. C., & Hood, R. W. (Eds.). (1999). *Measures of religiosity.* Birmingham, Alabama: Religious Education Press.
Hood, R. W. (1975). The construction and preliminary validation of a measure of reported mystical experience. *Journal for the Scientific Study of Religion, 14*, 29–41.
James, W. (1902). *The varieties of religious experience.* New York: Longmans Green.
Pargament, K. I. (1997). *The psychology of religion and coping: Theory, research practice.* New York: Guilford Press.
Putnam, R. D. (2000). *Bowling alone: The collapse and revival of American community.* New York: Touchstone.

Chapter 1
Ways of Studying the Psychology of Religion and Spirituality

Ralph W. Hood, Jr.

Abstract Psychology is far from a unified discipline. There are strongly differing opinions on how it is to be defined. One consequence of this diversity is methodological pluralism. Methodological pluralism includes the descriptive fact that different schools of psychology favor different research methods as well as the philosophical position that psychology cannot and ought not be defined in terms of a single methodology assumed appropriate for all investigations. Thus, while some would argue for the experimental method combined with the quantitative assessment of change in measured variables as the gold standard for research in religion and spirituality, this position must be balanced by a consideration of a wide variety of other methods used in the study of religion and spirituality. These include quasi-experimental methods when participants cannot be randomly assigned to treatment groups and ethnographic and participant observation often focused on qualitative assessments. The psychological study of religion and spirituality has always been identified with questionnaires and scales designed to measure particular phenomena of interest. Phenomenological studies are of descriptive value in their own right, as well as providing means to operationalize and measure reports of religious and spiritual experiences. Advances in neurophysiological imaging techniques are providing a rich database for correlating brain states with the report of religious and spiritual experiences. Finally, survey research allows the placing of religious and spiritual phenomena within a normative cultural context. A commitment to methodological pluralism assures that both religion and spirituality can be studied in ways appropriate to the richness and diversity that these terms connate.

The psychology of religion has since its inception struggled with what are the appropriate methods for studying religion and spirituality. As we shall see the questions of methods remain controversial among contemporary psychologists. However, rather than applaud a single method our purpose in this chapter will be to explore the range of methods available to psychologists who study religion and spirituality. Our presentation of various methods necessarily focuses on American psychology of

R.W. Hood, Jr. (✉)
Department of Psychology, University of Tennessee, Chattanooga, TN 37403, USA
e-mail: Ralph-Hood@utc.edu

religion dominated until recently by studies of largely Protestant college students (Gorsuch, 1988). While this is unfortunate, it characterizes, as we shall soon discuss, the American turn to experimental methods as the gold standard by which to judge psychological research as well as the American reliance upon undergraduate psychology students for their dominant subject pools (Sears, 1986). Thus we will provide some critical discussion of mainstream American psychology's adaptation of the experimental method as exemplars of scientific psychology and American psychology's compromise appeal to quasi-experimental methods as the ideal method for the psychology of religion. We do not accept this claim and argue for the expansion of methods within the psychology of religion. Furthermore, we will note that the methods used in the psychology of religion are additive in that older methods such as correlation and measurement are not abandoned but rather used alongside new ones. We accept a variety of methods, only some of which are quantitative. Qualitative methods add insights into the psychology of religion that quantitative methods miss. Furthermore, we applaud the use of mixed methods in the study of religion and spirituality where both quantitative and qualitative methods are used *simultaneously* in a single study (Kohls, Hack, & Walach, 2008).

In one of the earliest reviews of the psychology of religion, Dittes (1969) identified four conceptual options available to those who study the psychology of religion and spirituality. Each has methodological implications.

Two of Dittes' options are reductionistic. The first is the claim that the only variables operating in religion are the same that operate in mainstream psychology. Therefore the psychology of religion need have no unique methodologies as its subject matter is not unique. The second option is that, while the variables operating in religion are not unique, they may be more salient in religious contexts and thus their effect is greater within rather than outside religion. However, they remain purely psychological variables.

The other two of Dittes' conceptual options suggest something is unique about religion and thus it may need methods that mainstream psychology ignores. The least controversial of these is that established psychological variables uniquely interact in religious contexts and thus there is a unique contribution from the interaction of psychological with religious variables to the total variance explained. The final option is that there are unique variables operating in religion that either do not operate in or are ignored by mainstream psychologists. We will confront Dittes' various conceptual options as we gradually explore methods in terms of our additive comments above.

Method 1: Personal Documents and Questionnaires

Many of the techniques employed today were first used by the founding fathers of our discipline. William James (1902/1985) focused on personal documents describing the experiences of individuals who felt themselves to be in the presence of the divine. His focus on the *varieties* of religious experience left open all of Dittes' four options. He also relied on questionnaires employed by Edward Starbuck in his study of the growth of religious consciousness (Starbuck, 1899). The method is simply to ask persons to describe their religious experiences, either in an open-ended fashion or by responding to specific questionnaire items. Perhaps most congruent with the James and Starbuck tradition of the use of personal documents to understand religious experience has been the work associated with what was originally known as the Religious Experience Research Unit of Manchester College, Oxford University. This unit continues as the Alister Hardy Religious Experience Research Centre at the University of Wales, Lampeter. Alister Hardy achieved scientific accolades as a renowned zoologist. Yet his lifelong interest in religious experience led him upon retirement from his career in zoology to form a research unit in 1969 devoted to the collection and classification of religious experiences, for which he was awarded the Templeton Prize for research in religion. Hardy's basic procedure, stemming from his zoological training, was to solicit voluntary reports of religious experiences and to attempt to classify them into their natural types. Typically these reports were solicited via requests in newspapers, as well as newsletters distributed to various groups, mostly in the United Kingdom. Requests were not simply for the more extreme and intense types of experiences favored by James, but for the more temperate variety of religious experiences as well. Often individuals simply submitted experience unsolicited. In *The spiritual nature of man*, Hardy (1979) published an extensive classification of the major defining characteristics of these experiences from an initial pool of 3,000 experiences. Here the method is to impose classifications upon a set of data. A criticism often applied to classifications concerns the lack of any systematic metric properties.

Hardy's major classifications included sensory or quasi-sensory experience associated with vision, hearing, and touch; less frequent, but still fairly common, were reports of paranormal experiences. Most common were cognitive and affective episodes, such as a sense of presence or feelings of peace (Hardy, 1979). Not surprisingly, other surveys (discussed as Method 2 further) of a more scientific nature, such as Greeley's (1975) survey of 1,467 people, show some overlaps with Hardy's classifications, especially with the cognitive and affective elements but also reveal many differences. It seems that there is little agreement about exactly what might constitute the common characteristics of religious experience. Perhaps the term is simply too broad for agreement to be expected across diverse samples and investigators. The focus, then, must be on not simply religious experience, but the varieties of experience that are interpreted as religious. What makes an experience religious is clearly not the discrete, isolated components that can be identified in any experience as James long ago noted. Thus when persons are asked to describe their religious or spiritual experiences, the widest possible range of experiences are obtained. It is up to the psychologist to impose some order and classification on the diverse material.

Method 2: Survey Research

More sociologically oriented psychologists have used survey methods to determine the frequency and correlates of various types of spiritual and religious experiences. For instance, it has been over 40 years since Glock and Stark sampled churches in the greater San Francisco area using this question, "Have you ever as an adult had the feeling that you were somehow in the presence of God?" (Glock & Stark, 1965, p. 157, Table 8-1). With a sample size of just under 3,000 respondents (2,871), 72% answered "yes". Not surprisingly, the majority were religiously committed persons. However, Vernon (1968) demonstrated that even among those answering "none" in response to their religious identification, 25% answered "yes" to the Glock and Stark question. More recently, Tamminen (1991) in a longitudinal study of Scandinavian youth modified the Glock and Stark question slightly by omitting the phrase "as an adult," Tamminen asked, "Have you at times felt that God is particularly close to you." He found a steady decline in the percentage of students reporting experiences of nearness to God by grade level (and hence age).

The most frequently used survey question is associated with the General Social Survey (GSS) of the National Opinion Research Center. The GSS is a series of independent cross-sectional probability samples of persons in the continental United States, living in non-institutional homes, who are 18 years of age and English-speaking. The question most typically used is "Have your ever felt as though you were close to a powerful spiritual force that seemed to lift you out of yourself?" as first asked by Greeley (1974). The question has been asked to persons in Great Britain by Hay and Morisy (1978) with a 36% affirmative response. It was found that overall, in a GSS sample of 1,468, 35% of the respondents answered "yes" to this question (Davis & Smith, 1994).

Yamane and Polzer (1994) analyzed all affirmative responses from the GSS to the Greeley question in the years 1983, 1984, 1988, and 1989. A total of 5,420 individuals were included in their review. Using an ordinal scale where respondents who answered affirmatively could select from three options—"once or twice," "several times," or "often"—yielded a range from 0 (negative response) to 3 (often). Using this four-point range across all individuals who responded to the Greeley question yielded a mean score of 0.79 (SD = 0.89). Converting this to a percentage of "yes" as a nominal category, regardless of frequency, yielded 2,183 affirmative responses, or an overall affirmative response of 40% of the total sample who reported ever having had the experience. Independent assessment of affirmative responses for each year suggested a slight but steady decline. The figures were 39% for 1983 and 1984 combined ($n = 3,072$), 31% for 1988 ($n = 1,481$), and 31% for 1989 ($n = 936$).

The major consistent findings based on survey studies can be easily summarized in terms of Dittes' first two conceptual options. Women report more religious and spiritual experiences than men; the experiences tend to be age-related, increasing with age; they are characteristic of educated and affluent people; and they are more likely to be associated with indices of psychological health and wellbeing than with those of pathology or social dysfunction. Finally, Religious and spiritual experiences are common and reported by at least one-third of the populations in the United States, the United Kingdom, and Australia. The focus on belief ignores any actual ontological claims, so that belief in God as well as parapsychology and contact with the dead is found to be common. Such issues are best explored by phenomenological methods discussed later in this chapter.

Method 3: Scales, Measurement, and Correlation

The diversity of experiences reported in surveys and open-ended questionnaires can be ordered by the use of scales that operationalize a particular researcher's definition of religious and/or spiritual experiences. As opposed to survey research that typically uses one or a very limited number of religious questions, scales can have many items. Combined with exploratory factor analysis, items can be clustered together metrically leading to various sub-scales. These factored scales can be correlated with other scales to identify relationships. Most religious variables are multidimensional. One example is the Religious Orientation Scale first devised by Allport and Ross (1967) and perhaps the widest used scale in the psychology of religion (Donahue, 1985; Kirkpatrick & Hood, 1990).

However, Gorsuch (1984) noted how measurement via the use of scales was a mixed blessing for the psychology of religion. It emerged in the 1960s as American psychologists began to return to an interest in religion. On one hand, it proved to be as easy to measure religious and spiritual constructs as any other psychological constructs. However, on the other hand, a focus on measurement could inhibit systematic programs of research involving other than correlational methods. Hill and Hood (1999) have collected the most commonly used measures of religion and to a lesser extent of spirituality. Readily available are scales to measure religious belief and practices, religious attitudes, religious coping and problem solving, and concepts of God, to mention only a few. The important point here is that one ought to consult existing measures before constructing new ones. Likewise, once religious or spiritual measures are identified, they can be correlated with a wide variety of existing measures in mainstream psychology. Most of this research stays within the first two conceptual options noted by Dittes.

Method 4: Clinical Psychoanalysis and Object Relations

The measurement of God concepts has been a concern of the empirical psychology of religion with its re-emergence in the 1960s. This is relevant to the second wave in the study of religion after the founding fathers. Here the influence was from psychoanalysis with the imposition of its clinical methods and a focus on unconscious processes. Few psychoanalysts remained silent or neutral on the subject of religion. Thus, while academic psychology remained largely quiet on religion and spirituality after the founding father's interest, psychoanalysts explored it fully with their own methods. They ranged from Freud's well-known reductionist treatment of religion, placing the psychoanalytic study of religion within Dittes' first two conceptual options (Hood, 1992) to Jung's treatment of religion squarely within Dittes' options 3 and 4 (Halligan, 1995). The methods employed by psychoanalysts and analysts have seldom been championed by academic psychologists, but the focus on therapeutic transformation as a criterion of success does allow for some assessment that these are legitimate human sciences.

The second generation of psychoanalysts moved from purely Oedipal considerations to early infant/human interactions, including those with the mother. Object relation theorists have been accused by some as being apologists for religion (Beit-Hallahmi, 1995). Most are clearly within Dittes' third and fourth conceptual options and their methods are not unrelated to methods discussed latter in this chapter. While the methods of object relation theorists stay within the psychoanalytic hermeneutics of therapeutic transformation, they have produced some contemporary classics in the psychology of religion (Pruyser, 1976; Rizutto, 1979).

Interlude: The Question of the Experiment as Privileged Method

There have been only two reviews of the psychology of religion in the highly influential *Annual review of psychology* series. The first identified and ushered in measurement and correlation as the dominant paradigm in the academic psychology of religion (Gorsuch, 1988). Fifteen years later, the second review of the psychology of religion in the *Annual review of psychology* by Emmons and Paloutzian (2003) focused on experimental, not correlational research. This shift marked in some eyes the heeding of Batson's plea from over a quarter of a century earlier for achieving respect for the psychology of religion (Batson, 1977, 1979). His plea went largely unheard as American psychology of religion was dominated by measurement and correlational research. Achieving respect for the psychology of religion would require courting mainstream methodologies of American psychology. More precisely, a single methodology was then, and for many still is, privileged: the experimental method. Batson's argument was that, if true experimental research was impossible (largely due to violating the requirement of random assignment of subjects), then quasi-experimental research would at least assure the psychology of religion a silver medal and respect in mainstream journals.

In the decade prior to Gorsuch's (1988) identification of a measurement paradigm, Capps, Ransohoff, and Rambo (1976) noted that, out of a total of almost 2,800 articles in the psychology of religion to that date, only 150 were empirical studies. Of these 90% were correlational. Dittes (1985)noted the same dominance of correlational studies in the only review chapter on the psychology of religion to appear in the *Handbook of social psychology* (which has gone through four editions with only the second carrying a chapter on the psychology of religion). This is evidence for the dominance of Gorsuch's (1984) measurement paradigm that some have criticized (Batson, 1977, 1979).

The Emmons and Paluotzian review does not abandon the correlational paradigm nor the measurement paradigm but simply embeds correlational and measurement studies in research methods exhibiting the characteristic of mainstream psychology. Persons trained in experimental research (typically social or personality psychologist) do much of the current empirical research in the American psychology of religion. Not surprisingly then, the theme that dominates the contemporary empirical psychology of religion is for research modeled after what is acceptable to the flagship journal in American social psychology, *The Journal of Personality and Social Psychology* (JPSP).

Emmons and Paloutzian call for a new *multilevel interdisciplinary paradigm* to replace the measurement paradigm (2003, p. 395 emphasis in original). This multilevel interdisciplinary paradigm is accompanied by the assertion of the value of using data at multiple levels of analysis as well as the value of non-reductive assumptions regarding the nature of religious and spiritual phenomena. This suggests the possibility of all levels of Dittes' conceptual options, depending on what and how variables are selected and measured. The call for this new paradigm is echoed again in the *Handbook of the psychology of religion and spirituality* (Park & Paloutzian, 2003).

The history of interdisciplinary paradigms in American psychology suggests that, in terms of methodology, experimental paradigms trump all others. Thus interdisciplinary efforts with a plurality of methods have seldom succeeded. Jones reminds us that Harvard's Department of Social Relations established in 1946 as an interdisciplinary department (clinical psychology, cultural anthropology, sociology, and social psychology) is now but "a concession to nostalgia" (Jones, 1998, p. 4). Other interdisciplinary efforts such as the University of Michigan's Institute for Social Research, as Jones also reminds us, has more to do with funding and space than "intellectual convergence" (1998, p. 4). Stryker (1977) has identified two social psychologies, psychological social psychology (PSP) emphasizing quantitative experimental methods and sociological social psychology (SSP) emphasizing qualitative methods such as symbolic interactionism and ethnomethodology. House (1977) identifies a third SSP that is quantitative but focused on data derived from survey studies rather than experimentation. This would make for four social psychologies if historical studies are also acknowledged (Gergen, 1973).

Efforts to create a specifically interdisciplinary social psychology have as poor history as the interdisciplinary efforts noted above. In one of the most widely adopted social psychology textbooks of the 1960s, a team comprising a psychologist (Paul F. Secord) and a sociologist (Carl W. Backman) tried to create an interdisciplinary social psychology noting that "social psychology can no longer be adequately surveyed by a person trained in only one of its parent disciplines" (Secord & Backman, 1964, p. vii). However, both *Annual Reviews* discussed above attest to the fact that even within social psychology the literatures of one social psychology seldom reference the other. Furthermore, it is worth noting that when the criticisms of laboratory-based research were most intense by sociologically oriented social psychologists (in the decades of the 1960s and 1970s), the percent of experimental studies in JPSP *increased* (Moghadam, Taylor, & Wright, 1993, p. 26). Thus, American psychological social psychology has become a unitary subdiscipline of psychology with a singular ideal methodology, the laboratory experiment. This has occurred despite telling conceptual criticisms of the limits of a laboratory-based psychology and the philosophical assumptions that support it (Belzen & Hood, 2006; Hood & Belzen, 2005). In reviewing the history of social psychology, Gordon W. Allport noted that it had become a subdiscipline of general psychology, just as many today proclaim the psychology of religion to be a subdiscipline of psychology.

However, Allport noted that by defining the laboratory-based experiment as the gold standard what we identify as psychological social psychology has the obvious *disadvantage* that it can seldom generalize beyond the laboratory setting. In Allport's words:

> Even if the experiment is successfully repeated there is no proof that the discovery has wider validity. It is for this reason that some current investigations seem to end up in elegantly polished triviality – snippets of empiricism, but nothing more (Allport, 1985, p. 68).

Allport, widely acknowledged as one of the major early academic psychologist's of religion did not attempt to apply the experimental method to the psychology of religion.

Method 5: The Experimental Paradigm as an Unachievable Ideal

It may seem ironic that we include here as our fifth method a negative exemplar. Psychologically oriented social psychologists applaud the experiment as the single best source of legitimate scientific data. Aronson, Wilson, and Brewer (1998, pp. 118–124) identify four steps to the true experiment: (1) setting the stage for the experiment, (2) constructing an independent variable, (3) measuring the dependent variable, and (4) planning the post-experimental follow-up. Included in the follow-up is a concern that the "cover story" of the experiment was accepted by the participant since many experiments utilize deception. Deception, while guided by APA ethical codes and University IRB boards, nevertheless raises serious ethical issues (Kelman, 1967, 1968). Laboratory social psychology is almost totally deception based, and this as we will note became a concern in laboratory-based dissonance research. When deception is extended to field work it arguably raises even more serious ethical issues. Richardson (1991) has noted this with respect to a classic field study in the psychology of religion, When prophecy fails (Festinger, Riecken, & Schachter, 1956), and Hood (1995) has raised similar concerns with Dennis Covington's Salvation on sand mountain (Covington, 1995) dealing with deceptive participatory research with the contemporary serpent handlers of Appalachia. Likewise, Jones (1998) noted that ethical concerns with increasingly deceptive laboratory experiments attempting to induce cognitive dissonance was a factor in the eventual waning of interest in laboratory studies. Ironically, Festinger acknowledged that the type of laboratory research that he and his colleagues did in the "good old days" would be unlikely to be allowed today (Festinger, 1999, p. 384). As he succinctly states the case, "I don't know how we would have gotten anything through ethics committees" (Festinger, 1999, pp. 384–385).

Method 6: Quasi-Experimental Studies

Batson in seeking respect for the psychology of religion noted, "Although an experimental psychology of religion does not exist; one seems badly needed" (Batson, 1977, p. 41). However, he recognized that a true experimental design requires random assignment of participants to experimental and control conditions. This is not possible using religious variables, if for no other than ethical reasons. However, this is not unique to the psychology of religion. In his presidential address to the APA, Campbell (1975) noted that in some areas we are "unable to experiment" (p. 1193). However, if one is precluded from random assignment of participants to groups, one can still do quasi-experimental designs (Campbell & Stanley, 1966; Deconchy, 1985). Quasi-experimental designs can be done both in the laboratory and the field, fulfilling most of the requirements of internal validity regarded as the "sine qua non of good experimental research" (Aronson et al., 1998, p. 129). Criticisms that experimental and quasi-experimental designs often lack external validity (the ability to generalize to the non-experimental settings) are no longer prominent among psychologically oriented social psychologists, but are often raised by sociologically oriented social psychologists whose research occurs in a real world context. As laboratory-oriented experiments confront "realism" there is a radical shift in the meaning of the term.

Aronson and his colleagues have taken the lead in identifying three basic kinds of realism, all of which we subsume under the term *contextual realism*: mundane, experimental, and psychological realism. Mundane realism is the extent to which the experimental task is similar to the one that occurs in everyday life, while experimental realism is the extent to which participants take the experiment seriously (Aronson & Carlsmith, 1968). Psychological realism is the extent to which the processes that occur in the experimental situation are the same as those that occur in everyday life (Aronson, Wilson, & Akert, 1994). Contextual realism is equally relevant to both experimental and quasi-experimental designs. These realisms operate in quasi-experimental designs in research on the psychology of religion. For those with a more positivistic orientation to psychology they provide the best evidential base for establishing causal determinants of religious phenomenon viewed as dependent variables. While there are numerous examples of quasi-experimental research in the psychology of religion (Hood, Hill, & Spilka, 2009), we will focus on one area where the research is now state of the art and yet the area of investigation is not without controversy: the use of chemicals to facilitate mystical experience.

The first and most widely cited study of the uses of entheogens to facilitate mystical experience is a doctoral dissertation by Pahnke (1966). It has become widely known as the "Good Friday" experiment as 20 graduate students at Andover-Newton Theological Seminary met to hear a Good Friday service after they had been given either psilocybin (a known entheogen) or a placebo control (nicotinic acid). Participants meet in groups of four, with two experimental and two controls, all matched for compatibility. Each group had two leaders, one who had been given psilocybin. Immediately after the service and 6 months later the participants were assessed on a questionnaire that included all of Stace's common core criteria of mysticism. Results were impressive in that the experimental participants scored high on all of Stace's common core criteria while the controls did not.

In what is also a widely quoted study, Doblin (1991) followed the adventures of the original Good Friday participants. He was able to locate and interview nine of the participants in original experimental group and seven of the participants in the original control group. He also administered Pahnke's original questionnaire, including Stace's common core criteria of mysticism. In most cases, comparison of Doblin's result with both of Pahnke's results (immediately after the service and 6 months later) reported that participants in the experimental group showed *increases* on most of Stace's common core criteria of mysticism after almost a quarter of a century. Despite serious critiques of the Good Friday study (Doblin, 1991; Nichols & Chemel, 2006, pp. 10–11), it has until recently been the most significant study attempting to facilitate mystical experience in a religious setting.

The benchmark study in the tradition of the Good Friday experiment is the recent study by Griffiths, Richards, McCann, and Jesse (2006). They replicated Pahnke's original experiment with individual rather than groups sessions, using a more rigorous experimental control, a more appropriate placebo (methylphenidate hydrochloride). The double blind study was effective at two levels: first, the double blind was not broken in what is a very sophisticated between group crossover design that involved two or three 8-h drug sessions conducted at 2-month intervals. While the complexity of the research design need not concern us here, suffice it to say that of 30 adult volunteers, half received either the entheogen first, followed by the placebo control; half the placebo control first, followed by the entheogen. Six additional volunteers received the placebo in the first two sessions and unblinded psilocybin in the third session. This was to obscure the study design and protect the double blind. Unlike the Good Friday experiment, the double blind in this John Hopkins study was successful (Griffiths et al., 2006, p. 274).

While the Good Friday participants took psilocybin in a specifically religious setting, volunteers in the John Hopkins study had all session in an aesthetically pleasant living room like setting. While the volunteers had spiritual interests the setting itself did not contain religious artifacts or cues. All session were monitored by an experienced male guide who had extensive experience with entheogens. However, unlike the Good Friday experiment, the experienced male guide nor a companion female guide took psilocybin while serving as guides. Second, numerous measures and observations were involved in this study, including Pahnke's original questionnaire and Hood's *Mysticism Scale*. Results indicated that the experimental controls had higher mysticism scores than the active placebo controls. Further, in a follow-up study, only scores as measured by Hood's M-Scale predicted meaningfulness of the experience, judged by all experimentals as to be one of, if not, the most significant experience in their life (Griffiths, Richards, Johnson, McCann, & Jesse, 2008).

Method 7: Neurophysiological Measures

Closely related to entheogens being used to facilitate religious experience are studies employing new technologies to identify neurological processes that occur during spiritual and religious experiences. Many of these are advancements over previous nuerophysiological methods. All neurophysiological studies essentially use the older correlational paradigm, but correlate a given experiential state with ongoing neurological processes. Among the functional neuroimaging techniques are single photon emission tomography (SPECT), positive emission tomography (PET), and functional magnetic resonance (fMRI). These procedures vary in how they assess glucose and oxygen consumption in the brain. What is crucial is that these techniques are relatively non-invasive and can allow researchers to determine which areas of the brain are active when individuals are in various spiritual or religious states. The correlation of brain activity with specific religious and spiritual states is best viewed as merely correlational, not causal (Azari, 2006, pp. 34–35). Functional magnetic imaging can be used in quasi-experimental studies to facilitate religious and spiritual experiences by activating relevant brain areas thought to be involved in such experiences (see McNamara, 2006, for reviews). As with our discussion of research employing entheogens, research employing neuroimaging techniques indicates that psychology of religion can use quasi-experimental methods and advanced technologies to develop research programs in the psychology of religion and spirituality that are as rigorous as any in mainstream psychology. However, there are voices cautioning against this as an ideal or preferred method. Hood & Belzen (2005) have provided and suggested yet another paradigm for the psychology of religion, one that is hermeneutically based. Under this broad umbrella we can cite several other methods used in studying religion and spirituality.

Method 8: Ethnography, Participant Observation and Field Research

While there are various approaches to field and participant observation research in the psychology of religion we can note one major distinction. Field research occurs in a natural as opposed to a laboratory setting. The difference does not, however, mean that measurement or quasi-experimental studies cannot occur in these settings. For instance, in two separate studies Hood (1977, 1978) measured anticipatory set stress and assessed actual setting stress in a program that required students to spend a week in various activities from canoeing to a night alone without shelter other than a tarp. In addition, since on some days it stormed and other it did not, Hood was able to use this naturally occurring difference to test variations in setting stress that were planned (canoe versus solo night alone) and simply occurred (solo during storm versus solo without storm). The thesis that setting/set stress incongruities facilitates mystical experience was supported. Mystical experience was measured after each activity in the natural setting.

Ethnography overlaps considerably with participant observation research. Ethnographers are more committed to "thick" descriptions of phenomena from many points of view of the various participants. An example is Poloma's and Hood's 4-year study of an emerging Pentecostal church dealing with the poor in the inner city of a major American city in the deep south (Poloma & Hood, 1908). Similar to field and ethnographic research is participant observation research. This research tends to be less detailed in its descriptions but like ethnography it occurs in a natural setting. Both participant observation and ethnographic research differ from field research in that the investigator participates and observes the participants he or she is studying. Importantly, participant observation research often yields diametrically opposite results to laboratory-based research on the same topic. For instance, studies of failed prophecy employing Festinger's theory of cognitive dissonance are often supported by laboratory-based studies, but not by participant observation studies (Hood & Belzen, 2005).

Participant observation and ethnographic studies are especially useful when investigators wish to understand rather than explain religious phenomena and practices. Recent examples in the psychology of religion are Belzen's (1999) participant observation research on the "bevindelijken" and Hood and Williamson's (2008) study of the contemporary Christian serpent handlers of Appalachia.

Method 9: Phenomenological Research

Phenomenological research is another in the hermeneutical tradition broadly conceived. It seeks to describe the appearance of phenomena to participants. There are variations in precisely how investigators utilize phenomenological methods, but what is significant for the study of religion and spirituality is that judgments as to the ontological status of objects experienced are not made. This has led to significant studies of phenomena long associated with spirituality such as near-death experiences, out-of-body experiences, and psi or parapsychological experiences (see Cardeña, Lynn, & Krippner, 2000). The bracketing of ontological claims allows psychologists to study the condition under which such experiences occur as well as to describe their significance and meaning to those who have them. This has led phenomenological researchers to identify set and setting effects that influence the report of religious and spiritual experiences. Set effects include the state of the participant just prior to the experience. The two most studied set effects are mood and expectation. Setting effects refer to the location of the experience. Setting effects can be separated into proximate and distal. Proximate setting includes the immediate location and interpersonal environment where the experience occurs. Distal setting expands to include the historical period and culture within which experiences are encouraged or discouraged. Thus, phenomenological methods have merged for some into cultural psychology which seeks to understand religious phenomena in their historical and cultural context (Belzen, 1999; Belzen & Hood, 2006; Gergen, 1973).

Method 10: Confessional Research

As a final method of research in religion and spirituality, reference must be made to what can be identified as confessional investigators. By confessional we identify researchers who explicitly identify their own religious convictions as part of their investigative process. Porpora (2006) has noted that a methodological agnosticism is more adequate to the study of religious and spiritual phenomena than methodological atheism assumed by those who wish to restrict the social sciences to natural science methods. Agnosticism allows religious phenomena to reveal themselves, perhaps more so to investigators sensitized to them by their own participatory faith commitments. Examples including Poloma's (2003) own acknowledge Pentecostal commitment and how it facilitated her participatory observation study of the Toronto Blessing. Another example is provided by the confessional scholars of mysticism who have used their own experiences to affirm that mystical experiences occur and that, among what appear to be different descriptions of mystical experiences, an underlying commonality nevertheless exists (Barnard, 1997; Forman, 1999). Confessional methodologists applaud the value of returning psychology to the researcher as a subject that characterized psychological research at its inception as a laboratory science (Danziger, 1994). They also tend to support Dittes' conceptual option asserting that there are religious variables that uniquely interact with psychological variables such that religion cannot be explained by reductionistic theories. They also assert that some religious variables are unique, such that part of the sense of God may indeed come from God (Bowker, 1973; Porpora, 2006; Smith, 2003). The psychology of religion and spirituality in America is beginning to be dominated by confessional research due to the influence of The John Templeton Foundation. With over 1 billion dollars in assets this foundation gives out roughly 60 million dollars annually (www.templeton.org). The shifting to research in the psychology of religion and spirituality by those with a confessional stance has been criticized by Wulff (2003). However, the history of the psychology of religion in America has always been driven by powerful interests and individuals who often had either confessional or antagonistic stances toward religion (Hood, 2000). This issue is not whether one takes a confessional stance or not, but simply the quality of the research done.

Summary and Conclusion

We have far from exhausted the methods available to psychologist who study religion and spirituality. However, it is our position that the psychology of religion is not well served by an appeal to a single method. The choice of a method is dependent on what question is being asked. All four conceptual options proposed by Dittes are relevant to the psychology of religion. If this is accepted, then our appeal to an additive approach is more than appropriate. One can derive measurement from conceptual criteria established by other methods, such as Hood (1975) did operationalizating of Stace's (1961) phenomenologically derived common core of mysticism or as Francis and Louden (2000) did with operationalizing Happold's (1963) seven criteria of mysticism. In both cases, factor analyses confirmed the metric validity of the classifications. Thus phenomenology and measurement are used to complement one another.

Especially relevant cases are when different methods lead to contradictory results (Hood & Belzen, 2005). It may be that the mundane realism of laboratory settings is too controlled to allow more complex interactions that characterize life outside the laboratory. Hence, the precision and control of laboratory studies may be of limited usefulness when the questions are of a broader cultural concern, as they often are in religious studies where field research and participant observation may be more veridical to what is actually the case. The elicitation of mystical experiences under quasi-experimental conditions still must be explored in terms of longitudinal research designed to examine what people, who have these experiences, actually do in terms of their own religious and spiritual development as they live their lives out in particular cultural contexts.

Finally, if phenomenological methods bracket ontological claims, they serve to remind us that religious and spiritual experiences are interesting in their own right and deserving of a thick description. They are contrasted to confessional methods primarily on the basis of ontological claims. Confessional methods provide the intriguing option that what psychologists study may be real. The old sociological dictum that things believed to be true are true in their consequences is perhaps but a partial truth. Methodological agnosticism acknowledges that what confessional methods claim might also be not simply consequentially true, but true.

References

Allport, G. W. (1985).The historical background of social psychology. In G. Lindzey & E. Aronson (Eds.), *The handbook of social psychology* (2nd ed., Vol. 1, pp. 1–46). Reading, MA: Addison-Wesley.
Allport, G. W., & Ross, J. M. (1967). Personal religious orientation and prejudice. *Journal of Personality and Social Psychology, 5*, 432–443.
Aronson, E., & Carlsmith, J. M. (1968). Experimentation in social psychology. In G. Lindzey & E. Aronson (Eds.), *The handbook of social psychology* (Vol. 2, pp. 1–79). Reading, MA: Addison-Wesley.
Aronson, E., Wilson, T. D., & Akert, R. M. (1994). *Social psychology: The heart and the mind.* New York: HarperCollins.
Aronson, E., Wilson, T. D., & Brewer, M. B. (1998). Experimentation in social psychology. In D. T. Gilbert, S. T. Fiske, & G. Lindzey, G. (Eds.), *The handbook of social psychology* (Vol. 1, pp. 99–142). New York: Oxford University Press.
Azari, N. P. (2006). Neuroimaging studies of religious experience: A critical review. In P. McNamara (Ed.), *Where God and science meet* (Vol. 2, pp. 33–54). Westport, CT: Praeger.
Barnard, G. W. (1997). *Exploring unseen worlds: William James and the philosophy of mysticism.* Albany, New York: State University of New York Press.
Batson, C. D. (1977). Experimentation in psychology of religion: An impossible dream? *Journal for the Scientific Study of Religion, 16*, 413–418.
Batson, C. D. (1979). Experimentation in the psychology of religion: Living with or in a dream? *Journal for the Scientific Study of Religion, 18*, 90–93.
Beit-Hallahmi, B. (1995). Object relations theory and religious experience. In R. W. Hood, Jr. (Ed.), *Handbook of religious experience* (pp. 254–268). Birmingham, AL: Religious Education Press.
Belzen, J. A. (1999). Religion as embodiment. Cultural-psychological concepts and methods in the study of conversion among the "bevindelijken." *Journal for the Scientific Study of Religion, 38*, 236–253.
Belzen, J. A., & Hood, R. W., Jr. (2006). Methodological issues in the psychology of religion: Toward another paradigm? *Journal of Psychology, 140*, 5–28.
Bowker, J. (1973). *The sense of God: Sociological, anthropological, and psychological approaches to the origin of the sense of God.* Oxford: Clarendon Press.

Campbell, D. T. (1975). On the conflicts between biological and social evolution and moral tradition. *American Psychologist, 30,* 1103–1126.
Campbell, D. T., & Stanley, J. C. (1966). *Experimental and quasi-experimental designs for research.* Chicago: Rand McNally.
Capps, D., Ransohoff, R., & Rambo, L. (1976). Publication trends in the psychology of religion to 1974. *Journal for the Scientific Study of Religion, 15,* 15–28.
Cardeña, E., Lynn, S. J., & Krippner, S. (Eds.). (2000). *Varieties of anomalous experience.* Washington, DC: American Psychological Association.
Covington, D. (1995). *Salvation on sand mountain: Snake handling and redemption in Southern Appalachia.* New York: Penguin.
Danziger, K. (1994). *Constructing the subject: Historical origins of psychological research.* Cambridge: Cambridge University Press.
Davis, J. A., & Smith, T. W. (1994). *General social surveys, 1972–1994* [Machine-readable data file]. Chicago: National Opinion Research Center [Producer]; Storrs: Roper Center for Public Opinion Research, University of Connecticut [Distributor].
Deconchy, J.-P. (1985). Non-experimental and experimental methods in the psychology of religion: A few thoughts on their implication and limits. In L. B. Brown (Ed.), *Advances in the psychology of religion* (pp. 76–112). Oxford: Pergamon Press.
Dittes, J. E. (1969). The Psychology of religion. In G. Lindzey & E. Aronson (Eds.), *The handbook of social psychology* (Vol. 5, pp. 602–659). Reading, MA: Addison-Wesley.
Dittes, J. E. (1985). Psychology of religion. In G. Lindzey & E. Aronson (Eds.), *The handbook of social psychology* (2nd ed., Vol. 5, pp. 601–659). Reading, MA: Addison-Wesley.
Doblin, R. (1991). Pahnke's "Good Friday" experiment: A long-term follow-up and methodological critique. *Journal of Transpersonal Psychology, 23,* 1–28.
Doblin, R. (1991). Pahnke's "Good Friday" experiment: A long-term follow-up and methodological critique. *Journal of Transpersonal Psychology, 23,* 1–28.
Donahue, M. J. (1985). Intrinsic and extrinsic religiousness: Review and meta-analysis. *Journal of Personality and Social Psychology, 48,* 400–419.
Emmons, R. A., & Paloutzian, R. F. (2003). The psychology of religion. *Annual Review of Psychology, 54,* 377–402.
Festinger, L. (1999). Appendix A. Social communication and cognition: A very preliminary and highly tentative draft. In E. H. Jones & J. Mills (Eds.), *Cognitive dissonance: Progress on a pivotal theory in social psychology* (pp. 355–379). Washington, D.C.: American Psychological Association.
Festinger, L., Riecken, H. W., & Schachter, S. (1956). *When prophecy fails.* Minneapolis, MN: University of Minnesota Press.
Forman, R. K. C. (1999). *Mysticism, mind, consciousness.* Albany, New York: State University of New York Press.
Francis, L. J., & Louden, S. H. (2000). The Francis-Louden mystical orientation scale (MOS): A study among Roman Catholic priests. *Research in the Social Scientific Study of Religion, 11,* 99–116.
Gergen, K. (1973). Social psychology as history. *Journal of Personality and Social Psychology, 26,* 309–320.
Glock, C. Y., & Stark, R. (1965). *Religion and society in tension.* Chicago: Rand McNally.
Gorsuch, R. L. (1984). Measurement: The boon and bane of investigating the psychology of religion. *American psychologist, 39,* 228–236.
Gorsuch, R. L. (1988). The psychology of religion. *The Annual Review of Psychology, 31,* 201–221.
Greeley, A. M. (1974). *Ecstasy: A way of knowing.* Englewood Cliffs, NJ: Prentice-Hall.
Greeley, A. M. (1975). Sociology of the paranormal: A reconnaissance. *Sage research papers in the social sciences* (Vol. 3, No. 90–023). Beverly Hills, CA: Sage.
Griffiths, R. R., Richards, W. A., Johnson, M. W., McCann, U. D., & Jesse, R. (2008). Mystical-type experiences occasioned by psilocybin mediate the attribution of personal meaning and spiritual significance 14 months later. *Journal of Psychopharmacology, 22,* 621–632.

Griffiths, R. R., Richards, W. A., McCann, U. D., & Jesse, R. (2006). Psilocybin can occasion mystical experiences having substantial and sustained personal meaning and spiritual significance. *Psychopharmacology, 187*, 268–283.

Halligan, F. R. (1995). Jungian theory and religious experience. In R. W. Hood, Jr. (Ed.), *Handbook of religious experience* (pp. 231–253). Birmingham, AL: Religious Education Press.

Happold, F. C. (1963). *Mytsticism: A study and an anthology.* New York: Penguin.

Hardy, A. (1979). *The spiritual nature of man: A study of contemporary religious experience.* Oxford: Clarendon Press.

Hay, D., & Morisy, A. (1978). Reports of ecstatic, paranormal, or religious experience in Great Britain and the United States: A comparison of trends. *Journal for the Scientific Study of Religion, 17*, 255–268.

Hill, P., & Hood, R. W., Jr. (1999). *Measures of religiosity.* Birmingham, AL: Religious Education Press.

Hood, R. W., Jr. (1975). The construction and preliminary validation of a measure of reported mystical experience. *Journal for the Scientific Study of Religion, 14*, 29–41.

Hood, R. W., Jr. (1977). Eliciting mystical states of consciousness with semi-structured nature experiences. *Journal for the Scientific Study of Re*ligion, *16*, 155–163.

Hood, R. W., Jr. (1978). Anticipatory set and setting stress incongruities as elicitors of mystical experiences in solitary nature settings. *Journal for the Scientific Study, 17*, 279–287.

Hood, R. W., Jr. (1992). Mysticism, reality, illusion and the Freudian critique of religion. *The International Journal for the Psychology of Religion, 2*, 141–159.

Hood, R. W., Jr. (1995). (Review) Salvation on sand mountain: Snake handling and redemption in Southern Appalachia. *Appalachian heritage* (Summer, pp. 54–56). Reading, MA: Addison-Wesley.

Hood, R. W., Jr. (2000). American psychology of religion and the journal for the scientific study of religion. *Journal for the Scientific Study of Religion, 39*, 531–544.

Hood, R. W., Jr., & Belzen, J. A. (2005). Research methods in the psychology of religion. In R. Paloutzian & C. Parks (Eds.), *The handbook of religion and spirituality* (pp. 61–79). New York: Guilford.

Hood, R. W., Jr., Hill, P. C., & Spilka, B. (2009). *The psychology of religion: An empirical approach,* 4th ed. New York: Guilford.

Hood, R. W., Jr., & Williamson, W. P. (2008). *Contemporary Christian serpent handlers.* Berkeley, CA: University of California Press.

House, J. (1977). The three faces of social psychology. *Sociometry, 40*, 161–177.

James, W. (1902/1985). *The varieties of religious experience.* Cambridge, MA: Harvard University Press.

Jones, E. E. (1998). Major developments in five decades of social psychology. In D. T. Gilbert, S. T. Fiske, & G. Lindzey, G. (Eds.), *The handbook of social psychology* (4th ed., Vol. 1, pp. 3–47). Boston, MA: McGraw-Hill.

Kelman, H. C. (1967). Human use of human subjects: The problem of deception in social psychological experiments. *Psychological Bulletin, 67*, 1–11.

Kelman, H. C. (1968). *A time to speak.* San Francisco: Josey-Bass.

Kirkpatrick, L. A., & Hood, R. W., Jr. (1990). Intrinsic-extrinsic religious orientation: The boon or the bane of contemporary psychology of religion. *Journal for the Scientific Study of Re*ligion, *29*, 442–462.

Kohls, N., Hack, A., & Walach, H. (2008). Measuring the unmeasurable by ticking boxes and opening Pandora's box? Mixed methods research as a useful tool for investigating exceptional and spiritual experiences. *Archiv für Religionspsychologie, 30*, 155–187.

McNamara, P. (Ed.). (2006). *The neurology of religious experience.* In P. McNamara (Ed.), *Where God and science meet* (Vol. 2, pp. 33–54). Westport, CT: Praeger.

Moghadam, F. M., Taylor, D. M., & Wright, S. C. (1993). *Social psychology in cross-cultural perspective.* New York: W. H. Freeman.

Nichlos, D. E., & Chemel, B. R. (2006). The neuropharmacology of religious experience: Hallucinogens and the experience of the divine. In P. McNamara (Ed.), *Where God and science meet* (Vol. 3, pp. 1–34). Westport, CT: Praeger.

Pahnke, W. N. (1966). Drugs and mysticism. *International Journal of Parapsychology, 8*, 295–320.

Park, C., & Paloutzian, R. (2003). One step toward integration and an expansive future. In R. Paloutzian & C. Parks (Eds.), *Handbook of the psychology of religion and spirituality* (pp. 550–564). New York: The McGraw-Hill.

Poloma, M. M. (2003). *Main street mystics: The Toronto blessing and reviving Pentecostalism.* Walnut Creek, CA: Alta Mira Press.

Poloma, M. M., & Hood, R. W., Jr. (1908). *Blood and fire: Godly love in a Pentecostal emerging church.* Rochester, NY: New York University Press.

Porpora, D. V. (2006). Methodological atheism, methodological agnosticism and religious experience. *Journal for the Theory of Social Behavior, 36*, 57–75.

Pruyser, P. (1976). *A dynamic psychology of religion.* New York: Harper & Row.

Richardson, J. T. (1991). Experiencing research on new religions and cults. In W. Swatos & R. Stebbins (Eds.), *Experiencing fieldwork* (pp. 62–71). Newbury Park: Sage.

Rizutto, A. M. (1979). *The birth of the living god.* Chicago: University of Chicago Press.

Sears, D. (1986). College sophomores in the laboratory: Influence of a narrow data base on social psychology's view of human nature. *Journal of Personality and Social Psychology, 51*, 515–530.

Secord, P. F. & Backman, C. W. (1964). *Social psychology.* New York: McGraw-Hill.

Smith, C. (Ed.). (2003). *The secular revolution: Power, interests, and conflict in the secularization of American public life.* Berkeley, CA: University of California Press.

Stace, W. T. (1961). *Mysticism and philosophy.* Philadelphia: Lippincott.

Starbuck, E. D. (1899). *The psychology of religion: An empirical study of the growth of religious consciousness.* New York: Charles Scribmner's Sons.

Stryker, S. (1977). Development in "two social psychologies": Toward an appreciation of mutual relevance. *Sociometry, 40*, 145–160.

Tamminen, K. (1991). *Religious development in childhood and youth: An empirical study.* Helsinki: Suomalainen Tiedeakatemia.

Vernon, G. M. (1968). The religious "nones": A neglected category. *Journal for the Scientific Study of Religion, 7*, 219–229.

Wulff, D. M. (2003). A field in crisis. Is it time to start over? In H. M. Poelofsma, J. M. Corveleyn, & J. W. van Sane (Eds.), *One hundred years of the psychology of religion* (pp. 11–32). Amsterdam: VU University Press.

Yamane, D., & Polzer, M. (1994). Ways of seeing ecstasy in modern society: Experimental-expressive and cultural-linguistic views. *Sociology of Religion, 55*, 1–25.

Chapter 2
Measuring Religiousness and Spirituality: Issues, Existing Measures, and the Implications for Education and Wellbeing

Peter C. Hill and Lauren E. Maltby

Abstract This chapter consists of three major parts. The first part discusses general issues related to measurement in the psychology of religion. The second part reviews major measures of religiousness and spirituality by general religious and spiritual domain, concentrating on those areas and measures that have been (or might be) associated with educational processes and outcomes as well as general wellbeing. Only those measures judged to meet adequately acceptable standards for research purposes on the following criteria are discussed: theoretical basis, representative sampling and generalization, reliability, and validity. The final section talks about new developments in the measurement of religion and spirituality and alternatives to self-report or paper-and-pencil measures and offers guidance in choosing a measure for research in education and wellbeing.

In 1770, Pieter Camper, a Dutch scholar and one of the first proponents of craniometry, invented the concept of the "facial angle" as a way to measure intelligence among various races. A "facial angle" was formed by drawing two lines—one horizontally from the nostril to the ear and another perpendicularly from the upper jawbone to the forehead. Camper maintained that the closer the angle of the lines was to 90°, the more intelligent a person was. He claimed that Europeans consistently had angles of 80°, Africans of 70°, and orangutans of 58°. Samuel George Morton extended Camper's work by using cranial capacity (the volume of the interior of the skull) as a measure of intelligence. He, too, concluded that European Americans were the most intelligent, followed by African-Americans and Native Americans. These "scientific" findings were used to perpetuate racial stereotypes and justify racist practices for decades.

Clearly, measurement matters. As the means by which one tests a hypothesis or an idea, measurement is often the bridge between theory and practice; it not only allows us to test our conceptual framework and assumptions, but often does so in various practical and applied settings. How a particular concept is defined and measured significantly impacts understandings of the world, and influences not

P.C. Hill (✉)
Rosemead School of Psychology, Biola University, La Mirada, CA 90639, USA
e-mail: peter.hill@biola.edu

only subsequent research questions, but also the answers found in relation to those questions. This is especially true in a field such as the psychology of religion, which in essence looks at the measurable effects of such abstract experiences as religion and spirituality (RS).

If, indeed, interest in and attention to measurement is a sign of a field's scientific development (see Hill, 2005), then the psychology of religion has achieved some degree of maturity, though not without the experience of growing pains. It is now a quarter century since Gorsuch (1984) claimed that the dominant paradigm in psychology of religion was then one of measurement. Although near obsession with measurement by RS researchers meant that there existed a measure for virtually any RS research question, it also led to a proliferation of scales, some of which certainly overlap conceptually. Gorsuch (1990) later suggested that new scales should not be established unless (a) existing measures are not psychometrically sound; (b) new conceptual or theoretical advances require changes to current measures; (c) a measure is needed for use with a new population; or (d) a new construct needs to be measured. Hill (2005) also dissuaded researchers from constructing unnecessary new scales and suggested modifying current measures to adapt to new needs if at all possible. That being said, as the psychology of religion grows and is applied to an ever increasing set of questions and to more heterogenous RS populations, we should expect some continued development of new scales. To be sure, any inability of the field to move forward will *not* be due to a lack of attention to issues of measurement.

By 2003, Emmons and Paloutzian suggested that the psychology of religion was operating by a *multilevel interdisciplinary paradigm* that "recognizes the value of data at multiple levels of analysis while making non-reductive assumptions concerning the value of spiritual and religious phenomena" (p. 395). Some (e.g., Belzen & Hood, 2006), it should be noted, have questioned whether the psychology of religion is, in fact, operating by an interdisciplinary paradigm. At the very least, it can be argued that the substantial increase in recent years of various publications (such as this volume) suggests that the application of RS research to various domains is gaining momentum. For the implications of RS research to such applied domains, such as education and wellbeing, to be fully realized, issues of measurement must be seriously considered. To this end, this chapter will first discuss general issues to be considered in relation to measurement of RS variables, then review some existing RS scales, and finally discuss the application of measurement in psychology of religion to education and wellbeing.

General Issues Related to Measurement

Although researchers with applied interest in RS variables may choose to use any of the measures reviewed in this chapter, as they all represent "good" (or good enough) measures, any educator knows that this is only a temporary solution. As the old maxim goes, *give a man a fish and you've fed him for a day; teach a man to fish and you've fed him for life*. And so the more important question than "which measures are good measures?" is "what makes a measure good?" There are three major issues with which all measures must interact. Their successful navigation of these issues is what makes them "good."

Theoretical Considerations

Without conceptual clarity about what one is measuring, the significance of one's findings is severely constrained. Although the 1980s and the 1990s saw a continued proliferation of RS measures, a conceptual or theoretical focus to provide a coherence and unity to the field was often missing. During the measurement paradigm, the pull toward establishing a strong empirical framework often led to measures that, while psychometrically sound, were lacking a clear theoretical grounding. As a result, there are many empirical findings that lack the theoretical coherence necessary for real scientific progress. For example, the most dominant theoretical framework of psychology of religion has no doubt been Allport's (1950) distinction between intrinsic and extrinsic religious orientation. Although it was promising, systematic research did not further elucidate these orientations, and by 1990, Kirkpatrick and Hood claimed that the model was "theoretically impoverished and has really taught us little about the psychology of religion" (p. 442), largely because the intrinsic–extrinsic framework had become enmeshed in psychometric issues with little, if any, theoretical guidance.

Without well-defined conceptual frameworks, systematic, top-down research programs are difficult to maintain. As a result issues of scale validity are difficult to assess, and there is almost a complete absence of normative data for many scales.[1] However, as the field matures, we are beginning to see notable exceptions, where systematic programs of research are emerging: religious questing (see Batson, Schoenrade, & Ventis, 1993), mysticism (see Hood, 1975, 1995, 1997), religious coping (see Pargament, 1997), forgiveness (see Worthington, Berry, & Parrott, 2001), and attachment processes (see Granqvist & Kirkpatrick, 2004). The strong theoretical base of such systematic research programs will yield measures used with greater frequency across a broader population range.

When choosing an RS measure, theoretical clarity cannot be emphasized enough. No one scale will be the most appropriate for every study, and it is important that the concept which the researcher intends to study is well represented in the measure. Of course one can only be certain that this is the case if the scale itself and the research to which the scale is applied, were both designed from clear, conceptual frameworks. Thus, when choosing a measure, theoretical clarity is essential.

Psychometric Considerations

If theoretical considerations seem broad and abstract, the additional psychometric considerations that a scale must address are at the other end of the spectrum. The two most important psychometric considerations are that of validity and reliability.

Validity refers to whether a scale is measuring the thing it is trying to measure. A careful read-through of the scale's items should give you some idea of what the scale is measuring, and this is referred to as *face validity*. However, this is not an objective or empirical form of validating a scale and therefore not as useful as other types of validity. For instance, *convergent validity* refers to the extent to which a given scale is correlated with measures of similar or related construction. For example, one would expect religious identification to correlate with what type of religious institution one attends. Hand in hand with convergent validity is *discriminant validity*. This is the degree to which a given scale is not correlated with measures of constructs that it should not, in theory, be similar to. Two other important types of validity are *criterion* and *content*. The former refers to the correlation between a given scale and some other standard or measure of the construct of interest. The latter, content validity, refers to the degree to which a given scale includes all the facets of the construct under investigation. For example, if one wanted to measure spiritual practices, but only asked questions about prayer and attendance at religious services, one would have neglected other spiritual practices such as reading a holy text, giving alms, etc. A validity concern unique to RS scales pertains to construct validity. Because RS correlates highly with other constructs (such as physical and mental health; Koenig, McCullough, & Larson, 2001), it is important to establish RS construct validity in order to avoid faulty conclusions.

Consideration of *reliability*, or the extent to which a scale is consistent, is also important. Ideally, a scale should be both *internally consistent* and *consistent across time*, though typically the reliability of a scale is measured by only one of these two criteria. Internal consistency refers to the degree to which all of the items on the scale are measuring the same thing. It is measured by the statistic Cronbach's alpha, and can have a value ranging from zero to one; the higher the value the more internally consistent. Additionally, scales should ideally be consistent across time. This is referred to as *test–retest reliability*, and is generally measured by the correlation coefficient between individual's scores on the same test given on separate occasions (the time elapsed between testing can range from 2 weeks to 6 months; Hill, 2005). For practical reasons, Cronbach's alpha is used much more frequently than test–retest reliability when establishing the reliability of a scale.

Sample Representativeness and Cultural Sensitivity

The proliferation of measures in RS research has not protected the psychology of religion from one of measurement's most baleful banes: unrepresentative samples. Although psychology of religion has amassed quite an impressive amount of information throughout its development, perhaps there is no group we know more about than young, middle class, American (and to a lesser extent British) college students (Hill & Pargament, 2003). Such *convenience samples*, so called because they are easily accessible for study purposes at academic institutions, are highly problematic since age, SES, and education are three variables quite strongly correlated with religious experience (Hill, 2005). Therefore the unrepresentative sample upon which a large number of measures have been validated may fail to represent accurately the population at large with which the measures are eventually used. Age and education are not the only two variables biasing samples, however. Most RS research and measuring instruments have, until recently, assumed a Judeo-Christian context, with a disproportionate focus on White Protestants (Gorsuch, 1988; Hill, 2005; Hill & Hood, 1999). Caution is necessary should one choose to use such a scale for a population with a different demographic or outside the Judeo-Christian context.

Scales created on the basis of either unrepresentative samples or samples representing a narrow population (e.g., a single denomination) are usually insensitive or inapplicable to broader groups. Furthermore, RS scales are certainly not exempt from a lack of cultural sensitivity (Chatters, Taylor, & Lincoln, 2002). For example, Protestant African Americans emphasize community service (Ellison & Taylor, 1996) as well as the notion of reciprocal blessings with God (Black, 1999), both of which are often overlooked in traditional measures of Protestantism in favor of other issues that may even be irrelevant in these religious communities.

The difficulty of generalizing scales to other groups is not only a problem when measuring tradition-specific constructs within a religious group (such as Protestantism), or when using scales in the United States or Great Britain. Many RS scales, although purporting to measure a trans-religious construct, are culturally insensitive and do not generalize well to other cultures and religious traditions outside of that with which it was first created. For example, Hill and Dwiwardani (in press) have chronicled their difficulty in applying the widely used Religious Orientation Scale (ROS; Allport & Ross, 1967) with an Indonesian Muslim population. In order to make the scale applicable, more than just the language of the scale needed to change (e.g., changing church to mosque). Because Islam is such a strong pillar in the overall collectivistic culture in Indonesia, the concept itself of extrinsic-social religious orientation was not as applicable to Muslims as to Christians. However, careful research has yielded the Muslim–Christian Religious Orientation Scale (MCROS; Ghorbani, Watson, Ghramaleki, Morris, & Hood, 2002), with which researchers demonstrated "incremental validity of their new ... [s]cale (MCROS) beyond the Allport and Ross's (1967) ROS when the extrinsic social dimension was measured in relation to the broader community and culture rather than to the mosque" (Hill & Dwiwardani, in press). RS research must continue to move in this direction in order to create measures that can be utilized in more applied and diverse settings than has traditionally been the case. Sample representativeness when creating a measure and its cultural sensitivity are important factors to examine when picking a measure for use with a new population.

Review of Measures

Clearly the theoretical framework, the psychometric properties, and the sample representativeness/cultural sensitivity of a scale are all important aspects to consider when choosing a measure. Although a basic understanding of these issues will aid researchers in picking a measure independently, we offer some guidance by reviewing measures which we feel have successfully navigated the three issues discussed above. Of course, a thorough review of all or even most of the RS scales available is beyond the scope of this chapter, and the reader looking for a scale to serve an already specified purpose is pointed toward Hill and Hood's (1999) comprehensive review for scales developed prior to 1999, and Hill (2005), for a more updated list. Here, however, we will utilize Tsang and McCullough's (2003) two-level hierarchical model as a way to organize RS measures conceptually.

Tsang and McCullough (2003) propose that RS researchers think about RS variables on two levels. Level I represents a trait-like quality of religiousness or spirituality. This level represents a higher level of organization, or a disposition of, religiousness. Level II, on the other hand, represents a more behavioral or functional quality of religiousness or spirituality. This level includes measures that assess how RS functions in people's lives: the motivation toward RS, utilization of RS to cope with life demands, etc. Of course Level I and Level II interact, as dispositions influence behaviors and vice versa.

The measures reviewed here will be grouped into Level I and Level II categories. Only measures that have met three criteria are included for review. First, all scales reviewed in this chapter were grounded in at least some sort of theoretical framework (which was at least plausible, if not necessarily consensual). Second, all scales have demonstrated at least good reliability (alpha > 0.70) across two or more studies, and have demonstrated a good correlation ($r > 0.70$) across multiple samples on at least two of the five types of validity. And lastly, the measures we review represent a more broadly construed population (e.g., the scales do not apply only to Mormons, only to Evangelicals, etc.).

Measures of Dispositional Religiousness

Tsang and McCullough (2003) argue for a disposition of general religiousness or spirituality based on three factors. First, various indicators of religiousness are consistently correlated in research (e.g., attendance at a religious service, prayer, reading of sacred text, etc.). Second, factor analytic studies on measures of religiousness reveal factors that are intercorrelated, suggesting the presence of a higher order factor, such as a disposition toward religiousness. Third, some research has suggested that religiousness may be heritable to some degree. Finding and including a measure of dispositional religiousness in a study of RS variables is especially important for researchers in the study of education and wellbeing. By statistically controlling for dispositional variables, the relationship between other more functional RS variables and outcomes is better clarified. In order to design appropriate interventions or strategies in the fields of education and wellbeing, one must be able to disentangle specific factors from more general dispositional differences between individuals.

Assessment of General Religiousness or Spirituality

Scales assessing general religiousness or spirituality often use very broad language, thereby increasing the likelihood that they would be appropriate for use with a diverse sample. Measures such as these are often used in conjunction with measures of other constructs, and used to correlate religiosity with some over variable. For instance, researchers in education may consider using any of the following scales as predictors of various educational outcomes, or test for interactions between general levels of religiosity and type of educational intervention. Of all the scales designed to measure a general religious disposition, perhaps the best-validated and most widely used is the Spiritual Wellbeing Scale (SWBS; Paloutzian & Ellison, 1982). The SWBS consists of two, 10-item subscales measuring Existential Wellbeing (EWB) and Religious Wellbeing (RWB). The 10 items comprising the RWB subscale consistently load together in factor analytic studies, which suggest that it is indeed measuring a general RS factor. Although some may be put off by the scale's title as a measure of *wellbeing*, it has been used as a general RS measure in many studies. The Spiritual Transcendence Scale (STS) developed by Piedmont (1999) measures the ability of an individual to "stand outside of their immediate sense of time and place to view life from a larger more objective perspective" (p. 988). Overall, the STS has demonstrated good reliability and validity. It consists of three subscales measuring universality, prayer fulfillment, and connectedness. Although the STS was originally tested with American Christian samples, recent research has demonstrated its generalizability to populations in India (Piedmont & Leach, 2007), Malta (Galea, Ciarrocchi, & Piedmont, 2007), and the Philippines (Piedmont, 2007). And finally, Hood's Mysticism Scale (1975) has also been widely used and is applicable across religious traditions.

Assessment of Religious or Spiritual Commitment

Although many people identify themselves with a given religious tradition, the importance of that identification varies from person to person. Measures of RS commitment seek to ascertain how invested a person is in their given RS beliefs, whether within or outside a religious tradition. RS commitment measures often conceptualize the religiously or spiritually committed person as having developed a spiritual lens through which they perceive and understand the world and their circumstances. People who filter the majority of their experience through an RS lens may have a higher meaning-making potential (Park, 2005; Silberman, 2005), and the ability to create meaning has been significantly related to subjective and physical wellbeing (Brady, Peterman, Fitchett, Mo, & Cella, 1999). The Religious Commitment Inventory-10 (RCI-10) measures religious commitment outside of a specific religious tradition (Worthington et al., 2003). The RCI-10 has demonstrated excellent test–retest and internal reliabilities, as well as criterion, construct, convergent, and discriminant validity. It has also fared well on student samples of Buddhists, Hindus, and Muslims. The Santa Clara Strength of Religious Faith Questionnaire (Plante & Boccaccini, 1997) is another measure of RS commitment, and uses language that is broad enough to apply to the general public (as opposed to simply the "religious"). Although the original scale was comprised of only 10 items, a shortened 5-item version of the Santa Clara scale has been developed (Plante, Vallaeys, Sherman, & Wallston, 2002). Both the original and shortened forms have demonstrated good reliability and validity (Storch et al., 2004), although some research has suggested that it is susceptible to a ceiling effect among the religiously committed (Plante & Sherman, 2001).

Assessment of Religious or Spiritual Development

In as much as education is the process of growth, change, and maturity, educators should be interested in RS development. The broader question regarding RS development and maturity is one of conceptualizing growth, change, and maturity in spiritual and religious terms. How one conceives of RS maturity should certainly guide their choice of measure. The psychometrically sound Faith Maturity Scale (Benson, Donahue, & Erickson, 1993) is recommended if one defines religious maturity through mainstream Protestant traditions. The Religious Maturity Scale (Leak & Fish, 1999) measures religious maturity as conceptualized by Allport (1950). Within Allport's framework, religious maturity is marked by a commitment that directs one's life, a deep understanding of religious issues, the ability to doubt, and tolerance. Empirical studies have shown the scale to have excellent convergent, discriminant and predictive validity, as well as internal and test–retest reliabilities. It also appears that the scale can be used across denominations in Christianity. However, the degree to which it is generalizable to other religious traditions, even in modified form, has yet to be tested.

The Faith Development Scale (FDS; Maiello, 2005) is based on the assumption that there exists a core set of beliefs that transcends religious and cultural differences. Therefore, the FDS measures a participant's level of core religious belief, and uses this as an indication of maturity. The scale was initially developed on a sample of various European nationalities and religious traditions. Despite this, the scale requires additional research to verify its psychometric properties. However, because this scale was designed to transcend cultural differences the verification of its psychometric properties would offer another promising measure for cross-cultural RS research.

Two measures of reported RS experiences with the transcendent are worth noting. First, the 23-item Spiritual History Scale (SHS; Hays, Meador, Branch, & George, 2001) measures four dimensions (God-helped, Family History of Religiousness, Lifetime Religious Social Support, and Cost of Religiousness). Its validity and reliability are adequate among samples from a theistic background. Interestingly, it was developed on samples consisting primarily of the elderly, and was intended to be used as a measure of the relationship between its four factors and health in later-life. Therefore, its continued use with the elderly and/or in health research is strongly recommended. The degree to which it is useful with other populations has yet to be well established. Second, the Daily Spiritual Experience Scale (DSES; Underwood & Teresi, 2002) measures reported RS experience with the transcendent among those who do not necessarily come from a theistic background. The developers claimed that spirituality exists as a more stable internal construct than religiousness, and therefore attempted to design a scale that would measure the extent to which one feels the transcendent is a part of their daily lives (as opposed to extraordinary or miraculous encounters with the transcendent) as manifested in such experiences as awe, joy, and inner peace.

Two measures of religious maturity based on theories of development include the Attachment to God Inventory (AGI; Beck & McDonald, 2004) and the Spiritual

Assessment Inventory (SAI; Hall & Edwards, 1996, 2002). The AGI measures attachment to God based on Bowlby's (1969/1973) notion of infant attachment; it assesses the degree to which one exhibits fear of abandonment and/or avoidance of intimacy with God. Although attachment theory provides a rich conceptual framework from within which to develop measures and conduct research, the AGI has yet to receive much interest from outside a Western, Judeo-Christian tradition. However, within this population, evidence of internal reliability and convergent and construct validity have been consistently demonstrated. The SAI, designed for a Christian population, is a closely related measure based in object-relations theory. Specifically it measures awareness, instability, grandiosity, realistic acceptance, and defensiveness in the participant's relationship to God. The SAI has shown incremental validity above and beyond Paloutzian and Ellison's (1982; Ellison, 1983) Spiritual Wellbeing Scale (SWBS) and Gorsuch and McPherson's (1989) Intrinsic–Extrinsic Religious Motivation Scale.

Measures of Functional Religiousness

Assessment of Religious Motivation

As any educator knows, a major factor in successful education and development is the motivation of the individual; how one approaches the task is paramount in predicting the outcome. The same is true for RS. Among frameworks for understanding RS motivation and orientation, Allport's (1950) distinction between intrinsic (I) and extrinsic (E) motivation has been the most widely accepted. Allport's original Religious Orientation Scale (ROS; Allport & Ross, 1967) is still widely used, despite many well-documented methodological and theoretical criticisms and problems (Hill & Hood, 1999). Researchers have tried to improve on the ROS (see Hill & Hood, 1999 for a description of these measures) with perhaps the Revised Religious Orientation Scale (Gorsuch & McPherson, 1989) emerging as the most psychometrically sound. This does not mean it has escaped criticism, however. The entire I–E concept has been criticized by Batson and colleagues (Batson et al., 1993) as too simplistic, and they propose religious questing as an overlooked process necessary for religious maturity. During this quest, people ask challenging questions of their own faith and must ultimately reconcile themselves to the realization that the answers to such penetrating questions are often not black and white. In order to measure religious quest, the Batson and Schoenrade (1991a, 1991b) Quest Scale measures whether "an individual's religion involves an open-ended, responsive dialogue with existential questions raised by the contradictions and tragedies of life" (Batson et al., 1993, p. 169).

Assessment of Religious or Spiritual Practices

Researchers are often interested in the practical and applied questions of how outcomes are affected by what one *does*. As a result, several measures exist to assess both the public and private aspects of RS participation and activities. The Religious Involvement Inventory (RII; Hilty & Morgan, 1985), for example, measures participation in church activities beyond Sunday attendance for those who identify with the Christian tradition. The scale consists of 14 items and has demonstrated reasonably good validity and reliability. Similarly, the Christian Spiritual Participation Profile (CSPP; Thayer, 2004) measures one's involvement with each of the four spiritual development modes (which consist of both private and corporate spiritual disciplines). The Springfield Religiosity Scale (Koenig, Smiley, & Gonzales, 1988) also distinguishes between regular service attendance and additional involvement in religious group activities (e.g., Bible study groups, Sunday school class, and religious discussion groups). However, like the RII and the CSPP, the Springfield Religiosity Scale was created only for use with a Christian population. None of these scales have been modified and validated for use outside of this religious tradition.

By way of measuring more private RS practices, such as reading a sacred text, meditation, and solitary prayer, the Duke Religious Index (DUREL; Koenig et al., 1988) uses only one item. The entire DUREL consists of only five items, but the brevity of this measure has not diminished its psychometric properties, and it has continued to demonstrate strong reliability and validity. The Religious Background and Behavior Scale (RBB; Connors, Tonigan, & Miller, 1996), developed for use with a clinical population, is not tradition specific and measures more solitary RS behaviors.

Assessment of Religious and Spiritual Supports

Researchers have frequently posited social support as a mediator in the oft found linkage between religion and positive health outcomes. Measures of religious and spiritual supports attempt to get at the unique benefits of religious support, which may extend beyond just general social support. For example, Kahn and Antonucci (1980) described a collection of like-minded people with compatible worldviews who function to support each other through prayer and companionship as a *support convoy*. Because people within the same religious tradition are likely have similar or compatible worldviews, fellow congregants may be uniquely suited to function as a support convoy. The Religious Support Scale (RSS; Fiala, Bjorck, & Gorsuch, 2002) was created to measure perceived religious support among those in the Christian tradition. The scale consists of three subscales—support from God, support from the congregation, and support from church leaders. The RSS demonstrated adequate validity and excellent reliability. More research with scales such as these are needed to ascertain the unique contribution of religious support above and beyond general social support.

Assessment of Religious and Spiritual Coping

Education is more than the transmission of information; it is also the process whereby an individual is changed by the gained information, and good education always involves the teaching of how to apply that information appropriately.

Although many people hold RS beliefs and values, how they use and apply their RS to cope with demanding life circumstances is equally important as the other variables previous discussed. In fact, the ability of the individual to apply their RS framework successfully to cope with demands of life is likely a significant factor in the adaptiveness or maladaptiveness of their RS. Perhaps the most comprehensive and frequently used measure of RS coping is the Measure of Religious Coping (RCOPE; Pargament, Koenig, & Perez, 2000). The RCOPE has been tested on both physically healthy and ill patients and has moderate to high reliability and good validity. Recently, alternative versions of the RCOPE have been created and validated for use among Asian Indians in the United States (Tarakeshwar, Pargament, & Mahoney, 2003) and Pakistani Muslims (Khan & Watson, 2006). Not all use of RS to cope with circumstances outside of one's control is adaptive, however. In order to assess maladaptive religious coping, Pargament and colleagues created the Negative Religious Coping Scale (Pargament, Smith, Koenig, & Perez, 1998). Both the RCOPE and the Negative Religious Coping Scale assess styles of religious coping. Wong-McDonald and Gorsuch (2000) suggested a surrender style of coping in addition to the styles represented in the RCOPE. The Surrender Scale has good psychometric properties and has demonstrated incremental validity above and beyond the RCOPE.

Among groups frequently studied in conjunction with religious coping are the chronically ill. The Functional Assessment of Chronic Illness Therapy—Spiritual Wellbeing Scale (FACIT-Sp; Peterman, Fitchett, Bardy, Hernandez, & Cella, 2002) was designed for use specifically with this population and is applicable across religious traditions. The FACIT-Sp consists of two subscales: Faith and Meaning/Peace, both of which have sound psychometric properties. The Faith subscale has been associated with religiousness, while the Meaning/Peace subscale seems to measure RS independent of specific religious identification. Given that religiousness has some overlap with spirituality, but also some distinctiveness (Hill et al., 2000), this measure is useful for assessing RS in association with a religious tradition and that which is independent from it.

Alternatives to Self-Report

Up until this point, only paper-and-pencil self-report measures of RS have been reviewed. In addition to the use of such measures as standard fare in much social scientific research, the extensive reliance on self-report measures in RS research may be in part due to a Western Protestant paradigmatic belief that RS is personal and subjective (Cohen & Hill, 2007). Furthermore, self-reports are based on the assumption that (a) participants have the ability to self-assess accurately, and (b) participants are willing to disclose the results of their self-assessment to the investigator—two assumptions that may seriously limit the validity of scientific research. Psychologists, particularly social psychologists, have spoken to both issues extensively and have concluded that (a) self-assessment is biased by both intentional and unintentional distortions, and (b) honest disclosure is especially vulnerable to such common impediments as evaluation apprehension, demand characteristics, and impression management. Self-report measures may be especially limited when studying RS due to the importance of RS beliefs and practices and the power of the RS social context (i.e., persons may feel a certain social pressure to affirm certain religious beliefs; Burris & Navara, 2002). Finally, self-report measures may require a reading and comprehension level beyond that of some targeted participants, and may sometimes fail to engage the interest of the respondent—thus making the measure more vulnerable to a response set (e.g., agreeing with every item, even when logically inconsistent). In light of this, alternatives to self-report measures are needed in order for RS research to progress and expand.

Implicit Measurement

Implicit measures attempt to use indirect measurement techniques to assess a given variable. RS researchers have just begun to use techniques from social and cognitive sciences. Researchers in social cognition (e.g., Fazio, Sanbonmatsu, Powell, & Kardes, 1986) proposed that an attitude's accessibility is representative of underlying cognitive structures. In RS research, judgment speed has drawn strong interest, where participants are asked to identify an object as good or bad. Hill, as early as 1994, recommended that this technique of measuring attitude accessibility be extended to the psychology of religion. This recommendation was taken by Gibson (2006), whose findings indicated that reaction time is a good indicator of the accessibility of one's God schema. Cohen, Shariff, and Hill (2008) found that participants who held stronger religious opinions (i.e., clearly a religious or non-religious ideology) had more accessible attitudes as measured by response times, again offering support for the use of implicit measures of RS attitudes. The Implicit Association Test (IAT; Greenwald & Banaji, 1995; Greenwald, McGhee, & Schwartz, 1998) is one such cognitive timing measure, but is still in its early stages of use with RS research.

Another form of implicit assessment involves memory recall. Symons and Johnson (1997) demonstrated that people recall a higher number of adjectives when describing a target if the target is intimate (as opposed to familiar, but not intimate). In applying this notion to RS experience, Gibson (2006) found that evangelicals, whose image of God was more intimate (but not necessarily more familiar) than non-evangelicals and atheists, recalled adjectives that describe God at the same rate as self-reference adjectives, assumed to be both intimate and familiar. In contrast, non-evangelical and atheist participants recalled adjectives related to the self (again, assumed to be both familiar and intimate) with higher frequency than those related to God (familiar but not intimate). These findings tentatively suggest that memory recall can be used to assess certain qualities, such as intimacy and familiarity, in one's relationship to God. However, not all are in agreement that such measures are useful. Kinoshita and Peek-O'Leary (2005) raise doubt about what implicit and indirect measurements are actually assessing, and the lack of empirical research on RS variables using such measures suggests caution in using implicit and/or indirect measures for purposes other than research.

Other Alternative Forms of Measurement

RS research generally has not relied on other forms of measurement, but extending RS research into other, more applied fields may warrant reconsideration of alternative research methodologies. For example, qualitative research can be useful in fleshing out quantitative findings or for developing a theory, which can then be tested quantitatively. The complex nature of RS suggests that mixed-method designs may be useful in studies taking a more robust approach. Reports from others (e.g., friends, family members, and fellow members of a religious organization) are rarely used in RS research and may be beneficial to the study of religious practices and behaviors. Physiological indicators (e.g., fMRI and immunology) of RS experience are another method of measurement that would likely add significantly to the body of RS research. As the psychology of religion is applied in more diverse settings, one can expect the methods of measurement to expand as well.

Guidance in Choosing a Measure

There are several factors that must be considered with choosing a measure (Hill, Kopp, & Bollinger, 2007). First, one must choose a measure that serves the purpose of the research. For example, if one is conducting a study for experimental purposes only, a new or less validated measure, though less than desirable, may be used if nothing else is available. Again, however, one should thoroughly review the literature, since there is a vast array of measures now available. In contrast, if one is working in a more applied setting and hoping to use an RS measure to screen or identify participants with certain characteristics, then a more psychometrically sound and well-validated measure is likely necessary. Second, one must have a well-articulated notion of what RS construct they hope to study. Because RS is a robust and multidimensional construct, one must be sure to select a measure that coincides with the way one's hypotheses have defined the said construct. For instance, researchers who think that religiousness is manifested in religious behaviors (e.g., attendance at weekly religious services, prayer, and meditation) may choose a measure of religious behavior and draw conclusions about general religiousness. This would be a faulty conclusion, as their findings relate to only one dimension of RS—religious practices and behavior. Because RS is so broad and complex, it is wise to conceptualize it along various dimensions. However, in so doing, one must be sure to choose a measure that matches the said dimension. Third, the psychometric properties of the scale are important. If a scale has not demonstrated at least two types of validity beyond face validity, it is probably unwise to select it for use in other than experimental research.

Fourth, researchers should select measures which are appropriate for their given sample and/or population. As discussed throughout this chapter, there are relatively few RS measures that have been cross-culturally validated, or are applicable outside of one or two religious traditions. This will likely change in the years ahead, not only as many cultures become increasingly religiously pluralistic, but as RS research itself continues to grow and is conducted in different cultures. RS exists within a social and cultural context, and researchers would be wise to consider the context of their sample as compared to the context in which the measure was created in judging the appropriateness of the measures they intend to use. Lastly, researchers are admonished to be flexible. Although there has been a proliferation of measures in psychology of religion, it is still not guaranteed that one will find a scale that was created for the exact purpose of one's own research. Therefore, it is imperative that researchers have a strong conceptual understanding of both their own research and the measures they consider. Pilot studies may be necessary to confirm the applicability of the measure on one's sample or population of interest. If a scale is assessing a construct of interest, it may be worth the added effort to test ways of altering the measure to make it applicable to one's targeted population.

Conclusion

Colonel Jessep, the fictional character played by Jack Nicholson in the movie *A Few Good Men*, will long be identified by his statement "You want answers? You can't handle the truth!" RS researchers not only want answers, but are firmly convinced they can handle the truth about the complex and sometimes paradoxical nature of religion and spirituality. Frequently, that research has important implications for education and wellbeing. The quality of such empirical research is only as good as the quality of the measurement instruments that it utilizes. Though not breathtakingly exciting with widespread appeal, good measurement is absolutely necessary not only to move the field forward, but also to help understand and handle the truth.

Note

1. It should be noted, however, that such normative data are usually not necessary for research purposes and since most scales are used for research, it is unlikely that norms for most instruments will ever be established.

References

Allport, G. W. (1950). *The individual and his religion*. New York: Macmillan.
Allport, G. W., & Ross, J. M. (1967). Personal and religious orientation and prejudice. *Journal of Personality and Social Psychology, 5*, 432–443.
Batson, C. D., & Schoenrade, P. A. (1991a). Measuring religion as quest: I. Validity concerns. *Journal for the Scientific Study of Religion, 30*, 416–429.
Batson, C. D., & Schoenrade, P. A. (1991b). Measuring religion as quest: II. Reliability concerns. *Journal for the Scientific Study of Religion, 30*, 430–447.
Batson, C. D., Schoenrade, P., & Ventis, W. L. (1993). *Religion and the individual: A social-psychological perspective* (revised ed.). New York: Oxford University Press.
Beck, R., & McDonald, A. (2004). Attachment to God: The attachment to God inventory, tests of working model correspondence, and an exploration of faith group differences. *Journal of Psychology and Theology, 32*, 92–103.

Belzen, J. A., & Hood, R. W. (2006). Methodological issues in the psychology of religion: Toward another paradigm? *The Journal of Psychology, 140*, 5–28.

Benson, P. L., Donahue, M.., & Erickson, J. A. (1993). The faith maturity scale: Conceptualization, measurement, and empirical validation. In M. L. Lynn & D. O. Moberg (Eds.), *Research in the social scientific study of religion* (Vol. 5, pp. 1–26). Greenwich, CT: JAI Press.

Black, H. K. (1999). Poverty and prayer: Spiritual narratives of elderly African-American women. *Review of Religious Research, 40*, 359–374.

Bowlby, J. (1969). *Attachment, Vol. 1 of attachment and loss*. London: Hogarth Press; New York: Basic Books.

Bowlby, J. (1973). *Separation, Vol. 2 of attachment and loss*. London: Hogarth Press; New York: Basic Books.

Brady, M. J., Peterman, A. H., Fitchett, G., Mo, M., & Cella, D. (1999). A case for including spirituality in quality of life measurement in oncology. *Psycho-Oncology, 8*, 417–428.

Burris, C. T., & Navara, G. S. (2002). Morality play – or playing morality: Intrinsic religious orientation and socially desirable responding. *Self and Identity, 1*, 67–76.

Chatters, L. M., Taylor, R. J., & Lincoln, K. D. (2002). Advances in the measurement of religiosity among older African Americans: Implications for health and mental health researchers. In J. H. Skinner & J. A. Teresi (Eds.), *Multicultural measurement in older populations* (pp. 199–220). New York: Springer.

Cohen, A. B., & Hill, P. C. (2007). Religion as culture: Religious individualism and collectivism among American Catholics, Jews, and Protestants. *Journal of Personality, 75*, 709–742.

Cohen, A. B., Shariff, A. F., & Hill, P. C. (2008). The accessibility of religious beliefs. *Journal of Research in Personality*, 1408–1417.

Connors, G. J., Tonigan, J. S., & Miller, W. R. (1996). A measure of religious background and behavior for use in behavior change research. *Psychology of Addictive Behaviors, 10*, 90–96.

Emmons, R. A., & Paloutzian, R. F. (2003). The psychology of religion. *Annual Review of Psychology, 54*, 377–402.

Ellison, C. G. (1983). Spiritual well-being: Conceptualization and measurement. *Journal of Psychology and Theology, 11*, 330–340.

Ellison, C. G., & Taylor, R. J. (1996). Turning to prayer: Social and situational antecedents of religious coping among African-Americans. *Review of Religious Research, 38*, 111–131.

Fazio, R. H., Sanbonmatsu, D. M., Powell, M. C., & Kardes, F. R. (1986). On the automatic activation of attitudes. *Journal of Personality and Social Psychology, 50*, 229–238.

Fiala, W. E., Bjorck, J. P., & Gorsuch, R. L. (2002). The Religious Support Scale: Construction, validation, and cross-validation. *American Journal of Community Psychology, 30*, 761–786.

Galea, M., Ciarrocchi, J. W., & Piedmont, R. L. (2007). Child abuse, personality, and spirituality as predictors of happiness in Maltese college students. *Research in the Social Scientific Study of Religion, 18*, 141–154.

Ghorbani, N., Watson, P. J., Ghramaleki, A. F., Morris, R. J., & Hood, R. W., Jr. (2002). Muslim-Christian religious orientation scales: Distinctions, correlations, and cross-cultural analysis in Iran and the United States. *The International Journal for the Psychology of Religion, 12*, 69–91.

Gibson, N. J. S., (2006). The experimental investigation of religious cognition. Unpublished doctoral dissertation [available from http://www.divinity.cam.ac.uk/pcp/personnel/nicholas.html#PhD], University of Cambridge, England.

Gorsuch, R. L. (1984). Measurement: The boon and bane of investigating religion. *American Psychologist, 39*, 228–236.

Gorsuch, R. L. (1988). Psychology of religion. *Annual Review of Psychology, 39*, 201–221.

Gorsuch, R. L. (1990). Measurement in psychology of religion revisited. *Journal of Psychology and Christianity, 9*(2), 82–92.

Gorsuch, R. L., & McPherson, S. E. (1989). Intrinsic/extrinsic measurement: I/E revised and single-item scales. *Journal for the Scientific Study of Religion, 28*, 348–354.

Granqvist, P., & Kirkpatrick, L. A. (2004). Religious conversion and perceived childhood attachment: A meta-analysis. *The International Journal for the Psychology of Religion, 14*, 223–250.

Greenwald, A. G., & Banaji, M. R. (1995). Implicit social cognition: Attitudes, self-esteem and stereotypes. *Journal of Personality and Social Psychology, 102*, 4–27.

Greenwald, A. G., McGhee, D. E., & Schwartz, J. L. K. (1998). Measuring individual differences in implicit cognition: The Implicit Association Test. *Journal of Personality and Social Psychology, 74*, 1464–1480.

Hall, T. W., & Edwards, K. J. (1996). The initial development and factor analysis of the Spiritual Assessment Inventory. *Journal of Psychology and Theology, 24*, 233–246.

Hall, T. W., & Edwards, K. J. (2002). The Spiritual Assessment Inventory: A theistic model and measure for assessing spiritual development. *Journal for the Scientific Study of Religion, 41*, 341–357.

Hays, J. C., Meador, K. G., Branch, P. S., & George, L. K. (2001). The Spirituality History Scale in Four Dimensions (SHS-4): Validity and reliability. *The Gerontologist, 41*, 239–249.

Hill, P. C. (1994). Toward an attitude process model of religious experience. *Journal for the Scientific Study of Religion, 33*, 303–314.

Hill, P. C. (2005). Measurement in the psychology of religion and spirituality: Current status and evaluation. In R. F. Paloutzian & C. Park (Eds.), *Handbook of the psychology of religion and spirituality* (pp. 43–61). New York: Guilford.

Hill, P. C., & Dwiwardani, C. (in press). Measurement at the interface of psychiatry and religion: Issues and existing measures. In P. J. Verhagen, H. M. Van Praag, & J. J. Lopez-Ibor (Eds.), *Psychiatry and religion: Pushing back the boundaries. Explorations at the interface*. New York: Wiley & Sons.

Hill, P. C., & Hood, R. W., Jr. (1999). *Measures of religiosity*. Birmingham, AL: Religious Education Press.

Hill, P. C., Kopp, K. J., & Bollinger, R. A. (2007). A few good measures: Assessing religion and spirituality in relation to health. In T. G. Plante & C. E. Thoresen (Eds.), *Spirit, science and health: How the spiritual mind fuels physical wellness* (pp. 25–38). Westport, CT: Praeger Publishers/Greenwood Publishing Group.

Hill, P. C., & Pargament, K. I. (2003). Advances in the conceptualization and measurement of religion and spirituality. *American Psychologist, 58*, 64–76.

Hill, P. C., Pargament, K. I., Hood, R. W., Jr., McCullough, M. E., Swyers, J. P., Larson, D. B., et al. (2000). Conceptualizing religion and spirituality: Points of commonality, points of departure. *Journal for the Theory of Social Behavior, 30*, 51–77.

Hilty, D. M., & Morgan, R. L. (1985). Construct validation for the Religious Involvement Inventory: Replication. *Journal for the Scientific Study of Religion, 24*, 75–86.

Hood, R. W., Jr. (1975). The construction and preliminary validation of a measure of reported mystical experience. *Journal for the Scientific Study of Religion, 14*, 29–41.

Hood, R. W., Jr. (1995). The facilitation of religion experience. In R. W. Hood, Jr. (Ed.), *Handbook of religious experience* (pp. 568–597). Birmingham, AL: Religious Education Press.

Hood, R. W., Jr. (1997). The empirical study of mysticism. In B. Spilka & D. N. McIntosh (Eds.), *The psychology of religion: Theoretical approaches* (pp. 222–232). Boulder, CO: Westview Press.

Kahn, R. L., & Antonucci, T. C. (1980). Convoys over the life course: Attachment, roles, and social support. In P. B. Baltes & O. G. Brin (Eds.), *Life span development and behavior* (pp. 253–286). New York: Academic Press.

Khan, Z. H., & Watson, P. J. (2006). Construction of the Pakistani Religious Coping Practices Scale: Correlations with religious coping, religious orientation, and reactions to stress among Muslim university students. *International Journal for the Psychology of Religion, 16*, 101–112.

Kinoshita, S., & Peek-O'Leary, M. (2005). Does the compatibility effect in race Implicit Association Test reflect familiarity or affect? *Psychonomic Bulletin & Review, 12*, 442–454.

Kirkpatrick, L. A., & Hood, R. W., Jr. (1990). Intrinsic-extrinsic religious orientation: The boon or bane of contemporary psychology of religion. *Journal for the Scientific Study of Religion, 29*, 442–462.

Koenig, H. G., McCullough, M. E., & Larson, D. B. (2001). *Handbook of religion and health.* New York: Oxford University Press.

Koenig, H. G., Smiley, M., & Gonzales, J. A. P. (1988). *Religion, health, and aging: A review and theoretical integration.* Westport, CT: Greenwood.

Leak, G. K., & Fish, S. B. (1999). Development and initial validation of a measure of religious maturity. *The International Journal for the Psychology of Religion, 9,* 105–124.

Maiello, C. (2005). Degrees of belief in God: A measure of belief for use in cross culture. *Mental Health, Religion & Culture, 8,* 87–95.

Paloutzian, R. F., & Ellison, C. W. (1982). Loneliness, spiritual well-being and quality of life. In L. Peplau & D. Perlman (Eds.), *Loneliness: A sourcebook of current theory, research and therapy* (pp. 224–237). New York: Wiley Interscience.

Pargament, K. I. (1997). *The psychology of religion and coping.* New York: Guilford Press.

Pargament, K. I., Koenig, H. G., & Perez, L. (2000). The many methods of religious coping: Development and initial validation of the RCOPE. *Journal of Clinical Psychology, 56,* 519–543.

Pargament, K. I., Smith, B. W., Koenig, H. G., & Perez, L. M. (1998). Patterns of positive and negative religious coping with major life stressors. *Journal of the Scientific Study of Religion, 37,* 711–725.

Park, C. L. (2005). Religion and meaning. In R. F. Paloutzian & C. L. Park (Eds.), *Handbook of the psychology of religion and spirituality* (pp. 295–314). New York: Guilford Press.

Peterman, A. H., Fitchett, G., Bardy, M. J., Hernandez, L., & Cella, D. (2002). Measuring spiritual well-being in people with cancer: The Functional Assessment of Chronic Illness-Spiritual Well-Being Scale (FACIT-Sp). *Annals of Behavioral Medicine, 24*(1), 49–58.

Piedmont, R. L. (1999). Does spirituality represent the sixth factor of personality?: Spiritual transcendence and the five factor model. *Journal of Personality, 67,* 985–1013.

Piedmont, R. L. (2007). Cross-cultural generalizability of the Spiritual Transcendence Scale to the Philippines: Spirituality as a human universal. *Mental Health, Religion and Culture, 10,* 89–107.

Piedmont, R. L., & Leach, M. M. (2007). Cross-cultural generalizability of the Spiritual Transcendence Scale in India: Spirituality as a universal aspect of human experience. *American Behavioral Scientist, 45,* 1888–1901.

Plante, T. G., & Boccaccini, B. F. (1997). The Santa Clara strength of religious faith questionnaire. *Pastoral Psychology, 45,* 375–385.

Plante, T. G., & Sherman, A. C. (Eds.). (2001). *Faith and health: Psychological perspectives.* New York: Guilford.

Plante, T. G., Vallaeys, C. L., Sherman, A. C., & Wallston, K. A. (2002). The development of a brief version of the Santa Clara strength of religious faith questionnaire. *Pastoral Psychology, 48,* 11–21.

Silberman, I. (2005). Religion as a meaning system: Implications for the new millennium. *Journal of Social Issues, 61,* 641–663.

Storch, E. A., Roberti, J. W., Bagner, D. M., Lewin, A. B., Baumeister, A. L., & Geffken, G. R. (2004). Further psychometric properties of the Santa Clara Strength of Religious Faith Questionnaire—Short-form. *Journal of Psychology and Christianity, 23,* 51–53.

Symons, C. A., & Johnson, B. T. (1997). The self-reference effect in memory: A meta-analysis. *Psychological Bulletin, 121,* 371–394.

Tarakeshwar, N., Pargament, K. I., & Mahoney, A. (2003). Initial development of a measure of religious coping among Hindus. *Journal of Community Psychology, 31,* 607–628.

Thayer, O. J. (2004). Constructing a spirituality measure based on learning theory: The Christian Spiritual Participation Profile. *Journal of Psychology and Christianity, 23,* 195–207.

Tsang, J., & McCullough, M. E. (2003). Measuring religious constructs: A hierarchical approach to construct organization and scale selection. In S. J. Lopez & C. R. Snyder (Eds.), *Positive psychological assessment: A handbook of models and measures* (pp. 345–360). Washington, D.C.: American Psychological Association.

Underwood, L. G., & Teresi, J. A. (2002). The Daily Spiritual Experience Scale: Development, theoretical description, reliability, exploratory factor analysis, and preliminary construct validity using health-related data. *Annals of Behavioral Medicine, 24*, 22–33.

Wong-McDonald, A., & Gorsuch, R. L. (2000). Surrender to God: An additional coping style? *Journal of Psychology and Theology, 28*, 149–161.

Worthington, E. L., Jr., Berry, J. W., & Parrott, L., III (2001). Unforgiveness, forgiveness, religion, and health. In T. G. Plante & A. C. Sherman (Eds.), *Faith and health: Psychological perspectives* (pp. 107–138). New York: Guilford Press.

Worthington, E. L., Jr., Wade, N. G., Hight, T. L., Ripley, J. S., McCullough, M. E., Berry, J. W., et al. (2003). The Religious Commitment Inventory-10: Development, refinement, and validation of a brief scale for research and counseling. *Journal of Counseling Psychology, 50*, 84–96.

Biographical details

Peter C. Hill and Lauren E. Maltby, Rosemead School of Psychology, Biola University, California, USA.

Chapter 3
Examining Religious and Spiritual Development During Childhood and Adolescence

Chris J. Boyatzis

Abstract What does "spirituality" look like in a child? Does religion make a genuine difference in the lives of children and youth? How do we measure spiritual and religious development in children and adolescents? How can we characterize religious and spiritual development in its processes, sequences, and stages? These are a few daunting challenges facing our field, and I will address them here (to varying degrees of thoroughness). I first examine the historical neglect and recent attention regarding spirituality and religion and childhood and adolescence. Second, I explore definitional challenges inherent in this field. I then offer a selective review of very recent research literature that illuminates key issues in three emphases in the field: children's religious concepts, social dynamics that influence religiosity and spirituality, and religion's role in adolescent wellbeing and thriving. In addition, I problematize some assumptions about religious and spiritual development by challenging their implicit foundations derived from developmental theory.

What does "spirituality" look like in a child? Does religion make a genuine difference in the lives of children and youth? How do we measure spiritual and religious development in children and adolescents? How can we characterize religious and spiritual development in its processes, sequences, and stages? These are a few daunting challenges facing our field, and I will address them here (to varying degrees of thoroughness).

I first examine the historical neglect and recent attention regarding spirituality and religion and childhood and adolescence. Second, I explore definitional challenges inherent in this field. I then offer a selective review of very recent research literature that illuminates key issues in three emphases in the field: children's religious concepts, social dynamics that influence religiosity and spirituality, and religion's role in adolescent wellbeing and thriving. In addition, I problematize some assumptions about religious and spiritual development by challenging their implicit foundations derived from developmental theory.

C.J. Boyatzis (✉)
Department of Psychology, Bucknell University, Lewisburg, PA 17837, USA
e-mail: boyatzis@bucknell.edu

A New Day for Religious and Spiritual Development

Of the mountainous research conducted on children's development, a conspicuously small portion addresses religion and spirituality. A recent PsycINFO search revealed that less than half of 1% of research on children addressed religion, and an even smaller proportion addressed spirituality (see also Benson, Roehlkepartain, & Rude, 2003; Boyatzis, 2003a).

Fortunately, scholars are now heeding the call to "honor spiritual development as a core developmental process that deserves equal standing in the pantheon of universal developmental processes" (Benson, 2004, p. 50). For example, there were more dissertations on children and religion from 2000–2005 than in the 1990s, and more in the 1990s than the previous two decades combined. Dissertations on children and spirituality have surged, as more than half of the dissertations ever done on this topic have appeared since 2000. At the other end of the scholarly pipeline, many volumes have appeared in a brief interval. I highlight one seminal work that is "must reading"—*The Handbook of Spiritual Development in Childhood and Adolescence* (Roehlkepartain, King, Wagener, & Benson, 2006)—but also recommend other recent edited volumes (e.g., Allen, 2008; Dowling & Scarlett, 2006; Ratcliff, 2004; Rosengren, Johnson, & Harris, 2000; Yust, Johnson, Sasso, & Roehlkepartain, 2006). In addition, a journal (*International Journal on Children's Spirituality*) and a spate of special issues have examined child and adolescent spirituality in various journals: *Review of Religious Research* (Boyatzis, 2003b), *Applied Developmental Science* (King & Boyatzis, 2004), *The International Journal for the Psychology of Religion* (Boyatzis, 2006), *New Directions for Youth Development* (Benson, Roehlkepartain, & Hong, 2008), and *Research in the Social Scientific Study of Religion* (Boyatzis & Hambrick-Dixon, 2008). Finally, the most recent edition of the prestigious *Handbook of child psychology*, long viewed as the "bible" of child development scholarship, has an entire chapter on religious and spiritual development (by Oser, Scarlett, & Bucher, 2006); in contrast, the preceding edition in 1998 had, among its thousands of pages, a skimpy three references in the subject index to religion and spirituality. Therefore, it is clear that religious and spiritual development is working toward the mainstream like never before.

Defining Spiritual Development is Difficult

A fundamental task for our field is to generate valid definitions of our constructs, but this is easier said than done. First, there are stubborn historical and semantic tensions between "spirituality" and "religion"; there are many treatments of these debates (e.g., Zinnbauer & Pargament, 2005) so they will not be repeated here. Here I tentatively define religious development as the growth of understanding of and engagement in an organized religious tradition's beliefs, creeds, values, and practices (see also Reich, Oser, & Scarlett, 1999). This definition is inclusive for children in myriad religions and generates questions about children's relationships with the tradition's divine entity (God, Allah, etc.), how the children understand the religion's formal creeds and doctrines and participate in its formal events (e.g., religious worship or milestone events such as a Christian's first communion, a Jew's bar mitzvah, and a Muslim's first participation in the hajj).

In contrast, it is more difficult to define spirituality, especially "spiritual development." If children develop spiritually, *what* develops? There has been more effort to define "spirituality" than "spiritual development" (Roehlkepartain, Benson, King, & Wagener, 2006). The organizers of the landmark *Handbook of Spiritual Development in Childhood and Adolescence* wisely conclude that "there is no consensus about what 'this domain' (of children's spirituality) really is" (Roehlkepartain, Benson, et al., 2006) and went further to say it is "premature—and potentially dangerous—to propose that a single definition could capture the richness, complexity, and multidimensional nature of spiritual development" (Roehlkepartain, Benson, et al., 2006, p. 4).

To build an empirically based definition of spirituality, scholars at The Center for Spiritual Development, situated within the Search Institute in Minnesota, USA, and funded by the John Templeton Foundation, have collected data on more than 5,000 young people between the ages of 12 and 25 (Search Institute, 2008). These data arise from surveys and focus groups around the world: Australia, Cameroon, Canada, India, Thailand, Ukraine, the United Kingdom, and the United States. The Center is analyzing this data goldmine. Previously, Search Institute scholars offered this definition: spiritual development is growth in "the intrinsic capacity for self-transcendence, in which the self is embedded in something greater than the self, including the sacred.... It is shaped both within and outside of religious traditions, beliefs, and practices" (Benson, Roehlkepartain, & Rude, 2003, pp. 205–206). This definition seems fruitful because it recognizes spirituality (a) as a natural propensity (a view consistent with what some have named the "biological argument," Hay, Reich, & Utsch, 2006), (b) as socialized and shaped by multiple experiences within and outside organized religion, and (c) characterized by connection and relationality to what is beyond the self. On this last point, this definition is not restricted to a particular religious doctrine or sacred entity and also accommodates the "biological argument" claim (Hay & Nye, 1998) that children's relational consciousness emerges prior to religious socialization and beliefs: children are spiritual beings first and then are acculturated (or not) into a religious tradition that narrows intuitive spiritual dispositions, practices, and experiences. This view suggests, for example, that God (or some theistic version thereof) is not a priori the only transcendent entity with which a child experiences a relationship. I find this definition's inclusiveness helpful, especially at this embryonic point in the field, and it engenders many questions: What are the developmental trajectories of a spiritual relationality to whatever one perceives to transcend the self? What forces and entities beyond the self engage or attract the child in meaningful (or dysfunctional or dangerous) relationality? What experiences inside and outside religion foster, and which impede, this self-transcendent growth? As the study of children's spiritual development evolves, it will be crucial to examine how development in this domain is related to and/or distinct from development in other domains (religion, cognition, emotion, neurology, etc.). Finally, in our pre-consensus era, scholars should interrogate their own work (and others') by asking: what are the implications of my (your) definition of spirituality? What might be systematically excluded by a particular definition? This kind of intellectual honesty and humility will help the field advance.

I believe one major reason for our current difficulty in defining children's spirituality is the long-standing dominance of cognitive-developmental models of growth that posited an invariant march toward logical, rational thought, and away from other modes of thought. The post-Enlightenment Piagetian emphasis on rational thought brought a dismissive attitude toward other forms of knowing. Of course, many scholars have argued for a more inclusive approach and a richer understanding of children's spirituality. In his classic, *Will Our Children Have Faith?*, John Westerhoff (2000) argued that "two modes of consciousness are possible.... One is intellectual.... The other is intuitional ... experiential, and is characterized by nonverbal, creative, nonlinear, relational activities. The development and integration of both modes of consciousness is essential to the spiritual life" (p. 70). Robinson (1983) also makes this point in his collection of children's spiritual experience, *The Original Vision*: "What I have called the original vision of childhood is no mere imaginative fancy, but a form of knowledge and one that is essential to the development of any mature understanding" (p. 16).

These more inclusive views are consistent with claims, described below, by many contemporary cognitive-developmentalists who no longer embrace a Piagetian model (see Johnson & Boyatzis, 2006). The decline of Piagetian assumptions and the ascent of more inclusive, flexible models will engender a better understanding of children's spirituality.

Cognitive Approaches to Spiritual Development

Cognitive-developmental theories launched two waves of research on the development of religious concepts. In the 1960s, scholars applied Piagetian theory to children's concepts of God and prayer (e.g., Elkind, 1970; Goldman, 1964; Long, Elkind, & Spilka, 1967). A second wave, beginning in the 1990s, was sparked by new theories of cognitive development that emphasized the intuitive, domain-specific nature of thinking (Boyer, 1994). Both waves concluded that children's religious concepts operate under the same principles and tendencies of nonreligious cognition.

Recently, Johnson and Boyatzis (2006) suggested that spiritual development proceeds from intuitive understanding to increasingly reflective thought. Young children possess powerful inference mechanisms for intuitively sorting out reality and the supernatural, and this intuition is integrated with increasing reflection. These maturations are scaffolded by increasing cultural practices that orient the child to cultural modes of spiritual knowing and being. Thus, spiritual development arises not from mere acquisition of knowledge about the transcendent but from increasingly meaningful and organized connections of the self to the "something more" (see also Johnson, 2000; Roehlkepartain, Benson, et al., 2006).

The most studied topic in spiritual and religious cognition is children's concepts of God (e.g., Hyde, 1990), so this review will focus on more recent cognitive approaches in this research. In contrast to the older view that children possess solely anthropomorphic notions of God—a big person in the sky—recent research suggests that children and adults are not so different. Even adults tend to anthropomorphize, using a "fundamental cognitive bias" (Barrett & Keil, 1996, p. 223) that extends an intuitive folk psychology to supernatural figures (Boyer, 1994, 2001). In addition, children and adults hold God concepts featuring both natural and supernatural properties. Work by Barrett challenges the view that children are unaware of God's distinctly supernatural powers (Barrett & Keil, 1996; Barrett & Richert, 2003). His studies demonstrate that pre-schoolers view God as a special kind of agent who, unlike other agents, is not constrained by natural laws. In one study (Barrett, Newman, & Richert, 2003) 5-year-olds believed that their mothers would not immediately understand ambiguous drawings but God would; Woolley and Phelps (2001) similarly found that most children 5 years and older felt that God "just knows" what people are praying without needing to hear them. Barrett has posited that children are prepared conceptually at early ages to view God as *unique*, not humanlike, which helps explain why children easily distinguish God's special status.

These studies fit with broader accounts (see Boyer & Walker, 2000; Johnson & Boyatzis, 2006, for elaboration) explaining that children (and adults) are drawn to supernatural agents such as God or angels due to their "counterintuitive" nature (i.e., they violate ordinary expectations, as in the case of spiritual entities who are immortal, omniscient, or can pass through physical objects). These counterintuitive religious beliefs operate within an implicit backdrop of theory of mind, which provides children or adults with a prepared set of agentic qualities to extend to religious agents (e.g., "My supernatural God has wishes and thoughts and worries [just like all beings with minds do]"). The agents' counterintuitiveness, combined with the individual's belief that the agents are *real*, makes the beliefs all the more *salient* and memorable and potent. This salience increases the likelihood of religious beliefs being transmitted and shared with others.

There are additional perspectives from current cognitive-developmentalists that challenge the Piaget-inspired account of the march away from immature irrational, magical thinking to mature rational, abstract, scientific thinking. Children's (and adults') mental processes are believed to include multiple thought processes that coexist and often compete (e.g., Subbotsky, 1993; Woolley, 1997). As Woolley (2000) asserted, "Children's minds are not inherently one way or another—not inherently magical nor inherently rational" (pp. 126–127). As Callanan (2005) noted, in the minds of children and many adults the ontological boundaries between "empirical" entities (those with an objective evidential basis) and "nonempirical" entities—say, the differences between animals and angels—are probably much fuzzier and fluid than scholars who study such things seem to presume.

Researchers have documented cognitive propensities underlying ideas of immaterial spirit and life after death, which are widespread across cultures (Bering & Bjorklund, 2004). Children's beliefs about the afterlife are connected with an early distinction between minds and bodies (Bering & Bjorklund, 2004). Children know that death stops physical/biological functions but have difficulty imagining that death similarly ceases all mental and emotional functions. In other words, a mind–body distinction appears in children's afterlife beliefs. Such thinking is easily assimilated with religious beliefs, evident in most traditions, that at death a spirit or soul exists separately from the body and continues to live. If children possess early intuitions about the afterlife, or God, or the efficacy of prayer, there are also surrounding familial and cultural practices that provide ample testimony, dialogue, and rituals to reify, scaffold, and elaborate them.

Social influences have been shown in numerous studies. For example, Heller (1986) found that Hindu children, more than Jewish, Baptist, or Roman Catholic children, described a multifaceted God that feels close and like a person in some ways yet is also an abstract and intangible form of energy. These Hindu beliefs reflect their doctrine about different God with different natures and functions. Taken together, these studies suggest that children extend a folk psychology and theory of mind to their God images but are influenced by their surrounding cultural and religious influences.

In an important study, Evans (2000) analyzed children's beliefs about the origins of species and of the world in two kinds of families: secular or Christian fundamentalist; in the latter group children also attended religious schools or were home-schooled. A striking finding was that young children aged 7–9 in both types of families—fundamentalist *and* secular—espoused creationist views of the origin of species and the world. In secular homes, not until the children reached adolescence did they begin consistently to espouse their families' evolutionist cosmologies. These findings suggest that children are intuitive theists (and challenge the antiquated view of children as blank-slate recipients of parental input) who may revise their implicit theories when exposed to conflicting evidence in parental testimony or experiences (e.g., trips to science museums) that supports secular scientific accounts (Harris & Koenig, 2006).

Corroborating evidence comes from studies of children's and parents' beliefs about mythical figures (e.g., Santa Claus, Tooth Fairy). Although these figures are invoked in very specific circumstances in contrast to the more common yet also profound uses of religious deities or spirits, mythical figures are like God concepts in that they include supernatural features and have widespread cultural endorsement. Parents' endorsement of mythical characters such as Santa, the Easter Bunny, and the Tooth Fairy was positively related to their children's belief in them (Prentice, Manosevitz, & Hubbs, 1978). However, the correspondence between parents' and children's beliefs was not so strong as to suggest children think what their parents want them to think. In Prentice et al. (1978), of the parents who encouraged their children to believe in the Easter Bunny, 23% of their children did *not* believe, and of the parents who discouraged the belief 47% of children *did* believe in the Easter Bunny. In interviews with fundamentalist Christian families, Clark (1995) also found that many children believed that Santa was real even though their parents discouraged such belief. Collectively, the data indicate that children are influenced by cultural norms and parental input but also possess ample independence of thought. To speak in terms of two venerable ideas, the child is raised by a village, but the child comes with conceptual propensities and is *not* a tabula rasa.

A Social-Ecology Approach to Children's Spirituality

A social-ecology model (Bronfenbrenner, 1979) illuminates the many influences on children's spiritual development by analyzing diverse contexts of growth. Scholars should not only assess different systems that have immediate and proximal impact (e.g., family, church, peer group, school) but the interactions between them. Although there are many social contexts in which children develop, length limits preclude discussion of them, so here the discussion will be on the family and peer contexts. Although social-ecology models posit that it takes a village to raise a child, the family is "the first village" of RSD. Readers are referred to other sources on the family (e.g., Boyatzis, Dollahite, & Marks, 2006) and the focus here will be on some theories and mechanisms of family influence on religious and spiritual development.

One theoretical framework is a sociocultural model that emphasizes the influence of knowledgeable adults who use scaffolding and guided participation in culturally meaningful practices to help the child move to higher understandings (Vygotsky, 1978). In this view, parents, clergy, and other adults can be seen as mentors who guide apprentices—children—to more advanced levels of understanding and engagement in religious practices, creeds, and modes of expression. A second framework is a transactional model of development that posits that children and parents influence each other (P $\longleftrightarrow$ C) in recurrent reciprocal exchanges (Kuczynski, 2003). This characterization of bi-directional family interaction contrasts sharply with traditional views that presume parents influence children in a unilateral P $\rightarrow$ C fashion; unfortunately this "transmission" model has dominated socialization research for decades, but scholars now endorse a more dynamic conceptualization of the family as having bi-directional and multidirectional flows of influence. In transactional models it is difficult to determine when parent influence ends and child influence begins (in Yeats' apropos phrase, it is impossible to separate the dancer from the dance). In the family, whatever input children receive from their parents not only must be processed through the child's inherent cognitive structures but may also be mediated through external factors such as sibling relationships. In this view, children's beliefs may undergo initial revision due to parent testimony (Harris & Koenig, 2006) but also may show ongoing revisions due to "secondary adjustments" through "third-party discussions" that are common in family life (Kuczynski, 2003, p. 10). Our field knows far too little about these complex and crucial bi- and multidirectional dynamics in which parents and children influence *each other's* spiritual growth. When these dynamics are examined, it is likely (see Boyatzis, 2004) that some families reveal a distinct "parent-as-mentor, child-as-apprentice" role structure; in other families, there may be more fluidity between these roles. In some families the child may be viewed as something of a "spiritual savant." The typical family may display all of these interactional configurations at different times in a child's (and parent's) maturation and in response to specific topics under discussion. For example, we might expect that parents and children would use very different communication styles and roles when discussing, at one time, a worship ritual at church or temple but, at another time, ruminating on exactly what happens to us when we die. The prevalence and psychological functions of these various communication styles must be studied.

Within these dynamics, it is likely that parents influence their children as in other realms, through induction of beliefs, disciplinary tactics, rewards and punishments, and behavioral modeling. Recent work on parent–child communication confirms that parents do not typically try explicitly to teach specific beliefs but instead offer more subtly piecemeal fragments of knowledge (Boyatzis & Janicki, 2003; Callanan, 2005; Harris & Koenig, 2006). Other processes that have been recently proposed are parents' spiritual modeling and children's spiritual observational learning (Bandura, 2003; Silberman, 2003). For example, work from England has underscored the power of parental modeling as a key influence on the prayer behavior of children (Francis & Brown, 1990) and adolescents (Francis & Brown, 1991). Retrospective reports from religious adults confirm that "embedded routines"—regular family rituals such as mealtime prayer—were frequent in their childhoods and helped form the narrative structure of religious meaning in family life (Wuthnow, 1999). Scholars must attend more to how children influence their parents in these activities. This child→parent dynamic is a dark void in our literature.

Ongoing conversation about religion may also be an important mechanism through which parents and children influence each other and co-construct religious and spiritual meanings (see Boyatzis, 2004). One study of Christian families with children ages 3–12 used surveys and diaries of parent–child conversations about religious topics and found that children are active participants—they initiate and terminate about half of conversations, they speak as much as parents do, and they ask questions and offer their own views (Boyatzis & Janicki, 2003). The data challenge the view that children are passive recipients who merely consume parental input and instead show the family to have reciprocal influence; these findings also support the claim that children ask questions to actively seek adult input, especially on issues that children find puzzling (Harris & Koenig, 2005). Adults' retrospective reports also suggest that conversations about religion in childhood were important family interactions (Dudley & Wisbey, 2000; Wuthnow, 1999). Recent qualitative work (Dollahite & Thatcher, 2008) on highly religious Jewish, Christian, and Muslim families shows that when family conversations about religious issues are youth-centered (vs. parent-centered), the experience for both children and parents is more positive.

A social-ecology approach allows the scientist to assess various social contexts in which children's religion and spirituality develops; this approach also often entails the use of multiple measures of multiple religious and spiritual constructs. This is sorely needed in the field, as one review of research found that more than 80% of studies on religion and family used only one- or two-item measures of religiosity (Mahoney, Pargament, Swank, & Tarakeshwar, 2001). Let me illustrate the value of multiple measures of related constructs.

Parents with conservative Christian affiliations approve of spanking and use it more often with their children, but research has shown that a stronger predictor of spanking (than religious affiliation per se) is the parents' theological conservatism (e.g., Biblical literalism, thinking that children possess original sin) (Gershoff, Miller, & Holden, 1999). Of course, it should not surprise us that continuous psychological variables would be more informative than nominal/categorical ones. This religiosity-spanking link has been further elucidated by a superb recent study. Murray-Swank, Mahoney, and Pargament (2006) measured several indices of religious belief in mothers including their theological conservatism (vs. liberalism) and their sanctification of their roles as parents. Sanctification refers to how much mothers imbued their roles with sacred and holy qualities and saw themselves as doing "God's work." The results illuminated the value of using multiple measures. Neither conservatism nor sanctification was related independently to the mothers' use of spanking. However, regressions showed that spanking was predicted by the *interaction* between mothers' conservatism and sanctification scores. Specifically, mothers who were theologically conservative were *more* likely than other conservative mothers to spank their children if they also viewed their parent role as sacred and holy; in contrast, mothers who were theologically liberal were *less* likely than other liberal mothers to spank their children if they also viewed their role as sacred and holy. Thus, "the link between sanctifying one's role as a parent and using corporal punishment ... was moderated by how conservative or liberal a mother was in her interpretation of the Bible" (p. 283).

Thus, our scientific understanding of religious and spiritual development will be enriched by multiple measures of multiple relevant religious constructs. This work will be especially helpful to measure the *interactions* between variables.

A social-ecology approach also examines interactions between different social contexts in children's lives. Schwartz (2006) measured adolescent spirituality in relation to parent and peer religiosity. Data were collected at a large international Christian youth conference in Canada; campers were 16 years old on average and provided data on religious belief and commitment and "perceived faith support" from parents and friends, with items such as "my parents (friends) and I talk about how we are doing as Christians" and "my parents (friends) show me what it means to be an authentic Christian." Not surprisingly, the teenagers' own religiosity was predicted by their parents' and friends' religiosity; teens with stronger faith had parents and peers with stronger faith. But the interesting finding was that parents' influence was mediated by friends' religiosity: After controlling for friends' faith support, parents' faith support predicted teens' religiosity less strongly. Thus, our understanding of adolescent spirituality is enriched by measuring the interplay of different contexts in which youth develop. This conclusion emerges from a national study of US youth by Gunnoe and Moore (2002) on childhood and adolescent predictors of religiosity in early adulthood. Mothers' religiosity and religious training in childhood were predictors of young adult religiosity, but one of the most potent predictors was the frequency of worship attendance by one's peers during adolescence.

In a similar study, Regnerus, C. Smith, and B. Smith (2004) analyzed data from the National Longitudinal Study of Adolescent Health, a database of youth from grades 7 to 12. The surveys included two religiosity outcomes for youth: worship attendance and importance of religion. Relative influences were computed of the religiosity of parents, peers, the youths' schools, and the local county norms (of worship attendance). As expected, teens' worship attendance was related most strongly to their parents' attendance but peers' religiosity and local county worship norms also had strong relations to youth attendance. Also, the importance of religion in the youths' schools turned out to be the strongest predictor of the importance that the adolescent subjects themselves placed on religion. Together, these studies confirm the value of a social-ecology approach that analyzes links between multiple influences on youth religiosity.

Nevertheless, let us remember that "the map is not the territory." Large-scale survey studies are invaluable for charting structural relations between variables, but truly knowing *how* and *why* these variables affect each other is another matter. Deeper work—in-depth qualitative work with multiple informants within multiple social contexts—is needed to understand the dynamics between individuals' religious and spiritual development and their social and interpersonal contexts. I concur with the proposal for the "need for qualitative and quantitative studies that go both deep and wide" (Roehlkepartain & Patel, 2006, p. 333). In my view, truly to understand the richness of children's and adolescents' religiosity and spirituality, our field requires time-intensive, qualitative work (see Boyatzis & Newman, 2004; Coles, 1990; Hay & Nye, 1998).

Adolescent Wellbeing

A major research area is adolescent wellbeing and positive development. Here I describe recent studies that help us further understand religion's role in adolescent wellbeing and begin to address why religion might matter in teenagers' lives.

In a study that illustrates the value of studying multiple social contexts in teenagers' lives, Regnerus and Elder (2003) found that youth who live in high-poverty areas were more likely to stay on track academically if they were also high in church attendance. In contrast, those youth living in the same high-poverty areas and who were low in church attendance were more likely to fall behind academically. Thus, religious involvement can ameliorate broader risk factors such as community poverty.

Although longitudinal design is unfortunately rare in our field, Kerestes, Youniss, and Metz (2004) studied American youth from grades 10–12 (roughly 15–16 and 17–18 years of age). Changes in youth religiosity across that interval were linked to changes in risk behaviors (e.g., drug use) and civic involvement (e.g., desire to perform volunteer service). The most positive behavioral profile (high civic involvement, low drug use) occurred in the youth who scored as highly religious at both grade levels. The more telling finding from the longitudinal design was that youth who went from high to low religiosity over that 2-year interval also sharply increased in use of marijuana and alcohol, whereas going from low to high religiosity was linked to higher desire for civic involvement.

While the above study echoes the common findings that religion is linked in healthy ways to adolescent wellbeing, some studies are revealing why. For example, Furrow, King, and White (2004) assessed identity, meaning, and prosocial concerns in a diverse sample of 800 American public high school students. Structural equation analyses supported a model in which religious identity was significantly linked to stronger and more positive "personal meaning," which in turn predicted higher prosocial concern. This concern was manifested in higher scores for personal responsibility, empathy, and helpfulness toward others. In a national survey of 20,000 American adolescents, Wagener, Furrow, King, Leffert, and Benson (2003) found that teenagers' religious involvement made a positive impact on their wellbeing through the mediating mechanism of giving the youth exposure to increased social capital and developmental assets within the religious community. Social engagements with youth and adults in religious communities, in turn, reduced youth's risk behaviors and increased their psychosocial thriving and wellbeing.

In conclusion, it seems that involvement with religion can promote many aspects of adolescent wellbeing and identity and enhance one's sense of purpose and meaning in life and thus service toward others. This is a clear example of a strong connection between "religion" and "spirituality," in that engagement with organized religious tradition (and all that entails in beliefs, rituals, community, etc.) seems to promote a greater sense of personal connectedness with what is beyond the self and a deeper understanding of the self. Thus, youth who are engaged in a value-laden and moral context that religion can provide will emerge with an enhanced spiritual sensibility that promotes attitudes and actions to contribute to the greater good (Lerner, Dowling, & Anderson, 2003).

Moving Beyond Stage Theory

The paradigm of cognitive-developmentalism and its focus on age-related cognitive processing has dominated the study of children's religious and spiritual development and still underlies many scholars' thinking (Spilka, Hood, Hunsberger, & Gorsuch, 2003). I assert that this cognitive-developmental hegemony has impeded our understanding of religious and spiritual development (see Boyatzis, 2005). As developmental psychology has substantially outgrown stage theory (see Overton, 1998), the study of children's spiritual and religious development should as well. An "obsession with stages" impedes our understanding of both the gradualness and the "complexity and uniqueness of individual religious development" (Spilka et al., 2003, p. 85).

Another problem with cognitive-developmental stage theory is that its narrow focus on the "typical kid at a given age" fails to account for the substantial variability between and within individuals at any given age. Individuals—children and adolescents—enjoy sudden spiritual gains and spurts (due to dramatic experiences or revelatory insights) as well as regressions (due to trauma or despair); for many people, including children and teens, there are long seasons of stillness. Different individuals experience a different mix of these different experiences—growth, loss, stasis—at different times, in different ways, due to different causes, and with different consequences. An egregious flaw of stage theories is their failure to account for these varieties of religious and spiritual experiences within and between individuals at any age.

For some empirical meat in this critique, consider one of our most famous theories: James Fowler's stages of faith (Fowler, 1981). While this emphasizes modal stages characteristic of each age, Fowler's own data prove that *variability* commonly occurs within a single age. Drawing from Fowler's data (1981, Table B.3), while 72% of children in middle childhood possessed the "age-appropriate" mythic-literal faith, in that age group children scored in *four* different stages or combined adjacent stages. In the subsequent stage of synthetic-conventional faith (allegedly typical of teenagers), only 50% of adolescents sampled scored in this stage, and teens in this sample scored in *five* different stages or substages. (The variability is even greater at older ages.) I find it disappointing that Fowler, a truly great theorist whose book is a monumental achievement, has yet to recognize this empirical problem in his stage theory (see, e.g., Fowler & Dell, 2006). Let us question our veneration of stage theories that lump into tidy ages the myriad messy diversities of religiosity and spirituality.

Stage theory has constrained our understanding of children's spirituality and thus our work with children. I assume that religious educators and youth ministers have ample experiences with children who were considerably more mature spiritually than some (or many) older individuals, who, in contrast to standard theorizing, seemed less mature then they "should" have been. (Fowler has now recognized these possibilities; Fowler & Dell, 2006.) Consequently, our grasp of young children's spirituality and our modes of religious education and faith formation have been impeded due to mistaken assumptions of stage theory.

Let me note that it is indeed likely that *specific domains* of religion or spirituality reflect stage-like change (e.g., in God concepts, feelings about and understanding of prayer). However, these changes are not yoked so tightly to specific age ranges to justify calling them developmental stages. Stage models often have assumptions of wide-sweeping changes in the holistic cognitive structures children use. Most research supports an alternative view that cognitive changes are not so far-reaching and holistic as they are more narrow, specific, and local, or domain specific (Overton, 1998). Therefore, my hope is that scholars will spend more time exploring developmental *sequences* in different domains. I assume that individual domains show sequential growth that is at times incremental and orderly and other times more random with growth punctuated by stasis or regression. Looking across domains, there may be little uniform change (as predicted by older stage theories) but instead variation in trajectories of domains due to factors such as children's own cognitive propensities, family influences, local cultural support, and so on.

A theoretical framework that would enhance our field is Siegler's (e.g., 1994, 1996) overlapping waves model. Siegler analyzes children's "on-line" cognitive processes to solve individual mathematical problems. Based on years of research, Siegler argues that at any moment children have available to themselves several ways of thinking. These are strategies that compete with each other, and over time and experience (as some yield more parsimonious or palatable answers), some ways of thinking will become more common while others less common, and some will oscillate frequently. This model seems more consonant with children's actual thinking than do theories that posit children growing dramatically in sweeping change from one global stage to another. Siegler's claim that "cognitive change is better thought of in terms of changing distributions of ways of thinking than in terms of sudden shifts from one way of thinking to another" (Siegler, 1994, p. 3) seems to describe how children (and adults) often vacillate in their religious views and beliefs and spiritual connectedness to what is beyond them, perhaps never totally jettisoning one way of thinking but prioritizing some ways more than others at various times. In some circumstances, one form of thinking can become dominant that might not show up in other circumstances (e.g., a parent using prayer to plead for God to "help me out just this one time" in, say, the case of a sick child). In sum, the complexities of thought and behavior require us to move beyond stage theory. As leading theorists in developmental psychology have said, "the inability of stage theory to account for … variability has led to a virtual abandonment of stage theory as a framework for research and interpretation" (Fischer & Bidell, 1998, p. 470).

Conclusion

Children's religious and spiritual development is receiving attention from scholars like never before. While much work has revealed valuable lessons about religious and spiritual development, we have a lot to learn, and I have attempted here to identify recent areas of growth, empirical works that are yielding valuable information and pointing us in good directions, and theoretical contentions that call us to replace some long-standing but erroneous ways of thinking. We will need more sophisticated theories and measures than used in the past to move forward to a deeper understanding of a dimension of life that, though challenging to understand, is central to child development and our humanity.

References

Allen, H. C. (Ed.). (2008). *Nurturing children's spirituality: Christian perspectives and best practices*. Eugene, OR: Cascade.

Bandura, A. (2003). On the psychosocial impact and mechanisms of spiritual modeling. *The International Journal for the Psychology of Religion, 13*, 167–174.

Barrett, J. L., & Keil, F. C. (1996). Anthropomorphism and God concepts: Conceptualizing a non-natural entity. *Cognitive Psychology, 31*, 219–247.

Barrett, J. L., Newman, R. M., & Richert, R. A. (2003). When seeing is not believing: Children's understanding of humans' and non-humans' use of background knowledge in interpreting visual displays. *Journal of Cognition and Culture, 3*, 91–108.

Barrett, J. L., & Richert, R. A. (2003). Anthropomorphism or preparedness? Exploring children's God concepts. *Review of Religious Research, 44*, 300–312.

Benson, P. L. (2004). Emerging themes in research on adolescent spiritual and religious development. *Applied Developmental Science, 8*, 47–50.

Benson, P. L., Roehlkepartain, E., & Hong, K. (Eds.). (2008). Spiritual development [Special issue]. *New Directions for Youth Development, 118*.

Benson, P. L., Roehlkepartain, E. C., & Rude, S. P. (2003). Spiritual development in childhood and adolescence: Toward a field of inquiry. *Applied Developmental Science, 7*, 204–212.

Bering, J. M., & Bjorklund, D. F. (2004). The natural emergence of reasoning about the afterlife as a developmental regularity. *Developmental Psychology, 40*, 217–233.
Boyatzis, C. J. (2003a). Religious and spiritual development: An introduction. *Review of Religious Research, 44*, 213–219.
Boyatzis, C. J. (2003b). Religious and spiritual development [Special issue]. *Review of Religious Research, 44*(3).
Boyatzis, C. J. (2004). The co-construction of spiritual meaning in parent-child communication. In D. Ratcliff (Ed.), *Children's spirituality: Christian perspectives, research, and applications* (pp. 182–200). Eugene, Oregon: Wipf & Stock.
Boyatzis, C. J. (2005). Children's religious and spiritual development. In R. F. Paloutzian & C. L. Park (Eds.), *Handbook of the psychology of religion and spirituality* (pp. 123–143). New York: Guilford.
Boyatzis, C. J. (Ed.). (2006). Unraveling the dynamics of religion in the family and parent-child relationships [Special issue]. *The International Journal for the Psychology of Religion, 16*(4).
Boyatzis, C. J., Dollahite, D. C., & Marks, L. D. (2006). The family as a context for religious and spiritual development in children and youth. In E. C. Roehlkepartain, P. E. King, L. Wagener, & P. L. Benson (Eds.), *The handbook of spiritual development in childhood and adolescence* (pp. 297–309). Thousand Oaks, CA: Sage.
Boyatzis, C. J., & Hambrick-Dixon, P. (Eds.). (2008). Adolescent spirituality [Special section]. *Research in the Social Scientific Study of Religion, 19*.
Boyatzis, C. J., & Janicki, D. (2003). Parent-child communication about religion: Survey and diary data on unilateral transmission and bi-directional reciprocity styles. *Review of Religious Research, 44*, 252–270.
Boyatzis, C. J., & Newman, B. (2004). How shall we study children's spirituality? In D. Ratcliff (Ed.), *Children's spirituality: Christian perspectives, research, and application* (pp. 166–181). Eugene, OR: Wipf & Stock.
Boyer, P. (1994). *The naturalness of religious ideas: A cognitive theory of religion*. Berkeley, CA: University of California Press.
Boyer, P., & Walker, S. (2000). Intuitive ontology and cultural input in the acquisition of religious concepts. In K. S. Rosengren, C. N. Johnson, & P. L. Harris (Eds.), *Imagining the impossible: Magical, scientific, and religious thinking in children* (pp. 130–156). Cambridge, UK: Cambridge University Press.
Boyer, P. (2001). *Religion explained: The evolutionary origins of religious thought*. New York: Basic Books.
Bronfenbrenner, U. (1979). *The ecology of human development*. Cambridge, MA: Harvard University Press.
Callanan, M. A. (2006). Cognitive development, culture, and conversation: Comments on Harris and Koenig's "Truth in testimony: How children learn about science and religion." *Child Development, 77*, 525–530.
Clark, C. D. (1995). *Flights of fancy, leaps of faith: Children's myths in contemporary America*. Chicago: University of Chicago Press.
Coles, R. (1990). *The spiritual life of children*. Boston: Houghton Mifflin.
Dollahite, D. C., & Thatcher, J. Y. (2008). Talking about religion: How religious youth and parents discuss their faith. *Journal of Adolescent Research, 23*, 611–641.
Dowling, E., & Scarlett, W. G. (Eds.). (2006). *Encyclopedia of spiritual development in childhood and adolescence*. Thousand Oaks, CA: Sage.
Dudley, R. L., & Wisbey, R. L. (2000). The relationship of parenting styles to commitment to the church among young adults. *Religious Education, 95*, 39–50.
Elkind, D. (1970). The origins of religion in the child. *Review of Religious Research, 12*, 35–42.
Evans, E. M. (2000). Beyond scopes: Why creationism is here to stay. In K. S. Rosengren, C. N. Johnson, & P. L. Harris (Eds.), *Imagining the impossible: Magical, scientific, and religious thinking in children* (pp. 305–333). New York: Cambridge University Press.

Fischer, K. W., & Bidell, T. R. (1998). Dynamic development of psychological structures in thought and action. In W. Damon (Series Ed.) & R. M. Lerner (Vol. Ed.), *Handbook of child psychology: Vol. 1. Theoretical models of human development* (5th ed., pp. 467–561). New York: Wiley.

Fowler, J. (1981). *Stages of faith: The psychology of human development and the quest for meaning.* New York: HarperCollins.

Fowler, J., & Dell, M. L. (2006). Stages of faith from infancy through adolescence: Reflections on three decades of faith development theory. In E. C. Roehlkepartain, P. E. King, L. M. Wagener & P. L. Benson, (Eds.), *Handbook of spiritual development in childhood and adolescence* (pp. 34–45). Thousand Oaks, CA: Sage.

Francis, L. J., & Brown, L. B. (1990). The predisposition to pray: A study of the social influence on the predisposition to pray among eleven-year-old children in England. *Journal of Empirical Theology, 3*, 23–34.

Francis, L. J., & Brown, L. B. (1991). The influence of home, church, and school on prayer among sixteen-year-old adolescents in England. *Review of Religious Research, 33*, 112–122.

Furrow, J. L., King, P. E., & White, K. (2004). Religion and positive youth development: Identity, meaning, and prosocial concerns. *Applied Developmental Science, 8*, 17–26.

Gershoff, E. T., Miller, P. C., & Holden, G. W. (1999). Parenting influences from the pulpit: Religious affiliation as a determinant of corporal punishment. *Journal of Family Psychology, 13*, 307–320.

Goldman, R. G. (1964). *Religious thinking from childhood to adolescence.* London: Routledge and Kegan Paul.

Gunnoe, M. L., & Moore, K. A. (2002). Predictors of religiosity among youth aged 17–22: A longitudinal study of the National Survey of Children. *Journal for the Scientific Study of Religion, 41*, 613–622.

Harris, P. L., & Koenig, M. A. (2006). Truth in testimony: How children learn about science and religion. *Child Development, 77*, 505–524.

Hay, D., & Nye, R. (1998). *The spirit in the child.* London: Fount.

Hay, D., Reich, K. H., & Utsch, M. (2006). Spiritual development: Intersections and divergence with religious development. In E. C. Roehlkepartain, P. E. King, L. Wagener, & P. L. Benson (Eds.), *The handbook of spiritual development in childhood and adolescence* (pp. 46–59). Thousand Oaks, CA: Sage.

Heller, D. (1986). *The children's God.* Chicago: University of Chicago.

Hyde, K. E. (1990). *Religion in childhood and adolescence.* Birmingham, AL: Religious Education Press.

Johnson, C. N. (2000). Putting different things together: The development of metaphysical thinking. In K. S. Rosengren, C. N. Johnson, & P. L. Harris (Eds.), *Imagining the impossible: Magical, scientific, and religious thinking in children* (pp. 179–211). Cambridge, UK: Cambridge University Press.

Johnson, C. N., & Boyatzis, C. J. (2006). Cognitive-cultural foundations of spiritual development. In E. C. Roehlkepartain, P. E. King, L. Wagener, & P. L. Benson (Eds.), *The handbook of spiritual development in childhood and adolescence* (pp. 211–223). Thousand Oaks, CA: Sage.

Kerestes, M., Youniss, J., & Metz, E. (2004). Longitudinal patterns of religious perspectives and civic integration. *Applied Developmental Science, 8*, 39–46.

King, P. E., & Boyatzis, C. J. (2004). Exploring adolescent religious and spiritual development: Current and future theoretical and empirical perspectives [special issue]. *Applied Developmental Science, 8* (1).

Kuczynski, L. (2003). Beyond bidirectionality: Bilateral conceptual frameworks for understanding dynamics in parent-child relations. In L. Kuczynski (Ed.), *Handbook of dynamics in parent-child relations* (pp. 3–24). Thousand Oaks, CA: Sage.

Lerner, R. M., Dowling, E. M., & Anderson, P. M. (2003). Positive youth development: Thriving as a basis of personhood and civil society. *Applied Developmental Science, 7*, 172–180.

Long, D., Elkind, D., & Spilka, B. (1967). The child's conception of prayer. *Journal for the Scientific Study of Religion, 6*, 101–109.

Mahoney, A., Pargament, K. I., Swank, A., & Tarakeshwar, N. (2001). Religion in the home in the 1980s and 90s: A meta-analytic review and conceptual analysis of religion. *Journal of Family Psychology, 15*, 559–596.

Murray-Swank, A., Mahoney, A., & Pargament, K. I. (2006). Sanctification of parenting: Links to corporal punishment and parental warmth among Biblically conservative and liberal mothers. *The International Journal for the Psychology of Religion, 16*, 271–288.

Oser, F., Scarlett, G. W., & Bucher, A. (2006). Religious and spiritual development throughout the life span. In W. Damon & R. M. Lerner (Eds.), *Handbook of child psychology: Vol. 1: Theoretical models of development* (6th ed., pp. 942–997). New York: Wiley.

Overton, W. F. (1998). Developmental psychology: Philosophy, concepts, and methodology. In W. Damon & R. M. Lerner (Eds.), *Handbook of child psychology: Vol. 1. Theoretical models of development* (5th ed., pp. 107–188). New York: Wiley.

Prentice, N. M., Manosevitz, M., & Hubbs, L. (1978). Imaginary figures of early childhood: Santa Claus, Easter Bunny, and the Tooth Fairy. *American Journal of Orthopsychiatry, 48*, 618–628.

Ratcliff, D. (Ed.). (2004). *Children's spirituality: Christian perspectives, research, and applications*. Eugene, OR: Cascade.

Regnerus, M. D., & Elder, G. H., Jr. (2003). Staying on track in school: Religious influences in high- and low-risk settings. *Journal for the Scientific Study of Religion, 42*, 633–649.

Regnerus, M. D., Smith, C., & Smith, B. (2004). Social context in the development of adolescent religiosity. *Applied Developmental Science, 8*, 27–38.

Reich, K. H., Oser, F. K., & Scarlett, W. G. (Eds.). (1999). *Psychological studies on spiritual and religious development: The case of religion, Vol. 2*. Lengerich, Germany: Pabst Science Publishers.

Robinson, E. (1983). *The original vision: A study of the religious experience of childhood*. New York: Seabury Press.

Roehlkepartain, E. C., Benson, P. L., King, P. E., & Wagener, L. (2006). Spiritual development in childhood and adolescence: Moving to the scientific mainstream. In E. C. Roehlkepartain, P. E. King, L. Wagener, & P. L. Benson (Eds.), *The handbook of spiritual development in childhood and adolescence* (pp. 1–15). Thousand Oaks, CA: Sage.

Roehlkepartain, E. C., King, P. E., Wagener, L., & Benson, P. L. (Eds.). (2006). *The handbook of spiritual development in childhood and adolescence*. Thousand Oaks, CA: Sage.

Roehlkepartain, E. C., & Patel, E. (2006). Congregations: Unexamined crucibles for spiritual development. In E. C. Roehlkepartain, P. E. King, L. Wagener, & P. L. Benson (Eds.), *The handbook of spiritual development in childhood and adolescence* (pp. 324–336). Thousand Oaks, CA: Sage.

Rosengren, K. S., Johnson, C. N., & Harris, P. L. (Eds.). (2000). *Imagining the impossible: Magical, scientific, and religious thinking in children*. Cambridge, UK: Cambridge University Press.

Schwartz, K. D. (2006). Transformation in parent and friend faith support predicting adolescents' religious faith. *The International Journal for the Psychology of Religion, 16*, 311–326.

Search Institute. (2008, September). *Spiritual development survey data collection nears completion in eight countries* (September 2008 Progress Report). Minneapolis, MN: Search Institute.

Siegler, R. S. (1994). Cognitive variability: A key to understanding cognitive development. *Current Directions in Psychological Science, 3*, 1–5.

Siegler, R. S. (1996). *Emerging minds: The process of change in children's thinking*. New York: Oxford University Press.

Silberman, I. (2003). Spiritual role modeling: The teaching of meaning systems. *The International Journal for the Psychology of Religion, 13*, 175–195.

Spilka, B., Hood, R. W., Jr., Hunsberger, B., & Gorsuch, R. (2003). *The psychology of religion: An empirical approach* (3rd ed.). New York: Guilford Press.

Subbotsky, E. (1993). *Foundations of the mind: Children's understanding of reality*. Cambridge, MA: Harvard University Press.

Vygotsky, L. S. (1978). *Mind in society*. Cambridge, MA: Harvard University Press.

Wagener, L. M., Furrow, J. L., King, P. E., Leffert, N., & Benson, P. (2003). Religion and developmental resources. *Review of Religious Research, 44*, 271–284.
Westerhoff, J. W., III. (2000). *Will our children have faith?* (rev. ed.). Toronto: Anglican Book Centre.
Woolley, J. D. (1997). Thinking about fantasy: Are children fundamentally different thinkers and believers from adults? *Child Development, 68*, 991–1011.
Woolley, J. D. (2000). The development of beliefs about direct mental-physical causality in imagination, magic, and religion. In K. S. Rosengren, C. N. Johnson, & P. L. Harris (Eds.), *Imagining the impossible: Magical, scientific, and religious thinking in children* (pp. 99–129). Cambridge, UK: Cambridge University Press.
Woolley, J. D., & Phelps, K. (2001). The development of children's beliefs about prayer. *Journal of Cognition and Culture, 1*, 139–167.
Wuthnow, R. (1999). *Growing up religious: Christians and Jews and their journeys of faith.* Boston: Beacon.
Yust, K. M., Johnson, A. N., Sasso, S. E., & Roehlkepartain, E. C. (Eds.). (2006). *Nurturing child and adolescent spirituality: Perspectives from the world's religious traditions.* New York: Rowman & Littlefield.
Zinnbauer, B., & Pargament, K. I. (2005). Religiousness and spirituality. In R. F. Paloutzian & C. L. Park (Eds.), *The handbook of the psychology of religion* (pp. 21–42). New York: Guilford.

Biographical details

Professor Chris J Boyatzis is Professor of Psychology at Bucknell University, Lewisburg, USA

Chapter 4
Understanding and Assessing Spiritual Health

John W. Fisher

Abstract This chapter explores awareness and compassion as essential elements in spiritual cultivation. Of the education of awareness, it describes the ideas of Aldous Huxley and J. Krishnamurthi as well as the Buddha's teachings on mindfulness. The practice of awareness would reveal a holistic experience and multiple dimensions of reality. This chapter briefly describes the author's view of "the five dimensions of reality" that include dimensions from the surface to the deepest, infinite reality. Drawing on Eastern perspectives, it explains that "pure awareness" is identical with infinite reality and that "great compassion" emerges as a manifestation of pure awareness. In addition, as for cultivating compassion, this chapter explores such concepts as the Four Immeasurable Minds, *bodhichitta, bodhisattva,* and also the mind training called *lojong* in Tibetan Buddhism. Finally, it suggests a vision of "the education of enlightenment," in which both awareness and compassion are of central importance.

Brief Introduction

There is a growing consensus that human spirituality is a real phenomenon, not just a figment of the imagination (Seaward, 2001; Moberg, 2002). Accurate assessment is needed to extend knowledge about spiritual wellness, and to help diagnose spiritual ailments, so that appropriate spiritual care might be provided to restore spiritual health (Moberg, 2002). This action is needed not only for individuals, but for the whole world, and also for the survival of the human race (Seaward, 2001).

Attempts at defining spirituality vacillate between the human and the divine. Many people claim that "spirituality" and "wellbeing" are both multifaceted constructs that are elusive in nature (e.g. de Chavez, Backett-Milburn, Parry, & Platt, 2005; Buck, 2006; McSherry & Cash, 2004). This has not prevented people from trying to define spirituality and wellbeing and their interrelationship in the form of spiritual wellbeing (SWB).

J.W. Fisher (✉)
School of Education, University of Ballarat, Ballarat Vic 3353, Australia
e-mail: j.fisher@ballarat.edu.au

This chapter provides a brief look at the nature of spirituality and health, then a definition and model of spiritual health and wellbeing. A presentation follows of a number of instruments for measuring aspects of spiritual health and wellbeing that have been developed from this model, with comment on other recent research on spirituality of youth. The last section provides some reflections on this research in spiritual health and wellbeing for pastoral care in schools.

Nature of Spirituality

The nature of spirituality has been debated for centuries. The literature reveals the difficulty writers have in defining the concept (Chiu, Emblen, Van Hofwegen, Sawatzky, & Meyerhoff, 2004; Diaz, 1993; Goodloe & Arreola, 1992; Seaward, 2001). Muldoon and King claim:

> Spirituality can mean many things in popular usage, and is often understood differently by different people. While retaining a certain ambiguity, its current range of application extends from traditional institutional religion to occult practices. In general, the term appears to denote approaches to discovering, experiencing, and living out the implications of an authentic human life (1995, p. 330).

There are 24 separate meanings for the word "spirit" listed in the *Oxford English Dictionary* (Brown, 1993). The general meaning underlying all the uses is that of an animating or vital principle which gives life, transcending the material and mechanical. It refers to the essential nature of human beings, strength of purpose, perception, mental powers and frame of mind. "'Spiritual' may refer to higher moral qualities, with some religious connotations and higher faculties of mind" (Hill, 1989, p. 170). An extensive survey of the literature reveals several points of agreement, as well as divergent opinions, that are worth noting.

Spirituality Is Innate

There is considerable support for spirituality being posited at the heart of human experience (McCarroll, O'Connor, & Meakes, 2005), and being experienced by everyone (Nolan & Crawford, 1997). Oldnall (1996) not only believes that "each individual has spiritual needs" (p. 139), he goes a step further, claiming that "human spirituality in a very real sense ... unifies the whole person" (p. 140). This view is supported by Leetun (1996), in whose opinion spirituality "is the dimension that permeates, deepens, shapes, and unifies all of life" (p. 60). Spirituality can be seen as a vital component of human functioning.

Spirituality Is Emotive

The notion of spirituality is emotive (Jose & Taylor, 1986). It touches people's hearts because it deals with the very essence of being. It is important for people in positions of influence to remember that they cannot be neutral or value free, but must try to be objective in examining the concepts of spirituality and spiritual health, especially as they relate to young people (Warren, 1988).

Spirituality and Religion

Opinions vary on the nature of any relationship between spirituality and religion. Some people equate spirituality with religious activity, or use the words interchangeably (Piedmont, 2001; Gorsuch & Walker, 2006), whereas others believe this assumption is not valid (Banks, Poehler, & Russell, 1984; Scott, 2006). Hill et al. (2000) discuss commonalities between spirituality and religion as well as differences (2000). Scott reports three polarisations between views held by behavioural scientists, differentiating spirituality and religion (Zinnbauer, Pargament, & Scott, 1999). Hill et al. (2000) argue that spirituality is subsumed by religion, but some see religion as one dimension of spirituality (Nolan & Crawford, 1997). Rather simplistically speaking, religion focuses on ideology and rules (of faith and belief systems) (Horsburgh, 1997), whereas spirituality focuses on experience and relationships which go beyond religion (Lukoff, Lu, & Turner, 1992).

Koenig, McCullough, and Larson (2001) include "a relationship to the sacred *or* transcendent" [my italics] (p.18) in their definition of spirituality. Taking this broader view, Seaward (2001) asserts that spirituality involves "connection to a divine source whatever we call it" (p. 77). But, spirituality does not have to include "God-talk" according to Jose and Taylor (1986).

Abraham Maslow, reputed by many to be the father of humanistic psychology, and John Dewey, a founder of the philosophical school of Pragmatism, both consider spirituality to be part of a person's being, therefore, prior to and different from religiosity (Fahlberg & Fahlberg, 1991). A number of authors have followed this humanistic line of thinking bringing attempts at defining secular spirituality as a spirituality without any need for a religious or God component (Harvey, 1996; Newby, 1996). Smith (2000) and Wright (2000) are among many Christian writers who raise arguments against removing religion and God from discussions of spirituality.

This kaleidoscope of viewpoints illustrates how people's worldviews and beliefs can influence their understanding of spirituality, a key feature in the model of spiritual health presented later in this chapter.

Spirituality Is Subjective

Spirituality has been seen as personal, or subjective, lacking much of the objective nature considered necessary for its investigation via the scientific method (Chapman, 1987). But, science can neither affirm nor deny metaphysical issues, such as spirituality, any more than it can aesthetics. Diaz (1993, p. 325) is concerned that proponents of *scientism*, those who exalt the scientific method to the unholy status of "science = truth", tend to dismiss spirituality, because it cannot be studied through current scientific methodology. "If we can accept concepts such as self-worth, self-esteem, and self-actualization, then it should be legitimate to explore ... spirituality, for these concepts are equally as intangible as spirituality" (Jose & Taylor, 1986, p. 18).

If one says that the use of the five physical senses and the empirical way of knowing is the only true science, then much of logic, mathematics, reason and psychology have no place in science. To focus too much on the sensory realm, and, from a spiritual perspective, to reduce a person to mere matter is a classic example of mistaking substance for essence (Fahlberg & Fahlberg, 1991). To balance an over-emphasis on the subjectivity of spirituality, Thatcher (1991, p. 23) argues that there is a "crippling price to pay for misidentification of spirituality as inwardness", and we need to go beyond the inner search to fully understand spirituality.

Spirituality Is Dynamic

According to Priestley (1985, p. 114), "The spirit is dynamic. It must be felt before it can be conceptualised". Terms like "spiritual growth" and "development" are used to express the vibrant nature of spirituality (Chapman, 1987). A person's spiritual health can be perceived to be high or low. If it is static, there is neither growth or development, nor spiritual life. The spiritual quest is like being on a journey: If you think you have arrived, you have not yet begun, or you are dead.

Understanding Spirituality

Koenig et al. (2001, p. 19) describe five types of spirituality in the United States, although these could just as easily be grouped into the three categories described by Spilka as "God-oriented, worldly oriented with an idolatrous stress on ecology or nature, or humanistic, stressing human potential or achievement" (cited in Moberg, 2002, p. 49).

Palmer (1999) attempts an integration of the above divergent views, by describing spiritually as "the ancient and abiding human quest for connectedness with something larger and more trustworthy than our egos—with our own souls, with one another, with the worlds of history and nature, with the invisible winds of the spirit, with the mystery of being alive" (p. 6). Palmer's definition has many similarities to my functional definition:

> Spirituality is concerned with a person's awareness of the existence and experience of inner feelings and beliefs, that give purpose, meaning and value to life. Spirituality helps individuals to live at peace with themselves, to love (God and)* their neighbour, and to live in harmony with the environment. For some, spirituality involves an encounter with God, or transcendent reality, which can occur in or out of the context of organised religion, whereas for others, it involves no experience or belief in the supernatural. (NB: *These words were placed in parentheses as they will be meaningless to those people who do not relate with God) (Fisher, 1998, p. 190).

Dimensions of Health

A comment on the nature of health is warranted before investigating the relationship between spirituality and health. Even in Greek times, educators considered the total health of each individual as having a sound spiritual base (Brown, 1978). Thus, "for Hippocrates, it is nature which heals, that is to say the vital force – *pneuma* (or spirit) – which God gives to man" (from Adams, 1939); while "healing" may be defined as "a sense of wellbeing that is derived from an intensified awareness of wholeness and integration among all dimensions of one's being" (Coward & Reed, 1996, p. 278), which includes the spiritual elements of life.

Writers suggest that there are six separate, but interrelated, dimensions that comprise human health (Hawks, 2004; Seaward, 2001). Health involves much more than *physical* fitness and absence of disease; it includes the *mental* and *emotional* aspects of knowing and feeling; the *social* dimension that comes through human interaction; the *vocational* domain; and, at the heart, or, very essence of being, the *spiritual* dimension. To Eberst, it is the spiritual dimension which seems to have greatest impact on overall personal health (1984).

Spiritual Health and Wellbeing

Ellison (1983, p. 332) suggests that spiritual wellbeing "arises from an underlying state of spiritual health and is an expression of it, much like the color of one's complexion and pulse rate are expressions of good [physical] health". Fehring, Miller, and Shaw (1997, p. 664) support this view by adding, "spiritual wellbeing is an indication of individuals' quality of life in the spiritual dimension or simply an indication of their spiritual health".

Four main themes appear in the framework definition proposed by the National Interfaith Coalition on Aging (NICA), in Washington, D.C., that spiritual wellbeing is "the affirmation of life in a relationship with *God, self, community* and *environment* that nurtures and celebrates wholeness" (NICA, 1975, italics added). An extensive review of literature reveals these four sets of relationships are variously mentioned when discussing spiritual wellbeing (references across the last three decades include Benson, 2004; Burkhardt, 1989; Como, 2007; Ellison, 1983; Martsolf & Mickley, 1998; Ross, 2006). These relationships can be developed into four corresponding domains of human existence, for the enhancement of spiritual health:

> relation with self, in the *Personal* domain;
> relation with others, in the *Communal* domain;
> relation with the environment, in the *Environmental* domain;
> relation with Transcendent Other, in the *Transcendental* domain.

Fisher (1998) developed detailed descriptions of these four domains of spiritual health from interviews with 98 educators from 22 secondary schools (State, Catholic and Independent) in Victoria, Australia. Up to five senior staff were interviewed in each school to elicit their views on the nature of spiritual health and its place in the school curriculum. Surveys were also collected from 23 Australian experts. The following definition was derived, in which spiritual health is described as:

> a, if not *the*, fundamental dimension of people's overall health and well-being, permeating and integrating all the other dimensions of health (i.e., physical, mental, emotional, social and vocational). Spiritual health is a dynamic state of being, shown by the extent to which people live in harmony within relationships in the following domains of spiritual well-being:
>
> *Personal* domain – wherein one intra-relates with oneself with regards to meaning, purpose and values in life. Self-awareness is the driving force or transcendent aspect of the human spirit in its search for identity and self-worth.
>
> *Communal* domain – as shown in the quality and depth of interpersonal relationships, between self and others, relating to morality, culture and religion. These are expressed in love, forgiveness, trust, hope and faith in humanity.
>
> *Environmental* domain – beyond care and nurture for the physical and biological, to a sense of awe and wonder; for some, the notion of unity with the environment.
>
> *Transcendental* domain – relationship of self with some-thing or some-One beyond the human level (i.e. ultimate concern, cosmic force, transcendent reality or God). This involves faith towards, adoration and worship of, the source of Mystery of the universe (1998, p. 191).

This definition outlines the inter-connective and dynamic nature of spiritual health, in which internal harmony depends on intentional self-development, coming from congruence between expressed and experienced meaning, purpose and values in life at the personal level. This often eventuates from personal challenges, which go beyond contemplative meditation, leading to a state of bliss, perceived by some as internal harmony.

Morality, culture and religion are included in the Communal domain of spiritual health, in accord with Tillich's (1967) view that the three interpenetrate one another, constituting a unity of the spirit, but "while each element is distinguishable, they are not separable" (p. 95). Tillich adds that separation of religion from morality and culture yields what is generally called "secular" (p. 97). In this work, religion (with small "r") is construed as essentially a human, social activity with a focus on ideology and rules (of faith and belief systems), as distinct from a relationship with a Transcendent Other, such as that envisioned in the Transcendental domain of spiritual health.

A Model of Spiritual Health

Figure 4.1 depicts the dynamic interrelationships between the component parts of the definition of spiritual health given above. Here, each DOMAIN of spiritual health is comprised of two aspects – knowledge and inspiration. **Knowledge** (written in **bold** type under the heading for each DOMAIN) provides the cognitive framework that helps interpret the *inspirational* or transcendent aspect (in *italics* in the centre of each domain), which is the essence and motivation of each domain of SH. Here we see the metaphorical "head" and "heart" working together, striving for harmony. Once achieved, this harmony is reflected in the expressions of wellbeing, written in Arial type at the bottom of each cell.

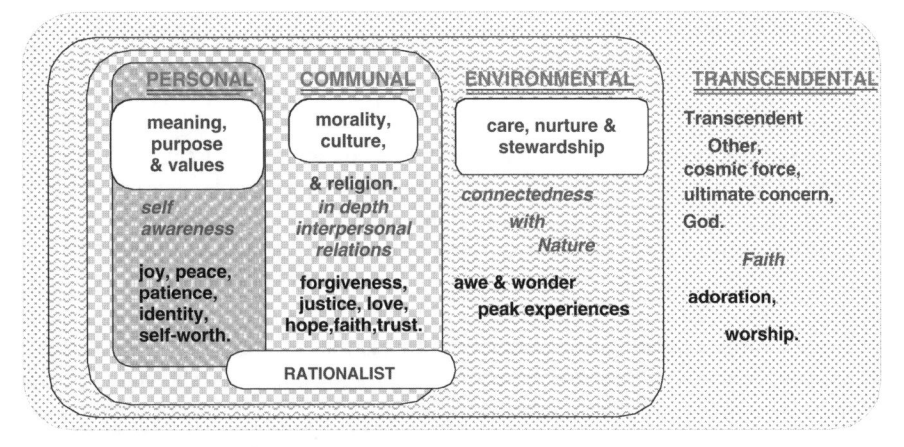

Fig. 4.1 Four domains model of spiritual health and wellbeing

[Figure contents:
- PERSONAL: meaning, purpose & values; self awareness; joy, peace, patience, identity, self-worth.
- COMMUNAL: morality, culture, & religion; in depth interpersonal relations; forgiveness, justice, love, hope, faith, trust.
- ENVIRONMENTAL: care, nurture & stewardship; connectedness with Nature; awe & wonder, peak experiences.
- TRANSCENDENTAL: Transcendent Other, cosmic force, ultimate concern, God; Faith; adoration, worship.
- RATIONALIST]

In this model, people's worldviews are seen to filter the knowledge aspects, while their beliefs filter the inspirational aspects. A key feature of this model is the partially distinct nature of, yet interrelation between, the "knowledge" and "inspirational" aspects of each of the four domains of spiritual wellbeing.

The quality, or rightness of relationship, in each of the four domains constitutes a person's *spiritual wellbeing* in that domain. An individual's *spiritual health* is indicated by the combined effect of spiritual wellbeing in each of the domains embraced by the individual. Spiritual health is thus enhanced by developing positive relationships in each domain, and can be increased by embracing more domains.

The notion of *progressive synergism* is proposed here to help explain the interrelationship between the domains of spiritual wellbeing. As the levels of spiritual wellbeing in the domains are combined, the result is more than the sum of the quality of relationships in the individual domains. Progressive synergism implies that the more embracing domains of spiritual wellbeing not only build on, but also build up, the ones they include. The figure depicts the progressive synergistic relationship between the four domains of spiritual wellbeing.

When relationships are not right, or are absent, we lack wholeness or health; spiritual disease can grip our hearts. The quality of relationships in each of the domains will vary over time, or even be non-existent, depending on circumstances, effort, the personal worldview and beliefs of the person. Not many people hold the view that they are sole contributors to their own spiritual health (relationship in the Personal domain only); most at least include relationships with others in their worldview of spiritual wellbeing. The notion of progressive synergism states that development of the personal relationships (related to meaning, purpose and values for life) is precursor to, but also enhanced by, the development of the communal relationships (of morality, culture and religion).

Ideally, unity with the environment builds on, and builds up, the personal and communal relationships. Cultural differences apply here: Many people from western societies do not hold the same view of environment as other people groups, for example, Australian Aboriginals and New Zealand Maoris. Westerners are more likely to have some awareness of environmental concerns rather than the deep connection or a sense of wonder and oneness that is evidenced in some non-Western cultures.

The figure also shows the relationship of a person with a Transcendent Other as embracing relationships in the other three domains. For example, a strong faith in God should enhance all the other relationships for SWB. "As persons go out from or beyond themselves, the spiritual dimension of their lives is deepened, they become more truly themselves and they grow in likeness to God" (Macquarrie, cited in Best, 1996, p. 126).

In this figure, the so-called rationalists are willing to embrace the knowledge aspects of "spiritual" wellbeing, but not the inspirational aspects (shown in balloon boxes). These people would be atheistic or agnostic.

As spiritual health is a dynamic entity, it is through the challenges of life that the veracity and viability of a person's worldview and beliefs will be tested, together with the quality of relationships in the domains of spiritual health and wellbeing considered important. Spiritual health will flourish or flail. If we had a way of assessing the current state of spiritual health, as friend, counselor, parent or teacher, we would have a basis from which to help nurture relationships appropriately, to enhance our own, and others', spiritual wellbeing.

Assessing Spiritual Health and Wellbeing

Many attempts at assessing spirituality and SH/WB are reported in the literature (e.g. Egbert, Mickley, & Coeling, 2004; Hill & Pargament, 2003; King & Crowther, 2004; Koenig et al., 2001; MacDonald & Friedman, 2002; Moberg, 2002). A major difficulty in trying to make sense of this plethora of research is that the conceptual bases upon which the research is founded vary markedly between studies (Berry, 2005). Much of the research confounds spirituality and religion. Although there are commonalities between these two constructs, they are not synonymous (see arguments above).

All measurement devices are built on a values base (generally the researcher's), and most instruments present norms for populations studied. Norms vary so much between groups that what appears to be positive for SWB in one group might have negative implications in another (Moberg, 2002). That is not all. Each group believes that its own criteria for "true" spirituality is better than everyone else's and should possibly be the normative base for all humanity. Moberg does not agree that, because all people are spiritual, it is possible to use identical procedures to evaluate SWB of diverse populations, especially religious and minority groups. He adds that investigating spirituality is complicated because any measure cannot be perfect, and it only reflects the phenomenon or its consequences, because it cannot be measured directly.

Most measures are self-reports, but they might not reflect reality, because "*feeling well* is not necessarily *being well*" (Moberg, 2002, p. 55). It is essential to check the validity of any instrument used. Does it "genuinely measure spirituality or its components?" (p. 56). The power of a questionnaire depends on its theoretical base and the rigour with which it is developed and tested (Gray, 2006).

Nearly all available religiosity/spirituality measures ask people for a single response about "lived experience" on a series of questions (Ross, 2006). In the best instruments, these questions are built on theoretical frameworks of relationships between spirituality and health that are considered important by the developers of the scales. The "scores" thus obtained are arbitrary indicators of spiritual health or wellbeing, especially if they only have a handful of items (Boero et al., 2005). The notion of a group norm of spiritual health is also problematic. People's spiritual health depends on their worldview and beliefs as well as lived experience (Fisher, 1999; Hill et al., 2000), so development of a single measure, which purports to be an objective standard by which to compare people, challenges the multifaceted nature of spiritual health.

Up to 1998, some qualitative studies had been undertaken with school-age children (Coles, 1990; Hay & Nye, 1998), but I could not find any record of quantitative studies of spirituality and/or SWB with school children. Subsequent to my work described here, at least two other studies have used my model of SH to critique their surveys of adolescents (Francis & Robbins, 2005; Hughes, 2007) but neither of these reported on validity to show if their items cohered in the factors presented in my model. None of the other recent studies of youth spirituality have included the balance across the four domains of SH in my model.

Dowling et al. (2004) employed seven items that would fit in Communal SWB, as well as 11 others in a religiosity scale. Engebretson (2006) used nearly equal numbers of questions that would fit Personal, Communal and mixed Transcendental/religiosity domains, but no formal statistics. The studies by Harris et al. (2007) and the Australian, Generation Y Study (Mason, Singleton, & Webber, 2007) almost exclusively used questions about religion and relation with God, conflating spirituality with religion. Tirri, Nokelainen, and Ubani (2006) reported validity analyses, which rated as "fair" for the Spiritual Sensitivity Scale, with its 11 items in four sub-scales. Very few SH/WB measures include many items on the environment, with the exception of Hood's Mysticism Scale (1975), which was developed using university students.

Two recent studies with adolescents in the United States (reported in Wong, Rew & Slaikeu, 2006) used the Spiritual Wellbeing Survey (Ellison, 1983). The SWBS is a commonly used instrument in the United States, comprising two 10-item measures, one for Existential Wellbeing and the other for Religious Wellbeing. This scale was considered too God-oriented for use with increasingly secular Australians, although it was used to validate SHALOM during its development (see next section).

Overall, I found nearly 190 quantitative measures of spirituality and/or Spiritual Health/Wellbeing (SH/WB) in available literature published between 1967 and early 2009. Many more religiosity measures have been reported (Hill & Hood, 1999; Koenig et al., 2001). Application of my model of SH led to the following measures related to SH/WB, which add to this growing collection.

Instruments for Assessing SH/WB

Spiritual Health in Four Domains Index (SH4DI)

The Spiritual Health in Four Domains Index (SH4DI) was developed by overlaying my model on a selection from 150 items used to study spirituality among 311 primary teachers in the United Kingdom (Fisher, Francis, & Johnson, 2000). Exploratory factor analyses were used to establish four factors in the SH4DI, each comprised of six items, with response sets on a 5-point Likert scale. Another study of mainly pastoral carers (in 1998) in a variety of Victorian schools led to a refinement of the SH4DI, by introducing two levels of response for each item (Fisher, 2001). This study contained eight items representing each of the four domains with 5-point Likert scales (ranging from "very high" to "very low").

Spiritual Health and Life-Orientation Measure (SHALOM)

The title SHALOM was chosen to represent the very essence of SWB. The Hebrew word *Shalom* means "completeness, wholeness, health, peace, welfare, safety, soundness, tranquility, prosperity, fullness, rest, harmony, the absence of agitation or discord" (Strong's Concordance—Ref. 7965, 1979). The acronym SHALOM reveals its two components – Spiritual Health measure (SHM) And Life-Orientation Measure (LOM). The LOM elicits the "ideals" people have for SH in four sets of relationships with self, others, environment and/or God. The SHM asks people to reflect on "lived experience/how they feel each item reflects their personal experience most of the time".

SHALOM was developed in the belief that an instrument based on input from 850 secondary school students with diverse cultural and religious backgrounds should have appropriate language and conceptual clarity for studies of SWB within general populations and individuals, from teens to the twilight years (Fisher, 1999). An initial selection of 60 items derived from my model of spiritual health was reduced to the 20-item SHALOM using exploratory factor analysis. The five items in each of four *domains* of SH were scored using Likert scale responses from 1 = very low to 5 = very high (Fig. 4.2):

Subsequent confirmatory factor analyses were performed on SHALOM using data from 4462 nurses and carers, university students and staff, school students and teachers, employees in a manufacturing plant and church-attendees. SHALOM showed good reliability (Cronbach's alpha, composite reliability and variance extracted) as well as (construct, concurrent, discriminant, predictive) validity (Gomez & Fisher, 2003). Factorial independence from personality shown by SHALOM indicates that it does more than just "religify" existing personality constructs (see Piedmont, 2001, p. 4). The stringent process applied to the development of SHALOM yielded salient features of each of the domains to make the overall instrument a balanced, sensitive, flexible tool for assessing spiritual health of individuals and groups.

Fig. 4.2 Twenty items comprising the four domains of SHALOM

Personal	*Communal*
sense of identity	love of other people
self-awareness	forgiveness toward others
joy in life	trust between individuals
inner peace	respect for others
meaning in life	kindness toward other people
Environmental	*Transcendental*
connection with nature	personal relationship with the Divine/God
awe at a breathtaking view	worship of the Creator
oneness with nature	oneness with God
harmony with the environment	peace with God
sense of 'magic' in the environment	prayer life

With only 20 items, SHALOM cannot be considered an exhaustive measure of SH. If carers and clients had time, as well as a confidential relationship, it would be possible to use suitable qualitative procedures to mine the depths of people's SH (e.g. Burkhardt & Nagai-Jacobson, 1994). Rather than taking hours, in 5–10 min plus 5 min scoring time, SHALOM provides an effective means of indicating key aspects of these four domains of SH.

Each person's beliefs and worldview impact their understanding and commitment to the importance of each of these four domains for spiritual health. It is, therefore, important to gain some idea of a person's worldview before attempting to "measure" their SH. In SHALOM, each person is compared with themselves as their standard. No arbitrary group norms are employed to compare or rank people. The difference between their "ideals" and how they feel/"lived experience" gives an indication of their SH in each of the four domains. For example, if people do not think relating with the environment is important for SH, when they score "low" on the "lived experience" category, this is in harmony with their "ideals" in this domain of SH, thus not an immediate cause for concern.

Some people believe that a wholesome relationship with oneself is all that is necessary for SH (MacLaren, 2004). Other people believe that you can only truly be yourself in relation with others (Thatcher, 1991). People are beginning to note the importance of relating with the environment for sustenance and the wellbeing of humanity. Relating with a Transcendent Other/God is not restricted to religious practice. Some studies have introduced terms such as "higher power" to replace "God" in attempts to be more politically correct and/or less offensive to non-theists (Hungelmann, Kenkel-Rossi, Klassen, & Stollenwerk, 1985). In the development of SHALOM, terms such as "godlike force" and "supernatural power" were trialed but found wanting as they were not meaningful to teenagers (and therefore a range of adults?). Whether theistic or not, nearly all people have a concept of "God." As they compare their ideals with their lived experience, it is up to each person to define their own meaning for each notion under investigation. For example, many different religions and denominations exist because of people's differing views. A brief question about religion is asked in the demographic section of my surveys, along with gender and age, but religion per se is not included in SHALOM.

Feeling Good, Living Life

Following the success of SHALOM with secondary school students, in 2000, I developed Feeling Good, Living Life (FG/LL), by surveying 1,080 primary school students (aged 5–12) in State, Catholic, other Christian and Independent schools in Victoria and Western Australia (Fisher, 2004). This 16-item measure elicits students' ideals (Feeling Good) and lived experiences (Living Life) in four domains of SWB, reflecting relationships with self, family (their most significant "others"), the environment, and God. A 5-point Likert scale is used to answer questions about how good each of the following makes pupils feel (Fig. 4.3):

	Self	*Family*
	feel happy	know family love you
	hear people say you are good	love your family
	think life is fun	know you belong to a family
	know people like you	spend time with family
	Environment	*God*
	look at stars & moon	know your God is a friend
	go for walk in park	talk with your God
Fig. 4.3 Sixteen items comprising the four domains of feeling good, living life	spend time in garden	know your God cares for you
	watch sunset or sunrise	think about your God

Quality of Life Influences Survey

In 2002–2003, the Quality Of Life Influences Survey (QOLIS) was developed by considering how much each of the following helped students relate with self, others, nature and God, four areas which reflect their SWB. Responses on a 4-point Likert scale (0 = never, 1 = sometimes, 2 = often, 3 = always) were gathered from 372 upper primary (aged 10–12) and 1,002 secondary school students (aged 12–18) in Catholic, other Christian and Independent schools in Victoria, Australia. Twenty-two influencers were nominated from four *groups*, based on my pastoral involvement with young people over several decades (Fisher, 2006) (Fig. 4.4):

Home	*School*	*Community*	*Church*
mother	teacher	female friend	Sunday/Sabbath school teacher
father	RE teacher	male friend	youth leader
sister	principal	sport coach	religious leader (pastor/priest/rabbi)
brother	counselor	doctor	God
self	welfare staff	counselor	
grand-parent	office staff	musician	

Fig. 4.4 Twenty-two influencers in four groups of the Quality Of Life Influences Survey (QOLIS)

Reflections on Research in SWB for Pastoral Care in Schools

Assessing a person's state of spiritual health is one matter; using the information to help improve quality of life is another. In schools, hospices and hospitals, most staff do not have time for in-depth communication with individuals to ascertain their deepest needs, which impact their spiritual wellbeing. So, how can people be encouraged to share of themselves in a way in which concerned carers can obtain and use the information to help enhance quality of life in the spiritual dimension?

With over 20 students in a class or many hundred in a school, how can a teacher or counselor effectively and efficiently identify students who may be experiencing spiritual dis-ease or distress? It would take hours, if not months or years to interview each student individually. Education policy documents indicate that staff are responsible to care for the whole child, so after some time, we could expect that they might have an inkling about the SWB of each student, as well as their physical, mental, social, emotional (and vocational) wellbeing; see, for example, *The Melbourne Declaration* from MCEETYA (Ministerial Council on Education, Employment, Training and Youth Affairs, 2008). How much time this would take depends on the degree of student–teacher contact in class, extra-curricular activities and in the school yard, as well as the staff members' affinity for relating with students.

Deeply disturbed students are often visible through attention-seeking behaviour. However, some can and do withdraw behind a mask of introversion or quietness. SHALOM and other measures presented here can and have been used to identify students of concern with regards to SWB.

Vignettes from Development of Instruments

Whilst developing SHALOM, I undertook consultancies with selected classes of students in a variety of schools to help test the validity of this instrument. I wanted to know how the findings compared with views of experienced school staff. I had a gut feeling, call it intuition, that the difference between stated ideals and lived experiences in four domains of SWB would relate to behaviour. I could not find anyone else who had reported this type of survey method. As I was doing a consultancy with principals, students were asked to record a code on their surveys, which could be identified by principals. After analysis, detailed reports were written on approximately 10% of participants in each school. In two schools, principals and welfare staff thought the findings from SHALOM added weight to concerns they had about all students identified.

Year 9 Surrogate Mum – Improved Maths and General Wellbeing

During the development of SHALOM, a teacher in a secondary school was drawn to the results from a year 9 girl, who was having trouble keeping up with maths in class as well as homework. Let us call her Jan. Jan was one of three girls in a lower ability class, with a cohort of boisterous boys. Jan showed low scores on her ideal states and even lower scores on how she felt (lived experience) for the Personal and Communal domains of SWB. Through my work with university students it has since been shown that these results correlate with depression (Gomez & Fisher, 2003).

The teacher did not reveal that the principal had told him of her results on SHALOM. He approached Jan quietly and asked, "How are things going?" Her response was to break into tears and inform the teacher that her mum was in hospital, dad was working night shift and she was responsible for looking after her two little brothers, and the housekeeping, cooking, etc. Jan had not told anyone at school about her situation. The teacher immediately offered lunchtime classes for Jan and any other interested students who wished to attend. A small group responded to this offer. Within 2 weeks, Jan's demeanour had improved as had her maths. She was happier now that she had support from school, which was also coming from her pastoral carer, who had been informed with Jan's permission.

Hollow Leader – Family Façade

A year 9 girl in another school scored highly on ideals for Personal and Communal SWB, but considerably lower on how she felt. In my written report to the principal, I expressed concern about this girl (let us call her Cathy) and others. The results suggested to me that Cathy was an outgoing person, who was feeling very empty inside. To me, she was calling out for help. Cathy had not scored very highly on either the Environmental or Transcendental domains (both ideal and lived experience categories), so she did not have either of these two aspects of life to support her spiritual wellbeing.

During a meeting with this school's Principal to discuss results, he questioned the accuracy of my interpretation of data for Cathy, but not other students "of concern". From his point of view, Cathy was fine. She was one of the school leaders. The Principal knew the family, who appeared to be supportive of her, so, "No worries." I had suggested the possibility of a simple, subtle approach such as the one used with Jan. But, no follow-up action was taken with Cathy because the Principal thought he knew the family.

When I had coffee with this Principal a couple of years after this event, he recalled Cathy and my comments. Her family had broken up less than 6 months after she had completed SHALOM and she was quite distraught at that time. What appeared on the surface to be "Happy families" was in fact a façade. SHALOM had the sensitivity to pick up Cathy's inner state of being, her potential hurt in the heart, without apparently causing any emotional distress, as completing SHALOM did not precipitate any adverse reaction in Cathy. Cathy had this state of being, but we do not know how effectively concerned counseling might have brought it to the fore, to help her prepare for the family breakup.

These examples show how SHALOM can be used to provide insight into over-compensating extraverts as well as those who are very quiet.

Whole School Environmental Education Program

Teachers in a Christian school were not happy that their students had scored "low" on the Environmental domain of SHALOM. They instigated an environmental awareness program, based on texts such as, "The Earth is the Lord's and the fullness thereof" (Psalm 24:1). The course went beyond stewardship for nature to an appreciation of Creation by the Creator and man's [sic] place in it. A post-test 6 months later using SHALOM, showed high levels of correlation with pre-test results, indicating stability of students' views, on the Personal, Communal and Transcendental domains, but significant "improvement" on the Environmental domain scores – the desired result.

General Comments on My SWB Research

Four Domains

My recent studies have shown that nearly all people are prepared to accept that relating with themselves and others has the capacity to influence spiritual wellbeing. These relationships can be positive or negative and quite often it is in dark times that people are thrown onto their inner strength to find answers to meaning, purpose, etc. in life, i.e. personal and communal spiritual pursuits (often referred to as existential

(Ellison, 1983), humanistic (Spilka, in Moberg, 2002) or non-theistic (Haber, Jacob, & Spangler, 2007)).

Fewer people think about how relating with the environment can enhance spiritual wellbeing. To some, even suggesting this sounds "New Age", and some practices are. But, many have "peak experiences" in special places or events that transcend emotional enjoyment and enhance spiritual wellbeing.

A marked divergence of views emerges when looking at relating with a Transcendent Other, often referred to as God, for spiritual wellbeing. Some people blame God for the hurt they experience from other people, many of whom are religious. So, in an attempt to minimise this hurt by removing the cause, they deny God's existence even though attributing blame in that quarter. Others believe that humans have the power to understand and solve all challenges by exercising power of the mind, so eliminating the necessity to introduce the notion of a Transcendent Other. We are still waiting to define clearly what the "mind" is, as well as "transcendent realities."

The 1990s were labelled the "Decade of the Brain" by US Congress. Some hypotheses, conjecture and cautious interpretations of empirical studies suggest that regions of the brain might hold keys to understanding how our spirits relate with self-transcendence and how the brain might have evolved to locate a God-factor. None of this work is definitive and it is all highly influenced by the researchers' worldviews. But, it is fascinating reading (e.g. *The God Gene* by Dean Hamer, 2004 and *The Spiritual Brain* by M. Beauregard & D. O'Leary, 2007).

Spiritual Dissonance

Spiritual dissonance is described in my work as a significant difference between the ideal and lived experiences in any of the four domains of spiritual wellbeing. In my studies, the level of dissonance for secondary school students is close to 8% in the Personal, Communal and Environmental domains and over 20% in the Transcendental domain, with significant variation among school types (Fisher, 2006). Of at least equal or, maybe, greater concern is the finding that similar percentages of teachers show dissonance between their ideals and lived experiences (12% Personal, 10% Communal, 5% Environmental, 17% Transcendental) (Fisher, 2008). Teachers' lived experiences are major predictors of how much help they provide to students in schools for SWB (Fisher, 2007) and so this finding has implications for the workplace.

Conclusion

Young people need help to guide them in their search for meaning, purpose and values in life from a personal perspective. From a communal perspective, their quest for in-depth relationships with others will build on their personal search, by clarifying and embracing aspects of morality, culture (and religion, among those for whom it is important). This human journey is set in an environment that is teetering on the brink of regression, facing major physical challenges, in terms of energy, finance, global warming, pollution and water shortage, apart from the threat of terrorism and tension between religious groups threatening world peace in hot spots around the globe. How much time they take to embrace the mystical aspects of environmental wellbeing may well be a moot point. On top of all this is the perennial question about the existence, or otherwise, of a Divine Creator/Transcendent Other/God or Ultimate Concern who/that has the potential for an over-arching influence on the quality of relationships and development in the other three (Personal, Communal and Environmental) domains of spiritual health.

These quests never end. They are an integral part of life, of being human. Very few people stand alone in life's quest. Parents, educators, youth workers and counselors have the immense privilege of spending quality time with young people as they develop and grow.

This chapter has shown ways in which we can reach into the heart of young people (and ourselves) to catch a glimpse of ideals and reported lived experiences, which reflect spiritual health. As we stand with each other, in and through education, beyond the confines of subject matter and religious persuasion, and are prepared to spend time and be sensitive, we will hopefully nurture our own and each other's spirits in ways that will sustain us in, and for, life.

References

Adams, F. (1939). *The genuine works of Hippocrates* [(trans. from the Greek, p. 299 (Aphorisms, I.1)]. London: Bailliere, Tindall & Cox.
Banks, R., Poehler, D., & Russell, R. (1984). Spirit and human-spiritual interaction as a factor in health and health education. *Health Education, 15*(5), 16–19.
Beauregard, M., & O'leary, D. (2007). *The spiritual brain: A neuroscientist's case for the existence of soul*. New York: Harper Collins.
Benson, P. L. (2004). Emerging themes in research on adolescent spiritual and religious development. *Applied Developmental Science, 8*(1), 47–50.
Berry, D. (2005). Methodological pitfalls in the study of religiosity and spirituality. *Western Journal of Nursing Research, 27*(5), 628–647.
Best, R. (Ed.). (1996). *Education, spirituality and the whole child*. London: Cassell.
Boero, M., Caviglia, M., Monteverdi, R., Braida, V., Fabello, M., & Zorzella, L. (2005). Spirituality of health workers: A descriptive study. *International Journal of Nursing Studies, 42*, 915–921.
Brown, I. (1978). Exploring the spiritual dimension of school health education. *The Eta Sigma Gamman, 10*(1), 12–16.
Brown, L. (Ed.). (1993). *Oxford English dictionary*. Oxford: Clarendon Press.
Buck, H. G. (2006). Spirituality: Concept analysis and model development. *Holistic Nursing Practice, 20*(6), 288–292.
Burkhardt, M. A. (1989). Spirituality: An analysis of the concept. *Holistic Nursing Practice, 3*(3), 69–77.
Burkhardt, M. A., & Nagai-Jacobson, M. G. (1994). Reawakening spirit in clinical practice. *Journal of Holistic Nursing, 12*(1), 9–21.
Chapman, L. (1987). Developing a useful perspective on spiritual health: Wellbeing, spiritual potential and the search for meaning. *American Journal of Health Promotion, 1*(3), 31–39.

Chiu, L., Emblen, J. D., Van Hofwegen, L., Sawatzky, R., & Meyerhoff, H. (2004). An integrative review of the concept of spirituality in the health sciences. *Western Journal of Nursing Research, 26*(4), 405–428.

Coles, R. (1990). *The spiritual life of children.* Boston: Houghton Mifflin Co.

Como, J. M. (2007). A literature review related to spiritual health and health outcomes. *Holistic Nursing Practice, 21*(5), 224–236.

Coward, D. D., & Reed, P. G. (1996). Self-transcendence: A resource for healing at the end of life. *Issues in Mental Health Nursing, 17*(3), 275–288.

de Chavez, A. C., Backett-Milburn, K., Parry, O., & Platt, S. (2005). Understanding and researching wellbeing: Its usage in different disciplines and potential for health research and health promotion. *Health Education Journal, 64*(1), 70–87.

Diaz, D. P. (1993). Foundations for spirituality: Establishing the viability of spirituality within the health disciplines. *Journal of Health Education, 24*(6), 324–326.

Dowling, E. M., Gestsdottir, S., Anderson, P. M., von Eye, A., Almerigi, J., & Lerner, R. M. (2004). Structural relations among spirituality, religiosity, and thriving in adolescence. *Applied Developmental Science, 8*(1), 7–16.

Eberst, R. M. (1984). Defining health: A multidimensional model. *The Journal of School Health, 54*(3), 99–104.

Egbert, N., Mickley, J., & Coeling, H. (2004). A review and application of social scientific measures of religiosity and spirituality: Assessing a missing component in health communication research. *Health Communication, 16*(1), 7–27.

Ellison, C. (1983). Spiritual well-being: Conceptualization and measurement. *Journal of Psychology and Theology, 11*(4), 330–340.

Engebretson, K. (2006). God's got your back: Teenage boys talk about God. *International Journal of Children's Spirituality, 11*(3), 329–345.

Fahlberg, L. L., & Fahlberg, L. A. (1991). Exploring spirituality and consciousness with an expanded science: Beyond the ego with empiricism, phenomenology, and contemplation. *American Journal of Health Promotion, 5*(4), 273–281.

Fehring, R., Miller, J., & Shaw, C. (1997). Spiritual well-being, religiosity, hope, depression, and other mood states in elderly people coping with cancer. *Oncology Nursing Forum, 24*(4), 663–671.

Fisher, J. W. (1998). *Spiritual health: Its nature and place in the school curriculum.* Doctoral thesis, University of Melbourne (http://eprints.unimelb.edu.au/archive/00002994/).

Fisher, J. W. (1999). Helps to fostering students' spiritual health. *International Journal of Children's Spirituality, 4*(1), 29–49.

Fisher, J. W. (2001). Comparing levels of spiritual well-being in State, Catholic and Independent schools in Victoria, Australia. *Journal of Beliefs and Values, 22*(1), 113–119.

Fisher, J. W. (2004). Feeling Good, Living Life: A spiritual health measure for young children. *Journal of Beliefs & Values, 25*(3), 307–315.

Fisher, J. W. (2006). Using secondary students' views about influences on their spiritual well-being to inform pastoral care. *International Journal of Children's Spirituality, 11*(3), 347–356.

Fisher, J. W. (2007). It's time to wake up and stem the decline in spiritual well-being in Victorian schools. *International Journal of Children's Spirituality, 12*(2), 165–177.

Fisher, J. W. (2008). Impacting teachers' and students' spiritual well-being. *Journal of Beliefs and Values, 29*(3), 252–261.

Fisher, J. W., Francis, L. J., & Johnson, P. (2000) Assessing spiritual health via four domains of well-being: The SH4DI. *Pastoral Psychology, 49*(2), 133–145.

Francis, L. J., & Robbins, M. (2005). *Urban hope and spiritual health: The adolescent voice.* Peterborough, UK: Epworth.

Gomez, R., & Fisher, J. W. (2003). Domains of spiritual well-being and development and validation of the Spiritual Well-Being Questionnaire. *Personality and Individual Differences, 35*(8), 1975–1991.

Goodloe, R., & Arreola, P. (1992). Spiritual health: Out of the closet. *Health Education, 23*(4), 221–226.

Gorsuch, R. L., & Walker, D. (2006). Measurement and research design in studying spiritual development. In E. C. Roehlkepartain, P. E. King, L. M. Wagener, & P. L. Benson (Eds.), *Handbook of spiritual development in childhood and adolescence* (pp. 92–103). Thousand Oaks, CA: Sage Publications.

Gray, J. (2006). Measuring spirituality: Conceptual and methodological considerations. *The Journal of Theory Construction and Testing, 10*(2), 58–64.

Haber, J. R., Jacob, T., & Spangler, D. J. C. (2007). Dimensions of religion/spirituality and relevance to health research. *The International Journal for the Psychology of Religion, 17*(4), 265–288.

Hamer, D. (2004). *The God gene: How faith is hardwired into our genes*. New York: Doubleday.

Harris, S. K., Sherritt, L. R., Holder, D. W., Kulig, J., Shrier, L. A., & Knight, J. R. (2007). Reliability and validity of the brief Multidimensional Measure of Religiousness/Spirituality among adolescents. *Journal of Religion and Health, 47*, 438–457.

Harvey, C. L. (1996, June). *The role of the soul*. Paper presented at "Whose Values?", the Third Annual Conference on "Education, Spirituality and the Whole Child", Roehampton Institute, London.

Hawks, S. (2004). Spiritual wellness, holistic health, and the practice of health education. *American Journal of Health Education, 35*(1), 11–16.

Hay, D., & Nye, R. (1998). *The spirit of the child*. London: Fount.

Hill, B. V. (1989). "Spiritual development" in the Education Reform Act: A source of acrimony, apathy or accord? *British Journal of Educational Studies, 37*(2), 169–182.

Hill, P. C., & Hood, R. W. (Eds.). (1999). *Measures of religiosity*. Birmingham, Alabama: Religious Education Press.

Hill, P. C., & Pargament, K. I. (2003). Advances in the conceptualization and measurement of religion and spirituality. *American Psychologist, 58*(1), 64–74.

Hill, P. C., Pargament, K. I., Hood, R. W., McCullough, J. P., Swyers, D. B., Larson, D. B., et al. (2000). Conceptualizing religion and spirituality: Points of commonality, points of departure. *Journal for the Theory of Social Behaviour, 30*(1), 51–77.

Hood, R. W. (1975). The construction and preliminary validation of a measure of reported mystical experience. *Journal for the Scientific Study of Religion, 14*, 29–41.

Horsburgh, M. (1997). Towards an inclusive spirituality: Wholeness, interdependence and waiting. *Disability and Rehabilitation, 19*(10), 398–406.

Hughes, P. (2007) *Putting life together*. Melbourne: CRA/Fairfield Press.

Hungelmann, J., Kenkel-Rossi, E., Klassen, L., & Stollenwerk, R. (1985). Spiritual well-being in older adults: Harmonious inter-connectedness. *Journal of Religion and Health, 24*(2), 147–153.

Jose, N., & Taylor, E. (1986). Spiritual health: A look at barriers to its inclusion in the health education curriculum. *The Eta Sigma Gamman, 18*(2), 16–19.

King, J. E., & Crowther, M. R. (2004). The measurement of religiosity and spirituality. *Journal of Organizational Change, 17*(1), 83–101.

Koenig, H. G., McCullough, M. E., & Larson, D. B. (2001). *Handbook of religion and health*. Oxford: Oxford University Press.

Leetun, M. C. (1996). Wellness spirituality in the older adult. Assessment and intervention protocol. *Nurse Practitioner, 21*(8), 65–70.

Lukoff, D., Lu, F., & Turner, R. (1992). Toward a more culturally sensitive DSM-IV. Psychoreligious and psychospiritual problems. *The Journal of Nervous and Mental Disease, 180*(11), 673–682.

MacDonald, D. A., & Friedman, H. L. (2002). Assessment of humanistic, transpersonal, and spiritual constructs: State of the science. *Journal of Humanistic Psychology, 42*(4), 102–125.

MacLaren, J. (2004). A kaleidoscope of understandings: Spiritual nursing in a multi-faith society. *Journal of Advanced Nursing, 45*(5), 457–464.

Martsolf, D. S., & Mickley, J. R. (1998). The concept of spirituality in nursing theories: differing world-views and extent of focus. *Journal of Advanced Nursing, 27*, 294–303.

Mason, M., Singleton, A., & Webber, R. (2007). *The spirit of generation Y*. Melbourne: John Garratt.

McCarroll, P., O'Connor, T., & Meakes, E. (2005). Assessing plurality in spirituality definitions. In A. Meier, (Ed.), *Spirituality and health: Multidisciplinary explorations* (pp. 43–61). Waterloo, ON, Canada: Wilfrid Laurier University Press.

McSherry, W., & Cash, K. (2004). The language of spirituality: An emerging taxonomy. *International Journal of Nursing Studies, 41*, 151–161.

Ministerial Council on Education, Employment, Training and Youth Affairs. (2008, December). *The Melbourne declaration on educational goals for young Australians*. Melbourne: MCEETYA.

Moberg, D. O. (2002). Assessing and measuring spirituality: Confronting dilemmas of universal and particular evaluative criteria. *Journal of Adult Development, 9*(1), 47–60.

Muldoon, M., & King, N. (1995). Spirituality, health care, and bioethics. *Journal of Religion and health, 34*(4), 329–349.

National Interfaith Coalition on Aging. (1975). Spiritual well-being: A definition. Athens, GA: Author.

Newby, M. (1996). Towards a secular concept of spiritual maturity. In R. Best (Ed.), *Education, spirituality and the whole child* (pp. 99–107). London: Cassell.

Nolan, P., & Crawford, P. (1997). Towards a rhetoric of spirituality in mental health care. *Journal of Advanced Nursing, 26*, 289–294.

Oldnall, A. (1996). A critical analysis of nursing: Meeting the spiritual needs of patients. *Journal of Advanced Nursing, 23*, 138–144.

Palmer, P. J. (1999) Evoking the spirit in public education. *Educational Leadership, 6*(4), 6–11.

Piedmont, R. L. (2001). Spiritual transcendence and the scientific study of spirituality. *Journal of Rehabilitation, 67*(1), 4–14.

Priestley, J. G. (1985). Towards finding the hidden curriculum: A consideration of the spiritual dimension of experience in curriculum planning. *British Journal of Religious Education, 7*(3), 112–119.

Ross, L. (2006). Spiritual care in nursing: An overview of the research to date. *Journal of Clinical Nursing, 15*, 852–862.

Scott, D. G. (2006). Spirituality and identity within/without religion. In M. de Souza, G. Durka, K. Engebretson, R. Jackson, & A. McGrady (Eds.), *International handbook of the religious, moral and spiritual dimensions in education* (pp. 1111–1125). Dordrecht, The Netherlands: Springer.

Seaward, B. L. (2001). *Health of the human spirit: Spiritual dimensions for personal health*. Boston: Allyn and Bacon.

Smith, D. (2000). Secularism, religion and spiritual development. *Journal of Beliefs and Values, 21*(1), 27–38.

Strong, J. (1979). *Strong's exhaustive concordance of the bible*. Nashville, TN: Thomas Nelson Publishers.

Thatcher, A. (1991). A critique of inwardness in religious education. *British Journal of Religious Education, 14*(1), 22–27.

Tillich, P. (1967). *Systematic theology, Vol. III: Life and the spirit history and the Kingdom of God*. Chicago: University of Chicago Press.

Tirri, K., Nokelainen, P., & Ubani, M. (2006). Conceptual definition and empirical validation of the spiritual sensitivity scale. *Journal of Empirical Theology, 19*(1), 37–62.

Warren, M. (1988). Catechesis and spirituality. *Religious Education, 83*(1), 116–133.

Wong, Y. J., Rew, L. R., & Slaikeu, K. D. (2006). A systematic review of recent research on adolescent religiosity/spirituality and mental health. *Issues in Mental Health Nursing, 27*, 161–183.

Wright, A. (2000). *Spirituality and education*. Florence, KY: Taylor & Francis.

Zinnbauer, B. J., Pargament, K. I., & Scott, A. B. (1999). The emerging meanings of religiousness and spirituality: Problems and prospects. *Journal of Personality, 67*(6), 889–919.

Chapter 5
The Contribution of Religiousness and Spirituality to Subjective Wellbeing and Satisfaction with Life

Ralph L. Piedmont

Abstract This chapter examines the numinous constructs of religiousness and spirituality relative to one another and to the five-factor model of personality (FFM). An empirical approach to defining numinous measures that involves the FFM will be outlined. The value of this approach will be highlighted through an examination of spirituality and religiousness' relations to subjective wellbeing. A review of the literature demonstrates that spirituality and religiousness have an unmediated impact on levels of life satisfaction. Two important conclusions will be developed from these findings. First, the numinous constructs represent universal human motivations that are not redundant with extant models of personality. Thus, any model of human functioning needs to include these constructs, if it is to be comprehensive. Second, because numinous constructs have the potential for impacting psychological functioning, the potential exists for the identification of a new class of intervention techniques that can promote durable psychological change.

Introduction

National surveys continue to show that large numbers of Americans profess a belief in God and consider themselves to be religious (e.g., Gallup, 1995). The salience of spirituality and religious involvement make these constructs of significant interest to researchers and clinicians in the social and medical sciences. A burgeoning research literature is empirically documenting the value of numinous constructs (i.e., psychological measures that capture aspects of one's sense of awe, hallowedness, and transcendence) for positively impacting a wide range of psychosocially relevant outcomes, such as treatment response to mental and physical interventions, recovery from illness, quality of life, and coping ability (e.g., Koenig, 1997; Koenig et al., 2001; Larson & Larson, 2008; Miller & Thoresen, 2003; Sawatzky, Ratner, & Chiu, 2005; Thoresen, 1999). This interest is truly interdisciplinary in nature and generates a vast empirical literature (Dy-Liacco, Piedmont, Leach, & Nelson, 2003). Because

R.L. Piedmont (✉)
Department of Pastoral Counseling, Loyola College in Maryland, Columbia, MD 21045, USA
e-mail: rpiedmont@loyola.edu

numerous reviews already exist in this area (e.g., Koenig et al., 2001; Sawatzky et al., 2005), this chapter will focus on distilling key conceptual and empirical findings rather than merely recounting all the results from this very large literature.

On the surface, the research literature shows the facilitative effect that religion and spirituality have on physical and mental health. Individuals with high levels of these constructs frequently are seen as experiencing less physical illness (or recovering quicker from disease) than those who score lower on these dimensions. Pargament and colleagues have shown how religious coping adds significantly to individuals' attempts to manage personal stress, burnout, and mortality (Pargament, 1997; Pargament, Koenig, Tarakeshwar, & Hahn, 2001; Pargament, Smith, Koenig, & Perez, 1998). However, these findings do not go unchallenged. Sloan and colleagues have criticized this research in this area on the basis of numerous methodological and statistical shortcomings (Sloan & Bagiella, 2002; Sloan, Bagiella, & Powell, 2001).

There are three particular issues that are most relevant to this chapter. The first major issue concerns how to operationalize the basic constructs of spirituality and religiosity. There is little consensus within the field as to how these constructs be defined. As a consequence, a plethora of instruments have been developed that capture a wide array of qualities, not all of which may be tapping into the same underlying dimension. Such diversity makes it difficult to compare results across studies and instruments (see Gorsuch, 1984, 1990). It also impairs the field's ability to develop a cumulative body of knowledge. As Hill et al. (2000, p. 65) noted:

> Without a clearer conception of what these terms mean, it may be difficult to know with any precision or reliability what researchers attribute to them. Also, communication within the social scientific study of these constructs and across other disciplines may be impaired by a lack of common understanding and clinical agreement. Finally, without common definitions within psychological as well as sociological research, it becomes difficult to draw general conclusions from various studies. Therefore, these definitions are in dire need of empirical grounding and improved operationalization.

The need for clarity in our constructs both conceptually and empirically perhaps ranks as the single most important effort for researchers in this area. It is hard to develop a field if you cannot agree on what your basic constructs are. Koenig (2008) provided an overview of some of these issues and asserted that if the field cannot create a unique, clear construct, it should be eliminated from research altogether.

Second, the majority of research in this area relies on simple, univariate paradigms. These studies merely correlate a measure of spirituality or religiosity with some set of outcome variables. The results of such studies are limited because they do not control for experiment-wise alpha levels; there is no control for spurious findings. When such studies employ multiple spiritual measures, they often fail to control for predictive overlap among these scales, resulting in the possibly erroneous conclusion that each of these measures has unique associations with the outcomes.

Third, research with numinous constructs rarely controls for the influence of other relevant predictors, such as social support or personality. As such, it is not clear whether spiritual constructs have any incremental predictive power over these other variables. This leads some to argue that spiritual constructs are merely stand-in variables for other, already established psychological constructs. Buss (2002, p. 203) has flatly stated, "A 'religious' phenomena may [be considered to] simply parasitize existing evolved mechanisms or represent byproducts of them." From this perspective, religious and spiritual constructs do not provide any insights into people that have not already been identified by current psychological measures. Consequently, numinous constructs add unwanted terminology and redundancy to a field already crowded with variables.

These criticisms are legitimate and raise important conceptual and empirical issues that the field needs to address. Consumers of research need to be aware of the limitations and potential confounds that exist in the current database. If these critics are correct, then the current body of knowledge which shows the predictive power of religious constructs can be explained away as merely Type I error and empirical redundancy. Researchers need to avail themselves of new methodologies and constructs so that a better evaluation of the effects of the numinous can be undertaken. Some new approaches for building a more rigorous database will be showcased below.

The purpose of this chapter is to provide an overview of the literature that addresses these specific criticisms. Three questions will be considered: (a) are spiritual and religious constructs sufficiently robust as to be measurable? (b) do numinous variables correlate with measures of life satisfaction? and (c) are these relationships maintained even after the predictive effects of personality are removed? Despite the potential problems noted by critics, it is hoped that this chapter will give readers renewed confidence in the empirical and conceptual value of numinous constructs. As will be seen, they do have something unique to contribute to our understanding of people. Some speculation as to why spiritual variables are so relevant to these psychosocial outcomes will be given. But before beginning, it is necessary to define the core variables of this chapter: religiosity and spirituality. A conceptual paradigm will be presented and its related measurement instrument will be introduced.

Defining and Measuring Spirituality and Religiousness

Because spirituality and religiousness are seen by many as being conceptually overlapping, in that both involve a search for the sacred (e.g., Hill & Pargament, 2003), some researchers prefer to interpret these two dimensions as being redundant (e.g., Zinnbauer, Pargament, & Scott, 1999). Musick, Traphagan, Koenig, and Larson (2000) have noted that in samples of adults, these two terms are highly related to one another. They question whether there is a meaningful distinction between these two constructs or if any disparities are ". . . simply an artifact of the wishes of researchers hoping to find such differences" (p. 80). Nonetheless, there are those who emphasize the distinctiveness between these two constructs (e.g., Piedmont, 2001; Piedmont & Leach, 2002). Here, spirituality is viewed as an attribute of an individual (much like a personality trait) while religiosity is understood as encompassing more of the beliefs, rituals, and practices associated with an institution (Miller & Thoresen,

1999, p. 6). Religiosity is concerned with how one's experience of a transcendent being is shaped by, and expressed through, a community or social organization. Spirituality, on the other hand, is most concerned with one's personal relationships to larger, transcendent realities, such as God or the Universe.

In an effort to operationalize these two constructs in a manner that would solidly ground them in mainstream psychological theory and measurement, the *Assessment of Spirituality and Religious Sentiments* (ASPIRES; Piedmont, 2005) scale was created. In this measure, spirituality was defined as an intrinsic motivation of individuals to create a broad sense of personal meaning within an eschatological context. In other words, knowing that we are going to die, spirituality represents our efforts to create meaning and purpose for our lives. This need for meaning is seen as an intrinsic, universal human capacity (see Piedmont & Leach, 2002). Assessing spirituality is the *Spiritual Transcendence Scale* (STS). The STS was developed to capture those aspects of spirituality that cuts across all religious traditions (see Piedmont, 2005, for how this scale was developed). This unidimensional scale contains three correlated facets: *Universality*, a belief in the unity and purpose of life; *Prayer fulfillment*, an experienced feeling of joy and contentment that results from prayer and/or meditation; and *Connectedness*, a sense of personal responsibility and connection to others.

Religiousness is not considered to be an intrinsic, motivational construct like spirituality. Rather, it is considered to represent a *sentiment*. Sentiment is an old term in psychology and reflects emotional tendencies that develop out of social traditions and educational experiences (Ruckmick, 1920). Sentiments can exert a powerful influence over thoughts and behaviors, but they do not represent innate, genotypic qualities like spirituality. That is why the expression of sentiments (e.g., religious practices) can and do vary over time and across cultures. There are two measures of religious sentiments on the ASPIRES. The first is the *Religiosity Index* (RI). The RI examines the frequency of involvement in religious rituals and practices (e.g., How often does one pray, How often does one attend religious services). It also queries the extent to which religious practices and involvements are important. *Religious Crisis* (RC) is the second measure and examines the extent to which an individual feels alienated, punished, or abandoned by God (e.g., I feel that God is punishing me). What is of interest about these items is that they address the negative side of religiousness, when faith and belief becomes sources of personal and social distress. This scale enables an examination of the extent to which disturbances in one's relationship to God can impact one's broader sense of psychological stability.

The five ASPIRES scales provide a relatively comprehensive assessment of the numinous dimension. Compared to most measures in this field, the ASPIRES has a rather large and comprehensive body of validity evidence. The increasing popularity of the ASPIRES can be attributed to its ability to address critical empirical questions about the utility of any measure of spirituality or religiousness. The next section will take a data-based approach that emphasizes the empirical value of numinous constructs for predicting satisfaction with life. For the purposes of this report, the Religious Crisis scale will not be included in these analyses. This measure captures aspects of distressed spiritual functioning and interested readers can obtain information on this scale elsewhere (e.g., Piedmont et al., 2007; Piedmont, 2009). The focus of this chapter will be on those positive aspects of spiritual and religious functioning that stress engagement in, and involvement with, transcendent realities. Three key empirical issues surrounding the spiritual assessment of these scales will be addressed in an effort to demonstrate the value of numinous variables for understanding life satisfaction.

Key Issues in Demonstrating Spirituality and Religiosity as Robust Predictors of Life Satisfaction

Issue 1: Spirituality and Religiosity as Robust Constructs

Spirituality has many definitions, in fact Scott (cited in Hill et al., 2000) identified 31 different definitions of religiousness and 40 for spirituality, which she classified into nine different content areas (e.g., experiences of connectedness, systems of thought or beliefs, and capacities for transcendence). Many of these definitions stress the unique, personal relationship one has with a transcendent reality. Given that spirituality is often conceptualized as a very personal and individualized relationship, a question that emerges is whether spirituality is merely a solipsistic characteristic of the person, a quality that only reflects idiosyncratic aspects of functioning that have limited interpretive and predictive value. In short, spirituality is often viewed as a private, personal reality that is uniquely defined by each person. Seen in this manner, spirituality would have limited scientific value because it would lack any consistent definition. If it cannot be defined, it would be impossible to discuss it or identify evidence of its influence.

It is surprising that very little effort has gone into addressing this fundamental issue. In some ways, the plethora of extant instruments supports this idiographic understanding of spirituality (see Hill & Hood, 1999). In order to demonstrate that spirituality and religiosity have substantive value as individual-difference qualities, it needs to be shown that there exists some level of consensual understanding among people of what "spiritual" means and the behaviors and goals that characterize such individuals. Such agreement provides support for the contention that spirituality does represent a generalized, substantive aspect of human function that has important implications for understanding human behavior. One way to show that spirituality is *not* "in the eye of the beholder" is to test for cross-observer convergence in ratings of spirituality and religiosity. Demonstrating that what individuals say about their own numinous qualities and motivations agrees with how knowledgeable others rate them on these qualities provides powerful evidence of just how overt and pervasive these qualities are.

The data to be presented in this chapter are a subset of the normative data on the ASPIRES found in Piedmont (2005). The information presented here is based on a sample of 416 individuals (289 women and 120 men, 7 indicated no gender), aged 17–62 (mean = 21.32). The majority (86%) were Caucasian, with 6% African-American, 3% Hispanic, 4% Asian, and 1% Arabic. In this sample, 391 obtained

Table 5.1 Correlations between self- and observer ratings on the ASPIRES dimensions

	Self-report scales ($N = 387$)				
Observer scales	PF	UN	CN	Rel	Observer, α
Prayer Fulfillment (PF)	**0.64*****	0..23***	0.21***	0.70***	0.95
Universality (UN)	0.38***	**0.32*****	0.11*	0.41***	0.80
Connectedness (CN)	0.21***	0.20***	**0.25*****	0.20**	0.61
Religiosity (Rel)	0.61***	0.41***	0.20***	**0.81*****	0.92
Self-report, α	0.94	0.78	0.47	0.89	

*$p < 0.05$; **$p < 0.01$; ***$p < 0.001$, two-tailed.

at least one observer rating on the ASPIRES. Raters knew subjects on average 8.3 years (SD = 7 years). Correlations between the self- and observer ratings are presented in Table 5.1. As can be seen, scores on the self-report ASPIRES correlated significantly with their corresponding observer ratings. Those correlations on the diagonal, which are in bold, provide evidence of the consensual validity for these spiritual constructs. The magnitude of these correlations (mean $r = 0.40$) compares favorably to peer-self convergence found with various measures of the five-factor model (FFM) of personality, a comprehensive taxonomy of personality traits (e.g., Goldberg, 1993), where average r's range from 0.30 to 0.48 (Funder, Kolar, & Blackman, 1995; McCrae & Costa, 1987; Piedmont, 1994). These data also provide evidence of discriminant validity as well: With the exception of Universality, each of the diagonal correlations is the highest in its respective row and column. This demonstrates that individuals have a clear, well-differentiated understanding of what spirituality is and its related aspects. Thus, despite whatever subjective nature spirituality may hold, it is clear that as a construct it represents a generalized quality that is consensually understood.

There are two important points to these data. First, the constructs contained in the ASPIRES represent constructs well understood by individuals in the general population. Spirituality is not solipsistic or completely subjective. Rather, spirituality represents a pervasive aspect of human psychological functioning, sufficiently overt and distinct that it can be recognized in one's behavior by others (see also Piedmont, 2001, 2007). Spirituality and religiosity represent robust, universal qualities of the individual (see Piedmont, 2007; Piedmont & Leach, 2002). Second, the use of observer data has an important role to play in research in this area that needs to be stressed. The singular reliance on self-report data found in current research creates potential problems concerning the interpretive and predictive value of numinous constructs.

One problem, addressed above, centers on the subjective nature of spiritual constructs. Do they represent a universal human motivation or merely reflect idiosyncratic aspects of individual functioning? The cross-observer paradigm directly addresses this issue and, as shown above, demonstrates the robustness of these constructs. A second problem associated with the use of only self-report data centers on correlated method error. When two self-report instruments correlate, it is not known to what extent that association is driven, or inflated, by the fact that the same person is completing both measures. We cannot be sure if that association reflects a truly substantive overlap between two constructs or if it reflects the individual associations (e.g., response styles, implicit theories) of the respondent being present in both sets of responses. The only way to disentangle response styles from substantive overlap is to employ multiple information sources (i.e., there are four sources: self-report, observer rating, life outcome, objective test data).

Although no information source is infallible and all have their unique weaknesses, the value in using multiple sources is that the weaknesses of one method are offset by the strengths of another. For example, in a particular context an individual may be motivated by a desire to appear in a certain light and will manipulate his/her responses accordingly. Raters do not share the same motivation to "look good" as the individual himself or herself. Therefore, their ratings will not contain this source of error. However, raters may have other natural biases in their ratings (e.g., halo effects), but these are not shared by the target of the rating, who can give more nuanced responses. Because the confounds found in each method are different, any correlation *across* two methods will not be spuriously inflated by a common source of error. As a result, correlations between a self-report and observer rating are frequently found to be smaller than the association between two comparable self-report measures. The magnitudes of these relations provide a more accurate estimate of the true association between two constructs.

Moving beyond a reliance on self-report data is critical to the field, because it will help develop the generalizability of our constructs. Also, it will help to encourage the application of spiritual and religious constructs into areas where self-report data are questioned (e.g., clinical assessment, medical/heath applications). In order to address this issue, observer ratings on the ASPIRES will also be included in all analyses. Replicating findings based on self-rated scores on the ASPIRES with observer ratings will refute criticisms that the predictive validity of spirituality is mostly based on common method error.

Issue 2: The Relational Fertility of Spiritual and Religious Constructs

Allport (1950) asserted that numinous qualities were central, organizing aspects of an individual's psychological world; spirituality and religiosity represented the core of the individual. One's spirituality reflected the fundamental manner in which a person positioned himself/herself adaptively to the world at large. As such, spirituality should be related to a wide range of psychosocially salient constructs. There is a growing research literature documenting the predictive validity of spiritual and religious constructs for understanding a wide array of mental and physical health outcomes (see Koenig et al., 2001; Paloutzian & Park, 2005).

Given the focus of this chapter on life satisfaction, data presented will demonstrate the construct validity of the ASPIRES scales with these types of constructs. Individuals in our data set completed a number of measures that together comprehensively sample what may be labeled "satisfaction with life." Six measures were selected for presentation: *The Hope Scale* (Snyder et al., 1996), which assesses the extent to which an individual feels that life is unfolding in a positive, encouraging manner; *Satisfaction with Life Scale* (Diener, Emmons, Larsen, & Griffin, 1985), a measure of the cognitive aspects of life contentment; *Affect Balance Scale* (Bradburn, 1969), a measure of the affective aspects of life satisfaction; it comprises two scales, Positive Affect and Negative Affect; *Delighted-Terrible Scale* (Andrews & Withey, 1976), a single overall rating of one's experience of life from *terrible* to *delighted*; and finally the *Self-Esteem Scale* (Rosenberg, 1979), the well-used index of personal self-comfort and belief in self. A factor analysis of these scales resulted in the emergence of a single dimension that explained 60% of the common variance. All the scales loaded significantly (i.e., > 0.58) on this dimension, suggesting that these different measures are capturing a single dimension of emotional stability and satisfaction.

Taken as a whole, these instruments provide a relatively broad operationalization of life satisfaction; including the cognitive and affective components of wellbeing, belief and comfort in oneself, and a positive, upbeat anticipatory outlook for the future. Correlations between these outcome indices and self- and observer ratings on the ASPIRES are presented in Table 5.2. As can be seen, there are numerous, significant associations across all the ASPIRES scales and all the outcome measures. Both the spiritual and religiosity scales are associated. In examining the self-report data, 21 of the 24 correlations (88%) are significant. The last row in this section provides the multiple R^2 between the four ASPIRES scales and each outcome. As can be seen, these measures explain from 3 to 9% of the variance in life satisfaction. When examining the results employing the rater scores from the ASPIRES, a very

Table 5.2 Correlations between self- and observer ratings on the ASPIRES scales and emotional satisfaction outcomes

ASPIRES scales	Hope	SWLS	POS	NEG	Delight	Esteem
Self-reports ($N = 407$)						
Prayer Fulfillment	0.18***	0.26***	0.19***	−0.16***	0.24***	0.21***
Universality	0.19***	0.22***	0.16***	−0.15**	0.21***	0.16***
Connectedness	0.11*	0.11*	0.16***	0.03	0.07	0.07
Religiosity	0.16***	0.23***	0.19***	−0.16***	0.27***	0.16**
R^2	0.05***	0.09***	0.02***	0.02***	0.05***	0.05***
Observer ratings ($N = 383$)						
Prayer Fulfillment	0.19***	0.27***	0.22***	−0.13**	0.23***	0.20***
Universality	0.20***	0.25***	0.17***	−0.17***	0.25***	0.20***
Connectedness	0.07	0.10*	0.14**	0.04	0.08	0.05
Religiosity	0.12*	0.20***	0.17***	0.14***	0.22***	0.11*
R^2	0.05***	0.06***	0.09***	0.03*	0.06***	0.05***

*$p < 0.05$; **$p < 0.01$; ***$p < 0.001$, two-tailed.
Note. Hope, Hope Scale; SWLS, Satisfaction with Life Scale; POS, Positive Affect Scale; NEG, Negative Affect Scale; Delight, Delighted-Terrible Scale; Esteem, Self-Esteem Scale.

similar pattern of findings emerges. Again, there are numerous, significant associations (20 of 24 correlations, 83%), and the pattern of findings replicates that found with the self-reports. Overall R^2 values are of similar magnitude. These data indicate that spirituality and religiosity have substantive associations with measures of life satisfaction and wellbeing.

Two issues emerge from these findings. First, it is clear that despite the prolific number of associations, their magnitude is only of low to moderate strength. The correlations in Table 5.2 do not show the ASPIRES scales to be overwhelmingly powerful predictors. Such modest correlations suggest limits on our ability to make predictions using current spiritual assessment tools. Thus, we need to avoid perceiving spirituality as the "answer" to all our questions about people. As I have noted previously (Piedmont, 2001), numinous variables should not be considered "Rosetta stones" that can unlock our understanding of human psychological functioning. Human behavior is much too complex to be explained by any single construct. Instead, numinous variables need to be used as part of a multidimensional assessment approach to understanding people. We need to construct multivariable models that link together in meaningful ways constellations of constructs that will maximize our understanding of any psychological outcome. Although single variables will only explain, on average, 5–10% of the variance in the outcome, linking together a set of such variables that are non-overlapping can drastically improve predictive accuracy.

Second, although these findings are an exemplar of a larger literature, it must be noted that the key criticism of these findings centers on the lack of evidence documenting the predictive power of religious and spiritual variables over and above other established constructs, like social support and personality. This failure to demonstrate *incremental predictive validity* for numinous constructs raises important concerns about their construct validity (see Joiner, Perez, & Walker, 2002). The question is, "To what degree are spiritual constructs merely the 'religification' of already existing personality constructs?" (Van Wicklin, 1990). To be of ultimate value, numinous constructs need to demonstrate that they possess predictive power even after the influences of other established constructs are controlled. Incremental validity studies will enable researchers to identify those individual-difference qualities unique to religious and spiritual constructs that are predictive of salient psychosocial outcomes. Such analyses will also help to stop interpretations of religious constructs as being "nothing more than..." (see Pargament, 2002). Because this question stands at the heart of research in spirituality, we turn our attention to it now.

Issue 3: Incremental Validity of Spirituality and Religiosity

It has been argued (Piedmont, 1999) that religious and spiritual constructs need to demonstrate that they carry significant predictive power over and above that of established personality constructs, like the dimensions of the five-factor model of personality (FFM; Goldberg, 1993; McCrae & John, 1992; Piedmont, 1998). This model has been well developed empirically and contains the dimensions of Neuroticism (a measure of negative affect), Extraversion (a measure of positive affect), Openness (a measure of permeability versus rigidity), Agreeableness (a measure of social interest), and Conscientiousness (a measure of personal reliability) (Costa & McCrae, 1992). Because much of the variance of these dimensions has been found to be heritable (Heath, Neale, Kessler, Eavers, & Kendler, 1992), these five dimensions are not mere summary descriptions of behavior, but genotypic tendencies of individuals to think, act, and feel in consistent ways (McCrae & Costa, 1995). These personality dimensions have been shown to be quite stable among normal adults, and predict a wide range of relevant life outcomes, including wellbeing and coping ability (see Piedmont, 1998, for a review).

Because the FFM represents a comprehensive taxonomy of personality constructs, the FFM is an ideal medium for managing information about religious and spiritual scales that will enable researchers to efficiently identify areas of content redundancy and uniqueness between numinous constructs and other personality variables. As Ozer and Reise (1994) noted, "[those] who continue to employ their preferred measure without locating it within the FFM can only be likened to geographers who issue reports of new lands but refuse to locate them on a map for others to find" (p. 361). In his meta-analytic review, Saroglou (2002) noted that various measures of religiosity and spirituality demonstrated significant associations with all five of the personality domains of the FFM, although the effect sizes were small. Current measures of spirituality and religiosity do contain, to varying degrees, qualities that are overlapping with established personality dimensions. To be scientifically useful, numinous constructs need to show that they represent something new about individuals.

One way to evaluate the incremental validity of measures of spirituality and religiosity is to conduct hierarchical multiple regression analyses. Once a suitable outcome criterion is identified (e.g., satisfaction with life), the FFM personality domains would be entered as a single block on the first step of the regression analysis. The resulting R^2 would represent the amount of variance in the criterion that is explained by constructs representing what is traditionally defined as "personality." On the second step of the analysis, the spirituality and religiosity variables can then be entered, using a forward entry method. This will identify those aspects of the numinous variables that are *independent* of personality that are related to the outcome. A partial F-test determines whether the amount of additional variance captured on the second step is significant. If a significant effect is found, then it can be demonstrated that the religious and spiritual constructs have incremental validity over personality.

Such an analysis was conducted with the current data set. A series of hierarchical regressions were conducted using each of the six satisfaction with life variables as the outcome criteria. On the first step of the analyses, individuals' scores on the FFM personality domains were entered. On the second step, the ASPIRES scales were entered. The results of these analyses are presented in Table 5.3. As can be seen, the FFM domains explained a significant amount of variance in each of the outcome

Table 5.3 Incremental validity of the ASPIRES scales in predicting emotional satisfaction outcomes over and above the FFM personality domains

Outcome	FFM, R^2	ASPIRES, ΔR^2	ASPIRES predictor
Self-report ASPIRES ($N = 405$)			
Hope	0.31***	0.02**	UN
Satisfaction with Life	0.31***	0.04**	UN, PF
Positive Affect	0.10***	0.01*	PF
Negative Affect	0.16***	0.01**	UN
Delighted-Terrible Scale	0.29***	0.01**	REL
Self-Esteem	0.38***	0.01**	UN
Observer ratings ASPIRES ($N = 381$)			
Hope	0.35***	0.01*	UN
Satisfaction with Life	0.34***	0.02**	PF
Positive Affect	0.15***	0.04***	PF
Negative Affect	0.25***	–	–
Delighted-Terrible Scale	0.31***	0.03***	REL
Self-Esteem	0.40***	0.01*	UN

Note. UN, Universality; PF, Prayer Fulfillment; REL, Religiosity.

measures (R^2s ranged from 0.10 to 0.38 with the self-report ASPIRES scales and from 0.15 to 0.40 with the observer ratings). These are moderate to strong effect sizes. Clearly personality has something significant to contribute to our understanding of life satisfaction. However, the third column presents the amount of variance that the ASPIRES scales contributed *over and above* the FFM domains. In all but one instance, the ASPIRES scales evidenced significant amounts of additional predictive variance.

Three points of interest are worth noting from these data. First, it should be noted that similar findings are obtained regardless of whether the self-report or observer-rating version of the ASPIRES was used. As noted earlier, such comparability provides confidence that the observed findings using self-reported scores on the ASPIRES are not an artifact of any type of correlated measurement error. The spirituality and religiosity scales do have reliable, substantive associations with life satisfaction that are not mediated by either personality or information source.

Second, it appears that Universality and Prayer Fulfillment are most relevant for understanding life satisfaction. Universality reflects the belief that there is a higher level of existence through which all of life is interconnected. Items reflect the idea that individuals are part of a larger social reality, a community of "oneness" that transcends the many differences we experience in this life. Higher scores on this scale have been shown to predict better treatment outcomes for substance abusers (Piedmont, 2004a). Prayer Fulfillment examines the extent to which one is able to create personal space that enables one to develop and maintain a relationship to the Transcendent that provides personal joy and contentment. Among clergy, high scores on this scale have been shown to reduce the likelihood of job-related burnout (Golden, Piedmont, Ciarrocchi, & Rodgerson, 2004). The former scale enables one to find a secure attachment within larger social networks, while scores on the latter scale reflect an ability to find emotional fulfillment within some larger, transcendent reality. Interestingly, Religiosity was only uniquely relevant in predicting the overall rating of feeling terrible or delighted with one's life. Perhaps religious involvement provides a structure for understanding life and an order for living it that enhances one's feelings of predictability, which in turn reduces anxiety and fear. Future research will need to plumb for conceptual explanations supporting why these relations hold.

Finally, the unique predictive contribution of the numinous constructs to life satisfaction was small. In one way, this was expected given the rather modest correlations noted in Table 5.2. Nonetheless, given that the average incremental R^2 noted in Table 5.3 is 0.03, concerns over practical significance are justified. Is it worth adding these two variables only to gain an addition 3% of the variance? The answer is, I believe, "yes." It should be kept in mind that the ΔR^2's are partial coefficients; they represent what each construct has to offer once the predictive effects of the *five* personality variables have been removed. Thus these values are low because there is little reliable variance left to explain in the criteria. Nunnally and Bernstein (1994) have observed that increases in R^2 are generally very small by the time a third substantive predictor is added to a regression equation. As more predictors are added, their incremental contributions will be increasingly smaller. Hunsley and Meyer (2003) suggested that an R^2 increase of between 0.02 and 0.04 would indicate a reasonable contribution for a variable entered on the third step. Given that the numinous variables in the present study are being added into the regression equations on the *sixth* and *seventh steps* (the five personality dimensions represent steps 1–5), the 3% additional variance appears to represent a quite robust contribution.

Theoretical Yield

These data should provide strong support for the value of spiritual and religious constructs as robust predictors of life satisfaction. The ASPIRES scales have been developed to reflect aspects of the individual that are non-redundant with established personality traits (Piedmont, 2005), and these data continue to support the empirical value of these measures. Because of its independence from the FFM, spirituality may well be considered a *sixth* factor of personality.

There is a growing literature that shows the psychometric and predictive value of the ASPIRES, evidencing both cross-denominational and cross-cultural generalizability (e.g., Goodman, 2002; Piedmont & Leach, 2002; Piedmont, 2007; Wilson, 2004). Such findings argue that the numinous represents a universal aspect of human functioning. Other research has shown its clinical utility across a wide range of groups, from predicting clergy burnout (Golden et al., 2004), to predicting outcome in a substance abuse treatment program (Piedmont, 2004a), to general wellbeing and health status among chronic arthritis sufferers (Bartlett, Piedmont, Bilderback, Matsumoto, & Bathon, 2003). As an aspect of the individual not contained in current personality models, numinous constructs provide new insights into who people are and the goals they are pursuing. Because religious and spiritual constructs play a significant role in adaptation and personal satisfaction, they offer the potential for the identification of entirely new therapeutic strategies and paradigms that are based on these types of motivations (e.g., Murray-Swank, 2003; Piedmont, 2004a). At a minimum, these data argue that any model of human behavior *must* include numinous constructs if that model were to be comprehensive.

The Psychological Value of Numinous Constructs

Why does spirituality and religiosity have relevance for levels of wellbeing and satisfaction with life? There are certainly many answers to this question ranging from a belief in the transforming power of God's grace to the perspective that spirituality represents a "master motive" that organizes the personality and brings coherence to its strivings. The position taken here is that spirituality is valuable because it serves as an antidote to narcissism. A materialistic, self-centered approach to life, where one is always concerned with obtaining gratification of personal needs and wishes, leads to an impulsive style that can be easily frustrated by the demands of life. Here, life goals are usually oriented to the short term and relationships are usually manipulative and emotionally superficial. Spirituality, on the other hand, represents a lifestyle that is transpersonal in nature, where one recognizes a transcendent reality that calls individuals to set personal goals along an eternal continuum. A spiritual perspective recognizes that birth and death are only developmental signposts along a much longer ontological process. Recognition of one's connections to all life, embracing one's responsibilities to care for others creates relationships that are emotionally deep, generative, and mutually satisfying.

Being able to step outside of the immediacy of one's life and to put it into a larger interpretive context can be emotionally healing and liberating. Committing to this larger vision allows individuals to find personal stability and coherence, even during times of fluidity and disjuncture. For individuals locked into their own narrow worlds of emotional pain, personal ineptitude, and interpersonal inadequacy, this broader meaning may provide ways of coping with stressful events or creating buffers against negative feelings. It may also represent a higher level of personality maturity. It is up to future research to examine these issues in more depth (see Piedmont, 2004b). Finding ways to promote spiritual growth may enable individuals to find more emotional security in life and to develop an enhanced capacity to find joy and emotional fulfillment through the many ups and downs of life.

Conclusion

Finding contentment, peace, and personal satisfaction with life are core goals that individuals strive to attain. We look to find fulfillment and completion in this life and pursue many paths to obtain it. Psychology has been successful in identifying many motivations and traits that are associated with wellbeing. Hopefully, this chapter has demonstrated that spiritual and religious variables represent *additional* constructs that contribute to one's sense of contentment. The data presented in this chapter have shown that well-conceived measures of the numinous can be developed and empirically demonstrated to represent unique aspects of the individual. Spirituality represents qualities of the person not represented in traditional individual-difference measures.

It is certain that the large literature documenting the predictive utility of spiritual and religious variables does indeed, despite potential methodological issues, represent a substantive effect. Studying the role of the numinous offers the exciting possibility of unlocking new perspectives on psychological functioning, including the identification of new motivations and personal goals. The opportunity now exists for the identification of new therapeutic interventions that capitalize on these dynamics. Helping individuals create a new sense of personal meaning that stresses relationships and connections created within an eternal framework may be useful for inducing durable personal change.

It is up to future research to identify these methods and to isolate the psychological mechanisms by which the numinous influences our sense of wellbeing.

Acknowledgments I would like to thank Rose Piedmont for her editorial assistance.

References

Allport, G. W. (1950). *The individual and his religion*. New York: Macmillan.
Andrews, F. M., & Withey, S. B. (1976). *Social indicators of well-being: American's perceptions of life quality*. New York: Plenum.
Bartlett, S. J., Piedmont, R. L., Bilderback, A. Matsumoto, A. K., & Bathon, J. M. (2003). Spirituality, well-being and quality of life in persons with rheumatoid arthritis. *Arthritis Care and Research, 49*, 778–783.
Bradburn, N. M. (1969). *The structure of psychological well-being*. Chicago, IL: Aldine.
Buss, D. M. (2002). Sex, marriage, and religion: What adaptive problems do religious phenomena solve? *Psychological Inquiry, 13*, 201–203.
Costa, P. T., Jr., & McCrae, R. R. (1992). *Revised NEO personality inventory: Professional manual*. Odessa, FL: Psychological Assessment Resources.
Diener, E., Emmons, R. A., Larsen, R. J., & Griffin, S. (1985). The satisfaction with life scale. *Journal of Personality Assessment, 49*, 71–75.
Dy-Liacco, G. S., Piedmont, R. L., Leach, M. M., & Nelson, R. W. (2003). A content analysis of Research in the Social Scientific Study of Religion from 1997 to 2001: Where we have been and where we hope to go. *Research in the Social Scientific Study of Religion, 14*, 277–288.
Funder, D. C., Kolar, D. C., & Blackman, M. C. (1995). Agreement among judges of personality: Interpersonal relations, similarity, and acquaintanceship. *Journal of Personality and Social Psychology, 69*, 656–672.
Gallup, G. (1995). *The Gallup Poll: Public opinion 1995*. Wilmington, DE: Scholarly Resources.
Goldberg, L. R. (1993). The structure of phenotypic personality traits. *American Psychologist, 48*, 26–34.
Golden, J., Piedmont, R. L., Ciarrocchi, J. W., & Rodgerson, T. (2004). Spirituality and burnout: An incremental validity study. *Journal of Psychology and Theology, 32*, 115–125.
Goodman, J. M. (2002). *Psychological well-being in the Jewish community: The impact of social identity and spirituality*. Unpublished doctoral dissertation, Kent State University.

Gorsuch, R. L. (1984). Measurement: The boon and bane of investigating religion. *American Psychologist, 39*, 228–236.

Gorsuch, R. L. (1990). Measurement in psychology of religion revisited. *Journal of Psychology and Christianity, 9*, 82–92.

Heath, A. C., Neale, M. C., Kessler, R. C., Eavers, L. J., & Kendler, K. S. (1992). Evidence for genetic influences on personality from self-reports and informant ratings. *Journal of Personality and Social Psychology, 63*, 85–96.

Hill, P. C., & Hood, R. W., Jr. (1999). *Measures of religiosity*. Birmingham, AL: Religious Education Press.

Hill, P. C., & Pargament, K. I. (2003). Advances in the conceptualization and measurement of religion and spirituality: Implications for physical and mental health research. *American Psychologist, 58*, 64–74.

Hill, P. C., Pargament, K. I., Hood, R. W., McCullough, M. E., Swyers, J. P, Larson, D. B., et al. (2000). Conceptualizing religion and spirituality: Points of commonality, points of departure. *Journal for the Theory of Social Behavior, 30*, 51–77.

Hunsley, J., & Meyer, G. J. (2003). The incremental validity of psychological testing and assessment: Conceptual, methodological, and statistical issues. *Psychological Assessment, 15*, 446–455.

Joiner, T. E., Perez, M., & Walker, R. L. (2002). Playing devil's advocate: Why not conclude that the relation of religiosity to mental health reduces to mundane mediators? *Psychological Inquiry, 13*, 214–216.

Koenig, H. G. (1997). *Is religion good for your health? The effects of religion on physical and mental health*. Binghamton, New York: Haworth Press.

Koenig, H. G. (2008). Concerns about measuring "spirituality" in research. *Journal of Nervous and Mental Disease, 196*, 349–355.

Koenig, H. G., McCullough, M. E., & Larson, D. B. (2001). *Handbook of religion and health*. New York: Oxford University Press.

Larson, D. B., & Larson, S. S. (2008). Spirituality's potential relevance to physical and emotional health: A brief review of the quantitative research. *Journal of Psychology and Theology, 31*, 37–51.

McCrae, R. R., & Costa, P. T., Jr. (1987). Validation of the five-factor model of personality across instruments and observers. *Journal of Personality and Social Psychology, 52*, 81–90.

McCrae, R. R., & Costa, P. T., Jr. (1995). Trait explanations in personality psychology. *European Journal of Personality, 9*, 231–252.

McCrae, R. R., & John, O. P. (1992). An introduction to the five-factor model and its applications. *Journal of Personality, 57*, 415–433.

Miller, W. R., & Thoresen, C. E. (1999). Spirituality and health. In W. Miller (Ed.), *Integrating spirituality into treatment* (pp. 3–18). Washington, D.C.: American Psychological Association.

Miller, W. R., & Thoresen, C. E. (2003). Spirituality, religion, and health: An emerging research field. *American Psychologist, 58*, 24–35.

Murray-Swank, N. (2003). *Solace for the soul: An evaluation of a psycho-spiritual intervention for female survivors of sexual abuse*. Unpublished doctoral dissertation, Bowling Green State University, Bowling Green, Ohio.

Musick, M. A., Traphagan, J. W., Koenig, H. G., & Larson, D. B. (2000). Spirituality in physical health and aging. *Journal of Adult Development, 7*, 73–86.

Nunnally, J. C., & Bernstein, I. H. (1994). *Psychometric theory* (3rd ed.). New York: McGraw-Hill.

Ozer, D. J., & Reise, S. P. (1994). Personality assessment. *Annual Review of Psychology, 45*, 357–388.

Paloutzian, R. F., & Park, C. L. (2005), *The handbook of the psychology of religion*. New York: Guilford.

Pargament, K. I. (1997). *The psychology of religion and coping: Theory, research, practice*. New York: Guilford Press.

Pargament, K. I. (2002). Is religion nothing but . . .? Explaining religion versus explaining religion away. *Psychological Inquiry, 13*, 239–244.

Pargament, K. I., Koenig, H. G., Tarakeshwar, M. A., & Hahn, J. (2001). Religious struggle as a predictor of mortality among medically ill elderly patients: A two-year longitudinal study. *Archives of Internal Medicine, 161*, 1881–1885.

Pargament, K. I., Smith, B. W., Koenig, H. G., & Perez, L. (1998). Patterns of positive and negative religious coping with major life stressors. *Journal for the Scientific Study of Religion, 37*, 710–724.

Piedmont, R. L. (1994). Validation of the NEO PI-R observer form for college students: Toward a paradigm for studying personality development. *Assessment, 1*, 259–268.

Piedmont, R. L. (1998). *The revised NEO Personality inventory: Clinical and research applications*. New York: Plenum.

Piedmont, R. L. (1999). Strategies for using the five-factor model of personality in religious research. *Journal of Psychology and Theology, 27*, 338–250.

Piedmont, R. L. (2001). Spiritual transcendence and the scientific study of spirituality. *Journal of Rehabilitation, 67*, 4–14.

Piedmont, R. L. (2004a). Spiritual Transcendence as a predictor of psychosocial outcome from an outpatient substance abuse program. *Psychology of Addictive Behaviors, 18*, 223–232.

Piedmont, R. L. (2004b). The logoplex as a paradigm for understanding spiritual transcendence. *Research in the Social Scientific Study of Religion, 15*, 263–284.

Piedmont, R. L. (2005). *Assessment of spirituality and religious sentiments, technical manual*. Baltimore, MD; Author.

Piedmont, R. L. (2007). Cross-cultural generalizability of the Spiritual Transcendence Scale to the Philippines: Spirituality as a human universal. *Mental Health, Religion and Culture, 10*, 80–107.

Piedmont, R. L. (2009). Personality, spirituality, religiousness and Axis II functioning: Predictive relations and treatment implications. In H. Koenig and P. Huguelet (Eds.). *The role of religion and spirituality in psychiatry* (pp. 173–189). New York: Cambridge University Press.

Piedmont, R. L., Hassinger, C. J., Rhorer, J., Sherman, M. F., Sherman, N. C., & Williams, J. E. G. (2007). The relations among spirituality and religiosity and Axis II functioning in two college samples. *Research in the Social Scientific Study of Religion, 18*, 53–73.

Piedmont, R. L., & Leach, M. M. (2002). Cross-cultural generalizability of the Spiritual Transcendence Scale in India: Spirituality as a universal aspect of human experience. *American Behavioral Scientist, 45*, 1888–1901.

Rosenberg, M. (1979). *Conceiving the self*. New York: Basic Books.

Ruckmick, C. A. (1920). *The brevity book on psychology*. Chicago, IL: Brevity Publishers.

Saroglou, V. (2002). Religion and the five-factors of personality: A meta-analytic review. *Personality and Individual Differences, 32*, 15–25.

Sawatzky, R., Ratner, P. A., & Chiu, L. (2005). A meta-analysis of the relationship between spirituality and quality of life. *Social Indicators Research, 72*, 153–188.

Sloan, R. P., & Bagiella, R. (2002). Claims about religious involvement and health outcomes. *Annals of Behavioral Medicine, 24*, 14–21.

Sloan, R. P., Bagiella, R., & Powell, T. (2001). Without a prayer: Methodological problems, ethical challenges, and misrepresentation in the study of religion, spirituality, and medicine. In T. G. Plante & A. C. Sherman (Eds.), *Faith and health: Psychological perspectives* (pp. 339–354). New York: Guilford Press.

Snyder, C. R., Simpson, S. C., Ybasco, F. C., Borders, T. F., Babyak, M. A., & Higgins, R. L. (1996). Development and validation of the state Hope Scale. *Journal of Personality and Social Psychology, 70*, 321–335.

Thoresen, C. E. (1999). Spirituality and health: Is there a relationship? *Journal of Health Psychology, 4*, 291–300.

Van Wicklin, J. F. (1990). Conceiving and measuring ways of being religious. *Journal of Psychology and Christianity, 9*, 27–40.

Wilson, T. (2004). *Ethnic identity and spirituality in the recovery from alcoholism among aboriginal Canadians*. Unpublished Masters Thesis, University of Windsor.

Zinnbauer, B. J., Pargament, K. I., & Scott, A. B. (1999). The emerging meanings of religiousness and spirituality: Problems and prospects. *Journal of Personality, 67*, 889–920.

Chapter 6
Culture, Religion and Spirituality in Relation to Psychiatric Illness

Kate M. Loewenthal

Abstract Religious and spiritual factors can affect mental health (Pargament, 1997; Koenig, McCullough & Larson, 2001; Loewenthal, 2007). There are many routes by which these effects operate. However, most of the work on these effects has been done in western, Christian cultures. Does work from other religions and cultures suggest new perspectives on the problems and conclusions? Using evidence from other cultural-religious contexts, some ideas are examined about the links between culture, religion, spirituality and mental health. This chapter will look at four issues in particular: somatisation, schizophrenia, obsessive-compulsive disorder and depression. There are hypotheses relating to each of these disorders and their links with religion or cultural factors. We look to see whether these hypotheses are supported by evidence from non-western and/or non-Christian cultures. Implications for education and wellbeing are considered.

Definitions

First, some definitions need to be offered.

Spirituality: This has been defined as the search for and experience of the sacred (Pargament, 1997, 2007). Spirituality is understood to be broader than any single formal religion and is reflected in the search for meaning, a sense of transcendence, and the practice of spiritual or mystical disciplines (Zinnbauer, Pargament, & Scott, 1999). Zinnbauer et al. (1997) have indicated that, at least for the North American adults they studied, all those who identify themselves as religious also see themselves as spiritual. Additionally there are people who identify themselves as spiritual but not religious and people who identify themselves as neither. Thus we can suggest that for this chapter, the term spiritual will apply to those who see themselves as engaged in spirituality—as for instance in the search for meaning and for the sacred—and will include those active in the formal religious sense. Popular

---

K.M. Loewenthal (✉)
Department of Psychology, Royal Holloway, University of London, Egham,
Surrey TW20 0EX, UK
e-mail: c.loewenthal@rhul.ac.uk

measures of spirituality include Ellison (1983) and King, Speck, and Thomas (1995). Measurement will be discussed elsewhere in this book.

Religiosity: There have been many attempts at definition and measurement of religiosity, with some scholars claiming that there will never be a satisfactory definition (Wulff, 1997; Hill & Hood, 1999; Loewenthal, 2007). However, there is some agreement about the basics. For instance, English and English (1958) suggested that religion is "a system of attitudes, practices, rites, ceremonies and beliefs by means of which individuals or a community put themselves in relation to G-d or to a supernatural world, often to each other, and derive a set of values by which to judge events in the natural world". Loewenthal (2000) suggested that the major religious traditions have a number of features of belief in common: the existence of a non-material (i.e. spiritual) reality, the purpose of life is to increase harmony in the world by doing good and avoiding evil, the monotheistic religions hold that the source of existence (i.e. G-d) is also the source of moral directives, all religions involve and depend on social organisation for communicating these ideas. We can see common themes underlying the beliefs and behaviours in all religious traditions. These are *spiritual reality, morality, purpose*, and finally the*communication* of these. A more basic definition of religiosity might involve identification with a religious group—and inherent in this would be the beliefs and behaviours outlined above. Elsewhere in this book are authoritative and more detailed accounts of the definition and assessment of religiosity. For our present purposes, we have said enough to indicate where spirituality and religiosity overlap.

Mental health: Mental health has been viewed as the absence of mental illness (or absence of symptoms). It can also be viewed as involving the features said to be characteristic of mental health. The former view has been more popular in studies of religion/spirituality and mental health, and particularly widespread has been the use of measures of depression and/or anxiety as indices of general mental health. However, measures of positive wellbeing are not simply in inverse relationship to measures of psychopathology. Their use in the study of religion, spirituality and mental health is on the increase. This has been alongside the rise of positive psychology, which is thought to be intimately and intricately connected with religion and spirituality (Seligman, 2002; Joseph, Linley, & Maltby, 2006).

How do cultural factors affect the relationships between religious and spiritual factors, and mental health? Are religious people better-off than others in terms of mental health? It is well established that there is a general overall weak but consistent relationship between measures of religiosity and measures of spirituality. This overall effect is the result of a plethora of effects, not all working in the same direction (Pargament, 1997; Koenig et al., 2001; Loewenthal, 2007). This chapter unpacks some of these effects, looking particularly at how the relationships are affected by culture. The addition of "culture" as variable involves difficulties, since religion and culture are intertwined.

Culture: Tylor's (1871) definition has remained popular and useful. He saw culture as "that complex whole which includes knowledge, belief, art, morals, law, custom, and any other capabilities and habits acquired by man as a member of society". Although there has been some concern over its vagueness and over-inclusiveness, for general social-scientific purposes, it remains in widespread use. In studies of culture in relation to psychological factors, the commonly used label for a particular social-cultural group is normally adopted, for example "Chinese" and "British".

We now turn to some examples of how cultural factors impact on the relations between religion, spirituality and mental health.

The Somatisation Hypothesis

This hypothesis arose from a suggestion that the expression of psychological distress is not always possible or understood in some cultures. Instead, distress is translated into bodily symptoms.

Early expressions of this hypothesis were frankly racist, implying that it was somehow more sophisticated to feel depressed than to have a backache. In *Aliens and Alienists*, Littlewood and Lipsedge (1997) review these suggestions, dismissing the claim that non-western people suffer from somatic disorders because their languages lack psychological categories in which to frame their misery. But racist descendants of the hypothesis can be seen for instance in the then-current South African opinion that "subjective depression" is rare among black people, though there may be observed a form of "primitive depression" with features of agitation and paranoia (p. 72). What is the current evidence?

The hypothesis would suggest that the expression of distress by bodily (somatic) symptoms is less common in countries which are privileged, i.e. wealthier, more technologically advanced, with higher levels of literacy and general education. There is little evidence to support this suggestion. There are great variations between cultures in the amount and types of organically unexplained somatic symptoms, and indeed some syndromes are completely culture-specific. Medical anthropologists and others have referred to these as *cultural idioms of distress* (Kirmayer & Young, 1998). Examples include "wind overload" (Hinton, Um, & Ba, 2001), common among Khmer refugees from Cambodia to the United States. The symptoms include rapid breathing, palpitations and fainting. The disorder appears to be a culture-specific form of panic attack, common among Khmer people with a history of severe trauma, and precipitated by stress. Cambodians have specific treatments for this disorder, particularly "coining": a coin is dipped in "wind oil" and rubbed along the arm or leg to displace the wind. Trollope-Kumar (2001) has described leukorrhea, a common condition in the Indian sub-continent, involving vaginal discharge in women and semen loss in men, together with other somatic complaints—headaches, backaches, weakness, dizziness. The condition is often preceded by social stress. Conventional Western treatment (antibiotics, tubectomy) is said to be less successful than Ayurvedic dietary or herbal treatments, based on the spiritual significance of the loss of genital secretions, purified *dhatu*. Loewenthal (2007) concluded that unexplained somatic symptoms are widely reported in the United Kingdom. The Western syndrome ME (Myalgic Encephalopathy), or CFS (Chronic Fatigue Syndrome), repeated bouts of fever and weakness, has so far defied attempts to identify organic causation, and is thought to be stress-related (Baumer, 2005).

There are some studies of culturally universal somatic symptoms, and these show no sign of being more common in less technologically advanced countries. Lack of ready access to health care does not seem to be an explanatory factor. For instance, in a recent World Health Organisation (WHO) study of medically unexplained pain (Gureje, Von Korff, Simon, & Gater, 1998), 25,000 primary care attenders were screened at 15 centres in Europe, Asia, Africa and the Americas. The eight centres in which unexplained pain was reported most frequently included five of the seven western centres. The seven centres in which unexplained pain was reported least frequently included all three of the Asian centres and the sole African centre in the study. In this and in many other studies (see Cohen, Pine, Must, Kasen, & Brook, 1998) somatic symptoms and psychological distress co-varied, ruling out the possibility that somatic symptoms are an *alternative* to psychological suffering as a way of expressing distress.

One form of the somatisation hypothesis suggests that some languages lack categories for psychological distress. This crude form of the hypothesis is not supported, but the study of culture-specific idioms of distress does indicate how language and religion play their roles. An example is described by Hollan (2004), of an Indonesian man suffering from chronic stomach pains and breathlessness. There was speculation that these symptoms were the result of guilt over youthful misdemeanours, which displeased his parents. But, says Hollan,

> He does not have a word for guilt...he would say that he has been in error ... (which) does not imply sinfulness or inherent badness. But it does imply that one has done something worthy of punishment if one is caught. Other humans may discover your misbehaviour, but so might the spirits or ancestors, who may then punish you or your family or descendants with countless forms of misfortune...many Toraja risk waiting to see whether their behaviour *has* been noticed and punished before changing their ways and making compensatory offerings.

Another factor which might account for the presentation of somatic symptoms is stigmatisation. Somatic symptoms are usually less stigmatised than are psychological symptoms. In small, tightly knit social groups—religious communities are outstanding examples—people are very reluctant to acknowledge psychological problems. For example,

> Our people do not go to the doctor (when depressed), in fact they hide it, because they think that if people know about it they will not accept them and they'll be laughed at and would be completely shut off because there is this prejudice (Muslim, in Cinnirella & Loewenthal, 1999).
>
> The one thing Black people hate is for anybody to find out there is any form of mental illness in their families ... what they try to do is shut that person away and deal with it by themselves as opposed to going through all the networks and being exposed (Black Christian, in Cinnirella & Loewenthal, 1999).
>
> I wonder what type of families need this (kind of help)? Is it just those who can't cope? I might feel ashamed to ask for such help (Orthodox Jewish, in Loewenthal & Rogers, 2004).

Apart from stigma, somatic symptoms may be simpler to deal with than psychological distress. Medical practitioners are much more accessible than psychologists and psychiatrists, they have quick-fix solutions (medication) for any psychological problems that may be apparent, and somatic symptoms may are less blameworthy and more intelligible than psychological problems. Perkins and Moodley (1993) reported that over half the psychiatric in-patients they studied reported only somatic symptoms. Among whites in particular, it was found that denial tended to take the form of somatisation, or the construction of problems in terms of social difficulties.

On the evidence reviewed so far, we cannot dismiss the idea that distress may be expressed somatically, but the factors influencing the form of expression are varied. Somatic complaints are not an alternative to psychological distress. Indeed there is much evidence that there are causal relationships in both distress – psychological distress, particularly depression, may affect immune system functioning with resultant effects on physical health, and physical illness may cause psychological distress (Loewenthal, 2007; Cohen et al., 1998).

Do religion and spirituality play any role in somatic symptoms and illnesses? Beliefs in spiritual forces as causing somatic distress have already appeared in some of the examples considered.

A correlational study among North American university students (Houran, Kumar, Thalbourne, & Lavertue, 2002) showed that malign spiritual experiences—poltergeists, hauntings, spirit infestations and other paranormal experiences—were related to hypochondriacal and somatic tendencies. We cannot be sure about causality here.

There is some ethnographic work which suggests that beliefs in spiritual forces may be heavily involved in shaping somatic disorders, for example, in the case described by Hollan (2004) above. Margolin and Witztum (1989) treated an Iranian father of three children:

> He had become impotent several days after the death of his father. He refused psychotherapy and asked for a medicine that would bring back his potency. However conventional pharmacological and behaviour therapy did not help and he left treatment because he did not believe anything could help him. Later the patient reported having improved following a dream whose content he would not reveal. The therapists consulted an Iranian colleague who suggested that the patient might believe that he had been "bound" by his vengeful deceased father as a punishment for failing to observe the religious laws of mourning properly, and who then unbound him in the dream, one year after his (the father's) death (when the prescribed mourning period was finished). Binding is a practice known to Christians, Muslims and Jews in Iran, involving witchcraft or sorcery, whose effect is to prevent male fertility. The therapist discussed this possibility tactfully with the patient, who said that now he felt the therapist understood him (based on the account by Margolin & Witztum).

Beliefs of this kind are clearly important in somatisation, even though causality is complicated. Some clinicians find it helpful to take these spiritual beliefs into account in developing their treatment plans. It can be helpful to consult and involve a religious leader or other spiritual advisor from the sufferer's own faith tradition. An example of a pragmatic and eclectic approach to somatic complaints is offered in MacLachlan's (1997) description of a treatment plan for "Mr Lin" who felt that his stomach complaints were the work of the spirit of his displeased, deceased father, concerned about Mr Lin's marital infidelities, and eating "foreign" food, among other factors. The treatment plan deals with these causes in ways that are acceptable to Mr Lin, for example, prayer and sacrifice to appease his father's spirit, recommitting himself to his wife and changing his diet to exclude "foreign" food.

We have seen that somatic complaints are often or always exacerbated by stress. They are not alternatives to psychological distress. Their patterning is the result of cultural and individual factors and has been usefully described as *cultural idioms of distress*. Beliefs in the involvement of spiritual forces are common, and many clinicians have found it helpful to take these beliefs into account, sometimes involving expert advice or other help from the sufferer's own faith tradition.

Afro-Caribbean Schizophrenia?

A problem which has caused some concern is the following: in the UK and North America, Afro-Caribbeans are more likely to be referred and diagnosed with schizophrenia than are members of other cultural groups (Davis, 1975; Littlewood & Lipsedge, 1981a; Ineichen, 1991; C. Thomas, Stone, Osborn, & P. F. Thomas, 1993; Comer, 1999). However, in Africa and in the Caribbean, schizophrenia is no more likely than it is in other countries. Why should Afro-Caribbeans be so much at risk when living in western countries? Are there effects of religion and spirituality?

There are two broad sets of explanations: first, differences in stress and other social factors and, second, misdiagnosis. There is some evidence to support the first possibility: in general, Afro-Caribbeans are more deprived and stressed than other social groups; some forms of stress have been shown to precipitate or exacerbate episodes of schizophrenia (McGovern & Cope, 1991; Sugarman & Crauford, 1994). What about misdiagnosis? Might approved or normative (religious) beliefs and behaviours, or a culture-specific syndrome, be mistaken for schizophrenia?

An Afro-Caribbean is defined as a West Indian person, a descendant of some of the approximately 10 million people of West African origin, forcibly shipped to the West Indies and North America as slave labourers in the seventeenth and eighteenth centuries, to replace the indigenous populations largely eliminated by desettlement, genocide and European-imported illnesses (Curtin, 1969) in plantations owned by European settlers. West Indians arriving in the United Kingdom as economic migrants expected a welcome in the Christian churches, but this was not forthcoming. Black churches—involving a blend of Christian and surviving African practices—evolved in the United Kingdom, the United States and the West Indies (Chatfield, 1989; Griffith & Bility, 1996; Howard, 1987). The proportion of Afro-Caribbeans in black-led religious groups is said to be high, and these groups often involve lively, charismatic forms of worship (Cochrane & Howell, 1995). Black-led religious groups are important sources of solidarity, identity and spirituality, and an enthusiastic style of religiosity is normative, but may be misconstrued as a sign of disturbance by outsiders.

Littlewood and Lipsedge's (1981a, 1981b, 1989, 1997) material is consistent with the idea that the high incidence of schizophrenia among Afro-Caribbeans in the United Kingdom could (at least partly) be accounted for by a normal prevalence of "true" schizophrenia, plus a number of further cases of culture-specific disorder. Among Afro-Caribbeans, a high proportion of cases diagnosed as schizophrenic have a "religious flavour", are of short duration with a relatively good prognosis, and are often preceded by a clear precipitating factor before admission. For example,

> M was descended from victims of the African slave trade. She lived in the United States, and employed in domestic work. She became unwell and could not afford professional medical attention. She went to a herbalist, who sexually abused her. Feeling defiled, she tried to purify herself by intensive prayer and bible study. She was too ill to work, and was sent to a psychiatric hospital, where her pious practices continued. She was diagnosed with schizophrenia (dementia praecox) (Evarts, 1914).

In Evarts' report, it appears that M's sole "symptom" was her fervent religious behaviour, with its understandable aim of self-purification. This example of (mis)diagnosis is a good example of the situation highlighted by the work of Siddle, Haddock, Tarrier, and Faragher (2002), and Bhugra (2002) whereby religious attempts to cope with stress are construed as symptoms of psychiatric illness. The following example from Fulford (1999) highlights the same point:

> A 40-year-old black American professional man, "Simon", a lawyer, from a Baptist background, had experienced occasional psychic experiences, which he used to discuss with his religious adviser, a man he consulted about major life events and decisions. More recently, Simon has been extremely troubled since a group of colleagues have brought a lawsuit against him. The complaint is unfounded, but it would be extremely expensive and risky to fight this. Simon took to praying at an altar set up in his living room at home. He discovered that the candles he lit to accompany his prayers dripped wax onto his bible, and he felt that the words marked by the wax had a special significance. Most people he showed this bible to, were not impressed, but Simon persisted in saying that the marked words had special symbolism, and that he was chosen and marked out for special responsibility by G-d. He also felt that often his thoughts were interrupted by sudden "thought insertion" from a higher source.

Fulford says that most medical students are likely to suggest a diagnosis of schizophrenia. In reality, Simon functioned well throughout his lawsuit, with no symptoms of disturbance other than these religious coping attempts. Once the lawsuit was resolved, his unusual religious practices declined, his career developed well and he became very successful.

Given that religious affiliation among Afro-Caribbeans is higher than that in whites, and religious behaviour is often more enthusiastic, could religious coping account for some misdiagnosis of schizophrenia?

The incidence of schizophrenia among Afro-Caribbeans in the United Kingdom is said to be rising. Black-led religious movements continue to flourish, providing social support, identity and cultural activity. Although there is evidence for other causal factors in schizophrenia among Afro-Caribbeans in western countries, particularly stress (McGovern & Cope, 1991; Sugarman & Crauford, 1994), there is still a strong cultural framework for the perpetuation of the kind of culture-specific disorder suggested by Littlewood and Lipsedge (Castillo, 2003; Loewenthal & Cinnirella, 2003). Further, as DSM-IV indicates, there is a risk of over-diagnosis in some ethnic groups. It would be premature to rule out the possibility that religious behaviour—particularly in the ecstatic or enthusiastic style favoured in black (and a few white) charismatic churches—may be misconstrued as symptomatic of schizophrenia, and this may help to account for the high rate of schizophrenia referral rate among Afro-Caribbeans in western countries.

Jewish OCD (Obsessive-Compulsive Disorder): Do Religions Which Encourage Scrupulosity as a Feature of Spirituality Foster OCD?

Obsessive-compulsive disorder involves uncontrollable, persistent and distressing repetitive thoughts and/or actions, to the extent that these interfere with everyday activities, work and relationships. Examples of unwanted thoughts and behaviours include fears and compulsions about dirt and cleanliness, for example, repeated hand-washing. Of course, scrupulousness is on a continuum from reasonable care and caution, to uncontrolled obsessionality. Does religion encourage perfectionism as a defence against anxiety? Can religion cause obsessive-compulsive disorder?

In 1907, Freud wrote a paper on the similarities between religion and obsessional neurosis. He described a woman who was obsessed with feeling dirty and compulsively washed her hands. The paper is interesting for two reasons. First, it argues very compellingly that the dynamics underlying religious ritual are similar to those underlying obsessional neurosis—those persons feel guilty if they do not carry out the prescribed action, and anxiety and guilt are relieved when the action is carried out. For a while! Then guilt surfaces once more and the action must be repeated. For both religion and neurosis, the deeper meaning or significance of the action is not usually apparent to the person carrying out the action.

The second point of interest in this paper that it does not suggest *anywhere* that religion *causes* (obsessional) neurosis. The paper merely makes the claim that the dynamics are similar. Still, Freud is credited with —or blamed for, depending on your perspective—the idea that religion causes neurosis, by engendering guilt, anxiety and scrupulosity. The idea has remained very popular.

Like schizophrenic symptoms, obsessive-compulsive symptoms often have a "religious flavour". For example,

> Ahmed, a pious Muslim, spends half an hour or more washing and checking himself before each of the five daily prayers. He recognises that this is excessive, but fears to go to a doctor or psychiatrist for help, since they may not recognise the spiritual importance of cleanliness before prayer (based on Al Soleim, 2005).
>
> Miriam, a strictly orthodox Jew, is very careful to avoid the mixing of foods containing meat with foods containing milk. The prohibition is an important aspect of Jewish dietary law, and it is a normal part of religious practice to have separate plates for milk and meat, and to wash these separately from each other. But Miriam has carried things to a degree

further than normal rabbinically recommended practice. Her family find her practices excessive and very difficult to live with. For example, most families use only one dustbin and one set of cooking spices, but Miriam insists on separate milk and meat dustbins, ketchup bottles, spices used in cooking, and she has insisted on a wall diving the kitchen into milk and meat areas, with family members washing hands and putting on designated overalls before moving from one to the other. Miriam believes she is carrying out the law with commendable strictness and her husband is having difficulty in persuading her to accept their rabbi's recommendation that her practices are excessive and inappropriate (based on Greenberg, Witztum, & Pisante, 1987, and the author's observations).

Both clinical observation and quantitative data indicate that religious and religiously derived themes (such as some forms of cleanliness) are common themes for obsessions (Greenberg & Witztum, 2001; Abramowitz, Huppert, Cohen, Tolin, & Cahill, 2002). Figure 6.1 gives some quantitative substance to these observations (based on Tek & Ulug, 2001).

We can see that contamination is a fairly constant theme, whereas other themes vary quite widely from country to country. Religious themes are most common in Israel, Saudi Arabia and Turkey—both Israel and Turkey are said to have a dominant "secular" culture. Concerns about cleanliness, aggression and sexuality may have a spiritual basis, but we can't tell in what proportion. Although the data in Fig. 6.1 indicate variation between the countries studied in the popularity of different themes in OCD, we do not know enough about levels and styles of religiosity in the different countries to discern any obvious patterns.

We must turn to other information to detect relations between religion and OCD. The most systematic analysis was reported by Lewis (1998) in a paper appropriately entitled "Is cleanliness next to G-dliness?" Lewis concluded that measures of religiosity related fairly consistently to measures of scrupulous or obsessional *personality*, but did not relate to obsessional *illness*. Thus, religion may make us careful and scrupulous, but does not apparently make us ill. To take a specific study, Sica, Novara, and Sanavio (2002) found that Italians who were more religiously active scored more highly on measures of obsessionality, overimportance of thoughts, control of thoughts, perfectionism and responsibility—but were not more likely to suffer from clinical OCD.

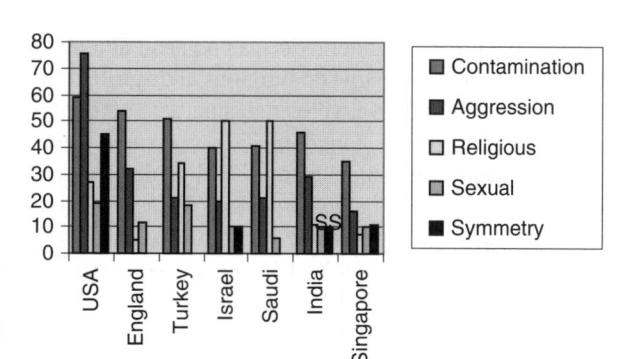

Fig. 6.1 Common themes of obsessions in different cultures (% frequency) based on Tek and Ulug (2001)

Tek and Ulug (2001) analysed OCD patients in Turkey. Religious symptoms were common across the whole sample (42% of symptoms)—but religious activity was not associated with a higher frequency of religious symptoms or with higher levels of disturbance. Tek and Ulug believe that religion is an arena in which OCD can express itself, but is not a determinant of OCD.

What about Jewish OCD? Jewish law is certainly scrupulous in its distinctions between what is religiously permitted and what is not. For example, more than one-sixtieth part of meat in milk food makes the food religiously unfit for consumption, and a person may not pray until he or she has washed their hands in a prescribed order, before walking more than four paces after waking. Leaves which are to be eaten must be carefully inspected to ensure that they harbour no wildlife—insects may not be eaten, and they can normally only be detected by holding each leaf up to a strong light.

Greenberg and Witztum (2001) offer compelling examples of cases in which OCD sufferers are aware that their compulsions have gone way over the boundaries of what is religiously required. Greenberg and Witztum believe that religion provides a means of expression for OCD, but does not cause or exacerbate it. Greenberg and Shefler (2002) studied 28 strictly religious Jewish patients suffering from OCD. They had many more (three times) religious symptoms than non-religious symptoms. They viewed their religious symptoms as their main difficulty. However their experiences of religious and non-religious symptoms were similar, with no differences in age of onset, length of time before seeking help, amount of distress caused, time spent on the symptom and other factors. This study indicated that religious OCD symptoms are no more (or less) entrenched or protected than other symptoms.

It is not clear that Jews—even strictly orthodox Jews—are more prone to OCD than other people. Religious teachings may indeed affect scrupulosity and other ways of thinking, but it is not clear that religion leads to obsessional pathology. Informed opinion suggests that obsessional pathology may be framed religiously, but not caused religiously.

Gender Differences in the Prevalence of Depression

Depressive illness is about twice as prevalent among women as it is among men. Is this always the case? How do religious and spiritual factors play a role?

In the mid-1990s we were analysing data on depression in community samples of Jews in the United Kingdom. To our surprise and alarm, our preliminary analysis indicated that major depressive disorder was about as prevalent among the men in our sample, as among women. We asked ourselves whether there was anything wrong with our methodology—we would have expected prevalence among women to be about double that among men (see for example Cochrane, 1993). Eventually we concluded that the findings were genuine. When we wrote up the work (Loewenthal et al., 1995) we suggested that the fact that there was no evidence of alcohol abuse, or even recreational alcohol use (other than for religious purposes) might bear some relationship to the relatively high prevalence of depression in Jewish men. We discovered that similar findings on prevalence of depression were being independently reported in Jewish samples in the United States and Israel (Levav et al., 1993; Levav, Kohn, Golding, & Weismann, 1997), and again it was suspected that low recreational alcohol use by Jewish men may be a factor in the raised prevalence of depression.

The alcohol-depression hypothesis—that depression varies inversely with alcohol use—has been explored with some success. Observant Jews drink limited amounts of alcohol on religious and festive occasions, and we confirmed that culturally carried beliefs do not support recreational drinking and drunkenness among Jews (Loewenthal, MacLeod, Cook, Lee, & Goldblatt, 2003a). For example, Jewish people envisaged catastrophic scenes consequent to loss of control—which they saw as a likely consequence of drinking:

> It can lead to immorality – getting into trouble with the police – getting into fights for no reason.
> It can lead to abuse or to violence ... it can cause husbands hitting wives...destroying furniture, things like this ... attacking wives and children.
> If you do go to the pub, you expect that there will be a lot of drunk people around and beer flying (from Loewenthal et al.).

British people of Protestant background, by contrast, saw (social) drinking as an aid to relaxation, and forgetting ones stresses and troubles:

> Fine, people need a chance to let their hair down.
> I find a drink might relax me.
> It drowns your problems.
> You lose your inhibitions so you might be able to socialise more (from Loewenthal et al.).

Indeed, there is some evidence that alcohol use up to a certain limit may be an effective way of coping with stress, resulting in a lowered prevalence of depression (Lipton, 2005), though of course beyond a certain limit, alcohol use generates a spiral of alcohol abuse and poor mental health.

We discovered that Jews do have a somewhat higher tolerance for depression than a comparison group of Protestant Christian background, and lower tolerance for suicide—both these factors may contribute to raised prevalence of depression among Jews (Loewenthal, MacLeod, Cook, Lee, & Goldblatt, 2003b; Loewenthal, MacLeod, Cook, Lee, & Goldblatt, 2002).

Alcohol use is religiously regulated, but alcohol use is only one of a number of factors—some of them religiously related—which may have an impact on depression. We know that alcohol use is generally frowned upon in Muslim countries, but the epidemiological evidence is that in most Muslim countries (for which evidence is available) women are generally more likely to be depressed than are men. Here, the alcohol-depression hypothesis does not seem to be supported. The patterns of depression by gender may be due to cultural factors, some of them religiously endorsed and supported, which place women in relatively powerless social, economic and political roles, and therefore vulnerable to depression-inducing losses such as widowhood. Employment opportunities for women may be very restricted, health and welfare provision limited, leaving widows with children to support, or with health problems, in a helpless situation (e.g. Dwyer, Bruce, & Cain, 1988; Mirza & Jenkins, 2004). A feature of life in many South Asian communities is upholding *izzat*—family honour. Women feel obliged to do this by being good wives, not complaining of any abuse and having reservations about seeking help for any mental health difficulties (P. Gilbert, J. Gilbert, & Sanghera, 2004):

> Izzat is the biggest issue in the Asian woman's life. It is not about yourself, it's about your family, it involves your relatives and the people you know. So it's you don't think about yourself, you've got to think about what other people are going to think.
>
> You have to be a good mother and a good wife and I think if you are not a good mother and not a good wife then you're not a good woman. And if you're not a good woman that's going to bring shame on your family.
>
> (if in an abusive relationship) "...one day it will get too much and...some women think it's better to commit suicide than to leave...I think from your point of view personally you would rather just die.
>
> (if in an abusive relationship)... if she goes away, she will be found again and brought back...shame does come into it if you are going to leave...it's because of izzat she's been taking the beatings (from Gilbert et al.).

As described in the opening phases of this chapter, religion is generally associated with lower levels of depressive illness, and of depression. The association is the result of several effects, some of which have working in opposite directions. There are more extensive discussions of many of these effects elsewhere in this volume. We have considered two effects of religion which may have differential impact on men's and women's mental health (alcohol use and gender role prescriptions). Other effects include religious coping—beliefs in a supportive, benevolent G-d predicts good mental health outcomes. Reports of gender differences in religious beliefs and religious coping styles are limited. Loewenthal, MacLeod, Goldblatt, Lubitsh, and Valentine (2000) found no differences between men and women (Protestants and Jews in the United Kingdom) in their religious coping beliefs. There have been very limited reports of gender differences in religious coping (Koenig et al., 2001), though Ferraro and Kelley-Moore (2000) reported an analysis of a national study in the United States which indicated that women were more likely than men to seek religious consolation when ill. Women, especially in Christian cultures, are generally more religiously active than men (Francis, 1993; Beit-Hallahmi & Argyle, 1997; Loewenthal, MacLeod, & Cinnirella, 2001), and even if there are no striking gender differences in religious coping style, the limited evidence suggests that women may be more likely than men to engage in religious activity such as prayer when ill or under stress. This may lead to better mental health outcomes among women.

There are other pathways by which religious factors may have a differential impact on women and men, and hence on depression—such as social support, caring and helping. These have been associated with lowered depression (Brown & Harris, 1978; Seligman, 2002), but the links with religion and gender remain to be systematically explored.

In this section we have seen that religious factors can impact differently on women and men, and some of these impacts may reflect on mood, particularly perhaps depression. The effects are mixed, and overall we must question the biological inevitability of women's depression-proneness. Sometimes the effects of religiously related factors may be strong enough to reduce or eliminate gender imbalance in depression.

Conclusions and Implications for Education and Wellbeing

This chapter has examined some common beliefs and questions about mental health, religion and culture. We have seen that somatisation is a culturally shaped and meaningful expression or idiom of distress, rather than a failure or inability to express distress in language. Schizophrenia can be affected by social and cultural factors, and we cannot dismiss the further concern that its diagnosis may be influenced by inadequately understood religious behaviour. The expression of obsessive-compulsive disorder can be in terms of religious behaviour and spiritual feelings, but there are strong reasons to suppose that religion does not cause obsessive illness. Finally, we have seen that religious and spiritual factors can have a strong influence on depression—even to the extent that the normal gender imbalance in depression prevalence disappears.

For those concerned with the education of children and adolescents, it is helpful to be aware that the conditions we have discussed can make their appearance in childhood. Very young children can suffer somatic complaints (Cohen et al., 1998), though the cultural shaping of these complaints during development has not been studied. Schizophrenia can be recognised in very early adolescence (Rapaport, 2000), and very young children have been diagnosed with OCD (Rutter & Taylor, 2002) and depression (Gotlib & Hammen, 2002). These psychiatric illnesses may not always be apparent to educators, to parents or even to mental health professionals. The commonest features of OCD in childhood may differ from those in adulthood—symmetry is common theme in childhood OCD for example. More problematic is that children may recognise that their obsession is abnormal, and they may be very furtive about it. The condition may go unrecognised until further symptoms develop and become uncontrollable. Childhood depression, while very common, may be unrecognised. Very quiet children may not draw enough attention to themselves to cause concern. Depressed mood may be masked by irritability (Butcher, Mineka, & Hooley, 2007). While teachers and others concerned with child and adolescent care and protection must be vigilant and concerned, it is appropriate to discuss concerns with other responsible and experienced professionals and to take respectful account of the child's social, cultural and religious background.

It is hoped that this chapter will have encouraged the reader to question some common assumptions and conclusions about religion and culture in relation to mental health. Religion is neither a universal destroyer of wellbeing nor a universal panacea. The effects of religion and spirituality on wellbeing are many and varied and, as we have seen, can definitely be modulated by culture.

References

Abramowitz, J. S., Huppert, J. D., Cohen, A. B., Tolin, D. F., & Cahill, S. P. (2002). Religious obsessions and compulsions in a non-clinical sample: The Penn Index of Scrupulosity (PIOS). *Behaviour Research and Therapy, 40*, 825–838.

Al Soleim, L. (2005). *Obsessive compulsive disorder among Muslim adolescents and young adults*. Doctoral dissertation, Royal Holloway, University of London.

Baumer, J. H. (2005). Management of chronic fatigue syndrome/myalgic encephalopathy (CFS/ME). *Archives of Disease in Childhood – Education and Practice, 90*, 46–50.

Beit-Hallahmi, B., & Argyle, M. (1997). *The psychology of religious belief: Behaviour and experience*. London: Routledge.

Bhugra, D. (2002). Self-concept: Psychosis and attraction of new religious movements. *Mental Health, Religion and Culture, 5*, 239–252.

Brown, G. W., & Harris, T. O. (1978). *The social origins of depression*. London: Tavistock.

Butcher, J. N., Mineka, S., & Hooley, J. M. (2007). *Abnormal psychology* (13th ed.). London: Pearson.

Castillo, R. J. (2003). Trance, functional psychosis, and culture. *Psychiatry, 66*, 9–21.

Chatfield, A. F. (1989). *A sociology of Trinidad Religion, with special reference to Christianity*. Master's thesis, Leeds University.

Cinnirella, M., & Loewenthal, K. M. (1999). Religious and ethnic group influences on beliefs about mental illness: A qualitative interview study. *British Journal of Medical Psychology, 72*, 505–524.

Cochrane, R. (1993). Women and depression. In C. A. Niven & D. Carroll (Eds.), *The health psychology of women*. Switzerland: Harwood Press.

Cochrane, R., & Howell, M. (1995). Drinking patterns of black and white men in the West Midlands. *Social Psychiatry and Psychiatric Epidemiology, 30*, 139–146.

Cohen, P., Pine, D. S., Must, A., Kasen, S., & Brook, J. (1998). Prospective associations between somatic illness and mental illness from childhood to adulthood. *American Journal of Epidemiogy, 147*, 232–239.

Comer, R. J. (1999). *Abnormal psychology* (2nd ed.). New York: Worth/Freeman.

Curtin, P. D. (1969). *The Atlantic slave trade: A census*. Madison: University of Wisconsin Press.

Davis, L. G. (1975). *The mental health of the black community: An exploratory bibliography*. Monticello, IL: Council of Planning Librarians.

Dwyer, D. H., Bruce, J., & Cain, M. (1988). *A home divided: Women and income in the Third World*. Palo Alto, CA: Stanford University Press.

Ellison, C. W. (1983). Spiritual well-being: Conceptualization and measurement. *Journal of Psychology and Theology, 11*, 330–340.

English, H. B., & English A. C. (1958). *A comprehensive dictionary of psychological and psychoanalytic terms: A guide to usage*. New York, London & Toronto: Longmans Green.

Evarts, A. B. (1914). Dementia Precox in the colored race. *Psychoanalytic Review, 1*, 388–403.

Ferraro, K. F., & Kelley-Moore, J. A. (2000). Religious consolation among men and women: Do health problems spur seeking? *Journal for the Scientific Study of Religion, 39*, 220–234.

Francis, L. J. (1993). Personality and religion among college students in the UK. *Personality and Individual Differences, 14*, 619–622.

Freud, S. (1907). Obsessive actions and religious practices. *Collected Papers*, 1907/1924. London: Hogarth Press.

Fulford, K. W. M. (1999). From culturally sensitive to culturally competent. In K. Bhui & D. Olajide (Eds.), *Mental Health Service Provision for a Multi-Cultural Society* (pp. 21–42). London: W. B. Saunders.

Gilbert, P., Gilbert, J., & Sanghera, J. (2004). A focus group exploration of the impact of *izzat*, shame, subordination and entrapment on mental health and service use in South Asian women living in Derby. *Mental Health, Religion and Culture, 7*, 109–130.

Gotlib, I. H., & Hammen, C. L. (2002). *Handbook of depression*. New York: Guilford Press.

Greenberg, D., & Shefler, G. (2002). Obsessive-compulsive disorder in ultra-orthodox Jewish patients: A comparison of religious and non-religious symptoms. *Psychology and Psychotherapy, 75*, 123–130.

Greenberg, D., & Witztum, E. (2001). *Sanity and sanctity: Mental health work among the ultraorthodox in Jerusalem.* New Haven and London: Yale University Press.

Greenberg, D., Witztum, E., & Pisante, J. (1987). Scrupulosity: Religious attitudes and clinical presentations. *British Journal of Medical Psychology, 60*, 29–37.

Griffith, E. E. H., & Bility, K. M. (1996). Psychosocial factors and the genesis of new Afro-American religious groups. In D. Bhugra (Ed.), *Psychiatry and religion* (pp. 82–96). London: Routledge.

Gureje, O., Von Korff, M., Simon, G. E., & Gater, R. (1998). Persistent pain and well-being: A World Health Organization study in primary care. *Journal of the American Medical Association, 280*, 147–151.

Hill, P. C., & Hood, R., Jr. (1999). *Measure of religiosity.* Birmingham, Alabama: Religious Education Press.

Hinton, D., Um, K., & Ba, P. (2001). *Kyol Goeu* ('Wind Overload') Part II: Prevalence, characteristics and mechanisms of *Kyol Goeu* and near – *Kyol Goeu* episodes of Khmer patients attending a psychiatric clinic. *Transcultural Psychiatry, 38*, 433–460.

Hollan, D. (2004). Self systems, cultural idioms of distress, and the psycho-bodily consequences of childhood suffering. *Transcultural Psychiatry, 41*, 62–79.

Houran, J., Kumar, V. K., Thalbourne, M., & Lavertue, N. E. (2002). Haunted by somatic tendencies: spirit infestation as psychogenic illness. *Mental Health, Religion and Culture, 5*, 119–134.

Howard, V. (1987). A report on Afro-Caribbean Christianity in Britain. Leeds: University of Leeds Department of Theology and Religious Studies Community Religions Project Research Papers.

Ineichen, B. (1991). Schizophrenia in British Afro-Caribbeans: Two debates confused? *International Journal of Social Psychiatry, 37*, 227–232.

Joseph, S., Linley, P. A., & Maltby, J. (Eds.). (2006). Mental health, religion and culture (Special issue).*Positive Psychology and Religion, 9*, 209–306.

King, M., Speck, P., & Thomas, A. (1995). The Royal Free interview for spiritual and religious beliefs: Development and standardization. *Psychological Medicine, 25*, 1125–1134.

Kirmayer, L. J., & Young, A. (1998). Culture and somatization: clinical, epidemiological and ethnographic perspectives. *Psychosomatic Medicine, 60*, 420–430.

Koenig, H. B., McCullough, M. E., & Larson, D. B. (2001). *Handbook of religion and health.* Oxford: Oxford University Press.

Levav, I., Kohn, R., Dohrenwend, B. P., Shrout, P. E., Skodol, A. E., Schwartz, S., et al. (1993). An epidemiological study of mental disorders in a 10-year cohort of young adults in Israel. *Psychological Medicine, 23*, 691–707.

Levav, I., Kohn, R., Golding, J., & Weismann, M. M. (1997). Vulnerability of Jews to affective disorders. *American Journal of Psychiatry, 154*, 941–947.

Lewis, C. A. (1998). Cleanliness is next to Godliness: Religiosity and obsessiveness. *Journal of Religion and Health, 37*, 49–61.

Lipton, R. I. (2005). The effect of moderate alcohol use on the relationship between stress and depression. *American Journal of Public Health, 84*, 1913–1917.

Littlewood, R., & Lipsedge, M. (1981a). Acute psychotic reactions in Caribbean-born patients. *Psychological Medicine, 11*, 303–318.

Littlewood, R., & Lipsedge, M. (1981b). Some social and phenomenological characteristics of psychotic immigrants. *Psychological Medicine, 11*, 289–302.

Littlewood, R., & Lipsedge, M. (1989). *Aliens and Alienists: Ethnic minorities and psychiatry* (2nd ed.). London: Unwin Hyman.

Littlewood, R., & Lipsedge, M. (1997). *Aliens and Alienists: Ethnic minorities and psychiatry* (3rd ed.). London: Oxford University Press.

Loewenthal, K. M. (2000). *A short introduction to the psychology of religion.* Oxford: Oneworld.

Loewenthal, K. M. (2007). *Religion, culture and mental health*. Cambridge: Cambridge University Press.

Loewenthal, K. M., & Cinnirella, M. (2003). Religious issues in ethnic minority mental health with special reference to schizophrenia in Afro-Caribbeans in Britain: A systematic review. In D. Ndegwa & D. Olajide (Eds.), *Main issues in mental health and race* (pp. 108–134). London: Ashgate.

Loewenthal, K. M., Goldblatt, V., Gorton, T., Lubitsh, G., Bicknell, H., Fellowes, D., & Sowden, A. (1995). Gender and depression in Anglo-Jewry. *Psychological Medicine, 25*, 1051–1063.

Loewenthal, K. M., MacLeod, A. K., & Cinnirella, M. (2001). Are women more religious than men? Gender differences in religious activity among different religious groups in the UK. *Personality and Individual Differences, 32*, 133–139.

Loewenthal, K. M., MacLeod, A. K., Cook, S., Lee, M. J., & Goldblatt, V (2002). Tolerance for depression: Are there cultural and gender differences? *Journal of Psychiatric and Mental Health Nursing, 9*, 681–688.

Loewenthal, K. M., MacLeod, A. K., Cook, S., Lee, M. J., & Goldblatt, V. (2003a). Drowning your sorrows? Attitudes towards alcohol in UK Jews and Protestants: A thematic analysis. *International Journal of Social Psychiatry, 49*, 204–215.

Loewenthal, K. M., MacLeod, A. K., Cook, S., Lee, M. J., & Goldblatt, V. (2003b).The suicide beliefs of Jews and Protestants in the UK: How do they differ? *Israel Journal of Psychiatry, 40*, 174–181.

Loewenthal, K. M., MacLeod, A. K., Goldblatt, V., Lubitsh, G., & Valentine, J. D. (2000). Comfort and joy: Religion, cognition and mood in individuals under stress. *Cognition and Emotion, 14*, 355–374.

Loewenthal, K. M., & Rogers, M. B. (2004). Culture sensitive support groups: How are they perceived and how do they work? *International Journal of Social Psychiatry, 50*, 227–240.

MacLachlan, M. (1997). *Culture and Health*. Chichester: Wiley.

Margolin, J., & Witztum, E. (1989). Supernatural impotence: Historical review with anthropological and clinical implications. *British Journal of Medical Psychology, 62*, 333–342.

McGovern, D., & Cope, R. (1991). Second generation Afro-Caribbeans and young whites with a first admission diagnosis of schizophrenia. *Social Psychiatry and Psychiatric Epidemiology, 26*, 95–99.

Mirza, I., & Jenkins, R. (2004). Risk factors, prevalence, and treatment of anxiety and depressive disorders in Pakistan: Systematic review. *British Medical Journal, 328*, 794–799.

Pargament, K. (1997). *The psychology of religion and coping*. New York: Guilford Press.

Pargament, K. I. (2007). *Spiritually integrted psychotherapy*. New York: Guilford Press.

Perkins, R. E., & Moodley, P. (1993). Perception of problems by psychiatric inpatients: Denial, race and service usage. *Social Psychiatry and Psychiatric Epidemiology, 28*, 189–193.

Rapaport, J. (2000). *Childhood onset of "Adult" psychopathology*. Washington, DC: American Psychiatric Publications.

Rutter, M., & Taylor, E. A. (2002). *Child and adolescent psychiatry*. Oxford: Blackwell.

Seligman, M. (2002). *Authentic happiness*. New York: Free Press.

Sica, C., Novara, C., & Sanavio, E. (2002). Religiousness and obsessive-compulsive cognitions and symptoms in an Italian population. *Behaviour Research and Therapy, 40*, 813–823.

Siddle, R., Haddock, G., Tarrier, N., & Faragher, E. B. (2002). The validation of a religiosity measure for individuals with schizophrenia. *Mental Health, Religion and Culture, 5*, 267–284.

Sugarman, P. A., & Craufurd, D. (1994). Schizophrenia in the Afro-Caribbean community. *British Journal of Psychiatry, 164*, 474–480.

Tek, C., & Ulug, B. (2001). Religiosity and religious obsessions in obsessive-compulsive disorder. *Psychiatry Research, 104*, 99–108.

Thomas, C. S., Stone, K., Osborn, M., & Thomas, P. F. (1993). Psychiatric morbidity and compulsory admission among UK-born Europeans, Afro-Caribbeans and Asians in central Manchester. *British Journal of Psychiatry, 163*, 91–99.

Trollope-Kumar, K. (2001). Cultural and biomedical meanings of the complaint of leucorrhea in South Asian women. *Tropical Medicine and International Health, 6*, 260–266.

Tylor, E. B. (1871). *Primitive culture*. London: Murray.

Wulff, D. M. (1997). *Psychology of religion: Classic and contemporary* (2nd ed.). New York: Wiley.

Zinnbauer, B. J., Pargament, K. I., Cole, B., Rye, M. S., Butter, E. M., Belavich, T. G., et al. (1997). Religion and spirituality: Unfuzzying the fuzzy. *Journal for the Scientific Study of Religion, 36*, 549–564.

Zinnbauer, B. J., Pargament, K. I., & Scott, A. B. (1999). Emerging meanings of religiousness and spirituality: Problems and prospects. *Journal of Personality, 67*, 889–919.

Chapter 7
Psychological Type Theory and Religious and Spiritual Experiences

Leslie J. Francis

Abstract Psychological type theory, originally proposed by Carl Jung and developed by instruments like the Myers–Briggs Type Indicator, the Keirsey Temperament Sorter, and the Francis Psychological Type Scales, provides a rich theoretical framework and a useful practical guide within which to understand and to promote religious and spiritual learning. This chapter defines and critiques psychological type theory, describes and evaluates measures of psychological type, reviews the growing body of research evidence linking psychological type with individual differences in religious and spiritual learning, and evaluates the relevance of the research literature for practice and application.

An Individual Differences Approach

The association between personality and religious experience has been a topic of long-standing interest both within psychology and within theology. The intention of this chapter is to engage with that debate, to extend the debate to embrace the emerging notion of spirituality, and to propose psychological type theory as a fruitful source for generating theoretical insight and empirical knowledge relevant to the debate.

For theologians, the debate concerning the association between personality and religious experience is classically established by appeal to teaching about the nature of God and by drawing on sources of divine revelation (say scripture) to explore the transforming impact of God on individual lives. On this account, the religious experience becomes the independent variable and human personality becomes the dependent variable.

For psychologists, the debate concerning the association between personality and religious experience is classically established by appeal to the psychological understanding of personality (variously conceived) and by drawing on psychological

---

L.J. Francis (✉)
Religions and Education, Warwick Religions and Education Research Unit, Institute of Education, University of Warwick, Coventry, CV4 7AL, UK
e-mail: leslie.francis@warwick.ac.uk

theory regarding ways in which given variation in personality may influence a range of other individual differences, including religious and spiritual experiences. On this account, human personality becomes the independent variable and religious experience becomes the dependent variable.

At this point an already complex debate becomes more complex by recognition of the variety of ways in which the term "personality" may be used both by theologians and by psychologists. In much of my own recent writings I have tried to cut through this complexity by distinguishing between three different constructs which I have wanted to define as character, as personality and as psychological type (see, for example, Francis, 2005). All three constructs are of central importance both to theologians and to psychologists, but I want to argue that it is the notion of psychological type theory that can provide the most efficient and effective starting point for a debate in which both psychologists and (Christian) theologians can engage.

The term "character" I take to be concerned with qualities that carry a moral valency. We can talk meaningfully about individuals who display a "good character" and about individuals who display a "bad character". Both theologians and psychologists may be properly concerned with distinguishing between such morally laden qualities. Within the Christian tradition, for example, Galatians 5 is often cited as contrasting the moral qualities of the good character (the so-called fruits of the Spirit) with the moral qualities of the bad character (the so-called works of the flesh). According to this tradition, the fruits of the Spirit include love, joy, peace, longsuffering, kindness, goodness, faithfulness, gentleness and self-control. The works of the flesh, by way of contrast, include lewdness, hatred, jealousy, outburst of anger, selfish ambitions, envy and drunkenness. It is a matter of proper empirical enquiry to test the extent to which religious and spiritual experiences may help to differentiate between individual differences in such qualities of character.

The term "personality" I take to be concerned with those aspects of the human psyche that psychologists review when they attempt to provide all-embracing and inclusive accounts and measurement of human personality. The problem with such a broad definition is that there is no consensus among personality psychologists regarding what should and what should not be included within such a definition. In fact the term "personality" is currently used among personality psychologists to include at least three areas: deep-seated value-free descriptions of normal personality, fundamental descriptions of abnormal personality and psycho-pathologies, and more surface and value-laden descriptions of individual differences. It is because of this wide range of usage that I prefer to draw on the notion of psychological type in order to generate dialogue between psychology and theology.

The term "psychological type" has been defined from within both a theological and a psychological framework. From a theological perspective, psychological type has been defined by reference to a doctrine of creation according to which human beings are created to reflect a divine image that embraces and models individual differences. According to Genesis 1:27 both male and female are created in the image of God. By extension other fundamental human differences, like ethnicity, must reflect the richness and diversity of the divine image. According to this principle, as a theologian, I define psychological type as embracing a small set of key individual differences which are largely immutable and go right to the heart of who an individual is (like sex and ethnicity). Such differences, it is argued theologically, reflect the intention and the diversity of the divine creator and are in effect non-negotiable. From a psychological perspective, psychological type has been defined by reference to the pioneering work of Carl Jung in his classic book *Psychological types* (Jung, 1971). It is to this body of work that attention will now be drawn.

Introducing Psychological Type

The model of psychological type, originally proposed by Carl Jung (1971), has been developed through a series of psychometric indices, including the Myers–Briggs Type Indicator (MBTI: Myers & McCaulley, 1985), the Keirsey Temperament Sorter (KTS: Keirsey and Bates, 1978) and the Francis Psychological Type Scales (FPTS: Francis, 2005). The choice to adopt the Jungian model of psychological type as the platform on which to construct a dialogue between psychology and theology may itself be controversial both among psychologists and among theologians. On the one hand, personality psychologists have been relatively slow to accord the same kind of esteem to the Jungian model of psychological type as accorded, say, to Raymond Cattell's notion of the 16 factor model of personality (R. B. Cattell, A. K. S. Cattell, & H. E. P. Cattell, 1993), or to Hans Eysenck's notion of the three-dimensional model of personality (Eysenck & Eysenck, 1991), or to the more recent Big Five factor model of personality (Costa & McCrae, 1985). The problem has been, in part, exacerbated by the comparative insularity and distinctive methodological procedures developed by pioneering researchers in the field of psychological type (including perhaps overreliance on the *Journal of Psychological Type* which both concentrates research in this area and keeps it apart from wider debate). In recent years, however, some real attempts have been made to mainstream research in psychological type theory, and such attempts are being largely successful (as evidenced by the symposia on psychological type convened by Section 36 of the American Psychological Association). On the other hand, theologians have either ignored or tended to be critical of the way in which psychological type theory has begun to penetrate the Christian community, as evidenced by the (somewhat superficial) collection of essays edited by Kenneth Leech under the title, *Myers–Briggs: Some critical reflections* (Leech, 1996). In recent years, however, some real attempts have been made to address such criticisms and to clarify some of the misunderstandings on which they have been based (Lloyd, 2007).

However, the choice to adopt the Jungian model of psychological type as the psychological platform on which to construct a psychological perspective on practical and pastoral theology is explicable in terms of the ways in which this particular psychological model of personality and individual differences has already been well established in church-related circles in Australasia (Dwyer, 1995), North America (Baab, 2000) and the United Kingdom (Duncan, 1993). In particular, in many places clergy are introduced to this way of thinking in initial ministerial training and in continuing professional development.

As popularised through books like *Gifts differing* (Myers & Myers, 1980) and *Please understand me: 2* (Keirsey, 1998), psychological type theory distinguishes between four bipolar psychological perspectives: two orientations (introversion and extraversion), two perceiving functions (sensing and intuition), two judging functions (thinking and feeling), and two attitudes towards the outer world (judging and perceiving). According to this model, the two orientations (introversion and extraversion) and the two attitudes (judging and perceiving) define the kind of context within which the individual human psyche functions. The two perceiving functions (sensing and intuition) and the two judging functions (thinking and feeling) define the mental processes involved in interpreting and making sense of the world.

The two orientations are concerned with where energy is drawn from and focused. On the one hand, extraverts (E) are orientated towards the outer world; they are energised by the events and people around them. They enjoy communicating and thrive in stimulating and exciting environments. They tend to focus their attention upon what is happening outside themselves. They are usually open people, easy to get to know, and enjoy having many friends. On the other hand, introverts (I) are orientated towards their inner world; they are energised by their inner ideas and concepts. They enjoy solitude, silence and contemplation, as they tend to focus their attention on what is happening in their inner life. They may prefer to have a small circle of intimate friends rather than many acquaintances.

The two perceiving functions are concerned with the way in which people perceive information. On the one hand, sensing types (S) focus on the realities of a situation as perceived by the senses. They tend to focus on specific details, rather than the overall picture. They are concerned with the actual, the real and the practical and tend to be down to earth and matter of fact. On the other hand, intuitive types (N) focus on the possibilities of a situation, perceiving meanings and relationships. They may feel that perception by the senses is not as valuable as information gained as indirect associations and concepts impact on their perception. They focus on the overall picture, rather than on specific facts and data.

The two judging functions are concerned with the criteria which people employ to make decisions and judgements. On the one hand, thinking types (T) make decisions and judgements based on objective, impersonal logic. They value integrity and justice. They are known for their truthfulness and for their desire for fairness. They consider conforming to principles to be of more importance than cultivating harmony. On the other hand, feeling types (F) make decisions and judgements based on subjective, personal values. They value compassion and mercy. They are known for their tactfulness and for their desire for peace. They are more concerned to promote harmony than to adhere to abstract principles.

The two attitudes towards the outer world are determined by which of the two sets of functions (that is, perceiving S/N or judging T/F) is preferred in dealings with the outer world. On the one hand, judging types (J) seek to order, rationalise and structure their outer world, as they actively judge external stimuli. They enjoy routine and established patterns. They prefer to follow schedules in order to reach an established goal and may make use of lists, timetables or diaries. They tend to be punctual, organised and tidy. They prefer to make decisions quickly and to stick to their conclusions once made. On the other hand, perceiving types (P) do not seek to impose order on the outer world but are more reflective, perceptive and open, as they passively perceive external stimuli. They have a flexible, open-ended approach to life. They enjoy change and spontaneity. They prefer to leave projects open in order to adapt and improve them. Their behaviour may often seem impulsive and unplanned.

According to Jungian theory, each individual needs access to all four functions (sensing, intuition, thinking and feeling) for normal and healthy living. The two perceiving functions (sensing and intuition) are needed to gather information about the inner and outer worlds inhabited by the individual. These are the irrational functions concerned with collecting information, with seeing reality and possibility. The two judging functions (thinking and feeling) are needed to organise and evaluate information. These are the rational functions concerned with making decisions and determining courses of action. Although each individual needs access to all four functions, Jungian theory posits the view that the relative strengths of these four functions vary from one individual to another. The analogy is drawn with handedness. Although equipped with two hands, the majority of individuals prefer one and tend to develop skills with that hand to the neglect of the other hand. Similarly, empirical evidence suggests that individuals will develop preference for one of the perceiving functions (sensing or intuition) and neglect the other and that they will develop preference for one of the judging functions (thinking or feeling) and neglect the other.

Moreover, according to Jungian theory, for each individual either the preferred perceiving function (sensing or intuition) or the preferred judging function (thinking or feeling) takes preference over the other, leading to the emergence of one dominant function which shapes the individual's dominant approach to life. Dominant sensing shapes the practical person; dominant intuition shapes the imaginative person; dominant feeling shapes the humane person and dominant thinking shapes the analytic person. According to Jungian theory, it is the function opposite to the dominant function which is least well developed in the individual (the inferior function). Thus, the dominant senser experiences most difficulty with the intuitive function; the dominant intuitive experiences most difficulty with the sensing function; the dominant thinker experiences most difficulty with the feeling function and the dominant feeler experiences most difficulty with the thinking function.

Measuring Psychological Type

Evaluation of the empirical evidence regarding the association between psychological type and religious and spiritual experiences must begin with an evaluation of the tools available for assessing psychological type. This includes consideration of the key psychometric properties of reliability and validity. Reliability concerns the extent to which a psychological tool produces a consistent reading of whatever it is that the tool measures. Validity concerns the extent to which a psychological tool actually measures what it sets out to measure. A highly reliable instrument may not, however, necessarily be a valid instrument.

The best known tool designed to assess psychological type is the Myers–Briggs Type Indicator (Myers & McCaulley, 1985). In an initial study, Francis and Jones (1999a) reviewed the extant research literature on the reliability and validity of the Myers–Briggs Type Indicator and concluded that there was good evidence for the internal consistency reliability and construct validity of the continuous scale scores, but that the use of the instrument to distinguish between discrete type categories remained considerably more problematic.

Recognising that no previous study had specifically explored the psychometric properties of the Myers–Briggs Type Indicator among a highly religious sample and acknowledging that some scale items may function differently among highly religious individuals, Francis and Jones (1999a) proceeded to test the scale properties of the Myers–Briggs Type Indicator Form G (Anglicised) among a sample of 429 adult churchgoers. Their data supported the general reliability of the eight scales intended to quantify preferences for introversion, extraversion, sensing, intuition, thinking, feeling, judging and perceiving. At the same time, the data highlighted ways in which all the scales, apart from sensing, contained some items which detracted from, rather than contributed towards, the homogeneity of the indices. They argued that some further refinement of the Myers–Briggs Type Indicator, giving particular attention to reassessing or reviewing those items which failed to achieve a corrected item total correlation of at least +0.30, would enhance the psychometric properties of the instrument.

As a second step in examining the psychometric properties of the Myers–Briggs Type Indicator, Francis and Jones (2000) and Francis, Craig, and Robbins (2007a) conducted two studies examining psychological type alongside the three-dimensional model of personality proposed by Hans Eysenck. The first of these two studies was conducted among 377 adult churchgoers who also completed the 90-item Eysenck Personality Questionnaire (Eysenck & Eysenck, 1975); the second was conducted among 554 undergraduate students who also completed the 48-item short-form Revised Eysenck Personality Questionnaire (S. B. G. Eysenck, H. J. Eysenck, & Barrett, 1985). The purpose of these two studies was to assess the extent to which dialogue could be established between research in the psychology of religion drawing on the Myers–Briggs Type Indicator and the growing family of studies in the psychology of religion drawing on Eysenck's model of personality, especially in light of the way in which both systems used the terms introversion and extraversion. The data demonstrated a number of statistically significant relationships between the two models of personality and drew attention to two substantively significant relationships. In Eysenckian terms, the Myers–Briggs Type Indicator constructs of introversion and extraversion translate as "neurotic introversion" and as "stable extraversion". In Eysenckian terms, the Myers–Briggs Type Indicator constructs of judging and perceiving translate as "low psychoticism" and as "high psychoticism".

There remain serious disadvantages in using the Myers–Briggs Type Indicator as a research tool. Properly developed as a refined and sensitive instrument for use in one-on-one situations, the Myers–Briggs Type Indicator is a cumbersome instrument in many research contexts, takes too long to complete, is inappropriate for postal surveys and remains expensive to purchase. Although not claiming to mimic the Myers–Briggs Type Indicator, the Keirsey Temperament Sorter, first published by Keirsey and Bates (1978) and revised by Keirsey (1998), offers a different operationalisation of the original Jungian constructs. The Keirsey Temperament Sorter provides an alternative, shorter and cheaper instrument which has been employed in a number of empirical studies. Francis, Craig, and Robbins (2007b) reviewed the research literature comparing these two instruments and were able to identify only three studies which had used the two instruments side-by-side (Quinn, Lewis, & Fischer, 1992; Tucker & Gillespie, 1993; Kelly & Jugovic, 2001). Building on these three studies, Francis et al. (2007b) invited their sample of 554 undergraduate students to complete both the Myers–Briggs Type Indicator (Form G Anglicised) and the Keirsey Temperament Sorter (1978 edition).

The data published by Francis, Craig, and Robbins (2007b) demonstrated that the underlying continuous scale scores generated by the two instruments are highly correlated and appear to be assessing similar psychological constructs. However, the methods proposed by the two instruments for assigning individuals to discrete psychological types are dissimilar and result in the generation of significantly different type profiles. When compared with each other, the Myers–Briggs Type Indicator tends to generate a significantly higher representation of sensing, thinking and perceiving, while the Keirsey Temperament Sorter tends to generate a significantly higher representation of intuition, feeling and judging. The current study points to the relative unreliability of the Myers–Briggs Type Indicator and the Keirsey Temperament Sorter as comparable type indicators but also to the relatively strong relationship between the Myers–Briggs Type Indicator and the Keirsey Temperament Sorter as indicators of continuous personality traits. Comparisons of type categorisations generated by the two instruments may need, therefore, to be treated with caution.

Although the Keirsey Temperament Sorter is more appropriate for self-completion survey work than the Myers–Briggs Type Indicator, there remain two major problems with using this instrument. First, the Keirsey Temperament Sorter is designed primarily as a self-assessment tool rather than as a research instrument. Moreover, the copyright holders are reluctant to allow researchers to reproduce the items separately from the published scoring mechanism. Second, reliability studies show some problems with a few of the Keirsey Temperament Sorter items. For this reason Francis (2005) published a new attempt to operationalise Jungian psychological type theory, claiming to mimic neither the Myers–Briggs Type Indicator nor the Keirsey Temperament Sorter. This instrument, the Francis Psychological Type Scales, was designed specifically for research purposes. A small but growing body of literature is now reporting on the psychometric properties of this new instrument.

Profiling Religious Professionals

One established way of examining the association between psychological type and religious and spiritual experiences has been through profiling religious professionals. In the mid-1980s, Macdaid, McCaulley, and Kainz (1986) published the following picture. In a sample of 2,002 sisters in Roman Catholic religious orders, the predominant types were ISFJ (27%) and ESFJ (16%). In a sample of 114 brothers in Roman Catholic religious orders, a similar pattern emerged, with ISFJ (23%) and ESFJ (14%) again predominating. This pattern continued in a sample of 1,298 Roman Catholic priests, with ISFJ (18%) and ESFJ (14%) followed by ENFJ (11%) and ENFP (11%). A slightly different pattern emerged for a sample of 102 Roman Catholic deacons, with ESFJ (23%), ENFJ (19%), ESTJ (14%) and ISFJ (13%). In a sample of 1,554 Protestant ministers, the predominant types were ENFJ (16%), ENFP (14%) and ESFJ (13%). A similar pattern emerged from a sample of 633 Protestant seminarians, with ESFJ (16%), ENFJ (14%) and ENFP (12%).

Other studies profiling religious professionals in the United States were published during the 1980s by Cabral (1984), Harbaugh (1984), Holsworth (1984) and Bigelow, Fitzgerald, Busk, Girault, and Avis (1988). The major point of consistency from all these studies concerns the clear preference among religious professionals for feeling over thinking. Preferences for intuition and sensing seem to be related to denominational allegiance, with a greater tendency towards sensing among Catholics and a greater tendency towards intuition among Anglicans and liberal Protestants. The majority of religious professionals prefer judging over perceiving. Introverts are more strongly represented among Catholic priests and among members of religious orders than among Protestant clergy.

Building on this research tradition initiated in the United States, a series of more recent studies have profiled the psychological type characteristics of religious professionals in the United Kingdom. The first study in this series was reported by Francis, Payne, and Jones (2001) drawing on data provided by 427 male Anglican clergy in Wales. The data demonstrated clear preferences for introversion over extraversion, for sensing over intuition, for feeling over thinking and for judging over perceiving. The two predominant types were ISFJ (20%) and ESFJ (13%). Commenting on the implications of these findings for ministry in the Church in Wales, Francis, Payne, and Jones (2001) made the following four points.

First, 59% of the clergy preferred introversion, compared with 42% who preferred extraversion. Introverts may bring many strengths to ministry, including the ability to work by themselves on tasks, to invest time in reading and in preparation, to welcome one-to-one encounters in counselling and in spiritual direction, to develop an inward life of prayer and spirituality. On the other hand, introverts may be drained by many of the social expectations of ministry: working with large groups of people, remembering names, visiting strangers and assuming a high profile in the local congregation and the wider local community.

Second, 57% of the clergy preferred sensing, compared with 43% who preferred intuition. Sensers may bring many strengths to ministry, including a fine awareness of the environment in which they serve and of the church in which they lead worship, a concern for the detail within the services they conduct and for the facts on which judgements and choices are made. On the other hand, sensers may find it more difficult to formulate a vision for their church's future, to welcome change and experimentation in liturgy, or to see new and imaginative solutions to old problems.

Third, 69% of the clergy preferred feeling, compared with 31% who preferred thinking. Feelers may bring many strengths to ministry, including the desire to affiliate with others, the gifts of empathy and sympathy, a commitment to harmony, a deep understanding of people and a respect for interpersonal values. On the other hand, feelers may find it more difficult to take tough decisions which affect other people's lives, to chair troublesome meetings, to be assertive on points of truth and justice, and to put other people in their place.

Fourth, 68% of the clergy preferred judging, compared with 32% who preferred perceiving. Judgers may bring many strengths to ministry, including the ability to organise their own lives, to organise the life of their parishes, to arrange services and events well in advance, to keep on top of administration and to manage local affairs. On the other hand, judgers may become too inflexible and restricted by their own strategies, plans and routines, too unwilling or unable to abandon their plans in order to respond to unexpected crises, emergencies or opportunities and too bound to the present structure to embrace new ideas and possibilities.

The Church in Wales is separated from the Church of England by a very porous boundary, although the policies and ethos of the two Churches are set in very different contexts. Francis, Craig, Whinney, Tilley, and Slater (2007) drew on data provided by 626 male Anglican clergy in England. In three ways these data reflected the same preferences as those found among male Anglican clergy in Wales: preferences for introversion over extraversion, for feeling over thinking and for judging over perceiving. In one crucial way, however, the profiles of the two groups of clergymen differed. In Wales 57% preferred sensing and 43% preferred intuition; in England, the balance was reversed with 62% preferring intuition and 38% preferring sensing. Francis, Craig, Whinney, et al. (2007) suggested that these differences in psychological type reflect a crucial difference in leadership styles between the two Churches and in the character of the two Churches. The Church in Wales tends to be more conservative than the Church of England and therefore a place in which leaders who prefer sensing may feel more comfortable. They suggested that clergymen who prefer intuition may become restless and impatient in the Church in Wales and cross the border to England, while clergymen who prefer sensing may become restless in the Church of England and cross the border into the Anglophone parts of Wales.

The two studies by Francis, Payne, et al. (2001) and Francis, Craig, Whinney, et al. (2007) both drew attention to the high proportions of feelers among male clergy: 69% in Wales and 54% in England, compared with 35% of men in the general population as reported by Kendall (1998). This finding is consistent with the view that the churches in the United Kingdom have become highly feminised communities (Brown, 2001) and that feeling characterises a feminised approach to life. According to Kendall (1998) 70% of women in the United Kingdom population prefer feeling. Such an analysis provides an important clue regarding why the churches may experience such difficulty in attracting individuals with a preference for thinking in general and in attracting men in particular.

A further study among 79 Roman Catholic priests reported by Craig, Duncan, and Francis (2006a) also found a clear preference for feeling (79%) over thinking (22%). However, a series of studies conducted among evangelical church leaders, in comparison with Anglican and Catholic church leaders, found a higher proportion of thinkers. For example, preference for thinking was found among 56% of the 81 male evangelical seminarians studied by Francis, Craig, and Butler (2007), by 54% of the 164 male church leaders studied by Craig, Francis, and Robbins (2004) at the evangelical Spring Harvest, by 50% of the 278 male Bible College students studied by Francis, Penson, and Jones (2001), by 56% of the 190 male Assemblies of God Bible College students studied by Kay, Francis, and Craig (2008), by 52% of the 130 male evangelical lay church leaders studied by Francis, Craig, Horsfall, and Ross (2005), by 62% of 42 male vergers studied by Craig, Duncan, and Francis (2006b) and by 70% of the 92 male evangelical missionary personnel studied by Craig, Horsfall, and Francis (2005). Taken together, these findings suggest that there may be more opportunities for men who prefer thinking within leadership roles in evangelical churches, although this conclusion is qualified by Francis and Robbins' (2002) study of 57 male evangelical leaders, of whom just 44% preferred thinking.

When compared with the population norms provided by Kendall (1998), there is a second way in which men engaged in Christian ministry differ from the profile of men in general. According to Kendall (1998), in the population as a whole just 27% of men prefer intuition. Although the proportions of intuitives found in studies among men concerned with Christian ministry vary considerably from one group to another, in most groups they exceed the proportion within the general population. The highest proportion of intuitives is found in the study by Francis, Craig, Whinney, et al. (2007) among 626 Church of England clergymen (62%). Then, in descending order, intuitives accounted for 49% in the study by Craig et al. (2006a) among 79 Roman Catholic priests, 43% in the study by Francis, Payne, et al. (2001) among 427 Anglican clergymen in Wales, 34% in the study by Francis, Penson, et al. (2001) among 278 male students in an Evangelical Bible College and 26% in the study by Kay et al. (2008) among 190 male students in a Pentecostal Bible College.

Three studies in this series also provided data on the psychological type profile of women engaged in or training for Christian ministry. The main conclusion from these three studies is that, like male church leaders, female church leaders are more likely to prefer intuition than is the case among women in the general population. According to Kendall (1998) in the general population just 21% of women prefer intuition. In a study of 237 Anglican clergywomen in England, 65% preferred intuition (Francis, Craig, Whinney, et al., 2007); in a study of 213 female students in an Evangelical Bible College, 34% preferred intuition (Francis, Penson, et al., 2001); and in a study of 122 female students in a Pentecostal Bible College, 38% preferred intuition (Kay & Francis, 2008). These data are considerably more limited in terms of quantity compared with the data available on male church leaders, simply because the full recognition of women into ordained ministry has only occurred quite recently in some denominations (for example, Anglicanism) and remains excluded by some other denominations (for example, Roman Catholicism).

The finding that the vocation to Christian ministry, among both women and men, attracts higher proportions of intuitives than are in the population as a whole deserves considered reflection. On the one hand, there is the practical gospel of pastoral care which may be attractive to the pragmatic concerns of individuals with a preference for sensing. Here are the people responding to the call to feed the hungry, to clothe the naked, to visit the sick, and to tend the dying. On the other hand, there is much more to the Christian gospel than the practice of good works in the here and now. The Christian gospel holds out a vision for the future, and faith in the future proclaims the unseen and the intangible. Here is a vision which may be grasped more easily by intuitives than by sensers. The Christian gospel continually challenges its adherents to work for change, to build a better future and to transform existing structures. Here are challenges which may be welcomed more easily by intuitives than by sensers.

In another study in this series, Francis, P. Nash, S. Nash, and Craig (2007) examined the psychological type profile of 155 male and 134 female professional Christian youth ministers. This group emerged as significantly more extraverted than ministers in general and significantly less judging than ministers in general. These findings are interpreted to illuminate some of the tensions between Christian youth ministers and other members of the ministry team.

While the majority of studies concerned with the psychological type profiling of religious professionals have been able to report only on the profile itself, a few innovative studies have also linked these profile data to other measures. For example, Francis and Payne (2002) examined the relationship between psychological type and ministry styles among a sample of 191 Church in Wales clergymen, using the Payne Index of Ministry Styles (PIMS). These data demonstrated both that there is an association between psychological type and ministry styles and that this association is in some ways complex. For example, the extraversion ministry style is correlated positively with a preference for extraversion and negatively with a preference for introversion. Extraverted clergy are energised by the public aspects of ministry, while introverted clergy are drained by these aspects of ministry. On the other hand, the introversion ministry style is not significantly correlated with preferences for introversion or for extraversion. Contrary to prediction, introverted clergy are not more likely than extraverted clergy to claim to be energised by the inward aspects of ministry. This finding may reflect two constraints placed on clergy by the public expectations of ministry. Such constraints may mean that ministry styles tend to be shaped as much by external influences as by individual personality predispositions. First, since Christian spirituality has been largely shaped by an introverted perspective, extraverted clergy may feel constrained to overemphasise the benefit they derive from such introverted activities as spending time alone in prayer. Second, since Christian ministry has been largely shaped by an extraverted perspective, introverted clergy may feel guilty about emphasising their preference for the inner world.

Two recent studies have examined the relationship between psychological type and work-related psychological health among religious professionals using the Francis Burnout Inventory (FBI). The first study, reported by Francis, Robbins, Kaldor, and Castle (in press), was conducted among a sample of 3,715 clergy from Australia, England and New Zealand; the second study, reported by Francis, Wulff, and Robbins (2008) was conducted among a sample of 748 clergy serving within The Presbyterian Church (USA). The data from both studies confirmed that the main association between work-related psychological health and psychological type among religious professionals is a function of the orientations (the source of psychological energy). Compared with clergy who prefer introversion, clergy who prefer extraversion display both higher levels of satisfaction in ministry and lower levels of emotional exhaustion in ministry. These findings are consistent with the theory that the extraverted nature of ministry requires introverted clergy to operate for considerable periods of time outside their preferred orientations, with the consequent loss of energy and the consequent erosion of psychological rewards.

Profiling Church Congregations

Another established way of examining the association between psychological type and religious and spiritual experiences has been through profiling church congregations, although this is a much less well-documented field than the study of religious professionals. Some pioneering studies in this field were reported in North America by Gerhardt (1983), Rehak (1998), Delis-Bulhoes (1990) and Ross (1993, 1995). Within the United Kingdom three exploratory studies of church congregations were reported by Craig, Francis, Bailey, and Robbins (2003), Francis, Duncan, Craig, and Luffman (2004) and Francis, Robbins, A. Williams, and R. Williams (2007) drawing on samples of 101, 327 and 185 churchgoers, respectively. The third of these studies specifically compared the profile of male and female churchgoers with the population norms provided by Kendall (1998). The main finding from this comparison concerned the undue weighting towards sensing, feeling and judging in church congregations. Among women ISFJ accounts for 32% of churchgoers, compared with 18% of the general population ($P < 0.001$), and ESFJ accounts for 28% of churchgoers, compared with 19% of the general population ($P < 0.01$). Among men ISFJ accounts for 19% of churchgoers, compared with 7% of the general population ($P < 0.001$), and ESFJ accounts for 27% of churchgoers, compared with 6% of the general population ($P < 0.001$). Over-representation of ISFJ and ESFJ among churchgoers leads to under-representation of other types.

Commenting on these findings, Francis, Robbins, et al. (2007) argued that analysis of the more visible demographic characteristics of rural Anglican churchgoers (in terms of sex and age) suggests that, although the invitation of welcome may be issued indiscriminately to both sexes and to all ages, women are more likely to respond than men and the post-retired are more likely to respond than the pre-retired. Analysis of the less visible psychological characteristics of churchgoers (in terms of the 16 discrete types) has also suggested that, although the invitation of welcome may be issued to all psychological types, individuals with a type preference for SFJ are more likely to respond than individuals with other type preferences.

In her booklet, *Introduction to Type* (Myers, 1998, p. 7) provides insightful profiles of the two SFJ types: ISFJ and ESFJ. The ISFJ profile is as follows:

> Quiet, friendly, responsible and conscientious. Work devotedly to meet their obligations. Lend stability to any project or group. Thorough, pains-taking, accurate. Their interests are usually not technical. Can be patient with necessary details. Loyal considerate, perceptive, concerned with how other people feel.

The ESFJ profile is as follows:

> Warm-hearted, talkative, popular, conscientious, born co-operators, active committee members. Need harmony and may be good at creating it. Always doing something nice for someone. Work best with encouragement and praise. Main interest is in things that directly and visibly affect people's lives.

There are important ways in which these two profiles describe the kind of people we might expect to have responded to the call of welcome to join the church congregation. The SFJ congregation possess a number of recognisable Christian strengths. The preference for feeling (F) characterises a community concerned with human values, interpersonal relationships and with a loving and caring God. Here is a community concerned with peace and with harmony. The population norms show that feeling is a feminine preference *par excellence* (reported by 70% of women and by 35% of men). A community shaped by such a dominant preference for feeling may, however, be quite alien to individuals who view the world through the lens of thinking (including the majority of men).

The preference for sensing (S) characterises a community concerned with continuity, tradition, stability, and with a God grounded in divine changelessness. Here is a community concerned with guarding what has been handed down by previous generations. The population norms show that sensing is the preferred mode of the British population (reported by 79% of women and by 73% of men). In this sense, the church congregation is in step with wider society. A community shaped by such a dominant preference for sensing may, however, be quite alien to individuals who view the world through the lens of intuition.

The preference for judging (J) characterises a community concerned with organisation, discipline, structure and with a God who welcomes a regular pattern to worship (whatever that pattern may be). Here is a community concerned with valuing regular commitment, advanced planning and respect for the guidelines (implicit as well as explicit). The population norms show that judging is the preferred mode of the British population (reported by 62% of women and by 55% of men). In this sense, the church congregation is once again in step with wider society. A community shaped by such a dominant preference for judging may, however, be quite alien to individuals who view the world through the lens of perceiving.

Building on this tradition, Village, Francis, and Craig (in press) in a study of 290 churchgoers found significant differences in type profiles between individuals attending evangelical Anglican churches and individuals attending Anglo-Catholic churches. There was a significantly higher proportion of intuitives in the Anglo-Catholic congregations. In a study of 2,658 churchgoers, Craig (2005) found significant differences in type profiles between individuals attending rural and urban churches. There was a significantly higher proportion of sensers in rural congregations.

Other studies in this tradition have reported on the psychological type profiles of 93 female and 65 male active members of the Anglican Church (Francis, Butler, Jones, & Craig, 2007), 246 male and 380 female participants in Christian programmes (Craig, Francis, & Barwick, in press), 74 female and 40 male members of Anglican church councils (Francis, Butler, & Craig, 2005), 104 student members of a university-based Christian Union (Craig, Bigio, Robbins, & Francis, 2005), 79 female churchgoers (Craig, Williams, Francis, & Robbins, 2006) and 30 volunteer workers in a rural Christian charity shop (Francis & Pegg, 2007). These studies generally confirm the strong SFJ preference in Christian communities. The study of the volunteer workers in the Christian charity shop showed a strong preference for extraversion, in contrast with the general preference for introversion among churchgoers. Francis and Pegg (2007) concluded from this finding that activities like the Christian charity shop may provide a focus of interest for those extraverted members of the community who may feel less at home in the normal introverted church congregation.

Different Expressions of Religious and Spiritual Experiences

The two research traditions concerned with the psychological type profile of religious professionals and with the psychological type profile of church congregations are clearly focused on a traditional "religious" understanding of spirituality. Within this definition, these studies have demonstrated that some psychological types are more likely than others to be attracted to church membership and to leadership roles within churches and that there are some significant variations between different church groupings. A third research tradition has explored in greater detail the association between psychological type preferences and individual differences in religious and spiritual experiences and expressions. Five different strands of research have been initiated within this context.

The first strand has examined the connection between psychological type and attitude towards Christianity, building on the well-established research tradition which had documented a stable link between attitude towards Christianity and the three-dimensional model of personality proposed by Hans Eysenck (Francis, Lewis, Brown, Philipchalk, & Lester, 1995), using the Francis Scale of Attitude towards Christianity (Francis, Lewis, Philipchalk, Brown, & Lester, 1995). The four studies in this series have been based on samples of 82 students (Jones & Francis, 1999), 367 students (Fearn, Francis, & Wilcox, 2001), 149 students (Francis et al., 2003), and 552 students (Francis, Jones, & Craig, 2004). The findings from these four studies are inconclusive and suggest that all types may develop a positive attitude towards religion, but in somewhat different ways.

The second strand has examined the connection between psychological type and mystical orientation, drawing on the conceptualisation and measurement proposed by Francis and Louden (2000a) in the Mystical Orientation Scale. The three studies in this series have been based on samples of 100 students and adult churchgoers (Francis & Louden, 2000b), 543 participants attending workshops concerned with personality and spirituality (Francis, 2002), and 318 individuals who frequented the retreat house associated with Ampleforth Abbey (Francis, Village, Robbins, & Ineson, 2007). The most secure conclusion to emerge from these studies is that mystical orientation is associated with the perceiving process: intuitives are more open than sensers to mystical orientation. This finding is consistent with the earlier finding of Francis and Ross (1997) among 379 participants attending spirituality courses that sensers record higher scores than intuitives on an index of traditional Christian spirituality, while intuitives record higher scores than sensers on an index of experiential spirituality. Francis and Ross (1997) argued that the recognition of different preferences between sensers and intuitives may help to explain some conflicting experiences between clergy and congregations. For example, worship leaders who have a clear preference for intuition may find it difficult to understand why their attempts to provide more creative or experientially based forms of worship are so strongly resisted by congregations which have a clear preference for sensing.

The third strand has examined the connection between psychological type and charismatic experience, building on an earlier set of studies concerned with locating charismatic experience within Eysenck's three-dimensional model of personality (Francis & Thomas, 1997; Robbins, Hair, & Francis, 1999; Louden & Francis, 2001; Francis & Robbins, 2003). These earlier studies tended to show that charismatic experience was associated with high extraversion scores and with low neuroticism scores. The two studies examining the connection between psychological type and charismatic experience were based on samples of 368 committed Christian adults (Francis & Jones, 1997) and 925 Christian adults attending workshops on personality and spirituality (Jones, Francis, & Craig, 2005). The data demonstrate that, compared with non-charismatics, the charismatic sample contains significantly higher proportions of extraverts, thinkers and perceivers. Compared with the non-charismatic sample, there is a significantly higher proportion of dominant thinkers among the charismatic sample. Among the charismatic sample there is a significant over-representation of ESTJ and a significant under-representation of ISFJ.

The fourth strand has examined the connection between psychological type and different styles of religious believing. The first study in this series examined the relationship between scores recorded on an index of conservative Christian belief and psychological type preferences among a sample of 315 adult churchgoers (Francis & Jones, 1998). The data demonstrated that Christians who preferred sensing and thinking were more likely to hold traditional beliefs than Christians who preferred intuition and feeling. In a second study drawing on the same database, Francis and Jones (1999b) examined the relationship between psychological type and tolerance for religious uncertainty. These data demonstrated that Christians who preferred intuition rather than sensing were more tolerant of religious uncertainty. Taking this question one step further, Francis and Ross (2000) examined the relationship between psychological type and the Batson and Ventis 6-item measure of quest orientation of religiosity (Batson & Ventis, 1982) among a sample of 64 active Catholic churchgoers. These data provided inconclusive results. The next study in the series, however, by Francis and Ross (in press) employed the quest measure proposed by the New Indices of Religious Orientation (Francis, 2007) among a sample of 481 weekly churchgoing Christians. These data confirmed a positive association between intuition and the quest orientation of religiosity.

The fifth strand has begun to examine the empirical evidence for some of the theoretical underpinning of the SIFT method of biblical hermeneutics and liturgical preaching (Francis, 2003, 2006). Drawing on a sample of 404 lay adult Anglicans from 11 different churches, Village and Francis (2005) invited the participants to read a healing story from Mark's Gospel and then to choose between interpretative statements designed to appeal to particular psychological type preferences. The data confirmed a match between preferred biblical interpretation and personality preferences in both the perceiving (sensing versus intuition) and the judging (feeling versus thinking) processes.

Other recent studies have examined the relationship between dogmatism, religion and psychological type among a sample of 422 female undergraduate students (Ross, Francis, & Craig, 2005); the relationship between psychological type and religious affiliation among a sample of 425 female undergraduate students (Ross & Francis, 2006); the relationship between psychological type and Christian belief about the bible and the Holy Spirit among 404 churchgoers (Village, 2005); the relationship between psychological type and attitude towards Celtic Christianity among 248 committed churchgoers (Francis, Craig, & Hall, 2008); and the relationship between psychological type and individual differences in experience and appreciation among 381 cathedral visitors (Francis, Williams, Annis, & Robbins, 2008).

This third research tradition has established the power of psychological type theory to predict and to account for certain key individual differences in religious and spiritual experiences and expressions. By so doing, the foundations have been laid on which future research can build to extend empirically based knowledge regarding individual differences in broad fields of religious and spiritual experiences and expressions.

Applications

One of the recurrent dangers within religious and spiritual traditions is the tendency to assume that one form of religious expression or one form of spiritual practice should be regarded as appropriate for everyone. What this chapter should have achieved, if nothing else, is the demonstration that any such monolithic view of religious and spiritual experiences ignores the rich diversity within human beings themselves. The Jungian notion of psychological type provides a theoretical framework against which diverse expressions of religion and spirituality may be tested.

Individuals shaped by the two orientations of introversion and extraversion may properly choose different paths of spirituality, reflecting their respective sources of energy. For example, long periods of solitary silent meditation may well enrich and energise the introvert, but exhaust and drain the extravert. Conversely, long periods of deeply meaningful spiritual group activities may well enrich and energise the extravert, but exhaust and drain the introvert.

Individuals shaped by the two perceiving processes of sensing and intuition may properly express their spirituality in different ways. For example, the careful study of sacred narrative (from whatever source) may satisfy the sensing person's thirst for detail, for facts, and for conformity, but quickly lose the interest of intuitives. Conversely, opportunities to speculate about the future and to build visions of a deeply transformed world may satisfy the intuitive person's quest for novelty and transformation, but quickly lose the interest of sensers.

Individuals shaped by the two judging processes of thinking and feeling may properly develop their spirituality in different ways. For example, the feeling person may come alive with a spirituality of the heart that would leave the thinker unmoved. Conversely, the thinking person may come alive with a spirituality of the head that would leave the feeler unmoved.

Individuals shaped by the two attitudes towards the outer world of judging and perceiving may properly long for very different characteristics in their preferred form of spirituality. For example, the judging person may need the structure that is provided by a disciplined spiritual practice in order to remain committed to or to sense benefit from a spiritual path. Conversely, the perceiving person may need to be given permission to follow spiritual practices in a relaxed and flexible manner so as not to feel overwhelmed or constrained by external structures.

Taking psychological type seriously could, therefore, challenge and transform our understanding of the very notion of spirituality itself.

Note

1. At an earlier stage of my thinking I attempted to make do with two terms (character and personality), but my fellow personality psychologists rebelled at the way in which I needed to restrict the term personality.

References

Baab, L. M. (2000). *Personality types in congregations*. New York: Alban Institute.
Batson, C. D., & Ventis, W. L. (1982). *The religious experience: A social psychological perspective*. New York: Oxford University Press.
Bigelow, E. D., Fitzgerald, R., Busk, P., Girault, E., & Avis, J. (1988). Psychological characteristics of Catholic sisters: Relationships between the MBTI and other measures. *Journal of Psychological Type, 14*, 32–36.
Brown, C. G. (2001). *The death of Christian Britain*. London: Routledge.
Cabral, G. (1984). Psychological types in a Catholic convent: Applications to community living and congregational data. *Journal of Psychological Type, 8*, 16–22.

Cattell, R. B., Cattell, A. K. S., & Cattell, H. E. P. (1993). *Sixteen personality factor questionnaire* (5th ed., 16PF5). Windsor: NFER-Nelson.

Costa, P. T., & McCrae, R. R. (1985). *The NEO personality inventory*. Odessa, Florida: Psychological Assessment Resources.

Craig, C. L. (2005). Psychological type preferences of rural churchgoers. *Rural Theology, 3*, 123–131.

Craig, C. L., Bigio, J., Robbins, M., & Francis, L. J. (2005). Psychological types of student members of a Christian Union in Wales. *Psychologist in Wales, 8*, 123–131.

Craig, C. L., Duncan, B., & Francis, L. J. (2006a). Psychological type preferences of Roman Catholic priests in the United Kingdom. *Journal of Beliefs and Values, 27*, 157–164.

Craig, C. L., Duncan, B., & Francis, L. J. (2006b). Safeguarding tradition: Psychological type preference of male vergers in the Church of England. *Pastoral Psychology, 54*, 457–463.

Craig, C. L., Francis, L. J., Bailey, J., & Robbins, M. (2003). Psychological types in Church in Wales congregations. *The Psychologist in Wales, 15*, 18–21.

Craig, C. L., Francis, L. J., & Barwick, J. (in press). Psychological type preferences of Christian groups: Comparisons with the UK population norms. *Journal of Psychological Type*.

Craig, C. L., Francis, L. J., & Robbins, M. (2004). Psychological type and sex differences among church leaders in the United Kingdom. *Journal of Beliefs and Values, 25*, 3–13.

Craig, C. L., Horsfall, T., & Francis, L. J. (2005). Psychological types of male missionary personnel training in England: A role for thinking type men? *Pastoral Psychology, 53*, 475–482.

Craig, C. L., Williams, A., Francis, L. J., & Robbins, M. (2006). Psychological type and lay ministry among women in the Church in Wales. *Psychologist in Wales, 19*, 3–7.

Delis-Bulhoes, V. (1990). Jungian psychological types and Christian belief in active church members. *Journal of Psychological Type, 20*, 25–33.

Duncan, B. (1993). *Pray your way*. London: Darton, Longman and Todd.

Dwyer, M. T. (1995). *No light without shadow*. Thornbury, Australia: Desbooks.

Eysenck, H. J., & Eysenck, S. B. G. (1975). *Manual of the Eysenck personality questionnaire (adult and junior)*. London: Hodder and Stoughton.

Eysenck, H. J., & Eysenck, S. B. G. (1991). *Manual of the Eysenck personality scales*. London: Hodder and Stoughton.

Eysenck, S. B. G., Eysenck, H. J., & Barrett, P. (1985). A revised version of the psychoticism scale. *Personality and Individual Differences, 6*, 21–29.

Fearn, M., Francis, L. J., & Wilcox, C. (2001). Attitude toward Christianity and psychological type: A survey among religious studies students. *Pastoral Psychology, 49*, 341–348.

Francis, L. J. (2002). Psychological type and mystical orientation: Anticipating individual differences within congregational life. *Sciences Pastorales, 21*(1), 77–93.

Francis, L. J. (2003). Psychological type and biblical hermeneutics: SIFT method of preaching. *Rural Theology, 1*(1), 13–23.

Francis, L. J. (2005). *Faith and psychology: Personality, religion and the individual*. London: Darton, Longman and Todd.

Francis, L. J. (2006). Psychological type and liturgical preaching: The SIFT method. *Liturgy, 21*, 11–20.

Francis, L. J. (2007). Introducing the New Indices of Religious Orientation (NIRO): Conceptualisation and measurement. *Mental Health, Religion and Culture, 10*, 585–602.

Francis, L. J., Butler, A., & Craig, C. L. (2005). Understanding the Parochial Church Council: Dynamics of psychological type and gender. *Contact, 147*, 25–32.

Francis, L. J., Butler, A., Jones, S. H., & Craig, C. L. (2007). Type patterns among active members of the Anglican church: A perspective from England. *Mental Health, Religion and Culture, 10*, 435–443.

Francis, L. J., Craig, C. L., & Butler, A. (2007). Psychological types of male evangelical Anglican seminarians in England. *Journal of Psychological Type, 67*, 11–17.

Francis, L. J., Craig, C. L., & Hall, G. (2008). Psychological type and attitude toward Celtic Christianity among committed churchgoers in the United Kingdom: An empirical study. *Journal of Contemporary Religion, 23*, 181–191.

Francis, L. J., Craig, C. L., Horsfall, T., & Ross, C. F. J. (2005). Psychological types of male and female evangelical lay church leaders in England, compared with United Kingdom population norms. *Fieldwork in Religion, 1*, 69–83.

Francis, L. J., Craig, C. L., & Robbins, M. (2007a). The relationship between psychological type and the major three dimensions of personality. *Current Psychology, 25*, 257–271.

Francis, L. J., Craig, C. L., & Robbins, M. (2007b). Two different operationalisations of psychological type: Comparing the Myers-Briggs Type Indicator and the Keirsey Temperament Sorter. In R. A. Degregorio (Ed.), *New developments in psychological testing* (pp. 119–138). New York: Nova Science Publishers Inc.

Francis, L. J., Craig, C. L., Whinney, M., Tilley D., & Slater, P. (2007). Psychological typology of Anglican clergy in England: Diversity, strengths and weaknesses in ministry. *International Journal of Practical Theology, 11*, 266–284.

Francis, L. J., Duncan, B., Craig, C. L., & Luffman, G. (2004). Type patterns among Anglican congregations in England. *Journal of Adult Theological Education, 1*(1), 65–77.

Francis, L. J., & Jones, S. H. (1997). Personality and charismatic experience among adult Christians. *Pastoral Psychology, 45*, 421–428.

Francis, L. J., & Jones, S. H. (1998). Personality and Christian belief among adult churchgoers. *Journal of Psychological Type, 47*, 5–11.

Francis, L. J., & Jones, S. H. (1999a). The scale properties of the MBTI Form G (Anglicised) among adult churchgoers. *Pastoral Sciences Journal, 18*, 107–126.

Francis, L. J., & Jones, S. H. (1999b). Psychological type and tolerance for religious uncertainty. *Pastoral Psychology, 47*, 253–259.

Francis, L. J., & Jones, S. H. (2000). The relationship between the Myers-Briggs Type Indicator and the Eysenck Personality Questionnaire among adult churchgoers. *Pastoral Psychology, 48*, 377–386.

Francis, L. J., Jones, S. H., & Craig, C. L. (2004). Personality and religion: The relationship between psychological type and attitude toward Christianity. *Archiv Für Religionspsychologie, 26*, 15–33.

Francis, L. J., Lewis, J. M., Brown, L. B., Philipchalk, R., & Lester, D. (1995). Personality and religion among undergraduate students in the United Kingdom, United States, Australia and Canada. *Journal of Psychology and Christianity, 14*, 250–262.

Francis, L. J., Lewis, J. M., Philipchalk, R., Brown, L. B., & Lester, D. (1995). The internal consistency reliability and construct validity of the Francis Scale of Attitude toward Christianity (adult) among undergraduate students in the UK, USA, Australia and Canada. *Personality and Individual Differences, 19*, 949–953.

Francis, L. J., & Louden, S. H. (2000a). The Francis-Louden Mystical Orientation Scale (MOS): A study among Roman Catholic priests. *Research in the Social Scientific Study of Religion, 11*, 99–116.

Francis, L. J., & Louden, S. H. (2000b). Mystical orientation and psychological type: A study among student and adult churchgoers. *Transpersonal Psychology Review, 4*(1), 36–42.

Francis, L. J., Nash, P., Nash, S., & Craig, C. L. (2007). Psychology and youth-ministry: Psychological type preference of Christian youth workers in the United Kingdom. *Journal of Youth Ministry, 5*(2), 73–90.

Francis, L. J., & Payne, V. J. (2002). The Payne Index of Ministry Styles (PIMS): Ministry styles and psychological type among male Anglican clergy in Wales. *Research in the Social Scientific Study of Religion, 13*, 125–141.

Francis, L. J., Payne, V. J., & Jones, S. H. (2001). Psychological types of male Anglican clergy in Wales. *Journal of Psychological Type, 56*, 19–23.

Francis, L. J., & Pegg, S. (2007). Psychological type profile of female volunteer workers in a rural Christian charity shop. *Rural Theology, 5*, 53–56.

Francis, L. J., Penson, A. W., & Jones, S. H. (2001). Psychological types of male and female Bible college students in England. *Mental Health, Religion and Culture, 4*, 23–32.

Francis, L. J., & Robbins, M. (2002). Psychological types of male evangelical church leaders. *Journal of Beliefs and Values, 23*, 217–220.

Francis, L. J., & Robbins, M. (2003). Personality and glossolalia: A study among male Evangelical clergy. *Pastoral Psychology, 51*, 391–396.

Francis, L. J., Robbins, M., Boxer, A., Lewis, C. A., McGuckin, C., & McDaid, C. J. (2003). Psychological type and attitude toward Christianity: A replication. *Psychological Reports, 92*, 89–90.

Francis, L. J., Robbins, M., Kaldor, P., & Castle, K. (in press). Psychological type and work-related psychological health among clergy in Australia, England and New Zealand. *Journal of Psychology and Christianity*.

Francis, L. J., Robbins, M., Williams, A., & Williams, R. (2007). All types are called, but some are more likely to respond: The psychological type profile of rural Anglican churchgoers. *Rural Theology, 5*, 23–30.

Francis, L. J., & Ross, C. F. J. (1997). The perceiving function and Christian spirituality: Distinguishing between sensing and intuition. *Pastoral Sciences, 16*, 93–103.

Francis, L. J., & Ross, C. F. J. (2000). Personality type and quest orientation of religiosity. *Journal of Psychological Type, 55*, 22–25.

Francis, L. J., & Ross, C. F. J. (2008). The relationship of intrinsic, extrinsic and quest religious orientation to Jungian psychological type among Christian church attenders. *Mental Health, Religion and Culture, 21*, 166–182.

Francis, L. J., & Thomas, T. H. (1997). Are charismatic ministers less stable? A study among male Anglican clergy. *Review of Religious Research, 39*, 61–69.

Francis, L. J., Village, A., Robbins, M., & Ineson, K. (2007). Mystical orientation and psychological type: An empirical study among visitors to Ampleforth Abbey. *Studies in Spirituality, 17*, 207–223.

Francis, L. J., Williams, E., Annis, J., & Robbins, M. (2008). Understanding Cathedral visitors: Psychological type and individual differences in experience and appreciation. *Tourism Analysis, 13*, 71–80.

Francis, L. J., Wulff, K., & Robbins, M. (in press). The relationship between work-related psychological health and psychological type among clergy serving in The Presbyterian Church (USA). *Journal of Empirical Theology*.

Gerhardt, R. (1983). Liberal religion and personality type. *Research in Psychological Type, 6*, 47–53.

Harbaugh, G. L. (1984). The person in ministry: Psychological type and the seminary. *Journal of Psychological Type, 8*, 23–32.

Holsworth, T. E. (1984). Type preferences among Roman Catholic seminarians. *Journal of Psychological Type, 8*, 33–35.

Jones, S. H., & Francis, L. J. (1999). Personality type and attitude toward Christianity among student churchgoers. *Journal of Beliefs and Values, 20*, 105–109.

Jones, S. H., Francis, L. J., & Craig, C. L. (2005). Charismatic experience and psychological type: An empirical enquiry. *Journal of the European Pentecostal Theological Association, 25*, 39–53.

Jung, C. G. (1971). *Psychological types: The collected works* (Vol. 6). London: Routledge and Kegan Paul.

Kay, W. K., & Francis, L. J. (2008). Psychological type preferences of female Bible College students in England. *Journal of Beliefs and Values, 29*, 101–105.

Kay, W. K., Francis, L. J., & Craig, C. L. (2008). Psychological type preferences of male British Assemblies of God Bible College students: Tough-minded or tender-hearted? *Journal of the European Pentecostal Theological Association, 28*, 6–20.

Keirsey, D. (1998). *Please understand me: 2*. Del Mar, California: Prometheus Nemesis.

Keirsey, D., & Bates, M. (1978). *Please understand me*. Del Mar, California: Prometheus Nemesis.

Kelly, K. R., & Jugovic, H. (2001). Concurrent validity of the online version of the Keirsey Temperament Sorter II. *Journal of Career Assessment, 9*, 49–59.

Kendall, E. (1998). *Myers-Briggs type indicator: Step 1 manual supplement*. Palo Alto, California: Consulting Psychologists Press.

Leech, K. (Ed.). (1996). *Myers-Briggs: Some critical reflections*. Croydon: The Jubilee Group.

Lloyd, J. B. (2007). Opposition from Christians to Myers-Briggs personality typing: An analysis and evaluation. *Journal of Beliefs and Values, 28*, 111–123.

Louden, S. H., & Francis L. J. (2001). Are Catholic priests in England and Wales attracted to the charismatic movement emotionally less stable? *British Journal of Theological Education, 11*, 65–76.

Macdaid, G. P., McCaulley, M. H., & Kainz, R. I. (1986). *Myers-Briggs type indicator: Atlas of type tables*. Gainesville, Florida: Centre for Application of Psychological Type Inc.

Myers, I. B. (1998). *Introduction to type: A guide to understanding your results on the Myers-Briggs type indicator* (5th ed., European English version). Oxford: Oxford Psychologists Press.

Myers, I. B., & McCaulley, M. H. (1985). *Manual: A guide to the development and use of the Myers-Briggs type indicator*. Palo Alto, California: Consulting Psychologists Press.

Myers, I. B., & Myers, P. B. (1980). *Gifts differing*. Palo Alto: California, Consulting Psychologists Press.

Quinn, M. T., Lewis, R. J., & Fischer, K. L. (1992). A cross-correlation of the Myers-Briggs and Keirsey instruments. *Journal of College Student Development, 33*, 279–280.

Rehak, M. C. (1998). Identifying the congregation's corporate personality. *Journal of Psychological Type, 44*, 39–44.

Robbins, M., Hair, J., & Francis, L. J. (1999). Personality and attraction to the charismatic movement: A study among Anglican clergy. *Journal of Beliefs and Values, 20*, 239–246.

Ross, C. F. J. (1993). Type patterns among active members of the Anglican church: Comparisons with Catholics, Evangelicals and clergy. *Journal of Psychological Type, 26*, 28–35.

Ross, C. F. J. (1995). Type patterns among Catholics: Four Anglophone congregations compared with Protestants, Francophone Catholics and priests. *Journal of Psychological Type, 33*, 33–41.

Ross, C. F. J., & Francis, L. J. (2006). Psychological type and Christian religious affiliation among female undergraduates in Wales. *Journal of Psychological Type, 66*, 69–78.

Ross, C. F. J., Francis, L. J., & Craig, C. L. (2005). Dogmatism, religion and psychological type. *Pastoral Psychology, 53*, 483–497.

Tucker, I. F., & Gillespie, B. V. (1993). Correlations among three measures of personality type. *Perceptual and Motor Skills, 77*, 650.

Village, A. (2005). Christian belief about the Bible and the Holy Spirit in relation to psychological type. *Research in the Social Scientific Study of Religion, 16*, 1–16.

Village, A., & Francis, L. J. (2005). The relationship of psychological type preferences to biblical interpretation. *Journal of Empirical Theology, 18*(1), 74–89.

Village, A., Francis, L. J., & Craig, C. L. (in press). Church traditions and psychological type preference among Anglicans in England. *Journal of Anglican Studies*.

Biographical details

The Revd Canon Professor Leslie J Francis is Professor of Religions and Education at the University of Warwick, UK

Chapter 8
Understanding the Attitudinal Dimensions of Religion and Spirituality

Leslie J. Francis

Abstract The social scientific study of religion appreciates the multidimensional nature of religion and spirituality and distinguishes between a number of well-defined dimensions, including affiliation (say Methodist, Catholic, Muslim), practice (say, personal prayer, public attendance), belief (say, life after death, hell), orientation (say, intrinsic, extrinsic), and attitude. This chapter concentrates on the body of research which has refined concern with the attitudinal dimension of religion and spirituality. The argument proceeds in five steps: defining and critiquing the concept of attitude; describing and assessing methods of assessing and measuring attitude; assembling and integrating the research evidence concerned with the correlates of the attitudinal dimension of religion and spirituality; antecedents and consequences of individual differences in the attitudinal dimension of religion and spirituality; and applying the research evidence to practice.

Introduction

The aim of this chapter is to profile an established research tradition concerned with understanding the attitudinal dimensions of religion and to suggest that this tradition may provide a fruitful model for examining broader understandings of spirituality. The research tradition discussed in this chapter has been informed by and influenced by an individual differences approach within empirically based psychology.

The individual differences approach in psychology is grounded on certain core assumptions including: the view that human behaviour is not entirely random, but patterned in discernable ways; the view that there are certain readily discernable factors that are core to organising and predicting individual differences (say, for example, the sex differences of being male or female); the view that deeper, more covert factors, can be accessed and measured by appropriately tailored psychometric

L.J. Francis (✉)
Religions and Education, Warwick Religions and Education Research Unit, Institute of Education, University of Warwick, Coventry, CV4 7AL, UK
e-mail: leslie.francis@warwick.ac.uk

instruments (say, for example, the personality differences of being introvert or extravert).

Within this individual differences approach, empirical research within the psychology of religion has made significant advances by recognising that religion is a multidimensional phenomenon and that effective research needs not only to distinguish between the different dimensions of religion but also to propose different methods for measuring the different dimensions.

Dimensions of Religion

One powerful model for distinguishing between different dimensions of religion well established in the social sciences discusses the dimensions of affiliation, belief, practice and attitudes. Each of these dimensions is of theological significance and of social significance and may be treated somewhat differently by empirical theologians and by social scientists of religion.

Religious affiliation is a measure of belonging and of self-identification with a religious tradition. This is the level of information which it is acceptable to assemble as part of a public census. For social scientists, religious affiliation is conceptualised as an aspect of individual identity, alongside, say, factors like sex and ethnicity. Religious affiliation does not function as a secure predictor of other dimensions like religious belief and religious practice, but nonetheless it remains of key interest to empirical theologians and to social scientists. For empirical theologians it is important to consider the theological significance of claiming affiliation without adopting the practice or belief systems of a religious tradition. For social scientists it is important to recognise the empirical evidence for the enduring power of religious affiliation (in the absence of practice and belief) to predict individual differences of considerable social significance. While social scientists may find it acceptable to group broad faith traditions (as demonstrated by inclusion of the broad category "Christian" within the 2001 census in England and Wales), empirical theologians may be much more aware of the implications of theological differences within the Christian tradition.

Religious belief is a measure of the cognitive component of religion. The ways in which religious belief is conceptualised and measured may vary considerably between theological and social scientific traditions. Individual differences in religious belief may be expressed very differently by the theologically naïve and the theologically trained and sophisticated. Early attempts by social scientists to conceptualise and to measure Christian belief tended to imagine that conservative belief defined the recognised norm. Such conceptualisation worked well to characterise those who scored high on such instruments as conservative Christian believers. It remained more problematic, however, to characterise low scorers on such instruments, where potential confusion exists between atheists, agnostics and liberal believers. A further confusion arises when the content of belief is confused with the manner in which belief is held. Conservative belief does not equate with dogmatic belief. Empirical theologians may be much more aware of the theological complexity involved in defining and calibrating the dimensions of Christian belief.

Religious practice is a measure of the behavioural component of religion. Again the ways in which religious practice is conceptualised and measured may vary considerably between theological and social scientific traditions. Distinctions, too, need to be made between the observance of public practice (say, church attendance) and the observance of private practice (say, personal prayer). Early attempts by social scientists to assess the psychological correlates of prayer concentrated primarily on assessing the frequency of prayer without differentiation among the different types or forms of prayers. Empirical theologians may be much more aware of the complexity and theological differences of prayer within religious traditions.

Attitude towards religion is a measure of the affective component of religion. A very long tradition in social psychology has developed considerable conceptual and methodological sophistication in defining and operationalising the attitudinal dimension of religion. This domain is concerned with how individuals feel (negatively and positively) towards religion. Early attempts by social scientists to provide measures of attitude towards religion may have been distracted by overemphasis on the outward and more visible aspects of religious traditions. Empirical theologians may be more aware of the inward and more spiritually salient aspects of religious traditions. The following sections argue why it is that this attitudinal dimension provides the strongest foundation for empirical research in religion and spirituality.

The Attitudinal Dimension

Reflecting on these four dimensions of religion in the early 1970s, I recognised that the attitudinal dimension was able to get closer to the heart of religion within individual lives and also that the measurement of attitude carried a number of important advantages over the measurement of affiliation, belief or practice.

First, although affiliation has been shown to be of conceptual and empirical value within both theology and social sciences, there are significant limitations for this construct within the individual differences approach. On the one hand, the level of measurement achieved is only that of discrete categories. Individuals are located either within one category or another. On the other hand, affiliation categories take on significantly different meanings within different denominational groups. While nominalism is high, say, among Anglicans; in another group, say among Baptists, nominalism is low.

Second, although practice may be easy to conceptualise and to measure on ordinal or (possibly) interval scales, the actual meaning of practice may vary according to a range of constraints. For example, an irreligious young person may attend church because of family pressures, while a highly religious elderly person may stay away from church because of health-related problems. Moreover, practice may convey different significances within different denominational environments.

Third, although belief may be open to clear conceptualisation and (in some senses) refined measurement on (probably) interval scales, the formulation of indices of religious belief is conceptually complex (both theologically and psychologically). It is this formulation of measures of belief which may distinguish one denominational group from another, the theologically educated from the theologically naïve, and so on. While such issues are of central importance to certain fields of theological enquiry, they may simply provide distraction to the broader individual differences approach concerned with comparative research dealing with the personal and social correlates of religion.

As a deep-seated underlying construct concerned with affective response (favourably towards or negatively against) religion, a well-developed attitude scale is able to calibrate individual differences in religiosity across age groups and across denominational divides. It is for this reason that in the 1970s I developed an instrument which has become known as the Francis Scale of Attitude towards Christianity and invited colleagues to join with me in building up a secure basis of empirical information regarding the correlates, consequences and antecedents of a positive attitude towards Christianity. By agreeing on the use of the same measure, colleagues could be clear that their independent studies fitted together to build an integrated tapestry of research concerning the contributions being made to individual lives of the form of spirituality being accessed by the Francis Scale of Attitude towards Christianity.

The Francis Scale of Attitude towards Christianity comprised 24 items concerned with affective responses to five aspects of the Christian tradition that transcend denominational divisions, namely God, Jesus, bible, church and prayer. The scientific basis for confidence in the assertion that studies conducted in different contexts could be joined together rested on the demonstration that the instrument functioned with comparable degrees of reliability and validity among different age groups, among different denominational groups and in different countries. This programme of establishing the reliability and validity of the Francis Scale of Attitude towards Christianity began in English-speaking contexts.

Research Across Linguistic Divides

Initially the tapestry of research constructed by means of studies agreeing on the use of the Francis Scale of Attitude towards Christianity was restricted by the English-speaking world. The second generation of studies conducted within this tradition began to explore the performance of the instrument in translation. In this way it becomes possible to test whether the correlates, antecedents and consequences of individual differences in attitude towards Christianity established in an English-speaking context remain consistent within other linguistic communities.

The advantages and difficulties of translating psychometric instruments across languages are now well discussed in the literature. It is recognised, for example, how the change of a single word within a psychometric instrument in one language may change the pattern of responding to that one item and consequently disturb the pattern of correlations between the items. Translation of a whole instrument may prove to be so much more disruptive. The first general principle in translating psychometric instruments is the conceptual task of ensuring that the concepts expressed in one language are adequately expressed in another language. This is much more complex than simply offering a word-for-word translation, although it may be relatively straightforward if the original instrument is itself expressed simply and in a clear manner. The process of translation is then followed by back translation into the original language. Discrepancies between the original wording and the back translation draw attention to potential problems with the translation.

The second general principle in translating psychometric instruments is the empirical task of examining whether the instrument displays comparable psychometric properties in the translated form to those established in the original form. Factor analyses and reliability analyses are able to examine whether the individual items perform in similar ways in translation. A family of studies has now reported on the satisfactory psychometric properties of the Francis Scale of Attitude towards Christianity translated into, for example, Arabic (Munayer, 2000), Chinese (Francis Lewis, & Ng, 2002), Dutch (Francis & Hermans, 2000), French (Lewis & Francis, 2003), German (Francis, Ziebertz, & Lewis, 2002), Greek (Youtika, Joseph, & Diduca, 1999), Norwegian (Francis & Enger, 2002), Portuguese (Ferreira & Neto, 2002), Romanian (Francis, Ispas, Robbins, Ilie, & Iliescu, 2009), Slovenian (Flere, Klanjsek, Francis, & Robbins, 2008), Spanish (Campo-Arias, Oviedo, Dtaz, & Cogollo, 2006), Swedish (Eek, 2001) and Welsh (Evans & Francis, 1996).

As a consequence of these studies, the horizons for comparative research in religion and spirituality have been enlarged against the background of a common religious heritage and an instrument that has the capability of operationalising the construct of attitude towards Christianity in a variety of languages.

Research Across Religious Traditions

Initially the tapestry of research constructed by means of studies agreeing on the use of the Francis Scale of Attitude towards Christianity was restricted, by very definition, to the Christian tradition. The third generation of studies conducted within this tradition began to explore how the basic attitudinal construct accessed by the Francis Scale of Attitude towards Christianity could be translated within other religious traditions. In this way it becomes possible to test whether the correlates, antecedents and consequences of individual differences in attitude towards Christianity remain consistent within other religious traditions. Thus, having established the usefulness of the attitudinal dimension within the individual differences approach to investigating the personal and social correlates of religiosity within a Christian context, an international group of scholars have begun to examine the potential for developing parallel instruments shaped within other religious contexts, namely (in chronological order of development), Islam, Judaism and Hinduism.

The core characteristics of the Francis Scale of Attitude towards Christianity are that it focuses on the affective response to the Christian tradition, that it identifies five key visible aspects of this tradition equally intelligible to children, adolescents and adults (God, Jesus, Bible, prayer and church) and that the construct is operationalised through 24 Likert-type items arranged for scoring on a five-point scale: agree strongly, agree, not certain, disagree and disagree strongly. The translation of this construct into other religious traditions involved proper theological awareness of the subtlety, complexity and diversity within these traditions.

The first of these instruments to be published was the Sahin–Francis Scale of Attitude towards Islam (Sahin & Francis, 2002). The items of the Francis Scale of Attitude towards Christianity were carefully scrutinised and debated by several Muslim scholars of Islam until agreement was reached on 23 Islam-related items which mapped closely onto the area assessed by the parent instrument. The psychometric properties of the instrument were assessed on 381 Muslim adolescents in England (Sahin & Francis, 2002) and later confirmed among 1,199 Muslim adolescents in Kuwait (Francis, Sahin, & Al-Failakawi, 2008).

The second of these instruments was the Katz–Francis Scale of Attitude towards Judaism (Francis & Katz, 2007). A similar process involving Jewish scholars of Judaism reached agreement on 24 Judaism-related items which mapped closely onto the area assessed by the parent instrument. The psychometric properties of the instrument were assessed on 618 Hebrew-speaking undergraduate students attending Bar-Ilan University.

The third of these instruments was the Santosh–Francis Scale of Attitude towards Hinduism (Francis, Santosh, Robbins, & Vij, 2008). A similar process involving Hindu scholars of Hinduism reached agreement on 19 Hinduism-related items which mapped closely onto the area assessed by the parent instrument. The psychometric properties of the instrument were assessed on 330 young Hindus in England (Francis et al., 2008) and 100 Hindus in India (Tiliopoulos & Francis, in press).

As a consequence of these studies, the horizons for comparative research in religion and spirituality have been enlarged against the background of a common understanding of the affective dimension of religion now operationalised within the framework of four major religious traditions: Christianity, Hinduism, Islam and Judaism.

Since I first invited colleagues to join with me in the late 1970s to develop a tapestry of studies specifically focusing on establishing the correlates, antecedents and consequences of individual differences within the attitudinal dimension of religion, over 300 studies have been published in what remains a developing programme of research. The scope of this research can be illustrated by two specific examples, concerned with the relationship between the attitudinal dimension of religion and mental health and concerned with the relationship between the attitudinal dimension of religion and wellbeing (positive psychology).

Religion and Mental Health

On a broader front, the psychology of religion has advanced two very different theoretical positions regarding the relationship between religion and mental health. One position has taken the negative view that religion is associated with lower levels of mental health, while the other position has taken the positive view that religion is associated with higher levels of mental health (see, for example, Batson, Schoenrade, & Ventis, 1993). The negative view is exemplified, for example, in the classic writings of Freud, who sees the Judaic-Christian tradition as capturing the human psyche in a state of infantile immaturity, leading to psychological vulnerability and neuroses (Freud, 1950; Vine, 1978). The opposite psychological view is exemplified, for example, in the classical writings of Gordon Allport, who sees the religious images of the Judaic-Christian tradition as providing powerful developmental tools promoting and leading to psychological health (Jung, 1938; Allport, 1950).

The empirical literature on the relationship between religion and mental health is also divided between some studies which report a positive association, some studies which report a negative association and some studies which fail to find association in either direction (Koenig, McCullough, & Larson, 2001). Such disparate findings suggest that the two constructs of religion and of mental health need careful definition before the problem concerning their relationship can be properly defined and operationalised.

One particularly attractive way of defining and operationalising the construct of mental health is provided by Eysenck's dimensional model of personality (H. J. Eysenck & M. W. Eysenck, 1985). Eysenck's dimensional model of personality, as operationalised through the Eysenck Personality Scales (H. J. Eysenck & S. B. G. Eysenck, 1991), maintains that abnormal personality is not discrete from but continuous with normal personality. Accordingly neurotic disorders lie at one extreme of a dimension of normal personality, ranging from emotional stability, through emotional lability, to neurotic disorder. Similarly, psychotic disorders lie at one extreme of another dimension of normal personality, ranging from tendermindedness, through toughmindedness, to psychotic disorder. Therefore, it is possible to define and operationalise the dimensions of neuroticism and psychoticism so that they appear to be orthogonal and independent of each other. Eysenck's dimensional model of personality adds a third orthogonal dimension which is not in itself concerned with psychological disorder. The third dimension ranges from introversion, through ambiversion, to extraversion.

A series of studies conducted in England over the past 25 years have mapped the relationship between attitude towards Christianity (as assessed by the Francis Scale of Attitude towards Christianity) and mental health (as assessed by the Eysenckian personality measures). Two main conclusions emerged from this series of studies.

The first conclusion concerns the relationship between attitude towards Christianity and neuroticism scores. H. J. Eysenck and S. B. G. Eysenck (1975) defined high scorers on the neuroticism scale as being anxious, worrying, moody and frequently depressed individuals who are likely to sleep badly and to suffer from various psychosomatic disorders. They are seen as overly emotional, reacting too strongly to all sorts of stimuli and finding it difficult to get back on an even keel after emotionally arousing experiences. Strong reactions interfere with their proper adjustment, making them react in irrational, sometimes rigid ways. Highly neurotic individuals are worriers whose main characteristic is a constant preoccupation with things that might go wrong and a strong anxiety reaction to these thoughts. After controlling for the expected sex differences, according to which females score more highly than males on both indices of religiosity (Argyle & Beit-Hallahmi, 1975) and neuroticism (Jorm, 1987), repeated analyses demonstrate no significant relationship between neuroticism scores and a positive attitude towards Christianity (Francis, Pearson, Carter, & Kay, 1981a; Francis, Pearson, & Kay, 1983a; Francis & Pearson, 1991).

The second conclusion concerns the relationship between attitude towards Christianity and psychoticism scores. H. J. Eysenck and S. B. G. Eysenck (1976) define high scorers on the psychoticism scale as being cold, impersonal, hostile, lacking in sympathy, unfriendly, untrustful, odd, unemotional, unhelpful, lacking in insight and strange, with paranoid ideas that people are against them. H. J. Eysenck and S. B. G. Eysenck (1976) also use the following descriptors: egocentric, self-centred, impersonal, lacking in empathy, solitary, troublesome, cruel, glacial, inhumane, insensitive, sensation-seeking, aggressive, foolhardy, making fools of others and liking odd and unusual things. H. J. Eysenck and S. B. G. Eysenck (1975) maintained that emotions such as empathy and guilt are characteristically absent in people who score high on measures of psychoticism. Repeated analyses demonstrate a significant negative relationship between psychoticism scores and a positive attitude towards Christianity (Kay, 1981a; Francis & Pearson, 1985a; Francis, 1992a). This finding lends support to the theory that Christianity is associated with higher levels of mental health and contradicts the theory that Christianity is associated with lower levels of mental health.

A subsidiary conclusion also emerged from this series of studies, but this conclusion provides no further indication of the relationship between Christianity and psychological health. The subsidiary conclusion concerns extraversion. Originally Eysenck defined high scorers on the extraversion scale as sociable, outgoing, impulsive, carefree and optimistic. This definition clearly combines the two notions of sociability and impulsivity (S. B. G. Eysenck & H. J. Eysenck, 1963). While both of these two components appear to have been well represented in the earlier editions of the extraversion scale, the more recent editions have been largely purified of impulsivity, which now relates more closely to psychoticism (Rocklin & Revelle, 1981). While according to the earlier operationalisations of extraversion, introverts emerge as holding a more positive attitude towards Christianity, according to the later operationalisations repeated analyses demonstrate no significant relationship between extraversion scores and attitude towards Christianity (Francis, Pearson, Carter, & Kay, 1981b; Francis, Pearson, & Kay, 1983b; Francis & Pearson, 1985b; Williams, Robbins, & Francis, 2005).

The consensus of these focused analyses is given further support by studies conducted among other samples of school pupils in the United Kingdom, using the

Francis Scale of Attitude towards Christianity, including 8–11-year-olds (Robbins, Francis, & Gibbs, 1995), 11-year-olds (Francis, Lankshear, & Pearson, 1989), 12–16-year-olds (Francis & Montgomery, 1992), 15–16-year-olds (Francis & Pearson, 1988) and 16–18-year-olds (Wilcox & Francis, 1997; Francis & Fearn, 1999). The findings have also been replicated among secondary school pupils in Germany (Francis & Kwiran, 1999).

Another set of studies have employed the Francis Scale of Attitude towards Christianity alongside the Eysenck measures of personality among students and adults, including studies in the United Kingdom (Francis, 1991, 1993, 1999; Francis & Bennett, 1992; Carter, Kay, & Francis, 1996; Bourke & Francis, 2000; Shuter-Dyson, 2000), Australia and Canada (Francis, Lewis, Brown, Philipchalk, & Lester, 1995), Northern Ireland (Lewis & Joseph, 1994; Lewis, 1999, 2000), Republic of Ireland (Maltby, 1997a; Maltby & Lewis, 1997), the USA (Lewis & Maltby, 1995a; Roman & Lester, 1999), France (Lewis & Francis, 2000), Greece (Youtika et al., 1999), Hong Kong (Francis, Lewis, & Ng, 2003) and South Africa (Francis & Kerr, 2003). Once again, the basic pattern was confirmed that attitude towards Christianity was negatively correlated with psychoticism, but unrelated to either extraversion or neuroticism. Moreover, more recent studies have reported similar results using the Katz–Francis Scale of Attitude towards Judaism (Francis, Katz, Yablon, & Robbins, 2004) and the Santosh–Francis Scale of Attitude towards Hinduism (Francis, Robbins, Santosh, & Bhanot, 2008).

Being purely cross-sectional correlational studies, the data currently available are not able to adjudicate on the direction of causality in the relationship reported. Eysenck's psychologically driven theory would argue for the priority of personality in shaping these relationships, seeing individual differences in personality to be biologically based. According to this account, individuals who record low scores on the psychoticism scale would be more drawn to the Christian tradition. Such a view is consistent with Eysenck's notion regarding the relationship between low psychoticism and greater conditioning into tenderminded social attitudes and the general location of religiosity within the domain of tenderminded social attitudes (Eysenck, 1975, 1976). On the other hand, such a psychologically driven theory may be hard-pressed to explain the lack of relationship between neuroticism scores and religion, since the psychological mechanism posited here suggests that religion provides an attractive escape for neurotic anxieties.

An alternative theologically driven theory would argue for the priority of religious experience in shaping the relationship between personality, mental health and religion, seeing religion as essentially transformative of individual differences. According to this account, individuals who record high scores on the scale of attitude towards Christianity would be challenged by their faith to transform and reject those qualities listed by Eysenck as characterising the high scorer on the psychoticism scale: egocentric, self-centred, impersonal, lacking in empathy, solitary, troublesome, cruel, glacial, inhumane, insensitive, sensation-seeking, aggressive and foolhardy (H. J. Eysenck & S. B. G. Eysenck, 1976). On the other hand, such theologically driven theory may be more hard-pressed to account for the lack of association between attitude towards Christianity and neuroticism. Throughout the Gospel tradition the Christian faith consistently proclaims the twin messages of "Fear not" and "Peace be with you" from the angelic annunciation preceding the Lucan birth narrative to the Johannine post-resurrection appearances. According to such theory the Christian disciple should be less troubled by those qualities listed by Eysenck as characterising the high scorer on the neuroticism scale: anxious, worrying, moody, frequently depressed, poor sleepers, suffering from various psychosomatic disorders and overly emotional (H. J. Eysenck and S. B. G. Eysenck, 1975).

Religion and Wellbeing

Once again, the empirical literature on the relationship between religion and positive psychology is divided between some studies which report a positive association, some studies which report a negative association and some studies which fail to find association in either direction. Taking the notion of happiness as a key indicator within positive psychology, Francis, Jones, and Wilcox (2000) undertook a thorough review of the available literature and concluded that a major problem with integrating and interpreting the findings was posed by the wide variety of ways in which the construct of happiness was defined and assessed.

Evaluating these empirical studies, Francis et al. (2000) argue that future studies need to agree on a more robust form of measurement. One particularly attractive way of defining and operationalising the construct of happiness is provided by the Oxford Happiness Inventory developed by Argyle, Martin, and Crossland (1989) on the basis of a thorough theoretical discussion of the nature of happiness. Drawing on earlier analysis, Argyle and Crossland (1987) suggest that happiness can be measured by taking into account three empirical indicators: the frequency and degree of positive affect or joy; the average level of satisfaction over a period; and the absence of negative feelings, such as depression and anxiety. The test constructors report for this 29-item scale an internal reliability of 0.90 and a 7-week test–retest reliability of 0.78. Validity was established against happiness ratings by friends and by correlations with measures of positive affect, negative affect and life satisfaction. A series of studies employing the Oxford Happiness Inventory in a range of different ways have confirmed the basic reliability and validity of the instrument and begun to map the correlates of this operational definition of happiness. For example, Hills and Argyle (1998a) found that happiness was positively correlated with intensity of musical experience. Hills and Argyle (1998b) found that happiness was positively correlated with participation in sports. Chan and Joseph (2000) found that happiness was correlated positively with self-actualisation, self-esteem, likelihood of affiliation, community feeling and self-acceptance.

The Francis Scale of Attitude towards Christianity has now been employed in a series of studies alongside the Oxford Happiness Inventory. The first study, reported by Robbins and Francis (1996), was conducted among 360 undergraduates in the United Kingdom. The second study, reported by Francis and Lester (1997), replicated the original study in a different cultural context among 212 undergraduates in the United States. The third study, reported by French and Joseph (1999), was conducted among 101 undergraduate students in the United Kingdom. The fourth study, reported by Francis et al. (2000), employed three separate samples drawn from the United Kingdom: 994 secondary school pupils during the final year of compulsory schooling; 456 first-year undergraduate students; and 496 members of a branch of the University of the Third Age, a relatively informal education network for senior citizens. The fifth study, reported by Francis and Robbins (2000), was conducted among 295 participants attending a variety of workshops and courses on the psychology of religion, ranging in age from late teens to late seventies. The sixth study, reported by Francis, Robbins, and White (2003), was conducted among 89 students in Wales. All eight samples employed in these six studies demonstrated a significant positive correlation between happiness and attitude towards Christianity, after controlling for the possible contaminating influence of personality. On the other hand, no significant relationship was found between attitude towards Christianity and happiness among a sample of 331 students in Germany reported by Francis, Ziebertz, and Lewis (2003).

In order to establish the extent to which the correlates of the attitudinal dimensions of religiosity established within a Christian or post-Christian context by means of the Francis Scale of Attitude towards Christianity held true within a context shaped by Judaism, Francis and Katz (2002) administered the Katz–Francis Scale of Attitude towards Judaism, alongside the Hebrew translation of the Oxford Happiness Inventory and the Hebrew translation of the short form of the Revised Eysenck Personality Questionnaire, to a sample of 298 female Hebrew-speaking undergraduate students. In a second study, Francis et al. (2004) administered the same set of instruments to a sample of 203 male Hebrew-speaking undergraduate students. The data from both studies confirmed a small but statistically significant positive association between attitude towards Judaism and happiness.

Broader Research Field

The two sets of studies reviewed in the previous sections, concerned with mental health and wellbeing, have provided good examples of how the tapestry of research-based knowledge has been developed regarding the correlates, consequences and antecedents of individual differences in attitude towards religion. Other research within this tradition can be best introduced within four main themes.

The first main theme has explored the relationship between the attitudinal dimension of religion and other key major personality-related constructs. These constructs include abortion-related attitudes (Fawcett, Andrews, & Lester, 2000), adjustment (Schludermann, Schludermann, Needham, & Mulenga, 2001), alcohol-related attitudes (Francis, Fearn, & Lewis, 2005), altruism (Eckert & Lester, 1997), Cattell's personality model (Francis & Bourke, 2003; Bourke, Francis, & Robbins, 2007), dissociation (Dorahy & Lewis, 2001), conservatism (Lewis & Maltby, 2000), dogmatism (Francis, 2001; Francis & Robbins, 2003), empathy (Francis & Pearson, 1987), gender orientation (Francis & Wilcox, 1996, 1998; Francis, 2005), general health (Francis, Robbins, Lewis, Quigley, & Wheeler, 2004), impulsivity (Pearson, Francis, & Lightbown, 1986), intelligence (Francis, 1998), intrinsic and extrinsic religiosity (Joseph & Lewis, 1997; Maltby & Day, 1998), just world beliefs (Crozier & Joseph, 1997), life satisfaction (Lewis, Joseph, & Noble, 1996; Lewis, 1998), mental health values (Tjeltveit, Fiordalist, & Smith, 1996), moral values (Francis & Greer, 1990), obsessionality (Lewis, 1994, 1996; Lewis & Joseph, 1994; Lewis & Maltby, 1994, 1995b; Maltby, 1997b; Maltby, McCollam, & Millar, 1994), openness to members of other religious traditions (Greer, 1985), operational thinking (Kay, Francis, & Gibson, 1996), paranormal belief (Williams, Francis, & Robbins, 2006), premarital sex (Francis, 2006), preoedipal fixation (Lewis & Maltby, 1992), Jungian personality type (Jones & Francis, 1999; Fearn, Francis, & Wilcox, 2001), prosocial values (Schludermann, Schludermann, & Huynh, 2000), psychological wellbeing (Francis, Jones, & Wilcox, 1997), religious orientation (Maltby & Lewis, 1996; Jones, 1997), schizotypal traits (White, Joseph & Neil, 1995; Diduca & Joseph, 1997; Joseph & Diduca, 2001), self-esteem (Jones & Francis, 1996), social desirability (Gillings & Joseph, 1996) and suicidal ideation (Lester & Francis, 1993).

The second main theme has explored the relationship between the attitudinal dimension of religion, attitude towards science, scientism and creationism among young people in Kenya (Fulljames & Francis, 1987; Fulljames & Francis, 2003), Scotland (Gibson, 1989; Francis, Gibson, & Fulljames, 1990; Fulljames, Gibson, & Francis, 1991; Francis Fulljames, & Gibson, 1992), England (Fulljames, 1996) and Northern Ireland (Francis & Greer, 2001). These studies highlight the ways in which both scientism and creationism can inhibit the development of positive attitudes towards *both* science *and* Christianity.

The third main theme has explored the social and contextual factors associated with the development of a positive attitude towards religion. Separate studies have focused on such factors as the possible influences associated with age (Francis, 1989a), church schools (Boyle & Francis, 1986; Francis, 1986a, 1986b, 1987; Francis & Carter, 1980; Rhymer & Francis, 1985; Francis & Gibson, 2001), conversion experiences (Kay, 1981b), denominational identity (Francis, 1990; Greer & Francis, 1990; Maltby, 1995; Francis & Greer, 1999), generational changes (Francis, 1989b, 1989c, 1992b; Kay & Francis, 1996), parental church attendance (Francis & Gibson, 1993b), parental marital happiness (Kay, 1981c), religious education syllabuses (Kay, 1981d), religious experience (Greer & Francis, 1992; Francis & Greer, 1993; Francis, ap Siôn, Lewis, Robbins, & Barnes, 2006), social class (Francis, Pearson, & Lankshear, 1990; Gibson, Francis, & Pearson, 1990), Sunday school attendance (Francis, Gibson, & Lankshear, 1991) and television (Francis & Gibson, 1992, 1993a).

The fourth main theme has employed the attitude scales to monitor changes in attitude towards religion or to describe attitude towards religion in specific situations. For example, Bennett and Rigby (1991) explored change during residence in a rehabilitation centre for female drug users. Greer (1981, 1982) profiled the religious attitudes of young people growing up in Northern Ireland. Kay (1981e) explored the relationship between attitude towards Christianity and subject preference among secondary school pupils. O'Keeffe (1992, 1996) explored the religious attitudes of pupils attending independent conservative Christian schools.

Conclusion

In my early paper entitled "Measurement reapplied" (Francis, 1978), I outlined an ambition of what could be achieved if a number of researchers agreed on employing a common attitudinal measure of religiosity across a wide range of studies. Thirty years later this chapter has demonstrated how the research programme has been broadened with a second generation of studies to embrace linguistic diversity and broadened further with a third generation of studies to embrace four different religious traditions. The potential contribution to knowledge made by this research programme has been illustrated by two detailed examples, concerning the associations between the attitudinal dimension of religion and mental health, and between the attitudinal dimension of religion and wellbeing, and by a more general overview of the research field.

The fruitfulness of this research tradition suggests that it would now be appropriate for a fourth generation of studies to face the challenge of developing a new family of measures capable of operationalising the attitudinal dimension of spirituality. Such measures would be able to help establish the extent to which the correlates, antecedents and consequences of individual differences in the attitudinal dimension of spirituality mirrored or contradicted the consensus of findings concerning the correlates, antecedents and consequences of individual differences in the attitudinal dimension of religion. Such research would also carry the additional bonus of helping to clarify the areas of continuity and discontinuity between religion as traditionally conceived and spirituality as conceived in the contemporary world.

References

Allport, G. W. (1950). *The individual and his religion*. New York: Macmillan.
Argyle, M., & Beit-Hallahmi, B. (1975). *The social psychology of religion*. London: Routledge and Kegan Paul.
Argyle, M., & Crossland, J. (1987). Dimensions of positive emotions. *British Journal of Social Psychology, 26*, 127–137.
Argyle, M., Martin, M., & Crossland, J. (1989). Happiness as a function of personality and social encounters. In J. P. Forgas & J. M. Innes (Eds.), *Recent advances in social psychology: An international perspective* (pp. 189–203). Amsterdam, North Holland: Elsevier Science Publishers.
Batson, C. D., Schoenrade, P., & Ventis, W. L. (1993). *Religion and the individual: A social-psychological perspective*. Oxford: Oxford University Press.
Bennett, G., & Rigby, K. (1991). Psychological change during residence in a rehabilitation centre for female drug misusers. *Drug and Alcohol Dependence, 27*, 149–157.

Bourke, R., & Francis, L. J. (2000). Personality and religion among music students. *Pastoral Psychology, 48*, 437–444.

Bourke, R., Francis, L. J., & Robbins, M. (2007). Cattell's personality model and attitude toward Christianity. *Mental Health, Religion and Culture, 10*, 353–362.

Boyle, J. J., & Francis, L. J. (1986). The influence of differing church aided school systems on pupil attitude towards religion. *Research in Education, 35*, 7–12.

Campo-Arias, A., Oviedo, H. C., Dtaz, C. F., & Cogollo, Z. (2006). Internal consistency of a Spanish translation of the Francis Scale of Attitude toward Christianity short form. *Psychological Reports, 99*, 1008–1010.

Carter, M., Kay, W. K., & Francis, L. J. (1996). Personality and attitude toward Christianity among committed adult Christians. *Personality and Individual Differences, 20*, 265–266.

Chan, R., & Joseph, S. (2000). Dimensions of personality, domains of aspiration, and subjective well-being. *Personality and Individual Differences, 28*, 347–354.

Crozier, S., & Joseph, S. (1997). Religiosity and sphere-specific just world beliefs in 16- to 18-year olds. *Journal of Social Psychology, 137*, 510–513.

Diduca, D., & Joseph, S. (1997). Schizotypal traits and dimensions of religiosity. *British Journal of Clinical Psychology, 36*, 635–638.

Dorahy, M. J., & Lewis, C. A. (2001). The relationship between dissociation and religiosity: An empirical evaluation of Schumaker's theory. *Journal for the Scientific Study of Religion, 40*, 317–324.

Eckert, R. M., & Lester, D. (1997). Altruism and religiosity. *Psychological Reports, 81*, 562.

Eek, J. (2001). *Religious facilitation through intense liturgical participation: A quasi-experimental study of Swedish pilgrims to Taizé*. Lund: University of Lund Studies in Psychology of Religion.

Evans, T. E., & Francis, L. J. (1996). Measuring attitude toward Christianity through the medium of Welsh. In L. J. Francis, W. K. Kay, & W. S. Campbell (Eds.), *Research in religious education* (pp. 279–293). Leominster: Gracewing.

Eysenck, H. J. (1975). The structure of social attitudes. *British Journal of Social and Clinical Psychology, 14*, 323–331.

Eysenck, H. J. (1976). Structure of social attitudes. *Psychological Reports, 39*, 463–466.

Eysenck, H. J., & Eysenck, M. W. (1985). *Personality and individual differences: A natural science approach*. New York: Plenum Press.

Eysenck, H. J., & Eysenck, S. B. G. (1975). *Manual of the Eysenck personality questionnaire (adult and junior)*. London: Hodder and Stoughton.

Eysenck, H. J., & Eysenck, S. B. G. (1976). *Psychoticism as a dimension of personality*. London: Hodder and Stoughton.

Eysenck, H. J., & Eysenck, S. B. G. (1991). *Manual of the Eysenck personality scales*. London: Hodder and Stoughton.

Eysenck, S. B. G., & Eysenck, H. J. (1963). On the dual nature of extraversion. *British Journal of Social and Clinical Psychology, 2*, 46–55.

Fawcett, J., Andrews, V., & Lester, D. (2000). Religiosity and attitudes about abortion. *Psychological Reports, 87*, 980.

Fearn, M., Francis, L. J., & Wilcox, C. (2001). Attitude toward Christianity and psychological type: A survey among religious studies students. *Pastoral Psychology, 49*, 341–348.

Ferreira, A. V., & Neto, F. (2002). Psychometric properties of the Francis Scale of Attitude toward Christianity among Portuguese university students. *Psychological Reports, 91*, 995–998.

Flere, S., Klanjsek, R., Francis, L. J., & Robbins, M. (2008). The psychometric properties of the Slovenian translation of the Francis Scale of Attitude toward Christianity: A study among Roman Catholic undergraduate students. *Journal of Beliefs and Values, 29*, 313–319.

Francis, L. J. (1978). Measurement reapplied: Research into the child's attitude towards religion. *British Journal of Religious Education, 1*, 45–51.

Francis, L. J. (1986a). Roman Catholic secondary schools: Falling rolls and pupil attitudes. *Educational Studies, 12*, 119–127.

Francis, L. J. (1986b). Denominational schools and pupil attitudes towards Christianity. *British Educational Research Journal, 12*, 145–152.

Francis, L. J. (1987). *Religion in the primary school*. London: Collins Liturgical Publications.

Francis, L. J. (1989a). Measuring attitude towards Christianity during childhood and adolescence. *Personality and Individual Differences, 10*, 695–698.

Francis, L. J. (1989b). Drift from the churches: Secondary school pupils' attitudes towards Christianity. *British Journal of Religious Education, 11*, 76–86.

Francis, L. J. (1989c). Monitoring changing attitudes towards Christianity among secondary school pupils between 1974 and 1986. *British Journal of Educational Psychology, 59*, 86–91.

Francis, L. J. (1990). The religious significance of denominational identity among eleven year old children in England. *Journal of Christian Education, 97*, 23–28.

Francis, L. J. (1991). Personality and attitude towards religion among adult churchgoers in England. *Psychological Reports, 69*, 791–794.

Francis, L. J. (1992a). Is psychoticism really the dimension of personality fundamental to religiosity? *Personality and Individual Differences, 13*, 645–652.

Francis, L. J. (1992b). Monitoring attitude towards Christianity: The 1990 study. *British Journal of Religious Education, 14*, 178–182.

Francis, L. J. (1993). Personality and religion among college students in the UK. *Personality and Individual Differences, 14*, 619–622.

Francis, L. J. (1998). The relationship between intelligence and religiosity among 15 to 16 year olds. *Mental Health, Religion and Culture, 1*, 185–196.

Francis, L. J. (1999). Personality and attitude toward Christianity among undergraduates. *Journal of Research on Christian Education, 8*, 179–195.

Francis, L. J. (2001). Christianity and dogmatism revisited: A study among fifteen and sixteen year olds in the UK. *Religious Education, 96*, 211–226.

Francis, L. J. (2005). Gender role orientation and attitude toward Christianity: A study among older men and women in the United Kingdom. *Journal of Psychology and Theology, 33*, 179–186.

Francis, L. J. (2006). Attitude toward Christianity and premarital sex. *Psychological Reports, 98*, 140.

Francis, L. J., ap Siôn, T., Lewis, C. A., Robbins, M., & Barnes, L. P. (2006). Attitude toward Christianity and religious experience: Replication among 16- to 18-year-old adolescents in Northern Ireland. *Research in Education, 76*, 56–61.

Francis, L. J., & Bennett, G. A. (1992). Personality and religion among female drug misusers. *Drug and Alcohol Dependence, 30*, 27–31.

Francis, L. J., & Bourke, R. (2003). Personality and religion: Applying Cattell's model among secondary school pupils. *Current Psychology, 22*, 125–137.

Francis, L. J., & Carter, M. (1980). Church aided secondary schools, religious education as an examination subject and pupil attitude towards religion. *British Journal of Educational Psychology, 50*, 297–300.

Francis, L. J., & Enger, T. (2002). The Norwegian translation of the Francis Scale of Attitude toward Christianity. *Scandinavian Journal of Psychology, 43*, 363–367.

Francis, L. J., & Fearn, M. (1999). Religion and personality: A study among A-level students. *Transpersonal Psychology Review, 3*(2), 26–30.

Francis, L. J., Fearn, M., & Lewis, C. A. (2005). The impact of personality and religion on attitudes toward alcohol among 16–18 year olds in Northern Ireland. *Journal of Religion and Health, 44*, 267–289.

Francis, L. J., Fulljames, P., & Gibson, H. M. (1992). Does creationism commend the gospel? a developmental study among 11–17 year olds. *Religious Education, 87*, 19–27.

Francis, L. J., & Gibson, H. M. (1992). Popular religious television and adolescent attitudes towards Christianity. In J. Astley & D. V. Day (Eds.), *The contours of Christian education* (pp. 369–381). Great Wakering: McCrimmons.

Francis, L. J., & Gibson, H. M. (1993a). Television, pop culture and the drift from Christianity during adolescence. *British Journal of Religious Education, 15*, 31–37.

Francis, L. J., & Gibson, H. M. (1993b). Parental influence and adolescent religiosity: A study of church attendance and attitude towards Christianity among 11–12 and 15–16 year olds. *International Journal for the Psychology of Religion, 3*, 241–253.

Francis, L. J., & Gibson, H. M. (2001). Growing up Catholic in a Scottish city: The relationship between denominational identity, denominational schools, and attitude toward Christianity among eleven to fifteen year olds. *Catholic Education: A Journal of Inquiry and Practice, 5*, 39–54.

Francis, L. J., Gibson, H. M., & Fulljames, P. (1990). Attitude towards Christianity, creationism, scientism and interest in science. *British Journal of Religious Education, 13*, 4–17.

Francis, L. J., Gibson, H. M., & Lankshear, D. W. (1991). The influence of Protestant Sunday Schools on attitudes towards Christianity among 11–15 year olds in Scotland. *British Journal of Religious Education, 14*, 35–42.

Francis, L. J., & Greer, J. E. (1990). Catholic schools and adolescent religiosity in Northern Ireland: Shaping moral values. *Irish Journal of Education, 24*, 40–47.

Francis, L. J., & Greer, J. E. (1993). The contribution of religious experience to Christian development: A study among fourth, fifth and sixth year pupils in Northern Ireland. *British Journal of Religious Education, 15*, 38–43.

Francis, L. J., & Greer, J. E. (1999). Attitude toward Christianity among secondary pupils in Northern Ireland: Persistence of denominational differences? *British Journal of Religious Education, 21*, 175–180.

Francis, L. J., & Greer, J. E. (2001). Shaping adolescents' attitudes toward science and religion in Northern Ireland: The role of scientism, creationism and denominational schools. *Research in Science and Technological Education, 19*, 39–53.

Francis, L. J., & Hermans, C. A. M. (2000). Internal consistency reliability and construct validity of the Dutch translation of the Francis scale of Attitude toward Christianity among adolescents. *Psychological Reports, 86*, 301–307.

Francis, L. J., Ispas, D., Robbins, M., Ilie, A., & Iliescu, D. (2009). The Romanian translation of the Francis Scale of Attitude toward Christianity: Internal reliability, re-test reliability and construct validity among undergraduate students within a Greek Orthodox culture. *Pastoral Psychology, 58*, 49–54.

Francis, L. J., Jones, S. H., & Wilcox, C. (1997). Religiosity and dimensions of psychological well-being among 16–19 year olds. *Journal of Christian Education, 40*(1), 15–20.

Francis, L. J., Jones, S. H., & Wilcox, C. (2000). Religiosity and happiness: During adolescence, young adulthood and later life. *Journal of Psychology and Christianity, 19*, 245–257.

Francis, L. J., & Katz, Y. J. (2002). Religiosity and happiness: A study among Israeli female undergraduates. *Research in the Social Scientific Study of Religion, 13*, 75–86.

Francis, L. J., & Katz, Y. J. (2007). Measuring attitude toward Judaism: The internal consistency reliability of the Katz-Francis Scale of Attitude toward Judaism. *Mental Health, Religion and Culture, 10*, 309–324.

Francis, L. J., Katz, Y. J., Yablon, Y., & Robbins, M. (2004). Religiosity, personality and happiness: A study among Israeli male undergraduates. *Journal of Happiness Studies, 5*, 315–333.

Francis, L. J., & Kerr, S. (2003). Personality and religion among secondary school pupils in South Africa in the early 1990s. *Religion and Theology: A Journal of Contemporary Religious Discourse, 10*, 224–236.

Francis, L. J., & Kwiran, M. (1999). Personality and religion among secondary pupils in Germany, *Panorama, 11*, 34–44.

Francis, L. J., Lankshear, D. W., & Pearson, P. R. (1989). The relationship between religiosity and the short form JEPQ (JEPQ-S) indices of E, N, L and P among eleven year olds. *Personality and Individual Differences, 10*, 763–769.

Francis, L. J., & Lester, D. (1997). Religion, personality and happiness. *Journal of Contemporary Religion, 12*, 81–86.

Francis, L. J., Lewis, J. M., Brown, L. B., Philipchalk, R., & Lester, D. (1995). Personality and religion among undergraduate students in the United Kingdom, United States, Australia and Canada. *Journal of Psychology and Christianity, 14*, 250–262.

Francis, L. J., Lewis, C. A., & Ng, P. (2002). Assessing attitude toward Christianity among adolescents in Hong Kong: The Francis scale. *North American Journal of Psychology, 4,* 431–440.

Francis, L. J., Lewis, C. A., & Ng, P. (2003). Psychological health and attitude toward Christianity among secondary school pupils in Hong Kong. *Journal of Psychology in Chinese Societies, 4,* 231–245.

Francis, L. J., & Montgomery, A. (1992). Personality and attitudes towards Christianity among eleven to sixteen year old girls in a single sex Catholic school. *British Journal of Religious Education, 14,* 114–119.

Francis, L. J., & Pearson, P. R. (1985a). Psychoticism and religiosity among 15 year olds. *Personality and Individual Differences, 6,* 397–398.

Francis, L. J., & Pearson, P. R. (1985b). Extraversion and religiosity. *Journal of Social Psychology, 125,* 269–270.

Francis, L. J., & Pearson, P. R. (1987). Empathic development during adolescence: Religiosity, the missing link? *Personality and Individual Differences, 8,* 145–148.

Francis, L. J., & Pearson, P. R. (1988). Religiosity and the short-scale EPQ-R indices of E, N and L, compared with the JEPI, JEPQ and EPQ. *Personality and Individual Differences, 9,* 653–657.

Francis, L. J., & Pearson, P. R. (1991). Religiosity, gender and the two faces of neuroticism. *Irish Journal of Psychology, 12,* 60–68.

Francis, L. J., Pearson, P. R., Carter, M., & Kay, W. K. (1981a). The relationship between neuroticism and religiosity among English 15- and 16-year olds. *Journal of Social Psychology, 114,* 99–102.

Francis, L. J., Pearson, P. R., Carter, M., & Kay, W. K. (1981b). Are introverts more religious? *British Journal of Social Psychology, 20,* 101–104.

Francis, L. J., Pearson, P. R., & Kay, W. K. (1983a). Neuroticism and religiosity among English school children. *Journal of Social Psychology, 121,* 149–150.

Francis, L. J., Pearson, P. R., & Kay, W. K. (1983b). Are introverts still more religious? *Personality and Individual Differences, 4,* 211–212.

Francis, L. J., Pearson, P. R., & Lankshear, D. W. (1990). The relationship between social class and attitude towards Christianity among ten and eleven year old children. *Personality and Individual Differences, 11,* 1019–1027.

Francis, L. J., & Robbins, M. (2000). Religion and happiness: A study in empirical theology. *Transpersonal Psychology Review, 4*(2), 17–22.

Francis, L. J., & Robbins, M. (2003). Christianity and dogmatism among undergraduate students.*Journal of Beliefs and Values, 24,* 89–95.

Francis, L. J., Robbins, M., Lewis, C. A., Quigley, C. F., & Wheeler, C. (2004). Religiosity and general health among undergraduate students: A response to O'Connor, Cobb and O'Connor (2003). *Personality and Individual Differences, 37,* 485–494.

Francis, L. J., Robbins, M., Santosh, R., & Bhanot, S. (2008). Religion and mental health among Hindu young people in England. *Mental Health, Religion and Culture, 11,* 341–347.

Francis, L. J., Robbins, M., & White, A. (2003). Correlation between religion and happiness: A replication. *Psychological Reports, 92,* 51–52.

Francis, L. J., Sahin, A., & Al-Failakawi, F. (2008). Psychometric properties of two Islamic measures among young adults in Kuwait: The Sahin–Francis Scale of Attitude toward Islam and the Sahin Index of Islamic Moral Values. *Journal of Muslim Mental Health, 3,* 9–24.

Francis, L. J., Santosh, R., Robbins, M., & Vij, S. (2008). Assessing attitude toward Hinduism: The Santosh-Francis Scale. *Mental Health, Religion and Culture, 11,* 609–621.

Francis, L. J., & Wilcox, C. (1996). Religion and gender orientation. *Personality and Individual Differences, 20,* 119–121.

Francis, L. J., & Wilcox, C. (1998). Religiosity and femininity: Do women really hold a more positive attitude toward Christianity? *Journal for the Scientific Study of Religion, 37,* 462–469.

Francis, L. J., Ziebertz, H.-G., & Lewis, C. A. (2002). The psychometric properties of the Francis Scale of Attitude toward Christianity among German students. *Panorama, 14,* 153–162.

Francis, L. J., Ziebertz, H.-G., & Lewis, C. A. (2003). The relationship between religion and happiness among German students. *Pastoral Psychology, 51*, 273–281.
French, S., & Joseph, S. (1999). Religiosity and its association with happiness, purpose in life, and self-actualisation. *Mental Health, Religion and Culture, 2*, 117–120.
Freud, S. (1950). *The future of an illusion*. New Haven: Yale University Press.
Fulljames, P. (1996). Science, creation and Christianity: A further look. In L. J. Francis, W. K. Kay, & W. S. Campbell (Eds.), *Research in religious education* (pp. 257–260). Leominster: Gracewing.
Fulljames, P., & Francis, L. J. (1987). Creationism and student attitudes towards science and Christianity. *Journal of Christian Education, 90*, 51–55.
Fulljames, P., & Francis, L. J. (2003). Creationism among people in Kenya and Britain. In S. Coleman & L. Carlin (Eds.), *The cultures of creationism: Anti-evolutionism in English-speaking countries* (pp. 165–173). Aldershot: Ashgate.
Fulljames, P., Gibson, H. M., & Francis, L. J. (1991). Creationism, scientism, Christianity and science: A study in adolescent attitudes. *British Educational Research Journal, 17*, 171–190.
Gibson, H. M. (1989). Attitudes to religion and science among school children aged 11 to 16 years in a Scottish city. *Journal of Empirical Theology, 2*, 5–26.
Gibson, H. M., Francis, L. J., & Pearson, P. R. (1990). The relationship between social class and attitude towards Christianity among fourteen and fifteen year old adolescents. *Personality and Individual Differences, 11*, 631–635.
Gillings, V., & Joseph, S. (1996). Religiosity and social desirability: Impression management and self-deceptive positivity. *Personality and Individual Differences, 21*, 1047–1050.
Greer, J. E. (1981). Religious attitudes and thinking in Belfast pupils. *Educational Research, 23*, 177–189.
Greer, J. E. (1982). Growing up in Belfast: A study of religious development. *Collected Original Resources in Education, 6*(1), fiche 1, A14.
Greer, J. E. (1985). Viewing "the other side" in Northern Ireland: Openness and attitudes to religion among Catholic and Protestant adolescents. *Journal for the Scientific Study of Religion, 24*, 275–292.
Greer, J. E., & Francis, L. J. (1990). The religious profile of pupils in Northern Ireland: A comparative study of pupils attending Catholic and Protestant secondary schools. *Journal of Empirical Theology, 3*, 35–50.
Greer, J. E., & Francis, L. J. (1992). Religious experience and attitude towards Christianity among secondary school children in Northern Ireland. *Journal of Social Psychology, 132*, 277–279.
Hills, P., & Argyle, M. (1998a). Musical and religious experiences and their relationship to happiness. *Personality and Individual Differences, 25*, 91–102.
Hills, P., & Argyle, M. (1998b). Positive moods derived from leisure and their relationship to happiness and personality. *Personality and Individual Differences, 25*, 523–535.
Jones, D. L. (1997). *Measuring the dimensions of religion: The Batson and Ventis scales*. Unpublished master's dissertation, Westminster College, Oxford.
Jones, S. H., & Francis, L. J. (1996). Religiosity and self-esteem during childhood and adolescence. In L. J. Francis, W. K. Kay, & W. S. Campbell (Eds.), *Research in religious education* (pp. 189–206). Leominster: Fowler Wright Books.
Jones, S. H., & Francis, L. J. (1999). Personality type and attitude toward Christianity among student churchgoers. *Journal of Beliefs and Values, 20*, 105–109.
Jorm, A. F. (1987). Sex differences in neuroticism: A quantitative synthesis of published research. *Australian and New Zealand Journal of Psychiatry, 21*, 501–506.
Joseph, S., & Diduca, D. (2001). Schizotypy and religiosity in 13–18 year old school pupils. *Mental Health, Religion and Culture, 4*, 63–69.
Joseph, S., & Lewis, C. A. (1997). The Francis Scale of Attitude towards Christianity: Intrinsic or extrinsic religiosity? *Psychological Reports, 80*, 609–610.

Jung, C. G. (1938). *Psychology and religion*. New Haven: Yale University Press.
Kay, W. K. (1981a). Psychoticism and attitude to religion. *Personality and Individual Differences, 2*, 249–252.
Kay, W. K. (1981b). Conversion among 11–15 year olds. *Spectrum, 13*(2), 26–33.
Kay, W. K. (1981c). Marital happiness and children's attitudes to religion. *British Journal of Religious Education, 3*, 102–105.
Kay, W. K. (1981d). Syllabuses and attitudes to Christianity. *The Irish Catechist, 5*(2), 16–21.
Kay, W. K. (1981e). Subject preference and attitude to religion in secondary schools. *Educational Review, 33*, 47–51.
Kay, W. K., & Francis, L. J. (1996). *Drift from the churches: Attitude toward Christianity during childhood and adolescence*. Cardiff: University of Wales Press.
Kay, W. K., Francis, L. J., & Gibson, H. M. (1996). Attitude toward Christianity and the transition to formal operational thinking. *British Journal of Religious Education, 19*, 45–55.
Koenig, H. G., McCullough, M. E., & Larson, D. B. (2001). *Handbook of religion and health*. New York: Oxford University Press.
Lester, D., & Francis, L. J. (1993). Is religiosity related to suicidal ideation after personality and mood are taken into account? *Personality and Individual Differences, 15*, 591–592.
Lewis, C. A. (1994). Religiosity and obsessionality: The relationship between Freud's "religious practices". *Journal of Psychology, 128*, 189–196.
Lewis, C. A. (1996). Religiosity and obsessionality. In L. J. Francis, W. K. Kay, & W. S. Campbell (Eds.), *Research in religious education* (pp. 219–227). Leominster: Gracewing.
Lewis, C. A. (1998). Towards a clarification of the association between religiosity and life satisfaction. *Journal of Beliefs and Values, 19*, 119–122.
Lewis, C. A. (1999). Is the relationship between religiosity and personality "contaminated" by social desirability as assessed by the lie scale? A methodological reply to Michael W. Eysenck (1998). *Mental Health, Religion and Culture, 2*, 105–114.
Lewis, C. A. (2000). The religiosity-psychoticism relationship and the two factors of social desirability: A response to Michael W. Eysenck (1999). *Mental Health, Religion and Culture, 3*, 39–45.
Lewis, C. A., & Francis, L. J. (2000). Personality and religion among female university students in France. *International Journal of Psychology, 35*, 229.
Lewis, C. A., & Francis, L. J. (2003). Evaluer l'attitude d'étudiantes universitaires françaises à l'égard du Christianisme: L'Echelle de Francis. *Sciences Pastorals, 22*, 179–190.
Lewis, C. A., & Joseph, S. (1994). Religiosity: Psychoticism and obsessionality in Northern Irish university students. *Personality and Individual Differences, 17*, 685–687.
Lewis, C. A., Joseph, S., & Noble, K. E. (1996). Is religiosity associated with life satisfaction? *Psychological Reports, 79*, 429–430.
Lewis, C. A., & Maltby, J. (1992). Religiosity and preoedipal fixation: A refinement. *Journal of Psychology, 126*, 687–688.
Lewis, C. A., & Maltby, J. (1994). Religious attitudes and obsessional personality traits among UK adults. *Psychological Reports, 75*, 353–354.
Lewis, C. A., & Maltby, J. (1995a). Religiosity and personality among US adults. *Personality and Individual Differences, 18*, 293–295.
Lewis, C. A., & Maltby, J. (1995b). Religious attitude and practice: The relationship with obsessionality. *Personality and Individual Differences, 19*, 105–108.
Lewis, C. A., & Maltby, J. (2000). Conservatism and attitude toward Christianity. *Personality and Individual Differences, 29*, 793–798.
Maltby, J. (1995). Is there a denominational difference in scores on the Francis scale of attitude towards Christianity among Northern Irish adults? *Psychological Reports, 76*, 88–90.
Maltby, J. (1997a). Personality correlates of religiosity among adults in the Republic of Ireland. *Psychological Reports, 81*, 827–831.
Maltby, J. (1997b). Obsessional personality traits: The association with attitudes toward Christianity and religious puritanism. *Journal of Psychology, 131*, 675–677.

Maltby, J., & Day, L. (1998). Amending a measure of the Quest Religious Orientation: Applicability of the scale's use among religious and non-religious persons. *Personality and Individual Differences, 25*, 517–522.

Maltby, J., & Lewis, C. A. (1996). Measuring intrinsic and extrinsic orientation toward religion: Amendments for its use among religious and non-religious samples. *Personality and Individual Differences, 21*, 937–946.

Maltby, J., & Lewis, C. A. (1997). The reliability and validity of a short scale of attitude toward Christianity among USA, English, Republic of Ireland and Northern Ireland adults. *Personality and Individual Differences, 22*, 649–654.

Maltby, J., McCollam, P., & Millar, D. (1994). Religiosity and obsessionality: A refinement. *Journal of Psychology, 128*, 609–611.

Munayer, S. J. (2000). *The ethnic identity of Palestinian Arab Christian adolescents in Israel.* Unpublished doctoral thesis, University of Wales (Oxford Centre for Mission Studies).

O'Keeffe, B. (1992). A look at the Christian schools movement. In B. Watson (Ed.), *Priorities in religious education* (pp. 92–112). London: Falmer Press.

O'Keeffe, B. (1996), Christian children at school: Their religious beliefs and practices. In L. J. Francis, W. K. Kay, & W. S. Campbell (Eds.), *Research in religious education*. Leominster: Gracewing.

Pearson, P. R., Francis, L. J., & Lightbown, T. J. (1986). Impulsivity and religiosity. *Personality and Individual Differences, 7*, 89–94.

Rhymer, J., & Francis, L. J. (1985). Roman Catholic secondary schools in Scotland and pupil attitude towards religion. *Lumen Vitae, 40*, 103–110.

Robbins, M., & Francis, L. J. (1996). Are religious people happier? A study among undergraduates. In L. J. Francis, W. K. Kay, & W. S. Campbell (Eds.), *Research in religious education* (pp. 207–217). Leominster: Gracewing.

Robbins, M., Francis, L. J., & Gibbs, D. (1995). Personality and religion: A study among 8–11 year olds. *Journal of Beliefs and Values, 16*(1), 1–6.

Rocklin, T., & Revelle, W. (1981). The measurement of extraversion: A comparison of the Eysenck personality inventory and the Eysenck personality questionnaire. *British Journal of Social Psychology, 20*, 279–284.

Roman, R. E., & Lester, D. (1999). Religiosity and mental health. *Psychological Reports, 85*, 1088.

Sahin, A., & Francis, L. J. (2002). Assessing attitude toward Islam among Muslim adolescents: The psychometric properties of the Sahin-Francis scale. *Muslim Education Quarterly, 19*(4), 35–47.

Schludermann, E. H., Schludermann, S. M., & Huynh, C.-L. (2000). Religiosity, prosocial values, and adjustment among students in Catholic high schools in Canada. *Journal of Beliefs and Values, 21*, 99–115.

Schludermann, E. H., Schludermann, S. M., Needham, D., & Mulenga, M. (2001). Fear of rejection versus religious commitment as predictors of adjustment among Reformed and Evangelical college students in Canada. *Journal of Beliefs and Values, 22*, 209–224.

Shuter-Dyson, R. (2000). Profiling music students: Personality and religiosity. *Psychology of Music, 28*, 190–196.

Tiliopoulos, N., & Francis, L. J. (in press). The internal consistency reliability and construct validity of the Santosh-Francis Scale of Attitude toward Hinduism among students in India.

Tjeltveit, A. C., Fiordalisi, A. M., & Smith, C. (1996). Relationships among mental health values and various dimensions of religiousness. *Journal of Social and Clinical Psychology, 15*, 364–377.

Vine, I. (1978). Facts and values in the psychology of religion. *Bulletin of the British Psychological Society, 31*, 414–417.

White, J., Joseph, S., & Neil, A. (1995). Religiosity, psychoticism, and schizotypal traits. *Personality and Individual Differences, 19*, 847–851.

Wilcox, C., & Francis, L. J. (1997). Personality and religion among A level religious studies students. *International Journal of Children's Spirituality, 1*(2), 48–56.

Williams, E., Francis, L. J., & Robbins, M. (2006). Attitude toward Christianity and paranormal belief among 13- to 16-year-old students, *Psychological Reports, 99*, 266.

Williams, E., Robbins, M., & Francis, L. J. (2005). When introverts ceased to be more religious: A study among 12- to 16-year-old pupils. *Journal of Beliefs and Values, 26*, 77–79.

Youtika, A., Joseph, S., & Diduca, D. (1999). Personality and religiosity in a Greek Christian Orthodox sample. *Mental Health, Religion and Culture, 2*, 71–74.

Biographical details

The Revd Canon Professor Leslie J Francis is Professor of Religions and Education at the University of Warwick, UK

Chapter 9
Social, Religious and Spiritual Capitals: A Psychological Perspective

Chris Baker

Abstract This article locates the concept of social capital and its faith-based correlates—religious and spiritual capital—within a psychological framework. Up to now, these correlates have been deployed primarily within a social policy and political science discourse. Having located these concepts, the article develops a hypothesis, based on qualitative case study material, that religiously based motivation (spiritual capital) and religiously based participation (religious capital) work in mutually reinforcing ways to produce a virtuous cycle (or feedback loop) of capitals (including bridging and linking forms of capital—as well as bonding).

The psychological dimensions of spiritual capital are typologised and then linked to a series of theological motifs and words that appear to trigger these psychological states. These psycho-theological motifs are then further examined for their potential contribution to what Donal Dorr refers to as a "balanced spirituality", which sees the possibility of change and transformation at a number of levels (including the social/political) and which also corresponds to classic understandings of the beneficial impact of social capital at micro, meso and macro levels (see Halpen and Putnam). The article concludes by linking this typologising to existing models of psychology of religion and measurement systems (e.g. Fisher, Allport and Ross) before raising some critical questions about the dominance of the capital paradigm as a sufficiently nuanced tool by which to evaluate the nature and psychological impact of faith-based engagement in civil society.

Introduction

The aim of this chapter is to locate the growing interest in the concept of social capital, and its "faith"-based correlates—religious capital and spiritual capital—within a specifically psychological framework. This is an underdeveloped use of capital theory, since the predominant deployment of social, spiritual and religious capital

---

C. Baker (✉)
William Temple Foundation, Luther King House, Brighton Grove, Rusholme, Manchester M14 5JP, UK
e-mails: chris.baker@wtf.org.uk; christopher.baker@manchester.ac.uk

has been in the political science and social policy fields. For example, within a UK context, notions of capital have been used to position the usefulness of "faith" in respect to a number of pressing political issues, including social cohesion, poverty and other multiple forms of exclusion. A "remoralising" Britain agenda is also emerging whereby faith groups are being encouraged by government to take a lead in promoting a set of common values to which all sections of an increasingly diverse and post-secular society can subscribe (see, for example, Lowndes & Chapman, 2005). This approach has been critiqued as a "functionalist" or "instrumentalist" approach to religion which tends to see faith groups as "repositories" of values and resources to be given freely (or at least more cheaply) to wider civil society (see Dinham, Furbey, & Lowndes, 2009).

Having outlined the current debate regarding definitions and applications of the concepts of social religious and spiritual capitals, I will then focus on qualitative research undertaken by the William Temple Foundation (WTF) in partnership with the Church Urban Fund with nine contrasting church groups (in terms of size and theological identity) engaging with civil renewal and urban regeneration in key redevelopment sites in the Northern English city of Manchester.[1] The main purpose of this approach is to highlight the new perspectives being brought to bear on the connection between spiritual/religious motivation and engagement in wider civil society by focusing on the relationship between theological tropes and psychological "triggers". This relationship appears to set up a virtuous cycle of "capital" production whereby theological motivations are interpreted by church members as provoking certain types of public engagement, the experience of which reinforces in turn feelings of happiness, belonging, usefulness, etc. The mechanisms for this virtuous feedback loop between "faith" and "action" will be explicated in terms of the link between religious and spiritual capital.

I will then attempt to theorise further on these Manchester case studies with reference to some psychology of religion, economic and spiritual growth literatures before offering a critical evaluation of the effectiveness of "capital" language to describe some of the psychological dimensions associated with spiritual and religious motivation and practice.

Mapping the "Capitals" Theoretical Terrain

Social, Religious and Spiritual Capitals—An Increased Foregrounding Social Capital

Academic and policy-based research into the nature and impact of social capital has mushroomed exponentially since the late 1980s. The chief exponents associated with its re-emergence in the last 20 years or so are Loury (1987), Coleman (1988), Woolcock (1988) and Bourdieu (1992). However, it is the work of political scientist Robert Putnam (2000) which has given the concept of social capital its most recent pre-eminence because of his thesis outlining the decline of social capital that is coinciding with the era of the neo-liberal globalisation. Although he traces the initial decline of social capital to the 1960s and the acquisition of a consumerist mentality by the "baby boomers" generation, he also implicates the growth of home-based entertainment systems and the pressure of wider patterns of mobility and longer working hours consistent with neo-liberal globalisation in the decline of American associations such as bowling clubs, trades unions, the family, Parent Teacher Associations. US churches are also declining albeit at a slower rate and within a more complex scenario (i.e. some dimensions of church life are in decline; some are on the increase). His thesis, therefore, backed up by a formidable battery of empirical social indicators, plays well into the overall social policy agenda of many European states who are also fearful of the erosion of public life and the decline of civil society (including common values) under the onslaught of large social upheavals generated by globalised capitalism.

In terms of definition of key terms therefore, and using Putnam as an authoritative source, social capital refers to "Features of social life—networks, norms and trust—that enable participants to act together more effectively to pursue shared objectives ..... Social capital, in short, refers to social connections and the attendant norms and trust." (Putnam, 2000, p. 22)

Emerging from this broad definition of social capital, Putnam identifies two different types of capital. *Bonding* social capital is a dense layering of norms and trust that is found in homogenous groups and tends to reinforce exclusivity and homogeneity. This type of capital "undergirds reciprocity and mobilises solidarity" and acts as a "kind of sociological superglue" in maintaining strong in-group loyalty and promoting robust identity (Putnam, 2000, p. 25). *Bridging* social capital occurs when individuals or groups manage to form linkages with groups different to themselves (i.e. more heterogeneous relationships), thus creating new spaces where power, information and communication can be shared. Putnam suggests that societies need this form of social capital to enhance productivity, creativity, new learning and diversity within society which would otherwise remain in fragmented and distinctive groupings. Thus he refers to bridging social capital as a form of "sociological WD 40" (Putnam, 2000, p. 25).

Putnam's original distinctions were later expanded by Michael Woolcock (2001) who added a third type of capital—*linking* capital which specifically addresses the power differentials within society and allows more marginal groups to link with the resources of more powerful groups (i.e. capital, information, knowledge, secondments) as a way of beginning to address the asymmetrical nature of power and influence in civil society.

Putnam's thesis of the decline of social capital in the United States, his typologies and his statistical methodology have had a profound impact on UK government social policy, amplified by other themes and dynamics specific to the UK. These include: the serious rioting apparently based on ethnic and religious lines in the Northern English cities and towns in 2000; the impact of both 9/11 and 7/7 on UK relations between government, secular and religious groups and especially the rise in Islamophobia; and the rise of the far-right British National Party (BNP) in local communities and the increased influx of both EU and non-EU workers into the

UK economy. These factors have combined to make the theme of social cohesion a key political and social policy priority, together with the search for a common set of British values to which both secular-based and faith/ethnic-based sectors can subscribe.

The increasingly complex and pressing socio-political agenda also largely explains the parallel growth in interest in concepts of religious and spiritual capitals, which has grown significantly within the last 5 years in both UK and US contexts. As I have already inferred, faith groups are increasingly seen by government as repositories of values and resources (for example, buildings, volunteers, paid sector workers, embedded community presences) to be used in the development of locally strong civil societies, a development which requires partnership working with other agencies, and therefore the need for religious literacy to help non-faith-based partners understand the distinctive aims and methods that faith groups bring to civil society. Thus the discourse of religious and spiritual capitals (as part of the ongoing debate about the nature and importance of social capital in general) has also arisen to meet this need.

We Now Move to Some Key Definitions of the Terms in Question

Spiritual Capital

This part of the social capital field is potentially the most widely theorised, not least because of the amount of money invested in researching it—for example, the $3 million Templeton Foundation research programme delivered by the Metanexus Institute entitled *The Spiritual Capital Research Network*. Current working definitions of spiritual capital range from the generic to the more culturally specific. An example of the former would be, "construed to refer to that aspect of social capital linked with religion and/or spirituality ... spiritual capital might be a subset of social capital [and is therefore] the effects of spiritual and religious practices, beliefs, networks and institutions that have a measurable impact on individuals, communities and societies". The breadth of this definition, whilst inclusive, is also imprecise, a feature that Iannaccone and Klick (2003) acknowledge is symptomatic of the concept of spirituality itself. The notion of spirituality, they assert, sidesteps negative images frequently associated with institutional religion, but is also elastic and popular enough to apply to existing traditional religions as well as new religions and a range of non-religious activities deemed virtuous or therapeutic. Meanwhile, an example of a more specific definition devised by Berger and Hefner as part of the Metanexus programme in a paper entitled *Social, Human and Spiritual Capital in Economic Development* describes spiritual capital as "referring to the power, influence, knowledge and dispositions created by participation in a particular religious tradition" (Berger & Hefner, 2003, p. 3).

Religious Capital (Including Religious Spiritual Capital)

A key exponent of the concept of religious capital is Pierre Bourdieu who sees it as functioning in a similar way to cultural capital, i.e. institutionalised specialists guard and maintain a "deliberately organised corpus of secret knowledge" whose knowledge of the religious field is translated into power as measured by the ability "to modify, in a deep and lasting fashion the practice and worldview of lay people" (Bourdieu, 1987, p. 127). Bourdieu's notion of religious capital is also closely linked to his idea of the habitus—the field of human religious and cultural activity that stands in between the theoretical structures and the every day action of life or the history of a community. Thus for Bourdieu, religious capital is the amount of knowledge and practice pertaining to the religious *cultus* one can bring to bear, and this knowledge and practice determine one's hierarchical status in the religious field.

Building somewhat on Bourdieu's understandings of religious capital other theorists have also added dimension of the human capital debate (initiated by the American economist Gary Becker (1964)) to suggest that religious capital is comprised of patterns of belief and behaviour repeated over the life cycle and between generations that influence current beliefs and behaviour. Iannaccone (1990), for example, formulates religious capital as a by-product of religious activity. He does not extrapolate how these personal or familial dimensions of religious capital can be transferred to a social or political dimension, but Starke and Finke (2000) and Smidt (2004) have attempted to do this more recently. Smidt, for example, in an edited collection of essays under the same title, uses the concept of "religious social capital" to describe the multifarious ways in which churches contribute to American civil society and political processes. He writes, "This volume [focuses] on a particular kind of social capital—social capital that is tied to religious life—and the kind of consequences that flow from its presence ... and our understanding of the complexity and richness of the interplay among religion, social capital and democratic life" (Smidt, 2004, p. 211).

Definitions of Spiritual and Religious Capitals (as Used in This Chapter)

For the purposes of this chapter we shall be using the definitions emerging from UK-based research which will feature later in this chapter. The William Temple Foundation, aware of previous working definitions but also having conducted in-depth qualitative research with a wide variety of Christian faith communities engaged in civil renewal and urban regeneration in Manchester, suggested the following as related but also distinctive concepts. Religious capital is "the practical contribution to local and national life made by faith groups" (Baker & Skinner, 2006, p. 9). Spiritual capital on the other hand, "energises religious capital by providing a theological identity and worshipping tradition, but also a value system, moral vision and a basis for faith" (Baker & Skinner, 2006, p. 9). Spiritual capital is often embedded locally within faith groups but also expressed in the lives of individuals.² In other words, what is being suggested here is that a virtual cycle of capital production can occur when values and theological motivation are connected to practical action.

WTF's definition of spiritual capital also stresses the "why" of spiritual or religious-based participation, not simply the "how". This emphasis on the why (i.e. the values, ethics and ethos that drive the praxis of a community or organisation) not only helps deepen the somewhat functionalist discourse on the engagement of faith groups within civil and secular society, but also emphasises the psychological dimensions to participation which all too often get ignored within official public policy. With the concern for motivations and the "why" factor firmly to the fore, I now move onto a consideration of the psychological perspectives of social, religious and spiritual capitals.

Psychological Perspectives on Social, Religious and Spiritual Capitals

Close linguistic examination of the qualitative data generated by the WTF research project shows a broad typology of different levels of psychological response. Within this broad, threefold structure a number of what I call trigger motifs can be identified, which appear to "trigger" sets of ever-deepening and more complex psychological response. These motifs not only correspond to affective words such as "love", "care", "acceptance", but are also linked to theological themes (which will be examined following this section).

A Threefold Structure of Psychological Response

Psychological features of responses from members belonging to church communities engaged in civil and urban regeneration in Manchester could be collated broadly under three types of heading:

- the security and support associated with belonging to a cohesive, close-knit faith community including the power of communal narrative and memory;
- the security and motivational belief in a personal pattern or meaning for life with reference to a transcendent source of love/authority; and
- the motivational and inspirational belief that wider change and/or transformation is possible and that one is somehow part of that process of transformation.

Case studies from WTF's research to exemplify each type could include the following. Under the first category (i.e. belonging to a cohesive faith community):

> ... this church aims to reflect that Jesus receives everyone – regardless of what they have done, regardless of where they are, and the church is an open door that whenever they come they should feel *received and accepted*, and this is their *home*, they *belong* here and

whenever they're in need as a family, we'd like to extend an open door that when they come in they *feel comfortable* (Baker & Skinner, 2005, p. 77 – emphasis mine).

... the thing I talked about, the supporting of people who have times in their life that are very hard ... [the church] is such an *accepting* place to be, you know, *they will grieve with you*, but here's not much condemnation ... I don't want to come over like it's a utopian vision ... we have as much church politics as anywhere else, but there is a sense in which *people listen to each other* (Baker & Skinner, 2005, p. 55 – emphasis mine).

A further aspect of psychological impact associated with belonging to a faith community includes the sense of being incorporated into a wider narrative of community history, identity and belonging. For example:

And, I was talking to people at church saying... we have got to get across to people our beginnings – how we started, where we came from and hopefully where we are going (Baker & Skinner, 2005, p. 39).

What I've heard is that the Church started in one of the member's cellars and that's the place that they used to worship. One day one of the members saw a local church [building] being advertised [for sale] in the newspaper and the rest is history (Baker & Skinner, 2005, p. 39).

Under the second category (personal pattern or meaning from life with reference to a transcendent source), a number of interesting case studies emerge.

... last night my daughter rang me up and we ended up talking about God and the church and how things that happened to her didn't just happen like that, it must be God who is working through her ... during that discussion I said to her "Don't forget there's a Guardian Angel" ... according to the Psalm 90 there is a spirit of God within each and every human being ... each of us have a spirit of God keeping us ... whatever I do I like it to be known that I do something for God (Baker & Skinner, 2005, p. 73).

I always think he [God] is working with people ... my daughter's mother in law came for the first time a couple of weeks ago. I don't think she's ever set foot in a church in her life, and why she came I don't know ... And she came again on Sunday ... we're obviously doing something right. God's obviously working in her to make her want to come back. I mean he's sort of, he's obviously working in people; working in us as well as working in these newcomers for them to come and stay (Baker & Skinner, 2005, p. 73).

The next quotation comes from a priest whose church had decided to enter into a lifelong learning partnership with the local council as part of a national government initiative (Learn Direct) to provide high-quality post-16 learning for those with few skills and qualifications and therefore unlikely to participate in traditional forms of learning. The church hall was repeatedly burgled and church members even carjacked as local gangs stole computers and other equipments associated with the scheme. The church council made the decision to persist with the scheme despite the high levels of crime and abuse. The vicar of the church reflects:

you accept the suffering that you are involved with because there is something more important and better ... reality is what that means ... to take up our cross, but that that was what we as a Christian community were called to do. And I was very proud of them [the church council] because we did think about it and we did talk about it. But they were absolutely agreed that we had to do it again ... despite what the cost would be (Baker & Skinner, 2005, p. 47).

The wider point to be made concerning this range of quotations is that despite contrasting psychological moods of joy or despair, the notion that there is a pattern or meaning behind the events or experiences which trigger these moods is seen as a source of comfort and reassurance. Within a typology of congregational narratives devised by Hopewell some of these case studies (especially the last one) would fit into a *tragic* typology of story which is closely linked with the narrative of Christ's own passion. "When portrayed as tragic hero, Christ accepts the cross .... Those who follow the way of Christ live their lives tragically in the shadow of the cross. They suffer; they die to self and gain justification, only beyond, and through, Christ's death and their own" (Hopewell, 1987, p. 60). In other words, faith in the ultimate goodness of God not only makes sense (or justifies) life's suffering, but locates the present pain within a promise of ultimate reward (or in psychological terms perhaps, a form of delayed gratification).

Under the third category, a number of case studies emerge to show the direct motivational power of belief in the possibility of change and transformation that begins at a personal level, but also occurs at a transpersonal level, reaching into social and political structures at local, national and even international levels.

> I think it's a case of, I think, God's been stirring us, you know, individually and collectively ... we'll look around the community and these are the needs and that we need to do something about it. We can no longer stay within the four walls of the church (Baker & Skinner, 2005, p. 73)
>
> ... it's not just about what we can do for the community, but also recognising that all of the members of the congregation are members of this community, and the more that they feel empowered and validated by their membership of the church, the more they can take that home and live that everywhere else in this community and that's what it means to be salt or yeast or light... what I think I'm doing on a Sunday, is actually giving them a place to bring the brokenness that is so much part of this community, but also refreshing and renewing them and enabling them to take something of the might and glory of God out with them, and be able to share that with their neighbours (Baker & Skinner, 2005, p. 41).

However, to put some of these quotations into a more meaningful psychological context, it is important to locate them alongside key theological themes that were simultaneously expressed as underpinning the feelings and motives for the engagement expressed. I would like to extrapolate four theological themes which I think are important indicators into the psychological motives associated with spiritual and religious capitals.

Service, Hospitality, Self-Emptying

This cluster of themes is associated with the persistent allusion in WTF's interviews and focus groups of traditional biblical images such as the "beacon" (set upon the hill) and an "open door", "salt" and "yeast"—which themselves are symbolic shorthand for an unconditional hospitality verging on unconditional love in response to what is perceived as the foundational role model established by Christ in his own ministry, culminating in the ultimate act of reconciliation—namely his self-sacrifice on the Cross. In more modern academic parlance, the concept of unconditional hospitality is also reflected in terms of the importance of encountering the stranger or the Other (for example, Derrida, 1996; Levinas, 1969) who comes in the guise of the poor and the marginalised. This approach was particularly exemplified by a small and elderly congregation whose increasingly dilapidated building is at the epicentre of a regeneration area and whose premises had a compulsory purchase order placed on it. One church member describes the activities and ethos of the church community and its building thus:

> On Sunday we have a luncheon club, but that's for people who have a psychiatric illness, and that's once every month they come and have a meal, they cook it themselves in the church premises ... and we now have a club for the people who live alone or are lonely ... and they can meet on a Tuesday afternoon ... and they run the club themselves (Baker & Skinner, 2005, p. 54).

In addition to these opportunities, the church has received a small health grant to provide an open aromatherapy and reflexology session with a qualified practice nurse who sets her massage table up in the church's sanctuary. What appears to lie at the heart of this simple DIY philosophy is the principle of self-empowerment and simply producing an open space for local groups to use, without condition or a sense of the need to control. Amongst the "client group" who are drawn to these so-called "services" are the frail elderly, those suffering poor mental health, asylum seekers and refugees. What is offered in a remarkably effective way (because of its inclusive and non-threatening ambience) springs from a psychological motivation to seek a sense of pleasure and meaning through a form of altruism (or what in Christian terminology is often referred to as a self-emptying love) which appears to go to a deeper level of openness and access than that associated with more traditional community development projects.

Vocation

The theme of vocation as a psychological driver is also expressed in a variety of different ways. One is closely linked to the Parable of the Talents located in the New Testament (Matthew 25: 14–30) and the sayings of Jesus about the good tree bearing good fruit (e.g. Matthew 12: 33–37). Particularly within the black-majority churches (BMCs) who participated in the WTF research considerable psychological motivation for getting engaged with the wider community was generated by a sense of duty. This sense of duty was partly derived by the need, as quasi-independent churches, to be self-sufficient. But there was also a strong sense of pride that this sense of obligation with regard to how one deployed the resources of time and money was creating a surplus that could be "ploughed back" into the wider community for the benefit of the common good. One interviewee from a BMC, a second generation church member who had recently qualified as a lawyer, places this psychological motivation within its socio-economic context:

> A couple of decades ago, our area was made up of a majority of semi-skilled blue collar workers who struggled to make ends meet. Those same families now have children who

are white-collar professional workers like solicitors, lawyers, local government officials . . . all of whom are able to volunteer their services and sort of plough back into the wider community in terms of advising [people] with regards to maximising benefit entitlements, filling in forms, holding health and well-being workshops, counselling and so on (Baker & Skinner, 2005, p. 71).

Choosing the Narrower Road

This category is linked to vocation in the sense that as well as being called to serve others by a higher moral authority, one can also be called to exercise one's conscience in respect of prevailing cultural norms and expectations. The psychological gains associated with this strategy can be explained in terms of deriving a sense of identity and significance through being different, as well as a sense of wellbeing and satisfaction derived from the congruence between action and core belief—one is not in a position of having to deal with emotional or cognitive dissonance. Two examples from WTF's case studies show how a partial and negotiated withdrawal from social norms can lead to a successful reintegration of core beliefs and public identity. One case study involves a young member of a BMC who has volunteered to become a Street Pastor in Manchester, a scheme which seeks to engage with young people involved in gangs or other forms of violent street crime. The main purpose is "to be a listening ear and someone who can offer wise counsel and advice" and is predicated on the assumption that BMCs (from which most Street Pastors are drawn) are still sufficiently respected and engaged with disaffected black youth to have a positive influence. The opportunity for personal evangelism and prayer is not discounted, although "that is not the predominant underlying motive behind why Street Pastors is around". A serious dilemma for this black church member is the way the Street Pastors scheme has been seized upon by Greater Manchester Police and Manchester City Council, who see it as an effective way to reduce crime and "solve a lot of their crime-related problems". He continues, "My concern is . . . 'whose agenda is it?' How am I going to be perceived by people who are in gangs or whatever . . . is this person (i.e. himself) an informer?" The BMC member concludes, "There's a fine line between the social agenda and a pressing need that needs to be spoken out against and the agenda of the church which is preaching the gospel and making disciples of men" (Baker & Skinner, 2005, p. 58).

What is significant in this quote is the degree of discomfort experienced by this church member brought about by what he sees as the moral and political compromises being asked of him by engaging with secular authorities such as the police and local authorities. However, this psychological sense of discomfort does lead to withdrawal from the complexity of engagement in the public realm but paradoxically is a spur to a continuing but honest and critical assessment of the contradictory nature of faith-based capital in a secular, multi-disciplinary context.

This scenario is complemented by an analysis of engagement carried out by another Christian faith group, albeit one with a more liberal theology influenced by liberation theology and its neo-Marxist social critique. This particular faith-based organisation (FBO) runs a series of community-empowerment networks within marginalised communities in Manchester. The main purpose of these networks is to create a space for those local communities most affected by the trauma of rapid regeneration, whereby plans and documents can be properly understood and scrutinised, and strategies for engagement devised. This has led the FBO to develop a sustained critique of colonialisation which assesses the methods and impacts associated with swift and aggressive urban regeneration. Referring to the attitude of local residents towards a major regeneration figure, one member of the FBO wryly remarks:

> I describe it [i.e. regeneration] as a colonial process and I imply, within that, a kind of missionary dimension ... I don't mean this nastily, personally, but look at Mr X at the New Deal for Communities programme ... as a missionary kind of figure, you know, in all kinds of terms. The man has come to save this part of Manchester and the way the residents relate to him is like a priest in some respects, they defer to his wisdom. And he comes and resides at meetings, there's loads of imagery like that (Baker & Skinner, 2005, p. 76).

This development of this political critique reflects the appeal of the prophetic—the psychological pleasure derived from consciously going against the flow of perceived wisdom for the sake of a purer or at least more spiritually authentic tradition which sets itself against the wisdom of this world. One FBO member summarises this dynamic thus by deploying the common image attributed to Jesus in the Gospels (e.g. Mathew 7.8)—that of making the choice between the narrow and thus more challenging road or path that leads to salvation, over the broad and easy road chosen by the majority that leads to perdition. She says, "lest we go down the road that has been made for us, [which] appeared like a collusion or compromise" (Baker & Skinner, 2005, p. 74). Whilst not necessarily explicitly referring to the notions of judgement or salvation contained within the original text, the quotation nevertheless reflects the idea that the road of spiritual and moral integrity is the harder road to choose. The temptation for this FBO to collude with the regeneration sector's agenda (often based on the principles of bidding and competition) is reflected perhaps in the biblical allusion to walking the wide path of ease, comfort and status. This path, however, does not lead to true happiness or transformation. Thus related to the image of the "road less travelled" is that of the "martyr"—literally one who bears witness to the coming of the way of the Lord (e.g. Isaiah 40: 1–5). The FBO leader acknowledges wryly that when applied to his team, the concept has a double edge—being a "martyr to the cause" of working too hard and occasionally too obsessively on the issue of community empowerment, but also in the sense of being "about a witness, you know, if you go back to the origins of the word" (Baker & Skinner, 2005, p. 75). The concept of martyrdom is therefore another theological driver to explain the psychological motivation of religious capital—making a sacrifice (in this case, time, effort and nervous energy rather than actual death) for the sake of a noble cause, but also seeking (and possibly enjoying) the public attention that such a sacrifice can bring.

Being Channels of Grace

Several church members we researched alongside referred to the notion of the unconditional nature of God's love (found within various strands of the Judeo-Christian tradition) as a motivational factor behind their various activities aimed at reaching out into the wider community. Although some churches referred to the proselytising potential of some of these wider engagements, all were quite clear that the offering of more "bridging" forms of capital was offered for its own sake—an end in itself rather than a means to an end. The word or concept that emerged across the theological spectrum in relation to this kind of activity was that of grace. Creating "spaces" of grace was an opportunity to express compassion—a form of non-judgemental action based on ideas of solidarity, especially with those suffering most at the hands of poverty and multiple forms of exclusion:

> ... it's the God of love ... unconditional love ... and by having that approach then there's more room for grace as well. Because it's all about the grace of God, and because the fact that I'm in church doesn't make me any different, it's just that I'm a forgiven sinner. And it's only through the grace of God. So through love you're also expressing the grace (Baker & Skinner, 2005. p. 77).

This idea of grace removing the "barriers" associated with past mistakes is one which is profoundly liberative at a psychological level—especially if perceived as a "gift" from a transcendent force (i.e. God). Within Christian and other faith traditions, one simply needs to accept the gift of grace in a spirit of genuine repentance for new growth (i.e. transformative change) to begin at a personal level. The feeling of being released from past patterns of behaviour, or the power of past events, and the opportunity to take up a new identity (as one who is now "saved", chosen or simply loved) is immensely powerful and can be life changing. However, members of the church groups WTF engaged with were also clear that the operation of grace had a role to play at the neighbourhood and community level as well—especially for those communities negatively impacted by previous waves of regeneration. "I feel strongly as faith-based communities we already hold within our grasp this language of transformation. Within repentance there is that joyful point where things can be changed and there is no longer a need to continue down a road that's leading to destruction ...so much baggage and there's so much maybe unforgiven". This interviewee envisages that repentance could form some sort of public community event containing a liturgical or ritualised element; "... a sort of dedication service or ceremony or prayers or just something that would help the process ... otherwise the hurts and resentments and the unforgiveness goes with us into the future" (Baker & Skinner, 2005, p. 24).

Theology, Psychology and Languages of Capital

We now connect some of the ideas concerning social, religious and spiritual capitals which we outlined in the first section with the psychological/theological typologies outlined in section *Psychological Perspectives on Social, Religious and Spiritual Capitals*.

The first connection one can make is to link ideas of spiritual and religious capitals to those of bonding, bridging and linking capitals. One can interpret ideas of bonding, bridging and linking capitals as representing expanding radii of trust and action. The social cohesiveness of society and the strengthening of civil society are predicated on the ability of citizens and community groups to move from the security of the bonded type of social capital (based on familiarity and homogeneity) to the unfamiliarity of the bridging type of capital. This involves a potentially risky journey as one chooses or finds oneself in a situation of forming bridges with individuals or groups unfamiliar to yourself. The idea of taking the risk and journeying out to increase the number of different experiences and people one knows is also related to the idea of linking capital, as a more strategic and politically motivated move to engage in partnership working or knowledge sharing between unequal sectors of civil society. Nevertheless, the risks to individual identity are high, and the intended outcomes are often either not met or changed radically which can carry high possibility of resentment and mistrust.

When ideas of religious and spiritual capitals are overlaid on these categories of bonding, bridging and linking we see the possibility of developing a theory which sees spiritual capital in particular as pivotal in the development of these widening radii of trust and risk. If we work with the theory that spiritual capital (i.e. values, visions, worshipping traditions but also theological ideas and identities) provides the psychological motivation which energises religious capital (i.e. the public contribution of faith groups to wider civil society including the use of buildings, and the deployment of volunteers and paid members in leadership and service provision roles) then clearly the psychological impact of spiritual capital in developing further radii of trust and deeper levels of relationships across different groups is crucial. Equally, an opposite effect could be created if one's spiritual capital was developed more in the service of bonding rather than bridging capital.

Those case studies analysed in section *Psychological Perspectives on Social, Religious and Spiritual Capitals* were clearly examples of a positive correlation (or virtuous cycle) between spiritual and religious capital which produced further enhancement of other capitals. The spiritual capital dimension of this virtuous cycle was reflected primarily in theological categories—namely how certain key theological ideas and images or symbols associated with the biblical and Christian tradition were portrayed as providing the motivation and justification (or trigger points) for social engagement beyond the bonded relationships and activities of the faith group. The motivation and justification generated by spiritual capital led to sometimes risky but creative engagement with the wider community for the common good. Thus ideas and images associated with Christian theological motifs such as grace, martyrdom, hospitality, self-emptying love (or dying to self), vocation, talents, open doors, salt, yeast, a beacon on a hill, repentance and forgiveness, future reward (or salvation) generated psychological symptoms associated with a variety of feelings and activities: security and affirmation, support and recognition, risk-taking within a sense of overall purpose, cognitive resonance (rather than dissonance), public recognition, delayed gratification. We observed that these feelings and activities produced a psychological outlook based on wellbeing, satisfaction, moral superiority (but less pronounced than might be expected), emotional stability and hope in the future (despite or especially when events might conspire to create adversity or tragedy).

Another way of analysing the psychological dimension of spiritual and religious capitals is to see life as a series of concentric or overlapping circles of activity incorporating three levels of psychological integration which when taken together, rather than in isolation, reflect an holistic or all-encompassing definition of wholeness and wellbeing. These levels I will call the micro, meso and macro levels of psychological integration, categories which are themselves borrowed from theoretical models of social capital which refer to its impact at micro (i.e. individual level), meso (i.e. group and neighbourhood level) and macro (i.e. national and global level)—see Halpern (2005, p. 25). I shall link these ideas to the threefold structure of psychological response identified earlier (see pp. 9–13).

I am also indebted to the ideas of educator and researcher Donal Dorr who also discerns three areas of psycho-spiritual "conversion" based on categories derived from his reading of the Hebrew prophet Micah (Micah 6; 8). These categories are the personal ("walk humbly"), the interpersonal ("love tenderly") and the structural ("act justly"). These three areas he contends need to be present for a balanced spirituality, which we might read as shorthand for the different elements that need to be present in a person's life for a well-integrated personal psychology that contributes significantly to that person's sense of wellbeing and happiness.

I now create a theoretical model, drawn from the sources identified above, to show (albeit in a stylised fashion) a set of connections whereby spiritual capital could, under favourable circumstances, energise religious capital to create impacts at ever wider more complex levels of civil society and partnership working.

The Micro, Bonding, Personal Level of Psychological Integration

This level of psychological integration is linked to what we have already identified as the personal security and support associated with belonging to a cohesive and close-knit group such as a faith community. This micro level has close links with what has already been defined as bonding capital—namely ties and relationships that relate to common identities—i.e. people who are similar to each other. These ties are usually strong, can reinforce exclusive identities and tend to revolve around the performing of common and shared purposes within civil society. These understandings of the micro coincide with the first circle of Dorr's first level of psychological conversion—namely at the level of personal, whereby traditional notions of God's providence cease to become an abstract theological theory and instead become "a living experience. God is acting in my life to carry out his will for me; and what God wills is my salvation" (Dorr, 1984, p. 9). Dorr further reflects on some of the psychological effects associated with this level of conversion—a sense of "peace and tranquillity", a "sense of forgiveness", "the awareness of being loved and accepted in spite of, and even in a sense because of, my weakness, my faithlessness..." (Dorr, 1984, p. 10).

The Meso, Bridging, Interpersonal Level of Psychological Integration

This level of psychological integration I am calling the meso level because it is the level of response that begins to move out from the personal to the interpersonal. Within the Christian tradition, for example, it is that point in the spiritual journey when one begins to engage in the world by following the steps of Jesus, or emulating aspects of his ministry—a journey that carries with it the possibility of a pattern and meaning to one's life and a set of commands or ethical principles that begin to shape one's behaviour towards notions of service and obedience. We saw these dynamics emerging from some of the earlier case study quotations—"doing something for God", "God working in us" and "taking up one's cross". Many of the church groups in our survey saw themselves as carrying out principles and ethics of love, hospitality, etc., within their local communities—at the local neighbourhood level.

The concept of the meso is also picked up in social capital theory within its ideas of bridging social capital. As we saw, bridging social capital occurs when an individual or group take the risk in investing in social capital with individuals or groups different to themselves and creating bridges of relationships based on heterogeneity rather than homogeneity. Instead of loving one's neighbour who is broadly the same as you, one now moves beyond bonding capital to love (or at least acknowledge) the neighbour who is different to you—who is the Other is a vital task which government and local authorities assume faith groups have a distinctive contribution to make.

The concept of a meso (or intermediate) level of psychological integration also resonates with Dorr's second level of psychological conversion—namely Micah's command to "love tenderly". Dorr suggests that this interpersonal level of psychological conversion carries within it strong moral dimensions (rather than simply religious). Psychologically it encourages the attitude of openness to others, which of itself also implies a willingness to take risks—of being vulnerable to "rejection or hurt" (Dorr, 1984, p. 13). This level also presupposes a deepening of response whereby initial openness to the Other will be followed by the enactment of he calls "fidelity". "Moral conversion involves not merely the power to reach out to others, but the power to 'stay with' them, to be loyal even in the difficult times" (Dorr, 1984, p. 14). This ability is based on an acceptance of one's own weakness and inadequacy which religious conversion (or the personal level of psychological conversion) brings.

The Macro, Linking, Structural Level of Psychological Integration

This level of integration I suggest is associated with the third level of psychological response explored earlier—namely the belief in the possibility of wider change or transformation, and that one is somehow part of that process of transformation. We could refer to this as "macro" level in the sense that the scope of the radius of transformation extends from the personal and the neighbourhood levels to embrace the national, international or even cosmic impacts of change and transformation wrought by divine initiative embedded in human action. In social capital terms there is an implicit comparison between belief in the possibility of macro change, with the notion of linking capital, whereby one as an individual or group moves beyond bonding and bridging capitals deliberately to engage with networks that transcend your place in the social and cultural capital hierarchy. As already discussed, this form of capital acknowledges the inbuilt asymmetrical access to power that exists within society and between societies and is thus concerned to bring into being the possibility of a more just and equitable transformation at a deeper and wider level than simply the personal or the local.

The concept of a macro dimension of engagement with the world links closely with Dorr's notion of "acting justly"—of working for change at a structural level "in public life, the political sphere", and thus to attempt "to build a society that is intrinsically just" (Dorr, 1984, p. 15). It also involves making "an option for the poor" and resisting the escapist elements of a personalist religion that promises only restitutions of justice and equality before God in heaven (Dorr, 1984, p. 15). This structural form of psychological conversion, involving "the challenge to change my priorities (especially concerning notions of success), my hopes, concerns and...my lifestyle", engages feelings of empathy and solidarity, which is, in Dorr's opinion, only possible in the light of the other two levels of conversion—namely the religious and the moral, especially if the level of political conversion is to successfully avoid what he calls "the frenzy of quasi-political activity" (Dorr, 1984, p. 17).

Drawing Together the Threads

This stylised schema is perhaps inevitably somewhat crude and in places inconsistent in terms of exact fit.

However, there are some alternative theories that focus on the positive contributions of spiritual and religious beliefs to psychological wellbeing that could also be drawn in to this structure. For example, there might be some overlaps between understandings of spiritual capital and Fisher's Spiritual Health in Four Domains Index and based on the National Interfaith Coalition on Aging definition of spiritual health as "the affirmation of life in a relationship with God, self, community and environment that nurtures and celebrates wholeness" (quoted Francis & Robbins, 2005, p. 33). Then there is a connection to the work of Allport and Ross on extrinsic and intrinsic religious orientation, a typology later supplemented by Batson and Ventis (1982) and their notion of a questing orientation. Within current definitions of these three typologies, the cluster of interpretations reflecting *intrinsic* orientation is perhaps the most salient in seeking to posit the idea of a close psychological connection between spiritual and religious capital with its emphasis on "integration or the close relationship between religion and the rest of life" (quoted by Francis, 2007, p. 590), or as Allport stated in his original case for intrinsic orientation "a religious sentiment of this sort floods the whole life with motivations and meanings—religion is no longer limited to single segments of self-interest" (Allport, 1966, p. 455).

Finally the economist Richard Layard, in seeking to move mainstream economics from the "gospel" of neo-liberalism, identifies a growing sense of dissatisfaction with contemporary life, which he traces to the collapse of a sense of a common good and a normative set of boundaries, in the face of the relentless quest for self-realisation. His central finding is that despite five decades of sustained economic growth, society is no happier than it was 50 years ago. He also claims that beyond a modest level of income that guarantees our subsistence needs, our happiness does not increase in proportion to our salary rise (Layard, 2005, p. 49). In seeking to move mainstream economics to more ethical and moral ends, Layard invokes seven sources of happiness towards which economic activity could take a more active role in promoting, including family life, financial security, work, etc. Personal values are also a key element in human happiness, by which he means a "philosophy of life" that could include anything from cognitive therapy, Buddhist mindfulness, the 12 steps of alcoholics anonymous through to the *Spiritual Exercises* of St Ignatius (Layard, 2005, p. 72). He summarises thus, "...one of the most robust findings of happiness research: [is] that people who believe in God are happier" (Layard, 2005, p. 72).

Conclusion

What this psychological framing of the categories of social, religious and spiritual capitals has done highlights the importance of seeing a virtuous link (or loop) between spiritual/religious motivation and engagement within both the community of faith and the wider community. Thus the ideas of social capital (i.e. the notion of investing in relationships and expecting to receive something by return) are enhanced by understandings of spiritual and religious capitals which suggest the possibility of transcending rational choice theory (see Coleman et al.) by offering the alternative notion of investing in social connections in the expectation that one might get nothing back in return. In other words this is a form of "unconditional capital"—i.e. a self-emptying, self-giving openness to the world (but which in some traditions nevertheless believes in an ultimate "payback" on some future, transcendent horizon). The notion of spiritual capital (in particular) also allows key theological themes to enter the discourse in a relatively neutral and scientific way as a means of understanding further the psychological triggers or mechanisms which motivate faith-based engagement in bonding and bridging contexts. These theological themes could expand the number of indices available for measuring the impact of psychological motivation on civil engagement than are currently available (see, for example, Schwadel for current debate, 2005, p. 168).

The relative weakness of this capital-based approach is that although it advances some further understanding of the complex nature of the motivational link between "faith" and "action", the hegemonic nature of its discourse (i.e. the language of capital) and its tendency to simplify mundane, everyday encounters into neat sociological and policy categories can be distorting. In what I have already noted as an overdependence on functionalist interpretations and discourses, the language of capitals is thus unlikely to uncover alternative paradigms by which to describe the nature and scope of psychological motivation for faith-based engagement in civil society. Neither is it likely to drill down in sufficient depth into the highly dialectical nature of spirituality and religion within the current post-Christian but also increasingly post-secular context of Western European and similar societies.

Notes

1. The research programme was entitled *Regenerating Communities—a theological and strategic critique* (2002–2005) and produced three annual reports: *Mapping the boundaries* (2003), *Telling the stories—how churches are contributing to social capital* (2005), *Faith in action—the dynamic connections between religious and spiritual capital* (2006). All are available to download on www.wtf.org.uk
2. This research has since appeared in a number of other UK discourses and policy documents including CULF (2006); Lowndes and Smith (2006); Farnell, Hopkinson, Jarvis, Martineau, and Hein (2005); Miller (2007); Finneron, Dinham, Chapman, and Miller (2008); and Baker (2009).

References

Allport, G. (1966). Religious context of prejudice. *Journal for the Scientific Study of Religion, 5*, 447–457.
Baker, C. (2009). Blurred encounters? Religious literacy, spiritual capital and language. In A. Dinham, R. Furbey, & V. Lowndes, V. (Eds.), *Faith in the public realism: Controversies, policies and practices*. Bristol: The Policy Press.
Baker, C., & Skinner, H. (2005). *Telling the stories: How churches are contributing to social capital*. Manchester: William Temple Foundation.
Baker, C., & Skinner, H. (2006). *Faith in action: The dynamic connection between spiritual and religious capital*. Manchester: William Temple Foundation.
Batson, C., & Ventis, W. (1982). *The religious experience*. Oxford University Press: Oxford.
Becker, G. (1964). *Human capital*. New York: National Bureau of Economic Research.
Berger, P. L., & Hefner, R. W. (2003). *Spiritual capital in comparative perspective*. Paper prepared for the Spiritual Capital Planning Meeting downloaded (www.metanexus.net/spiritual_capital/pdf/Berger.pdf) Accessed 29 March 2006.
Bourdieu, P. (1987). Legitimation and structured interests in Weber's sociology of religion. In C. Turner (Trans.), S. Whimster, & S. Lash (Eds.), *Max Weber rationality and modernity*. London: A & U.
Bourdieu, P. (1992).*The logic of practice*. Stanford: Stanford University Press. (Original publication 1980).
Coleman, J. (1988). Social capital in the creation of human capital. *American Journal of Sociology, 94*, 95–120.

Commission on Faith and Urban Life. (2006). *Faithful cities, a call for celebration, vision and justice*. London: Methodist Publishing House and Church House Publishing.
Derrida, J. (1996). Remarks on deconstruction and pragmatism. In S. Critchley, J. Derrida, E. Laclau, & R. Rorty (Eds.), *Deconstruction and pragmatism*. London and New York: Routledge.
Dinham, A., Furbey, R., & Lowndes, V. (Eds.). (2009). *Faith in the public realm: Controversies, policies and practices*. Bristol: The Policy Press.
Dorr, D. (1984). *Spirituality and justice*. Dublin: Gill and MacMillan.
Farnell, R., Hopkinson, J., Jarvis, D., Martineau, J., & Hein, J. R. (2005). *Faith in rural communities: Contributions of social capital to community vibrancy*. Warwickshire: ACORA Publishing.
Finneron, D., Dinham, A., Chapman, R., & Miller, S. (2008). *Report for communities and local government in connection with the CLG Framework for inter faith dialogue and social action 'Face-to-Face and Side-by-Side'*. London: Faith Based Regeneration Network.
Francis, L. J. (2007). Introducing the New Indices of Religious Orientation (NIRO): Conceptualization and measurement. *Mental Health, Religion and Culture, 10*, 585–602.
Francis, L. J., & Robbins, M. (2005). *Urban hope and spiritual health: The adolescent voice*. Epworth: Peterborough.
Halpern, D. (2005). *Social capital*. Cambridge and Malden, MA: Polity Press.
Hopewell, J. (1987). *Congregation: Stories and structures*. Philadelphia: Fortress Press.
Iannaccone, L. (1990). Religious practice: A human capital approach. *Journal for the Scientific Study of Religion, 29*, 297–314.
Iannaccone, L., & Klick, J. (2003). *Spiritual capital: An introduction and literature review*. George Mason University and American Enterprise Institute.
Layard, R. (2005). *Happiness: Lessons from a new science*. London: Allen Lane.
Levinas, E. (1969). *Totality and infinity: An essay on exteriority* (A. Lingis, Trans.). Pittsburgh, PA: Duquesne University Press.
Loury, G. (1987). Why should we care about group inequality? *Social Philosophy and Policy, 5*, 249–271.
Lowndes, V., & Chapman, R. (2005). *Faith hope and clarity: Developing a model of faith group involvement in civil renewal*. Leicester, Local Government Research Unit: De Montfort University Leicester.
Lowndes, V., & Smith, G. (2006). *Mapping the public policy landscape: Faith-based voluntary action*. Swindon: Economic and Social Research Council.
Miller, S. (2007). *Keeping it together*. London: Faith Based Regeneration Network.
Putnam, R. (2000). *Bowling alone: The collapse and revival of American community*. New York: Simon and Schuster.
Schwadel, P. (2005). Individual, congregational and denominational effects on church members' civic participation. *Journal for the Scientific Study of Religion, 44*(2), 159–171.
Smidt, C. (Ed.). (2004). *Religion as social capital: Producing the common good*. Waco: Baylor University Press.
Starke, R., & Finke, R. (2000). *Acts of faith: Explaining the human side of religion*. Berkeley: University of California Press.
Woolcock, M. (1988). Social capital and economic development: Toward a theoretical synthesis and policy framework. *Theory and Society, 27*(2), 155.
Woolcock, M. (2001). The place of social capital in understanding social and economic outcomes. *Isuma: Canadian Journal of Policy Research, 2*(1), 1–17.

Biographical details

Dr Chris Baker is Director of Research at the William Temple Foundation, Manchester and part-time lecturer in Urban Theology, Department of Religions and Theology, University of Manchester, UK.

Chapter 10
Mystical, Religious, and Spiritual Experiences

Ralph W. Hood, Jr.

Abstract The study of experience has long been a dominant theme in the psychology of religion. Whether or not there is a form of experience that is uniquely religious is a contested theme within the field. Part of this is captured by whether individuals identify themselves as religious, spiritual, neither, or both. Spirituality has come to be identified with a largely private, individualized focus on transcendent experiences, while religion has largely been focused on institutional expression and explicit belief statements regarding such experiences. The entry into religion (conversion) and the exit from religion (deconversion) are often largely experientially based. Both conversion and deconversion have differing psychological consequences depending on whether or not they are sudden or gradual. The nature of the cultural context in which conversion and deconversion occur is an important factor. The importance of religion varies greatly between cultures. Almost any experience can be identified as religious if it is framed within a system of religious beliefs. Among the most commonly studied religiously framed experiences are glossolalia (tongues speaking) and varieties of prayer. Meditation is analogous to prayer in many ways, but more likely to be associated with persons who identify themselves as spiritual but not religious. Among the claims to a specifically unique form of religious experience, mysticism is most commonly cited. This experience of self-loss and of a sense of ultimate unity is found both within the major faith traditions where it is given a specific religious interpretation and outside of institutional religion where it is associated with spirituality.

The study of mystical, religious, and spiritual experiences has been a major theme in the psychology of religion since the publication of the one assured classic in the field, *The varieties of religious experience* (James, 1902/1985). It is useful to remind readers that the subtitle of this classic text is "a study in human nature" suggesting that religious experiencing is a fundamental aspect of what it means to be human. However, the current study of religious experience, especially in the United States, compels us to distinguish between religion and spirituality.

R.W. Hood, Jr. (✉)
Department of Psychology, University of Tennessee at Chattanooga, Chattanooga, TN 37403, USA
e-mail: Ralph-Hood@utc.edu

Religion and Spirituality

It has become customary in the study of religious experience to allow participants to identify themselves as "religious," "spiritual," "both," or "neither." There are variations in precisely how this is done that produce minor variations in the percent of persons who classify themselves in one of the forced-choice options. For instance, some allow a choice "religious but not spiritual" while others use "more religious than spiritual" (see Hood, 2003; Zinnbauer & Pargament, 2005; Streib, Hood, Keller, Csöff, & Silver, 2009). However, the general outcome of this research is summarized fairly easily. Most people who are religious see themselves as also spiritual. For these persons, religion is the conceptual system within which they are able to find meaning and give expression to their spiritual experiences. These persons tend also to score high on indicators of spiritual wellbeing and on measures congruent with conventional views of mental health (Hood, Hill, & Spilka, 2009). Few persons identify themselves as neither spiritual nor religious, or religious but not spiritual. However, of strong interest is that persistent finding that an emerging large minority of persons in the United States, and in Europe, identify themselves as spiritual but not religious. Furthermore, they are not simply "not religious," but stand in opposition to religion (Hood, 2003). These persons also score high on a wide variety of measures of openness to experience, fantasy proneness, or absorption. They also tend to have characteristics congruent with mental health professionals' own spirituality that have implications for the assessment of wellbeing.

Shafranske (1996) has reviewed the empirical research on the religious beliefs, associations, and practices of mental health professionals. His findings are congruent with those of Zinnbauer et al. (1997). Shafranske focused primarily on samples of clinical and counseling psychologists who are members of the American Psychological Association, Shafranske notes that psychologists are less likely to believe in a personal God, or to affiliate with religious groups, than other professionals or the general population. In addition, while the *majority* of psychologists report that spirituality is important to them, a *minority* report that religion is important to them (Shafranske, 1996, p. 153). Shafranske summarizes his own data and the work of others to emphasize that psychologists are more like the general population than was previously assumed. However, Shafranske (1996, p. 154) lumps together various indices as the "religious dimension," and this is very misleading. In fact, psychologists neither believe, practice, nor associate with the institutional aspects of faith ("religion") as much as they endorse what Shafranske properly notes are "noninstitutional forms of spirituality" (1996, p. 154). One could predict that in forced-choice contexts they would be most likely to be "spiritual" but not "religious." Empirically, three facts about religious and spiritual self-identification ought to be kept quite clear.

The implications of Shafranske's findings for education and wellbeing in the United States are important. We will list four major ones.

First, as noted above, most persons who are *not* mental health professionals identify themselves as *both* religious and spiritual. These are largely persons sampled from within faith traditions, for which it is reasonable to assume that spirituality is at least one expression of and motivation for their religion (e.g., institutional participation). Hence many measures of spirituality simply operate like measures of religion and tend to correlate with positive indices of mental health (Gorsuch & Miller, 1999; Hood et al., 2009).

Second, significant minorities of individuals use spirituality as a means of opposing religion, especially the authority of religious beliefs and normative demands. Many of these persons seek to move away from religion in order to become more developed spiritually. The move is from belief to experience, as Day (1994) perceptively notes. Streib et al. (2008) found these persons to be more open to experience in both Germany and the United States.

Third, religiousness and spirituality overlap considerably, at least in North American populations. The majority of the US population in particular is religious *and* spiritual, in terms of both self-identification and self-representations. Exceptions are easy to identify, but one ought not to lose sight of the fact that they are *exceptions*. Significantly, they include not only scientists in general, but psychologists in particular (Beit-Hallahmi, 1977; Shafranske, 1996). Among these people, a hostility to religion as thwarting or even falsifying spirituality is evident. This hostility is readily revealed in qualitative studies in which there is some degree of rapport between interviewer and respondents (Day, 1991, 1994; Roof, 1993, 1999).

Fourth, further clarification of the three points above has come from a major study done by Streib and his colleagues (2008) comparing individuals who left new religious tradition from their counterparts who remained. He and his colleagues have also introduced a new field of research they refer to as deconversion.

Deconversion

Strieb and his colleagues compared individuals in two cultures (Germany and the United States) who either stayed in or left the same religious tradition. The study is important as it also used mixed methods (qualitative and quantitative) which Kohls, Hack, and Walach (2008) have recommended for the psychology of religion and spirituality. However, for purposes of this chapter we will focus only on their quantitative data that have direct implication for wellbeing.

In both the United States and Germany, those who deconvert identify themselves as more spiritual than religious and are characterized by lower scores on measures of religious fundamentalism and higher scores on measures of *openness to experience*, a subscale of the Big 5 measure of personality (McCrae, 1992). However, most important for our present purposes is that Streib and his colleagues also found that there were variations in the mental health implications of deconverts in Germany and the United States. This was most evident when within each culture the deconverts were contrasted with those who stayed within the tradition: in other words, those who tended to identify themselves as both religious and spiritual.

In the German sample, deconverts differed from in-tradition members on all five subscales of the Big 5. Of particular significance is the finding that German deconverts scored significantly higher on *openness to experien*ce than in-tradition members, but lower on the remaining four subscales of the Big 5 (*agreeableness, emotional stability, conscientiousness,* and *extraversion*).

On a widely used measure of psychological wellbeing, which we will refer to as the Ryff scale (Ryff & Singer, 1996), the German deconverts scored lower on four subscales (*environmental mastery, personal relations with others, purpose in life,* and *self-acceptance*). However, they did not differ from in-tradition members in *autonomy* or *personal growth*. Finally, on independent measures of religious fundamentalism, German deconverts scored lower than their in-tradition counterparts. We will discuss the implications of these differences for wellbeing more fully below when we consider how German deconverts differ between the United States and Germany in Strieb et al.'s study of deconversion.

If we focus upon the similarities between the United States and Germany in Streib's study of deconversion two measures are identical. In both Germany and the United States deconverts are (1) lower on measures of religious fundamentalism and (2) higher on *openness to experience* than their in-tradition counterparts.

The results with the Ryff scale also revealed differences between deconverts and in-tradition members for Germany and the United Sates. US deconverts scored higher on the total Ryff scale in contrast to German deconverts who scored lower. Furthermore, in the US sample this is accounted for largely by two of the subscales, *autonomy* and *personal growth*. Thus deconverts in Germany and the United Sates show significantly different patterns from their in-tradition counterparts, something that has strong implications for psychological wellbeing which we will now address.

Cultural Implications for Religion, Spirituality, and Psychological Wellbeing

Streib's study of deconversion has advanced the study of religion and spirituality by confirming that the meaning of psychological measures must be placed within the cultural context of those assessed. For instance, in the United States religious fundamentalism is strongly negatively correlated with openness to experience on the Big 5 and with autonomy and personal growth on the Ryff measure of wellbeing. Assuming that much of the variance on measures of the Big 5 is due to genetics (DeYoung, Peterson, & Higgins, 2002), it is reasonable to conclude that members of religious groups who are high on this measure tend to explore the limits of their faith tradition and become likely deconverts seeking autonomy and personal growth outside a faith tradition and thus identifying themselves as spiritual but not religious, even anti-religious as noted by qualitative studies done by both psychologists (Day, 1991, 1994) and sociologists (Roof, 1993, 1999). Note, however, there is a gain/loss factor in deconversion. It is those who stay within their faith tradition that maintain a sense of meaning and purpose and thus we can note what has been established in the empirical literature, religion and spirituality differentially relate to measures of wellbeing, each with its pros and cons. Deconversion presents little in the way of psychological risk to Americans as they inhabit a culture where religious freedom provides a "free market" of options, including a spiritual questing outside of the established faith traditions (Roof, 1993, 1999).

In Germany Streib and his colleagues argue that there is a significant difference with strong implications for wellbeing. On the Big 5 measures, German deconverts scored lower on *emotional stability* often identified when reversed scored as *neuroticism*. Thus, German deconverts had higher scores in *neuroticism* than their in-tradition counterparts who are perhaps inoculated from neuroticism by their faith. German deconverts also have lower scores on *extraversion* suggesting lack of social support as noted above. Correspondingly, on the Ryff scale, German deconverts had lower scores on *positive relations with others*, *environmental mastery*, *self-acceptance*, and *purpose in life*. Streib and his colleagues conclude that deconversion is associated with a crisis for Germans unlike that for deconverts in the United States. The crisis for German deconverts is with regard to self (meaning, emotion, self-acceptance), others (positive relations, extraversion), and mastery of everyday life. Further longitudinal research is needed to see whether this crisis situation is worked through or simply results in a permanent reduction in psychological wellbeing.

The possibility of a crisis situation for deconverts in Germany must be balanced by its mirror image for in-tradition members. Analyses of the Big 5 subscales and the Ryff subscales suggest that for those who remain in-tradition, their faith provides them with a satisfactory meaning system in which *emotional stability*, *agreeableness*, *conscientious*, and *extraversion* work in opposition to openness to provide a stable meaning system. German in-tradition members must be judged psychologically stable in terms of Big 5 traits of *agreeableness, emotional stability, consciousness, and extraversion*. Recalling that in-tradition members score higher on measures of religious fundamentalism, a consistent picture is beginning to emerge that suggests fundamentalism is a meaningful form of life for many persons. Likewise, in terms of psychological wellbeing, the relevant differences of the Ryff subscales indicate that in-tradition members have *purpose in life*, *positive relations with others*, and a sense of *environmental mastery*.

Three conclusions derive from the study by Streib and his colleagues. First, the implications for the various possibilities of self-identification as religious/spiritual must be understood in terms of the larger culture in which these terms carry and provide various meaning options. Being religious/spiritual has trade offs with respect to which aspects of wellbeing are being assessed and how they are evaluated. They also differ in whether the culture is open to religious and spiritual options as in the United States or more linked to official government supported religions as in Germany.

Second, longitudinal research is needed to explore how even a crisis resulting from abandoning a faith tradition may be worked through to provide other sources of meaning than those framed by a particular faith tradition. In this sense, higher order factor solutions to the Big 5 are relevant. In the two-factor solution agreeableness, emotional stability, and conscientious provide one factor, and openness and extraversion the other factor. These two factors are related to distinct neurophysiological systems (DeYoung et al., 2002) and have been identified with stability and plasticity. Peterson (1999) has written masterfully on the balance that is needed between tradition (religion) and change that is likely in our view to be associated with spiritual questing. The tension between tradition and change is the mirror in which the data on religious/spiritual self-identification is best viewed as are the consequences for various patterns of psychological wellbeing.

Third, Streib and his colleague have created a new area of study, that of deconversion. The various trajectories that deconverts follow are crucial to determine, including identification with a new faith tradition, the move to a purely secular world view, as well as the development of a private eclectic spirituality where psychological constructs of self-realization function as a spiritual ladder of growth outside the faith traditions are only some options necessary to explore. Here deconversion mirrors earlier research on conversion.

Conversion

Research on conversion has found that crises may or may not be involved in conversion. Crisis tends to be associated with the more purely psychological driven paradigm. The "Pauline" paradigm of a crisis producing a conversion to a faith tradition may parallel the German example by Streib and his colleagues as deconversion precipitating a crisis (Hood et al., 2009). On the other hand, the movement to what Hood et al. (2009) call the contemporary paradigm of conversion emphasizes the active role of the convert and the influence of interpersonal relations on a continual quest for new patterns of personal growth and meaning. This is consistent with the study by Streib and his colleagues of deconverts in the United Sates. It is important to note that the classic paradigm acknowledged a series of contrasts between sudden and gradual conversion, although empirical research was focused on the more dramatic case of sudden religious conversion. Perhaps it was this narrowed focus in the empirical literature that allowed the contemporary paradigm to emerge. In addition, the emergence of new religious movements and their obvious appeal to converts altered that typical pattern of research, almost by definition. Thus intensification experiences within traditions that focused on intrapsychological processes (studied by psychologists) gave way to conversion to new religious movements focused on interpersonal processes (studied by sociologists and social psychologists). Long and Hadden (1983) have argued for a "dual-reality" approach, in which conversion may involve either sudden, emotional processes (associated with intrapsychological processes, which can be denigrated in terms of a "brainwashing" metaphor) or more gradual processes (associated with interpsychological processes). However, we need not assume conversion to be an either–or process, based upon dichotomies such as sudden–gradual or passive–active. The distinction primarily reflects differing psychological and sociological interests. Investigators would best profit from studying actual processes of conversion in particular cases, and the degree to which characteristics typically assumed to operate in what we have termed the classical and contemporary paradigms could be empirically identified. One may assume, as Rambo (1993) does, that there are no fundamental differences among the processes of conversion to various religions. However, we must be careful to identify the various factors that actually do operate in conversion before we can take such an assumption as proven.

Finally although admittedly some change must occur in conversion, the nature of that change must be carefully delineated. Psychologists frequently focus on personality change. Paloutzian, Richardson, and Rambo (1999) argue that the two distinct literatures on conversion and personality change ought to be related. Adopting contemporary views of personality that recognize levels or domains to personality (Emmons, 1995) suggests that one can organize the empirical literature on conversion by the extent to which it produces changes in particular domains or levels of personality. For instance, research at the basic personality level, using such indicators as the five-factor model of personality (McCrae, 1992), has produced little, if any, evidence that conversion changes basic personality. However, at other levels of personality functioning, changes resulting from conversion can clearly be identified. Paloutzian et al. (1999) have summarized this literature according to three levels of personality assessment. Level 1 refers to basic function (such as measured by the Big 5), here conversion and deconversion reveal little personality change as might be expected in measures referring to basic inheritable traits. However, at level 2, referring to attitudes, emotions, and behavior, both conversion and deconversion reveal significant change. Finally, at level 3, referring to purpose in life, meaning, and psychological wellbeing, one finds rather profound changes. All of this is embedded in our discussion of the relationship between self-ascribed religious and spiritual identities. However, psychologists have also studied religious and spiritual experiences by imposing definitions of their own which identify phenomena to be investigated that cover the widest possible range in the Jamesean sense of human natures.

Religious Experience and Human Nature

James's (1902/1985) classic work, *The varieties of religious experience*, has continued to influence psychologists since it was initially delivered as the Gifford Lectures at the beginning of the twentieth century. Although one can speculate as to the varying reasons why this book has remained in print since its first publication, the simple fact remains that James set the tone for contemporary empirical work in the psychology of religious *experience* that is nonreductive (Hood, 2000).

James's definition of religious experience for the purposes of the Gifford Lectures clearly revealed his sympathy for the extreme forms of religious experience. James defined religion as "*the feelings, acts, and experiences of individual men, in their solitude, so far as they apprehend themselves to stand in relation to whatever they may consider the divine*" (James, 1902/1985, p. 34; emphasis in original). The presence of something divine within all religious traditions can be debated. Buddhism is often cited as an example of a faith tradition without a god (Hong, 1995). However, one need not equate something divine with belief in God or in supernatural beings. James' clarification of what he meant by "divine" makes the case for the near-universal application of this concept. As he saw it, the divine is "such a primal reality as the individual feels compelled to respond to solemnly and gravely, and neither by a curse nor a jest" (James, 1902/1985, p. 39). Thus, influenced by James' notion of divinity, religious experience—ultimately, the experience of the solitary individual—is placed at the forefront of the psychology of religion.

Religious experience distinctively separates, from the vast domain of experience, that which is perceived to be *religious*. Thus we psychologists are free to identify religious experience as experience that is identified within faith traditions as religious. This tautology need not disturb us. Religious traditions define the distinctively religious for the faithful. What is religious within one tradition may not be so within another. With the possible exception of mystical experiences discussed below, it is probably not fruitful to define religious experiences by their inherent characteristics. Whether an experience is religious or not depends on the interpretation of the experience. It is in this sense that even if what is experienced is both immediately present and unquestionable to the experiencing subject, the epistemological value of the experience is dependent on discursive meanings that entail public interpretations (Sharf, 2000). Interpretations provide meanings not inherently obvious to those who stand outside the tradition that provides the context for meaningfully identifying any particular episode as a religious experience. Given the wide range of religious experiences, we will focus on three that have been extensively studied: glossolalia, prayer, and apparitions.

Glossolalia

Samarin (1972) claim that glossolalia, or speaking in tongues, is merely meaningless, phonologically structured human sound. However, Hutch (1980) claims that glossolalia aims to amalgamate the sounds of laughing and crying—signs of both the joy and pain of life supporting the view of Lafal, Monahan, and Richman (1974) that glossolalia is meaningless. Early psychologists attributed glossolalia to mental illness, but modern researchers have made a strong conceptual case for distinguishing glossolalia from what are only superficial clinical parallels (Kelsey, 1964; Kildahl, 1972). Empirically, glossolalia is normative within many religious traditions, including some Pentecostal and Holiness groups where it is widely accepted as the most crucial criterion of baptism of the Holy Ghost.

The real focus of research has been on whether or not glossolalia occurs only in a trance or altered state of consciousness. Goodman (1969) has documented the cross-cultural similarity of glossolalic utterances. She attributes this similarity to the fact that glossolalia results from an induced trance. The trance state itself, for neurophysiological reasons, accounts for the cross-cultural similarity of glossolalia (Goodman, 1972). She argues for induction techniques generated by religious rituals in believers (Goodman, 1988, 1990).

Samarin (1972) has challenged Goodman's cross-cultural data on the grounds that all her samples were from similar Pentecostal settings, even though the data were collected within different cultures. Samarin also points out that patterns identified in typical Appalachian Mountain setting are similar to those found in glossolalia. This is the case, even though such preaching does not occur in a trance state; hence there is no reason to infer that glossolalia can only be elicited in trance states. Extensive field research on Christian serpent handlers of Appalachia support Samarin's claim (Hood & Williamson, 2008). This view is also supported by Hine (1969). More recently, however, Philipchalk and Mueller (2000) demonstrated increased activation of the right hemisphere relative to the left in a small sample of participants who allowed infrared photography before and after speaking in tongues. The opposite was found before and after reading aloud. These data suggest the activation of the right hemisphere in glossolalia, and not necessarily the existence of a trance state.

Wacker (2001) has argued for a compromise view, that glossolalia is produced in a trance state that Pentecostals have learned to enter and exit based on social cues produced in the appropriate religious context. Among Pentecostals worldwide, the experience of glossolalia is both meaningful and contributes to their psychological wellbeing. However, it may be that outside Pentecostalism glossolalia per se may not be particularly useful in fostering personality integration. This is the conclusion supported by Lovekin and Malony (1977) in their study of participants in a Catholic charismatic program of spiritual renewal. Empirical studies comparing glossolalic with nonglossolalic controls have consistently failed to find any reliable psychological differences, including indices of psychopathology, between the two groups (Goodman, 1972; Hine, 1969; Malony & Lovekin, 1985).

Prayer and Meditation

Poloma and her colleagues have made significant contributions to the contemporary empirical study of prayer (Poloma & Gallup, 1991; Poloma & Pendleton, 1989). Not only have they reliably measured several types of prayer (colloquial, meditative, petitionary, and ritualistic), but they have focused on the more psychologically meaningful measures of (1) experiences during prayer and (2) subjective consequences of prayer. Thus much of Poloma et al.'s work is in the quality-of-life tradition, which meaningfully assesses the subjective aspects of human experience (Poloma & Pendleton, 1991).Like most of the studies of prayer, Poloma has focused on Christian prayer. Reviews of the empirical literature on Christian prayer are readily available (Francis & Evans, 2001; Hood et al., 2009). Here we simply emphasize that prayer is multidimensional, and that different types of prayer relate to different aspects of wellbeing. For instance, meditative prayer is most closely related to religious satisfaction and existential wellbeing. On the other hand, only colloquial prayer predicts the absence of negative affect, whereas ritual prayer alone predicts negative affect (Poloma & Pendleton, 1989). Thus not simply frequency of prayer, but the nature and type of prayer, determine the experiential consequences of prayer.

The multidimensionality of prayer has resulted in remarkably similar factors by independent research teams. For instance both Poloma and her colleagues, and Hood and his, have derived remarkably similar factors in their multidimensional approach to the measurement of prayer. Both Poloma's and Hood's groups have noted that "contemplative" (Hood's term) or "meditative" (Poloma's term) praying—a non-petitionary attempt merely to become aware of God. We will focus on meditative prayer as it is the one area in the contemporary psychology of religion where empirical research has been done on subjects from both Western and Eastern meditative traditions.

Among religious persons in the West devout individuals find a meaningful confrontation with a "deeper" or "higher" reality that is meaningfully framed within the beliefs of their faith tradition. Eastern traditions may simply assert that meditation provides a full appreciation of reality as it is. For instance, Preston (1988) has shown how converts to Zen are socialized into an interpretation of reality that is based on nonconceptual meditative techniques, which demand attentiveness to reality presumably as it is, in and of itself.

Naranjo and Ornstein (1971) distinguish between "ideational" and "nonideational" meditation. The former encourages and utilizes imagery that is common within a tradition; the latter seeks an imageless state and avoids attention to unwanted imagery that may occur during meditation. The fact that much imageless meditation is widely recognized as a spiritual practice has contributed to the psychophysiological study of meditation. Rather than assessing either verbal reports or behavior, investigators have focused on physiological measures, particularly of brain activity as measured by a wide variety of new technologies (Azari, 2006). However, seeking a precise physiology of either prayer or meditation may be one of those chimerical tasks that serve to satisfy those who will accept the reality of spiritual things only if they can identify their bodily correlates.

To cite but one example of a bodily correlate of meditative states we can note the relationship between brain wave patterns and modes of consciousness. For instance waking attentive states are associated with brain wave cycles ≥ 13 cps (beta). However, it is also obvious that despite this physiological correlate of attentive consciousness, this fact does not tell us much about what is being experienced. Reading a book, playing baseball, and watching a great movie would all probably register as "beta" states; yet this equates them only in a trivial sense with all activities a person engages in when awake and attending to something external.

Alpha states ranging from 8 to 12 cps are of particular interest as they are strongly correlated with nondiscursive experiences during prayer or meditation. While prayer and meditation states can be associated with either alpha or beta states, depending on whether or not one is consciously attending to images or thoughts. Imageless states are more likely to be associated with alpha; image with alpha or beta, depending upon the degree of focused awareness on specific imagery.

Many studies of meditative traditions have focused on the less-expensive technique of identifying brain wave correlates of prayer and meditation. For instance, Kasamatsu and Hirai (1969) compared those learning to meditate and those adept at meditation in terms of four stages that occur as participants advance in *zazen*.

They found that Zen masters' independent ratings of those most adept at *zazen* were clearly associated with brain wave patterns assumed to be indicative of the higher stages of *zazen*. It is also worth noting that these objective electrophysiological correlates of the quality of meditative stages support the claims within the Zen tradition that advancement in *zazen* can be identified appropriately by Zen masters. They also support earlier research by Maupin (1965), who found that those most adept at *zazen* had higher tolerances for anomalistic experiences and were able to take advantage of what, in psychoanalytic terms, were regressive experiences. Maupin noted that, if meditation is considered to foster such regression, each stage of meditation, successfully mastered, permits further adaptive regression. A sophisticated and comprehensive effort to develop a neurophysiology of meditative states within the Zen tradition has been provided by Austin (1998).

Associated with efforts to meditate or pray is the difficulty of attending to one's prayerful or meditative activity without not being disrupted by external stimuli. Research with yogis suggests that those with well-marked alpha activity in their normal resting states show a greater aptitude and enthusiasm for practicing *samadhi* (yoga meditation) (Anand, Chhina, & Singh, 1961). In laboratory studies, external stimuli can be introduced while persons meditate, and the effects of these on their alpha activity can be examined. In terms of brain wave patterns, external stimuli force attention so that alpha states are disrupted or blocked (alpha blocking), and beta waves are noted. Meditators must then attempt to return to their inward states, characterized by alpha waves. It has been postulated that those adept at meditation are less likely to exhibit alpha blocking when external stimuli are introduced. Investigators have confirmed this prediction, both with Zen meditators (Kasamatsu & Hirai, 1969) and with those who practice yoga (Bagchi & Wenger, 1957). Likewise, in their now-classic study, Anand et al. (1961) documented the ability of yogis in a laboratory setting to exhibit high-amplitude blocking during *samadhi*, as well as the ability to show no response to pain.

Although brain wave correlates of meditative states present a fairly consistent gross pattern, they can be misleadingly interpreted to carry more weight than they should in terms of documenting religious experiences. Experience is no more "real" because one can identify its physiological correlates than it is the case that identical physiological correlates of meditative states mean that the experiences are necessarily the "same." For instance, numerous differences exist between *samadhi* and *zazen*, not to mention varieties of prayer. These differences are not necessarily reflected in brain wave patterns (though they may be). A person's exhibiting alpha activity may not tell us whether they practice *zazen*, *samadhi*, or Christian contemplative prayer. The experience of meditation and prayer is more than its physiology.

Sundén thought that his role theory was particularly useful in addressing the question "How are religious experience at all psychologically possible?" (Wikstrom, 1987, p. 390). Jan van der Lans (1985, 1987) utilized Sundén's theory in a study of students selected to participate in a 4-week training course in Zen meditation. They were told simply to concentrate on their breathing for the first 14 sessions. Then they were told to concentrate without a focus on any object—a method called *shikantaza* in Zen. Participants were divided into those with ($n = 14$) and those without

($n = 21$) a religious frame of reference, based on intake interviews. Instructions varied for each group: The religious group was told to anticipate experiences common in meditation within religious traditions, and the control group was told to anticipate experiences common in meditation used for therapeutic purposes.

Dependent measures included writing down every unusual experiences after each daily session, and by filling out a questionnaire on the last day of training that asked subjects specifically whether they had had a religious experience during meditation. The daily experiences were content-analyzed according to a list of 54 experiences categorized into five types: bodily sensations; fantasies, illusions, and imagery (hallucinations); changes in self-image; new insights; and negative feelings. Responses per category were too low for any meaningful statistical analyses. However, the number of persons reporting a religious experience during their Zen meditation varied as a function of presence or absence of a premeditative religious frame. Half of the religious participants reported a religious experience during meditation, while none of the control group (those without a premeditative religious frame) did. In addition, all participants were asked a control question at the end of the study: Had their meditations made them feel more vital and energetic? The groups did not differ on this question.

The conclusion we may draw from this research is that the actual practice of meditation elicits a specifically religious experience only for those with a religious frame of reference. If we assume equivalent meditative states in both groups (e.g., achievement of alpha states), the meaningfulness of such a state is dependent upon the interpretative frame one brings to the experience. Of course, a paradox is that, within Zen, interpretative frames are minimized; hence this research employed a technique more compatible with prayer within the Christian tradition, in which interpretation plays a more significant role (Holmes, 1980). Still, it is clear that experience, meaningfully interpreted, is dependent on whatever framework for interpretation can be brought to or derived from the experience. Sundén's role theory simply argues that familiarity with a religious tradition is the basis from which religious experiences gain their meaningfulness—and without which *religious* experiences are not possible. While it is obvious that prayer provides meaning and solace to those who frame the experience in religious terms, it also may be a factor in facilitating what arguable is a unique state common to all faith traditions, mysticism. This aspect of prayer will be confronted when we discuss mysticism.

Mysticism

If there is the claim to an experience of universal concern to all faith traditions, it is mysticism. James (1902/1985, p. 301) referred to it as the "root and centre" of religion. Whether or not this claim is challenged partly depends on the empirical issue of how mysticism is measured. In the contemporary psychology of religion there are three measures of mysticism, each based upon a different conceptual model.

Barnard (1997, p. 63) has noted that ultimately James equates mystical experience with any submarginal or subliminal state which includes a wide variety of experiences that defy easy classification. Including in these submarginal experiences are James' diabolical mysticism, a "sort of religious mysticism turned upside down" (James, 1902/1985, p. 337). In this sense, the measure of transliminality developed by Thalbourne (1998) is the most nearly Jamesian measure of mysticism we have. It is a single factor scale measuring essentially subliminal states of consciousness. Thalbourne and Delin (1999, p. 25) have coined the term transliminal to refer to a common underlying factor that is largely an involuntary susceptibility to inwardly generated psychological phenomena of an ideational and affective kind. However, transliminality is also related to a hypersensitivity to external stimulation (Thalbourne, 1998, p. 403) such that transliminality becomes a Jamesian measure of the submarginal region, as noted above where "seraph and snake" abide there side by side (James, 1902/1985, p. 338). Lange and Thalbourne (2007) have developed a single factor measure of mysticism that is more restricted than transliminal domain, but is similar to James' treatment of mysticism in the *Varieties* as it allows for interval scaling of intensity of experiences, as an empirical mystical ladder of sorts.

Francis and his colleagues have developed a measure of mysticism based on seven aspect of mysticism delineated by Happold (1963). These include ineffability, noesis, transiency, passivity, oneness, timelessness, and true ego. There is both a 21-item (Francis & Louden, 2000a) and a 9-item short index of mystical orientation (Francis & Louden, 2004). Given Francis' established interest in Eysenck's personality theory, he and his colleagues have used these measures to demonstrate that mysticism is most related to extraversion but unrelated to neuroticism and psychoticism in a large sample of Roman Catholic priests (Francis & Louden, 2000a). This replicates earlier research with a sample of over 200 male clergy that found the same results (Francis & Thomas, 1996). In a study relevant to our discussion of Eastern and Western forms of meditation, Kaldor and his colleagues found a difference between a sample of Eastern meditators and a sample of Christians who prayed: Christian prayer was associated with low psychoticism scores, but Eastern meditation was associated with high psychoticism scores, as measured by the Revised Eysenck Personality Questionnaire (Kaldor, Francis, & Fisher, 2002).

In two earlier studies, Francis and his colleague attempted to test Ross' hypothesis that, in terms of Jungian theory as operationalized in the Myers-Briggs scale, the perceiving function is crucial for individual differences in religious expression (Ross, Weiss, & Jackson, 1996). Using the short index of mystical orientation both Francis (2002) and Francis and Louden (2000b) failed to find support for Ross' hypothesis. However, in a sample of over 300 individuals who stayed at a retreat house associated with Ampleforth Abbey, Francis, Village, Robbins, and Ineson (2007) found clear support for Ross' hypothesis using the long (21-item) form of the Index of Mystical Orientation.

However, by far the most empirical research on mysticism has been done using a measure of mysticism derived from Stace's (1961) common core hypothesis. Hood's Mysticism scale is an empirical approach that Seigfried (1990, p. 12) has identified as the empirical validation of phenomenologically derived classifications. For our present purposes, it is sufficient to note that introvertive mysticism emerges as a distinct factor, not only in exploratory factor analytic studies (Hood & Williamson,

2000) but also in confirmatory factor analyses in such diverse cultures as the United States and Iran (Hood et al., 2001).

Hood's mysticism scale narrows the measurement of mysticism to an experience of oneness or unity that can be either introvertive (an experience of pure consciousness) or extrovertive (an experience of unity in diversity) and an interpretative factor. However, for our purposes in this chapter, we will focus only upon the introvertive factor and confront the possibility that there is a common mystical core to both faith traditions and to those whose mystical experiences are not embedded in religious discourse.

Our approach assumes that Stace has correctly identified three issues relevant to the empirical study of mysticism. First, one can distinguish between experience and the interpretation of experience such that differently described experiences may have underlying commonalties that escape linguistic structuring (Hood, 1995a,b). Second, important to Stace's treatment of introvertive mysticism is that it is a phenomenologically distinct experience of pure consciousness that is necessarily atemporal, aspatial, and ineffable (Hood et al., 2009). Recently Forman (1990) has coined the term *pure consciousness experience* (PCE) for Stace's introvertive mysticism. Barnard (1997, p. 63) has noted that ultimately James equates mystical experience with any submarginal or subliminal state none of which are clearly pure consciousness experiences. Thus, Hood's mysticism measure is unique in that it focuses only on unity states of consciousness, regardless of how interpreted (Hood, 1995b).

The empirical issue that we wish to address now is the possibility that there is at least one experience that is neither linguistically structured nor culturally determined. Namely introvertive mysticism. We can address this by three areas in which the empirical research suggests that, in Almond's words,

> Now in the mystical case, and taking a theistic mystical experience as our example, what remains as the basic datum of mystical experience if the content of the experience, the experience of the self in union with God, is abstracted? The residue is a contentless experience, one in which there is neither awareness of the self (of normal consciousness) nor of "anything" standing over against the self – a state in which, unlike the waking and the dream-state, there is no subject-object polarity. It is, furthermore, a state in which there is neither incoporated paradigmatic beliefs or symbols, nor, *ergo* reflexive interpretation, for there are no beliefs, thoughts, symbols, dual awareness therein. In other words, it is a state in which the distinctions between the knower, the act of knowing, and what is known are obliterated (Almond, 1982, p. 174).

Almond's thesis is shared by Stace and informs the operationalization of the introvertive factor of the M-scale. Three pieces of evidence can be offered that this experience exists and is a candidate for a universal, something social constructionists and cultural psychologists, especially with a post-modern orientation deny as a form of essentialism. However, our claim is empirical and must be addressed.

As noted above, exploratory and confirmatory factor analyses reveal similar structure to the M scale in various cultures, some as distinct as Iran and the United States (Hood et al., 2001).

Second, as noted above, among the confessional scholars who incorporate their own introvertive experiences into critical discussion of the unity thesis, interviews with mystics in other traditions about the nature of the introvertive mystical experience reveal that despite difference in the linguistic and cultural expression of these experiences, they are, mutually recognized to be essentially the same experience. Forman, who has practiced a Neo-Advaitan form of meditation twice a day since 1969 noted that his experience of PCE was acknowledged as identical to a Zen abbot's account of the same experience and to a Siddha Yoga novice's account of her experience (Forman, 1999, pp. 20–30).

Third, independent scholars who have sought a common phenomenology between various traditions have been able to find it. This includes scholars whose work had not been cross-referenced and hence reached their conclusions independently. For instance, Brainard (2000) found this commonality in the mystical traditions as cultural diverse as Advaita-Vendānta Hinduism, Mādhyamika Buddhism, and Nicene Christianity, supporting a previous finding of Loy (1988) with respect to Advaita-Vendānta Hinduism and Mādhyamika Buddhism.

Fourth, there is a large body of empirical research on the quasi-experimental elicitation of introvertive mysticism in both field and laboratory conditions (Hood, 1995a). These studies indicate that regardless of the conditions that facilitate the mystical experience, the experiences are identical. This has been established for mystical experiences facilitated by set and setting stress incongruities in nature settings (Hood, 1977, 1978), mystical experience facilitated in laboratory-based isolation tank studies (Hood, Morris, & Watson, 1990), and in studies employed entheogens in both religious (Pahnke, 1966) and nonreligious settings (Griffiths, Richards, McCann, & Jesse, 2006).

Conclusion

Religious, spiritual, and mystical experiences are integral to any psychology of religion. We have suggested that almost any experience can be framed such that it is religiously meaningful. Both conversion and deconversion reveal how experiences can be differentially framed. Experiences without interpretation lack the meaningfulness that religious framing can provide (Hood, Hill, & Williamson, 2005). In most religions prayer remains one of the most powerful activities to foster such experiences. Glossolalia can be framed as a form of prayer that may, but need not, involve a trance state. Those who identify themselves as spiritual but not religious reveal that, for some, religious framing becomes too narrow and is abandoned for a personal, eclectic sense of transcendence outside the Church, Synagogue, or Mosque. Finally, mystical experience remains one of the experiences that, whether interpreted in religious or spiritual terms, has proven capable of facilitation by a variety of quasi-experimental means congruent with mystical experiences facilitated by prayer or that simply occur spontaneously.

References

Almond, P. (1982). *Mystical experience and religious doctrine: An investigation of the study of mysticism in world religions.* Berlin: Mouton Publishers.

Anand, B. K., Chhina, G. S., & Singh, B. (1961). Some aspects of electroencephalographic studies on yogis. *Electroencephalography and Clinical Neurophysiology, 13*, 452–456.

Austin, J. H. (1998). *Zen and the brain.* Cambridge, MA: MIT Press.

Azari, N. P. (2006). Neuroimaging studies of religious experience: A critical review. In P. McNamara (Ed.), *Where God and science meet* (Vol. 2, pp. 34–54). New York: Praeger.

Bagchi, B. K., & Wenger, M. A. (1957). Electro-physiological correlates of some yogi exercises. *Electroencephalography and Clinical Neurophysiology, 2*(Suppl. 7), 132–139.

Barnard, G. W. (1997). *Exploring unseen worlds: William James and the philosophy of mysticism.* Albany, NY: State University of New York Press.

Beit-Hallahmi, B. (1977). Curiosity, doubt, and devotion: The beliefs of psychologists and the psychology of religion. In H. N. Malony (Ed.), *Current perspectives in the psychology of religion* (pp. 381–391). Grand Rapids, MI: Eerdmans.

Brainard, F. S. (2000). *Reality and mystical experience.* University Park: Pennsylvania State University Press.

Day, J. M. (1991). Narrative, psychology and moral education. *American Psychologist, 46*, 167–178.

Day, J. M. (1994). Moral development, belief, and unbelief: Young adult accounts of religion in the process of moral growth. In J. Corveleyn & D. Hutsebaut (Eds.), *Belief and unbelief: Psychological perspectives* (pp. 155–173). Atlanta, GA: Rodopi.

DeYoung, C. G., Peterson, J. B., & Higgins, D. H. (2002). Higher-order factors of the Big 5 predict conformity: Are their neuroses of health? *Personality and Individual Differences, 33*, 533–552.

Emmons, R. A. (1995). Levels and domains in personality: An introduction. *Journal of Personality, 63*, 341–364.

Forman, R. K. C. (Ed.). (1990). *The problem of pure consciousness: Mysticism and philosophy.* New York: Oxford University Press.

Forman, R. K. C. (1999). *Mysticism, mind, consciousness.* Albany, NY: State University of New York Press.

Francis, L. J. (2002). Psychological type and mystical orientation: Anticipating individual differences within congregational life. *Pastoral Sciences, 21*, 77–99.

Francis, L. J., & Evans, T. E. (2001). The psychology of Christian prayer: A review of the empirical literature. In L. J. Francis & J. Astley (Eds.), *Psychological perspectives on prayer* (pp. 2–22). Herefordshire: Gracewing.

Francis, L. J., & Louden, S. H. (2000a). The Francis-Louden mystical orientation scale (MOS): A study among Roman Catholic priests. *Research in the Social Scientific Study of Religion, 11*, 99–116.

Francis, L. J., & Louden, S. H. (2000b). Mystical orientation and psychological type: A study among students and adult churchgoers. *Transpersonal Psychology Review, 4*, 36–42.

Francis, L. J., & Louden, S. H. (2004). A short index of mystical orientation (SIMO): A study among Roman Catholic priests. *Pastoral Psychology, 53*, 49–51.

Francis, L. J., & Thomas, T. H. (1996). Mystical orientation and personality among Anglican clergy. *Pastoral Psychology, 45*, 99–105.

Francis, L. J., Village, A., Robbins, M., & Ineson, K. (2007). Mystical orientation and psychological type: An empirical study of guests staying at a Benedictine Abbey. *Studies in Spirituality, 17*, 207–223.

Goodman, F. D. (1969). Phonetic analysis of glossolalia in four cultural settings. *Journal for the Scientific Study of Religion, 8*, 227–239.

Goodman, F. D. (1972). *Speaking in tongues: A cross-cultural study of glossolalia.* Chicago: University of Chicago Press.

Goodman, F. D. (1988). *Ecstasy, religious ritual, and alternate reality.* Bloomington: University of Indiana Press.

Goodman, F. D. (1990). *Where the spirits ride the wind: Trance journeys and other ecstatic experiences.* Bloomington: University of Indiana Press.

Gorsuch, R. L., & Miller, W. R. (1999). Assessing spirituality. In W. R. Miller (Ed.), *Integrating spirituality into treatment* (pp. 47–64). Washington, DC: American Psychological Association.

Griffiths, R. R., Richards, W. A., McCann, U., & Jesse, R. (2006). Psilocybin can occasion mystical experiences having sustained personal meaning and spiritual significance. *Psychopharcomology, 187,* 268–283.

Happold, F. C. (1963). *Mysticism: A study and an anthology.* New York: Penguin.

Hine, V. H. (1969). Pentecostal glossolalia: Toward a functional interpretation. *Journal for the Scientific Study of Religion, 8,* 211–226.

Holmes, U. T. (1980). A history of Christian spirituality. New York: Seabury Press.

Hong, G.-Y. (1995). Buddhism and religious experience. In R. W. Hood, Jr. (Ed.), *Handbook of religious experience* (pp. 87–121). Birmingham, AL: Religious Education Press.

Hood, R. W., Jr. (1977). Eliciting mystical states of consciousness with semistructured nature experiences. *Journal for the Scientific Study of Religion, 16,* 155–163.

Hood, R. W., Jr. (1978). Anticipatory set and setting: Stress incongruity as elicitors of mystical experience in solitary nature situations. *Journal for the Scientific Study of Religion, 17,* 278–287.

Hood, R. W., Jr. (1995a). The facilitation of religious experience. In R. W. Hood, Jr. (Ed.), *Handbook of religious experience* (pp. 569–597). Birmingham, AL: Religious Education Press.

Hood, R. W. Jr. (1995b).The soulful self of William James. In D. Capps & J. L. Jacobs (Eds.), *The struggle for life: A companion to William James' The varieties of religious experience* (pp. 209–219). Newton, Kansas: Mennonite Press.

Hood, R. W. Jr. (2000). American Psychology of Religion and The Journal for the Scientific Study of Religion. *Journal for the Scientific Study of Religion, 39*(53), 1–544.

Hood, R. W. Jr. (2003). Spirituality and religion. In A. L. Greil & D. Bromley (Eds.), *Religion and the social order: Vol. 10. Religion: Critical approaches to drawing boundaries between sacred and secular.* New York: Elsevier.

Hood, R. W., Jr., Ghorbani, N., Watson, P. J., Ghramaleki, A. F., Bing, M. B., Davison, H. R., et al. (2001). Dimensions of the mysticism scale: Confirming the three factor structure in the United States and Iran. *Journal for the Scientific Study of Religion, 40,* 691–705.

Hood, R. W., Jr., Hill, P. C., & Spilka, B. (2009). *The psychology of religion: An empirical approach* (4th ed.). New York: Guilford Press.

Hood, R. W., Jr., Hill, P. C., & Williamson, P. W. (2005). *The psychology of religious fundamentalism.* New York: Guilford.

Hood, R. W., Jr., Morris, R. J., & Watson, P. J. (1990). Quasi-experimental elicitation of the differential report of religious experience among intrinsic and indiscriminately pro-religious types. *Journal for the Scientific Study of Religion, 29,* 164–172.

Hood, W. Jr., & Williamson, W. P. (2000). An empirical test of the unity thesis: The structure of mystical descriptors in various faith samples. *Journal of Christianity and Psychology, 19,* 222–244.

Hood, R. W. Jr. & Williamson, P. W. (2008). *Them that believe: The power and meaning of the Christian serpent—handling tradition.* Berkeley, CA: University of California Press.

Hutch, R. A. (1980). The personal ritual of glossolalia. *Journal for the Scientific Study of Religion, 19,* 255–266.

James, W. (1985). *The varieties of religious experience.* Cambridge, MA: Harvard University Press. (Original work published 1902).

Kaldor, P., Francis, L. J., & Fisher, J. W. (2002). Personality and spirituality: Christian prayer and Eastern meditation are not the same. *Pastoral Psychology, 50,* 167–172.

Kasamatsu, M., & Hirai, T. (1969). An electroencephalographic study on the Zen meditation (*zazen*). In C. Tart (Ed.), *Altered states of consciousness* (pp. 489–501). New York: Wiley.

Kelsey, M. T. (1964). *Tongue speaking: An experiment in spiritual experience.* Garden City, NY: Doubleday.

Kildahl, J. P. (1972). *The psychology of speaking in tongues*. New York: Harper & Row.

Kohls, N., Hack, A., & Walach, H. (i2008) Measuring the unmeasurable by ticking boxes and opening Pandora's box? Mixed methods research as a useful tool for investigating exceptional and spiritual experiences. *Archiv für Religionspsychologie, 30*, 155–187.

Lafal, J., Monahan, J., & Richman, P. (1974). Communication of meaning in glossolalia. *Journal of Social Psychology, 92*, 277–291.

Lange, R., & Thalbourne, M. A. (2007). The Rasch scaling of mystical experiences: Construct validity and correlates. *The International Journal for the Psychology of Religion, 17*, 121–140.

Long, T. E., & Hadden, J. K. (1983). Religious conversion and the concept of socialization: Integrating the brainwashing and drift models. *Journal for the Scientific Study of Religion, 6*, 101–109.

Lovekin, A., & Malony, H. N. (1977). Religious glossolalia: A longitudinal study of personality changes. *Journal for the Scientific Study of Religion, 16*, 383–393.

Loy, D. (1988). *Nonduality: A study in comparative philosophy*. Amherst, New York: Humanities Press.

Malony, H. N., & Lovekin, A. A. (1985). *Glossolalia: Behavioral science perspectives on speaking in tongues*. New York: Oxford University Press.

Maupin, E. W. (1965). Individual differences in response to a Zen meditation exercise. *Consulting Psychology, 29*, 139–143.

McCrae, R. R. (Ed.). (1992). The five-factor model: Issues and applications [Special issue]. *Journal of Personality, 60*.

Naranjo, C., & Ornstein, R. E. (1971). *On the psychology of meditation*. New York: Viking.

Pahnke, W. N. (1966). Drugs and mysticism. *International Journal of Parapsychology, 8*, 295–320.

Paloutzian, R. F., Richardson, J. T., & Rambo, L. R. (1999). Religious conversion and personality change. *Journal of Personality, 67*, 1047–1079.

Peterson, J. B. (1999). *Maps of meaning: The architecture of belief*. New York: Routledge.

Philipchalk, R., & Mueller, D. (2000). Glossolalia and temperature change in the right and left cerebral hemispheres. *International Journal for the Study of Religion, 10*, 181–185.

Poloma, M. M., & Gallup, G. H., Jr. (1991). *Varieties of prayer: A survey report*. Philadelphia: Trinity Press International.

Poloma, M. M., & Pendleton, B. F. (1989). Exploring types of prayer and quality of life research: A research note. *Review of Religious Research, 31*, 46–53.

Poloma, M. M., & Pendleton, B. F. (1991). *Exploring neglected dimensions of quality of life research*. Lewiston, NY: Mellen.

Preston, D. L. (1988). *The social organization of Zen practice*. Cambridge, England: Cambridge University Press.

Rambo, L. R. (1993). *Understanding religious conversion*. New Haven, CT: Yale University Press.

Roof, W. C. (1993). *A generation of seekers: The spiritual journeys of the boom generation*. San Francisco: HarperSanFrancisco.

Roof, W. C. (1999). *Spiritual marketplace*. Princeton, NJ: Princeton University Press.

Ross, C. F. J., Weiss, D., & Jackson, L. M. (1996). The relation of Jungian psychological type to religious attitudes and practices. *The International Journal for the Psychology of Religion, 6*, 263–279.

Ryff, C. D., & Singer, B. H. (1996). Psychological well-being: Meaning, measurement, and implications for psychotherapy research. *Psychotherapy and Psychosomatics, 65*, 14–23.

Samarin, W. J. (1972). *Tongues of men and angels*. New York: Macmillan.

Seigfried, C. H. (1990). *William James's radical reconstruction of philosophy*. Albany, NY: State University of New York Press.

Shafranske, E. (1996). Religious beliefs, practices and affiliations of clinical psychologists. In E. Shanfranske (Ed.), *Religion and the clinical practice of psychology* (pp. 149–164). Washington, DC: American Psychological Association.

Sharf, R. H. (2000). The rhetoric of religion in the study of religious experience. In J. Andresen & R. K. Forman (Eds.), *Cognitive models and spiritual maps: Interdisciplinary explorations of religious experience* (pp. 267–287). Bowling Green, OH: Imprint Academic.

Stace, W. T. (1961). *Mysticism and philosophy*. Philadelphia: Lippincott.
Streib, H., Hood, R. W., Jr., Keller, B., Csöff, R.-M., & Silver, C. (2009). *Deconversion: Qualitative and quantitative results from cross-cultural research in Germany and the United States*. (Research in Contemporary Religion, Vol. 4). Göttingham, Germany: Vandenhoeck & Ruprecht.
Thalbourne, M. A. (1998). Transliminality: Further correlates and a short measure. *The Journal of the American Society for Psychical Research, 92*, 402–429.
Thalbourne, M. A., & Delin, P. S. (1999). Transliminality: Its relation to dream life, religiosity, and mystical experience. *International Journal for the Psychology of Religion, 9*, 35–43.
van der Lans, J. (1985). Frame of reference as a prerequisite for the induction of religious experience through meditation: An experimental study. In L. B. Brown (Ed.), *Advances in the psychology of religion* (pp. 127–134). Oxford: Pergamon Press.
van der Lans, J. (1987). The value of Sunden's role-theory demonstrated and tested with respect to religious experiences in meditation. *Journal for the Scientific Study of Religion, 26*, 401–412.
Wacker, G. (2001). *Heaven below: Early Pentecostalism and American culture*. Cambridge, MA: Harvard University Press.
Wikstrom, O. (1987). Attribution, roles and religion: A theoretical analysis of Sunden's role theory of religion and the attributional approach to religious experience. *Journal for the Scientific Study of Religion, 26*, 390–400.
Zinnbauer, B. J., & Pargament, K. I. (2005). Religiousness and spirituality. In R. F. Paloutzian & C. L. Parks (Eds.), *Handbook of religion and spirituality* (pp. 21–42). New York: Guilford Press.
Zinnbauer, B. J., Pargament, K. I., Cole, B., Rye, M. S., Butter, E. M., Belavich, T. G., et al. (1997). Religion and spirituality: Unfuzzying the fuzzy. *Journal for the Scientific Study of Religion, 36*, 549–564.

Chapter 11
The Spiritual Dimension of Coping: Theoretical and Practical Considerations

Kenneth I. Pargament

Abstract In this chapter, I suggest that religion is designed first and foremost to facilitate spirituality—that is, to help people achieve spiritual goals. Building on this premise, I maintain that attempts to understand religion in purely biological, psychological, or social terms can provide, at best, an incomplete picture and, at worst, a distorted view of religious life. In this chapter, I present a model for understanding spirituality as a natural and normal part of life. I then examine the spiritual dimension of coping with life stressors within the context of this larger model of spirituality. I conclude the chapter with a discussion of the practical implications of spiritual coping.

Introduction

As with many maxims, the old saying that there are no atheists in foxholes is not particularly accurate. In fact, many people do not believe in God before a crisis, hold to their religious unbelief throughout their ordeal, and remain disbelievers after (Brenner, 1980). Yet, like many maxims, this old saying contains a grain of truth. Empirical studies do reveal a link between religion and major life crises. In some groups, religion is the first resource drawn on in stressful times (Conway, 1985–1986). Some experiences are so stressful that they elicit a religious response in a large majority of individuals. Following the 9/11 terrorist attacks, 90% of a sample of people in the United States reported that they turned to religion for solace and support (Schuster et al., 2001).

Theorists and practitioners have long tried to explain the "quickening" of religion in times of stress. Freud (1927/1961) viewed religion as a response to the child-like need for protection and security from the destructive forces in nature and within oneself. Other social scientists have attempted to explain religion in less pejorative psychological and social terms. Geertz (1966), for example, maintained that religion

---

K.I. Pargament (✉)
Department of Psychology, Bowling Green State University, Bowling Green, OH 43403, USA
e-mail: kpargam@bgnet.bgsu.edu

Portions of this chapter, including Fig. 11.1 were adapted from Pargament (2007).

provides its adherents with a sense of meaning in life. "The effort is not to deny the undeniable," he wrote, "that there are unexplained events, that life hurts, or that rain falls upon the just – but to deny that there are inexplicable events, that life is unendurable, and that justice is a mirage" (pp. 23–24). Durkheim (1915) argued that religion is designed to unite its followers into a single moral community. More recently, Kirkpatrick (2005) has asserted that religion is a by-product of evolution.

Although these theories offer very different explanations for the connection between religion and life stress, they rest on a common assumption—that religion is best explained by a factor that is nonreligious in nature, be it anxiety reduction, meaning in life, community solidarity, or evolution. Certainly, we can find people who look to their faith for psychological or social purposes. Consider some examples drawn from our interviews with people from the community. One college student describes her images of God and Jesus in a manner consistent with the writings of Freud: "I view God as a loveable, protective, compassionate, generous father that loves to hold me in His arms and set me on His lap. Jesus I see as a shepherd and I envision myself as a little white lamb who is always following him around, who loves to be held by him and who sleeps next to him." A priest recounts the funeral of his mother and the feeling of community he experienced in a way reminiscent of Durkheim: "The funeral was astounding ... The whole church, everybody was there. Many, many friends were there. Students from here, and the liturgy was a real experience of the resurrection. It was terrific. My blind niece played the piano ... And my best friend David gave the homily ... So there were so many powerful religious expressions and family expressions. It is hard to separate one from the other." In yet another example, a quadriplegic accident victim talks about the meaning he has derived from his faith in language supportive of Geertz: "Well, I'm put in this situation to learn certain things, 'cause nobody else is in this situation.' It's a learning experience; I see God's trying to put me in situations, help me learn about Him and myself and also how I can help other people" (Bulman & Wortman, 1977, p. 358).

These anecdotes illustrate the variety of psychological and social roles religion can play in stressful situations. But do they tell the full story? To frame the question in another way, is religion simply a means of attaining psychological, social, or physical ends?

The Meaning of Spirituality

The concept of spirituality, as used in this chapter, does not refer to a fixed set of beliefs or practices. It is, instead, a process; a part of life that develops, shifts, and changes over the course of the lifespan. Spirituality is defined as "a search for the sacred" (Pargament, 1999, p. 12). Two terms are key to this definition: sacred and search. By sacred, I am referring not only to concepts of God or higher powers but also to other aspects of life that take on divine character and significance by virtue of their association with, or representation of, divinity (Pargament

& Mahoney, 2002, 2005). Many life domains can be perceived as manifestations of God or as imbued with divine attributes, such as transcendence, boundlessness, and ultimacy. For example, love and the products of love—marriage, sexuality, and family—can be perceived as sacred. Human virtues such as forgiveness, gratitude, justice, compassion, and courage can be understood as "signals of transcendence," signs of a reality that goes beyond the immediate situation (Berger, 1969). Time too can be elevated to sacred status as we hear in the words of theologian Abraham Heschel (1986): "Six days a week we live under the tyranny of things of space; on the Sabbath we try to become attuned to holiness in time. It is a day on which we are called upon to share in what is eternal in time, to turn from the results of creation to the mystery of creation; from the world of creation to the creation of the world" (p. 304). By focusing on the sacred as the central phenomena of interest, we are able to expand the subject matter of spirituality beyond traditional religious concerns, such as church attendance, prayer, religious affiliation, and dogma, to a wider range of domains, for virtually any aspect of life can become a sacred matter. It is important to add that perceptions of sacredness are not unusual. In a recent survey of Americans, 78% agreed that they "see evidence of God in nature and creation"; 75% agreed that they "see God's presence in all of life"; and 68% agreed that they sense that their spirit "is part of God's spirit" (Doehring et al., 2009).

The second key term in the definition of spirituality is "search." By search, I am referring to what people do to discover the sacred, develop and sustain a relationship with the sacred, and when necessary, transform their relationship with the sacred (Pargament, 2007). The search for the sacred is perhaps best illuminated by a case example.

The Story of Cindy

Cindy is a 40-year-old married mother of four children who agreed to share her spiritual story in an interview (see Pargament, 2007, for complete story). Though she dressed like a young woman, she had more than her fair share of wrinkles and it was clear that she had seen some hard times. Nevertheless, she spoke with energy, honesty, and deep feeling. For almost as long as she can remember, Cindy said, she felt a hunger for God. At the age of four, she had a life-changing spiritual experience: "I was sitting in a field behind our house, and the sun was going down, and I just felt like God had His arms around me." Cindy believed that this experience was a gift from God: "I think he knew ... that I would need that [gift] to carry me through some of the hard times." Important as it was, Cindy kept her spiritual experience to herself. Her father, a cold and distant man, had been embittered by what he felt was rejection from his church and would have little to do with religion. Her mother kept a bible at home but never broached the subject of religion and never encouraged Cindy to go to church. Cindy would occasionally accompany a friend to her small Protestant church, but there she learned about a divine figure quite different from the God she had encountered in the field. This was a God "sitting up on a throne someplace, and all He ever really did was throw fire balls down on people." Cindy moved into adolescence believing that her relationship with God depended on her ability to live a sin-free life. The stage was set for failure. "The first time I screwed up, I thought, 'That's it,' I blew it, and had nobody to tell me any different. What happened after that was my life really took a downward spiral."

Feeling that she'd lost her "Christian God," Cindy began to search for the sacred elsewhere. Over the next 15 years, she experimented with astrology, tarot card reading, witchcraft, the occult, and Eastern mysticism. She also married four times, gave birth to four children, became addicted to cocaine, and moved out leaving her children behind with her mother.

A turning point in Cindy's life occurred when her mother died 10 years ago. Returning home for the funeral, Cindy discovered that a former "partying" friend had become Christian. Cindy's friend recounted her conversion with the story now popularized in the "footprints poster." The poster depicts two sets of footprints in the sand that then become a single set of footprints in difficult times. The individual in the poster complains: "Lord, I thought that when things are rough you would never leave me." And the Lord responds, "Those were the times that I carried you, and that's why you only saw one set of footprints." Cindy was powerfully affected by the story: "I felt like that was written for me. And when she told me that, I just thought, my God, He's been there with me this whole time. He never left. Jesus has been standing right by me."

Over the next 10 years, Cindy made significant changes in her life. She was treated for her chemical addiction, returned home, regained custody of her children, and developed a new, more compassionate understanding of God: "[He] accepts you just the way you are. You don't have to attain a level of perfection ever. He doesn't expect that from you." Cindy's view of the sacred also broadened. "Now I see [God] more in people and how He affects people's lives."

Currently, Cindy tries to deepen her relationship with God by daily prayer, active involvement in her church, and her new vocation—working with chemically dependent adolescent girls. Though she feels more rooted and stable, she does not believe that her spiritual journey is over. Cindy continues to have some spiritual questions and concerns: "I'd like to know why God let me fall down that shaft with the drugs and the occult and all that. I don't understand why he didn't send anybody into my life at that point. There was nobody, and I don't understand why." However, Cindy is now able to place these questions into a more benevolent spiritual perspective. "[Maybe] He thought I needed the experience to make me a more capable counselor now. It's hard to tell. I mean you're dealing with God. He's a big guy. He knows what He's doing." Asked about the legacy she would like to pass on to her children, Cindy responds in a way reminiscent of her own childhood spiritual experience: "I'd want them to realize that they're not alone . . . that we don't walk this walk ourselves. Once we reach out, Jesus grabs your hand. He's always right there with you."

Cindy's spiritual journey is filled with drama, highs and lows, and critical moments. It is not a one-act play, but rather a series of unfolding episodes. It is not a one-person play, but instead a narrative involving a cast of protagonists set against a larger cultural backdrop. And like any good tale, it contains a plot that lends coherence to the story. It is not hard to discern the driving force in Cindy's story. From her first spiritual experience as a 4-year-old to the security in God's hand she hopes to pass on to her children, Cindy has been engaged in a search for the sacred. Of course, other motivating forces are at play in Cindy's journey. Her hunger for a warm, embracing God could have been a compensation for the coldness she felt in her father or an effort to find relief from the emptiness she felt in her mother. Yet, to reduce her spiritual quest to purely psychological or social factors would fail to explain fully her spiritual persistence in the face of numerous obstacles. It would also leave us with a story devoid of "soul," a story Cindy herself would find unrecognizable.

Cindy's story is only one of many. There is tremendous diversity in the pathways people take to the sacred as well as in the nature of their sacred destinations. How do we make sense of the diversity in the search for the sacred? We turn now to a theoretical model of spirituality (see Fig. 11.1 for a diagrammatic representation; Pargament, 2007).

We will briefly review the model as a whole, highlighting key terms, and then focus in greater detail on the role of spiritual coping in the context of this larger model.

A Theoretical Model for Understanding and Evaluating Spirituality

The search for the sacred begins with the process of *discovery*. People experience the discovery of the sacred in different ways. Cindy perceived that God came to her as young child. While some feel that they have been touched by the sacred, others reach out to something beyond themselves, as we hear in the words of one child's letter: "Dear God, how is it in heaven? How is it being the Big Cheese" (Heller, 1986, p. 31). These experiences are not rare. Moreover, they are consistent with recent work in cognitive-developmental psychology which suggests that children come into this world already equipped with a propensity to seek out, think about, and experience the sacred (Johnson & Boyatzis, 2006). However, the discovery of the sacred can also occur later in life, as Parker Palmer described:

> One night, in the middle of one of my depressions, I heard a voice I'd never heard before, and haven't heard since. The voice said, "I love you, Parker." This was not a psychological phenomenon, because my psyche was crushed. It was 'the numinous.' It was "mysterium tremendum".... That rare experience taught me that the sacred is everywhere, that there is nothing that is not sacred, therefore worthy of respect (Palmer, 1998, p. 26).

As Palmer's experience suggests, the discovery of the sacred has certain consequences. The encounter with the sacred elicits a wave of emotions—what Rudolf Otto (1928) described as the mysterium tremendum—made up of feelings of attraction, including emotions of gratitude, humility, and reverence, and feelings of repulsion, fear, and dread. Haidt (2003) demonstrated how emotions of elevation and awe can be induced spiritually. He exposed one group of participants to video

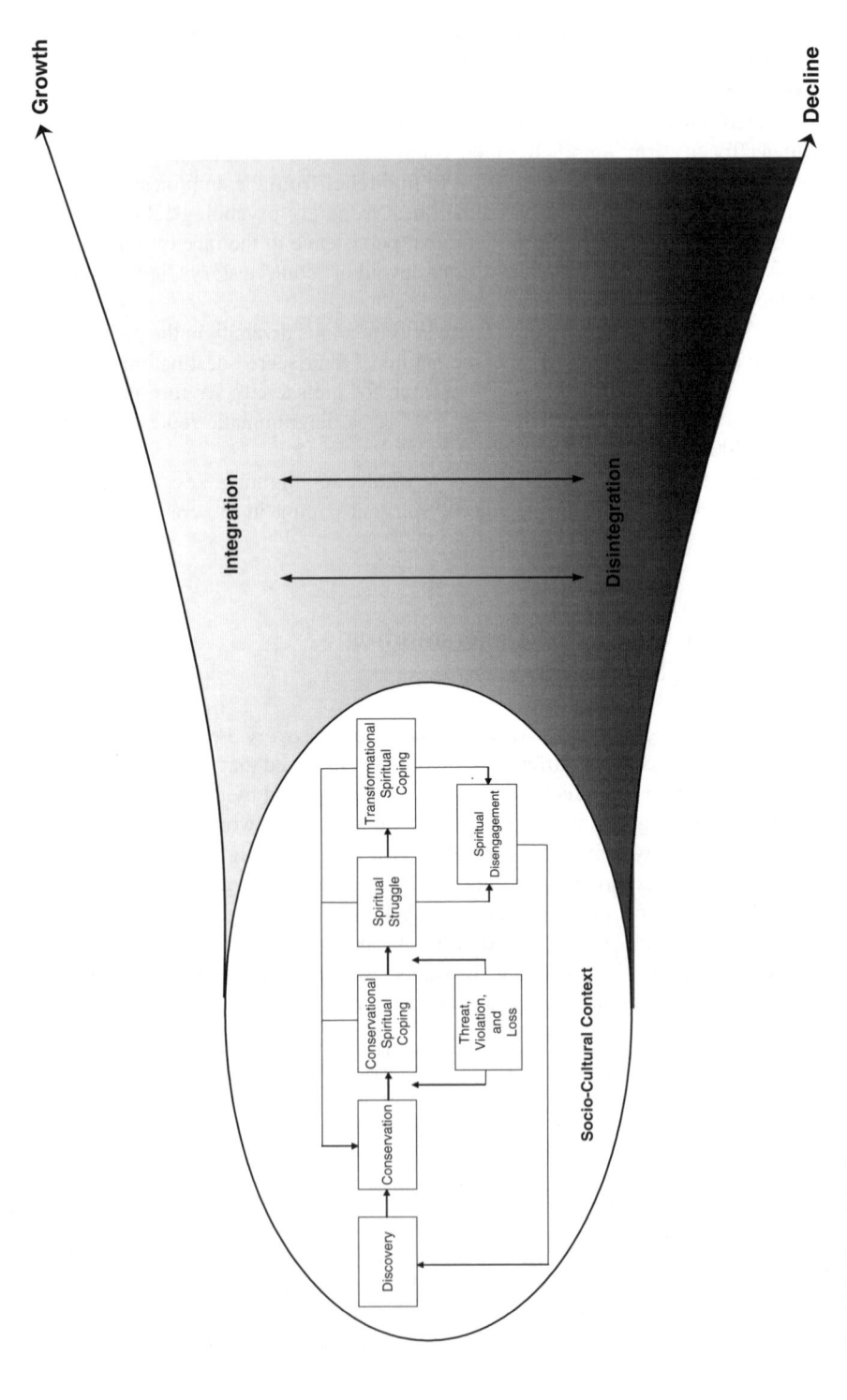

Fig. 11.1 The spiritual process

clips about the life of Mother Teresa. Other participants watched video clips from a neutral documentary and from a comedy sketch. People who watched the clips about Mother Teresa reported more warm, pleasant, and "tingling" feelings in their chests as well as a greater desire to help others and improve themselves. As the source of powerful emotions, the sacred becomes for many a passion and a priority, and as a result, they begin to invest more of themselves in sacred pursuits. For instance, in a study of a national sample of Presbyterians, we found that people who perceive the environment as sacred are more likely to invest their personal funds in environmental causes (Tarakeshwar, Swank, Pargament, & Mahoney, 2001).

Over time, the sacred becomes an organizing and directive force for many people, synthesizing their lives into a larger whole (Emmons, 1999). As Eliade (1957) noted, people want to remain in the sacred realm as long as possible. It is "the place to be." People take a number of pathways to develop and *conserve* their relationship with whatever they hold sacred. Bible study, religious rituals, relationships with clergy and church members, prayer, and meditation are a few of the diverse, traditionally religious ways people try to sustain and deepen their ties to the sacred. Yet, people can also form or follow nontraditional pathways to the sacred, including anything from scientific pursuits to quilting to volunteer services. Cindy, for example, experimented with astrology, witchcraft, and tarot card reading, in her effort to recapture a sense of God's presence in her life.

Empirical studies indicate that by and large people are quite successful in sustaining their relationship with the sacred over time. For instance, in a national survey in the United States, Gallup and Lindsay (1999) found that 97% of those who read the Bible stated that it helped them feel closer to God. Similarly, 95% of those who pray indicated that their prayers had been answered.

And yet, there are times when the search for the sacred may be put to test by trauma or transition. During these times of *threat*, *violation*, or *loss*, people may become spiritually "disoriented" and find it difficult to follow well-worn spiritual pathways. There are, however, a number of *conservational spiritual coping* methods that individuals can draw on to help them sustain their spirituality. These methods are quite effective in general, but not invariably so. Some life events throw the individual's spiritual world into turmoil and the individual then enters a period of *spiritual struggle*. For example, Cindy experienced an internal conflict between her desire to live a life of perfection and her natural adolescent impulses. Her sense of herself as a "child of God" was fundamentally shaken by her adolescent misdeeds that left her convinced that she was an "unforgiveable sinner." Spiritual struggles can be relatively short-lived experiences, followed by a return to established spiritual pathways. But they can also lead either to *spiritual disengagement* from the sacred quest, temporary or permanent, or fundamental *spiritual transformation* in the person's understanding and experience of the sacred. In Cindy's case, the death of her mother and exposure to the "footprint" poster, led to a profound transformation in her understanding of God. In essence, she re-discovered God. Once the sacred has been re-discovered, the task shifts once again to conservation and efforts to deepen a relationship with the sacred as it is now understood. Cindy, for one, is now involved in a variety of pathways, traditional and nontraditional, that help her build an ongoing connection with the divine. The search for the sacred is not time-limited; it continues over the lifespan in the context of situational, cultural, and psychological forces that both shape and are shaped by the nature of the search.

Spirituality as it is defined here is a natural and normal part of life. It is neither inherently good nor inherently bad. In Cindy's story, we can hear spirituality at both its best and worst. How do we distinguish between the highest and lowest forms of spirituality? Elsewhere, I have proposed process-based criteria for evaluating spirituality (Pargament, 2007). From a process point of view, the value of spirituality does not lie in a single belief, practice, affiliation, trait, or experience. It is instead a quality of a person in interaction with situations and his/her larger context. An effective spirituality is a *well-integrated spirituality*:

> At its best, spirituality is defined by pathways that are broad and deep, responsive to life's situations, and oriented toward a sacred destination that is large enough to encompass the full range of human potential and luminous enough to provide the individual with a powerful guiding vision. At its worst, spirituality is dis-integrated, defined by pathways that lack scope and depth, fail to meet the challenges and demands of life events, clash and collide with the surrounding social system, change and shift too easily or not at all, and misdirect the individual in the pursuit of spiritual value (Pargament, 2007, p. 136).

For much of her life, Cindy's spirituality lacked integration in several respects. As a child, her family and larger community were unable to provide her with the support and nurturance she needed to sustain her feeling of connectedness with God. Thus, the pathways she was able to take to the sacred were neither broad nor deep. She was exposed to a limited representation of God, a God who insisted on perfection and rejected those who failed to live up to this impossible standard. This was what Phillips (1997) has described as a "small god." In response to the spiritual vacuum in her life, Cindy's life spiraled down into drug use, promiscuity, and dabbling with witchcraft and the occult. In some sense, it might be said that she sought out "false gods" to fill the emptiness in her core. Following her transformational experience, however, Cindy's spirituality became more integrated. She was able to re-connect with a larger, more compassionate God and a sense of sacredness that expanded to include other people in her world. She developed a broader and deeper set of spiritual pathways to support and nourish her spiritual connection. And she has a newfound flexible understanding of spirituality as a process that is likely to continue to evolve as she moves forward in her life. Cindy does not downplay the challenges she is encountering. But she is now able to cope with these challenges more effectively by framing them within a larger, more benevolent spiritual perspective.

The Spiritual Dimension of Coping

With this theoretical model for understanding and evaluating spirituality in mind, we can now turn our attention more specifically to the role of spiritual coping in the search for the sacred. This discussion will focus on four processes that are central to this topic: spiritual trauma, conservational spiritual coping, spiritual struggles, and transformational spiritual struggle.

Spiritual Trauma

Major life stressors affect people on a number of levels. Empirical studies have documented robust links between stressors and physiological and psychological distress, disruptions in social relationships, shattered assumptions about the world, and questions about meaning and purpose in life (see Janoff-Bulman, 1992; Rabkin & Streuning, 1976). There is, however, another dimension to trauma.

Major life events can be understood spiritually as well as psychologically, socially, and physically. Consider the case of clergy sexual abuse. Certainly all forms of sexual abuse are traumatic. Clergy sexual abuse, however, adds another dimension to the abuse, for it is perpetrated by someone who is imbued with spiritual significance (Pargament, Murray-Swank, & Mahoney, 2008). Thus, clergy sexual abuse is likely to be perceived as a spiritual violation or a "desecration." First, it is a violation of the most sensitive parts of the individual's identity, the soul, or that which makes the person uniquely human. As one survivor of clergy sexual abuse wrote: "This guy had my soul in his hand. It was devastating to know that someone would step out of the powers of spiritual liberty to take over someone else's soul . . . I still have anger about a lot of that and I think more of the anger is about the spiritual loss than anything to do with the sexual abuse" (Fater & Mullaney, 2000, p. 290). Second, clergy sexual abuse is a violation of a sacred role and relationship, one that has been set apart from others. Perhaps for this reason, sexual abuse perpetrated by fathers and father figures has been linked to greater trauma than abuse committed by other perpetrators (e.g., Browne & Finkelhor, 1986). Third, it is a violation of a sacred institution that legitimated the cleric, possibly cloaking the acts of the perpetrator, and failing to come to the aide of the survivor. Fourth, clergy sexual abuse is a violation of a set of rituals and symbols that were intertwined with the offending clergy and institutions. One woman who had been abused by her minister at the age of 14 described her alienation from the rituals of her church: "I began to have dreams of communion wafers crawling with insects, of pearls oozing mucous, of the pastor blowing up the church just as I was about to serve communion for the first time" (Disch & Avery, 2001, p. 214). Finally, clergy sexual abuse can be perceived as a violation of the individual's understanding of God as a loving being who insures that bad things will not happen to good people.

The spiritual character of clergy sexual abuse is rather obvious. But other seemingly secular life events can also be perceived as threats to, violations, or losses of the sacred. For example, in one recent study of a community sample, my colleagues and I asked participants to describe a negative event they had experienced in the past 2 years, and then rate the event on the degree to which they perceived it as a desecration or a sacred loss (Pargament, Magyar, Benore, & Mahoney, 2005). The life events included personal illness, personal injury, death of a close family member, job loss, and divorce/separation. Approximately 25% of the sample perceived their event as a desecration and 38% of the sample perceived it as a sacred loss. Similarly, following the 9/11 terrorist attacks, we surveyed college students in New York and Ohio and found that 50% of the two samples agreed that the attacks were a desecration (e.g., "The event was both an offense against me and against God") (Mahoney et al., 2002).

Major life events that are perceived as spiritual threats, violations, or losses appear to have especially powerful implications for health and wellbeing. For example, perceptions of desecration have been tied to higher levels of anger, post-traumatic symptoms, and depression (Mahoney et al., 2002; Pargament, Magyar, et al., 2005). In the 9/11 study, students who perceived the attacks as a desecration were also more likely to endorse extremist reactions, such as the use of nuclear and biological weapons on countries harboring terrorists (Mahoney et al., 2002). Perceptions of sacred loss have also been associated with higher levels of depression and symptoms of post-traumatic stress (Pargament, Magyar, et al., 2005).

In addition, it is important to emphasizes that crises can affect the spiritual well-being of people. Cindy believed that she had "lost her Christian God." Similarly, we can find anecdotal accounts of the powerful negative spiritual effects of clergy sexual abuse on the individual's relationship with the church and God. As one survivor commented: "I don't think I'll ever step foot in a church again ... I lost my religion, faith, and ability to trust adults and institutions" (Matchan, 1992, p. 8). Other studies have shown that women with a history of childhood sexual abuse are more likely to report negative characterizations of God (Doehring, 1993). College students who report physical and emotional abuse as children are also less likely to maintain the religious beliefs of their families (Webb & Whitmer, 2003). Thus, spiritual traumas impact people, not only psychologically, socially, and physically, but also spiritually.

Conservational Spiritual Coping

Not everyone is devastated by major life stressors. In fact, many people are able to maintain their equilibrium and even thrive in the face of the most challenging of life situations (e.g., Goertzel & Goertzel, 1962). Whether critical life events lead to serious problems appears to depend, at least in part, on the resources the individual is able to bring to bear to these crises. Empirical studies have identified a number of forms of coping that are tied to less vulnerability and greater resilience to major life events (Lazarus & Folkman, 1984).

Spirituality is one potential resource to people grappling with their most difficult life situations. Pargament (1997, 2007) has identified and studied a variety of spiritual coping methods (see Table 11.1).

These methods of coping can help people sustain themselves psychologically and socially. For example, people can find meaning in negative events by reappraising them from a benevolent spiritual perspective, as we hear in the words of a woman who had been paralyzed in a car accident: "I know God doesn't screw up. He doesn't make mistakes. Something very beautiful is going to come out of this" (Baker

Table 11.1 Conservational methods of spiritual coping

Benevolent spiritual reappraisals:	Redefining a stressor through religion or spirituality as potentially beneficial
Seeking spiritual support:	Searching for love and care from the sacred
Seeking support from clergy/congregation members:	Seeking love and care from congregation members and clergy
Seeking spiritual connection:	Searching for a sense of connectedness with transcendent or immanent forces
Spiritual helping:	Attempting to provide spiritual support to others
Collaborative spiritual coping:	Seeking a partnership with the divine in problem solving
Spiritual purification:	Searching for spiritual cleansing through ritual

From Pargament (2007)

& Gorgas, 1990, p. 5A). Spiritual support can also be a source of psychological strength and empowerment. One older man with HIV/AIDS said: "I'm speaking to my higher power, my God. And I give thanks to that power. It has been a source of strength. You know, it's like tapping in to some sort of power source that I can recharge my batteries" (Siegel & Scrimshaw, 2002, p. 95).

These anecdotal accounts are not unusual. Moreover, they are supported by a number of empirical studies that tie spiritual coping methods to better psychosocial and physical health outcomes (see Ano & Vasconcelles, 2005). Consider a few recent examples. Murphy, Johnson, and Lohan (2007) reported that parents who made more use of religious coping methods following the violent death of their child were able to find greater meaning in the death five years later. Krause (2006) found that older church members who offered more spiritual support to fellow members were less vulnerable to the effects of financial strain on mortality. Working with a sample of patients undergoing major cardiac surgery, Ai, Peterson, Bolling, and Rodgers (2006) reported that pre-operative spiritual coping was associated with better post-operative, short-term, global functioning. These studies highlight the important role spiritual resources can play in sustaining people psychologically, socially, and physically when they are going through hard times.

Most importantly, however, these spiritual coping methods are designed to conserve spirituality itself. Many people in crisis speak to the vital spiritual function of these resources. For example, one Hindu woman disabled from birth with a neuromuscular disorder described how her benevolent spiritual perspective helped her not only psychologically but also spiritually: "I was told by the swamis early in my study of Vedanta that disability was present in my life so that I could grow in new ways and progress along the path to God consciousness. I have always had rebellious tendencies, and I am sure that, had I not had a disability, I would have easily succumbed to the temptations of the 60s. ... This life is riddled with physical frustrations but wealthy with opportunities for spiritual growth" (Nosek, 1995, pp. 174–175).

Are spiritual methods of coping effective in conserving spirituality? A number of studies suggest that they are. For instance, in one investigation of medically ill, hospitalized elders, those who made more use of the conservational methods of spiritual coping (e.g., benevolent religious reappraisals, seeking spiritual support, spiritual helping, spiritual purification) reported strong increases in their feelings of closeness to God, their sense of spirituality, and their closeness to their church over the following 2 years (Pargament, Koenig, Tarakeshwar, & Hahn, 2004). Other studies have shown that spirituality is generally quite resilient to the effects of major life crises. Brenner (1980) conducted a retrospective survey of Jewish Holocaust survivors and found that 61% reported no change in their religious behavior before the Holocaust, after the Holocaust, and at the time of the study.

Spiritual Struggles

Although spirituality is generally quite capable of withstanding the effects of major life events, there are times when an individual's spiritual resources are not capable of dealing effectively with the demands raised by internal transitions or external situations. During these times, the individual's system of spiritual beliefs, practices, relationships, experiences, and strivings may be shaken or shattered, and the individual undergoes a spiritual struggle—a period of spiritual uncertainty, tension and conflict.

We can distinguish among three types of spiritual struggle (Pargament, Murray-Swank, Magyar, & Ano, 2005). Interpersonal spiritual struggles involve conflicts among families, friends, tribes, and nations. For instance, in a study of older adults, Krause, Chatters, Meltzer, and Morgan (2000) identified several types of negative interactions among church members, including cliquishness, hypocrisy by clergy and members, and gossiping. One woman complained: "They get off in a corner and talk about you and you're the one that's there on Saturday working with their children and ironing the priest's vestments and doing all that kind of thing. . . . But they don't have the Christian spirit" (p. 519). These kinds of interpersonal conflicts are not uncommon. Nielsen (1998) reported that 65% of an adult sample voiced some sort of religious conflict in their lives, most of which were interpersonal in nature.

Intrapsychic spiritual struggles are defined by questions and doubts about matters of faith. These doubts may focus on one's own ultimate value or purpose in life, or on the claims of religious traditions, as we hear in the painful questions raised by one adolescent: "Is Christianity a big sham, a cult? If an organization were to evolve in society, it would have to excited people emotionally, it would have to be self-perpetuating, it would need to be a source of income, etc. Christianity fits all of these. How do I know that I haven't been sucked into a giant perpetual motion machine" (Kooistra, 1990, p. 95). In one study of a national sample of Presbyterians, only 35% indicated that they had never had any religious doubts (Krause, Ingersoll-Dayton, Ellison, & Wulff, 1999). Exline (2003) identified another intrapsychic spiritual struggle that deserves note—the tension between the desire to cultivate and pursue elevated ends and the temptations to satisfy more basic human appetites. This is the kind of struggle that Cindy experienced as an adolescent.

Perhaps most painful of all are struggles with the divine. These struggles include emotional expressions of abandonment and punishment by God as well as anger and fear toward God. One articulate 14-year-old illustrates this kind of struggle:

> Many times I wonder how there can be a God – a loving God and where He is ... I don't understand why He lets little children in Third World countries die of starvation ... I believe in God and I love Him, but sometimes I just don't see the connection between a loving God and a suffering hurting world. Why doesn't He help us – if He truly loves us? It seems like He just doesn't care? Does He? (Kooistra, 1990, pp. 91–92).

Again, this type of struggle is not unusual. Survey research indicates that 10–50% of various samples report divine spiritual struggles (Exline & Rose, 2005; Fitchett, Rybarczyk, DeMarco, & Nicholas, 1999).

Spiritual struggles appear to be a fork in the road to decline or growth. A number of studies among a variety of samples have linked higher levels of spiritual struggles to declines in mental health, physical health, and even greater risk of mortality (e.g., Ano & Vasconcelles, 2005; Burker, Evon, Sedway, & Egan, 2005; Pargament, Koenig, Tarakeshwar, & Hahn, 2001; Trevino et al., in press). For example, working with a large national sample of college students, Bryant and Astin (2008) found that intrapsychic and divine spiritual struggles were associated with significant increases in psychological distress and declines in self-reported health from freshman to junior years. In addition to their psychological and physiological effects, spiritual struggles can lead to problems or disengagement in the spiritual dimension. A survivor of childhood sexual abuse describes the impact of spiritual struggles this way:

> The death of our God-images causes us pain because we enter a period which is void of any image. Before a new one emerges, we reside in darkness and emptiness. We find it very difficult to pray, and we sense little comfort. We struggle intellectually and emotionally; we yearn for some felt experience of God, yet god is silent. Finally, we begin to wonder if there even is a God because our felt experience seems to be part of the past (Flaherty, 1992, p. 126)

Although spiritual struggles are clearly a source of significant distress for many people, there is some evidence that they may also be a source of personal and spiritual growth. A few investigators have reported that higher levels of spiritual struggle are associated with higher levels of post-traumatic growth. For instance, in a study of people who lived near the site of the 1998 Oklahoma bombing, those who indicated more spiritual struggle also reported greater stress-related growth (Pargament, Smith, Koenig, & Perez, 1998). What determines whether spiritual struggles lead to decline or growth? Certainly, many factors contribute to the direction people take at this fork in the road. One crucial determinant may be whether the individual engages in transformational spiritual coping efforts.

Transformational Spiritual Coping

As Piaget (1954) noted, people generally resist fundamental change. Only after their tried-and-true methods have proven to be less-than-effective are most people willing to entertain the possibility of transformation. This general point holds true for the spiritual domain. Here too people generally prefer to remain with what is familiar than venture off into new paths. Yet, critical life events and the spiritual struggles that follow may insist on change by pointing to the limitations in the individual's understanding of or approach to the sacred.

People can transform their spirituality in a number of ways (see Pargament, 2007). For example, in response to major life transitions such as childbirth, coming of age, marriage, and death, the religions of the world provide their adherents with a variety of rites of passage to mark and facilitate the movement toward new roles and identities. Individuals can also re-vision the sacred following critical life events, as Cindy did in shifting her view from a harsh divine figure that demanded perfection, to a Christian God who had abandoned her after her transgression, to a loving Jesus who had been with her throughout her life. Other people experience a spiritual conversion; a shift in the place of the sacred from the periphery to the very center of an individual's identity. This was the kind of transformation Gandhi was trying to foster in his encounter with a Hindu who confesses, "I am going to Hell. I murdered two Muslim children after the Muslims murdered my family." Gandhi replies, "You may indeed go to Hell. But there may be a way out. Find two orphaned Hindu children and raise them as Muslims" (Decker, 1993, p. 43). As this example also suggests, many people look to their faith for help in the process of forgiveness in which they seek a transformation from a life centered around anger, bitterness, and resentment to one of compassion, peace, and wholeness.

In spite of the central place of spiritual transformation in the narratives of major religious figures across diverse traditions and in the works of the founding figures in psychology, there has been relatively little research on this topic. Recently, however, researchers have begun to take a more serious look at spiritual transformation, including accounts of profound spiritual change (e.g., Miller & C'de Baca, 2001), forgiveness, (Worthington, 2005), and conversion (e.g., Zinnbauer & Pargament, 1998). These findings, preliminary as they are, suggest that people are capable of dramatic and long-lasting change in their spiritual lives. For example, in their study of people who had experienced transformation, what they call "quantum change," Miller & C'de Baca (2001) reported men and women experienced fundamental changes in their most five highly valued personal characteristics. Men changed from "wealth, adventure, achievement, pleasure, and be respected" to "spirituality, personal peace, family, God's will, and honesty." Women shifted in their values from "family, independence, career, fitting in, and attractiveness" before their quantum change to "growth, self-esteem, spirituality, happiness, and generosity" after. Similarly, in a retrospective study of three groups of college students, those who labeled themselves converts, more religious, and religiously unchanged over the past 2 years, Zinnbauer and Pargament (1998) found that the groups of converts and more religious students reported significant improvements in self-esteem, self-confidence, and personal identity, unlike the religiously unchanged students who reported no changes in their sense of themselves.

It is important to add that spiritual transformations are not necessarily positive. Recall that Cindy initially sought out drugs, the occult, and multiple sexual partners following her adolescent transgression and sense of divine abandonment. She herself saw these activities as negative transformations—attempts to replace her lost Christian God with other, admittedly flawed sacred objects. Cindy's personal story may be representative of a broader process at play here. Caprini-Feagin and Pargament (2008) tested the notion that spiritual struggles create a spiritual vacuum in the lives of individuals who then become more likely to engage in addictive behaviors to fill this inner void. Working with a sample of college students, they found that those who reported higher levels of intrapsychic, interpersonal, and divine spiritual struggles were more likely to develop greater addictiveness over 2 months in several domains, including food starving, gambling, prescription drugs, recreational drugs, sex, tobacco, and work. These findings point to the importance of carefully delineating what the individual holds sacred. Whether spiritual transformations are positive will depend in part on the character of the sacred the individual is moving toward the center of his/her life, and the degree to which the newfound spirituality is well-integrated.

The Practical Implications of Spiritual Coping

Building on the growing body of literature on spirituality and coping, practitioners have begun to attend more explicitly to the spiritual dimension in their efforts to promote change (see Pargament, 2007, for review). One direction they have taken has been to help people draw on their spiritual coping resources. Another direction has been to help people address spiritual struggles in their lives.

Helping People Access Spiritual Coping Resources

Practitioners have developed and evaluated a variety of psychospiritual interventions to assist people in the general population dealing with various critical problems. For example, several programs have been designed to foster forgiveness in response to interpersonal hurt, mistreatment, and victimization (e.g., Worthington, 2005). Even though they are still in their early stages of development, these programs have shown some promising results. Rye and his colleagues compared the effects of a religious forgiveness program with a secular forgiveness program for college students who had been hurt in romantic relationships (Rye & Pargament, 2002) and for ex-husbands and ex-wives struggling with anger toward their former spouses (Rye et al., 2005). The only difference between the two groups was that spiritual resources were explicitly interwoven into the religious forgiveness groups while the secular groups made no mention of religion or spirituality. Both groups proved to be helpful in promoting forgiveness. However, an interesting and important finding emerged when group participants were asked afterward what resources helped them the most in the forgiveness process. Members of the secular group indicated that two of the three most common resources they used to forgive were spiritual in nature (e.g., "I asked God for help and/or support as I was trying to forgive"). This finding suggests that even presumably secular approaches to change may have an implicitly spiritual character.

Other programs have helped people dealing with medical illness to draw on their spiritual coping resources. For example, Cole (2005) created and evaluated the efficacy of a manualized, spiritually focused therapy program for people diagnosed with cancer. The program, *Recreating Your Life*, encouraged participants to draw on their relationship with the transcendent for support in addressing four existential issues that people with cancer commonly face: the loss of control, loss of identity, loss of meaning, and loss of relationships. Over the course of the 6-week intervention, participants in a nontreatment control condition experienced significant increases in pain severity and depression; in contrast, those in the spiritually focused condition remained relatively stable. Working with a sample of college students with vascular headaches, Wachholtz and Pargament (2008) compared the effects of a spiritual mantra-based meditation to a secular meditation and progressive muscle relaxation. Participants were randomly assigned to the meditation groups which were taught to meditate in exactly the same way, with the exception of their mantras. Those in the spiritual group meditated to an explicit spiritual mantra (e.g., "God is peace" and "God is good"); those in the secular meditation groups meditated to internal or external secular phrases (e.g., "I am good " and "Sunshine is warm"). Measures were collected before the training, 1 month after the training, and 1 month later. The results were quite striking. In comparison to the other meditation and relaxation groups, those in the spiritual meditation group reported more significant declines in the frequency of headaches, negative mood, and trait anxiety, and more significant increases in existential wellbeing, mystical experiences, and pain tolerance as measured by the ability to keep their hands in ice water for longer periods of time.

Another set of programs has encouraged people with significant mental health concerns to access their spiritual resources. For instance, Richards, Berrett, Hardman, and Eggett (2006) developed and evaluated a spiritual treatment program for 122 women with eating disorders in an inpatient setting. They compared three groups: a spirituality group that read and discussed a spiritual workbook containing a variety of spiritual resources, a cognitive group that read and discussed a cognitive-behavioral self-help workbook, and an emotional support group that discussed nonspiritually related topics. Over the course of treatment, all three groups demonstrated positive changes, but the spiritual groups showed greater improvements in eating attitudes and spiritual wellbeing, and greater declines in symptom distress, relationship distress, and social role conflict. Avants, Beitel, and Margolin (2005) developed a spiritually integrated treatment to facilitate fundamental transformation among drug-dependent and HIV-at-risk clients. Spiritual Self-Schema (3-S) Therapy draws on Buddhist teachings and practices (e.g., self-affirmation, prayer, meditation, noble truths) to encourage clients to make a shift from an "addict self-schema" to a "spiritual self-schema". Initial evaluations of 3-S have been quite encouraging. In one study of treatment-resistant cocaine- and opiate-dependent clients, participants demonstrated a significant change in their self-schemas from the addict self to the spiritual self. In addition, they demonstrated significant declines in drug use and increases in the percentages of drug-free urines, spiritual experiences, spiritual coping, church attendance, and private religious practices.

Helping People Address Spiritual Struggles

A few practitioners have created innovative programs to assist people who are experiencing spiritual struggles in their lives. Although these programs are still in their infancy, they represent an important direction, given the significant implications spiritual struggles hold for health and wellbeing. *Solace for the Soul: A Journey towards Wholeness* (Murray-Swank, 2003) illustrates one such program targeted to the spiritual struggles of female survivors of sexual abuse. As noted earlier, sexual abuse often elicits perceptions of spiritual desecration and struggle. In this nondenominational program, a trained therapist implements a spiritually integrated intervention with a client for 8 weeks. *Solace for Soul* includes prayers to enhance a spiritual connection, focusing breathing to increase the sense of personal control, benevolent spiritual imagery (e.g., God's love as a waterfall within), two-way journaling to God (e.g., expression of feelings of anger and abandonment), spiritual rituals to reduce feelings of shame and self-loathing, and discussion. Using an interrupted time-series design with two survivors of sexual abuse, Murray-Swank and Pargament (2005) demonstrated significant changes in positive religious coping, spiritual wellbeing, and positive images of God over the course of the intervention. At the end of the program, one survivor commented: "This program has really helped me to come together with God a little more. I might go back to church and try praying and listening to God. Although I haven't let go of the anger completely, I am working towards God. Every day ... I notice the anger coming down. I see myself growing in that way. I know now that God is not the person to be angry at. I am angry at the person who's fault it is ... *my dad*" (p. 197).

Lighting the Way is another program that has been designed to address the spiritual struggles of women who have been diagnosed with HIV (Pargament, McCarthy, et al., 2004). As with survivors of sexual abuse, people infected with HIV often report feelings of negative feelings toward God, conflicts with church, feelings of shame, guilt, and punishment by God, and questions and doubts about religious matters. *Lighting the Way* is an eight-session group program that normalizes spiritual struggles, encourages their expression, and offers spiritual resources (e.g., gratitude, finding hope, forgiveness, religious support, spiritual surrender) for those interested in spiritual development. In an evaluation of a comparable program among HIV-infected men and women, Tarakeshwar, Pearce, and Sikkema (2005) found that participants reported significant declines in spiritual struggles and depression, and significant increases in positive religious coping over the 8 weeks of the program. Following one session, a woman in *Lighting the Way* commented, "I felt like something was missing in my life. All my life I was looking for something to fill that space. And I never found it. Friends, good friends, didn't fill that space. Drugs didn't fill it. And finally, I met God, and I feel like my whole chest is full of flowers" (Pargament, McCarthy, et al., 2004, p. 1204).

Conclusions

Spirituality has a dual character in the coping process: it can facilitate the process of change and it can interfere with human growth. In either case, as these programs have illustrated, there is much to be gained by attending more explicitly to the spiritual dimension in our efforts to facilitate health and wellbeing. Of course, these programs represent only a beginning. Exciting opportunities abound for the integration of spirituality into work with other populations as well. For example, spiritual struggles are commonplace and problematic among college students (Bryant & Astin, 2008). These struggles could be addressed more explicitly within the campus curriculum and student support services. Similarly, religious institutions could integrate spiritual struggles more formally in their educational programs, particularly as children move into adolescence when religious questions and doubts become more prominent. All too often religious education ends when it should be beginning, when adolescents are developing the cognitive abilities to grapple with the richness and complexity of spirituality. Efforts to normalize rather than stigmatize spiritual struggles and help young adults anticipate and deal with struggles *before* they occur would be particularly valuable.

In moving from theory to practice, it is vital to recognize that spiritual interventions are just that, spiritual in nature. They are not designed to meet exclusively psychological, social, or physical goals, but are tailored to foster the individual's relationship with the sacred. There is danger then in treating spirituality as merely a convenient tool to reach nonspiritual goals. At the same time, we have to be careful of distinguishing too sharply between spirituality and other spheres of life. Generally, change in one dimension is accompanied by change in another. Nevertheless, programs are likely to be more effective when they are based on a deeper understanding of spirituality itself—what it is, its distinctive function, how it develops and changes over the lifespan, how it can be helpful, how it can be harmful, and how it relates to other dimensions of life. Progress in this area will rest on more explicit attention to spirituality as a focus for change and as an outcome of the change process. This work will be undoubtedly challenging, not because spirituality is removed from everyday life, but because it is so deeply interwoven into human experience.

References

Ai, A. L., Peterson, C., Bolling, S. F., & Rodgers, W. (2006). Depression, faith-based coping, and short-term postoperative global functioning in adult and older patients undergoing cardiac surgery. *Journal of Psychosomatic Research, 60*, 21–28.

Ano, G. A., & Vasconcelles, E. B. (2005). Religious coping and psychological adjustment to stress: A meta-analysis. *Journal of Clinical Psychology, 61*, 1–20.

Avants, S. K., Beitel, M., & Margolin, A. (2005). Making the shift from "addict self" to "spiritual self": Results from a Stage I study of Spiritual Self-Schema (3-S) therapy for the treatment of addiction and HIV risk behavior. *Mental Health, Religion, and Culture, 8*, 167–178.

Baker, R., & Gorgas, J. (1990, July 19). Crash broke her back, but not her spirit. *News Journal* (Mansfield, OH), p. 5A.

Berger, P. L. (1969). *A rumor of angels: Modern society and the discovery of the supernatural*. Garden City, NY: Anchor Books.

Brenner, R. R. (1980). *The faith and doubt of holocaust survivors*. New York: Free Press.

Browne, A., & Finkelhor, D. (1986). Impact of child sexual abuse: A review of the research. *Psychological Bulletin, 99*, 66–77.

Bryant, A. N., & Astin, H. S. (2008). The correlates of spiritual struggle during the college years. *Journal of Higher Education, 79*, 18–27.

Bulman, R. J., & Wortman, C. B. (1977). Attributions of blame and coping in the "real world": Severe accident victims react to their lot. *Journal of Personality and Social Psychology, 35*, 351–363.

Burker, E. J., Evon, D. M., Sedway, J. A., & Egan, T. (2005). Religious and nonreligious coping in lung transplant candidates: Does adding God to the picture tell us more? *Journal of Behavioral Medicine, 28*, 513–526.

Caprini-Feagin, C. A., & Pargament, K. I. (2008). *Spiritual struggles as a risk factor for addiction*. Paper presented at American Psychological Society, Chicago, IL.

Cole, B. S. (2005). Spiritually-focused psychotherapy for people diagnosed with cancer: A pilot outcome study. *Mental Health, Religion, and Culture, 8*, 217–226.

Conway, K. (1985–1986). Coping with the stress of medical problems among black and white elderly. *International Journal of Aging and Human Development, 21*, 39–48.

Decker, L. R. (1993). The role of trauma in spiritual development. *Journal of Humanistic Psychology, 33*, 33–46.

Disch, E., & Avery, N. (2001). Sex in the consulting room, the examining room, and the sacristy: Survivors of sexual abuse by professionals. *American Journal of Orthopsychiatry, 71*, 204–217.

Doehring, C. (1993). *Internal desecration; Traumatization and representations of God*. Lanham, MD: University Press of America.

Doehring, C., Clarke, A., Pargament, K. I., Hayes, A., Hammer, D., Nikolas, M., et al. (2009). Perceiving sacredness in life: Correlates and predictors. *Archives for the Psychology of Religion, 31*, 55–73.

Durkheim, E. (1915). *The elementary forms of religious life*. New York: Free Press.

Eliade, M. (1957). *The sacred and the profane: The nature of religion*. New York: Harvest Books.

Emmons, R. A. (1999). *The psychology of ultimate concerns: Motivation and spirituality in personality*. New York: Guilford Press.

Exline, J. J. (2003). Stumbling blocks on the religious road: Fractured relationships, nagging vices, and the inner struggle to believe. *Psychological Inquiry, 13*, 182–189.

Exline, J. J., & Rose, E. (2005). Religious and spiritual struggles. In R. F. Paloutzian & C. L. Park (Eds.), *Handbook of the psychology of religion and spirituality* (pp. 315–330). New York: Guilford Press.

Fater, K., & Mullaney, J. A. (2000). The lived experience of adult male survivors who allege childhood sexual abuse by clergy. *Issues in Mental Health Nursing, 21*, 281–295.

Fitchett, G., Rybarczyk, B. D., DeMarco, G. A., & Nicholas, J. J. (1999). The role of religion in medical rehabilitation outcomes: A longitudinal study. *Rehabilitation Psychology, 44*, 1–22.

Flaherty, S. M. (1992). *Women, why do you weep?: Spirituality for survivors of childhood sexual abuse*. New York: Paulist Press.

Freud, S. (1961). *The future of an illusion*. New York: Norton. (Original work published 1927).

Gallup, G., Jr., & Lindsay, D. M. (1999). *Surveying the religious landscape: Trends in U.S. beliefs*. Harrisburg, PA: Morehouse.

Geertz, C. (1966). Religion as a cultural system. In M. Banton (Ed.), *Anthropological approaches to the study of religion* (pp. 1–46). London: Tavistock.

Goertzel, V., & Goertzel, M. G. (1962). *Cradles of eminence*. Boston: Little, Brown.

Haidt, J. (2003). Elevation and the positive psychology of morality. In C. L. M. Keyes & J. Haidt (Eds.), *Flourishing: The positive person and the life well lived* (pp. 275–289). Washington, DC: American Psychological Association.

Heller, D. (1986). *The children's God*. Chicago: University of Chicago Press.

Heschel, A. J. (1986). *The wisdom of Heschel*. New York: Farrar, Straus, and Giroux.

Janoff-Bulman, R. J. (1992). *Shattered assumptions: Toward a new psychology of trauma*. New York: Free Press.

Johnson, C. N., & Boyatzis, C. J. (2006). Cognitive-cultural foundations of spiritual development. In E. C. Roehlkepartain, P. E. King, L. Wagener, & P. L. Benson (Eds), *The handbook of spiritual development in childhood and adolescence* (pp. 211–223). Thousand Oaks, CA: Sage Publications.

Kirkpatrick, L. A. (2005). *Attachment, evolution, and the psychology of religion*. New York: Guilford Press.

Kooistra, W. P. (1990). *The process of religious doubting in adolescents raised in religious environments*. Unpublished doctoral dissertation, Bowling Green State University, Bowling Green, OH.

Krause, N. (2006). Church-based social support and mortality. *Journal of Gerontology: Social Sciences, 61B*, S140–S146.

Krause, N., Chatters, L. M., Meltzer, T., & Morgan, D. L. (2000). Negative interaction in the church: Insights from focus groups with older adults. *Review of Religious Research, 41*, 510–533.

Krause, N., Ingersoll-Dayton, B., Ellison, C. G., & Wulff, K. M. (1999). Aging, religious doubt, and psychological well-being. *The Gerontologist, 39*, 525–533.

Lazarus, R. S., & Folkman, S. (1984). *Stress, appraisal, and coping*. New York: Springer.

Mahoney, A., Pargament, K. I., Ano, G., Lynn, Q., Magyar-Russell, G., Tarakeshwar, N., et al. (2002, August). *The devil made them do it: Demonization and desecration of the 9/11 terrorist attacks*. Paper presented at the annual meeting of the American Psychological Association, Chicago, IL.

Matchan, L. (1992, June 8). Ex-priest's accusers tell of the damage. *Boston Globe*, pp. 1, 8.

Miller, W. R., & C'de Baca, J. (2001). *Quantum change: When epiphanies and sudden insights transform ordinary lives*. New York: Guilford Press.

Murphy, S. A., Johnson, L. C., & Lohan, J. (2007). Finding meaning in a child's violent death: A five-year prospective analysis of parents' personal narratives and empirical data. *Death Studies, 27*, 381–404.

Murray-Swank, N. (2003). *Solace for the soul: An evaluation of a psycho-spiritual intervention for female survivors of sexual abuse*. Unpublished doctoral dissertation, Bowling Green State University, Bowling Green, OH.

Murray-Swank, N., & Pargament, K. I. (2005). God, where are you?: Evaluating a spiritually-integrated intervention for sexual abuse. *Mental Health, Religion, and Culture, 8*, 191–204.

Nielsen, M. E. (1998). An assessment of religious conflicts and their resolutions. *Journal for the Scientific Study of Religion, 37*, 181–190.

Nosek, M. A. (1995). The defining light of Vedanta: Personal reflections on spirituality and disability. *Rehabilitation Education, 9*, 171–182.

Otto, R. (1928). *The idea of the holy: An inquiry into the nonrational factor in the idea of the divine and its relation to the relational*. (J. W. Harvey, Trans.). London: Oxford University Press. (Originally published in 1917).

Palmer, P. J. (1998, September). The grace of great things: Reclaiming the sacred in knowing, teaching, and learning. *The Sun*, Baltimore, Maryland, pp. 24–28.

Pargament, K. I. (1997). *The psychology of religion and coping: Theory, research, practice*. New York: Guilford Press.

Pargament, K. I. (1999). The psychology of religion and spirituality?: Yes and no. *The International Journal for the Psychology of Religion, 9*, 3–16.
Pargament, K. I. (2007). *Spiritually integrated psychotherapy: Understanding and addressing the sacred*. New York: Guilford Press.
Pargament, K. I., Koenig, H. G., Tarakeshwar, N., & Hahn, J. (2001). Religious struggle as a predictor of mortality among medically ill elderly patients: A two-year longitudinal study. *Archives of Internal Medicine, 161*, 1881–1885.
Pargament, K. I., Koenig, H. G., Tarakeshwar, N., & Hahn, J. (2004). Religious coping methods as predictors of psychological, physical, and spiritual outcomes among medically ill elderly patients: A two-year longitudinal study. *Journal of Health Psychology, 9*, 713–730.
Pargament, K. I., Magyar, G. M., Benore, E., & Mahoney, A. (2005). Sacrilege: A study of sacred loss and desecration and their implications for health and well-being in a community sample. *Journal for the Scientific Study of Religion, 44*, 59–78.
Pargament, K. I., & Mahoney, A. (2002). Spirituality: The discovery and conservation of the sacred. In C. R. Snyder & S. J. Lopez (Eds.), *Handbook of positive psychology* (pp. 646–659). New York: Oxford University Press.
Pargament, K. I., & Mahoney, A. (2005). Sacred matters: Sanctification as a vital topic for the psychology of religion. *The International Journal for the Psychology of Religion, 15*, 179–198.
Pargament, K. I., McCarthy, S., Shah, P., Ano, G., Tarakeshwar, N., Wachholtz, A., et al. (2004). Religion and HIV: A review of the literature and clinical implications. *Southern Medical Journal, 97*, 1201–1209.
Pargament, K. I., Murray-Swank, N., Magyar, G., & Ano, G. (2005). Spiritual struggle: A phenomenon of interest to psychology and religion. In W. R. Miller & H. Delaney (Eds.), *Judeo-Christian perspectives on psychology: Human nature, motivation, and change* (pp. 245–268). Washington, DC: APA Press.
Pargament, K. I., Murray-Swank, N., & Mahoney, A. (2008). Problem and solution: The spiritual dimension of clergy sexual abuse and its impact on survivors. *Journal of Child Sexual Abuse, 17*, 397–420.
Pargament, K. I., Smith, B. W., Koenig, H. G., & Perez, L. (1998). Patterns of positive and negative religious coping with major life stressors. *Journal for the Scientific Study of Religion, 37*, 710–724.
Phillips, J. B. (1997). *Your God is too small*. New York: Touchstone Books.
Piaget, J. (1954). *The construction of reality in the child*. New York: Basic Books.
Rabkin, J. G., & Streuning, E. L. (1976). Life events, stress, and illness. *Science, 194*, 1013–1020.
Richards, P. S., Berrett, M. E., Hardman, R. K., & Eggett, D. L. (2006). Comparative efficacy of spirituality, cognitive, and emotional support groups for treating eating disorder inpatients. *Eating Disorders: Journal of Treatment and Prevention, 41*, 401–415.
Rye, M. S., & Pargament, K. I. (2002). Forgiveness and romantic relationships in college: Can it heal the wounded heart? *Journal of Clinical Psychology, 58*, 419–441.
Rye, M., Pargament, K. I., Wei, P., Yingling, D. W., Shogren, K. A., & Ito, M. (2005). Can group interventions facilitate forgiveness of an ex-spouse?: A randomized clinical trial. *Journal of Consulting and Clinical Psychology, 73*, 880–892.
Schuster, M. A., Stein, B. D., Jaycox, L. H., Collins, R. L., Marshall, G. N., Elliott, M. N., et al. (2001). A national survey of stress reactions after the September 11, 2001 terrorist attacks. *New England Journal of Medicine, 345*, 1507–1512.
Siegel, K., & Scrimshaw, E. W. (2002). The perceived benefits of religious and spiritual coping among older adults living with HIV/AIDS. *Journal for the Scientific Study of Religion, 41*, 91–201.
Tarakeshwar, N., Pearce, M. J., & Sikkema, K. J. (2005). Development and implementation of a spiritual coping group intervention for adults living with HIV/AIDS: A pilot study. *Mental Health, Religion, and Culture, 8*, 179–190.
Tarakeshwar, N., Swank, A. B., Pargament, K. I., & Mahoney, A. (2001). The sanctification of nature and theological conservatism: A study of opposing religious correlates of environmentalism. *Review of Religious Research, 42*, 387–404.

Trevino, K. M., Pargament, K. I., Cotton, S., Leonard, A. C., Hahn, J., Caprini-Faigin, C. A., et al. (in press). *AIDS and Behavior*.

Webb, M., & Whitmer, K. J. O. (2003). Parental religiosity, abuse history, and maintenance of beliefs taught in the family. *Mental Health, Religion, and Culture, 6*, 229–239.

Wachholtz, A., & Pargament, K. I. (2008). Does spirituality matter?: Effects of meditative content and orientation on migraneurs. *Journal of Behavioral Medicine, 31*, 351–366.

Worthington, E. L., Jr. (Ed.). (2005). *Handbook of forgiveness*. New York: Routledge.

Zinnbauer, B. J., & Pargament, K. I. (1998). Spiritual conversion: A study of religious change among college students. *Journal for the Scientific Study of Religion, 37*, 161–180.

Chapter 12
The Psychology of Faith Development

Jeff Astley

Abstract James W. Fowler is a practical theologian whose main influence has been in shaping a theory of the development of faith in the context of a programme of empirical research. Although this theoretical framework and the research support for it have both been vigorously critiqued, many educators, pastors and counsellors have found their own thinking illuminated by Fowler's claims. This essay provides an overview of Fowler's theory. It begins by relating Fowler's broad account of human faith to a generic concept of "horizontal" spirituality. In describing Fowler's work in more detail, reference will then be made to its psychological and religious roots, its empirical support, and the critical literature that it has attracted. In its final part, the essay traces the relevance of Fowler's account of faith and its development for those concerned with pastoral care and spiritual counselling, as well as readers engaged in more educational contexts.

Introduction

Fowler's doctoral work was on H. Richard Niebuhr (Fowler, 1974), a theologian who remained an influence on his mature concept of faith (see Niebuhr, 1960, 1963) as did Paul Tillich and the religious scholar Wilfred Cantwell Smith. But it was his experiences of listening to people's spiritual stories that led Fowler to attempt an empirically founded developmental theory (Fowler, 1992a, 2004). Working with others at Harvard and later at Emory University, he built up a database of several hundred transcripts of semi-structured "faith development interviews", each lasting up to 3 hours. Heinz Streib, (2003a, pp. 23–24) estimates that approximately a thousand such interviews have now been undertaken by a variety of researchers. In them respondents answer questions about their relationships, experiences, significant commitments and beliefs; discuss what makes life meaningful and how they make important decisions; and give their views on the purpose of life and the meaning of death, as well as their religious views. The resulting transcripts have been

---

J. Astley (✉)
North of England Institute for Christian Education, 18 North Bailey, Durham City DH1 3RH, UK
e-mail: Jeff.Astley@durham.ac.uk

analysed in the light of Fowler's preconceptions about the structure of faith and a developmental hypothesis framed in dialogue with these data about the manner in which faith might change over a person's life.

What Is Faith?

It is important to be clear at the outset that Fowler is using the term "faith" in a wide, generic sense. We may think of this as "human faith" (Nelson, 1992, pp. 63–64), as Fowler claims that faith is an almost universal element of the human condition in that everyone "believes in" something or someone. Religious faith is only one species of human faith; it is faith directed to religious things, in particular to a transcendent God or gods. But everyone has their "gods" in the wider sense of realities and ideas that they value highly and to which they are committed, including their health, wealth, security, family, ideologies and their own pleasure.

For Fowler, the opposite of faith is not doubt, but "nihilism ... and despair about the possibility of even negative meaning" (Fowler, 1981, p. 31); he therefore writes that "anyone not about to kill himself lives by faith" (Fowler & Keen, 1978, p. 1). The human heart always rests *somewhere*.

Many critics have rejected this understanding of faith as theologically inadequate, contending that faith is fundamentally a religious (and for some, a specifically Christian) category. It has been argued that Fowler's view implies that even idolatry is a form of faith (Dykstra, 1986, p. 56) and that his concept is so broad as to be indistinguishable from knowing or "meaning making" in general. For many religious believers, faith is fundamentally a gift of God's grace rather than a human achievement and cannot be separated from the objects or content of faith (Avery, 1992, p. 127; Osmer, 1992, p. 141). But Fowler does allow that God may play a role, additional to the role of creating the natural laws of human development, in changing the content (and perhaps also the form?) of human faith by means of "extraordinary grace" (Fowler, 1981, pp. 302–303, 1984, pp. 73–75).

Despite the above criticisms, many accept that faith is an appropriate word for labelling a fundamental human category that is not restricted to religious people. Generic human faith may be regarded as a useful way of conceptualizing much of human spirituality, particularly when this is understood quite generally at what we may call a "human-horizontal" level as comprising those attitudes, values, beliefs and practices that "animate people's lives" (Wakefield, 1983, p. 549; see also Astley, 2003, pp. 141–144). Like spirituality, an individual's faith is understood here as having at its core a disposition or stance that informs his or her behaviour. It is "a way of moving into and giving form and coherence to life" (Fowler & Keen, 1978, p. 24), affecting how people lean into, meet and shape their experience of life. Faith is thus an activity, something that people do, rather than something that simply happens to them. Although grammatically a noun, faith has the logic of a verb; so that we may properly speak of human "faithing" (Fowler, 1981, p. 16).

Gordon Wakefield's definition also refers to a transcendent ("vertical") dimension or function of spirituality, which involves a person in "reaching out" to "super-sensible realities". Although some of the questions in the schedule for the faith development interview are specifically religious, including references to the interviewee's beliefs about the effect of "a power or powers beyond our control", this dimension of faith is more consistently represented in the more neutral and widely applicable vocabulary of Fowler's category of a "big picture" or an "ultimate environment" (Fowler, 1981, pp. 29–30). This is Fowler's terminology for whatever set of highly valued, indeed ultimately significant, objects—within this world or beyond it—functions as the target for a particular individual's faith, alongside the people who share that faith and to whom she is also committed in faith. These are the things, people, causes, ideals and values that give our lives meaning.

For Fowler, therefore, faith is essentially about "the making, maintenance, and transformation of human meaning" (Fowler, 1986, p. 15). It is the "generic consequence of the universal human burden of finding and making meaning" (Fowler, 1981, p. 33). Because of his focus on psychology, Fowler often expresses this in constructivist terminology, in terms of human meaning *making*; but this should not be taken to imply that this meaning has no objective reference. On Fowler's account, we may say that everybody creates and finds meaning in their lives as they know, value and relate to that which they take to be ultimately meaningful, in commitment and trust. In summary, faith is to be understood as

> the composing or interpreting of an ultimate environment and as a way-of-being-in-relation to it. [It] must be seen as a central aspect of a person's life orientation . . . . It plays a central role in shaping the responses a person will make in and against the force-field of his or her life. Faith, then, is a core element in one's character or personality (Fowler & Keen, 1978, p. 25).

Although most of Fowler's writings are concerned with changes in the *form* or structure of this faith, he also recognizes that over a lifetime important changes in its *contents* frequently take place. He labels these changes in faith content as a "recentring of our passion" (Fowler, 1984, p. 140) and a "conversion" (1981, pp. 281–286). It is significant that, on Fowler's view, it is possible to change the content of our faith while retaining its structural form. We may therefore be converted to Islam, Mahayana Buddhism or atheism, by coming to believe in different things, and yet we might still understand and relate to these new values and ultimate realities *in the same way* as we did within our previous commitment (say to fundamentalist Christianity). This situation is the mirror image of Fowler's more familiar claim that while we may continue to believe in the same things as we grow older, we often come to believe in them in a very different manner. In this case our faith is said to "develop". "One who becomes Christian in childhood may indeed remain Christian all of his or her life. But one's *way* of being Christian will need to deepen, expand, and be reconstituted several times in the pilgrimage of faith" (Fowler, 1986, p. 37).

Any attempt to separate the form from the content of faith in this way is bound to be contentious. At the empirical level, Fowler's research is based on research interviews in which people mostly reveal the mode of their believing through talking about what they believe. At the theoretical level, form and content are two parts of a single phenomenon (faith) that can only be separated by conceptual abstraction. Fowler accepts that the task is difficult. He also allows that changes in the form of faith that are brought about through human development will subtly modify a person's faith contents (ideas, stories, values, etc.), as these are "reworked" at the new stage of development (Fowler, 1981, pp. 275, 285–286, 288, 290–291), essentially by being thought about differently. Thus, while the child's faith may still be said to be "there" in the adult, in the sense that its contents are identifiably the same as before (provided that the adult believes in the same things that he believed in as a child), the faith of the child will have been "amended and adapted through the glass of later ways of faith" as it contributes to the adult's faith (Astley, 1991, p. 3). Similarly, a conversion that leads us to devote ourselves to different gods or causes—that is, different objects and contents of faith—may help trigger a developmental change in our way of being in faith. This usually leads to some sort of "recapitulation" of previous stages and a reorientation of the strengths and virtues of faith acquired at these earlier stages (Fowler, 1981, pp. 285, 287–291).

Fowler analyses the content (objects) of faith into three categories (1981, pp. 276–277). He writes that our images of our ultimate environment derive their unity and coherence from "a center (or centers) of value and power to which persons of faith are attracted with conviction" (Fowler, 1992c, p. 329). (Although Fowler often uses the rather different phrase, "centers of value and images of power", no real distinction is intended: cf. Fowler, 1981, p. 276.) The contents of a person's faith are what a person takes seriously, either because he or she honours and values them or because they are perceived as having power over that person.

The third category of faith content, "master stories" or "core stories", may be thought of in terms of one's personal mythology. This is an overarching narrative that functions as a metaphor for how one perceives and relates to life, particularly one's own life. Stories about God as the all seeing Judge may fulfil this specification, as may this more secular interpretation of life that was once told to Fowler:

> The way I see it, if we have any purpose on this earth, it is just to keep things going. We can stir the pot while we are here and try to keep things interesting. Beyond that everything runs down: your marriage runs down, your body runs down, your faith runs down. We can only try to make it interesting (Fowler & Keen, 1978, p. 23).

Aspects of Faith

How is the form of human faithing understood? Fowler's theory recognizes seven dimensions or *aspects of faith*, which he calls "windows or apertures into the structures underlying faith" (Fowler, 1976, p. 186). This is a useful analogy that allows us to claim that, like the windows of a house, each aspect gives only a restricted view of what lies within, and all of them together may not disclose everything about the house's furniture and occupants.

Although these seven aspects may lead us to focus on certain parts of faith at the expense of the whole, Fowler contends that faith is "an orientation of the total person" (1981, p. 14) and that both cognition and affection are "interwoven" in faith. He is frequently criticized for underplaying its social and affective components, but Fowler insists that he recognizes faith's role as a way of valuing and living in a committed way and that many of the aspects he identifies "represent psychosocial as well as cognitive content" (Moseley, Jarvis, & Fowler, 1986, p. 55; cf. Fowler, 2004, pp. 30–31). Faith gives shape to how people both construe *and relate to* the world, other people and whatever they take to be of ultimate value. Thus "to 'have faith' is to be related to someone or something in such a way that the heart is invested, our caring is committed, our hope is focused on the other" (Fowler & Keen, 1978, p. 18). Nevertheless, Fowler's aspects do seem to reflect the bias of his theory towards construing faith primarily as a way of knowing, thinking and judging.

Aspect A: Form of Logic. This aspect describes the characteristic pattern of thought that a person employs in making sense of the world. Fowler's Faith Stages 1–4 follow Piaget's account of a developmental movement from chaotic thinking to abstract ordered logic by way of concrete inferential reasoning (see Piaget, 1967; Astley & Kay, 1998). Stage 5 thinking is more dialectical.

Aspect B: Social Perspective Taking. This aspect is concerned with how each of us constructs the inner life of another person, seen in relation to knowledge of one's own self. As people develop they slowly become better at taking the perspective of a wider range of increasingly different people.

Aspect C: Form of Moral Judgment. This aspect is concerned with how a person thinks about morality and how he or she makes moral decisions. Fowler's account broadly follows the stages postulated in the work of Lawrence Kohlberg (cf. Kohlberg, 1969, 1986).

Aspect D: Bounds of Social Awareness. Faith is usually a shared activity, and this aspect captures the way in which, and the extent to which, an individual recognizes others as belonging to his or her own "faith community". As faith develops, the boundaries of this "faith church" widen.

Aspect E: Locus of Authority. This aspect describes how authorities are selected and how the person in faith relates to them: in particular, the authorities for this person's meaning making.

Aspect F: Form of World Coherence. This aspect describes how a person constructs his or her world, especially their "ultimate environment". How do people hold together the different elements of their experience and the different things in which they believe, so as to form one coherent *world*view?

Aspect G: Symbolic Function. This aspect relates to how we understand and use symbols. According to Fowler, this develops from regarding—and delighting in— symbols as sources of magical power at Stage 1, through a literal interpretation at Stage 2, to a "demythologizing" of symbols into concepts that are subjected to criticism at Stage 4. A further development is possible to a post-critical "second naiveté" at Stage 5, in which symbols regain something of their earlier power.

When is Faith?

Although the word "development" is used quite widely in educational circles to denote changes in learning brought about by experience, and Christian educators sometimes describe the learning process they are concerned with as "faith development", Fowler says relatively little about the development of faith in this sense. He is concerned, rather, with the psychologist's—and, more generally, the biologist's—notion of development as a change that is internally driven, rather than one dependent on external forces such as those that facilitate learning. Hence, faith development for Fowler is a progressive unfolding or maturation of faith.

Working within the theoretical paradigm of cognitive developmental psychology, Fowler postulated a sequence of discrete stages that progressively built on earlier stages. On this account of things a stage is an integrated system of mental operations ("structures") of thinking and valuing; in Fowler's case this is made up of the seven component aspects. These stages of relative stability or "equilibration" are said to alternate with periods of transition during which one or more of the faith aspects shifts in its form, until the whole structure (that is, all the aspects) changes and faith is restructured into a new, stable stage. This process may be thought of as losing (one way of being in) faith in order to gain (another way of) faith. Fowler writes that "to be 'in' a given stage of faith means to have a characteristic way of finding and giving meaning to everyday life". It is to have a worldview, "with a particular 'take' on things" (Fowler, 1996, p. 68).

While Fowler regards the sequence of stages as hierarchical (with each stage building on its predecessor) and invariant (one cannot "miss out" a stage), not everyone moves through all the stages. In fact very few interviewees have ever been designated at Stage 6; and in Fowler's original sample of 359 subjects of different ages, 65% were at Stages 3 or 4 or in transition between them. Seventy-two per cent of the 7–12 age group were at Stage 2; 50% of the 13– to 20-year-olds at Stage 3; and 56% of the 41– to 51-year-olds at Stage 4. Many may continue in Stage 3 for most of their adult lives, and a few will remain at Stage 2.

Pre-stage 0: Primal or Undifferentiated Faith (circa 0–4 years). The foundations of faith are laid down at this pre-stage, in which the child's ultimate environment is represented by her primary carer and immediate environment. In this context, faith begins with a disposition to trust, and our first *"pre-images* of God" are mediated through "recognizing eyes and confirming smiles" (Fowler, 1981, p. 121). (Clearly, this is not a stage that can be identified by formal interviews.)

Stage 1: Intuitive-Projective Faith (circa 3–7 years). This stage is characterized by the great influence of images and symbols, which are viewed magically and form a chaotic collage that makes up the child's ultimate environment. Thinking is intuitive, rather than discursive, and it is episodic—yielding an impressionistic scrapbook of thoughts, not an ordered pattern. The lack of control on the imagination makes faith at this stage very fertile, but sometimes dangerous.

Stage 2: Mythic-Literal Faith (circa 6–12). At this stage the child develops real skills of reasoning that enables him to order his experience so as to distinguish between true stories and fictions. Children at this stage thrive on stories and for them "the narrative structuring of experience ... provides a central way of establishing identity", through learning the stories of one's own community (Fowler, 1987, p. 61). However, the child—who is here reasoning at a concrete level—can become trapped in a story and in his literal, one-dimensional view of symbols.

Stage 3: Synthetic-Conventional Faith (circa 11–18, and many adults). The person at this stage (usually an adolescent) can now think abstractly and reflectively and has a new capacity for perspective taking that leads her to conform to a group of significant others. It is out of the convictions and values of these other people that the person at Stage 3 "welds together" (synthesizes) a form of second-hand faith: that is, a heteronomous, conformist and conventional worldview. At this stage, however, the person is not yet aware that she *has* a worldview, or where it comes from. "In this stage one is *embedded* in his or her faith outlook" (Fowler & Osmer, 1985, p. 184).

Stage 4: Individuative-Reflective Faith (from circa 17 or 18 onwards, or from one's thirties or forties onwards). When the adult can no longer tolerate the diversity of views and roles that make up Stage 3 faithing, individuals may truly become individuals by detaching from the defining group and (metaphorically or literally) "leaving home", enabling them to decide for themselves what it is they believe. At this stage one's faith can really be said to be an *owned* faith, as heteronomy gives way to autonomy. The transition to Stage 4 is frequently marked by some form of struggle and a vertiginous recognition of the variety of possible worldviews (Sharon Parks distinguishes two distinct stages within Fowler's Stage 4, the first being a post-adolescent, young adult stage of wary and tentative "probing commitment" before adulthood is reached: Parks, 1986, p. 76). The new capacity and impulse to judge for one's self, and to justify one's own truth, may make some who are at this stage unwilling to recognize the value of other voices, and rather over-reliant on their own reasoning powers.

Stage 5: Conjunctive Faith. (This is rare before age 30—only 7% of Fowler's total sample are at this stage, although another 8% are in transition towards it.) What Stage 4 "struggled to bring under consciousness and control", Stage 5 "must allow to become porous and permeable" (Fowler, 1986, p. 30). There is now a new openness to the interpretations of others and a new willingness to live with truths in tension, including the paradoxes and ambiguities of the mature life of faith (Fowler, 1984, p. 65). This is not, however, the easy relativism that claims that "all voices are true" (which is more characteristic of Stage 3, cf. Astley, 2000b), but a confidence in their own viewpoint that allows some people humbly to recognize both the multidimensionality of truth and that reason cannot decide everything on its own.

Stage 6: Universalizing Faith. (This is a very rare stage, represented by only 0.3% of Fowler's sample; its characteristics are usually only shown by those who are advanced in years.) Essentially an extrapolation from Stage 5, this form of faith involves a relinquishing and transcending of the self and discovers a new simplicity at the other side of complexity. In Stage 6, "a person more and more becomes herself as she increasingly widens her circle of concern and truth-finding" (Astley, 1991, p. 35).

(For more detail about the stages, see Fowler, 1981, Pt. IV.)

Criticisms

Despite some unease in a number of areas—including the generality and abstraction of Fowler's constructs, the wide-ranging nature of his hypothesis and the large number of unproven assumptions it involves—Nelson and Aleshire's review of Fowler's research concluded on a fairly positive note (Nelson & Aleshire, 1986, pp. 199–200), arguing that: (a) Fowler treats his data very tentatively; (b) the research is adequate "for the proposal of a theory", if not for its confirmation (although "to some extent this theory can be disconfirmed"); and (c) "his research methods are, by and large, quite consistent with his structuralist approach". John Snarey's statistical study, which used faith development analysis to study kibbutzim, very few of whom "considered themselves religious in any theistic sense" (Snarey, 1991, p. 289), supported several elements in Fowler's theory: (a) that there is indeed a general, unified dimension of faith development; (b) that variations in other relevant criteria (including moral and ego development) covary with faith development in a coherent manner; and (c) that the faith of non-Christians and non-theists is not undervalued by Fowler's model. Stephen Parker has recently concluded that the faith development interview "is clearly adequate for research purposes" (Parker, 2006).

Nevertheless, Fowler's claims have been widely criticized. Much of this criticism has focused on the difficulty of providing adequate empirical support for this "grand hypothesis" of faith development through his chosen methodology of analyzing transcriptions of semi-structured interviews. This process involves treating each interview response as expressing one of the seven aspects of faith and identifying the stage level of these aspects. The resulting scores are then "averaged out" for a given aspect and then again across all seven aspects to identify the interviewee's overall faith stage, which tends to flatten out scores. Interviews that span two, or even more, stages are taken to represent transition between stages.

It is also a weakness that very little longitudinal work has been done (although see Smith, 2003), leaving the pattern of faith development largely to be inferred from cross-sectional data. It has been further argued that scores on measures of religious judgment and faith reasoning lie too close to those of moral judgment for them to be treated as distinctive from them; and that there is such diversity in the "religious voice" that the idea of any underlying development of deep structures of meaning making seems implausible (Day, 2001, 2002).

Concern has also been expressed that Fowler's scheme fits male development better than that of females (see Slee, 1996, pp. 88–92), a view that parallels Carol Gilligan's critique of Kohlberg's stages of moral development (Gilligan, 1980, 1982). A number of studies of women's faith development argue that Fowler's account of Stage 4 is particularly inadequate. Karen DeNicola writes that "persons who fail to blend reason and feeling—specifically persons who rely solely on rational certainty—can too easily be scored at Stage 4" (Moseley, Jarvis, & Fowler, 1993, Appendix H). The work of Belenky, Clinchy, Goldberger, and Tarule (1986, chap. 6) distinguishes two ways in which females may move into what they call "procedural knowing" (which is akin to Stage 4): a "separate" style involving distancing and objective reasoning and a "connected" style that majors on reflection through participation and dialogue. Fowler admits (in Astley & Francis, 1992, pp. xii–xiii) that females—and some males—who tread this second path may be underscored in his analysis. Fowler also accepts that any claims to cultural *universality* for his faith development sequence, as opposed to his claim about the universality of human faith as such, would require the support of much more evidence from cross-cultural studies (see Slee, 1996, pp. 86–88).

A more theoretical critical question is often raised as to whether Fowler's developmental scheme is to be regarded merely as *descriptive* of how human faith does develop, or as representing an intentionally or unintentionally *normative* prescription of how faith—and therefore spirituality?—should develop. Certainly, Fowler's Stage 6, for which there is so little empirical support, must be regarded as a normative extrapolation from Stage 5. Fowler himself allows that his theory has

> established a normative thesis about the shape of human maturity and fulfillment.... [since] other things being equal, it is desirable for persons to continue the process of development, engaging in the often protracted struggles that lead to stage transition and the construction of new and more complex patterns of meaning making (Fowler, in Astley & Francis, 1992, pp. xi–xii).

Yet he also insists both that each stage has its own dignity and integrity and that each may be appropriate: that is, the right stage "at the right time" for a person's life (1981, p. 274). Certainly, people at later stages are not to be regarded as more valuable, nor as more "religious", "saintly" or "saved"—and, similarly, not as "more spiritual". Without doubt, however, people in these later stages reveal an increased capacity for understanding complex experiences and frequently a wider and more consistently human care for others.

Many scholars have insisted that Fowler is most vulnerable in his reliance on a framework of cognitive developmentalism based on Lawrence Kohlberg and Jean Piaget (see, e.g., Day, 2001; Heywood, 1992, 2008). Such theories, it is alleged, hardly do justice to the complex, multi-faceted nature and context of human development, or the influences that bear upon it. Fowler himself has recently admitted that "the most vulnerable feature" of formalist stage theories such as his own is "the tendency to overtrust the structuring power of the formally describable operations of knowing and construing", acknowledging that this can be "only half his story" of what shapes and maintains a person's worldview (Fowler, 2001, p. 169). The rest of the tale surely requires reference to a person's cultural environment and life history and perhaps to his or her personality as well. Fowler, with a nod to Heinz Streib (see below), even proposes his own theory of types (but of people rather than of faith—e.g. "rational critical", "diffuse"), which could "crosscut stages but not replace them".

It should be pointed out that, although Fowler's recent work has focused more on practical theology than on the psychology of religious development, there have been some shifts in his thinking on faith development. These include the integration of psychodynamic and psychosocial categories from the work of Robert Kegan (1982) in Fowler (1987) and of Daniel Stem (1985, 2000) and Ana-Maria Rizzuto (1991) in Fowler (1996). These modifications have begun to take the account of faith development beyond the narrow confines of pure structural developmentalism and the rather etiolated notion of faith that it generates.

Heinz Streib is another who criticizes faith development theory for its narrow point of view, resulting from its espousal of cognitive development as the motor of religious development (e.g. Streib, 2003b, pp. 124–126, 2003c, p. 7). He argues that faith development theory needs to account not only for structural diversity, but also for diversity in the content (especially the narratives) of faith (Streib, 1991, 2003a, p. 36). Drawing on his own empirical studies, Streib has proposed a reformulation of faith development theory. He prefers a typology of religious *styles of faith* that places more emphasis on narratives about a person's life history and accounts of her "life world", as well as research evidence from the psychodynamics of a person's representation of God. These faith styles are modelled as a series of overlapping curves, which replace Fowler's sequence of non-overlapping stages understood as structural wholes connected by periods of transition. The curves that represent each faith style rise from a low level and "descend again after a culminating point" (Streib, 2001, p. 149); each then persists at a lower level while succeeding styles come into their own. Each of these styles may begin to show its effect rather earlier than Fowler's theory of stages would allow, and each continues to be relevant after it has reached its biological peak. At any one time, then, an individual may have access to a range of different faith styles. Unlike the sequential, invariant and hierarchical typology of stages as structural wholes that are restructured and *trans*formed during development, this revised perspective sees development largely as a matter of an individual's operating through and coping with his or her integration of a number of faith styles.

Streib's theory designates five religious styles, each of which show obvious parallels with Fowler's stages:

(1) the *subjective* religious style of the infant;
(2) the *instrumental-reciprocal* religious style of later childhood, which is dominated by story telling;
(3) the *mutual religious* style characteristic of adolescence;
(4) the *individuative-systemic* religious style, which focuses on reasoned reflection and adopts a critical distance from matters of belief while at the same time hungering for intimacy and relatedness;
(5) the *dialogical* religious style, which is more open to beliefs different from one's own and involves a certain "letting go" of the self.

In the latest edition of the *Manual for Faith Development Research*, the authors write:

> While the perspective that faith development proceeds in a sequence of stages by which persons shape their relatedness to a transcendent center or centers of value is the basic framework of faith development theory and research, the assumption that a stage forms a 'structural whole' cannot be postulated a priori and prior to empirical investigation, when, besides cognitive development, the psycho-dynamic and relational-interpersonal dimensions of development, the (changing) relations to self and tradition, are included and when we theoretically allow for coexistence, for regressions to, or revivals of, earlier biographical forms of meaning-making. ... Thus, it cannot be excluded that individuals may revert to earlier styles, that elements of different styles are at the disposal of a person at the same time.
>
> Taking up and trying to integrate these recent contributions, faith development research accounts for the multidimensionality of faith development, including biographical, psychodynamic and social contexts (Fowler, Streib, & Keller, 2004, p. 13).

Writing some years before, and from a far less research-based perspective, the Christian educationalist John Westerhoff also proposed "four distinctive styles of faith": experienced, affiliative, searching and owned faith. He likened these to the annual rings of a tree, with the individual retaining the earlier faith style as a new one is added, and being capable of re-adopting the earlier style at any time (Westerhoff, 1976, pp. 89–103). In his later work, Westerhoff declared that he had moved on from speaking of faith development and (surprisingly) of "four stages of faith", expressing a preference for the metaphors of "pathways" or "trails" in the journey of faith: the affiliative-experiencing, illuminative-reflective and unitive-integrating ways. Unlike Fowler's understanding of sequential faith development, these may be travelled "at any time, in any order", with the individual returning at will to an earlier track (Westerhoff, 1983, pp. 44–46).

Relevance and Implications

Despite the criticism voiced by Nelson and Aleshire about the limitations of Fowler's research method, these authors concluded by asking whether the developmental journey that he traces "'rings true' with travellers who reflect equally seriously on their own constructions of meaning, values, relationships and centers of power" (in Nelson & Aleshire, 1986, p. 200). Many have responded to the question in the affirmative. Thus Nicola Slee writes that Fowler's work "continues to offer a rich resource to educators, pastors and others concerned with the development of spirituality" (Slee, 1996, p. 92). A number of areas of faith development theory and research have been cited as providing a relevant and illuminating perspective on human spirituality and wellbeing, and the work of the helping professions (see Streib, 2003a, pp. 16–19).

Religious education. Education into (rather than nonconfessionally "about") religion is the area of practice that has adopted the faith development conceptualization most enthusiastically (see Seymour & Miller, 1982, chap. 4; Hull, 1985, chap. 4; Fowler, Nipkow, & Schweitzer, 1992; Astley & Francis, 1992, sect. 8; Astley, 2000a; Fowler, 2004, pp. 413–415). This may seem surprising, given that Fowler's theory deals with human development rather than learning, but educators need to take account of the stage of development of learners in planning their teaching (see Stokes, 1982; Moseley & Brockenbrough, 1988; Blazer, 1989; Astley, 1991, pp. 70–77; Fowler, 1984, 1991a). In this context, for example, Fowler's work encourages religious educators to recognize the importance of images with learners at Stage 1 and of stories with those at Stage 2. It might also influence them to be more sensitive to the adolescent who is at Stage 3 and not yet ready to take responsibility for his or her own decisions about beliefs and value. They might also anticipate the rather rigid "Either/Or" ideology of the person at Stage 4, which contrasts so markedly with the "Both/And" openness of the more mature adult at Stage 5. We should note, however, that according to Fowler, "it should never be the primary goal of religious education simply to precipitate and encourage stage advancement.... Movement in stage development ... is a by-product of teaching the substance and the practices of faith" (2004, p. 417).

Much religious education in churches and elsewhere is targeted at groups rather than individuals and often needs to accommodate people at a variety of faith stages (as is the case with many sermons and services). For Streib, a religious styles perspective should release educators to get children and adults to "understand and anticipate the higher stages ... and [even] ... adopt them on a trial basis" (Streib, 2004, p. 432).

Pastoral work (including spiritual counselling) is the next most influenced area, with Fowler's monograph on faith development and pastoral care (Fowler, 1987) being a particular inspiration here. Those with both educational and pastoral interests are likely to take seriously Fowler's remarks about the importance of the "modal development level" of a congregation or other religious community (its average expectable level of adult faith development); as well as the significance of generating a "climate of developmental expectation" by providing "rites of passage and opportunities for vocational engagement that call forth the gifts and emergent strengths of each stage of faith" (Fowler, 1981, p. 296). Many of the mainstream topics in pastoral care—including the interaction of religion with health and coping—seem open to enrichment from a theory of faith stages or styles.

In brief, "the pastoral care of individuals needs to be informed by as full account as possible of 'where they are'" (Astley, 1991, p. 66; cf. Astley & Francis, 1992, sect. 7). Spiritual counsellors, like educators, will need to take account of people's developmental stage in seeking to help them walk their own spiritual paths (see Stokes, 1982; Fowler, 1984; Astley & Wills, 1999).

The family is another area where pastoral care and educational concerns overlap. The family has its own developmental history which overlaps with the faith development of its individual members; it also provides a paradigm of a social unit that comprises people at different faith stages (or styles), who need to live, work, care and learn together. The family with its shared stories, memories, celebrations and rituals—representing a shared faith content—may be viewed as a faith community or "domestic church", where both the problems and possibilities of unity with diversity may be helpfully informed by an account of the variety of ways of being in faith that it comprises (see Fowler, 1990, 1992c).

Public theology has been a growing interest of James Fowler in recent years. In this context he takes up Martin Marty's concern for a "public church" (Marty, 1981) that contributes towards understanding and enriching the common good of society. Faith development theory is relevant here if, as Fowler argues, a post-conventional (and, preferably, a Stage 5 faith) is necessary for a public church of this kind (Fowler, 1987, p. 97, 1991b, p. 191).

History of ideas. In some of his writings (see especially Fowler, 1992b, 1996), the sequence of faith development has been used by Fowler to illuminate the oft-remarked shift in cultural consciousness from a society structured by external authority (which parallels Stage 3), through the Enlightenment focus on reason and autonomy (Stage 4), to our current "post-modern" (Stage 5) outlook of openness to multiple, dialectical perspectives on the truth. This claim might illuminate the cultural and intellectual context of much contemporary spirituality.

References

Astley, J. (Ed.). (1991). *How faith grows: Faith development and Christian education*. London: National Society/Church House Publishing.

Astley, J. (2000a). Insights from faith development theory and research. In Astley (Ed.), *Learning in the way: Research and reflection on adult Christian education* (pp. 124–142). Leominster, UK: Gracewing.

Astley, J. (2000b). On gaining and losing faith with style: A study of post-modernity and/or confusion among college students. In L. J. Francis & Y. J. Katz (Eds.), *Joining and leaving religion: Research perspectives* (pp. 249–268). Leominster, UK: Gracewing.

Astley, J. (2003). Spiritual learning: Good for nothing? In D. Carr & J. Haldane (Eds.), *Spirituality, philosophy and education* (pp. 141–153). London: RoutledgeFalmer.

Astley, J., & Francis, L. J. (Eds.). (1992). *Christian perspectives on faith development: A reader*. Leominster, UK: Gracewing; Grand Rapids, Michigan: Eerdmans.

Astley, J., & Kay, W. K. (1998). Piaget and Fowler. In W. K. Kay & L. J. Francis (Eds.), *Religion in education* (Vol. 2, pp. 137–168). Leominster, UK: Gracewing.

Astley, J., & Wills, N. (1999). Adolescent "faith" and its development. *Youth and Policy: The Journal of Critical Analysis, 65*, 60–71.

Avery, W. O. (1992). A Lutheran examines James W. Fowler. In J. Astley & L. J. Francis (Eds.), *Christian perspectives on faith development: A reader* (pp. 122–134). Leominster, UK: Gracewing. (First published 1990).

Belenky, M., Clinchy, B. M., Goldberger, N. R., & Tarule, J. (1986). *Women's ways of knowing*. New York: Basic Books.

Blazer, D. (Ed.). (1989). *Faith development in early childhood*. Kansas City, Missouri: Sheed & Ward.

Day, J. M. (2001). From structuralism to eternity? Re-imaging the psychology of religious development after the cognitive-developmental paradigm. *The International Journal for the Psychology of Religion, 11*(3), 173–183.

Day, J. M. (2002). Religious development as discursive construction. In C. A. M. Hermans, G. Immink, & de Jong, A. (Eds.), *Social constructionism and theology* (pp. 63–89). Leiden, The Netherlands: Brill.

Dykstra, C. (1986). What is faith? An experiment in the hypothetical mode. In C. Dykstra & S. Parks (Eds.), *Faith development and Fowler* (pp. 45–64). Birmingham, Alabama: Religious Education Press.

Fowler, J. W. (1974). *To see the kingdom: The theological vision of H. Richard Niebuhr*. Nashville, Tennessee: Abingdon.

Fowler, J. W. (1976). Stages in faith: The structural developmental approach. In T. C. Hennessy (Ed.), *Values and moral education* (pp. 173–211). New York: Paulist.

Fowler, J. W. (1981). *Stages of faith: The psychology of human development and the quest for meaning*. San Francisco, California: Harper & Row.

Fowler, J. W. (1984). *Becoming adult, becoming Christian*. San Francisco, California: Harper & Row.

Fowler, J. W. (1986). Faith and the structuring of meaning. In C. Dykstra & S. Parks (Eds.), *Faith development and Fowler* (pp. 15–42). Birmingham, Alabama: Religious Education Press.

Fowler, J. W. (1987). *Faith development and pastoral care*. Philadelphia: Fortress.

Fowler, J. W. (1990). Faith development through the family life cycle. *Network Papers 31*. New Rochelle, New York: Don Bosco Multimedia.

Fowler, J. W. (1991a). Stages of faith consciousness. In F. K. Oser & W. G. Scarlett (Eds.), *Religious development in childhood and adolescence* (pp. 27–45). San Francisco, California: Jossey-Bass.

Fowler, J. W. (1991b). *Weaving the new creation: Faith development and public church*. San Francisco, California: Harper & Row.

Fowler, J. W. (1992a). Faith, liberation and human development. In J. Astley & L. J. Francis (Eds.), *Christian perspectives on faith development*: A reader (pp. 3–14). Grand Rapids: Eerdmans. (First published 1974).

Fowler, J. W. (1992b). The Enlightenment and faith development theory. In J. Astley & L. J. Francis (Eds.), *Christian perspectives on faith development*: A reader (pp. 15–28). Grand Rapids Michigan: Eerdmans. (First published 1988).

Fowler, J. W. (1992c). Perspectives on the family from the standpoint of faith development theory. In J. Astley & L. J. Francis (Eds.), *Christian perspectives on faith development*: A reader (pp. 320–353). Grand Rapids, Michigan: Eerdmans. (First published 1979).

Fowler, J. W. (1996). *Faithful change: The personal and public challenges of postmodern life*. Nashville, Tennessee: Abingdon.

Fowler, J. W. (2001). Faith development theory and the postmodern challenges. *The International Journal for the Psychology of Religion, 11*(3), 159–172.

Fowler, J. W. (2004). Faith development at 30: Naming the challenges of faith in a new millennium. *Religious Education, 99*(4), 405–421.

Fowler, J. W., & Keen, S. (1978). *Life maps: Conversations on the journey of faith*. Minneapolis, Minnesota: Winston Press; Waco, Texas: Word.

Fowler, J. W., Nipkow, K. E., & Schweitzer, F. (Eds.). (1992). *Stages of faith and religious development: Implications for church, education and society*. London: SCM.

Fowler, J. W., & Osmer, R. (1985). Childhood and adolescence – A faith development perspective. In R. J. Wicks, R. D. Parsons, & D. Capps (Eds.), *Clinical handbook of pastoral counseling* (pp. 171–212). New York: Paulist.

Fowler, J. W., Streib, H., & Keller, B. (2004). *Manual for faith development research* (3rd ed.). Bielefeld, Germany: Research Center for Biographical Studies in Contemporary Religion; Atlanta, Georgia: Center for Research in Faith and Moral Development.

Gilligan, C. (1980). Justice and responsibility: Thinking about real dilemmas of moral conflict and choice. In J. W. Fowler & A. Vergote (Eds.), *Toward moral and religious maturity* (pp. 223–249). Morristown, New Jersey: Silver Burdett.

Gilligan, C. (1982). *In a different voice: Psychological theory and women's development*. Cambridge, Massachusetts: Harvard University Press.

Heywood, D. (1992). Piaget and faith development: A true marriage of minds? In J. Astley & L. J. Francis (Eds.), *Christian perspectives on faith development: A reader* (pp. 153–162). Grand Rapids, Michigan: William B. Eerdmans. (First published 1986).

Heywood, D. (2008). Faith development theory: A case for paradigm change. *Journal of Beliefs and Values, 29*, 263–272.

Hull, J. (1985). *What prevents Christian adults from learning?* London: SCM.

Kegan, R. (1982). *The evolving self: Problems and process in human development*. Cambridge, Massachusetts: Harvard University Press.

Kohlberg, L. (1969). Stage and sequence: The cognitive developmental approach to socialization. In D. A. Goslin (Ed.), *Handbook of socialization theory and research* (pp. 347–480). Chicago, Illinois: Rand McNally.

Kohlberg, L. (1986). A current statement on some theoretical issues. In S. Modgil & C. Modgil (Eds.), *Lawrence Kohlberg: Consensus and controversy* (pp. 485–546). Philadelphia and London: Falmer.

Marty, M. (1981). *The public church*. New York: Crossroads.

Moseley, R. M., & Brockenbrough, K. (1988). Faith development in the pre-school years. In D. Ratcliff (Ed.), *Handbook of preschool religious education* (pp. 101–124). Birmingham, Alabama: Religious Education Press.

Moseley, R. M., Jarvis, D., & J. W. Fowler (1986, 1993). *Manual for faith development research*. Atlanta, Georgia: Emory University Center for Faith Development. (Amended by K. DeNicola, 1993).

Nelson, C. E. (1992). Does faith develop? An evaluation of Fowler's position. In J. Astley & L. J. Francis (Eds.), *Christian perspectives on faith development: A reader* (pp. 62–76). Grand Rapids, Michigan: Eerdmans. (First published 1982).

Nelson, C. E., & Aleshire, D. (1986). Research in faith development. In C. Dykstra & S. Parks (Eds.), (1986). *Faith development and Fowler* (pp. 180–201). Birmingham, Alabama: Religious Education Press.
Niebuhr, H. R. (1960). *Radical monotheism and western culture*. New York: Harper & Brothers.
Niebuhr, H. R. (1963). *The responsible self*. New York: Harper & Row.
Osmer, R. R. (1992). James W. Fowler and the Reformed tradition: An exercise in theological reflection in religious education. In J. Astley & L. J. Francis (Eds.), *Christian perspectives on faith development: A reader* (pp. 135–150). Grand Rapids, Michigan: William B. Eerdmans. (First published 1990).
Parks, S. (1986). *The critical years: The young adult search for a faith to live by*. San Francisco, California: Harper & Row.
Parker, S. (2006). Measuring faith development. *Journal of Psychology and Theology, 34*(4), 337–348.
Piaget, J. (1967). *Six psychological studies*. New York: Random House.
Rizzuto, A.-M. (1991). Religious development: A psychoanalytic point of view. In F. K. Oser & W. G. Scarlett (Eds), *Religious development in childhood and adolescence* (pp. 47–60). San Francisco, California: Jossey-Bass.
Seymour, J. L., & D. E. Miller (Eds.). (1982). *Contemporary approaches to Christian education*. Nashville, Tennessee: Abingdon.
Slee, N. (1996). Further on from Fowler. In L. J. Francis, W. K. Kay, & W. S. Campbell (Eds.), *Research in religious education* (pp. 73–96). Leominster, UK: Gracewing; Macon, Georgia: Smyth & Helwys.
Smith, M. (2003). *Ways of faith: A handbook of adult faith development*. Durham: North of England Institute for Christian Education.
Snarey, J. (1991). Faith development, moral development, and nontheistic Judaism: A construct validity study. In W. M. Kurtines & J. L. Gewirtz (Eds.), *Handbook of moral behavior and development, Vol 2: Research* (pp. 279–305). Hillsdale, New Jersey: Lawrence Erlbaum.
Stern, D. N. (1985, 2000). *The interpersonal world of the infant*. New York: Basic Books.
Stokes, K. (Ed.). (1982). *Faith development in the adult life cycle*. New York: W. H. Sadlier.
Streib, H. (1991). Autobiographical reflection and faith development: Prospects for religious education. *British Journal of Religious Education, 14*(1), 43–53.
Streib, H. (2001). Faith development theory revisited: The religious styles perspective. *The International Journal for the Psychology of Religion, 11*(3), 143–158.
Streib, H. (2003a). Faith development research at twenty years. In R. R. Osmer & F. Schweitzer (Eds.), *Developing a public faith: New directions in practical theology* (pp. 15–42). St. Louis, Missouri: Chalice Press.
Streib, H. (2003b). Variety and complexity of religious development: Perspectives for the 21st century. In P. H. M. P. Roelofsma, M. T. Jozef, & J. W. Van Saane (Eds.), *One hundred years of psychology of religion* (pp. 123–138). Amsterdam: Vrije University Press.
Streib, H. (2003c). Religion as a question of style: Revising the structural differentiation of religion from the perspective of the analysis of the contemporary pluralistic-religious situation. *Journal of Practical Theology, 7*, 1–22.
Streib, H. (2004). Extending our vision of developmental growth and engaging in empirical scrutiny: Proposals for the future of faith development theory. *Religious Education, 99*(4), 427–434.
Wakefield, G. S. (1983). Spirituality. In A. Richardson & J. Bowden (Eds.), *A new dictionary of Christian theology* (pp. 549–550). London: SCM.
Westerhoff, J. H. (1976). *Will our children have faith?* New York: Seabury Press.
Westerhoff, J. H. (1983). *Building God's people*. New York: Seabury Press.

Chapter 13
The Psychology of Prayer: A Review of Empirical Research

Tania ap Siôn and Leslie J. Francis

Abstract After years of comparative neglect, a renewed research interest developed in the field of prayer during the mid-1980s and has led to prayer being recognized as of central importance in understanding the role of religion and spirituality in human development and human functioning. In the context of this developing research agenda, the present chapter concentrates on three themes. The first theme focuses on research concerned with the subjective effects of prayer, looking at the correlates of prayer among those who engage in that activity. The second theme focuses on research concerned with the objective effects of prayer, giving particular attention to clinical trials of "prayer treatment", examining the medical outcomes of patients who do not know that they are being prayed for. The third theme focuses on the content of prayer as a window through which to view the religion and spirituality of ordinary people.

Introduction

From a theological perspective prayer is both an important and a problematic aspect of the Christian tradition (Le Fevre, 1981). Biblical theologians discuss the place and significance of prayer within the scriptures of the Old and New Testaments (MacLachlan, 1952; Coggan, 1967; Kurichianil, 1993). Historical theologians discuss the development of prayer in the church (Simpson, 1965; Kelly, 1966; Jasper & Cuming, 1987; Guiver, 1988). Philosophical theologians discuss the meaning and implications of the religious practice of prayer (Phillips, 1965; Baelz, 1968, 1982; Alhonsaari, 1973; Clements-Jewery, 2005; Brümmer, 2008). Pastoral theologians provide manuals and suggestions to promote the practice of prayer (Thornton, 1972; Harries, 1978; Leech, 1980; Miller, 2008; Davidson, 2008).

Reviewing this theological literature, it is difficult to escape the conclusion that many claims are being made about the efficacy, consequences or correlates of prayer

T. ap Siôn (✉)
St Mary's Centre, St Deiniol's Library, Hawarden, Flintshire CH5 3DF, UK
e-mail: tania.ap.sion@st-deiniols.org

and that such claims should properly become the subject of empirical investigation. This case was made succinctly and effectively by Galton (1883):

> It is asserted by some that men possess the faculty of obtaining results over which they have little or no direct personal control, by means of devout and earnest prayer, while others doubt the truth of this assertion. The question regards a matter of fact, that has to be determined by observation and not by authority; and it is one that appears to be a very suitable topic for statistical enquiry .... Are prayers answered or are they not? ... Do sick persons who pray, or are prayed for, recover on the average more rapidly than others.

This simple challenge is one which theologians meet in a variety of ways. Some, like Austin (1978) argue that theological concepts like the omniscience, omnipotence and all-loving character of the Christian God make divine arbitrary intervention into human situations in response to petitionary prayer inconsistent with the nature of God. Rosner (1975), speaking from the Jewish tradition, argues that the efficacy of prayer does not have to be scientifically proved to be trusted within the religious community. Others, like Wimber and Springer (1986) and Mac-Nutt (2005), document their personal involvement and experience in the ministry of healing.

One discipline which may properly concern itself with investigating empirical claims regarding the efficacy, consequences or correlates of prayer is psychology. In particular such claims should fall within the general remit of the psychology of religion. It is clear, however, from the major text books in the psychology of religion that the empirical study of prayer remained an underdeveloped field of research, at least until the mid-1990s. For example, there are just two references to prayer in the index of Batson, Schoenrade, and Ventis (1993), five in Argyle and Beit-Hallahmi (1975), five in Spilka, Hood, and Gorsuch (1985), six in Brown (1987), seven in Paloutzian (1983), eight in Brown (1988) and thirteen in Malony (1991). A similar impression is generated by reviews of the literature on the psychology of prayer undertaken during the 1980s and into the 1990s. For example, Finney and Malony (1985a) write

> Nowhere is the long standing breach between psychology and religion more evident than in the lack of research on prayer. Only a few studies of prayer exist in spite of the fact that prayer is of central religious importance.

Similar points are made in the reviews by Hood, Morris, and Watson (1987, 1989), Poloma and Pendleton (1989), Janssen, de Hart, and den Draak (1989) and McCullough (1995).

That lack of interest in research concerned with the psychology of prayer is particularly strange given the interest shown in the subject by early psychologists of religion. For example, James (1902) claimed that prayer "is the very soul and essence of religion." Coe (1916) wrote that "a history and psychology of prayer would be almost equivalent to a history and psychology of religion." Hodge (1931) argued in his study *Prayer and its psychology* that "prayer is the centre and soul of all religion, and upon the question of its validity depends the trustworthiness of religious experience in general."

Capps (1982) argued that prayer should once again be reinstated at the centre of the psychology of religion. During the 1990s there was some indication that psychologists of religion may be responding to this challenge. The number of index references to prayer grew to 37 in Wulff's (1991) *Psychology of religion: classic and contemporary views* and to 80 in Hyde's (1990) *Religion in childhood and adolescence*. The renewed interest in the psychology of prayer in the 1990s was heralded by Brown's (1994) major book, *The human side of prayer*, and by Francis and Astley's (2001) reader, *Psychological perspectives on prayer*.

This chapter, therefore, sets out to provide a map of empirical research concerned with aspects of the psychology of prayer, and to do so by focusing on three major themes. The first part reviews studies concerned with the subjective effects of prayer and examines the correlates of prayer among those who are themselves doing the praying. The second part reviews studies concerned with the objective effects of prayer and examines the correlates of prayer on objects for which or among people for whom prayers are offered by others. The third part focuses on the content of prayer as a window through which to view the religion and spirituality of ordinary people.

The Subjective Effects of Prayer

Empirical studies concerned with the correlates of prayer among those who themselves practise prayer begin with Sir Francis Galton's (1872) classic study published in *The Fortnightly Review*. He found that a sample of 945 clergy had a mean life value of 69.49 years, compared with a mean life value of 68.14 years among a sample of 294 lawyers and 67.31 years among a sample of 244 medical men. He argued that

> we are justified in considering the clergy to be a far more prayerful class than either of the other two. It is their profession to pray.

While on the face of it these statistics suggest at least a positive correlation between prayer and higher life expectancy, Galton rejected the conclusion that such data provide evidence for the efficacy of prayer on two grounds. First, he argued that the comparative longevity of the clergy might be more readily accounted for by their "easy country life and family repose." Second, he found that the difference in longevity between the professional groups was reversed when the comparison was made between *distinguished* members of the three classes, that is, persons who had their lives recorded in a biographical dictionary. According to this category, the average length of life among clergy, lawyers and medical men was 66.42, 66.51 and 67.04 years, respectively, the clergy being the shortest lived of the three professional groups. On the basis of this finding Galton concluded as follows:

> Hence the prayers of the clergy for protection against the perils and dangers of the night, for protection during the day, and for recovery from sickness, appear to be futile in result.

In a second attempt to assess the influence of a prayerful life on the constitution of the clergy, Galton (1869) reviewed the lives of 192 divines recorded in Middleton's *Biographical Evangelica* of 1786. The four volumes of this work set out to provide "an historical account of the lives and deaths of the most eminent and evangelical authors or preachers, both British and foreign." They included figures like John Calvin, John Donne, Martin Luther and John Wycliffe. On the basis of these biographies Galton concluded that divines are not founders of notably influential families, whether on the basis of wealth, social position or abilities; that they tend to have fewer children than average; that they are less long-lived than other eminent men; and that they tend to have poor constitutions.

Galton's early statistical study, published in *The Fortnightly Review* in 1872, was part of a significant debate stimulated by Professor John Tyndall's essay of the same year in *The London Contemporary Review*, under the title, "The prayer for the sick: hints towards a serious attempt to estimate its value." Much of the discussion was republished by John O Means (1876) in the collection of essays, *The Prayer Gauge Debate*.

A major strand in contemporary studies concerned with the subjective effects of prayer employ correlational techniques on data provided by cross-sectional surveys. For example, Morgan (1983) employed an interview survey to compare the self-reported personal behaviour of individuals who pray with that of individuals who do not pray. He concluded that

> Those who pray frequently, those who have integrated prayer into day-to-day life, seem to practise what they preach. The prayerful are less likely to "intensely dislike anyone," "to feel resentful when they don't get their way," to "like to gossip" or to get very angry or upset (i.e. "feel like smashing things"). On the other hand, the more prayerful are more likely to "stop and comfort a crying child," to be "a good listener" and even to "get along with loud-mouthed obnoxious people." They apparently "turn the other cheek" too. . ... Finally, our only chance to see if they actually practise what they preach occurs in the interview situation. In this context, interviewers judged the more prayerful as more cooperative and friendly.

In a series of three papers and a book, Poloma and Pendleton (1989, 1991a, 1991b) and Poloma (1993) discuss the findings of a telephone survey conducted among 560 individuals concerned with the relationship between different types of prayer and subjective perceptions of quality of life. From these data they identify four types of prayer, styled meditative, ritualistic, petitionary and colloquial, in addition to measures of frequency of prayer and prayer experience. Each type of prayer was found to relate differently to the five quality of life measures included in the survey. The index of prayer experiences generally proved the best predictor of quality of life. People who perceived themselves as having received a definite answer to a specific prayer request were more likely to enjoy a higher level of general satisfaction with life.

In a study of 208 couples, Gruner (1985) asked the question, "How often have you used prayer in connection with your personal problems, problems of your children, and problems between you and your mate?" He found a significant positive relationship between prayer use and marital adjustment. Butler, Stout, and Gardner

(2002) also studied the use of prayer during marital conflict among 217 couples, and found a significant positive relationship between prayer use and conflict resolution. In a study of 708 elderly people, Koenig (1988) found a significant inverse relationship between the use of prayer and religious beliefs during difficult times and death anxiety. On the other hand, Markides (1983) and Markides, Levin, and Ray (1987) failed to find a consistent relationship between prayer and life satisfaction in their longitudinal analysis of data on Mexican-Americans and Anglos. Similarly, Koenig, George, Blazer, Pritchett, and Meador (1993) failed to find a significant relationship between prayer or bible study and anxiety symptoms in a sample of 1,299 adults aged 60 or above, while Ellison, Boardman, Williams, and Jackson (2001) found a weak negative association between frequency of prayer and wellbeing and a weak positive association between frequency of prayer and distress in their analyses of data provided by the 1995 Detroit Area Study.

In a study conducted among 345 members of a non-denominational programme, Richards (1991) found a positive correlation between intensity of the prayer experience and self-reported purpose in life. In a study of 100 members of Alcoholics Anonymous, Carroll (1993) found a highly significant positive correlation between a variety of spiritual practices, including prayer, and purpose in life. In a study of 100 subjects, who were either HIV-positive or diagnosed with ARC or AIDS, Carson (1993) found a significant positive correlation between prayer and psychological hardiness.

Francis and Evans (1996) explored the relationship between personal prayer and perceived purpose in life among two samples of 12- to 15-year-olds. The first sample comprised 914 males and 726 females who never attend church. The second sample comprised 232 males and 437 females who attend church most weeks. The data demonstrated a significant positive relationship between frequency of personal prayer and perceived purpose in life among both groups. In other words, churchgoers who pray frequently report a greater sense of purpose in life than churchgoers who do not pray regularly. Similarly, non-churchgoers who pray regularly report a greater sense of purpose in life than non-churchgoers who do not pray regularly. This relationship between personal prayer and perceived purpose in life, after controlling for church attendance, is given further support in a study among 674 Roman Catholic adolescents by Francis and Burton (1994).

Francis (1992) explored the relationship between prayer and attitude towards school among a sample of 3,762 11-year-old pupils. After controlling for individual differences in church attendance he found that pupils who prayed reported a more positive attitude towards school, English lessons, maths lessons, music lessons and religious education, but not towards games lessons. Long and Boik (1993) found an inverse relationship between frequency of prayer and alcohol use among a sample of 625 pupils in grades six and seven.

A second strand in contemporary studies exploring the subjective effects of prayer is concerned with monitoring changes within individuals consequent upon the practice of prayer. For example, Parker and St Johns (1957) monitored the effect of prayer among a sample of 45 volunteers suffering from either psychosomatic symptoms or experiencing considerable subjective emotional stress. The volunteers were invited to indicate a preference for participation in one of three groups of 15 each. One group received weekly individual psychotherapy sessions. The second group agreed to pray daily that their specific problems would be overcome. They were styled *the random pray-ers*. The third group followed a programme of *prayer therapy*. At the beginning of the study all participants completed five psychological tests: the Rorschach Inkblot Test, the Szondi Test, the Thematic Apperception Test, the Sentence Completion Test and the Word Association Test. After a 9-month-period these tests were readministered. An "impartial tester" identified an average of 72% improvement from the prayer therapy group and a 65% improvement from the individual psychotherapy group, compared with no improvement among the random pray-ers. On the basis of this evaluation Parker and St Johns concluded that

> prayer therapy was not only a most effective healing agent but that prayer properly understood might be the single most important tool in the reconstruction of man's personality.

Elkins, Anchor, and Sandler (1979) monitored the effect of prayer on tension reduction after a 10-day training period among a sample of 42 individuals. Tension was measured both physiologically and subjectively. Prayer was found to reduce tension levels on both measures, but not sufficiently to reach statistical significance. Carlson, Bacaseta, and Simanton (1988) undertook a similar experiment among three groups of undergraduates enrolled in a Christian liberal arts college. Each group contained 12 students. One group followed a programme of progressive relaxation exercises. One group followed a programme of prayer and biblical meditation. One group served as a control. After a 2-week period members of the prayer and biblical meditation group reported less anger and anxiety than members of the other two groups.

Carson and Huss (1979) monitored the therapeutic effect of prayer among chronic undifferentiated schizophrenics resident in a state mental institution. Twenty clients were assigned to a student nurse in a one-to-one relationship. Ten clients and the students volunteered to use prayer and scripture readings. The other 10 clients and students used only the context of a therapeutic relationship without prayer. Both the clients and the students completed assessment tools before and after a 10-week experience. The findings showed that the students who participated in the prayer group perceived greater changes in themselves, including greater sensitivity to others. The major changes in the clients with prayer revealed an increased ability to express feelings of anger and frustration, a more positive outlook about possible changes in their lives and a decrease in somatic complaints.

Finney and Malony (1985b) studied the use of Christian contemplative prayer as an adjunct to psychotherapy among a sample of three men and six women. The authors conclude that the "results gave modest circumstantial support" for the hypothesis that the use of contemplative prayer would be associated with improvement in psychotherapy.

Ai, Dunkle, Peterson, and Bolling (1998) and Ai, Bolling, and Peterson (2000) examined the use of private prayer and psychological recovery among coronary artery bypass patients. The results showed that private prayer was associated with better post-operative emotional health, in terms of decreased depression and decreased general distress.

Helm, Hays, Flint, Koenig, and Blazer (2000) examined the relationship between private religious activity and survival. In a survey of 3,851 elderly adult participants were asked "How often do you spend time in private religious activities, such as prayer, meditation, or Bible study?" responses to which were placed alongside a range of sociodemographic and health variables. The results showed that elderly adults who engaged in private religious activity before the onset of impairment in activities of daily living (ADL) appeared to have a survival advantage over those who did not.

Meisenhelder and Chandler (2000, 2001) studied the relationship between frequency of prayer and self-reported health among 1,014 Presbyterian church lay leaders and 1,412 Presbyterian pastors over a 3-year period employing the Short-Form 36 Medical Outcomes Study (Ware & Sherbourne, 1992). The eight health subscales measured physical functioning, role functioning (physical), bodily pain, general health, vitality, social functioning, role functioning (emotional) and mental health. The results indicated a significant positive relationship between prayer frequency and mental health in lay leaders and between prayer frequency and general health, vitality and mental health in pastors.

Krause (2003) studied the relationship between the practice of praying for others and the effects of financial strain on self-reported physical health status among a sample of 1,500 older whites and older African Americans. The results suggested that praying for others significantly reduced the harmful effects of severe financial difficulties on self-reported perceptions of physical health.

A third strand in contemporary studies exploring the subjective effects of prayer is concerned with case studies. For example, Griffith, English, and Mayfield (1980) use this method to discuss the therapeutic aspects of attending prayer meetings, and Black (1999) also employs case studies to discuss the use of prayer by older African American women who have experienced long-term poverty.

Contrary to Galton's early contention, the consensus emerging from contemporary studies concerned with the correlates of prayer among those who themselves practise prayer suggests that there are certain positive psychological or behavioural concomitants of practising prayer or of living a prayerful life. While such findings may lead to the conclusion that prayer is beneficial for those who practise it, they do not lead to the conclusion that these positive benefits are necessarily generated by an influence, force or being outside the self.

The Objective Effects of Prayer

Empirical studies concerned with the objective effects of prayer on objects for which or on people for whom prayers are offered by others also began with Sir Francis Galton (1872). Galton observed that the formal state prayers offered throughout the Church of England made the petition on behalf of the Queen "Grant her in health long to live." He then argued that "the public prayer for the sovereign of every state, Protestant and Catholic, is and has been in the spirit of our own." Surely, he reasoned, if petitionary prayer is effective, then royalty should live longer than comparable groups.

To test this question empirically, Galton examined the mean age attained by males of various classes who had survived their 30th year, from 1758 to 1843, excluding deaths by accident or violence. The data comprised 1,632 gentry, 1,179 English aristocracy, 945 clergy, 569 officers of the army, 513 men in trade and commerce, 395 English literature and science, 366 officers of the royal navy, 294 lawyers, 244 medical professions, 239 fine arts and 97 members of royal houses. The highest mean age was among the gentry, 70.22 years. The lowest mean age was among members of royal houses, 64.04 years. Galton concluded as follows:

> The sovereigns are literally the shortest lived of all who have the advantage of influence. The prayer has, therefore, no efficacy, unless the very questionable hypothesis be raised, that the conditions of royal life may naturally be yet more fatal, and that their influence is partly, though incompletely, neutralised by the effects of public prayers.

A second major strand of research concerned with the objective effects of prayer was pioneered by the Revd Franklin Loehr (1959) and reported in his book, *The power of prayer on plants*. This body of research involved 150 people, 700 unit experiments and 27,000 seeds and seedlings. Loehr sets out the rationale for his series of studies in the following straightforward terms:

> A number of seeds are planted, any kind of seeds. Everything about them is kept just the same, except that half the seeds are given prayer and the other half are not. At the end of a set time, the growth of the seeds is carefully measured and the results are compared. If everything about them is kept the same except prayer, and if a difference in growth is produced, then prayer is indicated as the factor that produces the difference.

The original experiment began with the purchase of two sealed jars of water. One jar was brought to the Sunday prayer meeting and exposed to three prayer treatments. First, it was the subject of group prayer. Second, it was passed from hand to hand for personal prayer. Third, it was again subject to group prayer. Meanwhile, three pairs of test plantings were prepared under identical conditions. The three pairs contained eight kernels of corn, eight lima beans and an unreported number of sweet-pea seeds. Both sets of test plantings were given the same amount of water, one set form the water which had been exposed to the prayer treatment and one set from the water which had not been exposed to the prayer treatment. After 2 weeks seven of the corn prayer seedlings had sprouted, compared with three in the control pan; four of the prayer lima beans had sprouted, compared with none in the control pan; one of the prayer sweet-peas had sprouted, compared with three in the control pan. Repeated trials confirmed that two out of three times the prayed for plants came out ahead.

A second form of experiment involved the persons doing the praying coming into the laboratory and praying with as well as for the plants. Careful monitoring of the growth of these plants led to scientific conclusions like the following:

> Mrs Hoffman was an excellent helper and showed fine prayer power with her own plants in various experiments.

A third, more complex, form of experiment involved the same individual cultivating three identical pots, praying for growth in relationship to one, offering no prayer in relationship to the second, and praying for non-growth in relationship to the third. Mr Erwin Prust of Pasadena, for example, chose to plant three ivy clips in each of his three pots. After 5 weeks the non-growth prayer plants were quite dead.

A fourth form of experiment involved dividing one pot in half, giving positive prayer treatment to one side and negative prayer treatment to the other side. Erwin Prust, for example, planted 23 corn kernels in each side and administered the prayer treatment several times a day for 8 days. After this treatment he found that

> sixteen sturdy little seedlings greeted us on the positive side. On the negative side there was but one.

A fifth form of experiment was known as the 8-day prayer partnership trials. In this experiment 649 seeds for which positive prayer was offered produced a total of 34,409 mm of growth. By way of comparison 635 seeds for which no prayer was offered produced a total of 31,313 mm of growth. The overall prayer growth advantage was 8.74%.

A sixth form of experiment involved six teams of people. Each team was required to target three pots with three treatments: prayer for growth, prayer for non-growth and no prayer. This experiment involved a total of 720 seeds. The results demonstrated that the negated seedlings were running 10.95% behind the control plantings.

A seventh form of experiment involved sending out "a goodly number of home-experiment prayer kits." Loehr recognised that this technique lacked some of the objective control possible within the laboratory situation.

After investing so much energy in pot plants, Loehr (1959) turned attention to silkworm eggs. In spite of the remarkable claims made by Loehr's research for the objective effects of prayer, other researchers have generally failed to build on this tradition. Two exceptions are Miller (1972) and Lenington (1979). Miller (1972) employed what he describes as "a very accurate method of measuring plant growth rate by using a rotary transducer connected to a strip chart recorder." He selected rye grass as the experimental plant because "the new growth occurs at the bottom of the blades," with the consequence that a lever arm attached to the top of the blade of rye grass will measure total increase in length with accuracy. The prayer treatment was applied by Ambrose and Olga Worrell from their home some 600 miles away from the plants. The result was a growth rate increase of 840%. Lenington (1979) compared the growth rate of 12 radish seeds watered with holy water over which prayer had been offered with the growth rate of 12 radish seeds watered from the same source of water but without prayer. He found no significant differences in growth rate between the two conditions.

Also to this tradition belong *The Spindrift papers* which detail the series of experiments conducted between 1975 and 1993 and coordinated by Bruce Klingbeil and John Klingbeil (Spindrift Inc, 1993). Spindrift is a small group exploring ways to measure physically the effects of prayer on healing. Starting with seeds and yeast, they went on to cards, dice, and finally random event generators. Comments on this body of research are made by Benor (1992), Rockwell (1993) and Rush (1993).

A third major strand of research concerned with the objective effects of prayer is exemplified in two early studies by Joyce and Welldon (1965) and Collipp (1969). Joyce and Welldon (1965) studied 19 matched pairs of patients attending two outpatient clinics concerned with psychological or rheumatic disease. One patient from each pair was assigned to the prayer treatment group. Prayer was provided by 19 people, two as lone individuals and the rest in four groups which met as often as once in every 2 weeks for sessions of up to an hour. All the prayer was supplied at least 30 miles from the hospital. Neither the patients nor the physicians were aware that a trial was in progress. All medication and physical treatment prescribed by the consultant was continued in both groups. The clinical state of each patient was re-evaluated by the same physician between 8 and 18 months later. The final statistical analysis was based on the performance of 12 of the original 19 matched pairs. For the first 6 pairs of patients, those in the prayer group did better; for 5 of the next 6 pairs, the controls did better. The authors suggest that the prayers' interest and commitment may have waned in the latter part of the study. Overall 7 of the 12 results showed an advantage to the group for whom prayer had been offered. This is not a statistically significant finding.

Collipp (1969) studied the progress of 18 leukaemic children. The names of 10 of the 18 children were prayed for daily by 10 families. Each family was sent a weekly reminder of its obligation to pray. At monthly intervals, parents and physicians independently answered a questionnaire which asked whether the illness, the child's adjustment, and the family's adjustment were better, unchanged or worse. Neither the children, their families nor the physicians knew of the experiment. After 15 months of prayer, 3 of the 10 children in the prayer group had died, compared with 6 of the 8 children in the control group. This difference, however, does not reach statistical significance.

Byrd (1988) built on these two studies in an original way. Over a 10-month period, 393 patients admitted to the coronary care unit were randomised, after signing informed consent, to an intercessory prayer group (192 patients) or to a control group (201 patients). The patients, staff, doctors and Byrd himself were all unaware which patients had been targeted for prayer. The prayer treatment was supplied by "born again" Christians. After randomisation each patient was assigned to three to seven intercessors. The intercessory prayer was done outside the hospital daily until the patient was discharged from hospital. Under the direction of the coordinator, each intercessor was asked to pray daily for rapid recovery and for prevention of complications, and death, in addition to other areas of prayer they believed to be beneficial to the patient.

At entry to the coronary care unit, chi-square tests and stepwise logistic analysis revealed no statistical difference between the two groups of patients. After entry, all patients had follow-up for the remainder of their time in hospital. The group assigned to intercessory prayer had a significantly lower severity score after admission. The control patients required ventilatory assistance, antibiotics and diuretics more frequently than patients in the intercessory prayer group. In the prayer group

85% of the patients were considered to have a good hospital course after entry, compared with 73% in the control group. An intermediate grade was given in 1% of the prayer group, compared with 5% of the control group. A bad hospital course was observed in 14% of the prayer group, compared with 22% of the control group. The chi-square test confirmed that this difference was significant beyond the one percent probability level.

Byrd concluded his study with an appropriate *acknowledgement*, thanking both those individuals who had been involved in the research and "God for responding to the many prayers made on behalf of the patients."

More recent studies in the same tradition have produced mixed results. For example, Harris et al. (1999) studied the effects of intercessory prayer on the outcomes of 990 patients in a coronary care unit in a completely blind, randomised trial. The results showed that those assigned to the prayer group experienced lower overall adverse outcomes than the control group, although length of hospital stay remained unaffected. Aviles et al. (2001) studied the effect of intercessory prayer on cardiovascular disease progression in a coronary care unit using 762 patients (383 assigned to the intercessory prayer group and 379 to the control group). The results showed no significant difference in outcomes between the prayer group and the control group, although the trend favoured the prayer group. Benson et al. (2006) studied the effects of intercessory prayer on 1,802 cardiac bypass patients. The results showed that overall receiving intercessory prayer had no statistically significant effect on patient recovery, although the knowledge of receiving intercessory prayer was associated with a higher incidence of complications.

Cha, Wirth, and Lobo (2001) studied the effects of intercessory prayer on the success of in vitro fertilisation using 219 females who were receiving IVF treatment. The results showed that women assigned to the prayer treatment group had a statistically significant higher pregnancy rate (50%) than women assigned to the control group (26%). Marlowe, and MacNutt (2000) examined the effects of intercessory prayer on 40 patients with rheumatoid arthritis including both direct contact intercessory prayer and remote intercessory prayer. The results showed that patients who received direct contact intercessory prayer had a significant overall improvement in the 1-year follow-up, while there were no significant effects on those receiving distant intercessory prayer. Leibovici (2001) explored the effects of remote, retroactive intercessory prayer on the outcomes of 3,393 patients with bloodstream infections. The results showed that the group who received remote, retroactive intercessory prayer had statistically significant shorter stays in hospital and shorter duration of fever.

On the other hand, Matthews, Conti, and Sireci (2002) explored the effects of intercessory prayer, positive visualisation and expectancy on a range of medical and psychological measures in relation to 95 kidney dialysis patients. Neither intercessory prayer nor positive visualisation had an effect distinguishable from expectancy on any of the variables. Krucoff et al. (2005) explored the effects of intercessory prayer and music, imagery and touch (MIT) therapy on 748 patients undergoing percutaneous coronary intervention or elective catheterisation. Neither intercessory prayer nor MIT therapy demonstrated a significant effect on clinical outcomes.

Other relevant studies in this tradition include Walker, Tonigan, Miller, Corner, and Kahlich (1997), Sicher, Targ, Moore, and Smith (1998), Harris, Thoresen, McCullough, and Larson (1999), Krucoff et al. (2001), Furlow and O'Quinn (2002) and Mathai and Bourne (2004).

Contrary to Galton's early contentions, several more recent studies concerned with the objective effects of prayer on objects for which or on people for whom prayers are offered suggest that there may be certain positive consequences of prayer. While such findings may lead to the conclusion that prayers effect changes in the objective world, they do not lead to the conclusion that these positive benefits are necessarily generated by the activity of the God or gods to whom the prayers are addressed.

The Content of Ordinary Prayer

Empirical studies concerned with the content of prayer provide a window through which to view the religion and spirituality of ordinary people, and can be traced back to classic studies like the one reported by Pratt (1910), which are easily differentiated from the studies set within the developmental paradigm as evidenced by early work reported by Godin and van Roey (1959), Goldman (1964), Thouless and Brown (1964), Brown (1966, 1968), Long Elkind, and Spilka (1967) and Elkind, Spilka, and Long (1968). A good recent example of this genre of research is provided by the work led by Jacques Janssen in Radboud University, Nijmegen. For example, Janssen et al. (1989), Janssen, de Hart, and den Draak (1990) undertook a content analysis of the answers given by 192 Dutch high school pupils (mean age 16.8 years) to three open-ended questions: what does praying mean to you; at what moments did you feel the need to pray; how do you pray? On the basis of these data, they concluded that the common prayer of youth can be summarised in one sentence containing seven elements:

> because of some reason (1. need) I address (2. action) myself to someone or something (3. direction) at a particular moment (4. time), at a particular place (5. place) in a particular way (6. method) to achieve something (7. effect) (1989, p 28).

In a subsequent study, Janssen, Prins, van der Lans, and Baerveldt (2000) analysed the responses of 687 Dutch young people (mean age 23.9 years) who were asked to describe their praying behaviour and also to describe needs, actions, methods, times, places and effects. On the basis of these data they described four varieties of praying. In *petitionary* prayer the effect is central. Here individuals ask that "things will pass off as favourably as possible", that "relations will be improved", that "war will be prevented", that "things will be good", that there will be "a happy end" and that "we can make things happen". In *religious* prayer the direction towards God is central. Here individuals are talking with God, thanking God, hoping to experience God, building a relationship with God and inviting God to share their hopes and sorrows. In *meditative* prayer the action is central. Here individuals meditate, reflect, ponder, consider, concentrate and often looking inwards towards the inner-self. In *psychological* prayer the inner need is central. Here individuals pray "when my mother died", "when my father had a heart attack", "when my father and stepmother got divorced", "when my father attempted suicide", "when I was in crisis", "when my friend did not come home" or "when I got lost".

McKinney and McKinney (1999) explored the praying habits of 127 psychology and undergraduate students. Of the 107 who claimed on the screening questionnaire to pray at least a few times a year, 77 accepted the invitation to keep a proper diary for 7 days. A content analysis of the initial screening questionnaire identified six types of prayer within the students' definitions of prayer and in which they purported to engage adoration, petition, thanksgiving, reparation, communication and relaxation. When the prayers from the diaries were counted the following averages emerged:

> Over a 7-day period the average number of prayers of adoration was 1.18; petition, 12.75; reparation, 0.79; thanksgiving, 4.28; simple communication, 1.21; and prayer as relaxation, 0.91 (p. 204).

Of the petitionary prayers, most were requests for personal favours, such as "to get back into my schoolwork", "to get my job", "for my Lord to guide me", "to help me plan a date party", and "to afford graduate school and receive my financial loans". The remainder included requests for family and friends ("my grandfather who has cancer", "the prayer group") or for more global situations ("for the peace of the world", "for the local community"). Following these basic descriptions of the prayers, McKinney and McKinney (1999) proceeded to explore the texts from the perspectives of dramaturgical analysis (Goffman, 1959) and semiotic analysis (Eco, 1976).

Mountain (2005) employed the method of grounded theory to analyse the responses of 60 10-year-old children gathered through videotaped interviews, illustrations and written exercises. These data suggested four main functions for prayer defined as follows: finding help for self through individual connection to God; finding social identity through communal ritual, activity and belief; finding help for others, both close and distant; and expressing praise and thanksgiving.

A new research tradition is emerging concerned with the content and analysis of ordinary people's prayer requests in Christian contexts, and a number of exploratory studies have been conducted which identify the main themes and characteristics of prayer requests in terms of content and frequency. For example, Schmied (2002) analysed 2,674 prayers inscribed in the prayer intention books provided by seven Roman Catholic churches in Germany from the 1970s to the 1990s: four parish churches, one pilgrimage church associated with an education centre, a chapel of a university hospital, and a chapel of an international airport. The analyses examined four main issues: the addressees of the prayers; the kinds of prayers; the reference persons and groups; and the prayer intentions. First, just 72% of the prayers specified an addressee, which included 27% addressed to God, 21% to Mary and 5% to Jesus. Second, 91% of the prayers included some form of petition, while 23% included thanksgiving, 3% trust, 2% praise, 1% complaint, 1% love and 2% some other concept (acknowledging that individual prayers can contain more than one kind of prayer). Third, 59% of the prayers made petition only for others, 11% for self and others, 16% only for self, and the remaining 15% made no statement. Fourth, the prayer intentions were allocated to seven categories, with some prayers embracing more than one category. Over a quarter (28%) of the prayers referred to health or to recovery of health, 22% to protection in general, 16% to religious matters (including vocations and forgiveness), 9% to specific projects (including surgical operations and long journeys), 8% to peace, 7% to faith, and 34% to other issues (acknowledging that individual prayers can contain more than one intention).

Working on a much smaller scale, Brown and Burton (2007) analysed 61 prayer requests left in a rural Anglican parish church over an 8-month period in 2004. The majority of the prayers were for people who were ill, in hospital, about to undergo operations, or recovering from illness or operations (43%), or for people who had died (26%). The other prayer requests fell into the categories of general thanksgiving, other, strength to cope, world situations, and new personal situations.

ap Siôn (2007) analysed 917 prayer cards left in a rural Anglican parish church over a 16-month period in the mid-1980s employing a framework which consisted of three main constructs: prayer reference, prayer intention and prayer objective. Prayer reference distinguished between four key foci with which the individual authors were concerned: themselves, other people who were known personally to the authors, animals which were known personally to the authors and the world or global context. Prayer intention distinguished between nine key areas with which the individual authors were concerned: illness, death, growth, work, relationships, conflict or disaster, sport or recreation, travel, open intention and general. Prayer objective distinguished between two effects which the individual authors envisaged as a consequence of their prayers in terms of primary control and secondary control. In primary control prayer authors explicitly suggested the desired consequences of their prayers. In secondary control prayer authors placed prayers and their consequences entirely in the hands of another.

Results for prayer reference showed that the majority of prayer requests were for other people either known personally to the prayer authors or placed in a global context (90%) with very few written for the prayer authors alone (4%). For prayer intention, 29% were non-specific in terms of not offering a concrete, physical context for the prayer. The next three highest categories were illness (21%), death (16%) and conflict or disaster (14%). For prayer objective, there were more examples of secondary control (57%) than primary control (43%) with prayer authors employing primary control more often than secondary control in prayers relating to illness, growth, work and relationships, and prayer authors employing secondary control more often than primary control in prayers relating to death, conflict or disaster, and sport or recreation. In later studies the same reference, objective and intention framework were also used to explore the content of ordinary prayers from the perspectives of rural theology (ap Siôn, in press a) and implicit religion (ap Siôn, in press b), while modifications to the intention construct within the framework allowed a further focus on the relationship between ordinary prayers and health and wellbeing (ap Siôn, 2008a) and the relationship between ordinary prayers and the beliefs of "ordinary theologians" about the nature and activity of God and God's concern with and impact on the everyday world (ap Siôn, 2008b).

Outside church contexts, two studies have focused on prayer requests left in hospital settings. Grossoehme (1996) analysed 63 prayers in a chapel prayer book at a paediatric hospital in Ohio, USA, covering a 6-month period in an attempt to discover how the prayer authors viewed God and God's nature. Most of the prayers were intercessory prayers followed by thanksgiving. Grossoehme concluded that the majority of prayer authors, at particularly vulnerable times in their lives, appear to believe that God is able to act in response to prayer or at least to desire God's action, and that a special relationship is created between the prayer authors and the praying community.

A second hospital study was conducted by Hancocks and Lardner (2007) and involved the analysis of 939 prayers from prayer boards and books left in 2005 at the chapels and prayer/quiet rooms of three of the six hospitals which comprise Leeds Teaching Hospitals, England. Categorised according to type, 59% were concerned with specific intention (for named individuals who were sick), 7% for general intention (for the sick but of a more general nature), 20% for death (including people who were dying), 9% for thanksgiving (in instances of recovery, the life of the dead and the hospital), 2% for forgiveness (for themselves or others) and 3% for hospital staff and carers. In terms of addressee, 37% were addressed to God explicitly, 20% to God implicitly, 18% to the worshipping community, 17% to an uncertain addressee and 8% to a person or persons directly. The different names used for God were also identified and quantified as were 30 separate categories illustrating content. Hancocks and Lardner compared their results to Grossoehme's (1996) findings, concluding that they were largely similar although some differences were evident.

The consensus emerging from studies concerned with the content of ordinary prayers suggests that such prayers may provide valuable insights into the nature and role of prayer in ordinary people's lives from both psychological and theological perspectives. Whatever Galton may have assumed about the failure of prayer to survive within a modern and scientifically orientated world, there is ample evidence to support the view that prayer activity remains alive, well and conducive to human flourishing.

Conclusion

Since the mid-1990s there has been a renewed interest in conducting empirical studies in the area of prayer after a significant period of neglect, and this chapter has made it clear that useful foundations have been laid to influence the shape of future research. All three fields of empirical research identified in this chapter are now well-established and well-placed for further refinement and development.

The first type of study concentrates on monitoring the correlates of prayer among those who are themselves doing the praying. Existing studies in this tradition demonstrate a range of positive psychological or behavioural concomitants of practising prayer or of living a prayerful life. Great scope now exists to extend this tradition of research by studying the relationship between different forms of prayer and a variety of other factors. Particular opportunities exist for developing the insights of those studies concerned with the relationship between prayer and purpose in life, psychological wellbeing and aspects of mental and physical health.

The second type of study examines the correlates of prayer on objects for which or among people for whom prayers are offered by others. Existing studies in this tradition provide mixed findings. The challenge, however, has been clearly focused. It is simply not sufficient for psychologists of religion to be critical of the methodology of those studies which claim to have demonstrated the positive effect of prayer on the growth of pot plants or on the health of individuals. The scientific response to such claims rests in the area of replication and refinement of the studies themselves. Future studies in this contentious field, however, need to be conducted to the highest standards. If the findings of such studies are to be taken seriously by those who are theologically informed and by those who are psychologically informed, future research in the field needs both to observe the strict criteria of objective *empirical psychology* and to be alert to *theological* nuances regarding the actual claims made for the efficacy of prayer within the community of believers.

The third type of study concentrates on analysing the content of ordinary prayers. Existing studies in this tradition indicate that the content of such prayers provides important insights into the religion and spirituality of ordinary people. Future studies need to extend analyses of prayer content to a wider range of contexts and to engage in replication and refinement of existing analytical models.

References

Ai, A. L., Bolling, S. F., & Peterson, C. (2000). The use of prayer by coronary artery bypass patients. *The International Journal for the Psychology of Religion, 10*, 205–220.

Ai, A. L., Dunkle, R. E., Peterson, C., & Bolling, S. F. (1998). The role of private prayer in psychological recovery among midlife and aged patients following cardiac surgery. *The Gerontologist, 38*, 591–601.

Alhonsaari, A. (1973). *Prayer: An analysis of theological terminology*. Helsinki: Kirjapaino Tarmo.

ap Siôn, T. (2007). Listening to prayers: An analysis of prayers left in a country church in rural England. *Archiv für Religionspsychologie, 29*, 199–226.

ap Siôn, T. (2008a). Distinguishing between intention, reference and objective in an analysis of prayer requests for health and well-being: Eavesdropping from the rural vestry. *Mental Health, Religion and Culture, 11*, 53–65.

ap Siôn, T. (2008b). *Interpreting God's activity in the public square: Accessing the ordinary theology of personal prayer*. Paper presented at the ISERT conference, Würzburg, Germany in April 2008.

ap Siôn, T. (in press a). Ordinary prayer and the rural church. *Rural Theology*.

ap Siôn, T. (in press b). Implicit religion and ordinary prayer. *Implicit Religion*.

Argyle, M., & Beit-Hallahmi, B. (1975). *The social psychology of religion*. London: Routledge and Kegan Paul.

Austin, M. R. (1978). Can intercessory prayer work? *Expository Times, 89*, 335–339.

Aviles, J. M., Whelan, E., Hernke, D. A., Williams, B. A., Kenny, K. E., O'Fallon, M., et al. (2001). Intercessory prayer and cardiovascular disease progression in a coronary care unit population: A randomised controlled trial. *Mayo Clinical Proceedings, 76*, 1192–1198.

Baelz, P. (1968). *Prayer and providence*. London: SCM Press Ltd.
Baelz, P. (1982). *Does God answer prayer?* London: Dartman, Longman and Todd.
Batson, C. D., Schoenrade, P., & Ventis, W. K. (1993). *Religion and the individual: A social-psychological perspective*. Oxford: Oxford University Press.
Benor, D. J. (1992). *Healing research: Holistic energy medicine and spirituality* (Vol. 1). Deddington: Helix.
Benson, H., Dusek, J. A., Sherwood, J. B., Lam, P., Bethea, C. F., Carpenter, W., et al. (2006). Study of the therapeutic effects of intercessory prayer (STEP) in cardiac bypass patients: A multicenter randomized trial of uncertainty and certainty of receiving intercessory prayer. *American Heart Journal, 151*, 934–942.
Black, H. K. (1999). Poverty and prayer: spiritual narratives of elderly African-American women. *Review of Religious Research, 40*, 359–374.
Brown, A., & Burton, L. (2007). Learning from prayer requests in a rural church: An exercise in ordinary theology. *Rural Theology, 5*, 45–52.
Brown, L. B. (1966). Ego-centric thought in petitionary prayer: a cross-cultural study. *Journal of Social Psychology, 68*, 197–210.
Brown, L. B. (1968). Some attitudes underlying petitionary prayer. In A. Godin (Ed.), *From cry to word: Contributions towards a psychology of prayer* (pp. 65–84). Brussels: Lumen Vitae Press.
Brown, L. B. (1987). *The psychology of religious belief*. London: Academic Press.
Brown, L. B. (1988). *The psychology of religion: An introduction*. London: SPCK.
Brown, L. B. (1994). *The human side of prayer*. Birmingham, AL: Religious Education Press.
Brümmer, V. (2008). *What are we doing when we pray? On prayer and the nature of faith*. Aldershot: Ashgate.
Butler, M. H., Stout, J. A., & Gardner, B. C. (2002). Prayer as a conflict resolution ritual: clinical implications of religious couples' report of relationship softening, healing perspective, and change responsibility. *The American Journal of Family Therapy, 30*, 19–37.
Byrd, R. C. (1988). Positive therapeutic effects of intercessory prayer in a coronary care unit population. *Southern Medical Journal, 81*, 826–829.
Capps, D. (1982). The psychology of petitionary prayer. *Theology Today, 39*, 130–141.
Carlson, C. R., Bacaseta, P. E., & Simanton, D. A. (1988). A controlled evaluation of devotional meditation and progressive relaxation. *Journal of Psychology and Theology, 16*, 362–368.
Carroll, S. (1993). Spirituality and purpose in life in alcoholism recovery. *Journal of Studies on Alcohol, 54*, 297–301.
Carson, V. B. (1993). Prayer, meditation, exercise and special diets: Behaviours of the hardy person with HIV/AIDS. *Journal of the Association of Nurses in AIDS Care, 4*(3), 18–28.
Carson, V. B., & Huss, K. (1979). Prayer, an effective therapeutic and teaching tool, *Journal of Psychiatric Nursing, 17*, 34–37.
Cha, K. Y., Wirth, D. P., & Lobo, R. A. (2001). Does prayer influence the success of in vitro fertilization-embryo transfer? Report of a masked, randomized trial, *The Journal of Reproductive Medicine, 46*, 781–787.
Clements-Jewery, P. (2005). *Intercessory prayer: Modern theology, biblical teaching and philosophical thought*. Aldershot: Ashgate.
Coe, G. A. (1916). *The psychology of religion*. Chicago, IL: University of Chicago Press.
Coggan, D. (1967). *The prayers of the New Testament*. London: Hodder and Stoughton.
Collipp, P. J. (1969). The efficacy of prayer: a triple blind study. *Medical Times, 97*, 201–204.
Davidson, G. (2008). *Anyone can pray: A guide to Christian ways of praying*. London: SPCK.
Eco, U. (1976). *A theory of semiotics*. Bloomington, IN: University of Indiana Press.
Elkind, D., Spilka, B., & Long, D. (1968). The child's conception of prayer. In A. Godin (Ed.), *From cry to word: Contributions towards a psychology of prayer* (pp. 51–64). Brussels: Lumen Vitae Press.
Elkins, D., Anchor, K. N., & Sandler, H. M. (1979). Relaxation training and prayer behaviour as tension reduction techniques. *Behavioural Engineering, 5*(3), 81–87.

Ellison, C. G., Boardman, J. D., Williams, D. R., & Jackson, J. S. (2001). Religious involvement, stress, and mental health: Findings from the 1995 Detroit Area Study. *Social Forces, 80*, 215–249.
Finney, J. R., & Malony, H. N. (1985a). Empirical studies of Christian prayer: A review of the literature. *Journal of Psychology and Theology, 13*, 104–115.
Finney, J. R., & Malony, H. N. (1985b). An empirical study of contemplative prayer as an adjunct to psychotherapy. *Journal of Psychology and Theology, 13*, 284–290.
Francis, L. J. (1992). The influence of religion, sex and social class on attitudes towards school among eleven year olds in England. *Journal of Experimental Education, 60*, 339–348.
Francis, L. J., & Astley, J. (2001). *Psychological perspectives on prayer: A reader*. Leominister: Gracewing.
Francis, L. J., & Burton, L. (1994). The influence of church attendance and personal prayer on purpose in life among Catholic adolescents. *Journal of Belief and Values, 15*(2), 6–9.
Francis, L. J., & Evans, T. E. (1996). The relationship between personal prayer and purpose in life among churchgoing and non-churchgoing 12–15 year olds in the UK. *Religious Education, 91*, 9–21.
Furlow, L., & O'Quinn, J. L. (2002). Does prayer really help? *Journal of Christian Nursing, 19*(2), 31–34.
Galton, F. (1869). *Hereditary genius: An inquiry into its laws and consequences*. London: Macmillan and Co.
Galton, F. (1872). Statistical inquiries into the efficacy of prayer. *Fortnightly Review, 12*, 125–135.
Galton, F. (1883). *Inquiries into human faculty and its development*. London: Macmillan.
Godin, A., & van Roey, B. (1959). Imminent justice and divine protection. *Lumen Vitae, 14*, 129–148.
Goffman, I. (1959). *The presentation of self in everyday life*. New York: Doubleday.
Goldman, R. J. (1964). *Religious thinking from childhood to adolescence*. London: Routledge and Kegan Paul.
Griffith, E. E. H., English, T., & Mayfield, V. (1980). Possession, prayer and testimony: Therapeutic aspects of the Wednesday night meeting in a black church. *Psychiatry, 43*, 120–128.
Grossoehme, D. H. (1996). Prayer reveals belief: Images of God from hospital prayers. *Journal of Pastoral Care, 50*, 33–39.
Gruner, L. (1985). The correlation of private, religious devotional practices and marital adjustment. *Journal of Comparative Family Studies, 16*, 47–59.
Guiver, G. (1988). *Company of voices: Daily prayer and the people of God*. London: SPCK.
Hancocks, G., & Lardner, M. (2007). I say a little prayer for you: what do hospital prayers reveal about people's perceptions of God? *Journal of Health Care Chaplaincy, 8*, 29–42.
Harries, R. (1978). *Turning to prayer*. London: Mowbrays.
Harris, A., Thoresen, C. E., McCullough, M. E., & Larson, D. B. (1999). Spiritually and religiously orientated health interventions. *Journal Health Psychology, 4*, 413–433.
Harris, W. S., Gowda, M., Kolb, J. W., Strychacz, C. P., Vacek, L., Jones, P. G., et al. (1999). A randomised, controlled trial of the effects of remote, intercessory prayer on outcomes in patients admitted to the coronary care unit. *Archives of Internal medicine, 159*, 2273–2278.
Helm, H. M., Hays, J. C., Flint, E. P., Koenig, H. G., & Blazer, D. G. (2000). Does private religious activity prolong survival? A six-year follow-up study of 3,851 older adults. *Journal of Gerontology, 55A*, 400–405.
Hodge, A. (1931). *Prayer and its psychology*. London: SPCK.
Hood, R. W., Morris, R. J., & Watson, P. J. (1987). Religious orientation and prayer experience. *Psychological Reports, 60*, 1201–1202.
Hood, R. W., Morris, R. J., & Watson, P. J. (1989). Prayer experience and religious orientation. *Review of Religious Research, 31*, 39–45.
Hyde, K. E. (1990). *Religion in childhood and adolescence: A comprehensive review of the research*. Birmingham, AL: Religious Education Press.
James, W. (1902). *The varieties of religious experience: A study in human nature*. London: Fontana. (Reprinted 1960).

Janssen, J., de Hart, J., & den Draak, C. (1989). Praying practices. *Journal of Empirical Theology, 2*(2), 28–39.
Janssen, J., de Hart, J., & den Draak, C. (1990). A content analysis of the praying practices of Dutch youth. *Journal for the Scientific Study of Religion, 29*, 99–107.
Janssen, J., Prins, M. H., van der Lans, J. M., & Baerveldt, C. V. (2000). The structure and variety of prayer: An empirical study among Dutch youth. *Journal of Empirical Theology, 13*, 29–54.
Jasper, R. C. D., & Cuming, G. J. (1987). *Prayers of the Eucharist: Early and reformed* (3rd ed.). Collegeville, MN: Liturgical Press.
Joyce, C. R. B., & Welldon, R. M. C. (1965). The objective efficacy of prayer: A double-blind clinical trial. *Journal of Chronic Diseases, 18*, 367–377.
Kelly, F. L. (1966). *Prayer in sixteenth-century England*. Gainsville, FL: University Presses of Florida.
Koenig, H. G. (1988). Religious behaviours and death anxiety in later life. *The Hospice Journal, 4*, 3–24.
Koenig, H. G., George, L. K., Blazer, D. G., Pritchett, J. T., & Meador, K. E. (1993). The relationship between religion and anxiety in a sample of community-dwelling older adults. *Journal of Geriatric Psychiatry, 26*, 65–93.
Krause, N. (2003). Praying for others, financial strain, and physical health status in late life. *Journal for the Scientific Study of Religion, 42*, 377–391.
Krucoff, M. W., Crater, S. W., Gallup, D., Blankenship, J. C., Cuffe, M., Guarneri, M., et al. (2005). Music, imagery, touch, and prayer as adjuncts to interventional cardiac care: the Monitoring and Actualisation of Noetic Trainings (MANTRA) II randomised study. *The Lancet, 366*, 211–217.
Krucoff, M. W., Crater, S. W., Green, C. L., Maas, A. C., Seskevich, J. E., Lane, J. D., et al. (2001). Integrative noetic therapies as adjuncts to percutaneous intervention during unstable coronary syndromes: Monitoring and Actualisation of Noetic Training (MANTRA) feasibility pilot. *American Heart Journal, 142*, 760–767.
Kurichianil, J. (1993). *Before thee face to face: A study on prayer in the bible*. Slough: St Paul.
Leech, K. (1980). *True prayer: An introduction to Christian spirituality*. London: Sheldon Press.
Leibovici, L. (2001). Effects of remote, retroactive intercessory prayer on outcomes in patients with bloodstream infection: Randomised controlled trial. *British Medical Journal, 323*, 1450–1451.
Le Fevre, P. (1981). *Understandings of prayer*. PA: Westminster Press.
Lenington, S. (1979). Effects of holy water on the growth of radish plants. *Psychological Reports, 45*, 381–382.
Loehr, F. (1959). *The power of prayer on plants*. Garden City, New York: Doubleday.
Long, D., Elkind, D., & Spilka, B. (1967). The child's concept of prayer. *Journal for the Scientific Study of Religion, 6*, 101–109.
Long, K. A., & Boik, R. J. (1993). Predicting alcohol use in rural children: A longitudinal study. *Nursing Research, 42*(2), 79–86.
MacLachlan, L. (1952). *The teaching of Jesus on prayer*. London: James Clarke and Co.
MacNutt, F. (2005). *The prayer that heals: Praying for healing in the family*. Notre Dame, IN: Ave Maria Press.
Malony, H. N. (Ed.). (1991). *Psychology of religion: Personalities, problems and possibilities*. Grand Rapids, MI: Baker Book House.
Markides, K. S. (1983). Aging, religiosity, and adjustment: A longitudinal analysis. *Journal of Gerontology, 38*, 621–625.
Markides, K. S., Levin, J. S., & Ray, L. A. (1987). Religion, aging, and life satisfaction: An eight-year, three-wave longitudinal study. *The Gerontologist, 27*, 660–665.
Mathai, J., & Bourne, A. (2004). Pilot study investigating the effect of intercessory prayer in the treatment of child psychiatric disorders. *Australasian Psychiatry, 12*, 386–389.
Matthews, D. A., Marlowe, S. M., & MacNutt, F. S. (2000). Effects of intercessory prayer on patients with rheumatoid arthritis. *Southern Medical Journal, 93*, 1177–1186.

Matthews, W. J., Conti, J. M., & Sireci, S. G. (2002). The effects of intercessory prayer, positive visualization, and expectancy on the well-being of kidney dialysis patients. *Alternative Therapies, 7*, 42–52.
McCullough, M. E. (1995). Prayer and health: conceptual issues, research review, and research agenda. *Journal of Psychology and Theology, 23*, 15–29.
McKinney, J. P., & McKinney, K. G. (1999). Prayer in the lives of late adolescents. *Journal of Adolesence, 22*, 279–290.
Means, J. O. (1876) *The prayer-gauge debate*. Boston, MA: Congregational Publishing Society.
Meisenhelder, J. B., & Chandler, E. N. (2000). Prayer and health outcomes in church lay leaders. *Western Journal of Nursing Research, 22*, 706–716.
Meisenhelder, J. B., & Chandler, E. N. (2001). Frequency of prayer and functional health in Presbyterian pastors. *Journal for the Scientific Study of Religion, 40*, 323–329.
Miller, C. (2008). *The path of Celtic prayer: An ancient way to contemporary joy*. Abingdon: Bible Reading Fellowship.
Miller, R. N. (1972). The positive effect of prayer on plants. *Psychic, 3*(5), 24–25.
Morgan, S. P. (1983). A research note on religion and morality: Are religious people nice people? *Social Forces, 61*, 683–692.
Mountain, V. (2005). Prayer is a positive activity for children: A report on recent research. *International Journal of Children's Spirituality, 10*, 291–305.
Paloutzian, R. F. (1983). *Invitation to the psychology of religion*. Glenview, IL: Scott, Foresman and Company.
Parker, W. R., & St Johns, E. (1957). *Prayer can change your life*. Carmel, New York: Guideposts.
Phillips, D. Z. (1965). *The Concept of prayer*. London: Routledge and Kegan Paul.
Poloma, M. M. (1993). The effects of prayer on mental well-being. *Second Opinion, 18*, 37–51.
Poloma, M. M., & Pendleton, B. F. (1989). Exploring types of prayer and quality of life: A research note. *Review of Religious Research, 31*, 46–53.
Poloma, M. M., & Pendleton, B. F. (1991a). The effects of prayer and prayer experiences on general wellbeing. *Journal of Psychology and Theology, 19*, 71–83.
Poloma, M. M., & Pendleton, B. F. (1991b). *Exploring neglected dimensions of religion in quality of life research*. Lampeter: Edwin Mellen Press.
Pratt, J. B. (1910). An empirical study of prayer. *American Journal of Religious Psychology and Education, 11*(4), 48–67.
Richards, D. G. (1991). The phenomenology and psychological correlates of verbal prayer. *Journal of Psychology and Theology, 19*, 354–363.
Rockwell, T. (1993). The Spindrift papers: Exploring prayer and healing through the experimental test 1975–1993. *Journal of the American Society for Psychical Research, 87*, 387–396.
Rosner, F. (1975). The efficacy of prayer: Scientific vs religious evidence. *Journal of Religion and Health, 14*, 294–298.
Rush, J. H. (1993). A postscript on Rockwell's review of *The Spindrift papers*. *Journal of the American Society for Psychical Research, 87*, 397–398.
Schmied, G. (2002). God images in prayer intention books. *Implicit Religion, 5*, 121–126.
Sicher, F., Targ. E., Moore, D., & Smith, H. (1998). A randomized double-blind study of the effect of distant healing in a population with advanced AIDS. *Western Journal of Medicine, 169*, 356–63.
Simpson, R. L. (1965). *The interpretation of prayer in the Early Church*. PA: Westminster Press.
Spilka, B., Hood, R. W., & Gorsuch, R. L. (1985). *The psychology of religion: An empirical approach*. Englewood Cliffs, NJ: Prentice Hall.
Spindrift Inc. (1993). *The Spindrift papers: Exploring prayer and healing through the experimental test: 1975–1993*. Fort Lauderdale, FL: Spindrift Inc.
Thornton, M. (1972). *Prayer: A new encounter*. London: Hodder and Stoughton.
Thouless, R. H., & Brown, L. B. (1964). Petitionary prayer: Belief in its appropriateness and causal efficacy among adolescent girls. *Lumen Vitae, 19*, 297–310.

Walker, S. R., Tonigan, J. S., Miller, W., Corner, S., & Kahlich, L. (1997). Intercessory prayer in the treatment of alcohol abuse and dependence: A pilot investigation. *Alternative Therapies in Health and Medicine, 3*, 79–86.

Ware, J. E., & Sherbourne, C. (1992). The MOS 36-item short-form health survey (SF-36) (Vol. 1): Conceptual framework and item selection. *Medical Care, 30*, 473–481.

Wimber, J., & Springer, K. (1986). *Power healing*. London: Hodder and Stoughton.

Wulff, D. M. (1991). *Psychology of religion: Classic and contemporary views*. New York: John Wiley and Sons.

Biographical details

Mrs Tania ap Siôn is Senior Research Fellow at the University of Warwick, UK and Director of the St Mary's Centre at St Deiniol's Library, UK.

The Revd Professor Leslie J Francis is Professor of Religions and Education at the University of Warwick, UK.

Part II
The Role of Spirituality in Human Development and Identity: An Introduction

Daniel G. Scott

In this part we explore the role of spirituality in human development from several vantage points with a mix of perspectives, all based on a concern for the lack of consideration of the spiritual in existing developmental theory particularly in the lives of children and youth. As Glenn Cupit notes, "spirituality is generally ignored in human development texts and never treated as an essential component of development," while Kimball, Mannes, and Hackel point out there is a vacuum in this "important and understudied domain of human development." Aostre Johnson cites Roehlkepartain, King, Wagener, and Benson (2006) to suggest that:

> Spiritual development may be at a "tipping point" for becoming a major theme in child and adolescent development. A growing number of scholars in various fields have invested themselves in this field. The public imagination appears to be ready in numerous cultures, traditions, and contexts, all of which are struggling with social changes that threaten to undermine the spiritual lives of young people (p. 11).

The lack of models and theories for addressing spirituality in human development, after decades of life span development theory that did not include the spiritual, has created a need to identify and describe what constitutes spiritual development. There are theoretical gaps to be filled. In this part, the concern to establish theories grounded in existing literature and research efforts represents perspectives on spirituality and spiritual development that include academics and researchers from several disciplines. As well there are practitioners who observe the spiritual emerging in their therapeutic and educational work with children and youth and try to give conceptual structures or interpretative forms to assist in understanding spirituality as it seems to be experienced and expressed. The authors have questions that are shaping their inquiries: What role does the spiritual play in human maturation? What are the possible ways to study spirituality? Are there recognizable patterns of development, significant milestones, or common experiences that could be identified as spiritual and might indicate a process of spiritual development? What might count as evidence of the spiritual? Do existing theories and approaches offer insights or structures that might give us glimpses of spiritual development or formation? And of course the persistent question of what is meant by spirituality remains problematic and central to the conversation.

How one understands spirituality depends very much on one's context and on recognizing Jacques Derrida's (1988) insight that there is nothing outside of context. One's understanding of spirituality is rooted in one's cultural, religious/non-religious, social and personal locations, traditions, and experiences. In this part we have authors whose specialized interests, professional location, and training serve as lenses for interpretation. Some like Reimer, Dueck, Adelechanow, and Muto are rooted in and explore from the perspective of religious traditions and others, such as Perkins, Hoffman, and Ortiz, write from secular, humanist perspectives. King, Painton, and Cupit each draw on different psychological and therapeutic literature and traditions to inform their chapters.

The definitions chosen to represent the spiritual reflect the author's various sites and traditions. Perkins offers a clearly non-religious definition of spirituality calling it: "the inner felt experience of a connection to something greater than our thoughts, feelings and material existence or even the people and creatures with which we relate. It is described as energy and is defined uniquely by each of us." His definition represents one kind of understanding. Another tradition that more overtly includes a religious possibility comes from Kimball et al. who use a definition of spiritual development formulated by the Center of Spiritual Development in Childhood and Adolescence, an organization with strong Christian links who are striving to create a broad-based understanding of the spiritual rooted in religions:

> The process of growing the intrinsic human capacity for self-transcendence, in which the self is embedded in something greater than the self, including the sacred. It is the developmental "engine" that propels the search for connectedness, meaning, purpose and contribution. It is shaped both within and outside of religious traditions, beliefs, and practices (Benson, Roehlkepartain, & Rude, 2003, pp. 205–206).

This broader definition, which could encompass Perkins' definition, includes the religious and collective dimensions of spirituality. Similarly, in spite of his reluctance to define spirituality and to keep it an open concept, David Tacey comes to define spirituality as "an innate human capacity to experience transcendent reality."

Paul King recognizes that "spirituality is a concept that evades simplistic definition" but points out that the spiritual "as a natural dimension of the human person" is now recognized in educational aims in Irish legislation that in turn echoes the language of UN Convention on the Rights of the Child which acknowledges that spiritual development is one of the areas of development to which children and youth have an inherent right. King cites Rolheiser (1998) saying that: "Spirituality is about what we do with the fire inside us, about how we channel our eros" (p. 10) and then insists that spirituality not "something we *have*... it is something we *are*." Charlene Tan acknowledges the contextual shaping of spirituality by distinguishing between religiously "'tethered' and 'untethered' conceptions of spirituality," while Scott insists that "being human is being spiritual in the same way that being human is being physical or emotional. ..." What the authors hold in common is an insistence that the spiritual is part of human growth and development and that spirituality must be part of our understanding of human experience. The spirit as energy, as quest, as relationship, or as life force echoes throughout this part in a variety of ways.

As academics, researchers, educators, therapists, counselors, and practitioners attempt to evolve a field of study in spiritual development, they create theoretical models based on their research and/or professional experiences. Their perspectives contribute to a number of theoretical options for understanding the place and processes of spiritual formation or spiritual development in the lives of children and youth. Because they represent such different assumptions and contexts, their models do not fit neatly together. The rich variety of constructs proposed in this part immediately broadens the options, and therefore challenges those of us concerned with the spiritual development of the young to be thoughtful in making claims for definitive models of work with children and youth. We do not have a grand theory and need to respect the evolving diversity, resisting perhaps a singular definitive model. While each reader may have a preferred approach or a favorite theory, it may be important to keep concepts of spirituality and spiritual development open in recognition of its complexity, its cultural embeddedness, and its under-theorized state: it remains, in part, mysterious.

The Structure of the Part

The chapters that follow are written by researchers and educators from university faculty in Australia, Hong Kong, the UK, and the Americas as well as by practitioners from psychology, education, child and youth care, and counseling. Some of the writers are giving shape to insights that grew out of their practice-based experiences with children and youth. Others are looking at theoretical models from psychology offering options for re-thinking the spiritual within existing concepts and approaches. In addition others are drawing on literary and historical material and, of course, some are reporting on insights from research they have been conducting.

This part is structured in four clusters with chapters that share a common approach or focus placed together. The first cluster has three chapters that draw on psychological literature and traditions to make space for including the spiritual. Existing developmental theory has deep roots in developmental psychology and so it is useful to begin by opening some space in that domain. The first chapter, from David Tacey, calls for a recognition of spirituality in mental health and care across the whole of the life span. Tacey draws on his Jungian roots, traditional medicine, and rites of passage practices to claim the spiritual as central to healing for physical and mental health and calls for the spiritual to be recognized as a long-standing component of human wisdom and care. It is followed by Chapter 15; C. Glenn Cupit's offering of Dynamic Systems Theory as a lens to understand and explore spiritual development in the lives of children that recognizes the dynamic and complex non-linear processes of spiritual formation. The next chapter (Chapter 16) in the cluster offers Paul King's view that positive psychology can provide a place of hope and a perspective to address human suffering that can include the spiritual in our understanding of human development. He is concerned to create an open dialogue between religion and psychology that moves beyond fear and exclusion.

Because many of this part's authors turn their attention to experience to identify the forms and expressions that the spiritual takes in the lives of children and youth, the next cluster of chapters turns to research and practice. It begins with a grounded theory research project authored by Elisabeth M. Kimball, Marc Mannes, and Angela Hackel (Chapter 17) that foregrounds the voices of young people to ascertain how they speak of and understand the spiritual and its meaning in their own lives. This international study is part of a larger study conducted by the American-based Search Institute and uses focus groups and grounded theory methodologies to identify emerging theoretical constructs from the collected data.

The next three chapters present three different American practitioners working with children and youth in quite different settings. Chapter 18 takes us into an early childhood education and care setting with educator Mindy Upton where spirituality is seen in the daily interactions of children with one another, where the creation of an imaginative and open environment fosters connection, care, and means to interpret the events of life. Next Mollie Painton, who works as a children's therapist focusing on grief and loss, presents a model to understand children's spiritual journeys through difficulty based on a tree of life model. Her theoretical structure emerges from her interpretation of the different ways and means young children use to address their own wounds and their own life struggles. She accepts their identification of angels and monsters, totemic struggles, and imaginative play to describe their inner journeys. In Chapter 20, Peter J. Perkins explores the transitions of adolescent development as "portals to the spirit self." Perkins offers a "*Five Dimensions of the Self*" holistic model based on his therapeutic individual and group work with adolescents. Both Painton and Perkins are suggesting an interpretative construct emerging from their experiences and observations in practice to describe spiritual processes in the lives of their young clients and patients.

The next cluster of chapters focuses primarily on a particular spiritual discipline, practice, or theme that might inform our view of child and adolescent spiritual development. The cluster begins with Charlene Tan (Chapter 21) who turns her attention to the adolescent capacity for reflection which she sees as a significant capacity for spiritual development. Tan, an Indonesian educator, is careful to distinguish between "religiously 'tethered' and 'untethered' conceptions of spirituality" but sees self-reflection as promoting spiritual development in both contexts. She examines several curricular approaches and suggests some specific ways to promote reflection in adolescent educational settings across religious and non-religious settings. Aostre Johnson, in Chapter 22, highlights contemplative aspects of spiritual development. She sees contemplative practice evident in a multitude of traditions as "at the core of all human capacities" and therefore a vital concern for our pedagogy with children and adolescents. Like Charlene Tan in the previous chapter, Johnson addresses both religious and secular perspectives on contemplative practices in developing the spiritual capacity of children and adolescents. She draws on a range of theorists in arguing that children have the capacity for contemplative experiences that will connect them beyond themselves to the wonder of life and the universe.

In Chapter 23, Douglas Magnuson reports a study that listened for "accounts of spirituality interpreted through the theological framework of the idea of vocation, a calling" to see how adolescents might use a vocational sense to structure their lives. He embeds his argument in a comparison of four educational models to demonstrate "four ways of thinking about learning and growth, compared by organization of time, goals, values, data sources, methods and mechanisms of growth outcomes and metaphors." He sees spirituality as an educational ideology that promotes reflexivity, discernment, service, meaning making, and a sense of purpose and vocation that leads to "self-transcendence, responsibility, and authenticity."

The last chapter (Chapter 24) in this cluster is Scott's on coming of age through rites of passage as a model of spiritual development. Using the forms and practices of traditional rites of passage as a guide, Scott points out key qualities and characteristics of spiritual formation that adolescents may need to accomplish in coming of age. He also points out that cultural context and social engagement were critical in rites of passage and may be essential in contemporary spiritual development for adolescents. He implies that the absence of cultural recognition support and engagement may be hindering adolescent spiritual formation and development.

The fourth cluster in the part that follows focuses on defining experiences in the lives of children and adults. The first chapter of the cluster (Chapter 25) is part of an international study on childhood peak experiences. Edward Hoffman and Fernando Ortiz build on Abraham Maslow's (1959) concept of self-actualizing people and their capacity to "perceive reality more efficiently, fully, and with less motivational contamination than others do" (p. 64). Maslow (1970), just before his death, came to an interest in peak experiences and a recognition that "the great lesson from the true mystics... (is that) the sacred is in the ordinary, that is to be found in one's daily life, in one's neighbors, friends, and family, in one's backyard" (p. x). Hoffman and Ortiz report in some detail current research being conducted internationally gathering incidence of peak experiences based on a simple questionnaire developed by Hoffman. They examine results from Mexico, Canada, Norway, Indonesia, Japan, and the United States to explore the kinds of peak experiences adults report from their younger years.

In Chapter 26, Ann M. Trousdale, a specialist in children and adolescent literature takes a different track in bringing attention to life shaping peak experiences by turning to children's and young adolescent fiction. She identifies experiences based on the "relational consciousness" theories of Hay and Nye (1998) that she finds expressed in that fictional writing. Child–God consciousness, child–people consciousness, child–self consciousness, and child–world consciousness provide an interpretative map for a reading of children's literature as demonstrating spiritual experience. A considerable volume of youth literature has peak experiences that are central to the stories of the protagonists. Both boys and girls are shown to be making connections beyond themselves, reaching mystical heights in moments of insight and understanding and being swept away by the power of their experiences. The popularity of this literature demonstrates in part how it resonates with young readers and gives them a fictional context to process their own experience and characters with whom they can identify.

To conclude this cluster and this part, the final chapter (Chapter 27) presents the research of Kevin Reimer, Alvin Dueck, Lauren Adelchanow, and Joseph Muto.

They approach the question of the nature of spirituality and its expression through a project in which they interviewed exemplars from three religious traditions: Islam, Judaism, and Christianity, who were identified as having "exceptional spiritual maturity." For Reimer and his colleagues it is a way to demonstrate what spiritual life looks like as it is lived and practiced in the context of religious life. They claim that "spiritual experience is likely to incorporate categories of transcendent value reflecting a spectrum of relational influences". They recognize the challenges of defining spiritual life and use a naturalistic approach to describe the spiritual as expressed by the lived experiences of religious exemplars. Their study identifies five themes in common across the three faith perspectives: relational consciousness, vocational identity, stewardship, tradition, and the divine as omnipotent and leads them to concluding reflections on spiritual identity.

Across the four clusters of chapters that follow the reader will engage considerations of the spiritual development of the young through multiple lenses that draw on both religious and secular traditions and scholarship. Theoretical models from psychology, education, and therapeutic practice and various combinations of the three as well as proposals for understanding spirituality and spiritual development from research projects are offered as ways to open further the discourse of spiritual development. As a number of chapters suggest the intensity of childhood and/or adolescent experience is significant in human life and calls for a better understanding of those experiences as part of human development. There are current and historical reports of the events, beliefs, and ethos that shape the lives of spiritual exemplars and religious leaders as well as the lives of ordinary unacknowledged people. Many questions will remain: What are the best theories to describe spiritual development? What existing psychological or cultural theory can be adapted to make spirituality and its experiences comprehensible? What are the implications for educational practice? For therapeutic work? For mental health and wellbeing? And for understanding spiritual development as it happens in the lives of children and youth?

References

Benson, P. L., Roehlkepartain, E. C., & Rude, S. P. (2003). Spiritual development in childhood and adolescence: Toward a field of inquiry. *Applied Developmental Science, 7*, 204–212.

Derrida, J. (1988). *Limited Inc*. Evanston, IL: Northwestern University Press

Hay, D., & Nye, R. (1998). *The spirit of the child*. London: Fount.

Maslow, A. (1959). Cognition of being in the peak experiences. *Journal of Genetic Psychology, 94*, 43–66.

Maslow, A. (1970). *Religion, values, and peak-experiences*. New York: Viking.

Roehlkepartain, E. C., King, P. E., Wagener, L. M., & Benson, P. L. (Eds.). (2006). *The handbook of spiritual development in childhood and adolescence*. Thousand Oaks, CA: Sage.

Rolheiser, R. (1998). *Seeking spirituality: Guidelines for a Christian spirituality for the 21st century*. London: Hodder & Stoughton.

Chapter 14
Spirituality and Mental Health: The Mystery of Healing

David Tacey

> *Man creates in transcending himself, in revealing himself.*
> *He is not engaged in the discovery of what is there, not in*
> *production, nor even in communication, nor in invention.*
> *He is enabling being to emerge from non being.*
> – R. D. Laing (1967, p. 23)

Abstract The area of spirituality and health is developing as an academic field of enquiry, and this new perspective is beginning to be incorporated into training programs for medical doctors and health practitioners. A cloud of suspicion hovers over the issue of "spirituality" in the health and therapy professions. Part of the problem arises from the fact that a lot of activities go on under the umbrella term *spirituality*, and some of these warrant a critical eye. However, as an offspring of the Intellectual Enlightenment, medicine itself has had a materialist bias toward human nature and until recently has merely bracketed out the spiritual aspects of health and healing. There is a new air of receptivity today that was not evident even 10 years ago, and this is due to cultural changes wrought by postmodernism and to the sense that "spirit" can be understood apart from the hegemonic forms of the church that the Enlightenment opposed. Spirit can be claimed as part of the anthropology and psychology of human nature, and understood in its own terms, apart from any institutional authority. In this chapter, I review these problems and concerns, employing a perspective that derives from my professional background in Jungian depth psychology, spirituality studies and cultural studies.

The Changing Nature of Health

Spirituality does not have a hugely positive reputation in the medical and health-care professions. I have met professors of psychological medicine and psychiatry who have felt that spirituality is closer to mental illness than it is to mental health. It is true that what some people refer to as their "spirituality" can be a form of neurosis or a maladaptation to reality, as Freud argued in *The future of an illusion* (1927). But

D. Tacey (✉)
English Program, La Trobe University, Melbourne 3086, Australia
e-mail: D.Tacey@latrobe.edu.au

it has to be said that not all forms of the spiritual are pathological, and some forms of spirituality bring people to fuller health and renewed relationship with reality (Koenig, 2002). However, it is also true that our ideas about health and illness are constructed by historical values and conditions, and these ideas are subject to change and even to reversal.

We are living in a time in which notions of normality, health and illness are undergoing rapid change. What was regarded as strange or abnormal 20 years ago is being viewed with new eyes today, slightly less suspiciously. We are emerging from a long period of materialism and rationality, and just as our age is referred to as "postmodern", so it has been argued that it is "post-secular" as well (Caputo, 2001). We live in an era in which it is not uncommon for people to talk about their search for spiritual meaning, just as they might talk about personal relationships or employment conditions (Tacey, 2004). The spiritual is being included in the inventory of things that constitute our humanity. It is becoming normative and to be *spiritual* today is to be "nearly normal".

However, the spiritual is radically different to what it was in the past, when spirituality was felt to be the living heart or core of religion. Today, it is felt to be the living heart or core of the individual, and the location of spirituality has shifted from religious tradition to individual experience. This accords with the tenor of our times, which is individualistic and experiential. At present, religious traditions are displaced and take a secondary role in society. Today, that which was formerly outside has been taken inside, and this trend, if anything, looks like continuing into the future. It could be that the reductive logic and rationality that accompanied the "modern" period is being eclipsed. However, one can only hope that the eclipse of rationality does not result in a rise of destructive unreason. It is important that the spiritual is treated with care and respect, and not left to fester on the uninformed margins of society, where it can turn destructive (Wolin, 2004).

It behoves our health-care professionals and medical experts to re-educate themselves regarding the new discourses on spirituality and health. This area must be taken seriously as an important dimension of experience, and not left to the margins, where it is exploited on the one hand by right-wing religious fanatics and on the other by narcissistic forces of the New Age and sensation-seeking popular culture. The only reason why these movements thrive on the margins is because the centre of society, namely our medicine, our law, our education system, and even, ironically, our religion, does not include the spiritual element and does not integrate it as part of reality. What is suppressed at the centre re-emerges at the edges, and the worrisome edges will not go away until the centre of society and its professions have integrated this lost element of what it means to be human.

Our health-care professions and the discourses that support them have been shaped by a secular and humanist paradigm, and by a bio-psycho-social model that has largely ignored, or bracketed out, the spiritual. This model can hardly be expected to cope with the problem of spirituality, which emerges from a different set of assumptions about reality. It is not simply a matter of finding a few extra terms or concepts to add to our existing body of knowledge, but of opening to a broader horizon of possibility, with new values and ideas. We cannot just *add* spirituality and "stir in" with what we already know. The whole point of spirituality is that it challenges everything we know. Spirituality is unsettling to secular knowledge, and if we have never been disturbed by it, I doubt we have ever taken it seriously (Peterson, 1997).

The medical and healing professions have forgotten, or perhaps intentionally renounced, their roots in the spiritual origins of healing, origins which in our Greek heritage go back to the temples of Asclepius, the "Divine Physician", and to the dream incubation chambers of Cos, Pergamon and Epidaurus. The healing professions are suffering from a form of amnesia, and must force themselves to remember what they have forgotten through centuries of rationality and neglect (Swinton, 2001). Culturally, we are at a turning point, where we need to take a detour to the past, to gather up again what has been lost from our scientific model, which has privileged a purely rational kind of knowing (Capra, 1982).

Wisdom and Medicine

What has been lost to our knowledge is wisdom, which is broader and more intuitive than rational knowing. Wisdom teaches that there are forces at work in life that are greater than rational motivations and larger than the biological laws of cause and effect. Wisdom introduces us to the view that consciousness is not limited to the human being, but extends beyond the ego and includes forces that have not yet been imagined by us. In the past, such forces were mythologised as gods, angels and spirits. These forces have the capacity to heal and make us whole, which is why medicine has historically been linked with religion, cosmology and shamanism.

The medicine man or woman of ancient tribes was the person who was trained in the knowledge of the spirit as well as the body. By making adjustments to the reality of the spirit, by seeing what needed attention in the subtle realm, healing could take place and patients could be cured. For instance, in the temples of Asclepius, the priest would pay attention to the dreams of the patient, and carefully observe what spirit or force was asking for attention in the symbolic language of dreams. If these internal suggestions were respected and acted upon by the patient, a form of healing could take place.

Most of this wisdom has been lost, but it can be recovered again, albeit in a new way and using a language that is scientific rather than mythological. Instead of speaking of gods or spirits, we might speak (following Freud) of drives of the psyche, or (following Jung) of archetypes of the unconscious. Our language will have to remain poetic to some extent, to grasp the subtle nature of mental forces, but we will need to recognise that the spiritual dimension requires a language that changes with the spirit of the times. Because our time remains scientific, the language of spiritual healing will have to appear at least as vaguely scientific, even if, to some people, Jung's theory of archetypes seems just as *mystical* as the theory of gods and spirits that it seeks to replace.

But some re-appropriation of the non-rational side of human experience will have to take place. When I notice the resistance that the health professions seem to put up against this task, I often feel that the non-rational is confused with the *irrational*. The non-rational is not supernatural or occult, but is an entirely normal and natural element of human experience. The irrational, on the other hand, is contrary to rationality, and is potentially dangerous and disruptive to mental and physical health. These distinctions were made by Rudolf Otto in *The idea of the holy* (1923, p. 1). We need an appreciation of life beyond or outside the rational motivations, in order to understand the field of spirituality and its potential to heal or "make whole" the injured or diseased human psyche.

It is the rational approach to life and healing that causes some physicians to dismiss spirituality and regard it as lunatic or fringy. The haste with which many practitioners dismiss this matter in the clinical setting is sometimes justified as a desire to protect the client from delusional ideas. As London psychiatrist Andrew Powell (2005) concedes

> Patients' attempts to talk about their spiritual beliefs and concerns are often met with incomprehension and mistrust. Sometimes the chaplain will be called in but frequently the patient will be advised not to dwell on such matters, or else will find those experiences dismissed as delusions or hallucinations (p. 167).

But such dismissal might rather express a desire to protect the profession itself from a non-rational dimension that is too hard to cope with, given the model upon which the profession is founded. Andrew Powell (2005) continues

> The psychiatrist, frequently beleaguered and trying to maintain an emergency service with pitifully inadequate resources, relies first and foremost on medication, second on social support networks, third on psychological interventions where deemed appropriate and least of all on spiritual sources of strength. On top of that, he or she is three times less likely to hold a religious faith than the patient (p. 167).

There is frequently a significant gap between the assumptions and values of the health professional and the spiritual demands of the client, and this has been called the "spirituality gap" (Tacey, 2004). We can see from this sketch by a practising psychiatrist how difficult it is to bring the spiritual aspect into Western medicine. Spirituality appears to be operating on a different level, and is alien to the values of contemporary practice. To make matters worse, the hospital chaplain is often as confused and beleaguered as the psychiatrist, especially if he or she has not understood the all-important difference between religion and spirituality.

Professional therapists, like professionals in any field, like to be in control of a situation, and are reluctant to allow a meeting, of which he or she is purportedly "in charge", to drift off into areas of the unknown. Freud pointed out that therapists do not like to be "exposed" by their clients or found wanting. Freud talked of "the feeling of repulsion in us which is undoubtedly connected with the barriers that rise between each single ego and the others" (Freud, 1908, p. 153). How much more must this "feeling of repulsion" arise when clients try to take therapists into the unchartered waters of the spirit? When professionals sense they are losing control, they – we – are likely to pull back, and steer the conversation in a different direction. In this way, clients may be deprived of exploring spiritual questions. We have to face the fact that most therapists are not trained in spiritual matters, and are often "flying blind" in this realm. However, this is a flaw in our system of knowledge, and not necessarily a personal failing of individual practitioners.

Spirituality as a Life-Enhancing Factor

Spirituality is a cry for hope in the midst of despair and chaos. With so much collapsing in today's world, with the demise of traditions and structures that were central to life in the past, including moral norms and ethical guidelines, authority figures, religious institutions, youth clubs, family networks and social supports, many people are turning to "spirituality" to find something solid, secure and reliable in their lives. And why not? The winds of change are howling in the streets, and people seek solace in the spirit and communion with forces beyond the ephemeral forms that are collapsing. It has always been the case that when a social order is crumbling, the people seek, by way of compensation, to make a new pact with the forces of eternity, forces beyond time.

Some people want to define spirituality according to a definite set of meditation practices, religious rituals or exercises, but I believe that the seeking of the spiritual is a personal choice, and we cannot pin it down to any one tradition or code. It is best that we are not too prescriptive about it, and that our definitions are general and broad. For me, spirituality is not merely something we do when we are being self-consciously spiritual. It is the pursuit at all times – and not just at meditation or prayer times – of *a particular attitude* toward oneself, the world and others. The attitude is one of reverence, awe and openness to mystery. The spiritual attitude impels us to search for connectedness, and this search intensifies when we live in disconnected times. There are many kinds of connection, but spiritual connection seeks a relationship with something greater than ourselves, something that links us to the cosmos, but also to what is most genuine and true in ourselves.

Spiritual connectedness need not express itself in otherworldly ambitions, in a longing to live in the heavens, to fly above the world or a desire for death. Spirituality, if grounded in reality and affirmative of life, can arise through our connections with others, society, nature and existence. This connectedness can restore flow and meaning to lives, make us feel part of a whole, connect us to our ancestry and family line, enrich us by restoring faith in community, ground us in our particular time and place and alleviate the pain of being isolated, lonely and apart. These are precious and life-giving gifts, and it is little wonder that spiritual achievements have been associated through the ages with such symbols as gold, treasure, living water, the elixir, the boon, flow, joy, delight, bliss – in fact, every imaginable metaphor has been attributed to the achievement of connectedness with the spirit.

Client-Led Recovery of the Spiritual

According to recent medical research, it is often the suffering patient who brings the question of spirituality into the clinical setting (Roach, 1997). The person suffering from a neurosis, mental illness, addiction or compulsive disorder, tentatively expresses the barely formed view that a lack of "spiritual" meaning in his or her life might have something to do with their malady and feeling of despair. In our non-religious or post-Christian era, people often have inadequate language to express this feeling of spiritual absence, but they grope toward it, using their intuition and whatever resources they can find, whether these are drawn from organised religion, popular music, movies, conversations or the New Age movement. The attempt by suffering patients to express their illness in terms of a spiritual malaise is a problem that Jung first noted in "Psychotherapists or the clergy" (1932), but we are only becoming aware of this matter today.

Spirituality has arisen as a major item on the agenda of health and healing professions, not because university professors have had conversion experiences, but because suffering clients want to bring this vague and often ill-formed concept into the therapeutic setting. Today we can speak of a client-led or grassroots recovery of the spiritual dimension in health and healing (Swinton, 2001). It is a sign that civilisation is in transition, that man and woman "do not live by bread alone". The client-centred therapist has to learn to go along with this drift into spiritual discourse, even if he or she does not fully comprehend its meaning. If the spiritual has been raised as part of the healing process, there should be some acknowledgement that this element has crept into the professional setting, even if it makes both parties embarrassed, due to the secular paradigm.

If the professional happens to belong to a particular religious tradition or an evangelical church, he or she must, I believe, resist the temptation to turn the client into a new recruit, or to treat the disturbance as a sign that some particular religion is lacking. The problem is that postmodern spiritual hunger cannot always be nourished by traditional religious solutions (Moore, 1992). We live in fragmented, pluralist and diverse times, and can no longer assume that one spiritual solution fits all problems. There has to be receptivity to the particular case, a sensitivity that reaches out to the suffering patient and empathises with their condition and search (Orchard, 2001).

Spirituality and Suffering

Spirituality and suffering appear to go together. This is a theme found in all the world's religions and in all local indigenous traditions. Some of us find this theme to be morbid, and claim that the sacred should be experienced in joy and delight and not in negative ways. But the emergence of the sacred appears to demand a certain degree of suffering, as we find, for instance, in the rites of initiation into the mysteries of indigenous peoples. These rites of passage were felt to be savage and horrifying to some of the early explorers and missionaries who encountered these tribes in the history of Western exploration, and many tribes were encouraged to cease their initiatory practices. But the tribes seemed to know more than we know about the necessary suffering that is demanded of human beings if the sacred is to penetrate our lives.

In indigenous rites of passage, the profane self must be wounded, displaced, or symbolically put to death so that the spiritual self can emerge and replace the authority of the ego (Van Gennep, 1908). The fact that all indigenous systems of initiation place this tortuous experience at the beginning of adolescence, at around the age of 12 or 13, indicates that the coming into adulthood is synonymous with a need to enter a new state of being, often symbolised in tribal societies by a totemic animal or ancestor spirit. It is little wonder that so many youth today feel lost and at odds with themselves during their teens, because these are the years when, spiritually speaking, something big is supposed to happen, some life-changing event is supposed to take place. Secular youth seem to have an intuitive notion that they have been left out of the great design, and this is why "spirituality" looms large for many of them, even if they are completely secular and do not know where to start.

All experiences of birth and new life involve suffering, and the birth of the spiritual self is no exception. The more heavily defended the ego is against the life of the spirit, the more forcefully does spirit have to displace our egotism to make way for our participation in a larger life. In spiritual rebirth, the person effectively "dies" to his or her former self, and is reborn to a new plane of existence. Although the rites of passage have been lost today, for many of us a certain degree of suffering is still the "royal road" to entering into relationship with the spirit. This does not mean that we should make a cult out of suffering, but it does mean that whenever suffering befalls us, we must be alert to the spiritual potential that might be signalled by such suffering. Even if the spirit does not instigate our suffering, we might say that spirit uses our suffering as a way of deepening our lives toward the ground of being. As poet Leonard Cohen sings, "There is a crack, crack in everything, that's how the light gets in".

Spirit is paradoxical in this regard, because while spirit might be seen as the instigator of suffering, it is true that without spirit our suffering cannot be endured. Without the sense that our suffering is meaningful, it is hard to put up with it. We become demoralised and numbed to others, the world and ourselves. But with spirit, we are invited to use the pain and ruptures to explore the face of the deep. If "spirituality" is suddenly being discussed in numerous disciplinary contexts, in conferences and research seminars, it is because clients and patients are bringing questions of spiritual meaning into the clinical setting, often to the bafflement of some professionals. We are in the midst of a revolution from below, and it is often from below that real change takes place.

We must not assume that this interest in the spiritual is a marginal activity of sick individuals in need of healing. This hunger afflicts not only the patients in clinics and counselling rooms, but society as a whole. Beneath the broken promises of secular society, its promises of wealth, happiness and fulfilment, is a pervasive sense that life is not as meaningful as it once seemed to be. Prior to modernity, people had religion to help them make sense of the bigger picture. Today, without religion, people are taking matters into their own hands, and the phenomenon of "spirituality" is a response to disillusionment, an attempt to go in search of meaning and find the vision that adds depth and purpose to life.

It is not true that an unfortunate few are spiritually afflicted and the rest of us are healthy. To the extent that we are cut off from the reality of spirit and its healing capacity, we are all diseased at this level. Patients conduct these painful journeys of the spirit not only because their personal lives lack meaning but because modern consciousness as a whole lacks meaning. The mentally afflicted are the involuntary pioneers of a new dispensation, the human experiments, as it were, in which a new picture of reality is being forged.

The Mystery that Heals

Socrates said truth is not self-evident, and we have to say the same of the spirit. It has to be stirred to activity and awoken from its slumber at the core of our being. In the process of awakening, suffering is often the trigger. When life is proceeding normally, and the task of social adjustment is successful, there may not arise the need or opportunity to find a relationship with a spiritual core. But when the normal self has been ruptured, virtually the only option is to seek reunion with ourselves at a deeper level. By so doing, we turn to what is most profound in ourselves, and we ask it, implore it, to heal us, to close our gaping wounds and grant us new life.

This is why many recovery programs, or methods of dealing with addictions, alcoholism, drug dependency, eating disorders, depression and anxiety, as well as techniques to deal with grief and trauma, often find themselves moving into the spiritual domain, of which the AA movement is paradigmatic (Morgan & Jordan, 1999). This is not a move into "mystification", or an "escape into superstition" as some rationalists believe. It is an acknowledgement that what ultimately heals us and restores us to wholeness has a mysterious source.

Jung was one of the first psychotherapists to recognise this. In a letter of 1945, he wrote to his colleague, P. W. Martin, as follows:

> The main interest of my work is not concerned with the treatment of neuroses but rather with the approach to the numinous . . .. The fact is that the approach to the numinous is the real therapy (1945, p. 377).

Jung borrowed the word *numinous* from Rudolf Otto, who coined the term in 1923: "Omen has given us 'ominous', and there is no reason why from *numen* we should not similarly form a word 'numinous'" (1923, p. 7). The Latin *numen*, referring to a local deity, or the nod or will of a deity, is used to refer to the sense of an *other* that one might experience in intuitive, reflective or critical moments. Otto and Jung felt that the modern person living outside religion, and not only the traditional person living within a faith tradition, could experience the numinous in their lives. For Jung, the healing process of therapy begins in earnest not merely when the patient has understood the analyst's words, but when the patient has sensed the presence of an *other* at the core of his or her being.

Healing is ultimately self-healing, although the forces that initiate healing do come from outside the ego. The idea of an objective spiritual presence at the core of our subjectivity is new to Western medicine, which tends to externalise the healing process, seeing it as the result of one's encounter with the doctor, or the result of medical interventions and pharmaceuticals. The inward healing presence is often absent in Western religion as well, where it is felt that only the saint or the monastic, and not the ordinary human being, has access to the holy spirit. If common people claim this same kind of experience they are often treated with suspicion, or in the past regarded as witches, blasphemers or frauds.

In the West we have systematically downplayed the inward healing resources of the body–mind–spirit, which is why so many of us are at the mercy of the external forces of healing, especially prescription drugs and health experts. As we know, many in the community are turning away from conventional medicine toward the so-called complementary medicine, whose sources are found in the East or in the pagan and pre-Christian West (Powell, 1998). The internal healing capacity of the body–mind–spirit is new to the mainstream, but it is not new to the East, or to Western paganism, gnosticism, wicca or hermeticism.

Wave and Particle

Jung believed that the encounter with mystery is what heals us, and that it is the "real therapy". What, then, is the relationship between spirituality and healing? How does contact with mystery heal us?

Many of us imagine the self to be solid, formed and discrete. But the self can just as well be imagined as a process rather than a static object. To borrow a metaphor from quantum physics, what we had previously thought of as a solid entity may turn out to be a wave of potentially infinite extension. Physics discovered that the smallest elements of matter behave in one moment as particles, and in another as waves. As particles, they are discrete and separate, and can be "split" to release energy. As waves, they behave less like bits of matter and more like bands of light or energy, reaching out to eternity. They cannot be confined or boxed in by specific forms, but participate in the ocean of being.

I would like to suggest that our human existence is twofold, and we live as particles and waves. As particles, we are distinct human beings, physical and concrete, each with our unique personality and makeup. As waves, we are not so individual; we are similar to each other, and participate in the cosmos in predetermined ways. As waves, we are spiritual beings, fluid, open-ended and connected to other waves. We are especially receptive to archetypal currents that course through us, which Jung correctly identified as universal and collective. The wave-like connectedness is precisely what we call *spirituality*, namely, the ability to feel connected to the cosmos and to the entirety of life.

My contention is that as soon as we experience ourselves as waves, this has a soothing effect upon consciousness. When this connection is restored, we overcome ego-bound existence and its petty concerns, and feel ourselves to be reconnected to the totality. This experience renews and vivifies us. It is burdensome to be confined to the ego and its tiny world. We are not meant to dwell there all the time, in its confining prison. There is a large amount of us that is not about biochemistry, biology or cause and effect. We have a dimension that has a grander source, and that, I take it, is what creation myths mean when they claim that we are created by God in his image. When we transcend our ego-state in relationships, psychotherapy, rituals, art or spiritual experience we return to the ocean of being and are restored.

In normal life, as human beings going about our business, we live a "particle" existence. We behave like atomised entities, separate and autonomous, each concerned with his or her own self-interest or with a small family group. This is the only level that secular society knows us as human beings, and society imposes upon us its myth of the isolated individual. This is why secularism produces alienation, and barely knows how to create or sustain the bonds of community. But as waves, we seek connection to that which is beyond our ego. We extend beyond the particular, breaking its bounds, and reaching for eternity and the stars.

This wave-like participation is what all religions seek to engender. In ritual, liturgy, ceremony, our isolated selves are eclipsed, and we participate in ceremonies that connect us to the cosmos and each other. Religions and cosmologies build communities in ways that secular society never can, because they reach beyond the facade of individuality and draw from our depths the longing to connect with our mystical origin. At the same time, this impulse draws us closer to the healing centre and to each other.

Healing occurs when we no longer experience ourselves as a lone subject in a world of objects, but when we experience ourselves as a living subject in dynamic community. This is the formula that underpins the creation of human community, and it is the formula at the heart of the ecological vision. Thomas Berry (1988) said that ecological healing occurs when the world is no longer experienced as a collection of objects, but as a communion of subjects (p. 2). This is the winning formula for spirituality. The self may not realise its true nature, which releases bliss, until it experiences itself in relationship with a larger subject. The self "comes home" to itself when it glimpses the Other who is its origin. Longing is fulfilled when we recover our belonging.

Deep Security in the Other

Spirituality works toward healing by engendering a sense of security. The world of the ego, our atomised existence, is buffeted by the forces of change and subject to vulnerability and contingency. The particle self lives in the cycle of birth–death–rebirth, in the midst of coming to be and passing away. Our wave-like existence does not participate in the same reality, and exists as it were in the realm of the unborn, the realm prior to manifestation. When we contact our wave-like reality we feel detached from the tragedy of life and removed from the vulnerabilities that bring insecurity and anxiety. The particle self may try to find its security in the incarnate realm, by creating allegiances, traditions, networks, insurances, loyalties, plans and constitutions. But the world of manifestation is inherently unreliable and the things of this world do not assuage our need for a deeper spiritual security.

This is why the great spiritual teachings of all times have advised us not to look for security in the changing world. Rather, we are encouraged to look beyond the world (Christ) or beyond the normal categories of thought (Buddha), to find our true belonging and stable ground. Buddha insists that to attempt to find happiness in the normal world of experience is self-defeating and a category error. We must, he said, work with diligence on our enlightenment, because happiness can only be found once we have broken through the attachments of this world and discovered a connection to the eternal mind. Christ said his kingdom is "not of this world" and urged those who would be influenced by his teachings to direct their attentions to the eternal, not to the temporal. "Do not store up for yourselves treasures on earth, where moth and rust destroy them, and where thieves break in and steal" (Matthew 6: 19). The so-called Christian West decided not to take his advice, but to live primarily on the material level and seek satisfaction at this plane.

The deep security of the spiritual traditions is difficult to attain and involves effort and dedicated work. It seems to involve the cultivation of trust, spiritual confidence and faith, an ability to let go of the ego and its anxieties and allow oneself to be embraced and held by an Other. In Buddhism, the Other is the supreme consciousness and eternal mind, and in Judeo-Christianity it is personified as God the father, to whom one hands over one's life, as well as one's troubles and anxieties. All stress and tension are buried in the unfathomable depths of God, and this enables the ego to live free from debilitating stress or incapacitating anxiety. The existential writings of Søren Kierkegaard (1849) are especially illuminating on this point.

To experience the healing power of spirituality, the individual has to "fall in love" with the mysterious Other. In religious language, we need to experience a conversion. The psyche realises its depth when it sees that an Other loves it. In the same way that the newborn infant realises its identity in the context of a loving environment, the psyche realises its spiritual, wave-like potential only when it is drawn toward a loving spiritual reality that is perceived as larger than itself. Without the sense that love comes from the Other, I doubt that the soul could summon the confidence and trust to embark on the spiritual journey, or to take the leap of faith into reality. In this sense, the soul is by definition incomplete, and striving for a new wholeness or integration is written into its constitution. It finds its completion upon recognising its atonement with its creator. As St Augustine (c398) wrote, in the words immortalised by Johann Sebastian Bach, "our hearts are ever restless, until they find their rest in thee" (p. 346).

The Balance of Particle and Wave

We are emerging from an historical period in which our search for security in the wave-like dimension of being has been represented as pathological or deluded, as escapist or feeble-minded. Modern society has urged us to find security in the material world, and this has amounted to a disastrous shift in the course and direction of civilisation. The longing for security is innate, and without it we fall prey to various kinds of nervous disorders, obsessions and illnesses. It seems clear today that if we fail to care for the needs of the soul, we pay a great price for this at both individual and collective levels.

Freud (1930) wrote of what he called the "oceanic feeling", that is, a sense of fluid identity in which we feel buoyed along by the current of being. This was his attempt to describe the wave-like dimension of psychic existence. But as a materialist, Freud viewed the oceanic feeling as an expression of neurosis. He believed the oceanic feeling described the condition of the embryo in the maternal womb, and characterised the feeling that neurotic patients experience in states of regression. In other words, the deep unconscious is characterised by a wave-like or fluid state, whereas our socially adapted state is defined and differentiated. In periods of psychosis, the suffering person can be lost to the world of form and dropped into a formless chaos of undifferentiated life.

The waves of preconscious existence can be destructive, like a tsunami or tidal wave, but they can also bring healing if we relate to them in the right way. This is what Jung (1928) calls "finding a right relation to the unconscious". A right relation to the oceanic must avoid *denying* the reality of the wave-like dimension by pretending it does not exist. This leads to typical modern attitudes, such as atheism, rationalism, cynicism, intellectualism and so on. On the other hand, a right relation must avoid trying to swallow the ocean, as it were, in an act of assimilation. This leads to hubris, arrogance, spiritual inflation, mania, paranoia and the psychoses. A right relation to the ocean of being can be found in attitudes of reverence and awe toward that which is greater than ourselves.

Paradoxically, as soon as we admit we are not in control, the possibility of regaining control is discovered. This is the truth announced in the 12-step recovery program of Alcoholics Anonymous, which was based in part on Jung's comments made to Bill W. in the 1930s (Levin, 1998). Jung admitted to Bill W. that his alcoholism seemed hopeless and endless visits to therapists and analysts would probably not cure him. Jung told him squarely that only God could save him, and uttered the strange words that acted as a catalyst to the AA movement: *spiritus contra spiritum*. Only an authentic "spirit" could counter and combat the negative "spirit" of alcohol. After initial bafflement and confusion, this was taken on board as the credo for healing. As soon as we respect the greatness of the wholly Other, our lives take shape again, the tidal wave recedes, and we can rebuild our dwellings on dry land.

We have to learn to live beside the ocean of being and not allow it to overwhelm us. If we learn to attune ourselves to the wave-like dimension, we can allow ourselves experiences of unity, bliss and harmony, and these can have a positive effect on our state of mind, on the nervous system, immune system and mental condition (Koenig, 2002). The numinous can heal the body and the psyche, but we have to allow this to happen. By experiencing the more-than-human, we are released from our ego and returned to a deeper sense of our humanity, from which the water of life flows. It is contact with the non-human, the dimension beyond time, that makes us human again and allows us to be restored at our source, so we can live another day and meet the challenges before us.

Jung (1951) insisted that those who want to bathe at this source have to maintain their ongoing connection with the "reality principle" at the same time. It is important to maintain one's connection with society, normality and "time and space" if one wishes to live a balanced life in which ego and soul are nurtured and fulfilled (p. 45).

As ego we live as particles, and as soul we exist as waves. If we seek only the wave-like existence, which is often encouraged by the New Age and other cultic movements, Jung would agree with Freud that this is neurotic and has to be criticised (Tacey, 2001). Our ego-lives have to be protected against the desire to drown in the source and bathe continually in ecstasy, a pattern found in drug and alcohol addictions, in consumerism and in various kinds of mental illness.

Although our ego-lives can give us pain and need to be overcome from time to time, they have to be respected as a central part of our experience of being human. In secular society, a typical pattern is to attempt to dissolve the ego on Friday nights or at weekends, in bouts of drinking or festivity. There are better ways to transcend the ego, but secular society lacks imagination in this regard. Certainly, our ego existence calls for adjustment to social norms, family, friends, employment and morality. If we live only for the wave, we become esoteric, "mystical" in a negative sense and remote from humanity.

In a certain light, the wave does not care about the particle, and may even seek to annihilate it in the ocean of non-being. When that happens, the wave might say good riddance to the ego, because the particle is viewed as an illusion from the perspective of eternity. In the East, the ego's existence and its world of time and space is sometimes regarded as *maya*, illusion, and of little consequence in relation to the eternal. But the particle has to stick up for itself, and not allow itself to be annihilated. We might say the wave annihilates the particle only if the particle harbours a death-wish, and sees no point in its separate existence. If the particle is able to build self-esteem, it will experience the wave as healing and nurturing, and not as aggressively destructive.

For its part, the wave does not set out to extinguish the particle. To use religious terms, God does not set out to destroy creation. Without the particular, the wave has no way of entering time and space or of incarnating into this world. It is vital that the particle maintains its integrity, not only for its own sake, but for the sake of eternity, which needs the particular to establish itself in time.

Negative Capability, Wholeness and Healing

By way of conclusion, I want to return to basics: what is spirituality?

I don't believe I have yet defined spirituality in this essay. I am ambivalent about definitions, because while they satisfy the mind, and its desire to know and gain control, they do not satisfy the soul, which may feel boxed in and confined. The spiritual side of our nature perhaps asks for acknowledgement, rather than definition. If we spent as much time on acknowledgement as we do on asking for definitions, we might be in better shape. Having said that, I would nevertheless define spirituality as *an innate human capacity to experience transcendent reality*.

What this transcendent reality is, I don't know. If I did know it would not be transcendent. I just know that we live better lives if we acknowledge it and act as if it were real and close to us. I feel it is healthy if we adopt an attitude of humility; we should not attempt to know this reality too fully. An attitude of constant observance, matched with the art of not-knowing, or what Keats called "negative capability" is the best attitude to adopt. If we get too rational about the spirit and its substantive reality, chances are we have lost the plot and are heading into a kind of madness. It is simply not possible for our finite minds to grasp or know the infinite. When we think we know the divine nature, we can be sure, at that moment, we are far from genuine understanding. As Otto (1923) has said, "A God comprehended is no God" (p. 25).

The sacred makes claims on us and when we encounter the spirit we are called to a new life of commitment. In the past, such commitment was reserved for celibates and the priestly classes, but today, in our radically democratic world, everyone is called to commitment. No one can escape this encounter, because the self is incomplete and searches for completion. An encounter with spirit compels us to strive toward wholeness. Wholeness relates to the word "holiness", and the wholeness that spirit calls for leads to a search for connectedness (Sanford, 1977). We find ourselves searching for connectedness at various levels: to our inner selves (spirit or soul), to others and society, to nature and the cosmos and to transcendent reality – however it happens to be imagined.

A key break from the past is signalled by the shift from perfection to wholeness. Previously, it was felt by tradition that the best way to be holy was to become perfect, which entailed a moral piety and an extreme spiritual discipline which was antagonistic to the "flesh". The body and its desires were felt to be contrary to a spiritual life lived in pursuit of perfection. Today, this old ideal of holiness is in the process of being replaced by a new ideal of personal integration, in which body and spirit are brought together in relationship. There is a new "ecological" approach, and spirit and nature, or spirit and body, are no longer felt to be oppositional. This is another reason why the religious ideas of the past are often not suited to present need, which is to find a spiritual ideal in which the old moral conflicts are resolved in a new understanding of sexuality, desire and embodiment.

My sense is that spirit wants a new and more radical form of incarnation. It asks us to hold the tension between the heavenly, angelic aspects, and the earthly, sexual or instinctual aspects. To hold these elements together is an extraordinary feat, and we could not do it were it not for the support we receive from the spirit in giving us the courage to accommodate our contrary impulses. This support is what religion calls grace, and what Jung (1916/57) calls the transcendent function.

Acknowledgement of the spirit leads to healing, but not necessarily to cure. I think we have to be clear about this difference. Some believe that spirituality can lead to sudden or miraculous cures, and this is why they involve themselves in this pursuit. My belief is that miraculous cures do happen, but they are not our human province. We may receive them, as a boon or as grace, but we should not ask for them. The chances are that they will not occur, and if we beg for them, we will feel bereft and without hope. But healing is different. Healing may, for instance, give us the strength to endure what has to be endured. Healing and health share a common linguistic root, but the healing of the spirit may or may not bring cure. Spiritual experience may lead to a reduction of symptoms, but they are sought primarily to make our lives endurable. Viktor Frankl (1963) wisely said that "when a man has a 'why' he can handle almost any 'how'" (p. 9).

The Art of Spirituality in a Clinical Setting

My hope is that the health-care professions can emphasise spirituality and not organised religion. It is certainly not the job of professionals, whether academics, medical doctors, psychiatrists, psychologists or counsellors to foist their particular beliefs upon students, patients, clients and suffering people. Ought we think that patients are somehow "cured" when they have adopted the beliefs of their doctors? Are they "well" when they espouse the things that counsellors think are right? This is not the way to conduct healing, and it cannot be condoned.

What the healing professions need is to develop an interest in what could be called a *generic spiritual attitude*. The clinical discussions could draw the spiritual core out of the person, and allow him or her to choose the path that their spirituality will take. Therapy and consultation can help people find the courage to believe in an invisible level of support, but it is not up to the professionals to supply the specific language or creed. That is a personal matter and not the province of those in authority. This makes a generic spirituality all the more attractive and desirable in today's world, and especially important for professional life and ethical conduct.

The aim is to find a large healing framework, which is potent enough to evoke a sense of the sacred, but loose enough to allow variations on a theme. The professional's task is not to evangelise or proselytise, but to encourage people to discover what is life-giving and creative in their experience of the world. I have been arguing in this chapter that healing is achieved when the self connects to that which is "more than" itself. The therapist's belief system, however genuinely held, can act as a barrier to the healing forces within the client's immediate world.

The key for professional practice is to place the patient's experience before our own theories or beliefs, and use the patient's language, not our own, to access and mobilise the healing forces. This requires listening instead of preaching, and the results will be liberating rather than oppressive. The art of spirituality is the art of deep listening, of attunement to the Other within and beyond the self. This is spirituality in action, not only as therapeutic content but also as clinical method.

References

Augustine, Saint (c398) (1961). *Confessions*. R. S. Pine-Coffin (Ed.). London: Penguin.
Berry, T. (1988). *The dream of the earth*. San Francisco: Sierra Club Books.
Capra, F. (1982). *The turning point: Science, society and the rising culture*. London: Flamingo.
Caputo, J. (2001). *On religion*. London: Routledge.
Frankl, V. (1963). *Man's search for meaning* (4th ed.). Boston: Beacon Press, 1992.
Freud, S. (1908). Creative writers and day-dreaming. In J. Strachey (Ed. & Trans.), *Standard edition of the complete psychological works* (Vol. 9, 2001). London: Hogarth Press.
Freud, S. (1927). *The future of an illusion*. In J. Strachey (Ed. & Trans.), *Standard edition of the complete psychological works* (Vol. 21, 2001). London: Hogarth Press.

Freud, S. (1930). *Civilization and its discontents*. In J. Strachey (Ed. & Trans.), *Standard edition of the complete psychological works* (Vol. 21, 2001). London: Hogarth Press.

Jung, C. G. (1916/1957). The transcendent function. In H. Read, M. Fordham, G. Adler, & W. McGuire (Eds.), *The collected works* (Vol. 8, 2nd ed., 1969). London: Routledge, Kegan Paul.

Jung, C. G. (1928). The relations between the ego and the unconscious. In H. Read, M. Fordham, G. Adler, & W. McGuire (Eds.), *The collected works* (Vol. 7, 2nd ed., 1966). London: Routledge, Kegan Paul.

Jung, C. G. (1932). Psychotherapists or the clergy. In H. Read, M. Fordham, G. Adler, & W. McGuire (Eds.), *The collected works* (Vol. 11, 1958/1969). London: Routledge, Kegan Paul.

Jung, C. G. (1945). Letter to P. W. Martin. In G. Adler (Ed.), *C.G. Jung letters* (Vol. 1). Princeton: Princeton University Press, 1973.

Jung, C. G. (1951). Aion. In H. Read, M. Fordham, G. Adler, & W. McGuire (Eds.), *The collected works* (Vol. 9, Pt II, 1959/1968). London: Routledge, Kegan Paul.

Kierkegaard, S. (1849). *The sickness unto death*. London: Penguin, 1989.

Koenig, H. (2002). *Spirituality in patient care*. Philadelphia and London: Templeton Foundation Press.

Laing, R. D. (1967). *The politics of experience*. New York: Pantheon Books.

Levin, J. (1998). *Couple and family therapy of addiction*. Northvale, NJ: Jason Aronson.

Moore, T. (1992). *Care of the soul*. New York: Harper Collins.

Morgan, O., & Jordan, M. (1999). *Addiction and spirituality*. St Louis: Chalice Press.

Orchard, H. (Ed.). (2001). *Spirituality in health care contexts*. Philadelphia: Jessica Kingsley.

Otto, R. (1923). *The idea of the holy*. London: Oxford University Press, 1958.

Peterson, E. (1997). *Subversive spirituality*. Grand Rapids: Eerdmans.

Powell, A. (1998). Soul consciousness and human suffering. *Journal of Alternative and Complementary Medicine, 4*(1), 101–108.

Powell, A. (2005). Spirituality, healing and the mind. *Spirituality and Health International, 6*(3), 166–172.

Roach, M. S. (1997). *Caring from the heart: The convergence of caring and spirituality*. New York: Paulist Press.

Sanford, J. A. (1977). *Healing and wholeness*. New York: Paulist Press.

Swinton, J. (2001). *Spirituality and mental health care: Rediscovering a "Forgotten" dimension*. London and Philadelphia: Jessica Kingsley.

Tacey, D. (2001). *Jung and the new age*. London: Routledge.

Tacey, D. (2004). *The spirituality revolution: The emergence of contemporary spirituality*. London: Routledge.

Van Gennep, A. (1908). *The rites of passage*. Chicago: University of Chicago Press, 1960.

Wolin, R. (2004). *The seduction of unreason*. Princeton, NJ: Princeton University Press.

Chapter 15
The Dynamics of Spiritual Development

C. Glenn Cupit

Abstract Dynamic Systems Theory (DST) allows a description of spiritual development, applicable across a range of definitions of spirituality, without the paradigmatic limitations of traditional linear developmental theories which fail to account for the complexity of the phenomena associated with "spirituality". The concept of "Integrative Dynamic Systems" provides a powerful explanatory metaphor for "spirits" using concepts of "agency", "top-down causality", "emergence", and "attractors" which have direct parallels to terms commonly employed to explain spirituality. A DST stance allows us to transcend reductionism without losing scientific rigour. Through a DST lens, spiritual development exhibits sudden phase transitions from less to more functional organisation of the whole person, driven by "system parameters", ecological forces; organised by "attractors", patterns of behaviour which emerge regularly without clear causal factors; and responsive to the child's free choices. Children resist spiritual change, yet significant transitions may be precipitated by trivial events.

Introduction

While professional literature makes frequent reference to the spiritual (e.g., Crossley & Salter, 2005; Hodge & Bushfield, 2006; Josephson, 2007, Kvarfordt & Sheridan, 2007; Mercer, 2006; Miner-Williams, 2006; Moloney, 2006; Sayani, 2005), and non-scientific accounts recognise the ubiquity of spiritual experiences (e.g., Koulomzin, 1975; Gil'adi, 1992; Clinebell, 1996; Bunge, 2001; Cupit, 2006), spirituality is generally ignored in human development texts and never treated as an essential component of development. The lack of a developmental paradigm which marries humanity's phenomenological self-portrayal as free spiritual agent with the causal empiricism of normative science provides a rational justification for this. Current paradigms are limited by irremediable deficiencies in linear concepts

---

C.G. Cupit (✉)
Child Development, DeLissa Institute of Early Childhood and Family Studies, University of South Australia, Magill, South Australia, 5072, Australia
e-mail: glenn.cupit@unisa.edu.au

of scientific explanation that underpin contemporary developmental psychology. Human spirituality transcends the boundaries they can successfully explain and is accordingly ignored or dismissed.

While traditional approaches have been effective in understanding restricted aspects of human development, none encompass people's complex diversity. Being derived from different images of the human person, they are also essentially contradictory. "It appears that each of these theoretical traditions owe their family resemblance to a particular metaphor, emphasis, or viewpoint, not a scientific explanation ... Mechanistic theories compare developing humans to machines, organismic theories compare them to plants, and constructivist theories compare them to builders with a universal tool kit" (Lewis, 2000, p. 37). Lewis incorrectly assumes the issue is use of metaphors. Science is metaphor based; familiar and simplifying parallels reduce incredibly complicated phenomena to that which is readily recognisable and comprehensible, for instance, the "solar system" model of the atom.

However, effective metaphor requires passably analogous parallels to be a reasonable representation of reality. It fails in current developmental psychology because people are qualitatively different from traditional comparison objects. Humans do not resemble machines except in their most basic functions. While other organisms provide a closer analogy, they fail to parallel human consciousness and higher order mental and language functions (Hofstadter, 2007). Apart from specific distortions, each "tradition" misrepresents the human person in four identical ways.

Limitations of Previous Developmental Theories

Despite the demonstrable non-linearity of empirical data, traditional theories presume human behaviour is expressible by linear functions; that the development follows continuous straight or curved trajectories. Individual children's capacities vary over short and long terms with sudden accelerations, stable periods, regressions and oscillations. Conventional developmental research, "... draws its conclusions from results obtained after the moment-to-moment fluctuations and individual differences of behaviour have been partialled out by statistical smoothing procedures" (Wolff, 1993, p. 189). van Geert (1994) indicates "If a researcher repeatedly tests a child for the same developing variable ... and finds an irregular, oscillatory or downward path, it is usually assumed that this must reflect random fluctuations or measurement errors and that the true variable follows a path of linear or log-linear increase" (p. 38). An adequate model needs to represent the variability of individual developmental paths rather than conceal it behind presumed linearity.

The second misrepresentation is a revitalisation of the discredited philosophy of preformationism; that the final developmental outcome is laid down in pre-existing structures, specifically, the genes and/or environment. This means that there exists a prior "blueprint for development" and denies the possibility that anything genuinely novel can appear during development. Thelen and Smith (1998) outline some problems when one applies this to the complexity of factors which shape development: "... if the instructions to develop are in the genes, who turns on the genes? If the complexity exists in the environment, who decides what the organism should absorb and retain? ... Postulating an interaction of genes and environment merely assigns the pre-existing plans to two sources instead of one" (p. 564). One remarkable feature of the developing person is the incredible diversity of pathways of development and what appear to be genuinely novel solutions to developmental issues.

The third distortion lies in ignoring the unresolved anomaly that continuous stimuli to development lead to qualitatively discontinuous "stages"; prolonged periods of relative stability, interspersed with relatively brief periods of significant change. van Geert asks: "... how can a gradual mechanism that never ceases to operate explain a long-term process of stability penetrated by sudden changes?" (p. 7). It is a question standard theories do not answer.

Finally, by restricting themselves to particular developmental domains, established theories of child development omit consideration of facets of life which transcend the limits of their models. No theory presents a comprehensive picture of interactions between physical, social and conceptual development and the like, for instance, how thought and emotion mutually reinforce or hinder each other. Nor are higher level functions incorporated except, occasionally, through reductionist claims. Attempts to address moral, aesthetic, religious, creative and spiritual development generally extrapolate from structuralist theories of cognitive or social development. For instance, Kohlberg's (1984) theory of moral development and Fowler's (1981) theory of "faith" development are both derivative of Piaget's or Erikson's stage theories. Such argument by analogy may reasonably generate hypotheses but does not itself produce a valid theory of the more complex phenomenon.

Dynamic Systems Theory

Trenchant criticism of linear deterministic models of development comes from proponents of the new approach variously known as Dynamic(al) or Complex Systems Theory, Chaos Theory or Complexity Science (hereafter DST). DST claims to encompass the multifaceted intricacy of developing human "systems", using a metaphor based on highly complex phenomena, like weather, communities and information systems. As complex systems consist of systems of subsidiary systems, DST can deal simultaneously with the child as a whole, and as separate developmental domains.

The application of DST to human development has gained wide recognition following advocacy since the early 1990s (e.g., Kamm, Thelen, & Jensen, 1990; Thelen & Smith, 1996), recently justifying an entire volume of *Developmental Review* (2005, 25, passim). Albright (2000) and Goerner (1995) propose that it also provides a basis for understanding phenomena like spirituality.

It is not possible to fully represent DST in a brief summary. Reasonably accessible coverage is provided by Cupit (2002, 2005), Howe and Lewis (2005) and Lewis

(2000). While its essential character is clear, it is a new and growing approach, subject to ongoing modification. Most DSTists concede the theory is difficult to characterise, aggravated by their propensity for fanciful language such as "chaos", "butterfly effect", "strange attractor" and "magician system". Like relativity and quantum physics, it challenges our thinking because its outcomes contradict ways we have learned to see the world. I offer a limited description of its application to human development and how this may apply to spiritual development.

A Dynamic System Approach to Development

DST studies the behaviour of systems whose constituents are involved in complex mutual exchanges of influence. Such systems, including people, demonstrate behaviours unpredictable from their constituent parts (e.g., consciousness cannot be predicted from our chemical constituents or physiology). At each moment, every child confronts its "phase space", an imaginary region enclosing all its possible futures. These vary in probability (marriage is more likely than murder) and vary between children. The child's "trajectory" through its phase space, its actual rather than potential future, is shaped by three factors, "system (or control) parameters", "agency" and "attractors".

System Parameters

System parameters consist of all aspects of the child's genetic make-up, its environment (pre-empting nature-nurture arguments) and its history incorporating past learning. They both "determine" and "entrain" (cause works both "bottom up" as in reductionist theories and "top down" with more complex phenomena shaping the behaviour of less). For example, while, physiology determines thinking, thinking may equally entrain physiology; we may determine to ignore hunger. This is the first significant departure from traditional science. Despite their alternative name, system parameters do not "control" the child's trajectory but mutually interact to constrain and/or perturb it in directions consistent with their individual nature. They are not the only forces at work, nor do all work in concert. They "push" or "pull" the system but the system, the child, may well "push back".

Agency

Extremely complex systems, like people, are deemed "magician systems", though I prefer the less occult "integrative dynamic systems" (IDSs) (Cupit, 2002). These manipulate other systems, particularly their own subsystems, to maintain the integrity of their "whole". For instance, we deny pain from over-stressed muscles to fulfil a manual task and keep our partner content. Or, told we suffer from Type 2 diabetes, we engage muscles to exercise the body and deny impulses towards vanilla slices. This presumes agency, the ability to choose and act to bring choices to fruition. DST treats each child as an agent in its own development because its decisions mediate the impact of system parameters. Children internalise some influences, accept some and ferociously resist others. Their choices are important in shaping their development.

Attractors

The final factors can only be identified *ex post facto* by comparing many similar systems. Dynamic systems (DSs) are drawn into mysterious shared patterns of behaviour referred to as "attractors" (and recently "repellors"). So, while each child's trajectory is unique, all children's trajectories follow (or avoid) the same general pattern regardless of hereditary or environmental factors. Attractors are not determinable from the characteristics of the system itself. Examples include what other theories call "stages of development" and common behaviours like "crawling". Each child exhibits these but no two children in precisely the same way.

System parameters or children's choices perturb their paths away from attractors but, over time, they are drawn back. Systems resist shifting from an attractor even under significant pressure. A baby insists on crawling despite doting parents offering inducements to walk. Older children persist in inefficient approaches to problems despite being shown better resolutions. However, parameters which push the child towards more developed behaviour become progressively stronger and, when perturbations become irresistible, there is a brief chaotic period called a "phase transition" when the relevant behaviour becomes erratic. Then it settles down around a qualitatively different attractor. Children move from one favoured response to something totally different or from one developmental stage to a more advanced one.

This summary merely scratches the surface of a highly intricate and nuanced approach but concepts embedded in the characteristics of DSs are coherent with important aspects of children's spiritual development.

Spiritual Development Through a Dynamic Systems Lens

I have argued (Cupit, 2002, see also Hofstadter, 2007) that a hierarchy of complexity in species exists marked by the appearance of emergent capacities; for instance, life, adaptation, sexual differentiation and problem solving. But only with the complexity of human life does a superordinate integrative function (an IDS) emerge that is self-aware and seeks meaning for its existence. This novel system experiences itself as having a dimension which transcends less complex phases of being; it is more than just body and mind. From the way people describe this "dimension", it seems to entail a sense of mysterious yet discernible presence, at once immanent and ephemeral; unpredictable dynamism; strong beliefs, feelings and emotions; and the life or essential being of something. It recognises a similar dimension in other persons. It names itself, and them, as "spirits", or some equivalent, and debates the meaning of "spirituality".

The distinctiveness of the human spirit does not lie in having characteristics which other entities lack. It lies in the complex pattern of interactions of characteristics, particularly cognitive abstraction, symbolic language and self- and interpersonal-awareness, which generate an IDS able to conceive of itself as having a meaning or purpose for being; entering into relationships; and transcending simple hedonism and reproduction in favour of aesthetics, ethics and religion. This "spirit" is an unprecedented emergent mode of being which is distinct and autonomous even while identified with its components. It is marked by autopoietic stability (it persists despite component change) based on self-awareness and self-organising behaviours which it uses to avoid dis-integration, i.e. I know myself by name and as separate from other selves, and I remain myself despite changing. It is also able to combine its constituent elements to create novel outcomes. I create situations around myself which make me who I wish to be, and some of those creations are genuinely unique to me and unprecedented in other humans.

As intimated, a few DSTists indicate that DSs may serve as a metaphor for spirituality. Goerner (1995) says: "The oddest thing about the whole situation—the new science approach and deep ecology in its many guises—is that science, pragmatism, and spirituality are in fact becoming intertwined" (p. 17). Phenomena we designate as "spirits" fit well the criteria for IDSs. DST language is not "spiritual" but there are clear parallels between the highly complex systems it describes and spiritual entities. I will identify some resonances between IDSs and spirits which allow the scientific theory of the former to inform our understanding of how the latter develop.

Spirits and Integrative Dynamic Systems

Many common understandings of spirits suggest they share the following characteristics with IDSs (here expressed in the latter language):

- spirits behave in ways unpredictable by classical scientific theories;
- they are identified with the entities they integrate;
- spirits transcend the limits of corporeality. Nevertheless, as emergent properties of complexity both are instantiated in, and never exist apart from, material entities;
- spirits entrain subordinate systems to act as a coherent whole in ways unpredictable from those constituent elements;
- they exercise agency and self-organise to fulfil their objectives, managing their subsystems to achieve goals which reflect their perception of the best outcome for the whole person. They may shed or deny aspects of themselves, entrain components to behave differently, or gain control over systems not currently part of themselves;
- spirits retain their identity despite changes to component parts;

- they use the energy of the system to construct more functional self-organisation, in other words, to develop; they are "auto-catalytic";
- over time spirits demonstrate a pattern of resistance to change, followed by significant precipitate reorganisation into other modes;
- they organise themselves hierarchically and heterarchically, interacting with both higher and lower order systems, as well as systems of comparable complexity;
- spirits follow common patterns of behaviour which can be either sequential or alternative; they are influenced by attractors;
- they are deeply influenced by minor events, being highly sensitive to small changes in conditions.

As a consequence, both spirits and IDSs are predictable in general pattern but not individual detail. As we cannot foresee the behaviour of any IDS, we cannot forecast spiritual development in detail for any individual. However, their behaviour is not random but drawn to common and predictable patterns that allow us to state which behaviours are more likely and which less.

Applying the Dynamic Systems Theory Lens

A DST framework can be applied across a range of naturalistic, Romantic, or theistic definitions of spirituality (Cupit, 2002). I assume other spiritual entities are real and interact with children as system parameters, to their benefit or detriment. Depending on one's preferred metaphysic, these include persons (e.g., parents), social systems (e.g., school spirit), ideologies (e.g., materialism), cultures (e.g., national identity), immaterial "forces" (e.g., nature), "entities" (e.g., demons) and/or deities. Precise specification of spiritual influences is a matter for hermeneutical, philosophical and empirical research. However, as a metaphor, DST suggests the following: spiritual development is a process of phase transitions from less functional to more functional organisation of the whole person driven by system parameters, organised by attractors, and responsive to children's free choices. In spiritual terms "conversion", "apostasy", "enlightenment" or "backsliding" (or several alternative terms), indicate that a person has experienced a momentous (the DST term is "catastrophic") alteration to their spiritual life.

When we speak of our spirit, we speak of what we identify as the essential "me". Rather than being separable from my body or personality, my spirit is what integrates all the many aspects of me into a single self-aware entity. "My spirit" and "I" are coterminous, which contradicts the view that I "have" a spirit with its problem of identifying what the "I" is that "has". Some concepts of spirits depict them as acting independently of their body but it is more parsimonious to consider spirit as an expression of a physical/mental/social phenomenon with transcendent capacities derived from being a manifestation of the whole. A simple analogy is "team spirit" which is more than the performance of individual players and may well survive changes of personnel.

Stories abound of how sensitive to small changes spirits are, with significant spiritual reorganisation following an afternoon in the bush, hearing a story, a chance encounter with a child, an overheard slight. Our spirits are in constant flux as they respond to life experience yet, being spirits, they maintain a core integrity of identity. They not only entrain their own subsystems; they communicate and form relationships with like spirits in religions, cults, covens, clubs and the like. They also arrange relationships in hierarchies where more powerful spirits entrain the behaviour of subordinates.

As self-organising agents, spirits integrate physiological and psychological systems to shape their own development, perhaps by bodily exercises (e.g., mortification) or mental disciplines (e.g., contemplation). They may train, seek different companions, or develop martial arts (because spirits can be destructive). Spiritual development is also shaped by common patterns or attractors. While each spiritual life is unique, its distinctiveness lies in variations around identifiable patterns all follow. Some attractors relate to the way spirituality changes with age, e.g., with the achievement of language, and some represent alternate patterns of spirituality, e.g., solitary or communal.

At birth, children are minimally functional as IDSs, and consequently are "objectively helpless" (Buckland, 1977, 1988) as spirits, entirely "open" to spiritual influences. Spiritual development consists of gaining capacities to progressively discriminate between influences, accepting some and successfully resisting others. The mature spirit is an autonomous and accomplished player in its spiritual ecology.

Though it is rapidly progressing, the current application of DST to child development is yet to specify a detailed theory of the usual developmental domains, let alone of spiritual development. But it is possible to propose a notional framework upon which to build such a theory and to identify areas for theoretical or empirical study to substantiate it.

Principles of Spiritual Development Indicated by a DST Approach

As emergent IDSs, spiritual entities entrain other phenomena, that is, constrain them to behave to benefit the spirit. The child's spirit is entrained by its parents' spirits, and, in turn, entrains system parameters which are part of its context, e.g., by choosing peers. Other spirits also entrain system parameters external to the child, e.g., by shaping diet, church theology, and media.

System parameters maintain gradual progression within stable periods and stimulate phase transitions to new levels of self-organisation. Most are observable by existing empirical methods. I argue that the parameters of spirituality represent two metaphysical principles, one expressive of spiritual "good", the other spiritual "evil". The first organises parameters to optimise the child's developmental trajectory towards attractors representing health and wisdom, the alternative directs the child into trajectories leading to attractors of disorder and folly. Depending on one's philosophy these principles may be represented as mere reifications of the outcomes, emergent reflections of the good and evil in people or the world, or as signifying the existent of benevolent and malevolent supernatural beings. Both principles operate through common sources of spiritual encounter; nature, artefacts, relationships, ideas, etc.

Because of the dynamic interactions between the many factors that influence it, each child's spiritual development is unique and unpredictable in detail, and adults cannot prescribe how it will develop. However, broad conclusions can be drawn about children's response to spiritual parameters. Rather than continuous progression, intervals of stability will be interspersed with qualitative shifts, and even regressions. Trajectories will be marked by extreme sensitivity to changing parameters so that a small input (e.g., a song or a hug) at the right time may lead to significant change, and children raised in very similar contexts may follow different trajectories because of subtle variations unnoticed by adults.

Many religions propose a Divine intent that children follow sequential attractors towards "righteousness", however conceived. The reality of human life is that children are actually drawn towards alternative attractors, some which lead to God/goodness/positive spirituality, and others spiralling towards destructive spirituality/alienation/damnation, depending on your viewpoint. This duality of attractors expresses a moral bipolarity of spirituality rather than contrasting spirituality with unspirituality (Cupit, 2002, 2005).

In the early years, attractors are represented as wide and flat valleys separated by minimal medial saddles allowing easy transition from attractor to attractor, reflecting a spirituality readily deflected by contrasting system parameters. The most devout child in the Sunday school may be a tearaway in the playground. One mark of development is a decreased tendency to shift between attractors signifying greater spiritual stability; symbolically a narrowing and deepening of these basins. Nevertheless, attractors are not blueprints and no child's trajectory ever exactly matches them; the most "faithful" may not recognise the importance of tidying up.

Attractors and phase transitions in spiritual development will not exactly mirror those that occur in physical systems (Goertzel, 1997). In particular, "sudden" developmental transitions may be of extended duration. Previous organisation is not lost, but subsumed within the emergent organisation as a part of its more flexible functionality. After the phase change that allows walking, children can still choose to crawl; intuitive thought remains part of the toolbox of the more capable cognitive system capable of logical thinking. The developing person goes through many phase transitions of varied relevance to spirituality. For instance, the apparently neutral transition to walking allows rapid locomotion and consequent significant change in perceptual perspective, problem solving and agency. It is an important step towards the development of semantic symbolisation and, consequently, the emergence of concepts of truth and error.

Given the qualification that further empirical, phenomenological and philosophical/theological research is needed to articulate the actual transitions, some may be suggested a priori based on what we know from general developmental research and anecdotal accounts of those actively engaged with children, signalled by the emergence of qualitatively distinct patterns of global behaviour or phases of spiritual development (attractors) (Cupit, 2002). Each marks a significant transformation from "openness" or "helplessness" towards competence. This does not exclude other attractors which are either recursive, reappearing in varying forms across the growth process, nor attractors which are unrelated to developmental progress. But it is important to identify those attractors which mark the course of development to maturity.

Phases and Phase Transitions in Spiritual Development

Prenatal—the Symbiotic Phase

During the prenatal period the child is biologically dependent on the mother; the "mother–child" is a single system and the "child" is dissipated by separation, i.e. it dies. The developmental parameters are hereditary factors and ecological factors mediated by the uterine environment. The "child" only encounters environmental sources of spirituality through their impact upon the mother. Consequently, the mother's context and choices govern what parameters operate and how.

Children in utero are vulnerable and resilient. The dominant attractor creates trajectories leading to healthy development to birth except in extreme circumstances. Its basin is both very flat and wide. Consequently, while it is easy to jolt the child's trajectory away from close conformity, it requires an extreme perturbation to push the child so far that it is not drawn back. Nevertheless, some negative attractors are atypically very deep and narrow. The rubella virus creates such system disruption that it is impossible to exit its attractor to return to the positive attractor. The consequences are lifelong.

The foetus is not yet a separate IDS, so to apply the term "spirit" may be inappropriate, though this is contentious.

Phase Transition at Birth

The period is terminated by a separation of the mother–child system into two physically independent systems. Though children remain reliant on others, this need no longer be the biological mother. A consequence of this transition is a significant increase in sensory input as sense organs are freed from intra-uterine restrictions. Because their prenatal developmental trajectory provides the entry point for infancy, children do not enter on an equivalent footing.

Infancy—the Trust Period

Children are born as open IDSs, delivered into a world requiring transactions with systems ranging from simple physical environments, through complex biological structures, to immaterial principles (e.g., justice) instantiated in the material world through people and institutions.

Many parameters influential during the previous period remain so, though with reduced potency as the infant is less vulnerable to their effects. New parameters become important. The quality of caregiver nurture and of their relationships to infants comes to be of significance. The expression or denial of caregiver love in sustenance and interaction provides a powerful impetus towards the trajectory amongst spiritual attractors the infant will follow. Though access to other sources of spiritual encounters may occur, it is generally limited by caregiver decisions.

Psychologists and theologians have recognised the importance of a basic orientation to trust in infancy and the possibility of bifurcation into ongoing mistrust. For example, Erikson sees in the development of trust in the infant the beginnings of faith (whether religious or not) (Hill, 1995), and Bridger concurs from a Christian perspective:

> The foundations of faith are being laid even at this early stage. A child who does not learn how to trust adults now will have difficulty trusting anybody at more than a superficial level later on. This extends to trust in God (Bridger, 1988, p. 13).

Whether their world proves itself trustworthy or not has permanent spiritual consequences.

Koulomzin associates the importance of the infant period for spirituality with the development of the unconscious. What is learnt is not encoded in verbal symbols. Consequently, the person later finds it hard to articulate this learning, and to reconfigure it, as it is not susceptible to logical argument.

The infant is not only less dependent than the foetus but also exercises greater reciprocal influence on those systems which offer nurture. Usually, infants engender in caregivers the need to offer care:

> In this way the child, seemingly so helpless, performs the mighty work of awakening in us a tremendous appetite for understanding and so brings us to the table of love (Wolf, 1996, p. 28).

Transition to Pre-critical Linguistic Symbolisation

Infancy is destabilised by gradual contextual changes in system parameters, none of which is alone sufficient to bring about reorganisation. Significant contributors to the change include growing motor competence, identification as a "self" separate from others and of others as "selves" in their own right, weaning and toilet training. Most important is the emergence of language and, especially, its symbolic use, with the change in thinking that initiates. This transition is of reasonably limited duration and, being constrained by maturational factors, allows an approximate chronological designation of the end of infancy. Later periods vary more widely in their emergence and dissolution and consequently are specified functionally rather than by age.

Pre-critical Symbolic—the Period of Beliefs

With the emergence of symbolic language children are able to contemplate and articulate that which is beyond their immediate experience.

> In this linguistic symbolisation, we find the principle of transcendence, making the child gradually stand above the physical world mentally (Kao, 1981, p. 75).

They begin to assimilate the formative narratives of their family and community. They hear caregivers evaluate in terms of aesthetics, morality, manners and culture. Matters of spirituality begin to be articulated to and by them. However, apart from what they experience directly, what they "know", including how they interpret those direct experiences, is entirely dependent on their caregivers.

> Much depends on what they have learned at home or in church, what pictures of God they have seen – if any at all, and what vocabulary they have come to use (Hyde, 1990, p. 69).

Children's trajectory as they exit from infancy iterates into this period. They enter predisposed to trust what they are told unless, in infancy, they were drawn into a "mistrust" attractor. One would expect such prior attraction to be reinforced unless system parameters relevant to trust undergo their own phase transition, e.g. following a change of caregiver. As they progressively deepen, transition between the trust and mistrust attractors becomes less likely.

Consequently, the spiritual attractors and essential parameters of this period relate to believing those who offer care. Caregivers' control and children's continuing physical emotional dependence mean that caregivers are usually accepted by children as authorities; what they say is believed. Questions seek information (unless they are a game) rather than having any evaluative element. There are four cardinal parameters: increasing intellectual and linguistic competence; the commitment of caregivers to truth; their commitment to goodness; and the validity of what they say about each.

While children are responsive to all spiritual sources, those related to truth and deceit become particularly significant. What caregivers say will ideally draw children into an attractor marked by commitment to ideas which validly represent what is true and what is good. Children will also believe what they read, once they are able, and what they see on electronic media, which they evaluate only by perceptual appeal, if attractive then "good".

However, children are not passive recipients of caregiver beliefs. As active meaning makers, they construct their own explanations of spiritual encounters, but in the context of inability to appraise legitimacy in what they encounter. The attempt to make sense of complex ideas without the capacity to apply critical logic leads to the seemingly "quaint" nature of beliefs during this period. Far from being quaint, anecdotal reports often reveal in children a profound though naïve spirituality (Coles, 1990).

The first alternative attractor to learning truth from caregivers varies only a little; where caregivers value but misunderstand truth and goodness. Children accept mistaken parental ideas because they cannot discern right from wrong or true from false, except by what caregivers tell them. A far more significant alternative is failure to value truth or goodness based on adopting caregivers' devaluation of these. If one learns to cherish truth, then error is open to correction; if to appreciate "good", one can accommodate divergent ideas of virtue. It is much harder if children believe the very ideas of truth or goodness are vacuous.

How deep early attractors are depends on the resolution of the previous period. The more trusting the child, the deeper the attractor. Nevertheless, initially the saddles are low and children slip from one attractor to another depending on context, for instance, parental influences counteracted by grandparents or parents by educators. Ideally, trustful children are taught truth and goodness by trustworthy caregivers. The outcome is children able to believe, as well as to trust, dependable people. Not that beliefs in this phase have enduring stability. Rather they are extremely tenuous and mutable. The methodological difficulty in determining young children's religious beliefs reflects in part that there are no enduring beliefs to find (Tamminen, Vianello, Jaspard, & Ratcliff, 1988).

Neither ideal nor totally destructive caregivers exist. Rather all children experience caregivers who are both inconsistent with others and self-contradictory. So all children vary around identifiable attractors. Nevertheless, certain outcomes are far from optimal. Some children emerge committed to a distorted idea of, and others with little commitment to, truth and goodness. The former are likely to face disillusionment later; the latter follow an attractor which leads towards relativism and anomie. Children enter into the next period either following an attractor oriented to commitment to knowing the truth, or to a predilection to deny it.

Transition to Discernment

The acquired ability to recognise discrepancies between divergent accounts of reality and different moral demands precipitates the next phase transition. Although, previously, children accepted the truth of mutually exclusive claims, automatic acceptance of caretaker expertise now breaks down. Real questions begin to be asked. An increasing ability to evaluate alternative "realities" emerges with recognition that adults can and do err. Children begin to exercise the intellectual autonomy to choose between contradictory views, but in the context of significant constraint upon emotional and social independence.

Dependent Critical Symbolic—the Period of Discernment

This period is marked by recognition of alternative possibilities and development of the intellectual tools to discriminate between them, creating tension between the ability to decide what is true for themselves and continued socio-emotional dependence on caregivers. Children consider options and begin to use their experience and others' reactions to evaluate them. Exposed to a far wider range of spiritual sources, including multiple caregivers, they ask questions, often of different people, and weigh up the answers they receive. In particular, children begin to use repositories of human intellect beyond their caregivers in culture, religion, text, art, performance and especially in educative-care systems.

However, children are not self-sufficient individuals and retain strong emotional ties to caregivers, finding it hard to admit that they are wrong on important matters or to contradict them, despite increasing intellectual ability to do so. Consequently, they may become reticent about spiritual matters (Hay, 2000, p. 39).

The stability of this period is maintained against continuing exposure to important system parameters such as life experience and world knowledge, improving intellectual strategies and growing social competence, decreasing dependence on particular caregivers and increasing self-reliance. In the spiritual realm, these interact with the degree to which children are able and allowed to explore their beliefs, and how caregivers respond to their questioning. Authority can become authoritarian, insisting on unquestioning conformity; or children's questioning can be encouraged as an occasion to extend their understanding. Whether caregiver responses reflect a coherent and consistent spirituality, spiritual confusion or denial is also influential.

The primary attractor is a spirituality which discriminates between true and good spiritual influences and those which are distorted and destructive. Not that these children can fully resist either, but they demonstrate preferences and seek to be excused from some. They are very sensitive to discrepancies between what caregivers assert and what they enact. They may criticise aspects of caregiver spirituality even while socially involved. The contradiction of independent belief and social dependency is poignantly expressed by one of Hardy's respondents:

> My sense of conscious contact with the power at the heart of the universe dates from the age of 11 or 12 when I used to run as quickly as possible through the prayers I had been taught to say in order to get on with the real business of talking to someone who was 'there' (Hardy, 1979, p. 69).

Caregivers may find it increasingly difficult to penetrate children's spirituality from now on (Koulomzin 1975).

Once again there are two alternative attractors to healthy spiritual discrimination. One leads to unquestioning acquiescence to a particular version of "truth" or spiritual practice. This derives from caregivers who refuse to allow growing intellectual and social competence and enforce spiritual immaturity. The other assumes a similarly uncritical acceptance of all knowledge as equally legitimate and all spiritualities as uniformly acceptable, or as having no currency beyond the pragmatic. This stems from caregivers themselves lacking an articulate belief system or lacking respect for the importance of spiritual questions. Some children are accorded an ersatz maturity requiring them to address their questions without the guidance of trusted caregivers. In the extreme, the first leads to a spirituality of rigid codes having less to do with genuine concurrence than with the need to be accepted; the other to a spiritual life without cognitive content or ethical parameters.

Some caregivers arrest the development of personal competence so their children cannot conceive of themselves involved in spirituality different from that of their parents. Alternatively, being prematurely required to negotiate spiritual matters without caretaker guidance leaves children without the intellectual and social capital needed to recognise and accept mature spirituality. Any of these suboptimal attractors may prove sufficiently stable to resist subsequent parameter change. Consequently, subsequent phases are conditional rather than universal.

Transition to Exploration

For those who do transit to the following stable phase, the main precipitating factor is growing social independence from caregivers, even while physical reliance persists. For fortunate children, caregiver restraint is gradually withdrawn allowing freedom to make spiritual decisions without jeopardising important relationships. For others, autonomy has to be seized as caregiver restraint becomes intolerable. In either case, the system parameters relate to contextual and social factors which lead children to wish to disarticulate from spiritual dependence on the rest of the household, to make their own choices about what they believe and do.

Independent Constrained—the Period of Exploration

Many children traverse a period when they see themselves as sufficiently separate from their caregivers to consider a contrary approach to spirituality, even while, for pragmatic reasons, they have to comply with caretaker requirements. Avoiding irreconcilable conflict, some demonstrate this autonomy by symbolic choices about dress, hairdo, music and styles of speech. Those from a background without religious affiliation may experiment with religion. Children from religious backgrounds may resist attendance or participate sullenly. If caregivers recognise these as necessary to the process of maturing, they can help children reflect upon their experiences, recognising that their spirit can no longer be compelled, though it can still be placed under physical restraint where necessary. However, in some households and educative-care settings, children contemplating matters which cause caregivers grave discomfort creates considerable conflict. Certain caregivers experience great apprehension if children question the reality of the spirituality of their households (Hay, 1995, cited by Crompton, 1998, p. 51).

For the first time children are generally able to choose what sources of spirituality they are exposed to. Henceforth, caregiver mediation is superfluous and the critical system parameters are the direct spiritual encounters which occur. Children are close to spiritual competence but are not fully spiritually responsible as caregivers can still require participation in spiritual activities where they may be unable to resist the influences encountered. While a competent adult might flee influences they felt unable to resist, a constrained child cannot. Alternatively, caregivers may prevent children's chosen involvements.

The ideal attractor sees children choose to recognise and expose themselves to positive spiritual influences reflecting truth and goodness rather than growing alienation from these. Both attractors are wide and accommodate a diverse range of individual trajectories. Now they dramatically intensify and transition between attractors becomes increasingly problematic. In some cultures a dominant religion or ideology mandates its own spirituality and uses the instruments of state to enforce involvement. Though a person may not believe, they can be forced to participate in situations where the "national spirit" is inescapably encountered. The independent-constrained period can become a stable state from which it is hard to transit.

The Transition to Maturity

The final phase transition can be precipitated at any time that a child chooses to wholly accept the responsibilities of spiritual maturity with full awareness of the implications, which may include persecution or death. At that point the person ceases to be a child.

Spiritual Maturity

The final stable period is marked by the person being able to resist entrainment by other spiritual systems. Not that higher order IDSs; ideas, institutions, people and powers cease functioning to effect such entrainment, nor to transform or destroy the mature spirit; the system will still be entrained by other systems, but as a matter of voluntary choice among contending principles, a choice which can change, but can no longer be compelled.

The mature attractor ideal is a healthy, trusting person, with a personally owned commitment to truth and goodness and the intellectual, emotional and physical autonomy to exercise that commitment. Sub-optimal attractors include ill health, inability to trust, denial of truth and goodness, unresolved interpersonal dependence or enforced compliance with others. Given people's mixed developmental histories and situations, the ideal is never fulfilled. In dynamic terms, mature people's life trajectories vary from the ideal insofar as their subsystems are either entrained to, or, at least, are perturbed by, IDSs which exist beyond the person's system boundaries and control.

There are those who embrace life patterns associated with attractors antithetical to the ideal. They may express mistrust through angry suspicion of others, encysting their spirit in bitter fear of betrayal. They may live in denial of truth or advocacy of evil. They may be so determined to sustain the authoritative truth they received that they drift into bigotry or pharisaism, whether religious or secular. They may drift along accepting the group norm, committed to nothing except conformity.

In maturity to change trajectory requires a radical transformation justifying terminology like "new birth", "repentance", "regeneration" or "illumination".

Summary

This model represents spiritual development as an emergent phenomenon reflecting the complexity of children as integrative dynamic systems, and marked by qualitative changes in their encounters with other spiritual entities. Children move through a series of phase transitions from a state of unqualified openness to spiritual influences, to a mature state where they identify by choice with a particular spiritual orientation and are able to exclude alternatives. The dynamic for this development lies in all those factors which foster the general development of the child, but especially in the nature of their exposure to spiritual encounters. Of particular significance, at different times, are parental nurture, the validity of assertions of trusted authorities, caregiver response to attempts to exercise discernment and freedom to explore alternatives. Children pass through a series of stable periods separated by shorter periods of conflict which indicate the dissolution of previous patterns of spirituality to be replaced by emergent patterns of greater spiritual efficacy and autonomy. Though there is an order and consistency in the development of these patterns sufficient to allow general conclusions to be drawn as to characteristics and sequence of stable periods, each child follows an individual trajectory within the broad parameters set by this overarching order. This may include gradual change, plateaus and regressions. Their trajectories reflect the conflicting sway of spiritual principles underlying alternative constructive and destructive attractors. Initially children are unable to resist pressure from system parameters to shift between attractors. Increasing maturity is characterised by enhanced ability to recognise, discern between, and either identify with or counter these influences.

The relationship between stable periods and chronological age is highly variable and sensitive to societal and cultural, as well as personal, factors. However, the sequence is predictable even if each individual trajectory is anything but.

Conclusion

Current approaches to human development are not conducive to consideration of spirituality because they adhere to a linear paradigm incompatible with most conceptualisations of the nature of spirit. DST evades these limitations because complex entities behave in ways which transcend their components. While application of dynamic principles to development, and particularly spiritual development, remains nascent, the theory has considerable heuristic value, not least in approaching spiritual matters with the rigour expected of scientific enquiry.

DST provides a scientific approach to spiritual development compatible with many philosophical and theological understandings, while using principles of wide explanatory power across scientific fields. It offers predictions open to empirical investigation and computer simulation. The identification of actual "system parameters", "attractors", "phase transitions" and the like for spiritual development is far beyond the scope of this chapter, yet DST provides a tantalisingly realistic picture, sufficiently evocative to serve as a metaphor and also to contribute to an appreciation of how we may influence the development of children's spirituality in life affirming directions.

References

Albright, C. R. (2000). The "God module" and the complexifying brain. *Zygon, 35*(4), 735–744.
Bridger, F. (1988). *Children finding faith*. London: Scripture Union.
Buckland, R. (1977). *Children and the King*. Melbourne: ANZEA.
Buckland, R. (1988). *Children and God*. Homebush West: ANZEA.
Bunge, M. J. (2001). *The child in Christian thought*. Grand Rapids: Eerdmans.
Clinebell, H. (1996). *Ecotherapy, healing ourselves, healing the earth: A guide to ecologically grounded personality theory, spirituality, therapy, and education*. Minneapolis: Fortress.
Coles, R. (1990). *The spiritual life of children*. Boston: Houghton Mifflin.
Crompton, M. (1998). *Children, spirituality, religion and social work*. Ashgate: Aldershot.
Crossley, J. P., & Salter, D. P. (2005). A question of finding harmony: A grounded theory study of clinical psychologists' experience of addressing spiritual beliefs in therapy. *Psychology and Psychotherapy: Theory, Research and Practice, 78*, 295–313.
Cupit, C. (2006). *Come and follow Jesus: Practical ways to talk to children about faith*. Central Coast: Scripture Union Australia.
Cupit, C. G. (2005). *Perspectives on children and spirituality*. Central Coast: Scripture Union Australia.
Cupit, C. G. (2002). *A critical evaluation of biblical perspectives on spiritual development and of dynamic systems theory to identify major implications for public educative care of children*. Doctoral dissertation, Murdoch University, Perth. (Murdoch University Digital Thesis, URL: http://wwwlib.murdoch.edu.au/adt/browse/view/adt-MU20051129.114720)
Developmental review, 2005, *25*, passim.
Fowler, J. W. (1981). *Stages of faith: The psychology of human development and the quest for meaning*. San Francisco: Harper & Row.
Gil'adi, A. (1992). *Children of Islam: Concepts of childhood in medieval Muslim society*. New York: St Martins Press.
Goerner, S. J. (1995). Chaos and deep ecology. In F. D. Abraham & A. R. Gilgen (Eds.), *Chaos theory in psychology*. Westport: Greenwood.
Goertzel, B. (1997). *From complexity to creativity: Explorations in evolutionary, autopoietic, and cognitive dynamics*. New York: Plenum.
Hardy, A. (1979). *The spiritual nature of man: A study of contemporary religious experience*. Oxford: Clarendon.
Hay, D. (2000). Spirituality versus individualism: Why we should nurture relational consciousness. *International Journal of Children's Spirituality, 5*(1), 37–48.
Hill, B. V. (1995). Psychological considerations. In B. V. Hill (Ed.), *Studying the religious quest: Unit materials for E403 religious education*. Perth: Murdoch University.
Hodge, D. R., & Bushfield, S. (2006). Developing spiritual competence in practice. *Journal of Ethnic and Cultural Diversity in Social Work, 15*(3/4), 101–127.
Hofstadter, D. R. (2007). *I am a strange loop*. New York: Basic Books.
Howe, M. L., & Lewis, M. D. (2005). The importance of dynamic systems approaches for understanding development. *Developmental Review, 25*, 247–251.
Hyde, K. E. (1990). *Religion in childhood and adolescence: A comprehensive review of the research*. Birmingham: Religious Education Press.
Josephson, A. M. (2007). Depression and suicide in children and adolescents: A spiritual perspective. *Southern Medical Journal, 100*(7), 742–745.
Kamm, K., Thelen, E., & Jensen, J. L. (1990). A dynamical systems approach to motor development. *Physical Therapy, 70*(12), 763–775.

Kao, C. C. L. (1981). *Psychological and religious development: Maturity and maturation*. Washington: University Press of America.

Kohlberg, L. (1984). *The psychology of moral development: The nature and validity of moral stages*. San Francisco: Harper & Row.

Koulomzin, S. (1975). *Our church and our children*. Crestwood: St Vladimir's Seminary Press.

Kvarfordt, C. L., & Sheridan, M. J. (2007). The rôle of religion and spirituality in working with children and adolescents: Results of a national survey. *Journal of Religion and Spirituality in Social Work, 26*(3), 1–23.

Lewis, M. D. (2000). The promise of dynamic systems approaches for an integrated account of human development. *Child Development, 71*(1), 36–43.

Mercer, J. A. (2006). Children as mystics, activists, sages, and holy fools: Understanding the spirituality of children and its significance for clinical work. *Pastoral Psychology, 54*(5), 497–515.

Miner-Williams, D. (2006). Putting a puzzle together: Making spirituality meaningful for nursing using an evolving theoretical framework. *Journal of Clinical Nursing, 15*, 811–821.

Moloney, S. (2006). The spirituality of childbirth. *Birth Issues, 15*(2), 41–46.

Sayani, A. (2005). Spirituality, school leadership, and Islam. *Journal of School Leadership, 15*(6), 656–672.

Tamminen, K., Vianello, R., Jaspard, J.-M., & Ratcliff, D. (1988). The religious concepts of preschoolers. In D. Ratcliff (Ed.), *Handbook of preschool religious education*. Birmingham: Religious Education Press.

Thelen, E., & Smith, L. B. (1996). *A dynamic systems approach to the development of cognition and action*. Cambridge, MA: MIT Press.

Thelen, E., & Smith, L. B. (1998). Dynamic systems theories. In W. Damon & R. M. Lerner (Eds.), *Handbook of child psychology, Vol. 1: Theoretical models of human development* (5th ed.). New York: John Wiley and Sons.

van Geert, P. (1994). *Dynamic systems of development: Change between complexity and chaos*. New York: Harvester/Wheatsheaf.

Wolf, A. D. (1996). *Nurturing the spirit in non-sectarian classrooms*. Hollidaysburg: Parent Child Press.

Wolff, P. H. (1993). Behavioral and emotional states in infancy: A dynamic perspective. In L. B. Smith & E. Thelen (Eds.), *A dynamic systems approach to development: Applications*. Cambridge: MIT.

Chapter 16
Does Positive Psychology Have a Soul for Adolescence?

Paul King

Abstract The discipline of psychology is often presented as resistant to the insights of religion and spirituality. Psychology, with its emphasis on observable and measurable behaviour, can be seen as standing in opposition to religion, with its emphasis on faith and the ineffable. For young people, factors such as finding a purpose in life, building on personal strengths and developing emotional supports have become evermore important in the face of adversity in an increasingly complex society. The new movement of positive psychology with a research emphasis on positive states and dispositions offers a vehicle for the reconciliation of positive psychology, religion and spirituality with respect to understanding and contributing to the holistic development of young people. This chapter presents the common ground between the contemporary development of positive psychology and the ancient wisdom of Christian spirituality as mutually inclusive frameworks for helping young people find meaning and purpose in life.

Towards the Spiritual Path

Traditionally, psychology and spirituality have shared a fractured and polarised relationship where both spheres have demonstrated a mutuality of suspicion and antagonism. Spirituality, particularly within organised religion, has cast doubt on the introspection created by psychology, identified by an excessive humanistic and materialist orientation leading to self-centredness rather than other centred. Psychology has, in general, equally been distrustful of Christian religion and spirituality indicating its disposition for psychological and emotional abuse, namely focusing on people as hopeless sinners, promoting patriarchy, practising blind obedience and offering a naïve and false hope for an eternal life. Freud espoused this perspective insisting that religious experience was a regressive phenomenon. He declared it to be incompatible with the scientific mind since "religious beliefs were motivated by wish fulfilments derived originally in response to conditions of helplessness"

P. King (✉)
School of Education Studies, Dublin City University, Glasnevin, Dublin 9, Ireland
e-mail: paul.king@dcu.ie

(Shafranske, 2005, p.105). It is perhaps a desire for independence arising from a fear of submergence by each other and potential for the violation of boundaries that has warranted this unnecessary dualism between both disciplines. Yet, paradoxically, psychology and spirituality have been continuously united in a single unified ambition: How can suffering (pathos) in the human experience be transcended or eliminated?

Regrettably, however, this common theoretical heritage has orientated efforts in both domains towards a disease or sickness model in deference to the urgency for health and healing. Disintegration rather than integration has too often been the obsession of both psychology and spirituality with the ensuing loss of a creative tension respecting the mutuality of chaos and order. An integrationist spirituality and psychology cannot be built solely on the pathology of the human person. Neither can there be a divergence of the organic unity of mind and body, nor of the soul and heart. The mystery and complexity of life is such that it cannot be reduced to a singular unified interpretation of reality. In recent years this divorce between spirituality and psychology has been addressed with a renewed interest in matters of a spiritual nature on the part of psychotherapists (Shafranske, 2005). Historically, not all psychologists have ignored the significance of religion and spirituality in the human experience. Many key figures in counselling and psychotherapy with strong religious backgrounds—William James, Gordon Allport, Erich Fromm, Viktor Frankl, Abraham Maslow, Roberto Assagioli—have tried to forge some integration between their therapeutic work and the search for spiritual meaning in life (Strümpfer, 2005). Carl Jung identified spirituality to be of such an essential ingredient in psychological health that he could only heal those in middle age who embraced a spiritual or religious perspective. For Jung, every patient over 35 years "fell ill because he had lost that which the living religions of every age have given to their followers, and none of them has been really healed who did not regain his religious outlook" (Jung, 1933, p. 229).

Spirituality is a concept that evades simplistic definition, categorisation or measurement and yet it affects the social, emotional, psychological and intellectual dimensions of the lives of young people. This chapter reviews some of the evidence linking spirituality and religious expression with different aspects of positive psychology particularly as it applies to adolescence. The author argues that the development of positive psychology as "an umbrella term for the study of positive emotions, positive character traits, and enabling institutions" (Seligman, Steen, Park, & Peterson, 2005, p. 410) and the emanating research from the theory supplements and enhances the aforementioned contributions to the fields of spirituality and psychology and therefore can help to enable young people to transcend adversity or to cope with the sometimes harsh reality of living. The abundance of emerging themes—wisdom, courage, justice, temperance, transcendence, hope, resilience, optimism, happiness and wellbeing—do not replace what is known about human suffering, weakness and disorder. Positive psychology offers "a more complete and balanced scientific understanding of the human experience—the peaks, the valleys, and everything in between" (Seligman et al., p. 410).

It is apparent from the literature in positive psychology that it is a discipline which embraces the path of spirituality in order to emphasis a holistic world order where everything is assumed to be connected with everything else. Its classification as a social science does not lessen the value of its contribution to the field of religion and spirituality but rather as a science and a practice of psychology it includes an understanding of suffering and happiness, their correlation and valid interventions that both relieve suffering and increase happiness. The tendency of psychological research to focus on distress, pathology and maladaptive functioning rather than on strengths, abilities and optimal functioning is clearly demonstrated in the study of adolescence. Research has tended to focus on youth's problem behaviour and the prevention of negative outcomes, such as teen pregnancy, violence, eating disorders, academic difficulties and suicide, rather than on youth's strengths and abilities and the promotion of positive outcomes, such as happiness, life satisfaction, resiliency and initiative (Larson, 2000). Many areas of practice in educational psychology focus on identifying the origins of problems experienced by children and their families. By expending the totality of resources researching factors that lead to psychological distress rather than the preventive and protective factors that buffer against pathology, we may be shortsighted and hinder the advancement of the field. We may lack the knowledge necessary to teach students, parents and teachers the skills required to maximise their potential and indirectly alter their psychological distress. However, the growing body of scholarship focusing on supporting and enhancing the development of adolescents' strengths and abilities suggests that positive psychology has begun to foster change in the study of adolescence by directing increased attention to the importance of building on adolescents' strengths and abilities as a means to promote positive outcomes (Chafouleas & Bray, 2004). In particular, it is the concept of resilience, as presented later in this chapter, which best offers a point of convergence with terms, which are commonplace in spirituality such as courage, hope, meaning, fortitude and transcendence.

It seems that positive psychology has a natural empathy for matters of the spirit. It shares a language with spirituality that does not constrict it to a single, unilateral interpretation. Psychology, and especially positive psychology, has demonstrated a desire to cross the bridge to spirituality in recognition that inclusion of this aspect of the human condition allows young people to find meaning in life and achieve resilience in the face of adversity. This crossing first began with the journey to explore our shadow and now attention is called to help young people integrate their strengths, for the spiritual journey requires self-awareness and self-transformation. If, as the author argues, positive psychology serves to enhance a vision which augments rather than detracts from the immeasurable richness of the many world religions about what makes life worth living then the ensuing insights can only serve, in the words of the theologian Paul Tillich (1952), to help adolescents "accept our acceptability despite feelings of unacceptability" (pp. 164–165).

Spirituality or Spiritualities: A Babel of Languages

Christian spirituality will be the main focus for the purpose of this article in seeking to understand the influence of positive psychology on spirituality for young people. Though not true generations ago, a distinction is frequently made today between spirituality and religion, the latter focusing on defined structures, rituals and doctrines and how people exercise religious beliefs through their relationship with organised religion. Kenneth Pargament (1999) defines religion as "the search for significance in ways related to the sacred" (p. 11) and because this element of the sacred is core it separates religion from other human phenomena. There are obviously many ways through which young people search for meaning and significance. Pargament (1999) further clarifies that this search comprises two dimensions: a pathway and a destination with the sacred as part of either or both dimensions. Examples of the pathway include attendance at religious congregations, religious beliefs, involvement in prayer and rituals and are just a few of the many sacred pathways taken to find, hold on to or transform significance. If these pathways lead to sacred destinations then the search qualifies as religious, regardless of where it leads. The destination of a religious search may also be sacred. People may seek out God, transcendence, a spiritual mission, a religious community or any other number of sacred objects.

Spirituality evokes a plurality of definitions and the term *spirituality* is evidently an emotive and contentious one. For generations, religion as the sole mediator of spirituality has claimed a monopoly though religious spirituality and secular spirituality share common ground. Yet it is a contemporary bridge built on ancient foundations that renews the relationship between psychology and religion. Recognition of the spirit as a natural dimension of the person is expressed in how legislation in Ireland defines one of the aims of education to "foster an understanding and critical appreciation of the values—moral, *spiritual, religious*, social and cultural—which have been distinctive in shaping Irish society and which have been traditionally accorded respect in society" (Department of Education, Ireland, 1995, p. 10).

Philip Sheldrake (1991) notes that the Latin word for spirituality—*spiritualitas*, meaning breath—attempts to translate the Greek noun for spirit, *pneuma*, as it appears in the New Testament writings of St Paul. He is adamant that this understanding does not contain a dualistic contrast between the *physical* and *spiritual* or the body and soul as was evident in later classical Christian spirituality of the twelfth century. In tracing the evolution of Christian spirituality across two millennia he concludes that four characteristics of contemporary Christian spirituality can be classified. First, there is recognition that it is not exclusive to any tradition within Christianity or even to Christianity itself; second it is not the mere prescription of dogma; third it is concerned with the mystery of human growth in the context of relationship with the divine; and finally it is not limited to the interior life but integrated with all aspects of human experience (Sheldrake, 1991). Returning to Kenneth Pargament, he defines spirituality as the most central function of religion, and views spirituality "as a search for the sacred for it has to do with however people think, feel, act, or interrelate in their efforts to find, conserve, and if necessary, transform the sacred in their lives" (Pargament, 1999, p. 11). Thus we can see how spirituality goes further than religion and how in the context of the sacred it describes an awareness of relationships with all creation, an appreciation of divine presence and a search for purpose that includes a sense of meaning. The author considers it to be a more expansive term and differentiated from religion as an expression that speaks to the greatest of young people's capacities. Furthermore this differentiation between religion and spirituality is of particular significance in the understanding of young people's spirituality as argued by Daniel Scott: "spirituality is as normative and natural as physicality or emotionality" (Scott, 2006, p. 1118).

In describing the profusion of terminology for understanding the purposes of Religious Education, Finola Cunnane adopts the term "a Babel of Languages" (Cunnane, 2004, p. 17). This appropriate image captures too the complexity of spirituality. Distinctions are perhaps most evident in the concept of spirituality as mediated through the dominant world religions. A contemporary Christian writer on matters of Christian spirituality, Ronald Rolheiser (1998), offers a strikingly similar analysis to Augustine's invocation, "You have made us for yourself alone, and our hearts are restless 'til they rest in thee, O Lord'" when he writes that spirituality is what we do with our desires, our unrest. He develops the nuances of this description as follows:

> Spirituality is about what we do with the fire inside of us, about how we channel our eros. And how we do channel it, the disciplines and habits we choose to live by, will either lead to a greater integration or disintegration within our bodies, mind, souls, and to a greater integration or disintegration in the way we are related to God, others, and the cosmic world (Rolheiser, 1998, pp. 10–11).

Thus for Rolheiser and others spirituality is about what we do with our spirit, our souls. It is not something we *have* but more than this, it is something we *are*. The loss of soul is not eternal damnation but more principally the loss of meaning and falling apart in this life. Positive psychology seeks to address how human beings can search for greater integration and achieve meaning in life which comes from active engagement with the purpose of living, namely to achieve one's fullest potential. Its mission is particularly apt for young people on the cusp of all the opportunities and challenges of living precipitated by the phase of adolescent development.

What Is Positive Psychology? – From a Similar Lens to a Sharper Focus

In contemporary times positive psychology has a resonance with parts of humanistic psychology through the work of Carl Rogers and Abraham Maslow, particularly with the latter's concept of self-actualisation and the study of healthy individuals. As far back as 50 years Maslow (1954) lamented psychology's preoccupation with disorder and dysfunction:

> The science of psychology has been far more successful on the negative than on the positive side. It has revealed to us much about man's shortcomings, his illness, his sins, but little about his potentialities, his virtues, his achievable aspirations, or his full psychological height. It is as if psychology has voluntarily restricted itself to only half its rightful jurisdiction, and that, the darker, meaner half (p. 354).

According to Seligman and Mihaly Csikszentmihalyi (2000) this brief rebellion launched by Maslow failed to ignite into any degree of permanency because it lacked a solid empirical base. At least since the time of Aristotle, scholars, philosophers and religious leaders have pondered the question "How can we become lastingly happier?" This question has always been with us, even if lying dormant among a science of suffering but today its case for recognition "has been to consolidate, lift up, and celebrate what we do know about what makes life worth living, as well as carefully delineating the areas where we need to do more" (Linley, Joseph, Harrington, & Wood, 2006, p. 5). The distinctive essence of positive psychology, in contrast to the approach by the humanistic psychology movement of the 1960s and 1970s, is the use of empirical research as the substance for validity and reliability (Peterson & Seligman, 2004).

The contemporary explosion of interest in positive psychology can be attributed to the work of Martin E. P. Seligman. On becoming president of the American Psychological Association in 1998, he declared that the time had come for psychology not just to study pathology, weakness and damage but also to study the strengths and virtues of the human condition (Seligman, 2003). Other writers have designated the term "*Psychofortology*" to positive psychology, from the Latin *fortis* meaning strong, to indicate the focus on strengths (Strümpfer, 2005). Research in this area has attracted a great many investigators encompassing a substantial scope of topics evolving around the scientific study of happiness and human strength. The vastness of potential study in this area is reflected in how its influence has transferred to many other subdisciplines within psychology to include personality, developmental, educational, social, health and clinical psychology leading some to suggest that "positive psychology can truly be considered a general psychology" (Keith & Baumeister, 2005, p. 100).

The question arises: is positive psychology just a reconfiguration of the ancient wisdom present in the spiritual practices of many of the great world religions and therefore has nothing new to offer young people in their quest for meaning and understanding in life? Seligman et al. have acknowledged that positive psychology has not invented the good life but stresses that "the value of the overarching term *positive psychology* lies in its uniting of what had been scattered and disparate lines of theory and research about what makes life most worth living" (Seligman et al., 2005, p. 410). A simple yet fundamental principle of positive psychology is a focus on the ordinary and everyday circumstances where opportunities to maximise fulfilment and happiness are facilitated. This preventive approach is an obvious antidote to the general domain of many disciplines—health, education, social care, psychotherapy—usually preoccupied with crisis and dysfunction. Happiness is not considered as an exception but rather the norm. This preventive model asks: how can we maximise happiness and health and promote resilience rather than why do young people become physically or mentally ill or give up on life? Seligman does, however, distinguish between a superficial transient happiness that we usually associate with fleeting moments of satisfaction and a happiness that is enduring and built on character and strengths. He writes,

> The belief that we can rely on shortcuts to happiness, joy, rapture, comfort, and ecstasy, rather than be entitled to these feelings by the exercise of personal strengths and virtues, leads to legions of people who in the middle of great wealth are starving spiritually. Positive

emotion alienated from the exercise of character leads to emptiness, to inauthenticity, to depression, and, as we age, to the gnawing realization that we are fidgeting until we die (Seligman, 2003, p. 8).

In the research on positive psychology although there are many core themes with substantial overlaps there are also differences in emphasis and interpretation present. It is not possible here to identify all the elements of subjective experiences, positive individual traits and the enabling institutions which have implications for young people and their development. However, in order to appreciate the implications of positive psychology a brief reflection on the concept of resilience reveals its potential to promote an understanding of young people from a strength rather than from a deficit perspective.

Resilience from the Perspective of Positive Psychology

Psychology has yet to fully learn about protective factors (optimism, hope and resilience) that may buffer young people against adversity and pain. Adopting a strengths-based positive approach can expand our ability to promote the potential of all young people not just those who are in need of "being sorted". This requires a shift in areas for those working in close proximity with adolescents. It asks practitioners, trainers and researchers to think outside the traditional service delivery models. Enhancing the strengths and virtues of children can accomplish effective prevention. Focusing on children's strengths can increase the chances that they will successfully manage difficulties they confront in the present and how they will cope with future battles. Amplifying the target individual's strengths rather than focusing on repairing their weaknesses may lead to more effective treatment. Nurturing human strengths such as optimism, courage, present mindfulness, honesty and perseverance serve as more efficacious buffers against mental illness as compared to medication or therapy (Seligman, 2003).

The concept of resilience holds great potential for work with children in a preventive manner. During the last several decades, research on resilience has been widely conducted in the areas of developmental psychopathology, psychology, sociology and anthropology. Within secondary education, conceptual and empirical work on resilience has gained recognition as a framework for examining why some students experience success in school, while others from the same socially and economically disadvantaged backgrounds and communities do not. The development of such a framework is useful in helping educators design more effective educational interventions that take into account "alterable" factors that distinguish resilient students from non-resilient students.

The theoretical framework for understanding resilience emerged from longitudinal studies of "children at risk" illustrated by the work of Rutter, Maughan, Mortimore, and Ouston published in 1979 and that of Werner and Smith in 1988. Researchers since then have examined *risk* factors—conditions indicating increase that a child will develop a problem and *protective* factors—conditions militating against problems occurring. The findings of this research have indicated that adversity in childhood does not necessarily lead to adult pathology and have provided guidelines for developing services that foster resilience in children (Olsson, Bond, Burns, Vella Broderick, & Sawyer, 2003; Howard, Dryden, & Johnson, 1999). However, early intervention efforts focused on ameliorating the environmental adversities experienced by vulnerable children and attempted to provide remediation through reducing economic disadvantage and provide opportunities for mastery via early childhood education programs. In addition, they sought to enhance the nature and quality of the caregiver–child relationship by enhancing positive parental attitudes, increasing parental participation in relevant areas of the child's life and promoting age appropriate limits, consistent discipline and clear family structure. These remedial approaches tended to focus on the repair of pathology and were replaced with the quest to promote children's resiliency and competence to stressful life events from the beginning, rather than offering assistance once emotional and behavioural difficulties had emerged. Importantly, this perspective asserts that *early intervention* in multiple child contexts is of equal or greater importance than the implementation of treatment strategies later in the child's development (Weissberg et al., 1991).

Developmental theory is situated in the context of people's behaviour across the lifespan with a focus on terms such as *risk, vulnerability* and *protective factors*. The ecological perspective acknowledges the context or *multiple systems of influence* for the individual. Recognition is also given to the individual's *transactions* with a range of factors over time and their *relatedness* to others in their system. Finally, the strengths model adopts a move away from the emphasis on the client weakness to redefine resilience based on *capabilities, competences, knowledge, vision, optimism* and *hope*. More recently, the direction towards a strength-based model of resilience has received renewed impetus from the findings emanating from positive psychology as noted by Ann Masten who writes that "the message from three decades of research on resilience underscores central themes of the positive psychology movement" (Masten, 2001, p. 235). Seligman and Csikszentmihalyi, considered to be the driving force behind this movement, elaborate on such themes, writing:

> The field of positive psychology at the subjective level is about valued subjective experiences: well being, contentment, and satisfaction (in the past); hope and optimism (for the future); and flow and happiness (in the present). At the individual level, it is about positive individual traits: the capacity for love and vocation, courage, interpersonal skill, aesthetic sensibility, perseverance, forgiveness, originality, future mindedness, spirituality, high talent, and wisdom. At the group level, it is about the civic virtues and the institutions that move individuals toward better citizenship: responsibility, nurturance, altruism, civility, moderation, tolerance, and work ethic (2000, p. 5).

While encompassing the need to attend to the risk dimension of resilience, researchers and practitioners are recognising the benefits of a resilience model that equally takes account of factors, which optimise the strengths of young people and the institutions that are at the core of their lives.

Studies over the past four decades have identified characteristics and protective factors of individuals, families and communities related to resilience. While clinicians and researchers alike agree about the relevance of the construct, operational definitions of resilience have varied. Some researchers consider resilience to be a personal trait or attribute of an individual; others define it as a dynamic developmental process reflecting positive adjustment despite adversity (Luthar, Cicchetti, & Becker, 2000). Block described the construct "ego-resiliency" (1996). This refers to an individual's general capacity to adapt adequately to external and internal stressors. In this definition, ego-resiliency is a personality trait that offers individuals the opportunity to demonstrate the behaviour to which they are accustomed and to adapt it in line with the demands imposed on them by the environment. Here, resilience describes the personal qualities that make it possible for young people to grow and even to make headway in unfavourable circumstances. Resilience can therefore be regarded as a way of measuring emotional stamina. Generally speaking, it is assumed that resilience develops over time. Connor defines resilience as a way of measuring the ability to cope with stress. According to Connor (2006) the concept comprises various elements. Brook's (2005) definition echoes the trait dimension of resilience as:

> the capacity of a child to deal effectively with stress and pressure, to cope with everyday challenges, to rebound from disappointments, mistakes, trauma, and adversity, to develop clear and realistic goals, to solve problems, to interact comfortably with others, and to treat oneself and others with respect and dignity... [and as the]...ability to meet life's challenges with thoughtfulness, confidence, purpose, responsibility, empathy, and hope (pp. 297–298).

Representing resilience as a personal attribute is hazardous since it paves the way for perceptions that some children simply do not "have what it takes" to overcome adversity. As Reivich and Shatté (2002) argue, emphasis on the trait dimension is laden with limitations since resilience is not a one-dimensional, dichotomous attribute that children either have or do not have. Masten has challenged the notion that resilient children possess some rare and special qualities in favour of the "*magic of the ordinary*" and has questioned an overreliance on the trait factor suggesting that resilience stems from a healthy operation of basic human adaptational systems. If systems are cohesive, children should develop appropriately even if challenged. However, if children's basic adaptational systems are impaired, prior to or following challenge, the risk for problems in development is increased. She argues,

> Resilience does not come from rare and special qualities, but from the everyday magic of ordinary, normative human resources in the minds, brains, and bodies of children, in their families and relationships, and in their communities (Masten, 2001, p. 235).

Friborg, Hjemdal, Rosenvinge, and Martinussen (2003) regard resilience as a construct comprising various dimensions. The concept refers not only to psychological skills, but also to the possibilities for the individual child to take advantage of family, social and external support systems in order to cope better with stress. Generally speaking, resilient children are more flexible than vulnerable children and they protect themselves against stress by making use of various protective resources.

These resources may be internal or external. Various writers classify these protective resources as psychological/internal characteristics, support from family and friends and external support systems which develop over time. The attraction of the developmental process is that it does not overpromise. It does not imply perfection or constant invincibility but accepts the reality of fallibility and the probability of successful coping. It represents a capacity to rebound from adversity allied with renewed strength and resources. Resilience as a *process* is espoused by counselling psychologist E. J. Smith (2006) who attributes resilience to be a key dimension of her proposed strength-based counselling model. She describes resilience in this context as follows:

> the process of struggling with hardship, characterized by the individual's accumulation of small successes that occur with intermittent failures, setbacks, and disappointments. [and]... the process of an individual's persisting in the face of adversity ... an individual's manner of struggling with the hardship rather than the end goal or state (p. 53).

Smith's model represents a clear alignment with the strengths approach and a perspective that allows positive psychology to see the glass as half full rather than half empty, and a movement away from a deficit-focused context. In general, this author welcomes the orientation towards a strength perspective since it addresses the imbalance that was so often present in the past in various strata of the helping professions—teaching, counselling, psychology, health care—where the focus was primarily on failure, distress, fear and anxiety, disease and mental ill health. However, the author also expresses concern that this wellbeing emphasis on the positive dimensions of resilience must not fail to discount the reality of pain and suffering nor present a false dichotomy which represents resilience as existing in isolation from the context of adversity. Masten, Best, and Garmezy's definition of resilience as "the process of, capacity for, or outcome of successful adaptation despite challenging or threatening circumstances" (1990, p. 426) captures a key issue which is—how best can we measure successful adaptation to adversity? If resilience can be taught as much as it can be an innate capacity, as this author believes, then it can emerge from relatively ordinary adaptive processes that promote competency, restore efficacy in the face of adversity. It ought to be possible to have structures and practices, which facilitate these processes for individuals and especially for children. Thus it may be more helpful to address the concept in terms of "*positive adaptation*" or "living with" adversity rather than general notions of resilience that seek to remove the negative aspects or overestimate personal traits.

In conclusion, common threads have emerged from resilience research, suggesting three main clusters of variables that appear to facilitate positive adaptation under conditions of risk: (a) individual attributes or characteristics, including positive temperamental or dispositional qualities; good intellectual functioning; self-efficacy; positive self-worth; perceived competence; sound problem-solving skills; internal locus of control; accurate and realistic attributions of control; and positive future expectations or a sense of optimism; (b) a warm, nurturing family environment; quality parenting and a structured, stable home; a sound relationship with a primary caregiver; and (c) broader contextual variables such as positive extra familial support sources and identification models; links with extended family support networks; effective schools; connections to pro-social organisations; and neighbourhood qualities (Tedeschi & R. P. Kilmer, 2005).

Positive Psychology and Spirituality: Brother Sun, Sister Moon

Within positive psychology as a science there is evidence of strong correlations between religious belief and wellbeing where a higher rate of belief in a God is associated with higher average life satisfaction and lower rate of suicide. In addition to belief, church attendance is associated with higher reports of wellbeing across nations (Diener & Seligman, 2004). Positive psychology has rescinded from this adversity to spirituality and religion and has stridently recognised its pivotal importance. It is interesting how Seligman et al. (2005) speak of the "mission of psychology" (p. 421) with its purpose to offer scientific research on the entire breadth of human experience, from loss, suffering, illness and distress through connection, fulfilment, health and wellbeing. Nowhere is this sense of mission more manifest than in the *Character strengths and virtues: A handbook and classification* (CSV) by Peterson and Seligman (2004). In complete antithesis to the *Diagnostic and Statistical Manual of Mental Disorders* (*DSM*) this "manual of sanities" (Peterson & Seligman, 2004, p. 3) seeks to classify the strengths and virtues for optimum human functioning. The general scheme of the *CSV* relies on six overarching virtues: wisdom, courage, humanity, justice, temperance and transcendence. Under each virtue, they have identified 24 particular strengths, which meet 10 criteria and are classified in accordance with their capacity to enhance human striving. The authors of the CSV have also developed a *Values in Action* questionnaire (VIA) to empirically assess the 24 strengths.

It can be argued that all of the assigned virtues in positive psychology trace their origin from a historical and theological basis in scripture and the writings of the Church yet perhaps it is the virtue of *transcendence* and its accompanying strengths of *appreciation of beauty and excellence*, *gratitude*, *hope*, *humour* and *spirituality* that hold greater resonance with the broad concept of spirituality (Peterson & Seligman, 2004). Transcendence strengths are those that forge connections to the larger universe and provide meaning. Positive psychology holds that these are ubiquitously recognised and grounded in evolutionary process and identified as psychological ingredients thus setting them apart from how they are understood in theology. Another important distinction from how these virtues and strengths are understood in positive psychology is the emphasis on how these can contribute to fulfilment in living rather than as antidotes in facing adversity. In order to circumvent the notion of virtues and strengths "causing" fulfilment by their mere adoption the idea of "contribution" captures the effort, willful choice and pursuit over time of morally praiseworthy activities. The author strongly concurs with this distinction since the wisdom of Christian spirituality teaches us that complete fulfilment is not possible in this life.

In calling attention to the possibility of "authentic happiness" (Seligman, 2003) in the here and now of life, positive psychology speaks to the incarnational dimension of Christianity. As Rolheiser (1998) writes, "The incarnation is not a thirty-three year experiment by God in history, a one shot, physical incursion into our lives" (p. 79). This theology, that the Word did not just become flesh and dwell among us—it became flesh and continues to dwell among us, is at the heart of Christian spirituality. The author believes that positive psychology in establishing spirituality as a core strength under the virtue of transcendence is, at the very minimum, reminding young people of this essential aspect to human flourishing. The language employed provides a "different interpretative lens" (Linley et al., 2006, p. 5) through the vision of scientific definition. Yet this author believes that it is perfectly cogent for positive psychology and spiritual writers to have an awareness of each other's work and necessary that they should actively engage with areas of mutual interest. If positive psychology is basing virtue and strengths on the wisdom of a rich Christian heritage then this can only be a cause for hope and optimism. Positive psychology by honouring the value of spirituality as subject matter is tacitly admitting its authenticity in representing a legitimate proportion of normal human experience and a contributory element to optimal human functioning. Within education it will give legitimacy against those who argue that the study of religion and the experience of spirituality lie outside of the domain of measurement and assessment. For if science recognises and embraces a belief and commitment to the transcendent aspects of life then we can no longer accuse it of a reductionist, biological approach to life. Instead, there is opportunity for "spiritual thought to reassert itself, regain credence in the public's eyes, and, more important, help to create a more healthy and holistic understanding of our world and our life" (Sharpe & Bryant, 2005, p. 146).

Peterson and Seligman (2004) have claimed their perspective to be empirical and scientific in the realm of spirituality. However, they acknowledge that despite the evidence of data suggesting a link between religion, spirituality and positive outcomes in life there is an admission that the positive psychology field will benefit from greater attention to the role of theology in shaping the core beliefs, attitudes, behaviours, psychological and physical health outcomes experienced by individuals. This interpretation presents positive psychology as a fluid, complex and human activity and it is commendable for its rejection of dualism already alluded to in certain parameters of science. It recognises spirituality as one of humanity's strategies for dealing with the limitations of the life cycle, separation and loss, biological fragility, transience and non-existence as well as giving strength, hope and meaning to life. It is ironic that from the perspective of the hard sciences positive psychology might be perceived as having a more natural liaison with spirituality and religion than with science because of its subjective enterprise in dealing with virtues and strengths. Perhaps, it is in anticipation of this allegation that positive psychology aligns itself so closely to empirical research. There is a common theoretical heritage between spirituality and positive psychology, each offering a different interpreting lens on the subject of spirituality. Both scientists and spiritual thinkers need to adopt an overarching empirical framework that makes it possible to validate scientific and spiritual understandings of happiness. Spiritual thought must face science, adapting and recasting itself in the light of scientific discovery and science must recognise its own limitations, carefully considering the wisdom of ancient religions and spiritualities. The challenge will be to achieve integration and in doing so "we must demolish and reconstruct some of our most trusted conceptions" (Sharpe & Bryant, 2005, Introduction xi).

Neither domain need fear each other nor become possessive about their respective territories. All the evidence from reading positive psychology is that it is very favourably disposed to spirituality and religion. Positive psychology needs religion and spirituality to synthesise the positive and negative aspects of human experience providing an integrated understanding of human life. Perhaps, because it is rooted in optimism, long considered a recognisable facet of US culture, its focus on strength may have a tendency to be less appreciative of the full range of human functioning. The great religions have derived their essential validation by generations of mystics who have described their spiritual encounter with something beyond the self and by the provision of religious practices, beliefs and values that reflect the cumulative traditions of their religious faith. Many persons both inside and outside traditional religious structures report profound experiences of transcendence, wonder, awe, joy and connection to nature, self and others as they strive to make their lives meaningful and to maintain hope. Whether the value of this can be empirically validated should not be the obsession of positive psychology for commitment to spirituality facilitates engagement, participation and a commitment to something beyond the self. The emergence of a transcendent function may be far more difficult to study because the assumptions of traditional statistical methods remove the uniqueness of the individual. Specifically, if psychologists are looking for the one thing that a person can do better than ten thousand others then a wise, intuitive guide may be more appropriate than a multiple choice inventory. Qualitative approaches may better help positive psychologists to identify qualities that define the uniqueness of each person. For its part organised religion could consider the applications of positive psychology within religious settings, based on the principles that spirituality can serve as a point of connection between positive psychology's promotion of optimal human development and religious institutions that can serve as the vehicles for this development. The enduring task for both psychology and religion is to enable young people to live their lives with courage and optimism and to strive towards creating conditions that give then the strength to live well and that dispel beliefs and patterns which trap people in lives of misery. As Hayes and Cowie (2005) suggest, "A convergence, however, does not mean a merging" (p. 33).

A Dialogue for the Future

Although religious practice among young people, as traditionally indicated by attendance at church, is in decline across many Christian denominations in the Western world, many young people still consider themselves "religious". Spirituality continues to matter to them but the question of what spirituality is evokes much less clarity. Both psychology and religion have too often concerned themselves with pathologies of the soul: What aches me? Where is my life's meaning? Why am I unhappy? In contrast, a healthy spirituality and psychology seeks to address: What gives me energy? How can I live with hope? Where and how does my life have meaning?

Spirituality, although having a long history that sometimes, when mediated through religion, has emerged from the shadows in confusion and disillusionment, obscuring reality beneath superstition and control, has helped to promote justice, speak truth and offer hope. Spirituality is the unquenchable thirst in life at the heart of most great literature, poetry, art, philosophy and psychology. In Christian spirituality a desire for wholeness does not seek to have it all together but is rather a sense of being on the way: the journey holds precedence over the destination.

To evaluate positive psychology against the longevity of religion and spirituality is premature. As with any new direction in psychology, it is necessary to question whether current enthusiasm will result in broad, valuable contributions to the discipline or whether such interest is a temporary "fad" that will quickly fade. The ongoing dialogue between psychology and religion requires sharing wisdom and insight in parallel but distinctive ways. One source of encouragement is the mutual agreement that young people do not find true meaning in individual accomplishments and material accumulations, though these may bring some temporary satisfaction, but rather in family, faith and friends.

Now positive psychology invites mainstream psychology to come full circle to rediscover the place of hope, the importance of spirituality and the centrality of connections within the community of the young and the complex reality connections constitute. To arrive at a more complete understanding of the universe it is necessary to respect insights and approach each discipline with an open mind.

Currently the struggle for significance in an increasingly cyber-friendly but personally isolating society intensifies the need for young people to find meaning in the world and in their personal existence. Approaches to education which enhance student participation will be needed in reducing exclusion from schools and helping young people to develop coping skills for life. However, this education must speak to the fullest expression of what it is to be human embracing the physical, social, intellectual, moral and spiritual aspects of the adolescent. It must enable young people to wrestle with the questions of existence and meaning commensurate with their life experience and intellectual development.

Psychology has yet to fully learn about protective factors (optimism, hope and resilience) that may buffer young people in adversity and pain. Adopting a strengths-based positive approach can expand our ability to promote the potential of all young people not just those who are in need of "sorting out". This requires a shift for those working in close proximity with adolescents. It asks practitioners, trainers and researchers to think outside the traditional service delivery models. Enhancing the strengths and virtues of children can accomplish effective prevention. Focusing on children's strengths can increase the chances that they will successfully manage difficulties that they confront in the present and be able to cope with future battles. Amplifying individual strengths rather than focusing on repairing weaknesses may lead to more effective treatment. That is, nurturing human strengths such as optimism, courage, present mindfulness, honesty and perseverance serve as more efficacious buffers against mental illness as compared to medication or therapy (Seligman, 2003).

Religion/spirituality need not fear positive psychology. There will always be a role for religion to facilitate the experience of the sacred in the ordinary, to know the passion of existence that gives ourselves over to that which is greater than ourselves. The future of positive psychology and spirituality is a declaration of interdependence with a synthesis that does justice to the complexity of the human condition and can only be of immense richness and benefit to young people. If positive psychology can reliably teach young people how to become and remain happier, it will have made an important contribution to human life. Happiness is not in one fleeting moment; it is an unending process that has no guarantee. Its virtue is in the striving to surrender to moments where we give time for the creation of a space for the unexpected, to what cannot be bought or sold, to enduring love.

There is a human need to strive for "something more". We are impatient of being on the way to something unknown, something new. Yet, it is the law of all progress that it is made by passing through stages of instability even if it takes a very long time. We are told to live life with hope for this life is good even if, as the poet says, we tread on "slippery knowledge" (Levchev, 2003).

A Vision Along Salmon River
(*To Robert Bly*)

Sunset had lit up its X-rays to examine
the lungs and heart of the world.
Right then I thought I saw the angel:
crossing the river,
stepping on stones
although he wore wings.
Perhaps he had been sent
to explain in his
symbolic way just why
we too cross over our life
dancing on stones, on rocks
or even ruins.

Rapid currents roar
washing our naked feet.
We tread on slippery knowledge.
But on our shoulders, and higher up,
Something invisible spreads its wings
to give us faith and courage.

                        Lyubomir Levchev

References

Block, J. (1996). The construct of ego-resiliency. *Journal of Personality and Social Psychology, 70*(2), 349–361.

Brooks, R. (2005). The power of parenting. In R. Brooks & S. Goldstein (Eds.), *Handbook of resilience in children*. New York: Kluwer Academic/Plenum.

Carr, A. (2004). *Positive psychology: The science of happiness and human strengths*. Essex: Brunner-Routledge.

Cunnane, F. (2004). *New directions in religious education*. Dublin: Veritas.

Chafouleas, S., & Bray, M. (2004) Introducing positive psychology: Finding a place within school psychology. *Psychology in the Schools, 41*(1), 1–5.

Connor, K. M. (2006). Assessment of resilience in the aftermath of trauma. *Journal of Clinical Psychiatry, 67*(2), 46–49.

Department of Education, White Paper on Education. (1995). *Charting our education future*. Dublin: Government Publications.

Diener, E., Napa Scollon, C., & Lucas, R. (2003). The evolving concept of subjective well-being: The multifaceted nature of happiness. *Advances in Cell Aging and Gerontology, 15*, 187–219.

Friborg, O., Hjemdal, O., Rosenvinge, J., & Martinussen, H. (2003). A new rating scale for adult resilience: What are the central protective resources behind healthy adjustment? *International Journal of Methods in Psychiatric Research, 12*(2), 65–76.

Hayes, M., & Cowie, H. (2005). Psychology and religion: Mapping the relationship. *Mental Health, Religion & Culture, 8*(1), 27–33.

Howard, S., Dryden, J., & Johnson, B. (1999). Childhood resilience: Review and critique of literature. *Oxford Review of Education, 25*(3), 315.

Jung, C. G. (1933). *Modern man in search of soul* (Trans. W. S. Dell & C. F. Baynes). New York, London: Harcourt Brace & Company.

Keith, D., & Baumeister, R. (2005). Positive psychology at the summit. *Review of General Psychology, 9*(2), 99–102.

Larson, R. W. (2000). Toward a psychology of positive youth development. *American Psychologist, 55*, 170–183.

Layard, R. (2005). *Happiness: Lessons from a new science*. London: Penguin Books.

Levchev, L. (2003). And here I am (Trans. J. Harte). *Number 16, Poetry Europe series*. Dublin: Dedalus.

Linley, A., Joseph, S., Harrington, S., & Wood, A. (2006). Positive psychology: Past, present, and (possible) future. *The Journal of Positive Psychology, 1*(1), 3–16.

Luthar, S., Cicchetti, S. D., & Becker B. (2000) The construct of resilience: A critical evaluation and guidelines for future work. *Child Development, 71*, 543–562.

Maslow, A. (1954). *Motivation and personality*. New York: Harper Press.

Masten, A. (2001). Ordinary magic: Resilience processes in development. *American Psychologist, 56*(3), 235–253.

Masten, A., Best, K., &. Garmezy, N. (1990). Resilience and development: Contributions from the study of children who overcome adversity. *Development and Psychopathology, 2*, 426–439.

Olsson, C., Bond, L., Burns, J., Vella Broderick, D., & Sawyer, S. (2003). Adolescent resilience: A concept analysis. *Journal of Adolescence, 26*, 1–11.

Pargament, K. (1999). The psychology of religion and spirituality? Yes and no. *International Journal for the Psychology of Religion, 9*(1), 3–16.

Peterson, C., & Seligman, M. (2004). *Character strengths and virtues: A handbook and classification*. Washington, D.C.: American Psychological Association with Oxford University Press.

Rolheiser, R. (1998). *Seeking spirituality: Guidelines for a Christian spirituality for the 21st Century*. London: Hodder & Stoughton.

Reivich, K., & Shatté, A. (2002). The resilience factor. New York: Broadway Books.

Rutter, M., Maughan, B., Mortimore, P., & Ouston, J. (1979). *Fifteen thousand hours. Secondary schools and their effects on children*. Cambridge: Harvard University Press.

Scott, D. (2006). Spirituality and identity within/without religion. In M. De Souza, K. Engebretson, G. Durka, R. Jackson, & A. McGrady (Eds.), *International handbook of the religious, moral and spiritual dimensions in education* (pp. 1111–1125). Dordrecht, The Netherlands: Springer.

Seligman, M., & Csikszentmihalyi, M. (2000). Positive psychology: An introduction. *American Psychologist, 55*(1), 5–14.

Seligman, M. (2003). *Authentic happiness: Using the new positive psychology to realize your potential for lasting fulfillment*. London: Nicholas Brealey Publishing.

Seligman, M., Steen, T., Park, N., & Peterson, C. (2005, July–August). Positive psychology progress: Empirical validation of interventions. *American Psychologist, 60*, 410–421.

Shafranske, E. (2005). A psychoanalytic approach to spiritually oriented psychotherapy. In L. Sperry & E. Shafranske (Eds.), *Spiritually orientated psychotherapy* (pp. 105–131). Washington, D.C.: American Psychologist Association.

Sharpe, K., & Bryant, R. (2005). *Has science displaced the soul? Debating love and happiness.* Maryland: Littlefield Publishers Inc.

Sheldrake, P. (1991). *Spirituality and history*. London: SPCK.

Smith, E. J. (2006). The strength-based counseling model. *The Counseling Psychologist, 34*, 31–53.

Strümpfer, D. J. W. (2005). Standing on the shoulders of giants: Notes on early positive psychology (psychofortology). *South African Journal of Psychology, 35*(1), 21–45.

Tedeschi R., Kilmer R.P., (2005). *Assessing Strengths, resilence, and growth to guide clinical interventions*. Professional Psychology, Research and Practice *36*(3), 230–237.

Tillich, P. (1952). *The courage to be*. New Haven: Yale University Press.

Young, M. A. (2005). *Negotiating the good life: Aristotle and the civil society*. Hampshire England: Ashgate Publishing Ltd.

Weissberg, R.P., Caplan, M.Z., and Harwood, R.L. (1991). *Promoting competence enhancing environments: A systems-based perspective on primary prevention*. Journal of Consulting and Clinical Psychology, *59*, 830–841.

Werner, E., & Smith, R. (1988). *Vulnerable but invincible: A longitudinal study of resilient children and youth*. New York: Adams, Bannister and Cox.

Chapter 17
Voices of Global Youth on Spirituality and Spiritual Development: Preliminary Findings from a Grounded Theory Study

Elisabeth M. Kimball, Marc Mannes, and Angela Hackel

> *Spirituality is experienced in your own being. Most of religion is forced. Being spiritual means standing on a mountain with the wind blowing through your hair, and the feeling of being free.*
> (Youth, Africa)
>
> *I think spirituality is the way you look at something: the way you look at pictures, the way you look at nature, the way you read books, what kind of movies you like to look at.*
> (Youth, Israel)
>
> *Religion is more of a place ... it's there, [where] you're supposed to find spirituality.*
> (Youth, U.S.A.)
>
> *Spirituality strengthens the bond between the members of society ... it also strengthens the relationship between me and my Lord.*
> (Youth, Syria)

As these four quotes suggest, young people throughout the world have wisdom to share about a domain of human experience about which, as yet, the scientific community wrestles.

Abstract This chapter presents wisdom from international youth about their lived experience of spirituality and its relationship to religion. Eight robust constructs (themes) describing spiritual development in the lives of young people (12–19 years) emerged from a grounded theory analysis of context-sensitive data collected in 27 focus groups with 171 youth in 13 countries. The youth participants self-identified with a wide range of religious traditions, and a few had no religious affiliation. The theoretical constructs are offered with rich illustrative quotes and a through discussion of this preliminary study's contribution to the emergent field of adolescent

---

E.M. Kimball (✉)
School of Social Work, University of Minnesota, St. Paul, MN 55108, USA
e-mail: lkimball@umn.edu

spiritual development. In addition the study strongly suggests that young people desire more opportunities for intentional spiritual engagement, and it identifies the role of choice in active, sustained spiritual awareness. Both of these findings have significant implications for formal and non-formal educators.

Introduction

In 2006 Search Institute (Minneapolis, Minnesota, USA) launched the Center for Spiritual Development in Childhood and Adolescence[1] (CSD) as a global initiative to advance the research and practice of an important and understudied domain of human development. While inquiry into spirituality and spiritual development is conducted throughout the world, much of the research has been conducted primarily in Western contexts, with adults or children, and within specific (usually Christian) faith traditions. Although adolescent spirituality has in recent years garnered increased attention, the empirical research has, until now, focused on national samples of young people such as Christian Smith's National Study of Youth and Religion[2] (NSYR) in the United States or the Spirit of Generation Y Project in Australia[3] (a joint three-year venture of the Christian Research Association, Australian Catholic University and Monash University). With generous support from the John Templeton Foundation, the CSD initiated an ambitious research agenda to increase the understanding of what spirituality and spiritual development means across contexts (cultures, religions, continents, and disciplines), how they both manifest themselves in young people's lives, and what can be done to foster and support spiritual growth and expression among young people.

The CSD initially viewed spirituality as an active, engaging, life-long process articulated well by Hill and Pargament (2003), "A search for the sacred, a process through which people seek to discourse, hold on to and when necessary, transform whatever they hold sacred in their lives" (p. 65).

From that starting point, the CSD developed an operational definition of spiritual development that recognizes it as a universal domain of human capacity and as a fundamental developmental task:

> The process of growing the intrinsic human capacity for self-transcendence, in which the self is embedded in something greater than the self, including the sacred. It is the developmental "engine" that propels the search for connectedness, meaning, purpose and contribution. It is shaped both within and outside of religious traditions, beliefs, and practices (Benson, Roehlkepartain, & Rude, 2003, pp. 205–206).

One core line of inquiry within CSD's research agenda is a focus group study, "Exploring Understandings of Young People's Spiritual Development Around the World" in which more than 500 youth, parents, and youth workers in 13 countries on six continents participated in 73 focus groups. Focus group data are being analyzed to examine the three different groups' understandings of, and experiences related to, spirituality and spiritual development. The purpose of this line of inquiry was to collect and assess context-sensitive data (Way, 1998) as the basis for articulating an initial set of theoretical formulations of adolescent spiritual development.

This chapter presents one research team's contribution to that theory-building process. The authors describe the study's methodology and offer preliminary findings from a grounded theory analysis of the international youth focus group data. The intent is to identify key aspects of the emergent theory, describe its relationship to the emerging field in adolescent spiritual development, and suggest implications for further research and practice.

Methods

A focus group design was chosen to encourage individuals to share their particular experiences related to spirituality while engaging one another and the facilitator in a conversation about spiritual development as mutual learners. Members of the CSD's International Advisory Network[4] referred research partners with the capacity to conduct focus groups to the CSD. Final selection of sites were made based on partner's familiarity with adolescent development, their affinity with young people, and their ability to follow an established, comprehensive focus group protocol developed by the CSD staff. Each focus group lasted from 90 min to 2 h. The use of a generic protocol was intended to establish methodological consistency across groups and to improve the reliability of data gathered, while still affording the local facilitators some room to adapt the data collection process for cultural or practical reasons.

The protocol questions were designed to evoke rich descriptions of dimensions of young people's lives that had the potential to carry explicit and implicit understandings of spiritual development. To that end the protocol asked youth to (1) identify the spiritual aspects of times when they felt joy, wonder, hope, or experienced difficulties; (2) describe what "being spiritual" means; clarify how "being spiritual" is different from "being religious"; (3) describe people who seem spiritual and explain what they say or do which makes them spiritual; (4) generate words that can be used to define someone who is spiritual; (5) determine whether youth can be spiritual; (6) ascertain if being spiritual is seen as important and if so how it affects them; (7) clarify if being spiritual changes overtime; and (8) identify the factors that make it hard to be spiritual.

Awareness of being a spiritual person, having an understanding of the subject or the ability to articulate what spirituality means, were not criteria for youth participation. The focus groups included youth who are, and are not, actively part of religious traditions.

Sample

Twenty-seven focus groups were conducted with 171 young people aged 12–19 in 13 countries. The groups ranged in size from three participants to nine, and were conducted in English or translated into English in the field for analysis by the research team in Minnesota. The countries represented are Australia, Canada, China, India, Israel, Kenya, Malta, Nigeria, Peru, South Africa, Syria, the United Kingdom, and the United States. The participants self-identified with a broad range of religious traditions: Buddhism, Christianity (Roman Catholic, Orthodox, Protestant, and Reform), Hinduism, Judaism, Islam, Sikhism, and a few had no religious affiliation.

Selecting Grounded Theory

There are a number of different research and analytical approaches this study could have employed. Boyatzis (1998) specifies three distinct research orientations and the related steps for analyzing qualitative data that are summarized in Table 17.1.

This study decided to employ the "data-driven" orientation rather than a theory or prior research driven orientation for a number of reasons. First, a developmental perspective on spirituality among international youth has not been the subject of extensive inquiry. Second, the knowledge-base on the subject is especially thin. Third, conceptual and theoretical development, much less consensus, has yet to be reached. Fourth, scholarly writing on the subject in the disciplines that concentrate on child and adolescent development is generally lacking. By adopting the "data-driven" orientation, the study not only strengthens the empirically informed theoretical foundation of the emerging field, but also sidesteps theory developed deductively from the study of spiritual development in adulthood.

The next research decision involved selecting an appropriate "data-driven" analytic approach. "Grounded theory" (Glaser, 1992; Strauss & Corbin, 1998), a major analytic method for qualitative data that is increasingly employed in educational and social research, was chosen. In the simplest sense, grounded theory is an analytic approach for developing theory that is derived from data that has been gathered and systematically analyzed. Theory emerges from the interplay between analyzing the data and reflecting on the analytic process. As a result of utilizing the approach, theory is produced that is based upon a set of plausible relationships identified among concepts.

Grounded theory analysis was viewed as congruent with the CSD's research goal of building knowledge and theory about the spiritual development of youth across

Table 17.1 Grounded theory: three distinct orientations

Theory-driven orientation	Prior research driven orientation	Data-driven orientation
I. Generating a code for analysis based upon existing theory	I. Generating a code from previous research	I. Reducing the raw information
II. Reviewing and rewriting the code for applicability to the raw information	II. Reviewing and rewriting the code for applicability to the raw information	II. Identifying themes within the raw information
III. Applying the code to the raw information	III. Applying the code to the raw information	III. Creating a code

the world, and with the CSD's intent to foster field formation. The study operated on the assumption that the results of the grounded theory analysis of the focus group data would delineate an initial group of theoretical propositions that can be investigated more thoroughly in subsequent international research as the field grows and matures.

Practitioners of grounded theory also reinforce its relevance to and viability for analysis of the youth focus group data. For Bell and Bromnick (2003) grounded theory is tied to the described reality of individuals and rooted in their feelings. According to Sirin, Diemer, Jackson, Gonsalves and Howell (2004), the goal of grounded theory is to understand a person's experience through his or her own words. Ponterotto (2005) affirms that it embraces an "emic" perspective and Goulding (1999) highlights its ability to acknowledge multiple realities. For Fassinger (2005), grounded theory allows for innovative theory to be grounded in the data collected from participants on the basis of the complexities of their lived experiences in relation to social context.

Like Charmaz (2006), the research team tends to "view grounded theory methods as a set of principles and practices, not as prescriptions or packages" (p. 9). She and we treat grounded theory methods as a craft that we practice, recognizing that they naturally complement and are complemented by other approaches to qualitative data analysis. The CSD focus group research team remains especially sensitive to their intimate involvement in the construction of grounded theories, and the implications of their involvement in theory creation, in several salient ways. First, being especially receptive as to how the words, tones, and intentions of the focus group youth participant conversations might be influenced by team member's own past and present experiences as spiritual beings. Second, being cautious of any inherent biases and being fully accepting of the relevant social context from which each youth conversation came to the research team. Third, acknowledging that the youth conversations are being analyzed as an integral part of an actively expanding academic discourse among social scientists on the role of spirituality in human development. Ultimately, in the ontological language of Rorty (1979), the research team wishes to establish and continue a rigorous "conversation rather than [to] discover Truth" (p. 364). Grounded theory offered a dialogical analytic framework for reading the transcripts and to learn how our participants make sense of their spiritual experiences. More specifically, this research was conducted using Glaser's (1992) model of grounded theory that stresses the contextual, interpretive, and emergent nature of theory development.

Data Analysis

The focus group protocol questions were used as the basis for organizing the analytic plan and providing structure for the coding system. The questions remained the key standardized element of the inquiry amidst the international, cultural, and religious diversities.

Two members of the CSD research team began the qualitative data analysis process by reading the written transcripts of the 27 youth focus groups. In order to mediate the variability in focus group size, participant ages, facilitator styles, and transcript quality, the two researchers completed the following steps.

Step One: Conducting Line-by-Line Coding

Both researchers began by studying the data closely within the body of each focus group. They engaged in line-by-line coding as a way to stay close to and become familiar with the data before beginning to abstract and conceptualize any ideas. The readers thus learned about the participants' worlds. This careful beginning allowed the researchers to remain open to the data and to appreciate the nuances in it, including implicit concerns (such as a persistent struggle with the definition of spirituality) and explicit statements (such as "all spirituality is good"), without moving too quickly toward theorizing.

Step Two: Producing Focused Codes

After approximately 50% (12) of the transcripts had been read, both researchers met, reviewed their line-by-line coding, and confirmed an effective analytic rapport, by noting sufficient inter-rater agreement on what portions of the transcribed text were salient. At that point the researchers made the decision to move to the next stage of grounded theory, focused coding, using a dual approach. This meant they continued to conduct line-by-line coding for each transcript and undertook the process of separating, sorting, and synthesizing large amounts of data (Charmaz, 2006) in two distinct ways:

> Researcher A: Engaged in focused coding for all protocol questions by specific focus group or transcript.
> Researcher B: Engaged in focused coding for each protocol question across focus groups or transcripts.

The goal of focused coding is always to move from many initial data codes toward succinct, insightful, and complete categories. A concrete example will show how the use of a dual approach to the process unfolded and how inter-rater agreement was deemed acceptable. From the responses of a Peruvian focus group to the question, "Do you think people your age are or can be spiritual?" Researcher A, using line-by-line coding and transcript specific focused coding highlighted

> Yes, spirituality doesn't have to do with age. You can be 80,000 and be spiritual or be 12 or 13 or 15 and be spiritual too. It all depends on your heart and if we surrender it to God or not.
>
> Yes . . . it doesn't matter the age or . . . religion
>
> Any person can be spiritual. It doesn't matter the age because the only thing you need is open your heart to God and tell him what you feel.
>
> A person of any age can be spiritual . . . depends on his or her maturity and how they handle things and how they live their lives.

Meanwhile, Researcher B engaged in cross transcript focused coding identified very similar content:

> . . . doesn't have to do with age—depends on your heart—surrender it to God or not.
>
> Age or religion doesn't matter.
>
> Any person can be spiritual.
>
> Age is not defined.
>
> Open your heart to God and tell him what you feel.
>
> Maturity—how they handle things, live their lives.

Both researchers wrote memos along the way capturing moments of awareness, insight, and wonder. They also noted possible and emergent patterns and raised questions of concern. For example, "I'm aware of the 'me' quality of spirituality, especially when compared to religion . . . to what extent does this reflect cultural privilege? What if spiritual development really is personal, individualistic work to be done? Perhaps religion is just one way of doing spiritual development?" Or, in response to the comment, "the only time I talk about spiritual issues, sadly, is in church because that's the only time it's brought up. And I would like to talk about it a lot more" one researcher wrote, "Could this be a mandate to youth workers?" And, after a young person claimed, "I have faith in goodness. God to me is goodness. Do good and you'll get good," a margin memo reads, "This sounds very similar to the NSYR findings, all the while critically reflecting on the analytic protocol itself."

The researchers met regularly, exchanged memos, compared notes, discussed the ideas behind and the words used to describe the focused codes, and examined areas of agreement and disagreement regarding the focused codes. The interaction was intended to maintain coding exchanges between the two researchers and continually monitor the degree of consensus, or lack thereof, as the analysis proceeded.

Step Three: Generating Consolidated Categories or Themes

Over time the research team members became progressively more integrative. This required reconciling differences, affirming consensus, and building a conceptual crosswalk between the line-by-line and the two focused coding procedures. It entailed discussing and reconciling conceptual and/or wording differences that were present in the consolidated codes. It would also result in the elevation of certain focused codes to the level of consolidated categories (themes).

For example, in terms of Peruvian focus group responses to the protocol question about whether young people can be spiritual, Researcher A suggested the following consolidated categories:

> Being spiritual not correlated with age.
> Spirituality associated with openness to God.

Researcher B suggested somewhat similar and slightly different consolidated categories:

> Age is not a determinant of spirituality.
> Being spiritual implies action or choice on part of individual.

These consolidated categories/themes from both researchers were then compiled so that there were composite category sets derived from all 27 focus groups for each protocol question. Completion of this task set the stage for forging theoretical constructs.

An additional round of integration often occurred as focus group protocol questions that had come to be recognized as having a strong resemblance to one another (Wittgenstein, 1958/1968), and were producing logically related data, were incorporated into three distinct conceptual clusters that brought convergent data and congruent consolidated codes together:

A. Describing one's spiritual experiences
B. Reflecting on spiritual development
C. Considering the expression of spirituality.

It is important to mention that while the protocol questions could be naturally and usefully organized into these three clusters, the clusters and the data each contains are not mutually exclusive.

Step Four: Establishing Emergent Theoretical Constructs

The researchers took the consolidated categories established in Step Three and employed a process of "adapted" theoretical sampling in order to identify certain themes as emerging theoretical constructs. The term *adapted* theoretical sampling is used because, given the realities of this preliminary study, it was not possible to return to the empirical world to collect more data about the properties of our proposed categories. Standards of saturation were limited to the "fresh data" which could only be found within the body of existing transcripts. This distinction is made in response to Glaser's (2001) definition of saturation as a standard higher than simply observing described repetition of events, statements, and/or actions:

> Saturation is not seeing the same pattern over and over again. It is the conceptualization of comparisons of these incidents which yield different properties of the pattern, until no new properties of the pattern emerge. This yields the conceptual density that when integrated into hypotheses make up the body of the generated grounded theory with theoretical completeness (p. 191).

Glaser's standard must be considered in relation to Dey's (1999) assertion and Charmaz' (2006) supportive skepticism about the notion of saturation. They contend that saturation is a subjective standard because most grounded theorists produce categories through partial, not exhaustive, coding. The researchers did indeed "stop short of coding all the data" (Dey, p. 257) and "relied on conjecture that the properties of the category are saturated" (Charmaz, p. 114). Dey would contend that "rather than establishing categories saturated by data ... we have categories suggested by data" (Charmaz, p. 114). While recognizing the limitations of our process, the research teams believe that the adapted theoretical sampling process has produced consolidated categories and theoretical propositions much sturdier than mere collective suggestions.

To establish sturdier themes and theoretical constructs via the adapted theoretical sampling process, the emerging theoretical constructs were compared with the text of the original focus group transcripts, memos that had been written, and to both researchers' personal and professional knowledge of spirituality and spiritual development. The merits of the adapted theoretical sampling were tested by asking questions such as

- What sense do these comparisons make?
- What questions are raised and left unanswered by the comparisons?
- How well is actual experience (of the youth participants) reflected in the theoretical language? Would they see and/or hear themselves in the constructs we are proposing?
- What contradicts or challenges the theoretical constructs?

The following chart summarizes the structural logic of the focus group data analysis from 13 individual protocol questions to 8 emergent theoretical constructs. The consolidated categories were created from the systematic process of two researchers line-by-line coding each of the 27 focus group transcripts, then entering into their dual system of focused coding to generate proposed categories that ultimately informed one list of consolidated categories across groups. Note the three question clusters and the examples of consolidated categories that helped to shape the theoretical constructs (Table 17.2).

Table 17.2 Sample analytical process from protocol questions toward theoretical constructs

Protocol question clusters	Sample consolidated categories	Emergent theoretical construct
Describing one's spiritual experiences		
Moments experience spirituality?	Calming influence, not panicking	
Words to describe spirituality?		
Active S shapes purposeful orientation to life		
What does it mean to be spiritual?	Feeling sense of support, shield, inner power	S experienced as protection or comfort
	Overcoming adversity, doing well	S rooted in special connection
	The way you look at something	
	Beyond the senses, mystery, miracles	Capacity for S is natural
	Reflective – think before act	
	More to life than materialism	
	Having potential	
	Realizing who you are	
	Being connected	
	Doing something I love	
Reflecting on spiritual development		
People your age spiritual?	Yes and no, depends on environment	Being actively S is a choice
Different now than when younger?	Depends more on person than age	SD mediated by dynamics of context
How deepen your spirituality?	Awareness and appreciation grow with experience	
Important to you?	Provides roadmap, purpose	
	Being challenged—key to solving problems	
Hard to be spiritual?		SD not dependent upon age
	The more you are, the more you understand	
	Ideal—pleasing God	
	Requires more effort/responsibility with age	
	Fear of being judged, life urgency	
	It's a choice, can't be forced	
	Hard to talk about	
Considering the expression of spirituality		
	Way of living—who she/he is	Capacity for S is natural
Describe spiritual person		
Qualities of a spiritual person?	Sets an example, open to learning	
Hard to be spiritual?	Focus on right things	
Important to be spiritual?	Going beyond belief, motions	SD more expansive than R

17 Voices of Global Youth on Spirituality and Spiritual Development

Table 17.2 (continued)

Protocol question clusters	Sample consolidated categories	Emergent theoretical construct
Spirituality vs. religion	Loving, generous, self-motivated, wise; Able to forgive, virtuous, trusted	
	Enjoys life, hopeful	
	Search for answers	
	Attentive in the moment	
	Mental/inner peace	
	Accepting destiny	
	Beyond laws, beyond tangible	
	Deeply personal, just "is"	

S = spiritual city
SD = spiritual development
R = religion

Emergent Theoretical Constructs

As seen in the chart above, the researchers identified eight robust constructs from the youth focus groups data analysis. These theoretical constructs, resulting from this exploratory study, contribute to an initial delineation of the theoretical terrain of youth spiritual development. As the products of a grounded theory analysis it is important that each proposed construct be well supported by the raw data and this is illustrated here by the inclusion of rich quotes chosen from the original transcripts. It should be noted that voices from all 13 participating countries are "heard" supporting these constructs even though the particular experiences of individual focus group participants varied greatly.

Capacity for Spirituality Is Natural

The capacity for spirituality appears to be natural and readily available to all youth, although many can identify impediments.

The youth participants described an inherent capacity for awareness of, or awakening to, spirituality and active engagement with their own spiritual development, whether they were or were not growing up in a religious environment. The language they used to describe their capacity, and the experiences they offered to illustrate it, varied across cultural contexts. Some examples of their determination that spirituality is an innate part of being include

> Spirituality is important. If you lost your spirituality, you lost the attraction, you would become only flesh like a messy garlic; every day knocked here and there, eat and do not do work (Youth, China).
>
> I think spirituality is important to everyone. Maybe there's a section of people that doesn't realize they are following that path, but they are spiritual. And I think everyone has that kind of adaptability in themselves to go into that kind of path to being spiritual. Maybe

the word "spiritual" is more important in some people's lives, but the whole definition and the concept I think it's there in everyone (Youth, Pune, India).

I believe that every person has some spirituality within themselves because they believe in something, whatever it is they believe in (Youth, Peru).

Sometime I try too hard to find it, and don't just let it happen and just let it be natural. Like I try to force it. And I think my spirituality is better when it just happens (Youth, United States).

Being Actively Spiritual Is a Choice

As youth participants described their lives they often made a distinction between the natural capacity for being spiritual and being actively spiritual. For a number of youth worldwide, being spiritual requires an individual choice to activate their agency. Youth go on to explain this concept by asserting that

If one wants to become spiritual it will depend on the will of that person. If he wants to he can (Youth, Syria).

I used to think being spiritual meant having a rule to obey, but now I know I have to make a choice (Youth, Kenya).

You can be *religious* by coming to Jamat Khana (mosque) and doing your duty, but to be spiritual means that when you actually do your duty, you interact with Allah (Youth, England).

If you are not spiritual, then you don't ever struggle with things, you don't make a choice or ask, "why did this happen to me?" If you are not spiritual you will never learn anything ... goes together with wisdom ... you have to reflect on what's happening to you (Youth, South Africa).

If you don't want to be spiritual then can't nobody make you do it (Youth, United States).

Active Spirituality Shapes a Purposeful Orientation to Life

Spirituality affects the way a person looks at life, makes meaning, and/or lives his/her life with intention and direction. When asked about how spirituality impacts their lives and the lives of others, youth responded that

Spirituality is a force that helps you find your self and accomplish your goals (Youth, Peru).

I don't think you would find your way through this world without being spiritual. I don't think you would succeed (Youth, Israel).

Spirituality is dynamic. It will greatly inspire people and encourage them to progress (Youth, China).

Spirituality to me is finding meaning in life or finding beauty in the everyday (Youth, United States).

A person who vibrates positive energy, who teaches you how to stay calm and happy throughout all phases of life. That person is spiritual (Youth, India).

Spiritual Development Is Not Dependent Upon Age but Is Affected by Other Dimensions of Human Development

Youth participants gave ample statements which indicated that spiritual awareness and agency are not dependent upon age. Indeed their experience suggests spirituality and age are not correlated in meaningful and important ways.

When asked about one's ability to be spiritual at a certain age participants asserted that

> Spirituality doesn't have any age barriers. Depends more from person to person than the age group (Youth, India).
>
> I think sometimes we underestimate the spirituality of children...kids of 10 years old can be spiritual...I realize that there are people who are younger than I am who are examples for me (Youth, South Africa).
>
> You don't need an age to be a spiritual person (Youth, Peru).
>
> A person who has more experiences in life doesn't really mean that he's more spiritual than another person. I think a 17 year old can be more spiritual than a 44-year old man (Youth, Israel).

Spiritual Development Is Mediated by the Dynamics of Interpersonal Relationships and Social Contexts

The nature of interpersonal relations and the fluid contexts that youth experience in daily life (including the presence or absence of a religious tradition) are seen as encouraging or constraining to one's spiritual development. Many of the focus group participants were able to describe times when they had been particularly aware of their spirituality, and other moments when the demands or distractions of their lives made them oblivious to the spiritual domain.

> I mean one minute you are thinking spiritually, "This is what I'm supposed to do with my life. This is what I should do." The next minute your friend calls up, "Let's go to a movie!" and you're out there! (Youth, India).
>
> My being spiritual depends on whether my friends are good or not (Youth, Syria).

When describing their ability to articulate their own personal sense of spirituality youth responded that

> I think people feel comfortable talking about spirituality with anyone with whom we feel we are valued (Youth, England).
>
> To be spiritual you need to have an opinion. But here in this community, you always have to shut up. But in other communities, if you say something you will be appreciated for what you say (Youth, Israel).
>
> I know lots of people in my life are deeply spiritual, but I feel like that's something that's private almost-and I don't see that side of them (Youth, United States).

Spirituality Is Seen as Different from, and More Expansive than, Religion and Religious Observance

Participants discussed the relationship between spirituality and religion, but their descriptions revealed little consensus. For certain youth, religion and spirituality are synonymous, while for some religion is one practical dimension of, or context for, the expression of spirituality. For others religion and spirituality were best understood in contrast with each other. Respondents voiced their perceptions of the relationship between spirituality and religion explaining that

> The religion is somebody who has gone in depth into the religion and he knows a lot about his religion, while the spiritual is more in control of his soul (Youth, Syria).
>
> Spirituality is something open, without limitation (Youth, China).
>
> A person can, he is spiritual, by sitting down and meditating and goes in certain type of mediation. While another person can feel he is spiritual by doing good only. Another person feels that praying every day and building a relationship with God, another by not eating meat…Everyone has their own ways how to feel spiritual. Now to say that he is right, mine is right … wrong … is a bit difficult (Youth, Malta).
>
> Spirituality is the search for answers and religion provides the answers (Youth, England).

Spirituality Is Commonly Experienced as a Source of Protection and/or Comfort Especially During Troubling Times

Many youth indicated they experience spirituality as a source of protection or comfort in particular during difficult moments of their lives. When asked to elaborate on the role that spirituality plays in comforting them, youth asserted that

> Spirituality is the most important thing in life. It is the pillar of everybody's heart. It's like, with spirituality nothing will go wrong (Youth, India).
>
> Spiritual is when the human being feels happiness inside his heart. That is the time when he gets comfort (Youth, Syria).
>
> When I got hurt it was spiritual because when it happened, at the time the bomb exploded, I just stayed relaxed and I didn't panic and stuff (Youth, Malta).
>
> Spirituality, I believe I did become a lot closer to God after Katrina. Because you know, there was a lot of communication going on there…a lot of hoping and praying and pleading that my family, me and my mother who I was separated from would be okay…as long as you pray you can get through it (Youth, Louisiana, United States).

Spirituality Is Rooted in a Special Connection

While youth often had difficulty finding words to discuss spirituality, they still spoke of the experience as one of "being connected" to something or someone beyond oneself at a deep and mysterious level. Participants recognized others as being spiritual because of their capacity for connection, their ability to "make me stand in a proper way" (Youth, China). When asked about their experiences being spiritual, youth from India responded as follows:

> There is something connected from your soul to something. And that "something" can be called God or whatever. So sometimes you feel a connection between you and someone else (Youth, India).
>
> I think a connection of the soul to soul is spirituality (Youth, India).
>
> To me it's important to be spiritual because it's related to everything around me: my future, my family, the people around me, things to do with them, and how I'm going to be in the next ten years. It's all related to being spiritual (Youth, Israel).
>
> Spirituality strengthens the bond between the members of society…It also strengthens the relation between me and my Lord (Youth, Syria).
>
> With spirituality you have a sense of relationship (Youth, Malta).

An additional insight acquired from the grounded theory analysis is worth mentioning. While this is not presented as a theoretical construct it is shared for the contribution it can make to ongoing studies of spiritual development and practice in education and youth work.

Youth Are Open to Having Conversation About Spirituality

While few of the focus group participants had ever reflected on their experiences of spirituality or being spiritual beyond the doctrinal, programmatic or linguistic frameworks provided by their involvement in religious traditions, most welcomed the opportunity to explore the subject with intention and purpose, and without any fear of being judged as wrong. Despite uncertainty about the subject of spirituality most of the participants were highly engaged in the conversations and eager to learn more.

It was clear that the focus groups themselves offered a type of active intervention on the subject of spirituality—a place to become aware and then integrate holistically otherwise segmented or taken-for-granted dimensions of personal experience—a value-added benefit for most participants.

> I wasn't interested in this topic before [the focus group] but now I actually am (Youth, India).
>
> I would like to talk about this spiritual thing with all my friends, but when? (Youth, India)
>
> As we started to talk, I began to understand it. I think we need to understand it because not a lot of people know about it ... It's very important, especially in the Arab community. Because in our community, if you are different they start to blame you or if they are young, they blame the parents (Youth, Israel).
>
> It is possible one individual would come to discuss spirituality with another individual, like somebody else from another tradition. So he speaks to him about the soul and the other would tell him that if you are convinced about this idea then all your community is wrong (Youth, Syria).
>
> I would like to talk about it a lot more ... but the people I know are not really focused on talking about spiritual things. They're so busy ripping and running and trying to get their lives back together (Youth, USA).

Some young people like this 17-year–old Israeli were especially pragmatic about their level of interest in the subject of spirituality, "It's a weird subject, but I would like to know more information about it."

Contribution to Emergent Field of Adolescent Spiritual Development

The emergent theoretical constructs derived from this study of the life experiences of a diverse cross-section of young people on six continents offer strong support to the growing body of literature that recognizes spirituality as an innate, relational dimension of human development throughout the life-course (Groome, 1998; Harris & Moran, 1998; Hay & Nye, 1998/2006; Hill & Pargament, 2003; Roehlkepartain, King, Wagener, & Benson, 2006), distinguish spirituality from religiosity (Tacey, 2004/2007; Yust, Johnson, Sasso, & Roehlkepartain, 2006), and understand spirituality as opportunity for engaged, purposeful living (Crawford & Rossiter, 2006; Lantieri, 2001).

This study builds naturally on the foundation laid by Hay and Nye (1998) who successfully located children's spirituality as an essential dimension of child development. It honors the grounded theory approach Nye (1998) used to analyze conversations she conducted with children in particular political and social contexts and expands this listening tradition to adolescence.

Damon (1995) focused on moral development through the lifespan, suggested young people's need for spirituality is grounded in transcendence, an orientation of service to others, and an intimation of life's deeper meaning. By doing so, Damon confirmed the priority spirituality deserves in community youth development, and created a credible scholarly space between human development, education, and religion into which, these theoretical constructs now fit.

Five years later Lerner (2000), a progressive American Rabbi and social critic, published *Spirit Matters* in which he argues compellingly (for a popular audience) that spirituality is an essential and too often missing domain of human life. He called for a focus on emancipatory spirituality as a core dimension of personal and public purpose, a concept very similar to the core category of relational consciousness that Nye (1998) found "told the story" of the children she interviewed about their experience of spirituality.

The voices of the participants in this study suggest that young people not only experience spirituality as a process of emancipation—becoming fully alive and purposeful, but also demonstrate an unusual level of consciousness or perceptiveness in the context of relating to things, other people, themselves, or the transcendent, and recognize the importance of agency or choice in becoming actively spiritual.

> Realizing who you are is spirituality. It's not discovering myself, because I am already there. It's getting in touch with that. I mean it's like I am already whatever it is I am. But it is getting in touch with whatever it is. In response, yes, spirituality is "being what you are." (Youth, India)

It is the value-added dimension of reflective choice that seems to differentiate spirituality as many participants in this study experience it from rote religious observance or even right behavior. Spirituality seems to be beyond "God-talk" (Hay & Nye, 1998/2006). It appears to be something prior to religion (Tacey, 2007). According to the young people in this study, it is neither static nor passive. It is experienced in moments of protection, connection, mystery, and achievement but only "known" when consciously engaged. The extent to which participating in these focus groups triggered new awareness and understanding illustrates the iterative, episodic, and situational nature of spiritual development. It also suggests the importance of moving beyond the scholarly space of spiritual development to infuse spiritual consciousness into the everyday practice of youth work and youth education. Knowing about spirituality and living it may be as distinct as reciting a religious creed and actually believing it.

Limitations and Implications for Further Research

The preliminary nature of this study must be emphasized. The goal was to engage young people from as many countries, religious backgrounds, and cultural contexts as possible within the time and financial constraints of the study. Given the high costs and quality control issues of working across cultures and languages, and the complications introduced when research is conducted in multiple languages but the data are to be interpreted in one language, preference was given to conducting focus groups in English. Where this was not possible, transcripts were translated into English by local translators before being returned to Search Institute in Minneapolis. Youth participants were recruited through the CSD's international advisor network. These criteria limited the pool of eligible participants in non-English speaking countries to a convenience sample that was significantly middle/upper middle class and educated. Future studies should include youth from a much wider portion of the socio-economic spectrum.

Similarly, while there is significant religious diversity represented by the youth participants, the majority of the participants were Christian, and future studies should increase the participation rates of youth from other religious traditions and non-religious youth. Special care should be taken to recruit from non-theistic and beyond mono-theistic belief systems.

There was evidence in the focus group transcripts that spirituality could be interpreted as a form of culturally weighted individualism, a luxury of choice, an add-on in the developed world, perhaps most specifically in Western Christian capitalist contexts. While this concern is worthy of further consideration, the preliminary findings suggest something else. Perhaps the Western influence that needs to be recognized is the tendency to dichotomize—in this case to place religion and spirituality in an oppositional, either/or framework rather than one that is synergistic and in which religiosity and spirituality become inter-reliant. It is possible that spiritual development is indeed highly personal, inner work to be accomplished but in the rich cultural context of relationships and religious heritage.

Given the challenges inherent in facilitating conversation about a subject most young people have had little experience exploring, the fact that many participants were doing so in a second language and with adult facilitators who were often their religion teachers or youth leaders, it is not surprising that most of the conversations focused on the positive, almost idyllic dimensions of spirituality as expressed by this Syrian young man, "A spiritual person would have far-reaching vision, does not care for the shells but he cares about the essence. Generally his mistakes will be very few." In the next quote, a young South African girl captures the optimistic, positive view of spirituality many of the participants expressed, "Spiritual can be anything, except bad things ... Someone is very spiritual when they are in church 24/7."

There are hints in the transcripts such as, "Someone can be spiritual and still be a jerk" (Youth, Canada) that suggest, but do not make explicit, the possibility some experiences of spirituality may be other than positive—stirring conflict, distorting perspective, causing pain, stagnation, or just being value neutral. It will be important for future studies to move beyond the "niceness" of spirituality and, more importantly, an a priori assumption that spiritual development is always good.

A related conundrum this research points out is the common temptation to elevate "spirituality" to "all things pure" and denigrate "religion" to its immutable institutional reputation, thus falsely or over-simplistically defining spirituality as "religion minus doctrine" or "religion minus God" as articulated with confidence by this Syrian girl, "The spiritual has a soul ... A religious person is not a good one. The spiritual does not commit any mistakes, while the religious does."

Finally, despite thorough attempts to recruit experienced and neutral focus group facilitators, several of the groups were led by adults who knew the participants well, thus introducing the likelihood of reciprocal determinism (Bandura, 1986) and increasing the risk of social pleasing in the participant responses.

Summary

Despite the tremendous uncertainty among, and variation between, participating youths' understanding of the term "spirituality" the findings from this preliminary study confirm Tacey's (2007) observation that, "youth spirituality is alive and well, growing in strength and full of diversity ... a vast potential resource of spiritual vitality, and holds tremendous promise for the religious, moral and environmental renewal of society" (p. 75). The study also confirmed the existence of spirituality as a dimension of human experience and human development worthy of attention distinct from, and in relationship to, the other more established dimensions of human development. The apparent lack of importance of biological age as a determinant of spiritual experience became very clear, while the complex relationship between cognition and spirituality invites further study. The role of choice in active, sustained spiritual awareness suggests a degree of agency and stage of cognitive development not typical of younger children.

Perhaps one of the most important messages from the study findings is that spiritual development is mediated by the dynamics of interpersonal relationships and social contexts, and young people desire more opportunities for intentional engagement with their spirituality. This is a siren call to parents, educators, youth workers, clergy, and others engaged in the healthy development of young people. Many, if not most, youth have an unmet and often yet unrecognized hunger to experience spirituality as distinct from, or more expansive than, the religious tradition(s) they experience and within which they interact. Rather than having to break religion to release spirituality (Tacey, 2007) this study suggests that in most cases, there is room to nurture and build spiritual awareness alongside traditional religious practice. Healthy spirituality and active religious observance are neither mutually exclusive nor interchangeable. At best, in the context of 21st century global religious pluralism, spirituality and religion may have a synergistic relationship.

While this study endeavors to contribute to an increasingly coherent scientific picture of adolescent spirituality and spiritual development, it is important to remember that much of what Western scientists are now finding fundamentally supports certain core precepts that many aboriginal cultures never lost. These principles acknowledge that children are sacred beings; everyone is related in this world and beyond; discipline is used to teach courage not obedience; and spirituality is as fundamental to being alive as the air we breathe (Brendtro & Brokenleg, 2001).

Notes

1. www.spiritualdevelopmentcenter.org
2. www.youthandreligion.org
3. http://dlibrary.acu.edu.au/research/ccls/sppub/sppub.htm
4. 120 advisors from around the world who reflect a wide range of perspectives, disciplines, and ideologies, bringing scientific, theological, and practice expertise to the work of the CSD.

References

Bandura, A. (1986). *Social foundations of thought and action: A social cognitive theory.* Englewood Cliffs, NJ: Prentice Hall.
Bell, J. H., & Bromnick, R. D. (2003). The social reality of the imaginary audience: A grounded theory approach. *Adolescence, 38*(150), 205–219.
Benson, P. L., Roehlkepartain, E. C., & Rude, S. P. (2003). Spiritual development in childhood and adolescence: Toward a field of inquiry. *Applied Developmental Science, 7*, 204–212.
Boyatzis, R. E. (1998). *Transforming qualitative information: Thematic analysis and code development.* Thousand Oaks, CA: Sage.
Brendtro, L., & Brokenleg, M. (2001). The circle of courage: Children as sacred beings. In L. Lantieri (Ed.), *Schools with spirit* (pp. 39–52). Boston, MA: Beacon Press.
Charmaz, K. (2006). *Constructing grounded theory: A practical guide through qualitative analysis.* Thousand Oaks, CA: Sage.
Crawford, M., & Rossiter, G. (2006). *Reasons for living: Education and young people's search for meaning, identity, and spirituality. A handbook.* Camberwell, Victoria: ACER.
Damon, W. (1995). *Greater expectations: Overcoming the culture of indulgence in America's homes and schools.* New York: Free Press.
Dey, I. (1999). *Grounding grounded theory.* San Diego, CA: Academic Press.
Fassinger, R. E. (2005). Paradigms, praxis, problems, and promise: Grounded theory in counseling psychology research. *Journal of Counseling Psychology, 52*(2), 156–166.
Goulding, C. (1999). Consumer research, interpretive paradigms and methodological ambiguities. *European Journal of Marketing, 33*(9/10), 859–873.
Glaser, B. G. (1992). *Basics of grounded theory analysis: Emergence versus forcing.* Mill Valley, CA: The Sociology Press.
Glaser, B. G. (2001). *The grounded theory perspective: Conceptualization contrasted with description.* Mill Valley, CA: The Sociology Press.
Groome, T. H. (1998). *Educating for life: A spiritual vision for every teacher and parent.* Allen, TX: Thomas More.
Harris, M., & Moran, G. (1998). *Reshaping religious education: Conversations on contemporary practice.* Louisville, KY: Westminster John Knox Press.
Hay, D., & Nye, R. (1998/2006). *The spirit of the child.* London: Jessica Kingsley Publishers.

Hill, P. C., & Pargament, K. I. (2003). Advances in the conceptualization and measurement of religion and spirituality: Implications for physical and mental health research. *American Psychologist, 58*(1), 64–74.
Lantieri, L. (Ed.). (2001). *Schools with spirit: Nurturing the inner lives of children and teachers.* Boston: Beacon Press.
Lerner, M. (2000). *Spirit matters.* Charlottesville, VA: Hampton Roads Publishing.
Nye, R. (1998). Identifying the core of children's spirituality. In D. Hay & R. Nye (Eds.), *The spirit of the child* (pp. 108–128). London: Harper Collins.
Ponterotto, J. G. (2005). Qualitative research in counseling psychology: A primer on research paradigms and philosophy of science. *Journal of Counseling Psychology, 52*(2), 126–136.
Roehlkepartain, E. C., King, P. E., Wagener, L. M., & Benson, P. L. (Eds.). (2006). *The handbook of spiritual development in childhood and adolescence.* Thousand Oaks, CA: Sage.
Rorty, R. (1979). *Philosophy and the mirror of nature.* Princeton, NJ: Princeton University Press.
Sirin, S. R., Diemer, M. A., Jackson, L. R., Gonsalves, L., & Howell, A. (2004). Future aspirations of urban adolescents: A person-in-context model. *International Journal of Qualitative Studies in Education, 17*(3), 437–459.
Strauss, A., & Corbin, J. (1998). *Basics of qualitative research: Techniques and procedures for developing grounded theory.* Thousand Oaks, CA: Sage.
Tacey, D. (2004/2007). *The spirituality revolution: The emergence of contemporary spirituality.* New York, NY: Routledge.
Way, N. (1998). *Everyday courage: The lives and stories of urban teenagers.* New York: New York University Press.
Wittgenstein, L. (1958/1968). *Philosophical investigations* (3rd ed.). New York: Macmillan.
Yust, K. M., Johnson, A. N., Sasso, S. E., & Roehlkepartain, E. C. (2006). *Nurturing child and adolescent spirituality: Perspectives from the world's religious traditions.* Lanham, MD: Rowman & Littlefield.

Chapter 18
Moment to Moment Spirituality in Early Childhood Education

Mindy Upton

Abstract Younger children explore the world through curiosity, questions, and engaged excitement. This chapter, based on the author's experience of children in over 25 years of kindergarten practice, will look at the "twinkle" manifested in children's questions about the world: "Where does the water go after it goes down the bridge?" "If the sun is made up of fire fairies, how come it's round?" or the continual "Why?" "Why?" "Why?" Behind the questions is an ever-expansive quest for understanding that leads to an intimate relationship with the world. The questions are one way that children express their quest for connection. The road to a child's "truth" can be an exciting one, depending on their environment, school, peers, and family (karma).

Introduction

The day after the tragedy of 9/11, the children in my classroom started to build houses. Not just little houses. Big houses. They used every table, every chair, every wooden box and stool that they could find. The children were very careful during this process. They made sure it was a sturdy house that they were building. They all worked together, everyone having a special job. Some children were the gatherers, some were the construction workers, some were the helpers to the workers, some just sat and observed. Everyone was involved in some way. The teachers went about their daily work, but all the while they were sensitively watching the construction site evolve. When the buildings were completed and just the way the children wanted them, the oldest of the children in the group looked at each other very intently.

All was quiet. The teachers and the rest of the students turned to look. We watched as the older children knocked the houses down with determination and direction. The teachers watched and waited, not commenting but still. The little ones started to help knock down too, but the workers sent them back so they wouldn't get hurt.

M. Upton (✉)
Naropa Institute, Boulder Colorado, Mindy Upton, Blue Sky Kindergarten, Boulder CO 80304, USA
e-mail: www.blueskykindergarten.com

"This is the one," said one of the 4 year olds. "This is the building that fell." Other children asked, "Who did it?"

Someone else whispered a reply, "Someone made a mistake."

Just a moment's quiet pause...and then the process began anew. The workers gathered the blocks, the helpers started piling, the construction site was "built-up" once again, while the rest of the children in the room either watched or waited or went onto their own work and play.

Every morning for weeks, this process of "building and destroying houses" was repeated at playtime. In different ways on different days, the theme remained the same.

By the end of those weeks, every child in the class had a turn to be a worker, helper or watcher. Then it was over. As quickly as the "building up" theme arose, gently it seemed to be replaced by other little buildings and with the everyday business of the children's work. Little groupings of families moved into the houses together. Mommies and Daddies sat inside the houses with "babies." Animal play, with dogs and cats, became the next new theme. Before we knew it, spring arrived, and we were outside in the sand under the cottonwood trees making rivers and streams and feeling the warm breeze against our faces.

I have been honored to witness the richness of such profound play as a kindergarten teacher for the past 25 years. Each day the theme of the play was different, but here is one thing that has remained the same throughout all these years that I have noticed and observed on a daily basis in all children. I would call this children's "spirit." We have all used this word one way or another in our lives. Most commonly "spirit" has been used in mystical and religious contexts. Here, let us define "spirit" and the word "spirituality" as it is used in early childhood education. This spirit/spirituality is the impulse behind everything we as educators do and all that we offer to children in the classroom every moment that we are together.

This wonderful word "spirit" has its Latin root *spirare*, meaning breath—a perfect metaphor to use for the young child. Children breathe out into the world with all their senses. They thrust themselves into water. They fly into piles of snow. They roll in the mud. They sit and stare into the sky and then quickly run after a butterfly. They breathe in all that they have observed in their environment with their sensuality and curious minds. They can't help but see, be, and do whatever is in their environment. Children are always on the move, wanting to get somewhere, touch something, jump on what is near them, or connect to their closest adult. They are continually breathing out into the big world and then coming "home" to their own. They give their all, but very rarely stop until they fall off into dreamland at nighttime. We can see that within each child there are infinite possibilities for enjoying the wonderment of life. This joy is a unique characteristic of this age and it is the spirit of early childhood—to connect with one's world wholeheartedly.

Spirituality in early childhood is this: **Exuberance for life that fosters deep connections to family, friends, and nature. It is in this connecting to the wonder of daily life activities, beauty, and all creative endeavors that the child experiences his/her spiritual nature.**

The Child

Who Is this Spiritual Being?

The room was a lively workshop. Children were baking at the main table in the middle of the room, underneath was a family of mice. A bagel factory was being built off to the side, and I was busy with a crowd of bakers baking bread. I noticed the doll corner was empty. I looked up as Sam walked over and began gathering dolls into a pile. One at a time he piled them together. Once he had a huge pile of dolls he squished them as close together as possible on the floor, then intently sat on as many of them as he could.

When I saw he had taken every single doll in the entire classroom, I started to walk over to him to suggest that he might let a few dolls stay in their cradle for other children to play with. As I was walking over to him, I heard that he was "tweeting." I stopped a minute and listened closely. I listened to this "Papa bird" singing to his birdie babies. He sat on them in his nest quite content for a while, and then he flew away.

Childhood is filled with these rich sensual experiences of connections to oneself and the world. Children live deeply in their sensual experiences. Their whole bodies act as sense organs joining the outer world with their inner world. Impressions come into their bodies and are seeds for the human beings they will grow into. All their sense perceptions become information to be used later in life: their spiritual food.

Children, master imitators, learn how to be human from the humans that surround them—a reason to think deeply about what we offer their forming spirits as food for the foundation of their quest. Not only do they want to wash the dishes with us, wear our shoes, and sound like Mommy and Daddy, but also through this they continue to deeply connect with our inner being or spirit as well. From the moment they are born, they learn how to walk, talk, and live from us. Children's work in this magical time of life is to imitate all that is around them, connect with all of their environment, and use these forces to manifest their highest potentialities.

> There is in a child a special kind of sensitivity, which leads him to absorb everything about him, and it is this work of observing and absorbing that alone enables him to adapt himself to life. He does it in virtue of an unconscious power that only exists in childhood...this fashioning of the human personality is a secret incarnation (Montessori, 1988, p. 57).

The child is absorbing all the time, but he/she is not only absorbing the tangible world and events of life, but the living spirit—the spirare—of all he/she meets. This is the dreamy consciousness of childhood, a world in which everything has life.

This dreamy state of being is the spirit of childhood. Children are like butterflies tasting nectar from each flower, enjoying every little sip. The world is their flower. They fly from moment to moment with joy and wonder, very rarely stopping for rest—unless they need to hatch their eggs. Children are on a busy, magical quest of tasting every thing, every moment, filtering nothing, and digesting everything into the very heart of their being.

Healthy children must have the room to live in this dreamy state and sensually experience their world. This is only possible if caring adults are creating an environment for them that is predictable, safe, and protected so that they are not overwhelmed by life's challenges. Living this way is harder to manifest in our present world and is an important challenge for adults in this current culture with all of its pressures.

> Every thought is a living reality for the child. She (sic) sees the flower and experiences the inner reality of the flower. The child not only experiences the outlook but also the "in look", the inner being or the "I am" of the object perceived. The child is not awake like the adult is. She cannot separate the inner from the outer and think about the one or the other. She is neither fully awake, nor is she asleep. Her consciousness is in between, like a dream. Yet within that consciousness it is alert to the world and takes everything in (Glöckler, 2008, p. 73)

The Mindful Teacher

A cry came from the corner of the room. Two girls were fighting. They were tugging on the same doll. I slowly walked over and said:

"Mmmmmmmmmmmmmm,". "I wonder what's going on here?"

I sat and watched. I did not judge or evaluate. "Breathe. Take in. Sit. Breathe. Take in. Breathe out." This is how I connect with what's happened between the two children. I touched each child at her shoulders so she could feel me. We all sat together. There were some tears, and some screaming. I let that happen. I waited. I took in the crying, wiped the tears and just sent love. We all just sat together. Breathing, just breathing. And when the children were ready, the crying stopped.

Now the children are ready to tell their stories.

"She took my dolly!" one child says.

"I did not!" says the other.

"Yes, you did!"

Then the fun usually begins. I look at each of the children with the same curiosity. I say, "Looks like you both like that dolly!"

As a teacher my first goal beyond anything else is to be a loving and joyous human. This "living experience" that Rudolf Steiner talks about is inherent in every gesture, every word, and every interchange between the children and myself. I create an environment that fosters wonder in the children and teaches love, gratitude, and kindness. I acknowledge each child's unique spirit.

Then many things can occur. Most of the time, the children can work something out. I stay, I do not budge until they are both laughing and the dolly seems to be of little importance. Maybe some other child comes over and brings another dolly. That child is thanked and then the game can go on its way.

I practise meditation to cultivate this intimate connection to spirit. Through watching the thoughts that arise in my mind, their patterns, and allowing them to come forth and melt away, it is possible to stay present in *spirare* or nowness.

> In this kind of meditation practice the concept of nowness plays a very important part. In fact, it is the essence of meditation. Whatever one does, whatever one tries to practice, is not aimed at achieving a higher state or at following some theory or ideal, but simply, without

any object or ambition, trying to see what is here and now...for each respiration is unique, it is the expression of now (Rinpoche, 1996, p. 61).

This openness is the basis for the unconditional love that I have for every child in my classroom, regardless of if they are having a "good day." This love is the connecting piece that is needed for children to feel safe, and cared for, and for their learning to be able to take place.

I have experienced that the children occasionally imitate even the thoughts I have in my mind. I have experienced this before when children come to me and say: "Why are you sad?" when I haven't said a word or expressed a tear. Maybe there was a feeling of sadness in my thought at that moment. Children have that kind of spiritual empathy and they can appear to be mind readers.

Clearly, teachers need a quality of peace and tranquility in order to fully be present in the classroom, to be available and not overwhelmed. There are so many events in any moment of classroom life that the teacher can easily be pulled out of mindful presence. One has to have a "big mind" in order to sense the mood of the room and be able to guide the children. What is this "big mind" of the teacher? How does the teacher's big mind mold and sculpt the classroom environment?

Rachel was a dear little one with long braids, very large eyes and a sturdy physique. She was in my classroom for a full year. Her cheeks were always rosy. She played with the other children, ran happily around the house and loved dollies. There was one thing that was unique to Rachel—she never spoke. A three-and-a-half-year-old in a bustling classroom and not a sound from this dear child! The rest of us sang songs all through the day. I told many stories, while we had discussions around the snack table. The children would talk to Rachel, but she never spoke. I wondered on a daily basis what to do. She smiled and had a sparkle in her eye, and she ran to school every day. She seemed content and happy. Every day, every moment, I loved her within my inner spirit. Outwardly I would hug her. I would hold her hand on our walks, and I would also talk to her. Her parents said she talked at home and was a happy child. Most importantly, I did not judge her nor did I expect her to do anything other than what she was doing.

This experience with Rachel affirmed in me the importance of an environment of love without any words. As teachers, this is our first and foremost duty. Rachel, now a singer in her twenties, is a wonderful lively, talkative young woman. My meditation practice has given me the courage and confidence to create an environment in my classroom where even the unique can be fully loved and accepted without fear.

The big *mind* from meditation helps me face challenging situations like Rachel's silence without losing my composure, without losing my awareness of the whole room. I can be present for the next kindergarten situation that will, without a doubt, come up quickly. If something does occur that requires my attention, I move slowly toward the commotion. I walk toward the children who need some kind of attention, and with a *big mind* I sit down with them. I go in with an attitude of curiosity, nothing else.

> The discerning innocence of young children deepens my conviction that at every level of education, the selfhood of the teacher is key... In order to foster the magical spirit each

child possesses one must have a relationship with ones own inner life, one's own inner spirit. To educate is to guide students on an inner journey toward more truthful ways of seeing and being in the world. How can schools perform their mission without encouraging the guides to scout out that inner terrain? (Palmer, 1998, p. 5)

Allowing: Nurturing the Spiritual Moments

We were playing in the yard last week, when Leo came running over to me. He stood at my side silent for a moment. He then looked up at me and said,
   "Mindy where does the wind come from?"
   I looked up and down and behind me, and all the children around did the same. And there was Leo, looking too.

It is *big mind* that allowed me to be *with* Leo, to hear the depth of his awe and wonder, and to honor it. It allows me to listen with my heart. Allowing is an important practice that occurs in my classroom. Allowing connects with the concept of *spirare*. The give and take of the breath parallels the give and take of each interaction. Allowing creates an environment of acceptance and respect, honoring each child's unique expression and spirit. This allows this acceptance of the whole child that nurtures and honors his/her sense of wonder. When I emanate an atmosphere of acceptance, the children feel secure in their spirits. They are free to play and create with each other.

What allowing means is that we as teachers attend to the moment-to-moment experience of each child, without coming up with some adult solution for the situation. We do not have to impose or create peace. Instead, we allow space for peace to develop. Sadness, anger, disappointment, frustration, and glee are all part of a child's process of tuning into their own unique spirit. The way in which teachers can allow children to tap into the strength of their own spiritual moments of connection is a potent expression of our love for each and every one of our students. We allow children a moment to be fully in their experience.

To create visionaries in our world, one must allow a child his/her moment of wonder. Children need to know that they are listened to. If we adults can allow a moment of space before answering their questions, we nurture this moment of spiritual curiosity. Leo's chance to wonder openly was a tiny moment in time, yet so important. One can only imagine how it might impact who he will become. We acknowledge each question with our state of nowness. When the children feel this empathy from us, they connect with our hearts. We must be teachers with "listening hearts."

Moment to Moment Sounds of Spirit

Connecting with Language, Voice, and Song

Some girls in my class this past winter were excluding another child from their play, saying, "This is just a two person game."

I overheard their conversation. That afternoon I told a story, originally told by Isaac Bashevis Singer, of a family in Russia who cared for many children in their home. A starving little deer that had lost its way in the cold visited them. The old woman wanted to take the poor animal in to care for it.

She said to the children, "There's always room for one more."

Weeks passed, and I overheard the same girls say to another who wouldn't allow her classmate to play, "There's always room for one more."

"Once upon a time..." These words of wonder have, for centuries, taken us to distant lands in our minds. Through the power of story children see and hear with their minds' eyes and ears. When children listen to the storyteller there spirits are empowered to imagine pictures that might change from day to day. I tell many kinds of stories in the kindergarten to foster the theme "the world is good." I do this from moment to moment, day to day, season to season, in my classroom and in myself. This is the quest of early childhood teachers. From moment to moment we have to create a living spiritual environment that says to the children, "It is all right to remain in childhood. We will protect you, care for you, and honor your spirit with the message of goodness."

Stories can offer words and language—whole worlds—that have been passed on to us for many generations. This verbal lineage brings a spirit of life from the past as its gift. It is a moving experience for me to tell stories to children that have been told over and over again. I can feel the power of the past in the language of the story, which I live and breathe in my classroom over many days.

We also tell original stories in the Kindergarten. I have a squirrel that lives in my classroom—Squirrel Nutkin. She is a furry brown puppet that I have had for 20 years. Having her own particular spirit, she appears to connect with everyone and to love all children. She comes out to tell a story if something happens in the kindergarten that needs some attention.

A little girl was in the habit of pushing others. Squirrel Nutkin came out at story time, crying. I asked Squirrel Nutkin why she was so sad. She told a story about how her friend pulled her tail and hurt it. Stories such as these create pictures of the goodness we all possess. Children who are listening can absorb how to treat each other. Stories create a world where there is still plenty of magic and wonder, and the stories live on and on. The children in my class retell the story to each other at playtime. They make tickets and invite the little ones to come, creating a stage for all the actors or puppets. They have their own story time. They invite me to be part of the audience, as they create what is now their story. Sometimes it starts out to be the exact story they have heard the day before, but sometimes they just get everyone together and begin with their own story. It is quite the spirited moment when they all are offering their own little piece of magical truth. The audience is riveted. Children are honoring their connection to the world. Hearing stories, children become great storytellers.

Whether the stories come to us from long ago or are created on the spot, story is the breath of connection. The children sit and openly receive. They are transported to other worlds and other parts of themselves as they absorb the very essence of who I am. Sitting and receiving for children takes practice, but is an important life practice for learning and discovering inner spirit.

Tremendous power lives in our words. Our words are pathways to our hearts, our passion, and connection to our life experience. Stories are vital roads to learning about the spirituality of life and its complexities.

Singing Spirits

Children are moving music. They "become" the sounds they hear. Children inwardly feel the sounds. Watching children listen to music one can actually see the music in motion.

The teacher's joy of singing is a profound experience for young. Songs offer pictures of what is happening or going to happen in Mother Nature's world. We sing of the coming and goings of the changes in our world. We sing of the small little beetles and the sleeping bears. When we sing we are in harmony with each other. Our kindergartners become a chorus for all to hear. Some favorites are as follows:

Winter
  Rose red is the evening sky
  Milk white is the snow
  Let's go on our winter walk
  Do, do let us go.
  Tomorrow the sky may be dark and gray
  Tomorrow the snow may be gone
  So let's go on our Winter walk
  In the last rays of the sun (Swinger, 1972, pp. 22–23).
Spring
  Oh it is a happy morning
  There are blossoms on the trees
  There's a merry robin singing
  There's a golden flight of bees
  There's a tiny dew drop clinging
  Like a rainbow to a rose,
  And the sun is busy shedding
  Little freckles on your nose.
  Oh it is a happy morning
  There is joy in everything
  On such a happy morning
  All I want to do is sing (Swinger, 1972, pp. 22–23)
Summer
  When on a summer morning, As I go on my way,
  And hear the brown bird singing
  And blackbird whistling gay,
  And high the lark goes winging
  And call from sky so blue
  Then, oh, I must go singing
  And must go humming too! (Swinger, 1972, pp. 22–23)
Fall
  Golden in the garden

Golden in the glen
Golden golden golden
September is here again.
Golden in the treetops
Golden in the sky
Golden, Golden, Golden
September's flying by (Unknown author).

There are a myriad of songs for children. The songs we sing in my classroom are songs that evoke the spirit of the season and a reverence for the spirituality of life. We sing songs that bring pictures to the imaginations of children. They assure a refreshing and vibrant mood for the group. We become a chorus of little voices that ring through the neighborhood as we go by the apple tree or garbage truck. We are minstrels on a merry journey together. On our daily walk in the neighborhood we sing to the trees, to the squirrels, and to the wind. When the moon is out in the morning we sing:

Mister Moon, Mister Moon you're out too soon
The sun is still in the sky,
Go back to bed and cover your head
And wait for the day to go by . . .

Songs are nourishing to a child's spirit, and from that "food" for their spirit they can relax within themselves and with others. This aspect of heartfelt singing is part of the climate the teacher helps to create in the spiritual classroom.

The Classroom Environment

On Mondays we always bake, every Monday. When my children come into the room they always run for their aprons. Seeing the big bowl of dough rising on the table, they sit eagerly down. I don't say, "It's baking day!" They wait anxiously for the white powdery flour to drift down to the table. When the table is white with flour their little hands can slide across the maple and feel the luxury of the silky bread flour. The dough comes out and the pounding and molding can begin. The dough grasps every child's attention.

What I do as a teacher, I know that my little ones will do too. All I need to do is bake with love, connection, joy, and spirit. When the bread comes out of the oven the whole school community can enjoy the efforts of our happy classroom bakery. The smell permeates the entire neighborhood. Everyone knows it is baking day!...

The teacher creates an environment of safety and dependability in the children's day with a predictable daily rhythm. The day has many breathing in phases and breathing out phases. The children begin their day with breathing out into free play and walking in the neighborhood. Then when they come into the classroom they come into a "ring time" with story and songs in a group. Next is an open time of work and play, followed by an in phase of rest time and lunch. We go outside in the garden (breathing out), and then come back inside for our last breathing in phase of story and good-bye.

Between these there is also a moment of acknowledging the shift from one mood to the next. I sing the children in from their outside play to gently gather them together for their morning greeting which flows happily into our circle of singing together. Every part of our day has a song. We sing to all the children to gather for the morning walk, to tell them it's time to clean up, to warn them that going home time is soon. Songs bring the aliveness and spirit into the classroom and carry the children through the day.

We repeat this rhythm all year long because children thrive in this atmosphere of predictability and consistency. Their spirits can soar because they know what will happen. When my children come into the classroom in the morning, they take their shoes off, put on their slippers, go to the restroom, and then go to circle without any directions from me. We begin our day that way every day. They wait at circle with a joy in them knowing exactly what is coming next. They never say, "What are we doing now?" They come to circle carried by the rhythm of what they know.

> Simply put, life is a rhythmic event. It is the nature of our heartbeat, our breath, and our digestion. It is the child being rocked to sleep, the runner hitting his stride, the dancer at one with the music. It is the turning of the earth and the rise and fall of the tides. **There is no way that we can come into harmony with our world or ourselves unless we honor and work in harmony with the principles of rhythm**. Rhythm does not imprison, rather, it frees (Sutton, 2001, np)

The kindergarten is very much an extension of the home. Maria Montessori actually called one of her kindergartens "Casa." When we think of home, we think of a place of refuge, of love, of caring and of protection. The kindergarten/preschool should have the same qualities. A child's first experience away from home should offer the same happy impressions a home has. Great care should be given as to what is in the classroom "casa." We want to make sure that the materials and activities are from real life. Every day, life experiences and activities can be seen as spiritual moments with the exuberance of spirit. All activities that are domestic—polishing, sweeping, dusting, washing—are joyful spiritual activities that the children take pride in.

Everything that the children come in contact has a lively spirited quality. Each object that is in our classroom, whether it is a broom, piece of wood or doll is cherished. My love for each and every thing in our kindergarten world is a reflection of my spiritual connection to the children and their environment.

> Adults admire their environment, they can remember it and think about it, but the child absorbs it. The things he sees are not just remembered, they form part of his soul. He incarnates himself all in the world about him that his eyes see and his ears hear (Montessori, 1988, p. 56).

Our ordinary classroom activities engage in everyday are infused with this spirit. When I sweep, I use a broom that a friend has made me. Hand-carved, it has a little face of a bearded old man on the top of the handle. Early in the year I tell a story about my friend and how she chose the wood. How she asked the tree people in the forest if there was a spare branch. I tell how long it took her to carve the broom, and then tell a story about an old woman who uses her broom and "sweeps and sweeps all day, she never stops to play." After the telling of that story I lay out many pieces of wood and with tiny children's carving tools. As I sit and peel off bark, and many children come to join me. My broom becomes a lively tool with its own spirit. A simple tool can become "alive" because of my story and my connection to the broom itself.

Children love activity with purpose. The environment of the classroom is full of opportunities to satisfy this type of need.

Seasonal activities bring the children much excitement. Bags of wool that still smell of sheep give us a great opportunity for washing, drying, and carding the wool. This activity can take us days. In my classroom, I have children who can't wait to do the washing. Many children crowd around the sinks with washing boards and scrub all morning, happily singing "Baa, baa, black sheep," or "This is the way we wash the wool." After washing we dry the wool, brush it, spin it, and make it ready for knitting. Providing this type of process-oriented activity leads the children into a healthy picture of life. We can all participate in our environment. This process brings the community of the classroom together. Simple and natural materials can nurture our spirits. The message we present is that life is fun. The children experience that the world is literally at their fingertips.

Bits and pieces from nature as well as other beautiful objects are important for manipulating and using for play in the classroom. Materials from nature provide different textures and the spirit of the elements. The child's spirit blends with the shell, acorn, or pinecone to create magical use for inner spirits to play with. The wonder of daily existence is in itself a spiritual experience in the school setting.

Because children are such great observers of life, beauty has a strong component in the sensual environment of the classroom. Just like in the home, great care is given to the spirit and look of the classroom. Every season offers its own unique opportunities to evoke the color of the seasons. In my classroom we change the tablecloths and napkins every season. When the children come in for lunch and see the new seasonal lunch table, they ring with excitement.

Simple surroundings are an invitation to the spirit of the child. Walls should be simple, so the eye and mind can relax and the children can remain in a sensual place without too much stimulus. Natural wood and simple lines in furniture allow a freedom of movement and invitation for a child to explore the space. Open space is integral for any kind of building or dramatic play to occur. In my kindergarten we have an abundance of raw materials for the children to use to create whatever comes to mind. One day a blue cloth can be a roof of a house; the next day it is a river. With this kind of open-ended material, children's spirits can be satisfied with personal connection and fulfillment.

I love watching children build. Materials that do not have a predictable outcome feed children's imaginative forces. Pieces of wood, large and small provide an array of opportunities for visual and tactile play. Little villages and roads can be built. Train stations are constructed out of chairs and tables. Everything in the room can be used as a "prop" for the child's work. The whole classroom environment is transformed into a workshop of happy little bees. Everything in the room is used for the child's vision. What the children see, they use. The whole classroom world is at their fingertips.

I also have an array of tools so that my little carpenters can go to work. I have hammers, nails, wooden stumps, wood-handled saws and little pieces of wood. Each playtime the children have an opportunity to work with real tools.

We work therefore we clean, cleaning is an important component to play time. All the cleaning utensils come out. While we clean we sing or hum. Sometimes we just get down on the floors and wash. Children sometimes start arguing about who gets to be a sweeper or duster. Cleaning is done, as with every spiritual activity, with a sense of joy. Since I love my room; the children imitate this love and care. We are family! We use everything in our environment and we care for it as well. We have a "shining day" where we oil the wooden things in the room. Some children sit all morning and shine. I can see other children sitting on the floor washing with their wooden brushes. When all the furniture is put right side up, when the babies are tucked in, when the wood goes back to the wood pile, when the chairs are put in their places, when the crayons are back in their little houses, and the wool is wound for knitting, we look around the room for a moment and see if there is anything left to put away. The children take great care to find some little thing we have missed, and happily find its home too. The feeling in the environment is lively, happy, and purposeful, a true picture of connection for our sacred world.

The outside environment is vital to the appreciation of the magic of the world. My class and I walk every day to watch birds, greet the squirrels, welcome the garbage truck, watch the apple tree turn from bare to fruit, help the worms cross the street, and feel the wind on our faces. We walk in rain, sleet, and snow. We have the primal experience of nature as our walks provide a connection to the natural spirit of the season. In fall we collect golden leaves and make leaf crowns. In winter we slide down the ice-covered streets and watch the snowfall glittering to the ground. In spring we rejoice with the blossoms that grow on the apple and cherry trees, and in summer we enjoy the fruit from the plum trees. As we stroll through the neighborhood, the children watch the signs of the change that is about to happen. When the first apple arrives on the tree, the children dance for joy. The children's little hands find many things to hold and collect. Big and small treasures come back to our classroom to be used in artistic ways, and in play. Thanks to their power of spirit, imagination, and fantasy the children bring life to everything they find. When they find acorns, they make an acorn village. The leaves become beds and blankies for the fairies. Fairy flowers have houses, and the rock people need to rest somewhere in the classroom. Everything the children find in their world has a living sense to it. One can often see children talking to pieces of wood or little bugs. Tiny worlds arise out of the spirit that the children bring to each found thing. My special task as a teacher is to provide the rich, natural outdoor experience for the children to awaken the artistic aliveness in the children, and in myself as well.

18 Moment to Moment Spirituality in Early Childhood Education

Play: Vital Food for the Spirit

On our daily morning walk in our neighborhood my children and I watched a house being built over a year. First we watched a truck come and knock down the little white house down and haul it away. We watched the workers put old pieces of wood into the dump trucks. The next week we watched as they dug a space for a new basement and foundation was poured. Every day we passed by, watching with awe and wonder as the new house being built went through many transformations. We sat across the street watching and sometimes singing to the workers, who we got to know by name. When the house was complete, we were walking by one day and the construction manager, whom we had talked to all year, invited us into the house to see the completed project, my children were thrilled. They walked inside and pointed out all the places where they thought the pipes were and the wires were. Everything they saw they commented on as if they were professional builders. They talked about the day they saw the sheet rock delivered, and they shared their favorite stories of construction. They spoke of the construction as if they built it themselves. In a way they did. Every day in the classroom they would come back and imitate what they had seen. In their own play we had haulers and dump trucks. They used every play frame for walls and floors. We had roofers and cement workers. The children took wool and put it inside washbasins and made cement and covered the floor with it, they created their own homes. They did all this creative building because they had space to play. I watched as the children used their free imagination to use simple materials to manifest their unique ideas: ropes became wires: small pieces of wood became telephones: pillow, a helmet: chairs, a ladder.

The children's spirits had room to breathe into the environment. They were shaping their world from what they had seen. Every year I watch how children come into the class with a myriad of different things they like to do, knowing that it all has a similar enthusiasm and spirit. This spirit is the passion and love the children have for life and everything in it. They want to connect with all they see in their environment and use it to choreograph what they have seen from their life experiences and from the people around them.

What the children experience comes out dramatically in each child's play. This sacred space of "play time" is crucial for a child's inner spirit to synthesize what they have seen, heard, felt, and experienced in their short life. The child experiences the powerful aspect of feeling part of a whole is through play. When they feel part of a whole, their spirits relax. They can learn, play with each other, and love each other.

The children can come into the classroom and join in with what I am doing or choose to be in the group with what other children are playing. There is a happy buzz in the room. This part of the day is the "breathing out". The children's energy is lively and their spirits are engaged. They have many choices. They have space and freedom within a rhythm that is honored by the teacher, a rhythm that is dependable.

There are many themes in the classroom over the year. Some themes are universal: house building; playing house; playing mommy and daddy; being construction workers or zoo animals; being store keepers or restauranteurs; train conducting;

being kings, queens, and princesses; playing kitty or horsy or bunny; being cleaners or polishers or cobblers or street cleaners.

There are also very personal themes depending on what is going on in the home life or in the world: going on a trip; having a visitor for the weekend; having a new baby in the family; or becoming a baby again.

Allowing children's spirits the space and time for play in the classroom is vital for forming friendships with others and with one. Feeling that we are part of a tribe, be it large or small, is a rich and irreplaceable opportunity for the experience of connection to the world. In play we learn how to be human. The space for play is vital for the spiritual connection to each other and us.

> Play is the child's most useful tool for preparing himself for the future and its tasks...Play teaches the child, without his being aware of it, the habits most needed for intellectual growth (Bettleheim, 1987, p. 36).

Moment to Moment Spirituality in the Kindergarten

Little Moments, Many Times

Nola, a 5 year old little girl in my class last year came running over to me and said, "Mindy, look at my picture!" So that is what I did.

Nola sat down next to me.

She and I sat and looked at her picture.

We looked for what seemed to be a long time, maybe 3 minutes. Then she looked up at me and I looked at her. She looked at me as if to see what I was doing. I just kept looking.

We looked for another minute and then she spoke again. "Mindy."

I said, "What Nola?"

"I love you," she said.

"I love you too, Nola," I replied.

When we give children the space to connect to their own spirit, they are able to feel love within themselves and for others. Children rely on us to emanate love. We offer ourselves as a mirror for their self-love and spirituality. If they see themselves through their own eyes of love they can become the people that they want to be. This spirituality of connection is vital for confidence, a positive sense of wellbeing, the ability to receive, and the spirit of loving-kindness. All these qualities are necessary for human beings to create a peaceful and compassionate world for our future together.

The Latin root for education is *e-ducere*, "to lead out." As a teacher I lead my children through each day of the school honoring my own spirit, the spirit in the children, the classroom, and the environment. For spirituality in early childhood to thrive in our world, we must as educators work desperately to continually create a world of goodness for these most precious little ones. Our quest is to look deeply into what we offer these sensual, imitative, spiritual beings, so we do not bombard them with the overly mechanized world that stops their spiritual flourishing.

The children and myself, dance through the school year with our love and connection for each other to nature, to rhythm, singing songs, listening to stories, honoring day-to-day life experiences, and wholeheartedly engaging in our important work and play. This is a window into the world of Spirituality in Early Childhood.

References

Bettleheim, B. (1987). The importance of play. *The Atlantic Monthly*, March 1987.
Glöckler, M. (2008). Forces of growth and fantasy of the young child. *The Waldorf early childhood newsletter*. Spring Valley, NY: Waldorf Early Childhood Association of North America.
Montessori, M. (1988). *The absorbent mind*. London & New York: Oxford Press.
Palmer, P. (1998). *The courage to teach*. San Francisco: Jossey-Bass Publishers.
Rinpoche, C. T. (1996). *Meditation in action*. Boston/London: Shambhala Publications,
Sutton, B. (2001). *Enki foundation guides*. Providence, RI: Enki Education Inc. (8)
Swinger, M. (1972) *Sing through the seasons, ninety-nine songs for children* (The Society of Brothers, Eds.). Rifton, NY: The Plough Publishing House.

Chapter 19
Children's Spiritual Intelligence

Mollie Painton

Abstract The purpose of this chapter is to explore the evolution of a variety of intelligences, from IQ to emotional and social intelligences, with an emphasis on the emergence of awareness of spiritual intelligence. While a definition of spiritual intelligence is offered, it is found to be close in description to children's inner worlds. The author details the cost of oppressing spiritual intelligence in children and the aftereffects on adults. She also emphasizes the need for adults to be spiritual partners for the children in their lives. The illustrative stories of the Seven Branches of the Spiritual Tree of Life are taken from the author's clinical study of children in play therapy over a period of approximately 20 years. Much of the content is cited from the author Mollie Painton's book *Encouraging Your Child's Spiritual Intelligence*.

In recent years we have moved our understanding of intelligence from acknowledging one kind, IQ, to recognizing multiple intelligences. According to Howard Gardner (1998), multiple intelligences include visual–spatial, bodily kinesthetic, linguistic, logical–mathematical, musical, interpersonal, and intrapersonal. In the past 10 years, Daniel Goleman (1995) has introduced us to emotional intelligence, and more recently, social intelligence.

As stated in my article *Inner Worlds* in the September 2007 issue of the Rocky Mountain Parent Magazine,

> I would like for us to go one step further to really honor our children by being aware of their inner worlds, or spiritual intelligence. Without this knowledge, how can we honestly say that we know "what makes our children tick?" (Painton, 2007b, pp. 18–19)

At the same time, how can we be helpful to them as they grow and develop, navigating the rough waters of their transformation?

M. Painton (✉)
The Interplay Center and the SpiritPlay Institute, 1519 Rolf Court, Fort Collins, CO 80525, USA
e-mail: Pmollie@aol.com

Journey of Grief and Enlightenment

Let me begin the way I commonly introduce my work in a variety of settings by telling a story to shed light on what I am saying. In 1979 my husband Max, a clinical psychologist who started the Gestalt Institute of Phoenix, died of cancer leaving me a widow with two daughters, aged 3 and 7. As we moved through a grieving period that lasted several years, both my daughters reported seeing their dad on many occasions. The oldest was visited nightly for nearly a year after her father's death. While I was overwhelmed by my loss and aware of my daughters' pain, their wisdom and openness touched me.

One night my youngest daughter Sarah, who had recently turned 4, sat on my lap as I cried about her dad. She held my face in her hands and said, "Mom, at least we have life!" For about 2 years after her father's death my oldest daughter saw what she called "colors" around friends, family, and even strangers. These events began to shape my life, the life of my children, and my work as a therapist.

Children's Inner Worlds

Ten years later, when I was in private practice as a child psychologist and play therapist, my child clients told me similar stories that they were not comfortable sharing with many others:

> A ten-year-old boy disclosed that he is nearly incapacitated by his awareness of the pain of others, while feeling rejection from his peers ... A four-year-old boy told me that his deceased father visits him often in a variety of forms. A seven-year-old girl shared that after her grandmother died, she became the girl's guardian angel who watches over and protects her daily (Painton, 2007b, pp. 18–19).

During the course of my practice, many children have described their guardian angels and spiritual companions. A 9-year-old girl sees fairies dancing around her room every night when she goes to sleep. Another girl had a butterfly who was her spiritual companion. One child, who was in play therapy with me, interacted with nine different "ghosts" after having a near-death experience. His journey is similar to that of other children whose experiences have been acknowledged by clergy and documented by medical personnel as well (Painton, 2007a).

As child clients have disclosed their journeys to me, I realize that they live in a world that is incomprehensible to most adults. Exploring their own developed and developing identities, they are not confined to the limitations of life as we adults know it. They describe gaining entrance to other domains in which they coexist and prosper. From their stories, it is apparent that they journey easily, both in sleep and awake, from our everyday realities to profound worlds with an endless variety of fascinating, even magnificent, beings. They often appear to have an unconstrained rapport with these visitors who help them to survive while enriching their lives. As such their inner worlds are bursting with wisdom, guidance, and enriching experiences essential for their lives, and those of their parents, relatives, and friends.

According to these children, the angels, fairies, elves, deceased friends, and relatives who visit them, are, more often than not, advocates who watch over them. They enjoy a dynamic relationship with these helping spirits, many who are constantly at their sides, offering them a sense of protection and safety in a not-so-friendly world. Inevitably, children who have spiritual visitors report that they are greatly impacted by these guests. As they become accustomed to their presence, they are as much a part of the child's world as family members. Most importantly, their role in the healing of the child is paramount.

By healing, I am referring to a child's capacity to gravitate toward and benefit from an inner balance, while moving out of a state of conflict, developing more positive hopes and beliefs, and maturing to a developmentally appropriate state. Integral to healing is a sense of safety and protection that spiritual companions, as well as nurturing adults, can offer children. Awareness and validation are also central to the healing process. Much of this healing takes place in children's play as they creatively change the ingredients and outcome of the disturbing or traumatizing story to one with which they can comfortably live. Thus, they realize a shift from victimization to empowerment.

Picture children in their spiritual worlds as having their senses so finely tuned that they can hear a butterfly's wings flapping while standing next to a train moving full speed down the tracks. Everyone may see that butterfly, but few are able to not be distracted by the sounds of the train that drown out the butterfly's announcement, "I am!" Children are more finely attuned to stimuli that are present all the time. I remember watching my neighbor's 6-year-old daughter lay in the tall grass with her arms outstretched. Her legs were pointing up to the clouds, kicking gently with the rhythm of the wind. Her eyes were deeply focused on a small brown bug that she repeatedly rolled into a ball and shot across the wide expanse of meadow. "Roly-poly! Roly-poly!" she repeated with a giggle as she began to curl up in a ball and turn over and over in the wet grass. She continued this play for nearly half an hour, ingeniously mimicking the motions of the bug.

Children joyfully absorb every aspect of their environments. You may remember experiencing your world like these children. Unfortunately, for most people these experiences are unique to childhood. These moments may be ignored by adults who may have gradually lost touch with their gifts of sensitivity, intuition, and expanded consciousness, that can produce a deep capacity for compassion for all peoples of the world, a desire to be healing to themselves and others, while acting as peacemakers in a not always so peaceful world. To the extent that they restrict their awareness, adults become more narrowly focused with time as they lose their ability to be truly present.

Definition of Spiritual Intelligence

In Carl Jung's (1963) book *Memories, dreams, reflections*, he said

> Most people identify themselves almost exclusively with their consciousness, and imagine that they are only what they know about themselves. Yet anyone with even a smattering

of psychology can see how limited this knowledge is. Rationalism and doctrinarism are the disease of our time; they pretend to have all the answers. But a great deal will yet be discovered which our present limited view would have ruled out as impossible (p. 300).

After nearly 20 years of working with thousands of children, I have discovered that what I am observing is not pathology, and need not be a liability. It is a form of giftedness or a phenomenon called spiritual intelligence. *What is spiritual intelligence?* Spiritual intelligence is boys' and girls' capacity to be awake and aware of a deeper dimension of themselves that leads to wisdom and intuition, compassion, and other-worldly experiences. It refers to the inner world of the child.

Spiritual intelligence, related to human's struggle for meaning, vision, spiritual awareness, and worth. When children's spiritual intelligence is encouraged, their greatest gifts and potential for healing and happiness are realized. It is vital for their survival and human wellbeing.

The Cost of Oppressing Spiritual Intelligence

Unfortunately, boys and girls in Western cultures often find themselves lost in a world that does not believe in or support, much less nurture, their exceptional spiritual gifts. To the scientific mind "seeing is believing." It is perplexing to most Westerners to grasp that children encounter realities that cannot be seen by the ordinary (adult) eye and therefore, that which is unseen or unable to be precisely calculated is unthinkable. Worlds or realms that are invisible to some, simply do not exist for them.

As children feel that their inner worlds or spiritual intelligence is not valued, they live in fear of rejection. In his article, "Adults Who Had Imaginary Playmates as Children," John Connolly (1991) tells of a boy's cousin who was traumatized by his own father as he angrily put an end to his son's closest companion.

> I have a twelve-year-old cousin who had an imaginary friend when he was smaller. It drove his father crazy. One day his dad had had enough of it and asked him where his friend BoBo was, and when he pointed it out, my uncle stomped down as hard as he could and smashed BoBo into the ground. My cousin turned pale and wouldn't talk for the rest of the day. That is how he lost his imaginary friend (p. 118).

In contrast persons from many other cultures believe that contacting hidden realities and communicating with spirits are natural everyday occurrences. For instance, a boy in the Philippines saw a ghostlike woman at his home. After telling his family about what he saw, his grandmother asked him to identify the woman in their family picture albums. Feeling his family's support, respect, and validation, he readily found the person, clothing included, whom he had seen.

When spiritual intelligence is oppressed, it may lead to alcohol and drug abuse, as well as depression and suicide, panic disorders and anxiety, fearfulness and poor self-esteem, not to mention desperately unfulfilling lives. Major life decisions made without awareness and encouragement of a person's spiritual intelligence will inevitably lead to unhappiness. For teenagers their anger and sadness may be evidence of a vague sense of loss of their inner spiritual world. As they develop and move into adulthood, they may lose sight of their giftedness. If they have refused to let it flourish, they will inevitably live inauthentic lives, and gradually forsake their inner spiritual worlds. They may merely feel that something is "missing or wrong with them." Alienation from their inner worlds is a spiritual death that sets in motion a cycle of suffering that may last a lifetime. The source of this grieving is difficult for them to identify and therefore impossible to articulate.

Searching for heroes to lead them in their quests for truth, most children, fearing criticism and rejection, do not feel free to disclose to anyone the spiritual aspects of their extraordinary stories. They may consider these stories to be unusual, or even forbidden, especially when they include ongoing relationships with their spiritual visitors. When questioned, the greater majority respond, "Are you kidding? I would never tell my parents about that! They don't believe me. They don't believe in those things."

Many parents are critical of their children's spiritual gifts, characteristics, and encounters; fearful that others learning of their experiences will harshly judge, and perhaps shun, their children, as well as themselves. While their intention is to protect their child, this fear prevents boys and girls, as well as adults, from thriving emotionally and spiritually. Feeling like outcasts, they begin to suffer the destructive effects of isolation born of their spiritual giftedness.

The Spiritual Tree of Life

Boys and girls who share their spiritual intelligence with supportive significant others do not suffer from the same isolation. Reaching out for connection, they enrich the spiritual worlds of others. After a lifetime of being a privileged visitor in their worlds, I found myself in a limitlessly creative and fascinating universe—the inner spiritual realm of the child. In the center of their world I envisioned a grand, playful, and childlike tree that stood with great presence. Its massive and sturdy trunk provided support to the interconnected network of seven major branches, representing the seven spiritual themes most commonly manifested by girls and boys. As I pictured this astonishing tree that welcomes all children to play on its branches, the name *Spiritual Tree of Life* came to me.

The seven branches of the Spiritual Tree of Life, inspired by the children in play therapy with me, embody the gifts, rites of passage, and experiences associated with children's inner worlds or spiritual intelligence. As described in my book, *Encouraging your child's spiritual intelligence*,

> The first branch depicts children's spiritual gifts of wisdom and intuition; the second branch represents their profound compassion coupled with their need for belonging and connection. The third branch embodies children's belief that death is permanent only in a physical sense. On the fourth branch, they participate in a world, both invisible and incomprehensible to most adults, that primarily consists of spirit. Acting as spiritual warriors on the fifth branch, kids are sensitive to the notion of light and darkness, good and evil. On the sixth branch,

they spend much of their time in a world of metaphor, while engaging in healing play. The seventh branch concerns the transformative journey many spiritual boys and girls undergo as they shed their old lives on the road to spiritual rebirth (Painton, 2007a, pp. xxvi–xxvii).

First Branch – Wisdom and Intuition

Benjamin Hoff (1992) describes wisdom as the natural state of a child:

> Children are born with it; most adults have lost it, or a good deal of it. And those who haven't are, in one way or another, like children. Is it a mere coincidence that the Chinese suffix tse, which has come to mean "master", literally means "child"? (p. 195)

While children on the first branch are wise beyond their years, they are blessed with profound insights, understanding, and vision that come naturally and effortlessly to them. These insights take them beyond their ages and immediate experiences, allowing them to see outside the ordinary. In other words, these children have a natural wisdom that enables them to live an enriched life unexplained by the physical properties of science and beyond the confines of rationalism. This intimacy with truth is at the core of their spirituality.

While most children rest on at least one of the branches of the Spiritual Tree of Life, occasionally there is a child who is involved on each and every branch. Four-year-old Kyle, whose older brother James died in a car accident, is one of these children. He rests thoughtfully on the first branch of the Spiritual Tree of Life concerning the basic nature of children to be wise beyond their years. A few days after his brother James died, a neighbor approached Kyle and his mother asking if it were true that James had died in a car accident. Kyle's mother sadly told the neighbor, "Yes, we lost James." Kyle responded after listening closely, "Yes, he was lost, but now he is found. God found him!" At another point Kyle sent a message to the participants at a conference on the spiritual world of children. He insisted that I tell everyone, "People are really in good care, because they have angels and God."

The lives of the boys and girls on the first branch are enriched by their uncanny insights. I offer several examples drawn from hundreds of children who share Kyle's gifts on the first branch beginning with a Native American woman whose 4-year-old grandson predicted that he was going to die soon. He wanted to take his brother with him when he went to heaven. I was very touched by the grief of this grandmother, who remembered telling her grandson, "No, you are not dying! Both you and your brother will be here for a long time." Within 6 months the boy died of a brain tumor. Another child, Jonathan described his "inner voice" as keeping him safe. "I had a dream about my inner core. That inside part of me sometimes said, 'Jonathan, you have to be scared!' Then I would be very careful about what I was doing."

Boys and girls on each branch demonstrate strengths that are resources for their lives. The innate wisdom of children on the first branch makes them skillful candidates for journeying to great inner depths. While they are thinkers "outside the box" they may have an "inner voice" that guides them. As they value living, knowing, and telling the truth, they candidly and courageously face their own stories of major adjustments, destruction, and trauma. They desire to live their lives in the fullness they realize from their wisdom.

On the other hand, boys and girls on the first branch may suffer from a fear of exposure as they hide who they are in terms of their wisdom, intuition, and insights. Living with an expectation of rejection and criticism, they are likely to experience poor self-esteem, a sense of being weird, "not fitting in" and of course, a feeling of aloneness.

Second Branch – Compassion, Connection, and Belonging

On the second branch of compassion, belonging, and connection, children's love for their personal and global families, along with their need for a sense of belonging with people of all nations, colors, and creeds is as strong as their intolerance of the many inhumane acts of cruelty on our planet Earth. For instance, when the World Trade Center towers were destroyed, many deeply compassionate children felt a shared sense of sadness and hopelessness. They were moved to ask painfully thoughtful questions about the future of our world, the concept of hate and war, and the idea of killing people in retaliation for their attacks on our land. For many months they demonstrated their distress in their pictures, play, stories, and dreams.

Out of their compassion and need for belonging, they are sensitive to the fact that, despite differences among all people, there is a universal thread that connects all of us; our appearance of diversity quickly melts away as we join together in a hymn of the universe. Children on the second branch of the Spiritual Tree of Life reach out to the world of differing nations with an understanding and compassion that has no bounds. In fact they may become alarmingly distressed, physically ill, or even not want to live, if their purposeful goal of bringing about peace, inner and outer, is not reached.

During a group meeting with children his age, Kyle realized such a profound connection with all people in his global family. While in meditation with their eyes closed, I asked them who they saw standing in front of them. Kyle responded with excitement, "Mollie, I see all the people in all the world who have ever died—the Japanese are here too. And my brother is at the head of them all." Kyle reached out to his global family with love and comfort in his healing play announcing loudly, "I love people everywhere...all over the world. I feel really close to them. I hurt when others hurt...even people far away."

Other kids, like Brooke and Luke, who speak out in appreciation of children across the globe who suffer with handicaps, ask the pertinent question, "Why do children have to suffer?" Their answer is so complex, yet so simple—they do so in order to teach us about life, love, and our purpose here on earth! There are also children who have had near-death experiences. Their effortless, yet resounding, message is, "The most important thing is that you love one another!" They may live their lives playing out this desire for oneness, like Sean, who designed a community living peacefully together in a few homes that housed an entire city!

On the other hand, Sean envisioned the closeness of all people as a community living peacefully together in a few specially designed homes that housed an entire city! While these children may never travel beyond their own city, state, or country, their hearts are awakened to a compassionate connection with all peoples, even those beyond their immediate sphere. No matter how limited their actual contact with other nations, the healing they bring about has a force that is far-reaching!

On the second branch, children's need for connection and belonging, as well as their compassion, are tremendous resources for engaging with others in their lives. While these boys and girls are trusting and open by nature, they respond effortlessly to love and support. They are generous, cooperative, conscientious, scrupulously fair, and honest. When these boys and girls are involved in any activity, they are catalysts for establishing a sense of community. Rather than emphasizing differences, they create healing connections, working to change the world for the better.

Their innate ability to connect on such a deep level may create some vulnerability for them. As they bond so readily, they are likely to absorb others' pain and therefore become depressed and/or anxious. As a result of their sensitivity, they may tend to be overly responsible, even co-dependent in their relationships. Children on the second branch may be challenged to establish healthy boundaries without enmeshment. While they are overly compliant, they may find that they are easily taken for granted. If faced with rejection, these boys and girls may be prone to poor self-esteem, a feeling that "one is not enough," sometimes leading to hopelessness, anger, and suicidal ideation.

Third Branch – Physical Death

The third branch of the Spiritual Tree of Life describes "death" as permanent only in a physical sense. In the healing play of some of these children, the people, animals, and super heroes who die come back to life. In other cases the child actually realizes the presence of a deceased relative or friend. Spiritual children teach us that death is only permanent in a physical sense, and that death, as we commonly know it, does not exist.

Children's deeply spiritual practice of mourning can be understood as a communal process in loving union with those who have died. Thus their grief, although more often than not involving an immense amount of pain, can more easily give way to a realization of joy and completion. In this way, grieving by children takes on incredibly fresh and promising dimensions, especially when the person who is being mourned is part of the ongoing process.

In Kyle's case, he is always accompanied in the playroom by his deceased brother James. In fact, he says he is always with him. He commented on several occasions that James was not in the ground where they buried his body. He said, "He's in heaven...and here! He's always here, when I am. He's up there by that window. He likes it up there. James loves group!" Kyle continued, "I talk to James. I tell him, 'I love you' and all that stuff about everything going on. I told him he gets to go to see Ice Age with me and a neighbor and mommy. I tell him a lot how much I love him."

Many children suffer the loss of a sibling, parent, or grandparent through death. In countless cases the child says that the loved one who has died not only visits, but becomes a guardian or protector of the girl or boy. A spiritual boy, Sammy, describes his dad, "Sometimes I feel weird like my dad is around...he is always there, even though you can't see him! He is my guardian angel!" Another such child, Stephanie says of her deceased mother, "Even though she died, she still loves me and watches over me!"

Years after her mother's death, Renee felt blessed by her loving presence, saying with joy in her heart, "I know that my mother does not only visit once in a while, she is with me every minute of every day!" Another child, Devon, prayed that his dad would not die. While he was not granted his wish, he believed that God did give him a miracle! "He lets my dad talk to me sometimes, when I am alone in my room. He also lets him be in my dreams. We are always doing fun things together!" Meanwhile, Taylor spoke of her recently deceased father as "no longer being in his body," while enjoying an enriched relationship with him, including visits and dialogue.

Among the many resources of the children on the third branch is the innate ability to keep alive their connection with deceased friends, family, and others. Their grief is lessened by their gift of spiritual intelligence. As a result of their comfort with "death" they are willing to create, play, and dialogue around their unique circumstances. As they reenact their loss, they more readily come to terms with their grief while keeping their connection alive with the deceased one.

Children on the third branch may be vulnerable to feeling guilt for the death of a loved one. As they blame themselves, their fear of losing the surviving parent is intensified, while their ability to remain connected with the deceased person is diminished. During their time of mourning, they are likely to feel vulnerable, angry, and insecure faced with judgmental peers who make fun of them for having a deceased parent. Without a safe place to express their grief, their self-esteem will suffer.

Fourth Branch – World of Spirit

The fourth branch of the Spiritual Tree of Life is multi-faceted in its scope, emphasizing that spiritual children live in a world that primarily consists of spirit—a mystical territory wherein great potential for healing and happiness lies. On this branch the spiritual boys and girls are not necessarily "earthbound," while they play in worlds incomprehensible to most adults. For example, they report interacting with spirits such as angels, elves and fairies, deceased relatives and others, seeing lights, colors, and rainbows around people, and desiring to fly and/or remembering having done so at another time.

While Kyle demonstrated his ongoing relationship with a variety of unseen spirits and invisible worlds, his contact with angels was the most outstanding. He remarked excitedly, "Mollie, your angels are always with you in the playroom! You have dozens of them." Exuberantly he continued with his hands extended out to encompass the entire room, "There are lots of angels filling this whole room! Mom has lots of angels. My brother has lots, and dad has lots."

Even before James' death, Kyle's angel Velma went everywhere with their family. While she had been a family member for several years, Velma sadly disappeared when James died! Kyle described his loss, "Velma angel is in the angel hospital up in heaven. She's sick. She's with her family of angels. There's lots of different kinds. Every time they fly down and visit me. James is my one special angel. He stays with me all the time. James lives in our house, but he is just visiting. Velma came back to the world. She's not dead. She just moved back to her house in heaven for a while." In his healing play, Kyle unites two otherwise separate worlds—that of the seen and unseen, lending hope to a world greatly devoid of such numinous relationships.

Many more children, like Kyle, have dynamic relationships with unseen spirits and invisible worlds. Jane describes her angels, "I have angels who take care of me! There are at least three of them. Their names are Laurel, Nicole, and Mallory." Six-year-old Alex says that her fairy, which takes care of her, has a blue dress, green eyes, and pink wings. Thomas enjoyed a relationship with his grandmother, who was his spiritual companion who visited him all the time.

As to their resources, these girls and boys have at their disposal fascinating worlds of spirit that enrich their play. Their ability to see the unseen or to access worlds invisible to most adults provides an expansive support system that magnifies their potential for healing. Consequently, their dealings with trauma and loss take on a hopeful perspective.

At the same time their self-esteem may be poorly affected when their experiences or "truth" are not validated by the significant others in their lives. They may not only face lack of support, but disbelief and ridicule are common elements in their lives. As their integrity is undermined, they are likely to be ridden with anxiety, anger, hopelessness, powerlessness, and once again, a sense of isolation.

Fifth Branch – Light and Darkness, Good and Evil

The fifth branch on the Spiritual Tree of Life concerns children's sensitivity to the notions of light and darkness, good and evil. In their healing play they take on the role of spiritual warriors to help create a world of peace, harmony, and good will. They are compelled to design a battlefield wherein darkness is transformed into light and good defeats evil. They may play on this branch as super heroes, identifying perversion, destruction, and hate as evil forces they are compelled to overpower.

Sometimes the evil that boys and girls are fighting is both symbolic of someone or something that has set out to destroy them and represents an unbearable situation they have experienced. Occasionally, these children seem to have no reason to fight darkness in the world other than a natural tendency, often from birth, to be on a mission to save the world from the forces of evil. In all these boys' and girls' play, as the two opposing forces are eventually assimilated into one, they describe the evil they were fighting as "defeated" – meaning it no longer has power over them.

During several sessions Kyle rested steadfastly on the fifth branch. On at least one occasion, he insisted that I be a fairy who unlocked him from chains that were put there by the bad guys. Once he is unlocked, Kyle says, "The bad guys get me with a hook. I can't fight them, because they also took my gun away with the hook. They handcuffed my brother's arm to mine. Then I started to make a new house. I did what I had to do, and I played with my dog. Then my brother slid his hand out of the handcuffs. My brother and I both shot the bad guy's hand off and put the hook on him. It didn't work, because we did it all wrong. So we both threw the hook away. With the hook gone, the bad guy died and went away."

> During several sessions he (Kyle) ... acted out the role of a spiritual warrior compelled to create a battlefield where darkness is transformed into light and good defeats evil. Six-year-old Kyle spontaneously created the following picture. At the bottom of the large easel in the playroom he first drew a circle with a plus sign (+) inside of it. Connected to this circle and trailing upwards is what he referred to as a path. He said, "The circle with the plus sign inside is 'us' and we are OK, if we stay on the path where animals live, where there is a river, and lots of food, mostly in stores. We are safe there, until we get to the top of the path where there are more large circles, followed by similar circles surrounding the path." Pointing to the neighboring circles, Kyle said, "All of these circles are evil. It is all around us." He quickly added, "The food at the top of the path nearest the first circle of evil belongs to us, but it is being eaten by the evil ones." (Painton, 2007a, p. xxviii)

Jeremy is another child who, like Kyle, spends much of his time fighting the forces of evil. He is rare even among spiritual children on the fifth branch, as he is on a mission to save the world from the forces of darkness, even from an early age. He was a spiritual crusader in the purest sense of the word. As soon as he was able to speak, 18-month-old Jeremy enlightened our world in a most compelling way. "I am here to teach people. I teach everyone!" Years later as though it were a matter of life or death, he fought evil in the playroom and elsewhere for over 6 months. When he finally defeated the evil ones, he announced, "Now I'm free and I can take the stars and put them in my eyes, and my eyes sparkle, and all of me sparkles!"

The tremendous resources of children on the fifth branch include their gifted ability to be spiritual warriors who lovingly touch our world, softening the harshness of disparate forces of good and evil. While they determinedly promote peace and goodness, the energy they create is a life-sustaining force that is revitalizing to all of us.

On the other hand, by the very fact that they are compelled to overcome "darkness," they experience overwhelming anger, agitation, fear, frustration, and powerlessness. Their task is so daunting that they need a safe port to dock their ship and find refuge from the inevitable storm. While they are seeking support and understanding, they may be, more often than not, anxious that they will be rejected merely for their involvement in this frightening battle. As they journey through the dark waters, their loss of innocence, power, and hope may lead to depression.

Sixth Branch – Healing Play

On the sixth branch of the Spiritual Tree of Life children become focused on play that heals whatever distresses them. Their play stories are often metaphors that are not literal representations, but rather symbolic communications. In other words their metaphorical play is the language by which they implicitly convey their life story, along with their feelings and beliefs, in an amazingly meaningful and healing way. The healing play of spiritual kids comes from their intimacy with the truth, which is at the core of the spirituality of kids. Healing play as a spiritual process is boys' and girls' primary language. While they have an intrinsic ability to live within this spiritual realm, a great deal of their potential for wholeness lies within this branch.

While their play stories are at the heart of their enriched living, they are as powerful as what has actually happened to them in the "real" world. Girls and boys are able to transform their distressing stories in the nurturing milieu of a play setting, especially in the presence of a trained play therapist, who understands their inner spiritual worlds or intelligence.

Kyle's healing play involved the following, "All the farmers in Colorado will be washed away by a sand storm. The blue guy is me. He is getting sucked in by the sand storm, but he can dig his way out. Everyone can, so everyone is okay, but for now they are still getting sucked in. Sand storms are really bad! Then a big thing tried to stab our body parts, and the other guys. I think that's weird. Mollie, you and I will be on the same team. We are okay after the sand storm...right? Let's go to our house and have a celebration. We will have a ceremony. There's a trap box that I will stand on, because I don't speak very good. The trap box is my speaker box so everyone will hear me." In his healing play Kyle is celebrating his movement out of the sand storm of his grief, as well as that of his family's.

In addition to Kyle's story is that of a young girl whose parents were recently involved in a highly conflicted divorce. As her unique way of grieving and ultimately healing her wounds, she created a home with an idyllic family: a father, mother, and six children, who lived in a wonderful house, went to a great school and church, *never* fought, and did everything fun together *all* the time. Yet another story is that of Elizabeth, who has been physically abused by her babysitter. She plays out this sad story adding healing elements, such as her abuser is incapacitated one day, made to move far away, and later destroyed, while Elizabeth becomes powerful, playing as though she is the lion puppet, never again to be overcome by this perpetrator.

Interestingly, a boy whose sister was ill, created a family he referred to as "The First Family," who lived in the White House where his sister would *always* be protected by the soldiers. One more spiritual boy, whose father frequently visited him after recently dying, reached for the ghost figurine out of all the dozens of toys in the playroom. Keeping the connection with his father alive, he insisted that the ghost be a visitor in the play house along with his family and friends.

As healers in their play many spiritual children not only deal with their own concerns, but rather act as agents to help bring closure to their family's "unfinished business." Repeatedly, on their spiritual paths, children act as amazing sponges that soak up the unresolved pain. Because they are such creatures of love, their doors are open to honestly receive the truth of their existences, no matter how disturbing. Armed with this truth they go about their lives creating awareness and the need for change. They enlighten those near to them as they illuminate the issues hidden in the dark.

For instance, Rose repeatedly depicted the story of a young man who died in a fire. She added after a couple of weeks that the woman who was watching was finally able to say "Good-bye" to the man. When sharing my confusion about this play segment with Rose's mother, her eyes suddenly lit up, while she appeared both shocked and awestricken. I will never forget her amazing response! "I'm not sure what this could be about, except that when I was about six years old, my sixteen-year-old brother went to sleep while smoking in his bed, and he burned the house down, killing himself. I've always regretted the fact that I never said 'Good-bye' to my brother! But Rose knows nothing about this!"

In another case, my child client played that two babies had died! I was not too surprised when she did this, because her mother had recently miscarried. However, her daughter did not know anything about her pregnancy or miscarriage. Even more peculiarly, when I told the mother that I found it rather confusing that her daughter had played that *two* babies had died, rather than one, her face instantly flushed. She immediately disclosed to me that she had actually lost twins, but that no one, other than her doctor and the hospital staff, knew about this.

As catalysts for the expression and eventual healing of past wounds, boys and girls on the sixth branch stir up the issues "in the closet," so to speak, creating a powerful energy that will move those around them to expose their hidden or unconscious issues to the light of day. Once exposed, it is more likely that they will begin to honestly deal with their distress in a forthright fashion and eventually arrive at a place of peace and healing.

Children on the sixth branch of the Spiritual Tree of Life are fiercely imaginative individuals, who are natural creators of compelling metaphorical stories that are symbolic expressions of their lives. Through these stories they transform their troubled worlds, while softening the impact of their trauma by adding powerful elements to their play. In healing play they are their wisest, freest, and most balanced selves.

On the other hand, when overwhelmed by life events, children on this branch may suffer with poor self-esteem, feelings of insecurity, and hopelessness, while crying out in frustration for a safe place to creatively express their trauma, loss, or major adjustment.

Seventh Branch – Transformation

The seventh branch of the Spiritual Tree of Life holds within its supple boughs the agonizing journey children sometimes experience as they shed their old lives on the road to spiritual rebirth. Often having known abuse, exploitation, or neglect, these children feel alone and abandoned with nowhere to hide from their distress. They often play out themes of death that represent the devastation of their lives as they have known them. They are tormented by nightmares of mutilation, such as animals or monsters eating them, as well as fears of future losses. In their play they act out the trauma of their worlds falling apart, leaving them without a dependable foundation.

Resting with some apprehension on the seventh branch, children who have suffered deep losses and trauma, courageously find themselves in the depths of desperation and darkness. Their play is often represented by their interaction with skeletal or ghostly figures, or dismemberment of their dolls or superhero figures, all of whom are symbols of a frightening journey through an uncharted world of darkness. Their bravery and integrity allow them to successfully complete this challenging, and often excruciating, step toward healing themselves, along with their larger worlds and thus they gain a stronger, more authentic, sense of self.

Their new identity remains unshakeable until their life takes them to new crossroads, requiring more change and growth. In this process, boys and girls experience movement from an excruciating loss of everything to an unyielding recovery of their life force. At the end of this journey they find inner peace, as they build their new lives, with unearthed strength and vitality, on a strong spiritual foundation with all the richness of their never-ending resources.

Kyle played out stories of dismemberment and mutilation, as he traveled the agonizing road to spiritual rebirth. He was carrying a terrible burden of guilt about his brother, because they had fought only recently before James' death. He told me, "That was a bad day. It wasn't at all a fun day. James didn't want me to play with his castle. We had a big fight. I see pictures of us fighting every time I think of James. When James and I fought, things got broken. My stomach hurts. I begged my brother to forgive me for fighting with him over the castle?" Kyle paused adding sadly, "My heart is broken. James died, then there's no more fights."

Kyle also acted out the story of a shark that dismembered a woman's arm by eating it off. He ended his story with the assertion that now the woman is an angel. Immersed in his journey a couple of weeks later, Kyle was compelled to continue his story repeating, "The woman whose arm was eaten died. Then God turned her into an angel. Then he turned her back into a people and fixed her arm with a robot arm. Now her lives with a robot arm in a big house because she has a big family."

In close proximity to the session about the woman whose arm was torn off representing Kyle's powerlessness and upheaval, he enacted the play of a "dinosaur (symbolic of death) that took a big chunk out of one of the cavemen who didn't wear a shirt. When the police arrived, they turned the caveman's place into a jail." Kyle followed these sessions of mutilation and dismemberment by creating a safe home that symbolized a secure haven—a much needed retreat out of harm's way.

Luke much like Kyle, found himself in an agonizing situation. He felt he had lost his family when his baby sister was profoundly developmentally disabled from birth. Alone and abandoned as though his parents no longer cared about him. Luke was challenged to love, nurture, and feel compassion for one little girl, who had greatly robbed him of his peaceful life and nurturing home. He asserted that his happy home had become a "haunted, scary spooky house." As Luke and Kyle were struggling to survive the challenges of the seventh branch, Ashley and Michael were thrust into a painful journey of transformation as they lost contact with one another after Michael's sexual abuse was exposed. Ghosts, skeletons, and monsters haunted Ashley as her play was full of frightening events such as "scary picnics" with zombies that attacked her.

Boys and girls who journey through the seventh branch of transformation do so with honesty and courage, despite their heartache. Their journey strengthens their definition of self as well as their self-esteem, as they are transformed into extraordinary people with great resilience and in touch with incredible inner resources. They experience a deepening of spiritual depth and wisdom, an exaggerated desire and capacity for connection, and an awakened sensitivity to the pain of others.

During this difficult, yet enriching, transformation they are challenged to manage opposing forces within, such as love and caring versus anger and fear. Their insecurity as a part of feeling stripped of everything that is grounding to them, leads to a need for expression and validation, comfort, and support. As they redefine who they are in the light of their altered world, they may no longer have a will to live. Their spiritual and psychological turmoil are colored with the darkness of agonizing grief.

While playing on the Spiritual Tree of Life, children everywhere are hungering for support from spiritual partners on their unique journeys. They need significant adults in their lives, who are invested in their safety and wellbeing, to listen with a compassionate ear and communicate interest and acceptance of their innate spiritual nature or spiritual intelligence. While they share stories and information with these boys and girls, these spiritual partners are likely to benefit by allowing their own spirituality to blossom once again. Thus, spiritual partnership ignites a universal flame between adults and kids alike.

Bibliography

Axline, V. (1947). *Play therapy*. New York: Ballantine Books.
Baumeister, R. F. (1999). *Evil: Inside human violence and cruelty*. New York: Owl Books.
Campbell, J. (1988). *The power of myth*. New York: Doubleday.
Choquette, S. (1999). *Wise child: A spiritual guide to nurturing your child's intuition*. New York: Three Rivers Press.
Coles, R. (1990). *The spiritual life of children*. Boston: Houghton Mifflin Company.
Connolly, J. F. (1991). Adults who had imaginary playmates as children. In R. G. Kunzendorf (Ed.), *Mental imagery*. New York: Plenum Press.
Gardner, H. (1998). *Developing students' multiple intelligences*. Jefferson City, MI: Scholastic Inc.
Goleman, D. (1995). *Emotional intelligence*. New York: Bantam Books.
Gurian, M. (2002). *The soul of the child*. New York: Atria Books.
Hart, T. (2003). *The secret spiritual world of children*. Makawao, Maui, HI: Inner Ocean Press.
Hoff, B. (1992). *The Te of Piglet*. New York: Penguin Books.
Jung, C. (1963). *Memories, dreams, reflections*. New York: Random House.
Jung, C. (1968). *Man and his symbols*. New York: Dell Books.
Kubler-Ross, E. (1995). *Death is of vital importance*. New York: Station Hill Press.
Lama, D. (2001). *An open heart: Practicing compassion in everyday life*. New York: Little, Brown and Company.
May, G. (2004). *The dark night of the soul: A psychiatrist explores the connection between darkness and spiritual growth*. New York: HarperCollins.

Painton, M. (2007a). *Encouraging your child's spiritual intelligence.* Hillsboro, OR: Atria/Beyond Words.
Painton, M. (2007b). Inner worlds. *Rocky Mountain Parent Magazine, 12*(4), 18–19. Fort Collins, CO: Rocky Mountain Publishing.
Peck, M. S. (1985). *People of the lie.* New York: Simon & Schuster.
Schaefer, C., & O'Connor, K. J. (1983). *Handbook of play therapy.* New York: John Wiley and Sons.
Sinetar, M. (2000). *Spiritual intelligence: What we can learn from the early awakening child.* New York: Orbis Books.
Wolfelt, A. D. (1996). *Healing the bereaved child.* Fort Collins, CO: Companion Press.

Chapter 20
In Search of the Spiritual: Adolescent Transitions as Portals to the Spirit Self

Peter J. Perkins

Abstract Certain internal and external descriptions of youth during adolescence inspire inquiry into their development of the spiritual dimension. These descriptions are seen throughout developmental theories, while in clinical practice, there is growing interest in how the spiritual dimension may have promise, even urgency, in the key developmental years of adolescence. This chapter offers a selection of these developmental descriptions, my clinical observations, as well as first-hand accounts from youth themselves that support the call for education of the spiritual dimension during adolescent development. A holistic model of human development will be presented as a tool to set the context for adolescent education through mid- to late adolescence.

Opportunity for Deep Growth

Introduction

For many adults, recollections of adolescence conjure up a variety of responses, ranging from feelings of relief over its passing to sighs of recognition over the awkwardness of those first intimate relationships to unforgettable memories of risks taken with friends. I invite you to read this chapter with your own adolescent memories on your sleeve, ready to draw upon as we study and imagine the power of spirituality in the adolescent developmental journey.

Often 16-year-old boys and girls appear void of any spiritual dimension; rather, they seem steeped in their carnal awakenings and the discovery of material pleasures. This chapter suggests that, by stepping back a moment with a more holographic view, we can witness deeper manifestations of this developmental period—youth's essential odyssey toward becoming and more fully realizing their potential.

The theorists included here corroborate the wisdom of the youth with whom I have worked clinically, engaged in recreation or focus groups, and befriended over

---

P.J. Perkins (✉)
Global Learning Partners, Calais, Vermont 05648, USA
e-mail: peterp@globalearning.com

the years. These youthful illustrations give expression to the research and literature, suggesting that there is a real opportunity for youth to discover a portal into the spiritual dimension of life.

Description of Spirituality

In our most intimate public institutions of education, health care, and human service, we often find there is an important missing link. It is the link to the deeper or inner aspects of human development. It is access to the whole self including access to the non-material—the spiritual dimension.

The adolescent spirituality referenced here is the inner, felt experience of a connection to something greater than our thoughts, feelings, material existence or even the people and creatures with which we relate. It is described as energy and is defined uniquely by each of us. Our unique experiences essentially lead us all to a spiritual gestalt through the collective—an experience of something greater than our individual expressions of the spirit. This spiritual dimension resonates in many forms and results in varied impact on each individual life.

Everyone has a spiritual capacity from which to draw, while the twofold challenge often is becoming aware of it and learning how to access it. The spiritual has been part of the human condition from the beginning of time as evidenced by the suggestion of ancient belief in gods and goddesses (Eisler, 1987), religious practices, and rules of behavior all seen in early writings, archeological digs, or the history of humanity (Campbell, 1988). It is when and how one develops this capacity during adolescent development that is of most interest here.

In contrast to organized religious traditions, the spirituality we will explore in this chapter is secular in nature, personal in practice, hidden in each of us until tapped. Organized religion and its practices may well be the form some come to in order to develop their spiritual capacity, but not everyone taps into traditional religions to discover his or her inner dimension. For some, spirituality is deepened through a connection with nature, yogic breathing, spiritual teachers, meditation practices, or peak experiences. Many adolescents have not yet isolated their own spiritual experiences to allow for deeper exploration, and as a result they either resist or simply question organized religion. As a matter of fact, research (Wilson, 2004) with focus groups of middle to late adolescents in New England showed only 35% attended church regularly, while two-thirds of these youth also considered themselves to be religious. In addition, most (86%) considered themselves to be spiritual. One might infer that while these youth may recognize the value of spirituality and religion, they often have no guidance or opportunity to support an exploration of their spiritual dimension.

An adolescent on the journey to discover new opportunities is in the midst of a meaning-making time. He/she has to make sense of body changes, sexual feelings, deeper thoughts about the universe, ways to be in relationship to adults, or life's purpose—"Why am I here?" To make meaning is one basic element of spirituality.

Opportunities in Development

Much of our understanding of development focuses primarily on the cognitive development of the individual. This is sometimes complemented or enhanced by emotional, biophysical, psychosexual, psychosocial, or ego-specific development. Few writers directly discuss spiritual development as a determining aspect of the human developmental process.

More and more theorists approach the topic of development with ideas that reach beyond mechanistic explanations to focus on deeper systemic concepts that seem to reflect the real and complex life of a modern adolescent. When we recognize that the spiritual dimension is critical to healthy adolescent development, our thinking expands beyond categorical limitations.

Carl Jung (1933) acknowledges a deeper experience in development as he refers to the *consciousness of self*. He discusses this higher view of the self that youth can access in order to better understand who they are in order to grow a consciousness of life going on around them. The philosopher and psychologist William James (1952) describes the *Constituents of the Self* in his broad view of human development. He lays out three primary aspects of the self that are guided by what he calls pure ego: material self, social self, and spiritual self. Native American philosophy has long considered spiritual health as part of an individual's natural self-concept (Bopp, 1985). Spirituality is part of the icon of native teaching seen in the medicine wheel. Many Eastern philosophies such as Buddhism, Hinduism, and Sufism put great emphasis on the spiritual aspects of life. In these Eastern philosophies the spiritual dimension can hardly be distinguished from other aspects of being human. Even among the poverty and decay in Nepal, references and practices of the spiritual are everywhere in rituals, greetings, altars, icons, and simple day-to-day interactions.

In my 25 years of clinical practice as a substance abuse counselor with youth I have witnessed how significant the absence of the spiritual was for most of the youth with whom I worked. I found consistently that, although boys and girls could change their drug-taking behavior, it was not until they had experienced a deeper shift within themselves that more sustainable and more significant change would occur. It would not come from their thinking about the behaviors needed to change or from resolving the feelings they might have about their families as much as it would result from achieving a shifting perspective about themselves. This was often seen when they realized that maybe they are important in the world regardless of what their family says; maybe they do have a purpose in the world; maybe others do care about and need them; or that maybe life is about more than partying, drug taking, and sex. Call it what you will, but this deeper realization brought energy and hope into many youthful lives. It did not necessarily make everything all better, but it seemed to introduce a vitality and resilience that was not there previously.

On Adolescent Development

Introduction

In many ways spirituality is the experience of living one's life fully. It is the "human beingness" of life that Kegan (1982) describes. Joseph Campbell (1988) sets the stage for this adventure of exploring adolescent spirituality with this quote:

> People say that what we're all seeking is a meaning for life. I don't think that is what we're really seeking. I think that what we're seeking is the experience of being alive, so that our life experiences on the purely physical plane will have resonance within our own inner most being and reality, so that we actually feel the rapture of being alive (p. 3).

The rapture of being alive!—what a powerful segue into the busy and ever-changing world of the adolescent. Adolescents are truly in rapture with being alive. They could not hide it if they tried. Their lives are filled with exploited and missed opportunity after opportunity. It is a time for emerging completely out of the shell, shaking oneself off, and beginning to live with a true sense of one's own existence and control over that existence (Perkins, 1991).

Adolescence as a Spiritual Portal

Erik Erikson (1980) writes about adolescence as a crisis though not an affliction. This crisis characterizes the youthful development as an opportunity. Although there is a particular increase of internal conflict, this time possesses a high potential for growth and learning from the challenges presented. This potential is probably both the greatest beauty and tragedy of adolescence. Many who have embraced this potential by taking risks with what "could be" rather than what "appeared to be" have continually amazed adults with their successes, in what might otherwise have been written off as folly. While some adolescents explore their potential, others remain stuck, never moving beyond what is in front of them, not seeing the potential in moments, relationships, or decisions.

Italian psychologist, Vittorio Guidano (1987), indicates that adolescence is the beginning of a commitment to life. It is a time of new appraisal of the self. The world is actively "discovered" or experienced as volitionally imposing one's view upon reality, as opposed to passively "accepted" or experienced as adapting oneself to an externally defined view of the world as in childhood. Guidano goes on to discuss how adolescent integration experiences set the stage for future life span integration experiences. How a youth experiences the separation process, from the passive role of an infant or from the special parent relationship a child has known, will, to a large degree, determine separation patterns for the person in young adulthood and the rest of his/her life.

How those around her/him perceive the separation process itself will also influence life patterns. Carol Gilligan's perspective (1982) expands on the separation process of youth by suggesting that one knows oneself as separate only in being in connection with others. Along with that, one experiences relationship only to the degree that one can differentiate others from one's self. It is a wonderful moment for youth to come to the place in their development when they can recognize and even enjoy themselves being connected in meaningful ways to someone else while seeing both their uniqueness and separateness from that person. They can be intimate and still hold on to who they are as individuals. It is not necessary to give over the whole self and be what the other person wants; instead the individual comes to the place of knowing self through knowing another.

So when the adolescent moves through the natural process of separation, it can be a time of learning about the value of both attachment and separation and how these experiences can be meaningful. This experience of separation often results in a sense of alienation, arousing fear, and anger. This, Robert Kegan (1982) would say, stems from the natural fluctuations of the growth process, the duality of inclusion, and independence. This duality becomes the internal battle as one grows: "She loves me, she loves me not." The never-ending desire to be included in tension with a sense of too much inclusion rings the alarm for independence.

In adolescence we see a break in the time symmetry between past and future; an awareness of past and future develops, leading to life planning, future boundlessness, possibility, and even the feeling of immortality. Guidano (1987) uses the metaphor of the individual life span as a journey, with the "developmental pathway" being built during infancy and the preschool years. It is along the adolescent journey that youth recognize there is no turning back. The possibilities to the future are unending and one can plan for or manipulate these opportunities to achieve them. The future is a wide open highway. Note the recurrence of unrestrictive themes in music for adolescents such as wondering, openness in relationships, sexuality, drug use, traveling, movin' on, and riding down the highway.

Guidano joins with psychoanalytic theory in agreeing that the crucial aspects to life span development do not happen in the first 5 years of life. Rather, it is the integration of process that is or is not accomplished in adolescence. It is the genuine quality of this integration that most powerfully affects the life span developmental processes.

Furthermore, the adolescent is in a search for the "dynamic balance" of the "apparent self"—the way he/she behaves in situations, and the "real self"—the way he/she feels in situations, according to Guidano (1987). There is a constant struggle between being who one is versus being whom friends might want you to be.

There is also a balancing of the notions of "decentering and recentering" (Kegan, 1982). "Decentering from the world" is the experience of a newfound perception of oneness and uniqueness as separate from others. "Recentering on the self" is the pressure toward a steady commitment to that new unique sense of self. So adolescence is a time of tremendous balancing of all this new information about oneself and how one fits into the world. The adolescent tries balancing feelings and behaviors regarding her uniqueness, his oneness, the pressure to be him/herself, and the releasing from the old childhood self.

Jean Piaget (1958) calls adolescence the "metaphysical age par excellence." It is the time when one moves from the concrete thinking of childhood years ("concrete operational phase") to the abstract thinking processes ("formal operational phase"). The adolescent can reflect and speculate about concepts such as God, right and wrong, and ideals. He/she can distinguish between fantasy and reality.

This is a time where the formation of "identity" culminates according to Erik Erikson (1968). It is the first opportunity to become aware of the "self" as having control of one's destiny. It is a time for differentiating self from one's parents or siblings, for discovering what one thinks and feels about people, things, and issues. The question of "Who am I?" is prevalent.

Writing about youth, Carl Jung (1933) says "the individual finds himself (sic) compelled to recognize and to accept what is different and strange as a part of his own life as a kind of 'also I' " (p. 116). He seeks an identity bigger than him. Perhaps this at least partially explains teenagers' intrigue with the occult, heroes, mystery, rock and roll bands, dissidence, and anarchy. They are looking for that "also I," a larger identity beyond themselves. I would venture to say that this desire is present because the adolescent comes so abruptly into this new consciousness of self. Prior to this, as an infant and a child, he/she had been guarded, protected, dependent, and unconscious of his/her self.

Jung goes on to describe adolescence as a time of becoming conscious of problems in life. It would seem natural for a person at this point to seek company in order to diffuse the burden of the newly identified existence of problems. Identity is becoming clearer due in part to this new consciousness. He/she seeks comfort in relationships with peers who, at least to him/her, are the only ones who understand what it is he/she is feeling. The rest of the world (adults) is out of touch if not peculiar.

Jung (1950) puts his work on the phenomena of consciousness and soul immediately into perspective with these powerful words: "The art of life is the most distinguished and rarest of all the arts." He sees the human experience as something beyond simply observable, quantifiable, or even predictable. Like art, life develops through experience and reflection on that experience from one's unique perspective—one's soul. The main character, Cody (2007), in the film with the same title, shows her viewers this art in action as she explores relationship from her perspective as a pregnant teenager. Her soul deepens as the film progresses. Experience becomes the art of life.

Jung's metaphor has the "Dawn" of development finding the child to be essentially unconscious of problems around him/her. It is not until the "Morning" of youth that consciousness begins to develop; an awareness of the challenges, problems, and opportunities in life. The "Afternoon," or adulthood, is when conscious develops to its fullest with lots of doubts about oneself and the world and a recognition of being at "variance" with oneself; changing from who one thought one was to something new. Consciousness begins in youth and develops in adulthood. Adolescence bridges this divide between youth and adulthood and perhaps should be seen as the lunch hour of adolescence: a frenzied feeding indeed.

Holistic View of Adolescence

Meaning Making

Adolescents quickly and deeply respond to an invitation to explore the whole self. So much of their lives is spent in the superficial realms of their material worlds that they desire more in their lives. As an adolescent develops the search becomes increasingly about finding something more; finding meaning. It may be illusive and even unattainable, yet the search goes on. As one girl reflected during one of my short self-discovery workshops, "Wouldn't it be nice if my friends and I knew this much about each other? What we tell each other is just not deep like what we did here with strangers in half an hour."

During my own late teen years I hitch-hiked and drove many miles, meeting many youthful comrades who were looking for something. Often their comments were of a contemplative nature; they would express a longing for something more but were unable to articulate precisely what it was they sought: "...it was time to move on." When asked about their travels, a common response would be, "I don't know, just gotta' hit the road and see what I find ...," clearly a deeply felt and indefinable search for something different and in many something meaningful.

In early adolescence, there is certainly little to no overt awareness of the search for identity. There is, however, a tremendous amount of energy and excitement over the newfound feelings and sensations of being older and a bit more independent. It is often this first stage that catches a parent by surprise. Suddenly a daughter acts like she is her own person. A son makes many demands on how he will spend his free time.

These changes actually catch the young teenager by a bit of surprise. Like a child in a candy store, he/she is suddenly aware and overwhelmed by all the possibilities. It seems that an adolescent wants it all and assumes the right to have it all. This initial growth of self-awareness often comes in the early teen years with recognition of boundaries being both problematic and even advantageous. He/she begins to create boundaries in order to feel more comfortable in the chaotic world of early adolescence.

At a dinner with friends recently, I listened with amazement as my 14-year-old son described his own personal boundary at school, telling how he liked "fooling around in class at school just to the point that I won't get into too much trouble." He went on to describe his friends as not being the "cool group" or the "nerd group," but rather known as the group who likes to "have fun and not get too crazy."

By around 16 to 17 years of age, youth are generally quite ready to explore themselves more overtly. They have had some of the reckless experience of their earlier years from which to learn. They have already experienced tremendous emotions without necessarily understanding them. Mid-teens may know more about what they want, a little more about who they are as well as who they are not. There seems to be an opening toward self-awareness, a little more patience, and interest in deeper thoughts and ideas.

By about 19 years of age, they have experimented with many behaviors and feelings. They have pondered many things about their lives. They are beginning to realize there is life after high school. The desire to explore their deeper dimensions may increase dramatically and, if and when it does, rapid development of values and behaviors will lead into their first adventures with adulthood. There is a discovery of more than themselves in this bigger world. It is no coincidence that this is when youth are willing to join the armed services and fight a war, become political activists, or grow more outspoken about issues in the world. These older youth are playing out an important developmental challenge—a desire to make a difference in light of their feelings of immortality. *How old were you when you began to look for more meaning in your life?*

Build It and They Will Grow

There is much fertile ground to grow our work with holistic adolescent development. Solid theoretical conclusions speak to the urgency of adolescents accessing the resources they need to know themselves—to find that "also I" by expanding their view to include spiritual development.

In searching for a usable holistic view of human development for my work with youth and adults, I recalled the words of Kurt Lewin (1951): "There is nothing so practical as a good theory." But where was a good practical theory on human development from a holistic perspective? Theorists referred to the physical or material self as psychosexual, biophysical, or biological aspects of development. The intellectual or thinking self is referred to as cognitive processes, cognitive complex, personal cognitive organization, or ego. The social or community self is called psychosocial, social, or moral. The emotional or feeling self is referred to as affective, psychological, or as in emotional states. And the spiritual or conscious self is marginally referred to as self-awareness, consciousness of the self, or self-actualization. Collectively these theorists create a model of human development that suggests a multidimensional view of what it is to be a human being. Each dimension is reflected in specific theories that have proven to assist people in understanding aspects of themselves.

Five Dimensions of the Self

The *Five Dimensions of the Self* (Perkins, 1990) is an inclusive model of human development that describes our thinking and feeling processes, our material and human relationships, and our spiritual nature. Each dimension can be described, examined, and experienced individually, while in actuality all five dimensions are interconnected and do not operate in a vacuum; rather, they exist as a plethora of capacity in all of us. We are organic and open complex systems that draw on multiple resources. This model of *Five Dimensions of the Self* is a way to name and honor

The Five Dimensions of the Self: A Way of Looking at Ourselves (Perkins 1990)

Thinking self (mind)

Feeling self (heart)   Material self (body/stuff)

Spiritual self (non-material)   Social self (family/friends/community)

Fig. 20.1 The Five Dimensions of the Self: a way of looking at ourselves (Perkins, 1990)

the capacities that we all have. Capacities exist but they do not automatically come alive. They need to be acknowledged, nurtured, drawn out, developed, and affirmed (Fig. 20.1).

The Thinking Self: What Goes on in My Brain or Mind?

The thinking self is the dimension we rely on to consider possibilities and ultimately make decisions. It helps us create a perception of our world and how it operates. How we experience our world may well be created through our thoughts about it. The deepening thoughts of an adolescent often incite emotions of excitement, confusion, dismay, and frustration. The mind then draws conclusions from all the information it has about what is reality. Because the mind of the adolescent is not yet fully developed, the reality created in the mind of youth may well not be accurate.

To simply notice thoughts that pass through the mind, sometimes at a million miles per hour, is a critical step to distinguishing thoughts that are true about oneself from those that do not fit self-image. This sorting begins to help an adolescent stabilize his/her behavior and be more balanced in acting as he/she really wants to act as opposed to how others may want him/her to act. Journeying through adolescence, youth explore thoughts about fairness, injustice, politics, fun, how others view them, getting what they want when they want it, the universe, meaningfulness, and more immediate needs such as appearance and peers.

The thinking self has tremendous influence during the adolescent years with so many conflicting thoughts and desires leading to behaviors that may be peculiar, risky, and unpredictable. With more life experience and increased self-awareness this dimension begins to be more congruent. The balance of the apparent self and the real self begins to emerge so that the adolescent may act as he/she thinks and feels is right. *What thoughts dominated your mind at eighteen?*

The Feeling Self: What Goes on in My Heart?

An adolescent's feeling self is the dimension that helps him/her experience the quality of life. It recognizes deep and shallow responses to experiences and gives emotional description to it. It might be a quick angry reaction with little thought behind it when reacting out of pure emotion. It may be a thoughtful compassionate response that balanced the thinking and feeling self. Access to honest emotions challenges everyone. We are often told to put away feelings in exchange for rational thoughts.

It is common to confuse our thoughts with our feelings by describing feelings as thoughts, i.e., *I feel you are a good person*, rather than, *I feel so comfortable around you because you warm my heart*. Feelings can get masked by our thoughts. Learning to express the feeling self effectively brings a fuller experience to life and clarifies how thoughts and experiences feel to us and lead us to certain reactions. Through emotional responses to life, youth find a voice or expression for their chaotic experience. Consider an emotional, even bizarre outburst you may have witnessed from a teenager. There may be lots of confusion and there is likely rationale behind it. *How did you deal with strong feelings in early adolescence?*

The Material Self: What About My Body and All My Stuff?

Experiencing the adolescent world through the material self draws immediately on body sensation and image, life-support materials (headsets, iPods, and particular fashions), and physical expression through movement (sports and dance). What one sees (or thinks one sees) is what one gets. This perception of oneself in the world and the life circumstances that influence that perception together play a powerful role in developing the material self.

Our material perception also sets up our emotional responses to things in the world. That is to say, if I think I am fine just the way I am, an emotional response to life will most likely be from a confident perspective; for example, the adolescent who tells a friend offering a marijuana joint to smoke that he does not want to smoke it. In doing so, he is not afraid the friend will no longer be a friend. From a position of confidence, the notion of peer pressure is insignificant. Good material choices in adolescence come from a perception of confidence in being satisfied with who one is. On the other hand, for the adolescent who thinks of the self as not good enough, an emotional response that may follow is insecurity, leading to unhealthy choices. Peer pressure thrives when lack of confidence influences poor choice-making—smoking that pot even though it is not wanted; when fears dwarf confidence and reason.

The material life of an adolescent focuses on body image and possessions, "my stuff" as one 19-year-old put it in one of my workshops. What we wear—clothes, jewelry, or hair style—makes a statement to others about whom we are or what we believe. The emotional and social need to look a certain way, to feel a part of a peer group, or make a certain political statement determines the physical manifestation of this need. Tattoos, body piercing, hairstyles, or choice of clothing all can be deliberate ways to say "I am me," "I am different," "I believe a certain way of thinking," and "I am part of a certain group." However, the visible choices youth make regarding body and clothing often precedes their consciousness of a bigger process of identity development. Instead of a cognitive decision to be themselves, it is a reaction coming from the emotional need to be part of a group. This is what can lead to personal beliefs being compromised, such as choosing inappropriate or unsafe sexuality, drug use, gang membership, and criminal activity, since the need for belonging can dominate so much at this time of life. Photographer Carley Stevens-Mclaughlin (2002) captured thoughts about the adolescent material self, as with the following statement by "Travis," a male teen:

> I never considered myself gothic. I don't like to be categorized; I like to be myself. Everyone's different. Even if people dress the same it doesn't mean they're the same in anyway except appearance. I would wear dresses or skirts to school if there weren't people who would really dislike that and probably abuse me for it.

What was your' relationship to material possessions as a teen?

The Community Self: How I Connect with Others in the World

The adolescent community self is the dimension that draws on both peer and adult relationships influencing who one becomes throughout life. The community self is made up of relationships to people and the environment. It is through social interactions that we find meaning and opportunity and how healthy or unhealthy behaviors can be reinforced. Meaningful work gets recognized, leading to civic responsibility, and a sense of responsibility for self. The development of peer relationships through friends and lovers grows very strong, especially in early adolescence. The importance of peer relationships seems to diminish some in strength and intensity as independence is realized in later years. Intimate relationships, however, seem to continue and even deepen.

The larger community of friends and other relationships may vary in scope and intensity but are central to survival in an unfolding world. The discovery of the self and of the bigger world beyond childhood brings many other people into the adolescent world. Friends become essential for support and camaraderie as well as simple distraction, comfort, and fun. For the typical adolescent, friends may be seen as the only ones who understand what he/she is thinking. There is an urgency driving his/her belief that adults simply cannot know "what it is like for me. I must be with my friends now!" However, an apparent contradiction arises in that adolescents simultaneously have a growing desire to be recognized and engaged by adults; but the adolescent's peer bonds often dominate because of the lack, or perceived lack, of adults reaching out to engage and to recognize youth in a meaningful way.

Skills such as communication, conflict management, and self-expression and the desirable traits of good judgment and a sense of humor develop through social interaction and allow the individual to live a healthy life. *Which adults, other than parents, were important to you? What made them important?*

The Spiritual Self: What Goes on in My Soul?

The adolescent spiritual self varies for each person and is unlike the other dimensions in quality of description. When youth describe their spiritual self they tell of deep and very personal things such as their relationship to nature, music, their soul, God, their dead relatives, or feelings for which they can find no words. It seems to be the one aspect of ourselves that plays a role in each of the other dimensions. It may be the glue that holds all the dimensions together. It may be a religious form for some. It may be an earth-based form for others and even formless yet for others A common ingredient is relationship to something greater than only one's self; as described in Alcoholic Anonymous as the *Higher Power*. It is that non-material dimension of the self that is elusive and difficult to capture in description.

Exploring the self more deeply within, youth will describe an inner life that is a source of calmness, safety, comfort, and even guidance. It becomes evident through music, writing, sitting and thinking, talking with friends and, for some, a relationship with a higher being. It gets described as an energy that moves one to do good and to be interconnected with others. It is part of a bigger energy of some kind. One 16-year-old described his understanding of the soul as "It is like an inner body that tells you what to do." A high school senior girl described spirituality as "the morals that affect your thinking and your decision-making."

The inner world of the adolescent is alive. It may be dormant from a lack of self-awareness, yet it can be awakened with the right opportunity. From focus groups which I facilitated with various high risk (homeless, runaway, in state custody, gay, lesbian, or questioning) youth exploring spirituality (Wilson, 2004), a pregnant teen said "You have to believe in something. You don't know if it's really there or not. You can't see it or touch it, but you just have to believe" (p. 31). An 18-year-old male reflected, "I am only on this earth for a short period of time; If I can make somebody smile, even if my life is feeling like hell, at least I made somebody feel good about themselves" (p. 31).

"I am trying to figure that out right now – what it is we're living for. Like, why? It's really a hard thing for me, because it doesn't make any sense why people live for the things they do," a 17-year-old female thoughtfully considered (p. 31).
When did you first think about your spirituality?

A Context for Educating Youth

For the adolescent, there is fear, excitement, and tremendous conviction about the more mysterious aspects to life. The mysteries of the inner life rarely find opportunity to be explored through any means. The spiritual self often lacks exploration even with family, in peer conversations, or in youth programs and educational settings. When it does find its way into conversation, it seems to consistently resonate strongly through diverse thoughts about God or energy, a range of feelings like conviction or doubt, as well as physical reactions of quiet stillness or raucous dance.

Youth have the resources to look deeply at themselves; stand back and assess themselves; see their journey as an exciting opportunity to get to know the self; and find the portals into their self-discovery. Adults can help youth to find these portals as long as they too have done this internal exploration. Education that draws on the known to explore the unknown is at the heart of what Jane Vella (2002) calls Dialogue Education. It is through this kind of dialogue that we help youth first acknowledge what they already know or think they know and then move them deeper into their own understanding of the spiritual in their lives. The Five Dimensions of the Self provide a context to have the dialogue with youth about the whole self. We can start with the assumption that we all have all the capacities of all five dimensions. From there, exploring each dimension briefly leads to a dialogue about how they interconnect, moving on to what the spiritual can really look or feel like. I find youth will consistently delve into this kind of dialogue if we honor what they do indeed perceive regarding the spiritual before we facilitate in guiding them to what they may not know.

Consider how you describe each of your Five Dimensions of Self. Which are most prominent right now and which were least present during your adolescent years?

Adolescent Spiritual Self

How Does an Adolescent Make Sense of Spirituality?

A 16-year-old girl at the Alternative High School in Montpelier, Vermont (Perkins, 1991), wrote about her understanding of spirituality in a self-assessment at one of my workshops:

> My understanding of spirituality is ... life and your conscience which is the door way to God and to your soul and you can find it in anything you see beauty in. Love, music, colors, friends, God, thoughts, people, woods, feelings, yourself (p. 45).

These words are evidence that she is certainly familiar with the complexity of the concept of spirituality and knows where she can experience it in her life. She describes with ease many aspects of spirituality.

So let us now return to some of the theorists' points of view which support adolescent spiritual development. Erikson (1980) writes about the high "growth potential" of adolescence and as it being the time when the formation of her identity culminates. Spirituality inspires further growth potential and informs a youth's identity. So when the spiritual dimension is explored, we see deep and sustainable growth. When you meet a teenager who has this deeper sense of self you see it in his/her body, hear it in his/her words, sense it in his/her presence, and feel it in his/her compassion.

Guidano (1987) writes about adolescence as beginning a time of commitment to life; a time of first recognizing the differentiation of past and future; and a discovery of the uniqueness of the self and how one experiences oneself and is experienced by others in the world. A teenager needs this commitment to his/her life in order to give it meaning and direction. The search for meaning and direction can lead to discovering his/her spiritual sense of life. Meaning begins to take shape with this larger view of life—a view beyond one's material self alone.

Gilligan (1982) speaks of the value of attachment in relationship. In the spiritual sense it may be the youth's attachment to beliefs that fit who he/she thinks he/she is.

It may be attachment to a teacher or deity that gives a comforting relationship that he/she can rely on in difficult times.

Piaget (1958) refers to adolescence as a time when abstract thinking, reflection, and speculation begin. Spiritual discovery requires reflection or inner exploration. Many religious and secular practices support this kind of discovery—prayer, ritual, mediation, yoga, writing, or music. At a large high school in Vermont the health education curriculum has included mediation and yoga (www.talkaboutwellness.org, 2007). The students and faculty have embraced this opportunity in numbers exceeding what any of the school personnel could have imagined. The school recently sought funding for more yoga mats to meet the increasing demand. Youth long for time to reflect quietly and deeply as well as speculate about their lives.

Jung (1933) also emphasizes the discovery of what is different and strange about one's life but goes on to include the adolescent search for a connection to something else, the "also I." Youth dream. They look to potential and opportunity. They need to be part of something bigger than themselves. When given time to reflect and speculate on their spiritual dimension they can see how it can provide an "also I." It opens new doorways of understanding and ways of being in the world.

Youthful changes are acknowledged in some cultures through organized religion. The Jewish Bar Mitzvah and the Christian confirmation are two rituals that acknowledge this time of change for youth in early adolescence. In both of these there comes recognition of the young person by adults in the respective communities. Along with social and cultural affirmation, there is often a spiritual acknowledgment that manifests in these practices. In American Indian practices there is the Circle of Courage (Brendtro, 1990) that explores the spiritual nature of life.

Conclusion and Openings

All in all, adolescence is a monumental time of transition from childhood into adulthood when important thinking processes and emotional responses develop. Youth can come to consciousness and self-awareness and discover their identity. It is a time to begin looking outside of the self and to recognize the self as an active participant in the world—choosing sides with issues of importance. These powerful developmental events unfold in adolescent bodies, hearts, minds, and souls and especially in relationship to others in their lives. Adolescent development persists from about age 11 on into the late twenties and even thirties in some cases. Along this span of life are many portals into the spiritual dimension for these high energy and vulnerable youth. Portals will vary depending upon the path chosen as youth step cautiously through these turbulent years. They may have healthy or unhealthy beliefs and behaviors. They may delve into drug use, deeper relationships, sexuality, travel, new ways of being in the world, provocative questioning, deep listening, the natural wilderness, yoga or meditation, the mind–body–spirit connection, and/or explore other portals into the spiritual self.

One of my most influential spiritual portals came in Old Snowmass, Colorado, at the age of 19. I was growing weary of all the drug use and shallow relationships. I was looking for something more in this beautiful fun-loving valley. I signed up for a weekend retreat called "The Art of Loving" that a friend of mine was facilitating. This opportunity opened to me without my seeking; it just came to me and it was clear that I should step into it—a portal into myself. I left that intense weekend changed forever, especially in terms of how I viewed myself in the world. I differentiated myself from others in my life—even from my family and my best friend. To this day I count that portal as key to my personal growth. Prior to that event, drugs, sex, and Colorado were all that was on my mind.

Adolescents are prime candidates for the discovery of their spiritual selves. They may be developing this part of themselves as these changes are being experienced; or as their identity becomes more explicit; discovering their spiritual self. Adolescent youth are emerging from an identity with parents only to discover that there is a "cruel, crazy, beautiful world" (Clegg, 1990) out there, which is scary and wonderful all at the same time. They need much support to help them make this discovery within themselves.

As one parent ruminated about how she might help youth after she attended the Spirituality of Prevention Conference in Fairlee, Vermont (1994, p. 3). "I am. I'm worthy. I'm released from the earthly expectation. I'm acceptable. There is reason. If we were able to instill this in our youth, would they have the need to try to escape? Spiritually loving fully, completely, accepting all others for who they are without judgment. I pray that this will be ours and our children's way of life."

According to my clinical observations with youth in multiple settings, adolescents do wonder about the meaningfulness of life. They are interested in spirituality and what it means to them. They generally believe in God, life and death, willpower, right and wrong, and love. Several youths describe spirituality in complex ways. Based on their feedback, it is clear that this is important to them. It can act as that part of themselves that provides consistency and a sense of inclusion. It is also closely related to self-esteem. The more one takes charge of her life with a confident self-perception and embraces it, the more likelihood there is of having high self-esteem. Spirituality can either be a catalyst for this self-acceptance or an outcome of it.

In conclusion, the words one teenager provided on her workshop evaluation (Perkins, 1991) show how, when given the opportunity to explore the deeper dimensions of the self, adolescents are ready and waiting. She described what she liked about the spirituality workshop: "What I realized in myself that I didn't know" (p. 49). This statement emphasizes how important it is that we listen to and support youth in their developmental process and that we recognize spiritual development as part of that process. We can help them start with what they know and move them into an open dialogue about what they can know.

Bibliography

Berry, T. (1988). *The dream of the earth*. San Francisco, CA: Sierra Club Books.
Bopp, J., Bopp, M., Brown, L., & Lane, P. (1985). *The sacred tree*. Lethbridge, AB: Four Worlds Development Press.

Brentro, Larry K., M. Brokenleg, S. Van Bockern, (1990) National Educational Service, Bloomington, Indiana.
Bronowski, J. (1971). *The identity of man*. Garden City, NY. American Museum Science Books.
Campbell, J. (1988). *The power of myth: With Bill Moyers*. New York: Doubleday.
Capra, F. (1982). *The turning point: Science, society, and the rising culture*. New York: Simon & Schuster.
Clegg, J. & Savuka. (1990). Album entitled *"Cruel, crazy, beautiful world"*.
Cody, Diablo, (2007) Juna, Fox Searchlight Pictures.
Eisler, R. (1987). *The chalice and the blade*. New York: Harper and Row.
Erikson, E. H. (1968). *Identity: Youth and crisis*. New York: W.W. Norton Co.
Erikson, E. H. (1980). *Identity and the life cycle*. New York: W.W Norton Co.
Freud, S. (1961). *The future of an illusion*. New York: W.W. Norton Co.
Freud, S. (1949). *An outline of psychoanalysis*. New York: W.W. Norton Co.
Fromm, E. (1956). *The art of loving*. New York: Harper and Row.
Gilligan, C. (1982). *In a different voice*. Cambridge, MA: Harvard University Press.
Guidano, V. (1987). *Complexity of self*. New York: Guilford Press.
Helminiak, D. A. (1989). Self-esteem, sexual self-acceptance, and spirituality. *Journal of Sex Education and Therapy, 15*(3), 200–210.
James, W. (1952). *The principles of psychology*. Chicago: William Brenton Encyclopedia Britannica, Inc.
Jung, C. (1933). *Modern man in search of a soul*. New York: Harcourt, Brace and World.
Kegan, R. (1982). *The evolving self*. Cambridge, MA: Harvard University Press.
Kohlberg, L. (1969). Stage and sequence: The cognitive developmental approach to socialization. In D. Goslin (Ed.), *Handbook of socialization theory and research*. New York: Rand McNally.
Lewin, K. (1951). *Field theory in social science*. New York: Harper.
Loevenger, J. (1976). *Ego development*. San Francisco, CA: Jossey-Bass.
Maier, H. W. (1978). *Three theories of child development*. New York: Harper and Row.
Marx, K. (1844). Religion, the opium of the people. In J. Pelikan (Ed.), *The world treasury of modern religious thought*. Boston: Little, Brown and Co.
Maslow, A. H. (1954). *Motivation and human personality*. New York: Harper and Row.
May, G. G. (1982). *Will and spirit*. New York: Harper & Row.
Perkins, P. (1990). *EDAP: Facilitator's guide*. Montpelier, VT: Washington County Youth Service Bureau.
Perkins, P. (1991). *Human development assessment*. Santa Barbara, CA: Dissertation. Fielding Institute.
Perkins, P. (1997). *Adolescence. ah what a wild time!* Revised version. Vermont.
Perkins, P. (2003). *Five dimensions of the self*. Revised version. Vermont.
Piaget, J. (1958). *The growth of logical thinking from childhood to adolescence*. New York: Basic Books.
Prigogine, I. (1973). Irreversibility as a symmetry-breaking process. *Nature, 246*, 67–71.
Schuster, C. S., & Ashburn, S. S. (1980). *The process of human development: A holistic approach*. Boston: Little, Brown and Co.
Stevens-Mclaughlin, C. (2002). *Public faces private places: Photographs and interviews*. Vermont: National Institute for Community Innovations.
Spirituality of Prevention. (1994). *Conference participant thoughts and inspirations*. Prevention Unlimited. Vermont
Tylor, E. B. (1973). *Primitive culture: Researches into the development of mythology, philosophy, religion, language, art, and custom* (2nd ed.). London: John Murray.
Vella, J. (2002). *Learning to listen learning to teach: The power of dialogue in educating adults*. San Francisco, CA: Jossey Bass.
Wilson, M. (2004). *New England network for children, youth and families*. Burlington, Vermont.

Chapter 21
Reflection for Spiritual Development in Adolescents

Charlene Tan

Abstract Adolescence is a period characterised by a personal quest for purpose, meaning and relationships. This chapter distinguishes between religiously "tethered" and "untethered" conceptions of spirituality. The former is linked to or housed within the tradition of a religious faith, while the latter is concerned with beliefs and practices that are disconnected from religions. This chapter proposes that reflection is effective in promoting spiritual development in adolescents so that they can derive personal destiny and direction; develop their personal identity and ethical worldview; and build relationships with others. Given that adolescents are at the crossroads of life and face many issues and challenges that are unique, uncertain and value-conflict, they need to critically reflect on practical interests and examine broad issues on religiously tethered and untethered spirituality in their lives.

Introduction

Confronted with issues and concepts that are embedded in existential and transcendent realms, adolescents undergo major identity transformations during this period of life (Erikson, 1968; Benson, Roehlkepartain, & Rude, 2003; King & Boyatzis, 2004). They experience great ambiguity and uncertainty as they move beyond an absolute form of knowing based on authority towards multiple perspectives, critical self-awareness and construction of one's own beliefs and values (Love, 2001). Students in late adolescence in particular experience "heightened sensitivity about personal identity, relationships, ideology, and decisions about the future" when "concerns about individual purpose, meaning, and commitment interact with forces of cognitive development, maturation, and social expectations" (Dalton, 2001, p. 18).This chapter proposes that reflection is effective in promoting spiritual

---

C. Tan (✉)
Policy and Leadership Studies, National Institute of Education, 1 Nanyang Walk, Singapore 637616
e-mail: charlene.tan@nie.edu.sg

development in adolescents so that they can derive personal destiny and direction; develop their personal identity and ethical worldview; and build relationships with others.

Spirituality and Spiritual Development

It is important, at the outset, to distinguish between religiously "tethered" and "untethered" conceptions of spirituality (Alexander & McLaughlin, 2003). The former is linked to or housed within the tradition of a religious faith. It "takes its shape and structure from various aspects of religion with which it is associated and that make it possible for us to identify criteria for 'spiritual development' " (Alexander & McLaughlin, 2003, p. 359). Religion here is defined as an organised and shared system of beliefs and practices related to a transcendent entity such as God, higher power or ultimate truth or reality, and is closely linked to a particular faith institution (Reich, Oser, & Scarlett, 1999; Koenig, McCullough, & Larson, 2001; Love, 2001; Chae, Kelly, Brown, & Bolden, 2004; King & Boyatzis, 2004). Religiously untethered spirituality, on the other hand, is concerned with beliefs and practices that are disconnected from religions. This form of spirituality is not associated with any named supernatural power, institutionalised doctrines, or religious affiliations. It is about *transcendence*—where one reflects on things pertaining to one's spirit or soul. It propels the search for personal meaning, purpose and identity in life, connectedness with others (whether divine or human), and a commitment to contribute to others. In terms of the search for meaning, personal cultivation, manifestations of spirituality in life, responses to aspects of the natural and human world, and the collective domain, religiously untethered spirituality tends to be unstructured, less specific, more open-ended and diffused (Alexander & McLaughlin, 2003).

Spiritual development is a process of self-transcendence where the individual is an active agent in shaping his or her own spiritual growth (Benson et al., 2003; King & Boyatzis, 2004). Dowling et al. (2004) define adolescent spirituality as "seeing life and living in new and better ways, taking something to be transcendent or of great value, and defining self and relation to others in ways that move beyond the petty or material concerns to genuine concern for others" (p. 7). That adolescents show a high interest in spirituality is seen in the Search Institute's survey of 218,000 6th- to 12th-grade youth in public schools during the 1999–2000 school year in the United States. The survey informed us that 69% of 6th- to 12th-grade youth reported that "being religious or spiritual" is at least somewhat important, and 54% said it is quite or extremely important (cited in Benson et al., 2003, p. 208). In Singapore, adolescents have also increasingly turned to religion. According to Population Census 2000 for youth aged 15–24, Buddhism rose from 29.1% in 1990 to 38.9% in 2000 while Islam saw a slight increase of 0.9% from 17.7% in 1990 to 18.6% in 2000 (National Youth Council, 2007). The interest in religion is evident in the high percentage of religious conversions among adolescents. A survey by *The Straits Times* on 622 Singapore residents aged 15 and above showed that 27% of believers were converted when they were below 15 years old, 19% were converted when they were aged 15–19 years old, 26% between 20 and 24, and 12% when they were aged 25–29 years old (cited in National Youth Council, 2007). Love and Talbot (1999, p. 364) identify the following characteristics of spiritual development (SD):

1. Spiritual development (SD) involves seeking personal authenticity, genuineness and wholeness as an aspect of identity development.
2. SD involves continually transcending one's current locus of centricity.
3. SD involves developing a greater connectedness to self and others through relationships and union with community.
4. SD involves deriving meaning, purpose and direction in one's life.
5. SD involves increasing openness to exploring a relationship with an intangible and pervasive power or essence that exists beyond human existence and rational human knowing.

In short, spiritual development helps adolescents to derive personal destiny and direction; develop their personal identity and ethical worldview; and build relationships with others.

The Concept and Nature of Reflection

To see how reflection in spirituality is relevant to adolescents, it is instructive to clarify the concept and nature of reflection. Dewey (1933) defines reflection as the active, persistent, and careful consideration of any belief or supposed form of knowledge in the light of the grounds that support it and the further conclusions to which it tends. It involves a cycle of paying deliberate attention to one's own action in relation to intentions so as to expand one's options and make decisions about improved ways of acting. Dewey (1933) identifies three characteristics of a reflective learner: open-mindedness, whole-heartedness, and intellectual responsibility. Dewey views open-mindedness as the freedom from the prejudice, partisanship and other such habits as close the mind, and the willingness to consider multiple or novel ideas. It focuses on the learner's self-examination of aims, beliefs, assumptions and actions. This is premised on the belief that one's own experiences and knowledge are essential to reflection (Schon, 1987). This process of self-evaluation requires the learner to be open-minded.

Whole-heartedness refers to the genuine enthusiasm to channel one's mental, emotional and physical resources to resolve a problem (Dewey, 1933). It is essential for the learners to examine, frame and attempt to solve the dilemmas that one faces. Finally, intellectual responsibility refers to the consideration and adoption of the consequences of any proposed plan (Dewey, 1933). A reflective learner is one who constantly reviews and changes his or her goals and actions. Such reflection empowers the learners to connect the insights gained from the reflective process to changes they are making in real life.

There are two continua along which conceptions of the notion of reflection are located (McLaughlin, 1999; Tan, 2008a). The first continuum refers to the nature of reflection, while the second continuum refers to the scope and objects of reflection. McLaughlin (1999) identifies one view of reflection which stresses the explicit and the systematic, and one that emphasises the implicit and the intuitive. The type of reflection that is explicit and systematic involves "technical reason" or what Schon called "technical rationality". Under this notion, the focus of reflection is on possessing the technical knowledge and skills to apply to routinisable and pre-specifiable procedures and strategies. McLaughlin associates this to Aristotle's notion of *techne* which is "an activity of making or production (*poesis*), aimed at a pre-specifiable and durable outcome (a product or state of affairs) which constitutes its purpose (*telos*)" (McLaughlin, 1999, p. 12).

At the other end of the continuum is a type of reflection that is implicit and intuitive based on the ideas of Schon (1987). Arguing that one's daily decisions require judgements which go beyond the technical, Schon points out that they involve "reflection in action" which is tacit and intuitive. Given that adolescents face many issues which are unique, uncertain and value-conflicted, they need to set, frame, construct and solve problems based on their reflective judgements. McLaughlin (1999) sees a parallel between Schon's account of reflection and Aristotle's *praxis* which "involves the engagement of persons in activity with others which is non-instrumental in that it is not intended to realise goods 'external' to the persons involved but rather excellences characteristic of a worthwhile form of life" (pp. 14–15). *Praxis* requires "a kind of knowledge that was more personal and experiential, more supple and less formulable than the knowledge conferred by *techne*" (Dunne, 1993, p. 10, cited in McLaughlin, 1999, p. 15). Aristotle describes the knowledge of *praxis* as *phronesis* (or practical wisdom) which is a major ordering agency in our lives.

While the first continuum focuses on the nature of reflection, the second continuum along which views of reflection can be located refers to the scope and objects of reflection. McLaughlin distinguishes between reflection that involves specific and proximate matters, and that which involves general and contextual ones. The former relates to the present and particular concerns of the adolescents, while the latter focuses on matters viewed from a broader and less immediate perspective. These may include the overall aims and purposes of one's life, and questions of a philosophical, psychological, social and political kind.

McLaughlin's distinctions between the explicit and systematic versus the implicit and intuitive (in terms of the nature of reflection), and the specific and proximate versus the general and contextual (in terms of the scope and objects of reflection), are echoed by other writers. Elliot (1993) contrasts two main types of reflection: reflection that focuses on technical interest, and reflection that focuses on practical interest. Describing the first type of reflection as non-problematic, impersonal and non-critical, he notes that it involves clear and unambiguous standards, impersonal means-ends rules as the source of standards and instrumental thinking. On the other hand, reflection that has a practical interest involves intrinsically problematic standards, regards the person as the source of standards, and promotes critical self-reflection. The former serves a technical interest in controlling and predicting the material and social environment, while the latter serves a practical interest in acting consistently with human values. While McLaughlin, Schon and Elliot identify two main types of reflection, van Manen (1977, 2002) proposes three levels of reflectivity: technical reflection, practical reflection and critical reflection. Technical reflection is concerned with techniques and strategies for specific goals, while critical reflection examines broader ethical issues. Situated between these two types of reflection is practical reflection which goes beyond looking at skills, strategies and rules to question the goals themselves. Louden (1991) highlights four forms of reflection, from technical reflection at one end of the spectrum to critical reflection at the other end. The other two types of reflections are personal reflection which focuses on one's own life, and problematic reflection which aims at the resolution of the problems of professional action as explicated by Schon's account of the reflective practitioner (Elliot, 1993).

King and Kitchener's (1994) three levels of reflective thinking are also helpful for us to understand the stages of reflection. The first level is pre-reflective thinking (levels 1, 2 and 3) where the individuals justify their opinions in a simple fashion because they fail to perceive that answers to the problem at hand must contain some elements of uncertainty. Such learners often view the problems they face as having a high degree of certainty and completeness. The next level is quasi-reflective thinking (levels 4 and 5) where the individuals recognise that knowledge claims about ill-structured problems contain elements of uncertainty. While they can acknowledge differences between well- and ill-structured problems, they are often at a loss when asked to solve ill-structured problems because they do not know how to deal with the inherent ambiguity of such problems. The third level is reflective thinking (levels 6 and 7) where the individuals recognise that one's understanding of the world is not "given" but must be actively constructed and that knowledge must be understood in relationship to the context in which it was generated. This view presumes that judgments must not only be grounded in relevant data, but that they must also be evaluated to determine their validity.

Mclaughlin's notion of reflection that is explicit, systematic, specific and proximate corresponds to Elliot's technical interest, van Manen's and Louden's technical reflection. Such reflection falls under King and Kitchener's first two stages of reflective thinking: Pre-reflective thinking and quasi-reflective thinking. On the other hand, McLaughlin's conception of reflection that is implicit, intuitive, general and contextual corresponds to Elliot's practical interest, van Manen's practical and critical reflections and Louden's critical reflection. Such reflection matches King and Kitchener's reflective thinking where one actively constructs, assesses and evaluates judgements. Reflection for spiritual development in adolescents should go beyond the explicit and the systematic which emphasises expert knowledge and skills that are applied to predictable situations. Given that adolescents are at the crossroads of life and face many issues and challenges that are unique, uncertain and value-conflicted, they need to "reflect in action" (Schon, 1987) by setting, framing, constructing and solving problems based on their personal judgements. They also need to reflect beyond specific and proximate matters to consider general and contextual issues that concern their meaning in life, long-term plans and identity formation. By moving towards the third level of reflective thinking (King & Kitchener, 1994), adolescents will be able to reflect beyond technical concerns (Elliot, 1993; van Manen, 1977, 2002; Louden, 1991) and critically reflect on practical interests and examine broad issues on religiously tethered and untethered spirituality in their lives.

Reflection for Religiously Tethered Spiritual Development

Reflection is instrumental in the development of both religiously tethered and untethered conceptions of spirituality. Within a religious framework, reflection can help adolescents develop their personal ethical worldview and build relationships with others, thereby giving them a sense of personal destiny and direction.

Benefits for Adolescents

Within a religious context, educators should aim at providing a stable initial culture for the adolescents to reflect on their purpose of life, their relationship with the divine, and their desired personal values to guide them in their life journey. A number of writers have indeed pointed out how religion(s) can help a person to think and act morally. Moulavi avers that "it is a fact that moral education cannot succeed without religious education, because morality has its foundation and root in religion" (1987, p. 8). Haydon (1997) argues that religious beliefs provide the wider framework of meaning for moral demands to be experienced. Jesuit priest Dr (Rev) Robert Balhetchet, who was involved in preparing the secular moral education programme in Singapore, explains that there is an added dimension for Christians to be moral as they believe that goodness comes from God (*The Straits Times*, 22 October 2002). By underscoring things that are metaphysical and transcendent, most religions also promote "less pragmatic and utilitarian attitudes and dispositions [such] as faith, hope, charity, forgiveness, chastity and so forth" (Carr, 1995, p. 95). Some parents also share the belief that religious knowledge is salubrious for their children's moral development. It is reported that non-religious Chinese parents in Hong Kong are keen to send their children to religious schools because they perceive that these schools have more effective moral education (Cheng, 2004). In their research, Taris & Semin (1997) also conclude that the religious faith of mothers helps in the transmission of moral values to their children. They note that widely shared and objectively important core values such as caring, honesty and fairness are passed down from the mothers to their children.

However, it is important to note that the mere teaching of religious knowledge does not automatically translate into greater moral commitment. The positive effect of religion on morality depends on other factors such as religious orientation and level of education. In an empirical study on how religiosity affects moral development, Ji (2004) concludes that the degree of devout commitment to traditional religious doctrines and beliefs is conversely related to the likelihood that Christians act at the principled level of moral reasoning. This means that a fervent believer who holds dogmatically to teachings from his or her religious leaders is less likely to reason morally and act independently. This can be potentially dangerous if the religious beliefs are not shared by others in the society, or worse, are detrimental to society at large.

Besides developing the adolescents' ethical worldview within a religious framework, reflection on spirituality also encourages adolescents to build relationships with others, especially those of different faiths. Reflection should go beyond highlighting the commonality in religions and draw participants' attention to the disagreements among the religious traditions without leading adolescents to judgemental thinking. A dialogue among youth of different faith traditions is based on the common understanding that there exists a variety of moral traditions and legitimate moral differences (Runnymede, 2000). Reflections underscoring the ambiguous, controversial and dangerous are necessary to develop in students "religious literacy" which is crucial for the development of active citizenship (Ipgrave, 2003). By understanding and reflecting on the conceptual differences in religious worldviews and their influences on the motivations and behaviour of believers, students can develop their own beliefs and values critically (Erricker, 2006). Without such dialogues aimed at inter-religious polemics, interfaith dialogue exercises remain superficial as universal agreement is reached but is devoid of meaningful ethical, metaphysical, anthropological or theological content (Lindholm, 2004, cited in van Doorn-Harder, 2007). What is recommended is a culture of tolerance where religious education takes place in an open and inquiring way.

Reflections based on Dewey's open-mindedness, whole-heartedness and intellectual responsibility can be encouraged when teachers refer to universal themes and values from religious sources to get students to reflect on, discuss and apply the values learnt. For example, teachers could introduce moral teachings from different religions and ask students to reflect on their significance for each religion and draw comparative perspectives. For example, the golden rule in Christianity, "Do unto others as you would have others do unto you" finds parallels with the teachings in Islam: "No one of you is a believer until he desires for his brother that which he desires for himself", and in Buddhism: "Hurt no others in ways that you yourself would find hurtful".

Reflections can also be introduced when students of various faiths participate in school or community projects where they are encouraged to practically reflect on their learning experiences. Through working on shared projects such as environmental or service learning endeavours, they will be able to build friendships with those of different religious worldviews. This helps them to go beyond their preconceptions of people of other faiths, and dispels certain prejudices and stereotypes they may have about others. Schools can also introduce specific curriculum aimed at inter-religious education through critical reflection.

An example of inter-religious engagement is a special curriculum known as *(Re)embracing Diversity in New York City Public Schools: Educational Outreach for Muslim Sensitivity* to foster dialogue and process for public schools in New York. The curriculum aims to address and prevent intolerance towards Arab American and Muslim American students in the wake of the tragic events of 9/11; and promote interpersonal and intercultural dialogue based on tolerance and respect for ethnic and religious diversity by raising students' critical understanding of and sensitivity towards Muslims in America (Kenan, 2005). Through activities such as problem solving, critical reflection and collaborative learning, the students learn about topics such as "Towards Understanding Islam and Muslims"; "A Common Language for Discussing Bias and Hatred"; "Reflections on Prejudice" and "Field Trip to an Islamic Institution". Kenan (2005) points out that research has shown that the curriculum has succeeded in promoting and restoring the value of tolerance, peace and diversity in public school communities.

It is also essential to draw the students' reflection to the diversity within a religion so as to avoid stereotyping a particular religion as intolerant, radical or militant. In the aftermath of a series of terrorist acts by some Islamist groups, it is especially important to direct the adolescents' spiritual reflections to the different worldviews and trends within Islam. For example, students could engage in critical dialogue by learning about the teaching of pluralism and respect for all religions in many Islamic traditions. One Islamic scholar explains

> Islam is categorical: "Let there be no compulsion in religion" (*Surat al-Baqarah*, 2:256) and "To you be your Way and to me mine" (*Surat al-Kafirun*, 109:6). The Qur'an also reminds humankind that society, by divine design, is plural that is, multi-ethnic, multi-racial, and multi-religious (Moten, 2005, p. 233).

The students' attention could also be drawn to the critical humanist tradition in Islam which is a branch of Islamic thought that is often overlooked today due to the limelight given to the interpretations of Islam by some Islamist groups. The critical humanist tradition seeks to be open to new knowledge through the exercise of human reasoning while remaining rooted in Islam. It regards human beings as God's steward on earth who have been given the task to attain perfection in this life. This is achieved by exercising one's rational faculties given by God to integrate various branches of knowledge to become a virtuous person who is integrated into society. An Islamic scholar argues that "It is only with the recognition of the efficacy of human reasoning, an intellectual openness to enrich Muslim intellectual culture, and the consciousness to fulfill the task for humanity, that Muslims would be able to appreciate the tradition of critical humanism which was once explored and developed in the classical period" (Azhar, 2008, p. 130). Another Islamic scholar concurs that Muslims need to "work towards cultivating certain traits, such as the courage to live, willing to stand on their own, taking initiatives, sensitive toward others' rights and the common needs of humanity; willing to co-operate for common good, in the continuous process of social change, without fear of the changes taking place" (Soedjatmoko, 1985, p. 275, cited in Azhar, 2008, p. 130).

Religion and Indoctrination

In the context of religiously tethered spirituality where the problem of religious indoctrination is a concern, reflection is essential to develop the learners' rational autonomy and avoid indoctrination. There are three main approaches to religious education available to educators, namely, teaching *for* commitment (the confessional approach), teaching *about* commitment (the phenomenological approach) and teaching *from* commitment (Thiessen, 1993). The confessional approach tends to indoctrinate by paralysing one's intellectual capacity characterised by an inability to justify one's beliefs and consider alternatives (Tan, 2005, 2008b). Indoctrination is reprehensible because it makes a person incapable of thinking independently. In extreme cases, indoctrinated individuals are easily manipulated by others to inflict harm on themselves and/or others. Such an approach is inconsistent with the aim of parents and educators in a democratic society to develop rational autonomy in children. There is no reason why religious beliefs must be taught in an unthinking manner: rational autonomy is compatible with genuine religious commitment. After all, as Laura and Leahy (1988) put it, "an authentic faith is an autonomous faith" (p. 259).

Rejection of the confessional approach has given rise to the phenomenological approach, which teaches about commitment. This approach seeks to avoid indoctrination by rejecting any induction into substantial spiritual beliefs, and concentrating instead on different social and cultural expressions of spirituality. Rather than simply teaching one religion, children are exposed to a wide range of religious views in a neutral and objective fashion. The phenomenological approach has met with a number of objections (Tan, 2008c). The most common criticism is that it does not represent the true character of religion in its Herculean quest to avoid any religious point of view. Scraps and fragments of different religious traditions are presented which are meaningless, superficial and distortive of any real understanding of religion (Carr, 1996). Such an unreflective approach is not only inadequate in giving students a realistic picture of religion, it has the danger of misrepresenting the character of a faith. By making little or no reference to the lived experiences of religious believers, this approach also does not encourage students to see religion beyond its status as an academic subject. By presenting a truncated and superficial account of religion, it is also not favoured by parents and educators who want their children and students to have an empathetic awareness of religion. It is also questionable that indoctrination will inevitably occur when only one religion is taught, which is the presupposition for teaching a plurality of religious views to children. Whether indoctrination has taken place depends on how religious views are taught, not how many religions are addressed. A teacher could deliberately teach comparative and historical material on religions in a manner that amounts to the indoctrination of a particular religion. Hence, the phenomenological method, with its emphasis on neutrality and pluralism, cannot ensure a religious education that is non-indoctrinative. In fact, some have countered that religious liberals who embrace the phenomenological method can be as dogmatic as religious conservatives. For example, Alexander (1992) maintains that "religious liberals are attracted to their own dogmas, from the secularist denial of any value in theological discourse, to claims that ultimate authority for one's religious posture lie[s] in individual autonomy or the positivist historical study of tradition" (p. 385).

What is needed to avoid the problems associated with the confessional and phenomenological approaches is to promote a form of reflection that balances "openness" with "rootedness". An ethos of openness is needed for participants to explore critically the domains of religion. Alexander and McLaughlin (2003) explain that "open" refers to "the range of traditions and perspectives considered, the attitude that is invited toward them, and the forms of autonomous judgement and response sought on the part of students" (p. 365). This "openness" is accompanied by "rootedness" where students should be given the opportunity to acquire an insider perspective through an empathetic awareness of and critical approach towards religious traditions. Arguing for "openness with roots", Alexander and McLaughlin (2003) posit that participants should be "exposed to, and involved in, a form of education articulated by a particular conception of the good, but they are encouraged to put their formation into critical perspectives and to make any acceptance of it on their part authentic" (p. 369; also Thiessen, 1993; Tan, 2008c). Reflection through openness and rootedness both affirm the value and uniqueness of the adolescents and give them a sense of value in connectedness to a faith community:

> For example, if a religious tradition emphasises the faith community, without valuing the uniqueness of its members, youth may not have the necessary opportunities to explore different aspects of identity. When youth are not given the freedom to experience moratorium, and are either forced or pressured into adopting a specific ideology, social group, or expression of spirituality, identity foreclosure is at risk (King, 2003, p. 202).

In other words, reflection for religiously tethered spirituality is premised on an empathetic awareness of and critical approach towards various religions worldviews. Leirvik (1999) posits that "religions need to be approached both from the 'insider' as living sources for faith, morals and life orientation—and from the 'outsider', as objects for critical investigation" (p. 83, cited in Leganger-Krogstad, 2003, p. 179). Such a form of reflection can be achieved by providing the balance between openness and rootedness through the "teaching from commitment" approach (Tan, 2008b). In this approach, adolescents are introduced to a particular religion from *within* the religious system while developing the adolescent's reflective thinking and enhancing rational autonomy. Using the idea of a "primary culture" developed by Ackerman (1980), McLaughlin (1984) highlights the importance of parents' providing a stable and coherent primary culture as a precondition of the child's later development into an autonomous liberal citizen. A primary culture in the sense of a shared framework of fundamental beliefs is essential to the preservation of one's culture. The need to provide a primary culture is especially relevant to religious minorities in plural societies. Halstead (1995) notes that the cultures of minorities are threatened by prolonged exposure to liberal values. There is therefore a need for these communities to use education to maintain their shared framework of fundamental beliefs.

The initiation into a primary culture is not indoctrinative. On the contrary, initial commitment is necessary for children to develop their critical faculties for reflecting and evaluating the different alternatives presented. Without initial beliefs, there is no point of comparison and, when confronted with opposing views later in life, "an individual reared without parental instruction will likely be indifferent to the alternatives" (LaFollette, 1996, p. 165). The initiation of children in their early stages of development into a particular worldview is not indoctrinative as long as their autonomy is not stifled. The aim is to encourage them to gradually "reflect critically on the committed perspective into which they have been nurtured" within the religious context, knowing that "they will eventually make an independent choice" for or against the religious commitment (Thiessen, 1993, p. 255).

Likewise, McLaughlin (1984) argues for a need to balance the demands of stability and openness at the same time; he describes the intention of parents and teachers to achieve this balance as aiming at "autonomy via faith". The short-term aim is to develop faith within a stable primary culture, although this faith is not impervious to any change or rejection in the future. In the long run, the ultimate goal is for individuals to exercise their autonomy in making a personal decision about the faith. In embracing the "teaching from commitment" approach, which avoids the pitfalls of teaching for commitment (with its problem of indoctrination) and teaching about commitment (with its problem of a truncated and superficial account of religion), the aim is for religious faith to be acquired not indoctrinatively but reflectively and meaningfully.

Adapting suggestions from McLaughlin (1984, p. 81), educators should nurture the following attitudes and procedures to promote reflection in the adolescents:

- Encourage adolescents to ask questions and be willing to respond to their questioning honestly and in a way which respects the adolescent's developing cognitive and emotional maturity.
- Make the adolescent aware that religion is a matter of faith rather than universally, publicly agreed belief.
- Encourage attitudes of tolerance and understanding in relation to religious disagreement.
- Indicate that morality is not exclusively dependent upon religion.
- Be alert to even subtle forms of psychological or emotional blackmail.
- Ensure that the affective, emotional and dispositional aspects of the adolescent's religious development take place in appropriate relationship with the cognitive aspect of that development.
- Respect the eventual freedom of the adolescent to refuse to participate in religious practices.

Reflection for Religiously Untethered Spiritual Development

Reflection is also salutary for religiously untethered spirituality in adolescents so that they can derive personal destiny and direction; develop their personal identity and ethical worldview; and establish connectedness with others.

Benefits for Adolescents

First, reflection enables adolescents to develop themselves by exploring, clarifying and identifying their sense of personal calling and destiny, values and commitments for their future. Dalton (2001) avers that students' spiritual reflections are especially important in helping them to identify and commit to future goals and career choices:

> Self-understanding and acceptance are important outcomes of spirituality, but I think we fail as educators if we do not help students link the ethical claims of life and work with others to one's relationship with what is transcendent and sacred.... If we do our job well in higher education, then students inevitably reflect upon the greater purpose of their lives. They ask questions about worthy commitment, moral commitment, moral responsibility, and life's inevitable transcendent claims and experiences (p. 24).

Reflection propels adolescents to search for meaning, belonging and ultimate answers in life—an endeavour that is central to the task of identity exploration for adolescents (King, 2003; Benson, 1997; Hill et al., 2000). Adolescents experience great insecurity and uncertainty in their journey of faith development as it is a period where any "absolute form of knowing breaks down and other perspectives are heard and recognised, the individual grows in self-awareness, authorities may be resisted, and the definition and experience of the community become more diffuse" (Love, 2001, p. 10). Through reflection, the adolescents' personal identities are developed by combining intellectual knowledge and abilities with personal values and convictions, leading to a lasting and holistic experience that links knowing and feeling (Dalton, 2001). Given that adolescents are at the stage of developing and exercising their abstract reasoning and thinking, reflection on spirituality provides meaningful opportunities for them to reason critically and sceptically about previously held beliefs (King, 2003; Loder, 1998; Markstrom, 1999). Through philosophical questioning and responding to experiences of great sadness or joy, adolescents ponder the purpose of their lives, their personal journey and important life choices (Dalton, 2001).

Reflections on ideological frameworks can provide youth with the fundamental beliefs and values essential for their identity formation and societal roles (Furrow, King, & White, 2004; Damon, 1983; Erikson, 1968). Research shows that highly moral people were often recognised by religious or spiritual attributes, and that their morality was determined by their spiritual experience and thought (Wagener, Furrow, King, Leffert, & Benson, 2003; also see Walker, Pitts, Hennig, & Matsuba, 1995; Walker & Pitts, 1998). Underpinned by a moral and value-laden framework, youth "develop not only integrated civic and moral identities, but a transcendent or spiritual sensibility that propels them to contribute to the common good" (Furrow et al., 2004, p. 17; also see Lerner, Dowling, & Anderson, 2003). Reflections about one's commitment to values such as justice, fairness, respect for others and the common good will prepare students to build relationships with others and be active participants in social and civic communities (Dalton, 2001).

Through reflection, educators could encourage adolescents to explore spirituality by developing a greater connectedness to self and others as well as personal destiny, direction and identity. Guided by Dewey's (1933) open-mindedness, wholeheartedness and intellectual responsibility, adolescents can transcend the self to reason critically about previously held values, beliefs, feelings and behaviour. Relying on tacit and intuitive reflection (Schon, 1987), adolescents are free to ponder their feelings of personal destiny and decision-making about their goals and the means to achieve these goals. Reflective learning is also salubrious for identity formation as adolescents become active agents in seeking their individual authenticity and wholeness.

Promoting Spiritual Reflection in School

Spiritual development through reflection can be promoted in school through the school curriculum, ethos and climate. The overall aim is to use reflection to help adolescents discover personal destiny and direction; develop their personal identity and ethical worldview; and build relationships with others. Spiritual development could take place in various subjects across the curriculum, especially the arts—literature, poetry, drama, painting and music. Carr avers that the arts "have a key part to play in communicating or explicating the sense of a connection between the temporal and the eternal, the finite and the infinite, the material world and the world of the soul, in human affairs" (Carr, 1995, p. 95). Universal themes from a variety of sources may be introduced to encourage students to reflect on, internalise and apply the spiritual values learnt. For example, the poems of English Romantics such as Wordsworth and Coleridge could be used to help students freely explore the themes of love, self-fulfilment and worship, and the implications for their construction of their personal identity and destiny. Spiritual reflection can be nurtured in the students when appropriate feelings and a sense of connectedness are aroused, and desired spiritual values are inculcated. For instance, students can reflect on metaphysical and normative principles such as truth, human nature, justice, compassion and social responsibility.

Critical discussions can also take place when teachers refer to spiritual perspectives on social issues such as natural or man-made disasters and tragedies (Tan, 2008; Robson & Lonsdale, 1987). By discussing cases such as the Ethiopian famine, the Asia tsunami tragedy or the Bali bombings, students can debate on the different metaphysical concepts and interpretations of suffering, evil, justice and compassion from various spiritual worldviews. Such a reflective process will contribute towards adolescents developing their personal and ethical worldviews. Teachers can get students to be involved in projects where they choose a system of beliefs of their choice such as Confucianism or Humanism, research an aspect of that system of beliefs and present their insights and the lessons gained. The focus is not just information gathering, but a sincere exploration of the belief system in its teachings and everyday experiences. Such a task serves to help them to clarify their personal beliefs, life goals and identities.

In terms of pedagogy, educators can use different types of scaffolding to promote reflection in spiritual matters in adolescents. Among the strategies, watching films and writing journals are helpful in getting adolescents to reach a higher level of reflective thinking. Films, when appropriately chosen, are ideal in triggering the pre-service teachers to reflect on an issue of concern, ponder the meanings and implications for themselves, and finally change or modify their values, beliefs and actions. Recommended films which focus on spiritual themes include *Eternal Sunshine of the Spotless Mind* on love, memory and personal identity, and *Matrix* on reality, truth and destiny in life. Suitable religious films include *Jesus Camp* which raises issues on religious instruction and indoctrination in the United States, and *Sepat*, a Malaysian film which examines the interfaith romance between a Muslim Malay girl and a non-Muslim Chinese boy.

After watching a film, journal writing can be used to promote and facilitate reflections based on the film. A journal captures the free flowing personal interpretations and expressions of a diary where the writer documents his or her learning process. Critical thinking is also encouraged as the learner is required to discuss and integrate different insights in the drawing of coherent conclusions. Writing journals helps the learners to gain the most from the films and thereby facilitates reflective thinking. For example, students can write their reflections after watching *Sepat* on their views of love and religious differences, or they could reflect, after watching *Jesus Camp*, on whether they agree with the American pastor's claim that religious indoctrination is necessary and desirable for children.

Conclusion

Adolescence is a period characterised by a personal quest for purpose, meaning and relationships. This chapter distinguished between religiously "tethered" and "untethered" conceptions of spirituality. The former is linked to or housed within the tradition of a religious faith while the latter is concerned with beliefs and practices that are disconnected from religions. This chapter proposed that reflection is effective in promoting spiritual development in adolescents so that they can derive personal destiny and direction; develop their personal identity and ethical worldview; and build relationships with others. Adolescents are at the crossroads of life and face many issues and challenges that are unique, uncertain and value-conflicted. Hence they need to critically reflect on practical interests and examine broad issues on religiously tethered and untethered spirituality in their lives. The chapter further suggested how educators can promote spiritual development in adolescents through reflection.

Spiritual reflection is crucial as it focuses on the adolescent's own construction of meaning in his or her life through personal reflection, experience, exploration and construction of both religious and non-religious phenomena. It is a form of "deeper learning" because it touches on students' encounter with transcendence and ultimate meaning in their lives; as Dalton (2001) rightly avers: "Education that does not connect with and integrate these spiritual dimensions of learning and development is ultimately less engaging and lasting for a student" (p. 19). Through a liberating and self-fulfilling reflective process, spirituality—both tethered and untethered—could provide the humanising effect of education for adolescents in their holistic development.

References

Ackerman, A. B. (1980). *Social justice in a liberal state*. New Haven, CT: Yale University Press.
Alexander, H., & McLaughlin, T. H. (2003). Education in religion and spirituality. In N. Blake, P. Smeyers, R. Smith, & P. Standish (Eds.), *The Blackwell guide to the philosophy of education* (pp. 356–373). Malden, MA: Blackwell Publishing.
Alexander, H. A. (1992). Science and spirituality: Traditional interpretation in liberal education. *Curriculum Inquiry, 22*(4), 383–400.
Azhar, I. A. (2008). Critical humanism in Islamic educational philosophy. In C. Tan (Ed.), *Philosophical reflections for educators* (pp. 121–131). Singapore: Cengage Learning.
Benson, P. L. (1997). Spirituality and the adolescent journey. *Reclaiming Children and Youth, 5*, 206–209.
Benson, P. L., Roehlkepartain, E. C., & Rude, S. P. (2003). Spiritual development in childhood and adolescence: Toward a field of inquiry. *Applied Developmental Science, 7*(3), 205–213.
Carr, D. (1995). Towards a distinctive conception of spiritual education. *Oxford Review of Education, 21*(1), 83–98.
Carr, D. (1996). Rival conceptions of spiritual education. *Journal of Philosophy of Education, 30*(2), 159–178.
Chae, M. H., Kelly, D. B., Brown, C. F., & Bolden, M. A. (2004). Relationship of ethnic identity and spiritual development: An exploratory study. *Counseling and Values, 49*, 15–26.
Cheng, R. H. M. (2004). Moral education in Hong Kong: Confucian-parental, Christian-religious and liberal-civic influences. *Journal of Moral Education, 33*(4), 533–551.
Dalton, J. C. (2001). Career and calling: Finding a place for the spirit in work and community. In M. A. Jablonski (Ed.), *The implications of student spirituality for student affairs practice* (pp. 17–25). San Francisco: Jossey-Bass.
Damon, W. (1983). *Social and personality development*. New York: Norton.
Dewey, J. (1933) *How we think: A restatement of the relation of reflective thinking to the educative process*. New York, DC: Heath and Company.
Dowling, E. M., Gestsdottir, S., Anderson, P. M., von Eye, A., Almerigi, J., & Lerner, R. M. (2004). Structural relations among spirituality, religiosity, and thriving in adolescence. *Applied Developmental Science, 8*(1), 7–16.
Dunne, J. (1993). *Back to the rough ground: "Pronesis" and "techne" in modern philosophy and in Aristotle*. Nortre Dame, IN: University of Notre Dame Press.
Elliott, J. (1993). The relationship between "understanding" and "developing" teachers' thinking. In J. Elliott (Ed.), *Reconstructing teacher education: Teacher development* (pp. 193–207). London: The Falmer Press.
Erikson, E. H. (1968). *Identity: Youth and crisis*. New York: Norton.
Erricker, C. (2006). If you don't know the difference you are living with, how can you learn to live with it? Taking difference seriously in spiritual and religious education. *International Journal of Children's Spirituality, 11*(1), 137–150.
Furrow, J. L., King, P. E., & White, K. (2004). Religion and positive youth development: Identity, meaning, and prosocal concerns. *Applied Developmental Science, 8*(1), 17–26.
Halstead, M. (1995). Voluntary apartheid? Problems of schooling for religious and other minorities in democratic societies. *Journal of Philosophy of Education, 29*(2), 257–272.
Haydon, G. (1997). *Teaching about values: A new approach*. London: Cassell.
Hill, P. C., Pargament, K. I., Hood, R. W., McCullough, M. E., Swyers, J. P., Larson, D. B., et al. (2000). Conceptualising religion and spirituality: Points of commonality, points of departure. *Journal for the Theory of Social Behavior, 30*, 51–77.

Ipgrave, J. (2003). Dialogue, citizenship, and religious education. In R. Jackson (Ed.), *International perspectives on citizenship, education and religious diversity* (pp. 147–168). London: RoutledgeFalmer.

Ji, C. H.C. (2004). Religious orientations in moral development. *Journal of Psychology and Christianity, 23*(1), 22–30.

Kenan, S. (2005). Reconsidering peace and multicultural education after 9/11: The case of educational outreach for Muslim sensitivity curriculum in New York city. *Educational Sciences: Theory & Practice, 5*(1), 172–180.

King, P. E. (2003). Religion and identity: The role of ideological, social, and spiritual contexts. *Applied Developmental Science, 7*(3), 197–204.

King, P. E., & Boyatzis, C. J. (2004). Exploring adolescent spiritual and religious development: Current and future theoretical and empirical perspectives. *Applied Developmental Science, 8*(1), 2–6.

King, P. M., & Kitchener, K. S. (1994). *The development of reflective judgment in adolescence and adulthood*. Jossey Bass: San Francisco.

Koenig, H. G., McCullough, M. E., & Larson, D. B. (2001). *Handbook of religion and health*. Oxford, England: Oxford University Press.

LaFollette, H. (1996). Freedom of religion and children. In R. E. Ladd (Ed.), *Children's rights re-visioned: Philosophical readings* (pp. 159–169). Belmont, CA: Wadsworth.

Laura, S. R., & Leahy, M. (1988, April). The fourth dimension of space: A meeting place for science and religion. *Journal of Christian Education, Paper 91*, 5–17.

Leganger-Krogstad, H. (2003). Dialogue among young citizens in pluralistic religious education classroom. In R. Jackson (Ed.), *International perspectives on citizenship, education and religious diversity* (pp. 169–190). London: RoutledgeFalmer.

Leirvik, O. (1999). Theology, religious studies and religious education. In D. Chidester, J. Stonier, & J. Tobler (Eds.), *Diversity as ethos: Challenges for inter-religious and intercultural education* (pp. 75–83). Cape Town: University of Cape Town ICRSA.

Lerner, R. M., Dowling, E. M., & Anderson, P. M. (2003). Positive youth development: Thriving as the basis of personhood and civil society. *Applied Developmental Science, 7*, 171–179.

Lindholm, T. (2004). Philosophical and religious justifications of freedom of religion or belief. In T. Lindholm, Jr., W. C. Durham, & B. G. Tahzib-Lie (Eds.), *Facilitating freedom of religion or belief: A deskbook* (pp. 19–62). The Hague: Martinus Nijhoff.

Loder, J. E. (1998). *The logic of the spirit: Human development in a theological perspective*. San Francisco: Jossey-Bass.

Louden, W. (1991). *Understanding teaching: Continuity and change in teachers' knowledge*. London: Cassell.

Love, P., & Talbot, D. (1999). Defining spiritual development: A missing consideration for student affairs. *NASAP Journal, 37*, 361–375.

Love, P. G. (2001). Spirituality and student development: Theoretical connections. In M. A. Jablonski (Ed.), *The implications of student spirituality for student affairs practice* (pp. 7–16). San Francisco: Jossey-Bass.

Markstrom, C. A. (1999). Religious involvement and adolescent psychosocial development. *Journal of Adolescence, 22*, 205–221.

McLaughlin, T. H. (1984). Parental rights and the religious upbringing of children. *Journal of Philosophy of Education, 18*(1), 75–83.

McLaughlin, T. H. (1999). Beyond the reflective teacher. *Educational Philosophy and Theory, 31*(1), 9–25.

Moten, A. R. (2005). Modernisation and the process of globalisation: The Muslim experience and responses. In K. S. Nathan & K. H. Mohammad (Eds.), *Islam in Southeast Asia: Political, social and strategic challenges for the 21st century* (pp. 231–255). Singapore: ISEAS.

Moulavi, M. H. B. S. (1987). The Islamic view. In *Harmony Among religions*. Addresses given at the Parliament of Religions organised by the Ramakrishna Mission in Singapore (pp. 8–11). Singapore: Inter-Religious Organisation.

National Youth Council. (2007). *A to Z guide on youth in Singapore*. Retrieved June 13, 2008, from http://www.nyc.gov.sg/research/atoz.asp#Religion

Reich, H., Oser, F., & Scarlett, W. G. (1999). Spiritual and religious development: Transcendence and transformations of the self. In K. H. Reich, F. K. Oser, & W. G. Scarlett (Eds.), *Psychological studies on spiritual and religious development: Vol. 2. Being human: The case of religion* (pp. 57–82). Scottsdale, AZ: Pabst Science.

Robson, J., & Lonsdale, D. (Eds). (1987). *Can spirituality be taught?* London: ACATE & BCC.

Runnymede, T. (2000). *The future of multi-ethnic Britain: The Parekh report*. London: Profile Books.

Schon, D. (1987). *Educating the reflective practitioner*. San Francisco, CA: Jossey-Bass Publishers.

Soedjatmoko. (1985). *Etika pembebasan: Pilihan karangan tentang agama, kebudayaan, sejarah dan ilmu pengetahuan*. Jakarta: Lembaga Penelitian, Pendidikan dan Penerangan Elionomi dan Sosial.

Straits Times. (2002). Priest who's no Mr Morality. 22 October. *The Straits Times*.

Tan, C. (2005). Indoctrination. In W. Hare & J. Portelli (Eds.), *35 key questions for educators*. Halifax, Nova Scotia: Edphil Books.

Tan, C. (2008a). Improving schools through reflection for teachers: Lessons from Singapore. *School Effectiveness and School Improvement*, 19(2), 225–238.

Tan, C. (2008b). The teaching of religious knowledge in a plural society: The case for Singapore. *International Review of Education*, 54, 175–191.

Tan, C. (2008c). Religious education and indoctrination. In C. Tan (Ed.), *Philosophical reflections for educators* (pp. 183–192). Singapore: Cengage Learning.

Taris, T. W., & Semin, G. R. (1997). Passing on the faith: How mother-child communication influences transmission of moral values. *Journal of Moral Education*, 26(2), 211–221.

Thiessen, E. J. (1993). *Teaching for commitment: Liberal education, indoctrination and Christian nurture*. Montreal: McGill-Queen's University Press.

van Doorn-Harder, N. (2007). Teaching religion in the USA: Bridging the gaps. *British Journal of Religious Education*, 29(1), 101–113.

van Manen, M. (1977). Linking ways of knowing with ways of being practical. *Curriculum Inquiry*, 6(3), 205–228.

van Manen, M. (2002). The pathic principle of pedagogical language. *Teaching and Teacher Education*, 18, 215–224.

Wagener, L. M., Furrow, J. L., King, P. E., Leffert, N., & Benson, P. L. (2003). Religion and developmental resources. *Review of Religious Research*, 44, 271–284.

Walker, L. J., & Pitts, R. C. (1998). Naturalistic concepts of moral maturity. *Developmental Psychology*, 34, 403–419.

Walker, L. J., Pitts, R. C., Hennig, K. H., & Matsuba, M. K. (1995). Reasoning about morality and real-life moral problems. In M. Killen & D. Hart (Eds.), *Morality in everyday life: Developmental perspectives* (pp. 371–407). Cambridge, England: Cambridge University Press.

Chapter 22
Developing Contemplative Capacities in Childhood and Adolescence: A Rationale and Overview

Aostre N. Johnson

> *Ah, not to be cut off,*
> *not through the slightest partition*
> *shut out from the laws of the stars.*
> *The inner—what is it?*
> *if not the intensified sky,*
> *hurled through with birds and deep*
> *with the winds of homecoming.*
> Rainer Maria Rilke

Abstract This chapter articulates an overall definition of "contemplative" and reviews research on the benefits of contemplative practices. It suggests four overlapping but differing ways of defining contemplative development, including (1) attitudes and emotions, (2) intuitive knowing, (3) religious or spiritual knowing, and (4) rational cognitive reflection. Relevant developmental theories and developmental trajectories for children and adolescents in each of these categories are discussed, addressing the following questions: Do contemplative capacities "develop" and if so, in what ways? How does each definition relate to early consciousness? Is it valid to refer to "stages" of contemplative development? How can teachers and parents support rather than impede contemplative capacities in youth?

Introduction

I have been researching the multiple ways in which spirituality is interpreted and integrated in educational settings for many years. I read current literature and interview and surveyed teachers about their personal definitions and understandings of spirituality and how these impact teaching and learning environments. Distinct (yet interrelated) themes of definitions have emerged and I categorize them into the following: religious, reflective, meaning-making, creative, ethical, ecological, and

A.N. Johnson (✉)
Saint Michael's College, One Winooski Park, Colchester, Vermont 05439, USA
e-mail: ajohnson@smcvt.edu

contemplative. Although I list these as separate categories, they are really intertwining and overlapping. The central metaphor common to all of the categories is connections (Johnson, 1999a). Each way of thinking about spirituality and education emphasizes differing kinds of connections with self, others, world, and "spirit" or "God." In addition, each contains within it a number of more specific abilities and attitudes that I refer to as "capacities." These emerge and change in varying ways and rates.

Adults inside and outside of religious traditions are realizing that in this era of tumultuous cultural, social, and environmental upheaval, the emergence of fresh ways of understanding and supporting the inner lives of our youngest and most vulnerable members is necessary. As Roelkepartain, King, Wagener, and Bensen (2006) state, "Spiritual development may be at a 'tipping point' for becoming a major theme in child and adolescent development. A growing number of scholars in various disciplines have invested themselves in this field. The public imagination appears to be ready in numerous cultures, traditions, and contexts, all of which are struggling with social changes that threaten to undermine the spiritual lives of young people" (p. 11).

In this chapter, I will highlight *contemplative* aspects of spiritual development for several reasons. In one sense, contemplative capacities are at the core of all human capacities. In addition, most adults recall very formative contemplative experiences in their own childhood and adolescence—and current studies of children confirm the existence of many types of experience that can be labeled contemplative. Also, "contemplative" is an emerging focus of scholarly and popular concern that cuts across many disciplines and aspects of development. The growing body of literature on contemplative development and education across the life span draws on religious and secular, historic and current knowledge from nearly all disciplines. There is a dawning realization that contemplative capacities are critical not only for the wellbeing of youth but also for the survival of the human species and the planet. High-speed, high-stress, acquisition-oriented ways of living are taking an enormous toll on all forms of life. Emerging research suggests the benefits of contemplative educational practices and methods—and, therefore, the inclusion of contemplative perspectives on development and education has the potential to be effective and appropriate for secular, spiritual, and religious settings.

I will begin by reviewing the literature on definitions, including aspects of contemplative practice, briefly positing four ways of defining contemplative development. I will then turn to relatively recent research on the benefits of practices and educational methods that strengthen contemplative capacities. Next, I will look more closely at each of the four categories, considering relevant developmental theories and possible developmental trajectories for children and adolescents, with emphasis on the following questions: How does each way of defining "contemplative" relate to early consciousness? Do varying contemplative capacities "develop," and if so, in what ways? Does it make sense to talk about "stages" of development? How can teachers and parents support, rather than impede this development? What are the benefits of attempting to enhance contemplative capacities through education? Are there potential dangers? Which approaches are suitable for secular settings and which for more specific spiritual/religious settings?

Definitions and Practices

Contemplative derives from the Latin word *contemplari*, to gaze attentively or observe, and *attention* is at the root of many definitions. In defining contemplative, the idea of inner/outer is significant—while attention may be directed outward, it never excludes inner experience. In fact, *contemplative* implies focus on the "inner" or interior dimensions of being, or more often, seamless integration of inner and outer, as the opening Rilke poem illustrates. It sometimes means the opposite of action, a withdrawal from the active life. Definitions also vary along the following dimensions: They may distinguish between *single-pointed* ("narrow angle lens") or *diffuse* ("wide angle lens") *focus of attention*. They may include, highlight, or exclude *various aspects of the human being*, such as intuition, mystical knowing, emotions, attitudes, or the mind. They may fall along a *religion, spiritual, and secular continuum*, with a "divide" between definitions that assume that there is an "ultimate spiritual reality" or God and those that do not.

My four major categories of definitions are derived both from dictionary definitions and a literature review and vary in their implications for development and education. They are,

(1) a combination of *attitudes and emotions* that support the act of living with presence, attention, sensitivity, nonjudgmental awareness or "mindfulness";
(2) an *epistemology* or intuitive way of knowing;
(3) *religious or spiritual knowing* or meditation on spiritual or religious ideas;
(4) *a way of thinking or using the mind* when considering something deeply, i.e., deep thought, insight, pondering, examination, consideration, study, and reflection, including self-reflection and ethical reflection.

It is difficult to separate the definition of the word *contemplative* from practices to strengthen contemplative capacities since the latter are often used as aspects of definition. Practices noted vary widely from specific to general, as Roth (2006) expresses, "While various methods to attain contemplative states of consciousness can be found in such religious practices as chanting, prayer, ritual performance and meditation, such states can also be found in a wide variety of nonreligious practices, such as music, dance, drama, poetry and prose, painting, sculpting, and even mindful observation of the natural world" (p. 1789). The practice of contemplative reading and writing also has deep historical roots in all of the major religions. Some forms of contemplative practice are more bodily based, such as yoga, tai chi, walking meditation, or simply being aware of one's physical presence.

The most general contemplative methods include any activities in which we are slowing down, sitting quietly, relaxing, becoming more aware of our sensory experiences (including tasting, smelling, touching, listening, looking), reflecting, and/or responding with attention to any situation in daily life. In fact, in its most basic form, any activity we perform slowly and consciously can be seen as contemplative experience. For example, Krishnamurti (1969) suggests, "Meditation can take place when you are sitting on a bus or walking in the woods full of light and shadows, or listening to the singing of birds or looking at the face of your wife or child" (Blau, 1995, p. 241).

In many traditions, meditation techniques are used to increase contemplative skills or religious understanding and to disrupt the identification of self with personal ego. Some are very specific with the intention of connecting believers to a particular religious worldview. Others are more general, for example, breath practices such as awareness of breath or control of breath are used as a way to focus the mind. A popular contemporary approach to meditation is referred to as *mindfulness* meditation, stressing conscious awareness of the breath, body and surroundings and attentive self-examination of thoughts and feelings that arise during the practice. Trungpa Chogyam (1988) explains, "By meditation here we mean something very basic and simple that is not tied to any one culture. We are talking about a very basic act: sitting on the ground, assuming a good posture, and developing a sense of our spot, our place on this earth. This is the means of rediscovering ourselves and our basic goodness, the means to tune in to a genuine reality, without any expectations or preconditions" (p. 36).

While contemplative definitions and practices vary widely, they center on ways of accessing our "authentic" inner selves, including feelings and knowledge that may seem more "real" and true than those we ordinarily access. Another aspect of the literature revolves around why it is important that we do so, as well as the proof that it is.

Benefits of Developing Contemplative Capacities

Much recent research is attempting to validate contemplative practice, but from one perspective, this utilitarian focus violates its most profound truth. As Rockefeller (2006) says, "Contemplation is a form of human activity that possesses its own inherent value, and it may involve a beautiful experience that is a fulfillment complete in itself. In this sense, it is an end in itself" (pp. 1777–1779). From this view, contemplative activity is natural and beneficial by definition. Historically, in fact, the assumption that all education and intellectual study is by nature contemplative was characteristic from the time of the Greeks, including neo-Platonists and all religious traditions, which were generally the centers of schooling. In fact "contemplative" education was typical until the 12th and 13th centuries when scientific methods began to rival and eventually to eclipse contemplative/religious ones.

The recent awakening of interest in contemplative practice has resulted in many claims made for its efficacy, and an argument can be made that a research base is necessary for wider acceptance in light of the commonly accepted contemporary "scientific" worldview. While research on the results of contemplative practice is not new, up until recently it has been sparse and variable in reliability. Yet, it seems that a few conclusions are gaining clarity. Hart (2004) summarizes,

> "There are hundreds of studies of the effects of contemplative practice, particularly on meditation, offering varying degrees of methodological precision. Among the main trait effects (changes that endure over time) are improved concentration, empathy, perceptual

acuity, a drop in anxiety and stress symptoms, and more effective performance in a broad range of domains from sports and academic test taking to creativity.... What has been best documented is that contemplation of this nature affects physiology" (p. 31)

Among the most precise physiological studies have been in the field of medicine, as Stock (2006) articulates:

We know that stress reduction techniques like meditation lead to a positive state of the parasympathetic nervous system and meditation is increasingly used to help prevent and treat heart disease, autoimmune disorders, chronic lung disease, headaches, diabetes, eczema, asthma, allergies, infertility, and gastrointestinal problems, as well as panic, depression and hostility (p. 1763).

The second major area of research findings relates to focus of attention. A number of studies suggest that contemplative practice results in a greater ability to focus, sustain, and/or expand attention/concentration (e.g., Berggraf and Grossenbacher; 2007; Hart, 2004).

Other claims for the potential of contemplative practice relating to character and personality traits are less experimentally documented, but exist in the literature based on more qualitative observations and also on the "traditional wisdom" of contemplative practice traditions. For example, Berggraf and Grossenbacher (2007) suggest that contemplative practices have been found to enhance creativity, open-mindedness, the ability to hold paradox and compassionate civic engagement, suspension of judgment, compassionate listening, and a sense of awe. Rockefeller (2006) says, "Contemplative disciplines may help some people become less frenetic and more centered, more aware of goodness and beauty of their own being, more responsive to suffering, more attentive and mindful and more open to I–thou relationship and meaning" (p. 1777). And Thurman (2006) states,

We would like for people to develop contemplative states that increase contentment, detachment, tolerance, patience, nonviolence and compassion, which simultaneously decrease feelings of anger, irritation and paranoia. We would like them to develop more wisdom, more freedom and more capacity for freedom and responsibility by seeing through the constructed realities in which our materialistic culture has enmeshed us (p. 1766)

These capacities are naturally seen as desired educational outcomes by many parents and teachers. A body of literature is growing relating to the most effective methods of realizing them. The importance of the adult teacher or parent's contemplative consciousness is frequently emphasized. In keeping with the broadest definitions, any practice that supports adult capacity to focus attention and self-awareness on being fully engaged with each young person can be called contemplative educational practice.

In one example, in his graduate education classes, John P. Miller (1994) introduces his teacher students to many forms of contemplation practice, including meditation on the breath, mantra (a "sacred" word), visualization, concentration on poetry or sacred texts from any religious tradition, and "movement meditations." After selecting one of these and practicing it regularly, teachers observe any effects on their lives and teaching and record their observations in journals. In his study of approximately 400 educators engaged in this endeavor, several benefits clearly emerge. Teachers report increased self-acceptance, fuller perspective on their lives, more calmness, increased listening skills, and a growing sense of interconnectedness with others, with nature and with current issues. Some began to use contemplative practice with their own students. And in a teacher education program rooted in contemplative practice, Richard Brown (1998) reports that educators skilled in contemplative self-observation become extremely adept at child observation skills. Once grounded in this perceptual and reflective awareness, they become more able to engage in a genuine way with their students and with pedagogical practice.

Some studies have been conducted on young people in schools but the evidence is just beginning to emerge. For example, McLean (2001) qualitatively studied the benefits of 15–30 min a day of meditation in British elementary schools and found increased calmness of teachers and many benefits for students, including greater calmness, concentration, readiness to learn, ability to handle distractions and pressures, creative expression, awareness of the world around them and their place in it, awareness of the beauty of the world and sense of wonder. Brown (2007) reports that initial studies of effects of meditation in public elementary schools in the United States suggest increased control of attention, less "negative internal chatter," and improvement in "mood disorders." According to Lantieri (2008), studies by Schonert-Reichl in Canada suggest that children who practiced "mindfulness meditation" were less aggressive, more attentive in class, and more optimistic, and The Mindfulness Awareness Research Center at UCLA reports that meditation can help students with ADHD to focus better and experience less anxiety. Lantieri is currently conducting an empirical study of the effects of mindfulness meditation and calming techniques on children in New York City schools and reports similar preliminary results.

Further formal research as well as informal experimentation on developing contemplative capacities could be enhanced by greater clarity about the varied ways it is defined and understood. The following section offers an overview of this endeavor.

What is Contemplative Development?

There is a continuum of views of contemplative development with opposing visions at the extremes. In one, children are "natural contemplatives" who are, as the poet Wordsworth said, "trailing clouds of glory" because they are a manifestation of spirit or God; they are in touch with a deeper "ground" or "realm" of being that is their birthright since it is the very essence or nature of who they are. They are by nature loving, fluid and open, and able to live fully in the present. The other end of this continuum holds that true contemplative capacities are the highest form of development, and can only be reached by going through the complete developmental cycle, expanding our cognitive capacities until we are able to reach above or through them to deep, contemplative multidimensional states. According to this view, we cannot really call children contemplatives, although adolescents could be well on their way if they are being educated correctly. I suggest that both views are partially true and depend on one's definition of contemplative and one's assumptions and beliefs about the very idea of development. Each of the following four definitions fall somewhere on the above continuum; in the first two, children are natural contemplatives whereas in the second two, their contemplative potential must be developed. All four definitions have varying emphases on emotion, spirit, intuition, and/or mind—and it is not necessary to accept or embrace all of them. However, they are overlapping and intertwining.

The Act of Looking at or Attending Intently with Presence, Attention, Sensitivity, or "Mindfulness"

Nakagawa (2000) says, "the way of contemplation has been the royal road to Awakening in the traditions of Eastern philosophy for thousands of years" (p. 177). He goes on to define contemplation as "an art of awareness" in its basic forms; it is the art of being aware of that which is taking place in the present moment. The Buddhist teacher Thich Nhat Hanh (1999) suggests that contemplation in this sense is at the core of Buddha's teachings. He emphasizes two steps in the contemplative process. The first is stopping, calming and resting and the second is looking deeply (at self or world) once we have calmed down. This "looking deeply" or attentiveness is often referred to as mindfulness. Berggraf and Grossenbacher (2007), who teach in Naropa University's Department of Contemplative Psychology take their basic definition from William James's Principles of Psychology: "the faculty of voluntarily bringing back a wandering attention over and over again" (p. 1).

In this category, the focus of attention can be either inward or outward, focused or diffuse. We can focus attention outward on an object, on our surroundings, and/or on our own actions, thus highlighting a powerful sense of presence inherent in each concrete moment of our experience, awake to our full experience of the world around us. Alternatively, the focus may be inward on self, the state of our body, senses, emotions, or thoughts—or it can be both, an inclusive focus on everything in the present moment of our experience, a nonjudgmental acceptance of sensory experiences, thoughts, feelings, images, and physical sensations. The *awareness* of these rather than identifying with them is key. Duff (2003) defines contemplative as awareness: "something we are awake to...knowing our relationship with the world, ideas, people" (p. 230).

This definition emphasizes attitudes and emotions such as openness, peacefulness, relaxation, acceptance, fluidity, and a sense of living in the present, with a sense of integration between self and world, body, emotion, mind, and awareness of these. It does not assume a belief in ultimate spiritual reality or God, although it can coexist with this belief.

In *The Spirit of the Child*, David Hay and Rebecca Nye (1998) suggest three interrelated categories of spiritual sensitivity or awareness based on their study of spirituality and childhood. They are (1) *awareness-sensing* including *here-and-now* (living in the present), *tuning* (tuning into or feeling "at-one-with"), *flow* (intense and seemingly effortless absorption in activity), and *focusing* (a bodily based sense of feelings and reality); (2) *mystery-sensing* including *wonder and awe* and *imagination*, and (3) *value-sensing*, including delight and despair, ultimate goodness, and meaning. They point out that these are characteristics of young children's thinking, based on many sources that validate this. Hart (2003) has also researched the spiritual experiences of young children utilizing qualitative methods, autobiographical studies, and case studies. Two of the "domains," similar to Hay's, in which even very young children exhibit spiritual capacities are *wonder and awe* and *relational spirituality*.

I think that most people would agree that young children have the ability to focus attention intensely, even for a short time, to engage deeply with their senses with objects of interest to them, to relate very directly to people around them, to be in touch with their own emotions, to exhibit awe and wonder, and to freely use their imaginations. Under ordinary circumstances, these contemplative capacities seem to be "given" to us, an aspect of our human nature, but most contemporary cultures do not encourage or enhance them. The potential for these remains throughout life; stages of development are not highly relevant since we can encourage children to retain and sustain these qualities at any age or stage.

However, young children do not necessarily show awareness of their awareness. As cognitive abilities develop, especially in adolescence, the ability to be self-reflectively aware of all aspects of experience without identification with them can increase greatly in the appropriate environment and does have a developmental dimension, which will be discussed in the fourth category.

Children's natural contemplative capacities must be protected from the incursion of speed-driven, acquisition-oriented, stressful living. "Reclaiming childhood," an increasingly commonly used "mantra," is fitting here. The causes of the increasing frequency of ADD and ADHD in young people are uncertain, but many theories suggest a strong cultural influence.

The following recommendations for parents and educators are consistent with this view of contemplative: Infants and children should not be hurried, either in terms of time or developmental goals. As Wood (2007) expresses this, "Because young children spend so much time at school, rushing through school means rushing through childhood. Doing so stresses the children, their teachers and their parents" (p. 4). He suggests that even small changes—such as changing the order of the day to allow more "breathing room," giving children more time to complete and transition activities and to reflect on their learning—can make a significant difference. Children should be allowed as much time as possible for learning through play and delving deeply into investigations of topics that interest them. The natural world is usually fascinating for both children and adolescents and an effective place for nurturing contemplative capacities. We are now starting to hear about "nature deficit disorder," the contemporary problem resulting from children spending increasingly less time outdoors at all ages. Many studies about attention span and young children have been conducted and overall, have demonstrated that children's attention spans increase naturally as they grow older but are considerably longer when they are able to select objects they are interested in looking at or playing with. Adults often make the mistake of distracting children with one toy after another and surrounding them with an overabundance of material objects, which shortens the attention span. Technological toys, computers, and television often inhibit the contemplative capacities of young children because they tend to move rapidly, disrupt natural play rhythms, substitute externally imposed images from more spontaneously arising, inner play-based imagination and take away from the child's tendency to focus on the people, objects, and activities going on around them.

Howard Gardner's theory of multiple intelligences (1999) suggests that rather than being uni-dimensional, intelligence has a number of "frames" through which it can manifest, including logical–mathematical, linguistic, visual–spatial, bodily kinesthetic, musical, interpersonal, intrapersonal, naturalist, and existentialist. Engaging all of these can promote contemplative consciousness. Children should have access to an environment rich in "raw materials," of many types and be offered multiple opportunities to use these imaginatively and artistically to learn about themselves, others, and the world around them.

Ideally, young children would not need imposed meditation techniques to put them in touch with their contemplative nature or reduce their feelings of stress, but in the current cultural environment, it may be helpful to offer them simple contemplative practices as an "antidote." In the most general sense, this simply means helping them to slow down and pay more attention to their senses, their bodies, and natural world. Additionally, this may involve basic practices such as asking them to examine natural objects closely, leading them through exercises in which they focus on each of the senses, helping them notice the effects of stress on their bodies, offering a guided imagery experience, or simply asking them to sit quietly with eyes open or closed. As children get older, the above practices can be lengthened and made more specific and more explicit forms of mindfulness meditation can be introduced.

Some potential problems with these practices are that adults will get caught up in technique rather than consciousness and that practices will be artificially substituted for play and meaningful exploration, a slow rhythm, and nature-based experiences. Because of current cultural and educational tendencies that focus on outcome at the expense of process and experience, there is a real danger that they will be utilized in a way that, ironically, is the very opposite of contemplative.

Intuitive Knowing

Another way of understanding contemplation is as an epistemology. Hart (2004) calls it "a third way of knowing that complements the rational and the sensory" (p. 29). Many theories have contrasted two basic contrasting types of thinking or knowing, for example, William James' pure experience and reflective thought (1912/1971), the Buddhist concepts of the conditioned and unconditioned mind, John Dewey's qualitative and quantitative thinking (1931), and James Macdonald's meditative and calculative thinking (1981). These can all be seen as different words for the contrast I am making between contemplative and rational thinking and knowing. Meditative or contemplative understanding is the "ground" out of which more explicit, rational, intellectual thinking arises. Dewey explains. "Things, objects, are only focal points of a here and now in a whole that stretches out indefinitely. This is the qualitative 'background' which is defined and made conscious in particular objects and specified properties and qualities" (Dewey, 1958, p. 163). James describes this ground as infants or young children know it: "Experience in its immediacy seems perfectly fluent. The active sense of living which we all enjoy, before reflection shatters our instinctive world for us, is self-luminous and suggests no paradoxes" (p. 49).

The consciousness of infants is generally referred to as global and relatively undifferentiated. However, this may be seen as merely primitive or alternatively as an intuitive/contemplative way of knowing that is often forgotten as we grow older. Significantly, from this perspective, contemplative awareness is inherent in our being and does not have to be externally imposed. Infants are born with the ability to experience reality globally through a feeling-intuition in a direct, unmediated way. This knowing provides the motivating and integrating power for all of their subsequent ways of making meaning of the world, including rational understanding. The power of contemplative knowing in this sense connects infants and young children to the world around them in an unmediated and engaged way, also providing the motivation to explore it. We could say that infants come from the "inner realm" but add the "outer" as they interact with and learn about it. The challenge is to allow them to gain in their knowledge without losing their connection to the "inner." Various writers have articulated this dilemma for centuries. In one example, as Rockefeller (2006) points out,

> Two hundred years ago, Frederick Schleiermacher, the founder of the modern liberal Christian tradition.... noted that every person is born with a capacity to experience directly the mystery, wonder and beauty of the world, which is essential to human well-being and a sense of the joy and meaning of life. However, he lamented that this capacity is "crushed out" of children in the course of a their education by the modern rage for calculating and explaining... (p. 1779)

As in the previous category, it does not really make sense to talk about stages of development since this way of knowing is a "given" but it can become "crushed out" or obscured when it is not recognized and honored by the culture. There have been many words written on the way in which contemporary culture tends to force babies and young children to focus prematurely on rational thinking. One key is in allowing and supporting ongoing access to this capacity, with a gradual introduction of academics, using imagination and the arts as a bridge. All of the educational suggestions from the first category are relevant. A recognition of and respect for the reality of the intuitive knowing of young people is critical; I believe that this one practice can have a profound effect. Macdonald (1974) recommends the following educational processes: meditation, perceptual experiences, imagination, sensitivity to others, ecological awareness, meaning-making based on all aspects of patterning (especially, artistic forms, play, and playful experiences), and a wide range of physical experiences.

Mystical Knowing, Meditation on Spiritual, or Religious Ideas

Contemplation also has distinctive connotations in religious and mystical traditions. This definition can be seen as an extension or subcategory of the previous one, in that if we have a belief in God, a divine presence or an ultimate ground of being, our intuitive understanding links us directly to the "source." For example, Thomas Keating defines contemplation in Christianity as "the knowledge of God based on the intimate experience of his presence" (p. 20). Yust (2004) understands contemplative as the "inner" side of spiritual life... "the times we and our children spend pushing aside the noisiness of the world so we can attend to God's presence and God's voice. When we dwell in this space, we are in listening mode, inviting the silence or the word and images of others to 'speak' a word from God" (p. 145).

In a more general mystical sense, this definition of contemplation includes connecting to "the unseen world" that the philosopher William James called "something more," meaning more than is immediately obvious to the senses. As he says, "the visible world is part of a more spiritual universe from which it draws its chief significance." This is the realm of the mystics. Margaret Smith (1980) suggests that mysticism is "an attitude of mind, an innate tendency of the human soul which seeks to transcend reason and to attain a direct experience of God" (p. 20). All religious traditions have mystical branches that teach contemplative practices such as meditation or prayer. These enhance a "believer's" ability to feel a direct connection with God or spirit, although the type of mystical experience is mediated by beliefs of the religion and the forms of practice. In addition, these traditions often emphasize a withdrawal from the everyday world for varying time periods—brief times daily, regular monthly or yearly times for days or weeks or even months, or, in the case of "contemplatives" such as monks or nuns, permanent lives of relative removal from "the world" in order to live a life based on direct connection with God.

This category is based on a belief in God or a spiritual world. It can be understood as rooted in same epistemology as the previous one, but with the added assumption that all intuitive knowing is anchored in God or a spiritual "ground of being" that underlies but is fully present in the material/temporal world. Religious contemplation is experienced as a simultaneous insight/emotion and a profound knowing. It seems to confirm knowledge already possessed, an uncovering rather than an adding and leads to a deep sense of connection to God or source, shaped and modified by particular religious or spiritual beliefs.

Although it is impossible to "prove" that contemplative religious knowing exists, in certain circumstances, such as meditative experience, it can be seemingly "isolated." When perceptual or conceptual objects of consciousness are removed, as in deep meditative experience, the mind is "thrown back on itself" to experience itself directly. When this happens, there is a sense of locating oneself in relationship to the most existential aspects of the human condition as well as a sense of connectedness with all beings and the entire cosmos—classic characteristics of mystical experience. While it is logical that during meditative states of consciousness, brain wave activity can be recorded, traditional mystical and spiritual views of intelligence would say that it is not *reducible* to what can be measured in the brain. Nonetheless, this is a task of current interest to many researchers and in fact, "neurotheology," the study of the neurobiology of religion and spirituality, is an emerging field. For example, A. and S. Newberg (2005) research the neurobiology of spiritual experiences, "defining" them at base as "the sense of having a union with some higher power or fundamental state of being" (p. 185). In one study they conducted brain scans on Tibetan Buddhists and Franciscan nuns while they were meditating. Their research demonstrates that these kinds of experiences are accompanied by a blocking of input into the posterior parietal lobe of the brain and also by an "affective discharge via the right-brain limbic connections" (p. 186) with the amygdale and the hippocampus likely to be involved.

In comparing brain functioning during adult spiritual experience to brain functioning of infants regarding these unitary states of consciousness, the Newbergs suggest that there are differences due to the absence or the presence of sense of ego self. However, they also see "some remarkable similarities, and it has been remarked by a number of mystical traditions that the ultimate goal of spiritual pursuits is to return to a time in which the mind was at the beginning" (p. 189).

From this definitional perspective, humans are born with the capacity to be in direct contact with the God or spirit. But adults must offer children and adolescents a conscious religious or spiritual perspective with accompanying practices that allow them to remain in touch with and grow into a more profound and self-aware relationship or understanding of spiritual ground or God. Infants can *experience* but not fully *know* God. A number of theories suggest that there are clear stages that human beings must progress through to reach our full contemplative potential. I will give two examples.

Michael Washburn's (1988) theory of development is a "spiritualized" psychoanalytic view. It holds that emotion, not mind, is the critical organizing force in human development. Unlike Freud and most neo-Freudians, though, Washburn believes that emotion is rooted in spirit—he calls it "Dynamic Ground . . . The power of the Ground . . . is the very life of the soul" (p. 130). He believes that the newborn baby is absorbed and intoxicated by blissful feelings of this "Dynamic Ground." Washburn calls this *original embedment*. The baby's body is flowing with magnetic energy; she is bathed in the "water of life" (p. 48) and lives in a numinous, shimmering, meaning-filled, entrancing, "magical" world. Even though she is aware of the world and people around her, she is also so filled with this intense energy that she can be very contented and self-absorbed—in much the same way that "mystics"—or ordinary meditators—can become absorbed in their meditative states. Washburn says that we never really forget this feeling, that all adults, in a sense, yearn for embodied childhood bliss all of our lives, except for the few humans who do become spiritually fulfilled as adults. Washburn's stages of development are based on the assumption that our emotional–relational lives, as well as modernist cultural conditioning, lead to a rupture with Dynamic Ground. We develop a separate ego and identify with it, thinking that it is the entirety of ourselves rather than an ever-changing aspect of ourselves. Once the ego has emerged, the psyche is "bi-polar" in relationship to the Ground and the personal ego. The ensuing stages of development result from the relationship between these two poles of development, in a heroic journey of struggle. In the "highest" level of development, we return to a merging with the Ground, with a transformed but highly functioning ego. Adolescence is a critical time as the ego fully forms and begins to become capable of not only reflective, moral, and sexual awakening, but also spiritual transformation.

Ken Wilber (2002) has written a great deal about spiritual/contemplative development. His model integrates many approaches, but it is more rooted in a cognitive perspective, using Piaget as his base for the earlier stages. Wilber's view is that the psyche, or mind, is inherently endowed with basic structures that are universal to human experience, dependent on experience to draw them out. The structures emerge in a hierarchical order, one at a time, starting at the lowest, or physical level, and proceeding to the highest, or spiritual level, the level of "ultimate reality." The development of the consciousness of each human being, therefore, evolves from matter toward spirit. As each structure is dependent on the one before it in order to emerge, this means that no stages can be skipped—and no stages are ever completely left behind; rather, they are incorporated, or subsumed, into the next highest level. Thus, when we move from the "sensorimotor" to a higher level, we continue to use the evidence of our physical senses as raw data for our minds, but we add the ability to use our imaginations as data for our minds, an ability we do not have in a previous stage. Similarly, we do not lose our ability to use logic when we incorporate a profound contemplative level at a higher stage of development. From this view, a contemplative childhood consciousness either does not exist, or exists at a very low level. This is because reflective consciousness is such a significant aspect of this theory of spiritual development—we could not become contemplative without first having developed our logic. Each human being has the potential to develop to the highest levels of consciousness, but this is not given.

Thus both Washburn and Wilber believe that there is religious or spiritual "reality" which can be fully realized by adults as a result of what happens to children during each stage of development, although the nature of their proposed stages differs. Washburn's theory, leads us to honor infants and young children as "unconscious contemplatives," whereas Wilber is cautious about "elevating" childhood to a contemplative status.

Each of these theorists emphasizes the relevance of accepted contemporary developmental theories, both cognitive and emotional–social, as primary components of meeting children's needs that becomes the foundation for contemplative development. In other words, for example, infants and young children need loving, responsible, and responsive adults to interact with and the freedom to move safely and explore a variety of materials with all of their senses. In addition to these, school-age children should have access to guided, in-depth explorations in a variety of disciplines utilizing their varied intelligences and emphasizing the mastery of skills and knowledge. However, for optimal contemplative development, other experiences are critical. For example, 'William James' theory of mysticism leads to the inclusion of religious history and mystical experience in education (Johnson, 2002).

The way that adults regard children is key. Historically, all religious traditions see children as a reflection or manifestation of God, although to differing degrees.

In contrast to deficit models prevalent in many modernist educational systems, religious contemplative views offer the potential for seeing each child as a unique and sacred gift of the divine with valuable gifts to offer the world. (Johnson, 1999b)

While religious traditions vary, all "view children as spiritual beings able to connect to God" (Yust, Johnson, Sasso, & Roehlkepartain, 2006, p. 82) and each has some theory of significance of stages of development and of adult responsibility for ensuring that children have the appropriate experiences at each stage. Children must be taught practices of that religious tradition. Practices include individually based ones and communal ones, such as various types of meditations, prayers, scripture readings and chanting, services, stories, rituals, and ceremonies. Some of these mark transitions or passages in children's or adolescents' spiritual lives. In general, the practices become more specific as the child gets older, until the adolescent is incorporated into the adult community.

The Act of the Mind When Considering Intently—Deep Thought, Insight, Pondering, Reasoning, Study, Reflection, Self-Reflection

This category emphasizes more traditional rational aspects of thought and learning, including the capacity to think logically, lucidly, and self-reflectively. For example, Holland (2004) suggests that contemplative education promotes reflective thinking and personal insight. Since this definition does not assume a belief in God or spirit and aligns with capacities usually included in definitions of "an educated person," it would be reasonable to assume they are already being supported in public schools. Yet, many contemporary critics suggest that schools are not engaging students' critical, reflective, substantive intellectual thinking with much depth or frequency.

Historically, religions tend to value intellectual education highly, and the first formal schools were located within religious traditions. Developing a sharp mind along with compassion and ethical reasoning was seen as a critical aspect of religious formation in all major religious traditions. Stock (2006) emphasizes the historic link between contemplative practice, intellectual thinking, and ethical action, with an emphasis on self-knowledge, beginning with ancient Greek philosophy. The method for developing this type of thinking was direct conversation, with the teacher sharpening the students' intellectual understanding in order to introduce them to their ethical responsibility for the greater community's needs: "The exercises by which individuals were prepared for this challenge were not arid and abstract, although they were intensely cognitive" (p. 1761). As suggested above, intellectually oriented contemplative practice tends to include community involvement and social justice, rather than merely working toward individual fulfillment. It can lead to a growing awareness of the relationship between self and others, the effects of individual action on the whole. In this category the emphasis is on the type and quality of intellectual thinking; it is critical, insightful, self-reflective and ethically aware.

Content is relevant in this category. The mind is focused on topics worthy of consideration that can be classified as philosophical, existential or religious, such as "Why do we exist? What is the meaning of our time on earth? What is our origin? What happens when we die? What does it mean to be human? How can we live together equitably? How can we learn about the world around us and utilize that knowledge equitably? What is beauty and how can it be created and appreciated? What activities are most worthy of time and attention? How can humans best live a balanced, thoughtful, ethical, and beautiful life?" Religious traditions have historically posed these questions to children and youth while also supplying the answers.

But there is also a secular approach. Howard Gardner's (1999) idea of existential intelligence is one example of this. For some years he posited the possibility of a ninth spiritual intelligence but ultimately rejected it because of difficulties in defining its content, dealing with its truth claims, and proving its existence. He settled instead on existential intelligence, which includes the potential to think about cosmic issues and to ponder existential, philosophical and religious questions, but excludes any notion of knowing or attaining ultimate truth.

Mathews' (1980) research on young children's ability to reason and grapple with complex philosophical issues led him to suggest that, "for many young members of the human race, philosophical reasoning—including, on occasion, subtle and ingenious reasoning—is as natural as making music and playing games, and quite as much a part of being human" (p. 36). Robert Coles (1990) who writes about children's spirituality points out "how young we are when we start wondering about it all, the nature of the journey and the final destination" (p. 335). Similarly Hart's (2003) second two spiritual "domains" (introduced earlier) are *wondering* and *wisdom*. By wondering, he means the tendency for children to ask, ponder, and puzzle over the "big questions" and by wisdom, the ability of children to "come to the heart of the matter," to see issues or situations clearly and compassionately. His research suggests that some young children demonstrate remarkable strengths in these domains. All of these theorists are challenging the assumption that contemplative reason is not accessible to young children.

Clearly this is an area that is compatible with aspects of developmental stage theory. Piaget's theory of rational cognitive development is relevant, but with some qualifications. Mathew and others have critiqued Piaget as not understanding and therefore missing the philosophical responses of young children. Where Piaget believed that real philosophical understanding cannot take place until adolescence, Mathews, Hart, and Coles argue that many 5-, 6-, and 7-year-olds are philosophically astute. Yet, most people do develop in their ability to think contemplatively in terms of becoming more insightful, reflective, and self-reflective—and cognitive stage theory is relevant. Parents and teachers can focus the mind on existential topics worthy of deep consideration beginning at the preschool stage. By adolescence, meaningful philosophical reflection could be incorporated into most academic subjects. Noddings (1993, 2006) and Theodore Sizer and N. Sizer (2007) are representatives of many educational theorists who advocate for the inclusion of profound existential questions with strong ethical dimensions at the core of the curriculum. T. Sizer and N. Sizer (2007) say,

> A curriculum rich in content will teach young people that important matters of sensitive living have everything to do with hard, substantive, and often agonizingly painful thought. ...We're selling our children short when we believe that grappling is beyond them. In fact, most of them are dealing with questions of intense seriousness while we're looking the other way (p. 155).

Conclusion

By ignoring the development of contemplative capacities (in any way we define them), we are "looking the other way." All four of the above perspectives on definition assume that contemplative capacities not only exist but also are key elements of living fully, and it is possible to embrace them all in a "nondualistic" consciousness. Thomas Merton (1972) defines contemplation as follows:

> The highest expression of man's (*sic*) intellectual and spiritual life. It is that life itself, fully awake, fully active, fully aware that it is alive. It is spiritual wonder. It is spontaneous awe at the sacredness of life, of being. It is gratitude for life, for awareness (p. 1).

By consciously educating for contemplative capacities, we are embodying our hopes that our children will not be "shut out from the laws of the stars," will experience "the intensified sky hurled through with birds" with spirit, heart, mind, and senses and will feel again and again "the winds of homecoming."

References

Berggraf, S., & Grossenbacher, P. (2007). Contemplative modes of inquiry in liberal arts education. *Liberal Arts Online*, June, 2007, 1–9.
Blau, E. (1995). *Krishnamurti: 100 years*. New York: Stewart, Tabori and Chang.
Brown, P. (2007). In the classroom, a new focus on quieting the mind. *New York Times*, June 16, 2007.
Brown, R. (1998/1999). The teacher as contemplative observer. *Educational Leadership*, 56(4), 70–73.
Boyce, B. (2007, January). Please help me learn who I am. *Shambala Sun: Buddhism, culture, meditation, life*, 15, 66–73, 119.
Chogyam, T. (1988). *Shambhala: The Sacred heart of the warrior*. Boston: Shambhala Publications.
Coles, R. (1990). *The spiritual life of children*. Boston: Houghton and Mifflin.
Dewey (1958). Art as Experience. New York: C.P. Patnam's Sons
Dewey, J. (1931). *Philosophy and civilization*. New York: Milton, Balch.
Duff, L. (2003). Spiritual development and education: A contemplative view. *International Journal of Children's Spirituality*, 8(2), 227–237.
Gardner, H. (2006). *Multiple intelligences: New Horizons in theory and practice*. New York: Basic Books.
Gardner, H. (1999). *Intelligence reframed: Multiple intelligences for the 21st century*. New York: Basic Books.

Grossenbacher, P., & Parkin, S. (2006). Joining hearts and minds: A contemplative approach to holistic education in psychology. *Journal of College and Character, 7*(6), 1–13.

Hanh, T. N. (1999). *The heart of the Buddha's teaching*. New York: Broadway Books Random House.

Hart, T. (2004). Opening the contemplative mind in the classroom. *Journal of Transformative Education, 2*(1), 28–46.

Hart, T. (2003) *The Secret Spiritual World of Children*. Nouoto, CA: New World Library.

Hay, D., & Nye, R. 1998. *The spirit of the child*. London, UK: Harper Collins.

Holland, D. (2004). Integrating mindfulness meditation and somatic awareness into a public educational setting. *Journal of Humanistic Psychology, 44*(4), 468–484.

James, W. (1912/1971). *Essays in radical empiricism* and *a pluralistic universe* (R. Bernstein, Ed.). New York: E. P. Dutton.

Johnson, A. (2002). James' concept of mystical consciousness: Implications for curriculum theory and practice. In J. Garrison, R. Podeschi, & E. Bredo (Eds.), *William James and education*. New York: Teacher's College Press.

Johnson, A. (1999a). A postmodern perspective on spirituality and education: Hearing many voices. *Encounter: Education for Meaning and Social Justice, 12*(2), 41–48.

Johnson, A. (1999b). Teaching as sacrament. In J. L. Kincheloe (Ed.), *Democratizing intelligence: Confronting psychological assumptions about teaching and learning*. New York: Routledge.

Johnson, A. (1998) Meditations on James Macdonald's transcendental developmental ideology of education. *Journal of Curriculum Theorizing, 14*(1), 37–43.

Keating, T. (1986). *Open mind, open heart: The contemplative dimension of the Gospel*. New York: Continuum Publishing.

Lantieri, L. (2008). *Building emotional intelligence: Techniques to cultivate inner strength in students*. Boulder, Colorado: Sounds True.

Macdonald, J. (1974). A transcendental developmental ideology of education. In W. Pinar (Ed.), *Heightened consciousness, cultural revolution and curriculum theory* (pp. 153–172). New York: Peter Lang.

Macdonald, J. (1981). Curriculum, consciousness and social change. In B. J. Macdonald (Ed.), *Theory as a prayerful act: The collected essays of James B Macdonald* (pp. 153–172). New York: Peter Lang.

McLean, P. (2001, March). Perceptions of the impact of meditation on learning. *Pastoral Care in Education, 19*, 31–35.

Mathews, G. B. (1980). *Philosophy and the young child*. Cambridge, MA: Harvard University Press.

Merton, T. (1972). *New seeds of contemplation*. New York: New Directions Publishing Corporation.

Miller, J. (1994). *The contemplative practitioner*. Thousand Oaks, California: Corwin Press.

Nakagawa, Y. (2000). *Education for wakening: An eastern approach to holistic education*. Brandon, VT: Foundation for Educational Renewal.

Newman, A. B., & S. K. (2005). A neuropsychological perspective on spiritual development. In E. C. Roelkepartain, P. King, L. Wagener, & P. Bensen (Eds.), *The handbook of spiritual development in childhood and adolescence*. Thousand Oaks, CA: Sage Publications.

Noddings, N. (1993). *Educating for intelligent belief or unbelief*. New York: Teacher's College Press.

Noddings, N. (2006). *Critical lessons: What our schools should teach*. Cambridge, UK: Cambridge University Press.

RockeFeller (2006) Meditation, Social Change and Undergraduate Education. *Teacher's College Record, 108*(9), 1775–1786.

Roth, H. (2006). Contemplative studies: Prospects for a new field. *Teacher's College Record, 108*(9), 1787–1815.

Smith, M. (1980). The nature and meaning of mysticism. In R. Wood (Ed.), *Understanding mysticism*. New York: Image Books.

Sizer, T., & Sizer, N. (2007). Grappling. In A. Ornstein, E. Pajak, & S. Ornstein (Eds.), *Contemporary issues in curriculum*. Boston, MA: Allyn and Bacon.

Stock, M. (2006, September). The contemplative life and the teaching of the humanities. *Teacher's College Record, 108*(9), 1787–1815.

Thurman, R. (2006, September). Meditation and education: India, Tibet and modern America. *Teacher's College Record, 108*(9), 1765–1774.

Washburn, M. (1988). *The ego and the dynamic ground: A transpersonal theory of human development*. Albany, NY: State University of New York Press.

Wilber, K. (2002). *Integral psychology: Consciousness, spirit, psychology, therapy*. Boston, MA: Shambhala Publications.

Wood, C. (2007, August). Breathing in and breathing out. *Responsive Classroom Newsletter*. Vol, 19, No. 3, pp.1–3.

Yust, K. M. (2004). *Real kids, real faith: Practices for nurturing children's spiritual lives*. San Fransciso: Jossey-Bass.

Yust, K. M., Johnson, A. N., Sasso, S. E., & Roehlkepartain, E. C. (Eds.). (2006). *Nurturing child and adolescent spirituality: Perspectives from the world's religious traditions*. Lanham, MD: Rowman & Littlefield.

Chapter 23
The Contribution of Spirituality to "Becoming a Self" in Child and Youth Services

Douglas Magnuson

Abstract Spiritual development can be considered as a kind of educational ideology and compared with the constructive-developmental, romantic, and cultural transmission ideologies on the basis of their organization of time, goals, values, data sources, methods and mechanisms of growth, outcomes, and metaphors. One view of spirituality, originating in a theology of vocation, is based on discernment of self-transcendence, responsibility, and authenticity, in response to a calling, and youth programs can be organized to nurture discernment of a calling in the lives of youth.

In Don DeLillo's *Underworld*, a seminary instructor—a priest—and a student are conversing about the student's education. The priest looks down at the students' wet boots and says,

> "Name the parts. Go ahead. We're not so *chi chi* here, we're not so intellectually chic that we can't test a student face-to-face."
> "Name the parts," I said. "All right. Laces."
> "Laces, one to each shoe. Proceed."
> I lifted one shoe and turned it awkwardly.
> "Sole and heel."
> "Yes, go on."
> I set my foot back down and stared at the boot, which seemed about as blank as a closed brown box.
> "Proceed, boy."
> "There's not much to name, is there? A front and a top."
> "A front and a top. You make me want to weep."
> "The rounded part at the front."
> "You're so eloquent I may have to pause to regain my composure. You've named the lace. What's the flap under the lace?"
> "The tongue."
> "Well?"
> "I knew the name. I just didn't see the thing."

D. Magnuson (✉)
School of Child & Youth Care, Victoria, BC V8W 2Y2, Canada
e-mail: dougm@uvic.ca

> He made a show of draping himself across the desk, writhing slightly as if in the midst of some dire distress.
> "You didn't see the thing because you don't know how to look. And you don't know how to look because you didn't know the names."

The priest continues on to name the cuff, counter, quarter, welt, vamp, eyelet, aglet, grommet, and last.

Like this student's encounter with the shoe, what we see when we "look at" young people reflects how we have come to name and interpret. In formal and informal education, a small number of ways of naming things are common, and spirituality is the unadopted foster child of youth services. It is referred to, discussed, and desired, but outside of religious ministries the literature is small and practices tend to be individual rather than systemic or programmatic. Scott and Magnuson (2005) point toward one kind of integration of spirituality into child and youth services by describing the practices of forgiveness, gift-giving, and responding to suffering and pain as exemplars of spiritual development, especially in services for children and families who are distressed. That discussion did not include a comparison with alternative or related ideologies and practices of child and youth services or what might be required to have a fully developed child and youth services practice of spirituality. Here I take a step back to consider (a) common alternative conceptions and ideologies of practice in child and youth services and informal education, and (b) one perspective on the practice of spiritual development based on the historical and theological idea of "vocation."

This work begins with Kohlberg and Maier's (1972) explication of the constructive-developmental, cultural transmission, and romantic educational ideologies, which is still the most thorough explanation of educational ideologies in formal and informal education, and I compare to these one interpretation of the practice of spiritual development. This interpretation is derived from a post-Reformation Protestant theology. The data and literature review on which this discussion is based are from an exploratory study, the Project on Vocation, Work, and Youth Development (Baizerman, 1999). We interviewed 145 youth in long interviews, listening for accounts of spirituality interpreted through the theological framework of the idea of vocation, a calling. One purpose of that study was to think about how vocation might contribute to an understanding of spirituality as an organizational principle of daily life for young people.

A good place to begin the discussion is with a comparison of schools, since everyone has experience with some kind of formal education, and the ideas and practices related to each of the ideologies is easiest to access there.

A Comparison of Educational Practices

The first kind of school, the progressive school based on constructive-developmental principles, aims to "build a free and powerful character" (Kohlberg & Maier, 1972), and this is accomplished through the active, democratic participation of students in organizing daily life (Power, Higgins, & Kohlberg, 1989). Students take on roles in administering various components of the school, including the administration and maintenance of rules and guidelines, disciplinary actions, extracurricular activities, and project-based learning activities. They participate in service projects and peer-helping programs for students who need and want help with student work or with personal issues. With the guidance of teachers, in these activities students challenge and support each other, think and reflect, and students learn gradually to take the perspective of others, to actively coordinate between competing interests, values, and ideas. Conflict and disagreement are seen as means for deepening understanding of others and of moral principles. In these the exercise of judgment helps students move from a perspective embedded in their own needs and impulses to acting as principled moral agents. Students explore, test, and experiment in and with the world around them, like poets or scientists, and both success and failure are educational.

A second kind of school aims to nurture the creative, spontaneous, authentic self and help each student achieve self-actualization. Like Steiner Waldorf schools, it is believed that students are like flowers in that there is an innate biological imprint that needs nurturing—but not active management. In fact, it is believed that active management interferes with this innate growth. The most important educational role is to provide room to explore and play, "education toward freedom" (Steiner Waldorf Schools Fellowship, n.d.) to protect the rights of children to be themselves and to be unique, to allow the "inner good" to unfold, and there is great faith in this inner good. Like the progressive school, this kind of school encourages student exploration, but while progressive schools believe that growth requires encountering persons and minds more advanced and disciplined than oneself, here it is believed that discipline will result from the individual's emerging sense of self in exploration of the world. Conflict is more likely to be perceived as a violation of one's own or someone's rights and right to be an individual.

A third kind of school is most concerned with preparing students for future participation in adult life, and the goal is to help students internalize moral values, habits of successful living, and the content of the culture. Students are wax, and the cultural values are imprinted on the wax for life; it is believed that outputs depend on the quality of the inputs. These schools attend carefully to the building blocks of the culture and how they are transmitted to students. They will typically have careful programs of reward for achievement and consequences or discipline for failure. Moral values and the content of the curriculum are seen as similar—they must be explicitly taught; in some districts, these schools are called "traditional" schools, and the content is the three "Rs": "readin' ", "ritin", and "rithmatic." Successful living requires learning the specific skills of the academic, social, and moral curriculum. A common phrase for the moral curriculum is "character education," in which students are provided role models, shown the consequences of bad choices, and taught explicit skills for refusing bad choices and making good choices. Drug Abuse Resistance Education (D.A.R.E.) is a common program in these schools.

A fourth kind of school is also concerned with preparation for adult life, although its methods are to have students participate alongside adults in adult activities. The primary pedagogical method is to have available to students interesting adults who are doing interesting things and to invite students to participate with them. For example, science teachers may be working on a robotics project and students, when they see it, become interested in learning how to build and animate such a thing. They start hanging around the teachers, and if the project and the teachers are compelling enough, students ask to help and ask to be taught the necessary skills. The work is a craft, and like apprentices in any craft, the skills, values, attitudes, and expertise take time, commitment, and discipline to acquire. Students come first to identify with and try out adult activities, experiences, values, and points of view, and they do this primarily by identifying with the people who are the experts, and they also respond to the implicit practice wisdom, values, and techniques of the craft. In this they are responding to an invitation, a calling, that embodies particular and general ideals and identities, intrinsic values that are required in order to accomplish an expertise. The work requires interdependency and teaching occurs at all levels of expertise, not just from teacher to student but also from student to less experienced student. Learning activities, in this view, are embedded in a larger community that gives those activities meaning.

These four different kinds of practices, all based on actual schools, assume different things about the meaning of learning and of what it is to be a young person, and there is implicit in and assumed by each a kind of metaphor: The constructive-developmental model—the progressive school—assumes that youths' main learning project is testing oneself against the world and organizing what is learned into a system of meaning—the scientist-poet. The therapeutic/romantic model assumes that young people are flowering organisms, with an innate pattern of growth, and the learning project is finding one's authentic, self-actualized self. The cultural transmission model assumes that the goal is preparation for the future by learning the knowledge, skills, and attitudes necessary to be a successful adult. And, finally, this "situated learning" model assumes that learning is a craft and that young people are responding to a "call," a vocation, embedded in everyday life—including one's spiritual tradition—and in this response is, in some sense, a working out and expression of one's self-transcendent, authentic, and responsible commitment.

The Educational Psychology of Growth and Development

Table 23.1 shows some of the characteristics of these four ways of thinking about learning and growth, compared by organization of time, goals, values, data sources, methods and mechanisms of growth, outcomes, and metaphors.

Organization of Time

Cultural transmission programs are based on clock time, in which linear progress is the measure of growth, and expectations are synced with objective measures of time, such as grade and age. Hirsch (1988), for example, presented a schedule of when

23 The Contribution of Spirituality to "Becoming a Self" in Child and Youth Services

Table 23.1 Education psychologies of informal and formal education

	Constructive-developmental	Therapeutic/romantic	Cultural transmission	Spirituality
Organization of time	Developmental	Event time	Clock time	Rhythmic
Goals	–Becoming a "self" –Building of a free and powerful character –Reorganization of psychological structure –Nurture interaction with developing society	–Finding authentic self –Self-actualization –Spontaneous, creative, self-confident personality –Health and growth –Self-awareness	–Teaching strategies for avoiding trouble –Transmission of information, rules, and values collected in the past –Internalization	–Practice of spiritual disciplines –Experience of ultimate concerns –Spiritual discernment and listening for one's vocation
What is true?	–Resolved relationship between human actor and a problematic situation	–Curiosity –Intellectual reasoning –Natural and inner self –Innate patterning –Novel immediate, inner experience	–Patterning or association of events in the outside world –Repetitive and objective knowledge	–Congruence with one's spiritual tradition
Source of data	–Thought and valuing processes –Meaning of experience –Longitudinal, universal, qualitative states	–Freedom –Inner feelings –Happiness, inner awareness –Mental health –Enjoyment –Novel, intense, or complex experience	–Favorable response –Incorporation –Discipline –Performance –Conformity to cultural standard –Skills –Traits	–Spiritual value system –Evidence of transcendence, responsibility, authenticity

Table 23.1 (continued)

	Constructive-developmental	Therapeutic/romantic	Cultural transmission	Spirituality
Organization of time	Developmental	Event time	Clock time	Rhythmic
Methods and mechanisms of growth	–Nourish natural interaction with developing environment –Rights grounded in justice –Ethical universals –Democratic practices, decision making, participation –Role-taking, increasing complexity of experience	–Permissive enough to allow the inner "good" to unfold –Freedom –Respect and defend rights of children –Avoid interfering –What children want is what they should want	–Direct, explicit instruction –Imitation –Reward and punishment –Discipline –Conformity –Demonstration	–Commitment to a calling/vocation "gift-giving," conversion –Pursuit of expertise service, faith, hope, love
Outcomes	–Principled agency, including toward and about oneself –Empathy –Perspective-taking	–Acceptance of oneself –Insight –Flourishing –Self-care	–Staying out of trouble –Contributing to society	–Finding a "calling" –Transcendence –Conversion –Authenticity –Responsibility –Expertise at spiritual disciplines
Metaphors of the self	–Scientist-poet (experiments) –Philosopher (organizes meaning)	–Flower; organic growth	–Machine –Wax –Telephone switchboard –Computer	–Craftsperson

students should learn ideas and concepts. There is a right age for everything, and some things are wrong at any age. Moral values are conceived to be the same—and look the same—at all ages. Honesty looks the same at 5 years of age as it does at 25. In comparison, romantic programs function by event time (Levine, 1997), in which the right time for beginning and ending is when individuals and groups are ready. When developmental milestones happen, when learning occurs, is when they *should* occur.

Developmental time is a consequence of the interaction between persons and the environment, and it is close to event time, except that there is a linear progress that results from increasing complexity of experience. Our expectations of kindergarten students going away from home for several hours are different from our expectations of college students leaving home for months, and their sophistication in managing the transition is developmentally different. Unlike clock time, though, progress takes a more discerning eye to recognize, because in the dynamic movement from agency to communion—and back—connection and independence are emphasized and experienced to relative degrees (Kegan, 1982), and developmental progress may, on the surface, look like regression. A child who, at age 4, orders dinner items off a menu may, at age 8, be too shy to do so, even though developmentally he or she is far more advanced. That new shyness may be a result of increasing self-awareness.

Finally, rhythmic time is cultural and ritualistic, being keyed in religion to the rhythms of the church calendar, call, and response in the liturgy, the organization of the day in a monastery or religious summer camp, and the rituals of daily spiritual practices. In secular settings, there are rhythms of the seasons, the year, and daily life, and child and youth care organizations are increasingly attentive to these. Residential programs attend to the rituals of going to bed, for example. These rhythms give life order and significance. There are also rhythms—and patterns—of dysfunction, and good programs recognize and intervene with discordant rhythms.

Goals and the Methods and Mechanisms of Growth

It has already been mentioned that the goal of constructive-developmental programs is "building a free and powerful character." This is thought of as resulting from the interaction with the developing society and the continual "reorganization of psychological structure" (Kohlberg & Mayer, 1972, p. 457) that occurs as a result. Growth is registered as an increasing disembeddedness from context, the ability to recognize oneself, to "take a perspective on oneself," and to exercise agency over one's impulses, needs, and goals. These programs nurture qualities of experiential, social, and material interaction with the developing environment, and they provide opportunities for role-taking, increasing complexity of experience, reflection, continuity, and a balance of support and challenge (Reiman, Sprinthall, & Thies-Sprinthall, 1997). The therapeutic/romantic programs are aiming for psychological traits like confidence, self-actualization, and situated constructs like "health" as well as meeting one's own needs. In this view programs respond to what children want, believing this to be markers of what they need, and they aim to be just permissive enough to nurture the inner good as well as defending the rights of children. Cultural transmission programs aim for internalization of the values and habits of the culture, the lessons learned from the past.

In sum, the constructive-developmental program wants richness of interaction, with the content taking a subsidiary role, while the romantic–therapeutic approach wants richness of individual and individualistic experience. The cultural transmission programs want richness of content, and the content is transmitted through explicit, direct instruction, imitation, and behavioral and behaviorist discipline. For spiritual programs, the goals direct attention to what Mullen (1995) called "ultimate concerns," the goal of existence and how a spiritual tradition answers the questions about those concerns. This attention requires "discernment," the ability to distinguish and choose from signs and signals about how one is to live. Spiritual programs nurture commitment to a vocation, whether general or individual, and they attend to spiritual practices such as gift-giving, forgiveness, love, and faith (Scott & Magnuson, 2005).

Values and Sources of Data

Each ideology values something, and the sources of data about these values differ. The constructive-developmental tradition, with its focus on interaction, believes growth is shown by a "resolved relationship between a human actor and a problematic situation" (Kohlberg & Mayer, 1972, p. 460). Persons are problem solvers, and in the process of mastering problems, they achieve a new qualitative state of development, shown by longitudinal differences in sources of meaning and in qualities of valuing processes. What they value, and the richness of how they value it, changes in progressive, developmental ways. The romantic/therapeutic program values qualities of inner experience and the richness of immediate experience which are, in part, aesthetic criterion. How much one enjoys something is important, and the self-awareness, authenticity, and uniqueness with which one enjoys is a measure of its importance and one's own growth. The cultural transmission program values objective experience: behavioral outcomes, intellectual and factual knowledge, skills, traits, and expertise. It is measured by performance and achievement, by demonstrating its accomplishment. Spiritual programs, in contrast, value the quality of one's discernment in response to a calling, as measured by the historical values of self-transcendence, responsibility, and authenticity.

Vocation as a Foundation for Spirituality in Informal Education

The constructive-developmental and cultural transmission models aim for outcomes that are true for everyone. The romantic/therapeutic model values individual experience, and one looks within oneself for guidance. In contrast, the perspective on spirituality offered here directs attention to self-transcendence, to processes of discernment from outside oneself, but following Adams (1987) and Kierkegaard, the existential difficulties of being a person are not about understanding the general ethical rules or responsibilities that apply to everybody—the universal—but individual responses and responsibilities. "The cases in which I am most likely to be morally fragmented, crushed, or immobilized, however, are those in which this procedure [the application of ethical principles] fails to write my name legibly on any particular task" (Adams, 1987, p. 448). In Kierkegaard's terms, it is consideration of one's "absolute relation to the absolute" (Adams, 1987, p. 452), the ethical obligation that is unique to me. This is a vocation, Adams says in referring to Kierkegaard, "as part of what makes him who he is in the sense that it is part of what gives his existence, his life, a unity that is humanly and morally significant. It is part of what matters about being himself" (Adams, 1987, p. 455). The central existential question is, from the point of view of the idea of a vocation: "Who am *I* called to become, and what is *my* responsibility?" Historically, this question was answered through the interaction between an individual and his or her "station." I will briefly review the historical development of the idea of vocation as a way of describing vocation's contemporary role in spirituality, summarized as the experience of and commitment to self-transcendence, responsibility, and authenticity.

One's Station as the Site of a Vocation

Luther believed that one's vocation is mediated through a "station" in life, for example, the station of work. Work is a divine vocation, although not the only one. A "vocation is the specific call to love one's neighbor which comes to us through the duties which attach to our social place or 'station' within the earthly kingdom" (Hardy, 1990, p. 46). Work defined who one was, the moral commitments required, and it placed one within the social hierarchy in a community. The idea of a "station" in life—others include family, marriage, work, church, social role, or synagogue, community, or education—is a helpful metaphor for thinking about what it is that religious youth require in order to mature. A station is both a destination and a waypoint. It directs attention to the social roles, traditionally ascribed, and to the values and identities embedded in it. It is how one knows who and what one is, a road map that tells one how far there is to go. These social stations were believed to be sanctioned and chosen by God, and one's spiritual and moral responsibility was to accept that call and commit oneself to it. One cannot choose one's birth family or one's community, and only an elite few have been able to choose their schooling and work. One could, in many cases, choose one's spouse and those with whom one associated. But an understanding of one's station was relatively stable and came to resemble an ascribed identity, an identity about which one could hardly imagine being otherwise. Thus, individuals came to see themselves in the image of the stations in which they lived, whether religious, family, or occupational. Kohn and Schooler (1978), for example, have described how blue-collar and white-collar workers come to see themselves in ways that are uniquely consistent with their occupations. Individuals may have formerly had a more static image of their life chances and possibilities, and to step out of this was literally to step out of the self, to be another person—not one's self.

Stations as Humanly Organized

According to Hardy (1990), Calvin modified Luther's understanding of the origins of stations by suggesting that the stations were not necessarily divinely inspired but were themselves culturally shaped and humanly formed; thus they require reordering and transformation so that they are compatible with God's intentions and so that individuals can truly exercise God's purposes within those stations. In this the community exercises reason and good judgment. Since the station is the context of God's calling, "our calling itself must be brought into alignment with God's Word" (Hardy, 1990, p. 66). This introduced an element of human agency into the experience, although it was still true that stations were largely ascribed. Still, Calvin's interpretation was that the world, and one's place in it, needed to be evaluated by the standards of what one believed God wanted. This requires some discernment and wisdom about God's will and the willingness to act on the basis of one's discernment in ways that help make the world more just. And stations in life themselves became subject to reordering, tinkering, and creation of the new and elimination of others. This is one historical source of the Protestant roots of entrepreneurial activity and the idea that one's success in life was sanctified by God, and it is the source of the idea of the value of individual discernment and authenticity.

Calling: Divine, Social, and Individual Imperatives

Over the past few centuries, learning about and coming to know and choose one's calling has been historically a weaving of divine—as Luther understood it—social—as Calvin understood it, and individual imperatives (Healy, 1986), but knowing whether one's call is "right" (true to God's will) has always been a difficult matter of faith and belief, and that problematic has its roots in conflicting tendencies within Puritanism (e.g., Clapp, 1996; Healy, 1986). In addition, according to Healy, cultural changes in western and American society have influenced how one's calling is discerned. As divine, social, and imperative strands became unraveled, the idea of a calling became secularized and individualized. Its roots are no longer always considered to be in a divine relationship or in community goods and needs. More recently, an "individual" confirmation of one's calling has taken precedence over other methods, even for many Christians.

> One effect of a secularized concept of calling is a change in perspective, from outward—first listening for God's call and seeking confirmation of that call in the tangible things around one, then hearkening the voice of one's society and finding fulfillment in a life of service—to inward: Listening to the voice of one's true self and seeking confirmation in one's own sense of satisfaction, fulfillment, and inner peace...Hearing the voice of God,

after all, has not—at least since Biblical times—been a simple matter. *How* does God speak? As I have already indicated, the Puritans never satisfactorily resolved this question (Healy, 1986, p. 95).

One's ear must be tuned carefully in order to understand God's call as mediated through the world; it is just as difficult to "hear" the call of God when the search turns inward, a kind of "eavesdropping on the self" (LaMagdeleine, 1996) in order to listen to God, and the signals of this call that are authentic—to me—are not always easy to discern. Still, there is here a historical process of listening to transcendent voices, represented in secular terms by other people, and in religious terms by God, as well as listening to oneself.

The Authentic Self

In addition to self-transcendence and responsibility, a vocation in contemporary terms is often heard, chosen, and committed to as an expression of authenticity, a sense that "this is who I am." One example is Ruby, who shows how her idea of an authentic self is used as an instrument of discernment and engagement with God. She is an intelligent and energetic high school senior who has many friends. In school she is in advanced placement classes, participates in a variety of extracurricular activities, and she has leadership positions in school and in her youth group. Even so, she does not think her same-age friends are always comfortable with her; her theory is that because she likes to be in charge and is very vocal she intimidates others. Some of her closest friends are older than her. She also feels atypical because she has a peaceful and harmonious relationship with her parents and brother; she is puzzled by the stories of intense conflict and disagreement with parents that are related to her by friends and acquaintances. She has not had many opportunities to date because, she says:

> I think sometimes I give almost a picture of being perfect. I mean, I go to church. I love going to church. I love my activities with church. I love my activities with school, and with [peer counseling youth group], and I'm in Campfire. So I'm very involved in everything I do. And sometimes I think that kind of gives this.... I think I just give this image sometimes that I'm perfect and it takes a lot to be in my world, but it doesn't.

Despite her busy social and academic schedule, Ruby feels somewhat the emptiness of her public image and the barriers that image has created between her and others, both male and female. She believes, though, that to become more "accepted" and more typical of her peers might require changes in herself that she believes would compromise her self-integrity, specifically, to not be herself. She has lost friends and dating relationships because of it. In this she has truly chosen herself.

The process of choosing a self can be a monologue, and Ruby describes herself in early adolescence as someone who knew what she was about and thought everyone else ought to be similar to her. Instead of continuing with this monologue, Ruby chose to "dialogue." One of the ways her dialogue with the world engaged herself, her family, her peers, and her sense of life's possibilities was in her choice of a high school. Ruby's family and community is white and middle class, and students in her community have a choice between a high school that is white and middle class and a high school that is integrated and has few middle-class students. Ruby's family wanted her to go to the middle-class school because they were concerned about her academic opportunities and about her safety. Her friends also chose that school. However, Ruby felt that the choice of schools represented an opportunity to test herself, to test her faith and God, to test the world and in so doing to find an authentic expression of herself. Further, she intuited that trying this high school would reveal something inconsistent about herself and about her faith as it was framed by her church. Essentially, she was testing her experience against her beliefs, motivated in part by a search for herself, and a search for authentic and real experience that she had not yet discovered.

Her intuitions proved to be true. Her choice to go to an integrated school illuminated racist attitudes prevalent in her church, expressed in their concern for her, and she found herself teaching them about another way of thinking:

> Ruby: That's going to make my church sound bad, but there's even some people in my church that are prejudiced themselves.
> Interviewer: Well, church is filled with human beings.
> Ruby: Yeah, oh, I agree totally. By learning to see that.... By saying, "Well, look at their perspective," I've been able to show other people—"Why don't you maybe stop and think about what they're feeling?"

She found some of her former friends to be wanting, since she realized that some of their choices were made for reasons of comfort and ease of thought "...they had that same background. They were from the upper middle class. That's why they went there. We thought exactly the same. And then I went to [high school] and it was like, 'These people don't think the same way I do!' And it wasn't necessarily the color, the race issue. It was so many different ideas."

Another example of learning to dialogue is in Ruby's experience of debate.

> I think my being in debate, that has helped me also to be able to see both sides of things, because, oh, gosh. It was chaos! When I started debate, it was chaos! Me and a friend were the only two Christians in this class. And debaters, they just have this gung-ho, "Say whatever we want to say" attitude. It wasn't, "Well, okay, I'll respect that that's your place." It was, "Well, that's not right. I'm right and you're wrong." So I had to learn to see their side of things before I could show them mine.
>
> At first I was just like, "I'm right, you're wrong." So it took me a while to see that I'm going to have to look at how other people feel, sometimes before I can see what I feel. Before, I didn't think that there could ever be a possibility that they could be right. I was just right and that was the end of the story! So I really learned to see that they could be right. Yeah, I have to listen to what they think without.... I would listen, but I wasn't listening. I would hear them, but I would be thinking what my come-back was going to be, what I was going to say in return. I wasn't thinking, "Well, maybe I could think about this. Maybe they could be right." And another friend has taught me a lot about if I don't understand something, question it. And I always thought if I questioned something about my faith, then I wasn't having faith. I was, "Well, I can't question that, that's just the way God wants it to be." But without questioning it, I didn't understand it. And that's why I had questions. So now, if I have a question, I question it until I understand it, and then I understand and we go on.

She found that attending this high school was an essential expression of herself: "If I didn't go to [high school], I would not be who I am." This is an expectation of authenticity, of a self created in part through her own agency, in dialogue with her past, her family, and her community.

It is this demand for authenticity that is characteristic of how contemporary youth discern their call—God's call, if they are religious. Authenticity is a form of self-fulfillment that Taylor (1991) believes can be a moral ideal: "The moral ideal behind self-fulfillment is that of being true to oneself" (p. 15). A moral ideal is "a picture of what a better or higher mode of life would be, where 'better' and 'higher' are defined not in terms of what we happen to desire or need, but offer a standard of what we ought to desire" (p. 16). Ruby expresses an ideal that Taylor (1991) describes as new to modern consciousness:

> Before the late eighteenth century no one thought that the differences between human beings had this kind of moral significance. There is a certain way of being human that is *my* way. I am called to live my life in this way, and not in imitation of anyone else's. But this gives a new importance to being true to myself. If I am not, I miss the point of my life, I miss what being human is for *me*...Being true to myself means being true to my own originality, and that is something only I can articulate and discover. In articulating it, I am also defining myself. I am realizing a potentiality that is properly my own (p. 29).

My potentiality is the goal of the spiritual educational ideology based on discernment of one's vocation. Ruby accepts the moral invitations of her faith. She accepts her responsibilities as they are framed by her family and church. But Ruby also feels called to be an authentic person, and she has experimented with her life possibilities and her self-definition. Most importantly, *her experience of authenticity, of being herself, is a criterion for discerning God's will*. In secular terms, it is a requirement for discerning who she should be and, in Taylor's terms, being true to the moral ideal. Authenticity is an experiential criterion, the expectation that what I feel be real, make sense and, most importantly, that my experience live up to my ideals. In Ruby's case, the process of choosing a school, for example, was her interrogation of God; she wanted her life live to live up to the high-minded ideals of her faith.

Discerning the Transcendent

Baumeister (1986) points out that most of the stable markers of identity for adults are no longer stable such as parenting, marriage, employment, religion, even though successful adaptation to adult life requires stable aims. As a result, the underpinning of meanings that sustains everyday life is missing or obscure for many youth, and many interventions with youth misdiagnose the problem. Most activities in education have to do with the "economies of the culture-spheres ... which remain beholden to the metaphors of production and consumption, distribution and exchange" (Schrag, 1997, p. 135). This is typical of most youth development goals, such as the intent to "produce" mature youth, to create moral persons, to "get youth" to be responsible, to reduce risks for them and for society, to make them economically viable, to teach knowledge, skills, and attitudes, and to prevent social problems.

Spirituality's contribution that is unique is a transcendent point of view. Schrag (1997) argues that transcendence has the function of "providing a space and a dynamics for a transfiguration and transvaluation of the life of self and society within the intramundane culture-spheres" (p. 134). There is more to being a person, especially, than the immanent, mundane world, and there is more to raising young people than production values. Schrag argues that the metaphor of "gift-giving" is crucial to the idea of transcendence, corresponding to Kierkegaard's movement from Religiousness A to Religiousness B, from "religion as a cultural configuration of beliefs and practices tending toward institutionalization" (p. 120) to religion as the "rupture of immanence" (p. 120), a "transcendent dimension of depth" (p. 123). The immanent demand of a return on investment is what most youth development assumes. "Be good and the return on investment will be good." But one element of transcendence proposed by Schrag is the metaphor of a gift which, if is truly a gift, is given without expectation of being reciprocated.

> The point that carries the pivotal weight in the phenomenon of gift-giving and gift-receiving is that the gift as gift remains outside, external to, the economy of production and consumption, distribution and exchange. Indeed, the gift remains radically transcendent to the determinations of reciprocity within the economy of goods and services; and insofar as it does impinge upon and interact with this economy, the gift displays a surplus of significations that overflow the particulars within the cycle of putative gift exchange (Schrag, 1997, p. 140).

The stories youth tell us that are the most powerful almost always display this element of gift-giving—either as a recipient or as one who gives: A single mother gave up a lucrative career in favor of one which allowed her to be at home with her daughter; a family that chose to adopt a developmentally disabled child; a boy from a Hispanic community who, when given a car by his grandfather, restored it into a family symbol and turned down an offer of $100,000 for the car; a girl who chose to attend an integrated high school rather than the "safe" local high school; a boy whose family sacrificed to help the father go back to school; a 13-year-old girl who, with her 12-year-old sister, ran the family business when the father was suddenly disabled; a boy's commitment to creating a community center for other youth; tenacious friendships; teachers and youth workers who invite youth to be colleagues; creating a work of art, music, or poetry; caring for a sibling.

God can be heard, seen, and felt in these stories of grace and gracefulness. From an immanent point of view, these are stories about youth risk-taking and about youth "at-risk," about "resilience," about competencies and skills, about "assets." At its best, this point of view emphasizes the importance of a "caring adult in the lives of youth" and the value of service to others, but these are typically methods of ensuring outcomes and of reducing risk. From a transcendent point of view, the point of gift-giving is not ensuring the outcome. The aim is the act of rupturing immanence which for youth illuminates and provides access to grace.

Discernment of Discernment

David Foster Wallace (1998) writes that in his experience of teaching Kafka to college students, he finds that they have difficulty with the difference between the idea of a "self as something you have" and the difficulties of "being a self." The "call to selfhood," the struggle to be "a self," requires discernment. We propose that child and youth services, both formal and informal, give some thought to focusing on spirituality and one's vocation as a way to make a subtle but powerful shift from the goal of arriving at the structure and form of identity, exemplified by knowledge, skills, and attitudes, to a focus on the emerging "struggle to be a self." This is a shift from identity as the goal to identity as a reflexive process of growing to maturity: In short, it is a shift from the static goal to the dynamic goal of "development." As Goodman (1956) said, young people look for something in which to have faith. The advantage that religious youth have is the typically firm belief that there is a purpose to their lives, a destiny. They do not always know what it is, but they are intent on figuring it out through experience and with discernment. This search is the origin of a dialogue with the church and the content of that dialogue. In their own terms, secular youth services can also engage young people in a dialogue about "being a self," about the individual relationship to the absolute, about one's calling.

Few youth have mature adults in their lives with whom to talk. Only 4 of 145 youth said that they have an adult who really talks to them about the meaning of their lives for any length of time. These two concerns are experientially attached to each other, not only in the value of conversation for nurturing, therapeutic, and supportive purposes, but also because reflection and conversation are themselves the experience of a "productive hermeneutic" (Veling, 1996, p. 68). Not only can youth learn from adults how they interpret the meaning of experience, but inherent in this dialogue in contemporary terms is the developmental importance of youths' emergent and emerging new self-interpretations as a result of these reflections. These are acts of discernment.

Vocation in a Youth Program

> "Well you know, sometimes I look in the mirror and I say, the face is familiar, but what's my name?" (Member of an Exploring Post)

Developmentally, on occasion the anchors for knowing oneself come loose. Sociologically, Baumeister's (1986) suggestion that almost all anchors are now unstable means that linear processes of "growing youth" into adulthood have a more muddled target. Mead (1970) described contemporary society as pre-figurative, in which young people live in a different world than their parents, and Coleman (1972) said that the prescriptions and wisdom of the past are not much of a guide to young people in choosing what to do with their lives. Coleman and Mead may have overstated it, but it is true that less is fixed. In the Exploring program, described below, of 69 youth who were interviewed, only 9 expressed any interest in the occupations of their parents, and of these some were interested specifically in avoiding their parents lifestyle. Under these conditions, discernment may be even more important than in the past.

One example of how this might look in practice is illustrated by the Exploring program, a national co-education, experiential youth development program in the United States. This is a volunteer-run program in which individual youth groups—called "Posts"—are sponsored by organizations—businesses, churches, nonprofits, public agencies, and recreation services. The organization provides youth access to its resources, its personnel, and its expertise, and the youth learn that expertise and are expected to share it with others in service projects. The program is intended to be run by youth in collaboration with adults. When it works well, extraordinary things happen. Youth in an engineering post design robots, in an emergency medical services youth participate alongside adults in providing First Responder care, in cadets youth learn to fly planes, at a Living History farm youth do historical research and write articles for publication, and in outdoor adventure youth go spelunking, white-water canoeing, and rock climbing. These are concrete, linear activities, and they are attractive to youth.

In the interviews of youth from good programs there were signs of more than activity: Youth experience an invitation, a calling, that we interpret as a kind of spiritual vocation. One kind of invitation is to be an adult. "We get treated like adults...well, we're on the same level. I wouldn't say adults, but it's like we're all on the same level. I mean, they treat us like they respect us and we respect them, so I guess that's like adults." A second kind of invitation has to do with competence; the opportunity to associate with competent adults—competent professionally and interpersonally—to be friends with them, and to see what it is they do and how they do it, is important.

> Youth: We have police officers, we have counselors, social workers—just whatever deals with the issue that we're talking about. We get the highest person that we can get because we don't want any information to be false that we're giving to people.
> Interviewer: Got it.
> Youth: We get the pros.
> Interviewer: Get the pros, okay. You guys are the pros.
> Youth: Yeah! We like to think so.

Youth were excited about being measured against adult criteria, surprisingly. They found the challenge of it exciting, and when they measured up and were able to use those skills in meaningful situations, it was quite powerful. "But I guess I like to be counted on." There was an invitation to learning, and it was often tied to specific needs, as in this youth who said, "And he dragged me...he was like, 'I need your help with something.' I was like 'What?' And he goes, 'I need your help. Come help me.' " When youth respond to these invitations, they become and are repeatedly invited to become responsible and to accept responsibility—for teaching and caring for others, for the safety of community members, and for the leadership opportunities. There was an interesting dynamic among some interviewees, especially young women. The more troubled and difficult their own family life, the more serious and intense experience they desired.

Explorers also talked about "being themselves." Their Exploring Posts were places where they could try being authentic: "Personality. Every...see when you... the school I attend now, I met all the people in the seventh grade, so you know, you only make your first impression once and, unfortunately, kids are not very likely to drop the things that they remember from you in the seventh and eighth and ninth grade, even though I know I've changed a lot and I know they have. Most people change over a five year period of time. They're a lot different, but you go into the Post and you just pick out right where you want to be and you don't have to worry about, you know, things people already know about you, not necessarily bad things." This girl joined an Exploring Post where nobody knew her, and she deliberately kept it separate from her school life.

Finally, there is an invitation to try out a way of life. Many youth find that there is not very much help in their world for learning how to live. One young man expressed his family's hope for him to "be somebody." Being somebody in his world is to avoid jail and be able to support himself and a family. They were not very helpful in figuring out how to do so. He joined an Exploring Post, and he has been able to strategically put together pieces of an ideal and of goals that are based on lifestyles that he sees, lifestyles that he wants to avoid, and images of what life could be like. In his present life he appears to have two lifestyles: One is based in his city neighborhood with one set of friends and his high school. The other lifestyle is in suburbia where his jobs are, where his Exploring Post is, and where another set of friends lives. He has pieced them together in a way that allows him access to an interesting future without rejecting entirely the necessities of his present life. His growth into maturity is more complicated than simply being socialized into a culture or a world of work. For him it is literally "self-creation" and creation of a world. When asked to identify the sources of his values, his ideals, and his hopes, he says, "Myself." For some youth that answer might be disingenuous or developmental, but for him it is probably accurate.

> Interviewer: You're putting pieces together. You're tinkering with all kinds of options and figuring out...life is a kind of problem and you're strategizing solutions and paths.
> Youth: Yeah. Like testing myself. I kind of take a little bit from here and there.

"Being himself" is a process of trying things out. "Doing his life" is a process of self-control and self-monitoring. Exploring is where he is the person he is but also where he is trying out the lifestyle of the person he wants to be.

Spirituality as an Educational Ideology

In sum, how do the stories from these youth about their experience in Exploring illustrate spirituality? With other youth and with adults, youth reflect on the meaning of their experiences, exercising a kind of discernment. They think about who they are and who they want to be, and they are invited to commit to and learn from purposeful and meaningful experience, typically in service to others. The meaningfulness is created, in part, by encounters with ideas and purposes that transcend their own experience and are time-tested and proven worthy and interesting. These opportunities invite youth to accept responsibility for themselves and for others, and implicit in these are embedded values. These expectations are grounded in a concrete praxis. For example, an emergency medical service is a kind of craft in which there is an important and specific expertise that takes some time to acquire. There are also important expectations, for reasons of efficiency and reasons of maintaining relationships, for how members treat each other and how they care for equipment and for patients. There are expectations for planning and orderliness related to pre-emergency preparation and post-emergency wrap up. EMS workers know exactly what is negotiable and what is not. The consequences of mistakes in care are serious, and discipline about the work is crucial. At the same time, EMS workers are known for being friendly, for protecting each other, and for their sense of humor, albeit sometimes dark. They look out for each other. Moreover, the practice of EMS associated with expectations to use those skills to help and protect others and for the public good. Emergency workers frequently volunteer their time. There is, then, a kind of craft subculture, and this subculture is shared with young people: It becomes a calling that helps shape the identity, the development, and the practice of young people.

Thus, the practice of EMS is a concrete horizon that also serves as a horizon against which youth can measure themselves, in thought and action. Self-transcendence, responsibility, and authenticity are anchored in a specific, local world in which young people learn to "become themselves," to choose who they are and to what and whom they will commit. In so doing they are participating in a kind of conversion experience that is "ontic," as Lonergan (1978) puts it: "The convert apprehends differently, values differently, relates differently because he [or she] has become different. The new apprehension is not so much a new statement or a new set of statements, but rather new meanings that attach to almost any statement" (p. 13).

References

Adams, R. M. (1987). Faith and philosophy. *Vocation, 4*(4), 448–462.
Baizerman, M. (1999). *The call to selfhood*. St. Paul, MN, USA: College of St. Catherine.
Baumeister, R. F. (1986). *Identity: Cultural change and the struggle for self*. New York: Oxford University Press.
Clapp, R. (1996, October 7). Why the Devil takes Visa: A Christian response to the triumph of consumerism. *Christianity Today*, 19–33.
Coleman, J. (1972). *Innovations in the structure of education*. (ERIC Document Reproduction Service No ED015159).
Goodman, P. (1956). *Growing up absurd*. New York: Vantage Books.
Hardy, L. (1990). *The fabric of this world*. Grand Rapids, MI: Eerdmans.
Healy, D. J. (1986). *The cultural diffusion of the concept of calling and its impact on Protestant clergy*. Unpublished doctoral dissertation, University of Minnesota, Minneapolis.
Hirsch, E. D. (1988). *Cultural literacy*. New York: Knopf.
Kegan, R. (1982). *The evolving self*. Cambridge, MA: Harvard University Press.

Kohn, M. L., & Schooler, J. C. (1978). The reciprocal effects of the substantive complexity of work and intellectual flexibility: A longitudinal assessment. *American Journal of Sociology, 84*, 24–52.

Kohlberg, L., & Mayer, R. (1972). Development as the aim of education. *Harvard Educational Review, 42*, 451–496.

LaMagdeleine, D. (1996). *The crucibles of society: Public schools from a Durkheimian perspective*. Unpublished manuscript.

Levine, R. V. (1997). *The geography of time*. New York: Perseus.

Lonergan, B. (1978). Theology in its new context. In W. E. Conn (Ed.), Conversion: Perspectives on personal and social transformation (pp. 2–21). New York: Alba House.

Mead, M. (1970). *Culture and commitment: A study of the generation gap*. Garden City, NY: Natural History Press.

Mullen, J. D. (1995). *Kierkegaard's philosophy*. New York: New American Library.

Power, F. C., Higgins, A., & Kohlberg, L. (1989). *Lawrence Kohlberg's approach to moral education*. New York: Columbia University Press.

Reiman, A., Sprinthall, N., & Thies-Sprinthall, L. (1997). Service-learning and developmental education: The need for an applied theory of role taking and reflection. *International Journal of Group Tensions, 27*(4), 278–279.

Schrag, C. O. (1997). *The self after postmodernity*. New Haven, CT, USA: Yale University Press.

Scott, D., & Magnuson, D. (2005). Integrating spiritual development into child and youth care programs and institutions. In P. L. Benson, E. C. Roehlkepartain, P. E. King, & L. Wagener (Eds.), *The handbook of spiritual development in childhood and adolescence*. Thousand Oaks, CA: Sage Publications.

Steiner Waldorf Schools Fellowship. (n.d.). Recommended readings. Retrieved February 18, 2008, from http://www.steinerwaldorf.org.uk/reading.htm

Taylor, C. (1991). *The ethics of authenticity*. Cambridge, MA: Harvard University Press.

Veling, T. A. (1996). *Living in the margins: Intentional communities and the art of interpretation*. New York: Crossroad Publishing Company.

Wallace, D. F. (1998). Laughing with Kafka. *Harper's Magazine*, July.

Chapter 24
Coming of Age as a Spiritual Task in Adolescence

Daniel G. Scott

Abstract This chapter offers a framework for understanding expressions of spiritual development in the behaviours and experiences of young adolescents (aged 10–15). Drawing loosely on the wisdom and models of rites of passage traditions, links are made between the deliberate communal coming of age ceremonial processes and the personal experiences of contemporary adolescents who are often left to accomplish the same developmental tasks in peer groups or in individual processes. Rites of passage included a deliberate acknowledgement of their spiritual significance and specific tasks, activities and means to insure appropriate spiritual education in a coming of age process. The communal absence of these rites now does not diminish adolescent attempts to come of age in spiritual terms.

Introduction

In grappling with the nature of spiritual development across the early stages of a life journey it is useful to acknowledge that there are and have been a variety of cultural models to consider. Contemporary society is not the first to be concerned with the maturation processes of the young and the implications for and impact on culture. Many societies have evolved ways of assisting the young to become adults in the hope of preserving and passing on their way of life, beliefs, value structures, cultural knowledge and skills. As is pointed out in the literature on rites of passage (Eliade, 1958; Blos, 1979; Gutterridge, 1979; Mahdi, Foster, & Little, 1987), one of the acknowledged tasks in a culturally constructed and deliberate coming of age process is the passing on of adult values. It would appear (Raphael, 1988) that the primary cultural goal is to insure the formation of successful adults and it is understood that having an informed[1] value system is critical.

It appears that cultures that use coming of age ceremonies understand that the task of adult making requires the whole community to be involved. One can only make an adult with the support of mentors, elders, peers and families engaged in

---

D.G. Scott (✉)
School of Child and Youth Care, University of Victoria, Victoria, BC, Canada
e-mail: dgscott@uvic.ca

a public process. Becoming an adult is a change of social status that brings with it new responsibilities, roles and privileges. Becoming an adult requires not only that the person coming of age have an altered sense of place and status in the social hierarchy but also that his or her home community marks the border crossing into adulthood accepting, acknowledging and celebrating his or her new status.

The communal aspect of coming of age is paralleled in other cultural rites of passage. One of the most persistently practiced rites of passage is the celebration of marriage in which some form of communal ceremony acknowledges the formation of a long-term couple that brings together two (or more) families into new relationships. In contemporary culture where public rituals around births, deaths and marriage are less common, there are a number of legal structures now in place to protect partners involved in longer term couple relationships if public declarations or communal ceremonies have not happened. For example, common law unions are now legally sanctioned based on a time period of shared living to provide personal and legal protective structures regardless of public ceremony. The absence of public declaration and acknowledgement are now covered by different social processes so that the status change of being coupled is still recognized. Communal status still matters to cultures.

In addition to a public ceremony providing a basis for the shared recognition of new status, the rituals that are part of such declarations usually contain some form of spiritual or religious invocation. The blessings of marriage, funeral rites, infant baptisms, graduation exercises and other initiation ceremonies often include prayers, appeals to the Divine, or an acknowledgment of obligations and connections beyond the self. The obligations being established extend beyond the assembled community to the larger society and may include recognizing the presence of ancestors or a call to responsibility for the care of future generations. Some sense of the spiritual is present in ritual and ceremonial life regardless of the form it takes, the language used or the degree of deliberate spiritual consciousness that is part of constructing the ceremonial experience.

As an academic who frequently attends graduation ceremonies at a secular university, it is fascinating to note the number of symbols and practices that have spiritual history and significance that are used in convocation. They include a chaplain's prayer, the swearing of an oath and the wearing of special vestments to mark the significance of university graduation. Passage is being marked in a public declaration of achievement that indicates a shift in status and communal responsibility. Values are being underlined and reinforced in a ceremonial way that consciously or unconsciously duplicates traditional spiritual practices and has spiritual implications. Universities are maintaining a long tradition of using public ceremony—a rite of passage—to affirm their beliefs and the significance of their place in shaping communal life.

As a scholar curious about spiritual formation and development I am interested in the underlying spiritual potency of such ceremonies and our cultural interest in maintaining them. We continue to carry some sense of the importance of acknowledging passage in public ceremony but we seem to have set aside both the need for a deliberate cultural coming of age ceremonial process and the spiritual affect of rites of passage on human development. Let me turn now to the language of spirituality and spiritual development to clarify my approach.

Spiritual Development: Several Clarifications

It is difficult to speak definitively about spiritual development as it is one aspect of the human maturation process that has not been extensively studied and for which there is neither a strong and commonly acknowledged theoretical base nor a commonly accepted structural model. We do not have a shared understanding of how the spiritual develops in concert with other developmental processes. It is easy to witness and study the processes of physical development as infants become toddlers, young children, early adolescents, teenagers, adults, middle aged, older adults and seniors. We have established normative ranges of physical development, recognized types of developmental delays, and studied nutritional, cultural and social impacts on physical maturation. We have robust theories about cognitive development and models of emotional and social development. Our understanding of spiritual formation is much more tenuous.

It is important for me to declare that I see life span development as a complex matter. In spite of a tendency to divide areas of human development into discrete categories with linear progression through steps or stages, the lived experience of development is not tidy and often not linear. There is complex interplay amongst social, emotional, cognitive, physical and spiritual developmental processes. No one area of development happens in isolation and the rate of development varies from one person to another and the personal pace of areas of development can also be irregular. An adolescent who is a late physical developer, not achieving puberty or adult body size until 14 or 15 years of age may have had a much earlier cognitive or spiritual development. And similarly someone at 12 years of age who has an adult body may not have matured socially or emotionally. I believe development has a cyclical nature with early stages being repeated or reviewed especially at major points of transition. For example, during the coming of age period adolescents may repeat some of the processes that Erikson (in Berger, 1988) identifies as earlier life tasks. Issues of trust and mistrust, autonomy and doubt, initiative and guilt and industry and inferiority may all be part of establishing identity and intimacy and require reworking to move on. As Maslow (1970) recognized near the end of his life transcendence and self-actualization could happen in a peak experience that did not require all of the other stages of his own hierarchy of needs to be met (see also Chapter 25).

It may be possible to identify the characteristics of the physical, social, emotional and cognitive development of children based on common experiences and acknowledged signs of development formulated through our studies over the last century. We do not have the same signposts or markers of spiritual development or formation, much less than any agreed insight into the spiritual experiences of children and youth. What is the spiritual life of infants or children like in their early years? What markers might we recognize? Is spiritual development a stage process moving from one milestone to another? Is it linear or cyclical? Are there experiences or behaviours that we could recognize and classify as spiritual? How do we explain or understand the peak, mystical or spiritual experiences of children (Robinson, 1983; Coles, 1990; Hoffman, 1992; Scott, 2004; Hart, 2003)? Is the spiritual capacity of a child merely a younger and less developed version of adult capacity? Is the formation of a spirituality a similar process throughout the life journey? What is the process of moving from an immature to a mature spirituality? Is there a parallel process to physical puberty that is a dramatic shift in capacity, "shape" and potential? What are the differences or similarities between a child's spiritual capacities and those of an adult? I am not pretending that this chapter or any other in this book can answer all these questions but it is important to be clear that we are working in a context where there are many questions that need to be asked in the process of understanding spiritual development. This chapter is focused on the shift from child to adult spiritual experience and expression and is written with some of the questions about that transition in mind.

The reader will note that I am using a number of terms: spiritual development, spiritual formation, spiritual life and spirituality. Each of these terms has distinct implications that are important and, in my use, all are based on the following primary assumption: being human is being spiritual in the same way that being human is being physical, emotional, social or intellectual. The spiritual is a part of the nature of our character/personalities and beingness as humans. I assume that the spiritual is a dynamic part of our lives that changes and matures as we do in all our capacities as we age. How this dynamic functions in our lives, the processes used or the forms and stages it takes are not clear.

I use the terms listed above with deliberate intent. I use "spiritual development" because it suggests that the spiritual is part of the larger conversation on human and life span development. I am also aware that spiritual development is now beginning to be mentioned in life span developmental textbooks used in university and college courses. In the context of my home province (British Columbia) the provincial school curriculum for First Nations (Indigenous) students includes spirituality as a recognized theme of the curriculum, but curiously enough it is not part of the acknowledged themes in the mainstream curriculum.

I use "spiritual formation" as it links to the rites of passage literature and some traditions of religious education that see the spiritual as being about giving shape and form to a person through the shaping of values, meaning and inner life. I use this term also to counter the conservative idea of development as a step-by-step or stage process that moves gradually from one level to a higher level, each stage built on the accomplishments of the previous stage. I am suggesting by using spiritual formation that the human spirit is malleable and can be formed/re-formed over a life span or life journey, particularly at transitional moments.

I use "spiritual life" to imply that the spiritual is grounded in lived experience. It is not merely a concept or a set of beliefs, values or claims but is grounded in and played out experientially, that is, the spiritual is best noticed in how a life is being lived. It implies a "way"—a way of living and acting that expresses or enacts a sense of meaning, purpose and lived values. One of the challenges of spiritual life as lived is the maintenance of congruency between how one is living life and the beliefs and values that are being espoused. I also intend to suggest that the spiritual is other than being. In addition to the embodiment of values it includes who one is becoming and how that becoming is engaged. The process of being shaped and "in-formed" goes on. The work of making a self (or more accurately selves) is unfinished business and requires a number of life transitions or passages.

Lastly, I use "spirituality" because it is currently being taken up in a wide range of areas, including popular media and literature. In my view, it is the least satisfactory term in its imprecision but I use it occasionally to connect what I am writing to the larger cultural discourse. On the one hand, it is a useful term in that it implies a link to other descriptors of human experience that end in "ity": emotionality, sexuality, personality and physicality. All these words suggest a human quality that takes particular form or shape. On the other hand, I dislike the term because it has become a catch-all descriptor for almost anything that suggests beliefs, feelings, mystery, religion, esoteric practices, mystical and unusual experiences or claims. In this chapter, I intend to stay within the boundaries of development in using spirituality. It suggests some quality of embodied spiritual expression in the same way that sexuality is *the state of being sexual; involvement or interest in sexual activity; or sexual appeal or potency* (Encarta® World English Dictionary, 1999). Thus spirituality is the state of being or quality of being spiritual, or involvement in/interest in spiritual activity or spiritual strength, energy or attractiveness.

Coming of Age as Cultural Model

In assessing the mechanisms of coming of age cultural ceremonies and processes I will be generalizing from a number of examples but my goal in this section is to establish the spiritual and developmental significance of the most common practices in coming of age rituals. There are widespread variations across cultures and religions in marking the transition from being a child in a community to being/becoming an adult in the community.

The most recognizable vestiges of coming of age ceremonies remain in some religious communities in which children go through a period of preparation and study to learn the creeds, sacred texts or language of the sacred texts and then are presented in a confirmation, bar/bat mitzvah, baptism or other ceremony to mark the shift to full adult status in the community. This normally allows the child, now adult, to take part in the full ceremonial life of the community and in some cases to qualify for adult political and ceremonial roles. High school graduation ceremonies are the most common secular cultural practice that duplicates the techniques of rites of passage to mark changes in status (see Markstrom, Berman, Sabino, & Turner, 1998). I begin with these potentially familiar ceremonies in order to point out a number of features that have spiritual and developmental significance beyond deliberate religious instruction. It is important to acknowledge that these ceremonial practices have long and ancient lineages and therefore carry some of the main characteristics of coming of age rites of passage and traditional developmental knowledge expressed in cultural practices.

First, coming of age ceremonies are communal and very much a part of the ongoing life cycle of a community. The adult community has a role to play in welcoming and accepting new members and the very act of inclusion is a form of renewal for the community. New members mean new vitality and longer term survival for the community. Rites of passage are the ways of preserving a community and its values and form. They have an essentially conserving function. At the core of coming of age rituals is the passing on of adult values and beliefs (see Mahdi et al., 1987). In religious settings, the instruction is meant to instil the central beliefs at the heart of the community and to assure the community that the child has learned them. The public ceremony celebrates the learning and acknowledges ritually the passage to the new status, with the taking up of adult responsibilities in the community. The new adult, as a result of instruction, knows what is central to the community, what matters most in belonging and has through the ceremony, acknowledged his or her acceptance of and dedication to those values. Simultaneously, the community has recognized the new status of its new members and welcomed them into their adult roles and responsibilities.

The rite of passage, therefore, accomplishes several major developmental tasks. It provides the new adult with a strong sense of belonging through being welcomed and embraced. It also gives the new adult an inner basis or structure for further identity development and personal maturation. He or she has a home or base, a sense of meaning and values that are affirmed and supported and a site for an adult role that is acknowledged and celebrated. These developmental accomplishments are grounded in spiritual assumptions that are played out in rites, symbols and intends to create healthy relationships across the generations. The child is now an adult and relates to everyone in the community, including his or her parents as an adult. The whole life of the new adult is being woven into the community.

Second, the journey into adult life is usually done in a cohort or peer group process. The instruction is conducted by recognized community leaders, teachers or elders (a term still used in some religious communities) and the peer group goes through the process together, including the culminating ceremonial celebration. There is usually some kind of exam or public test to demonstrate that the required new knowledge or skills have been learned. For example, a Jewish child reads or recites from the Torah in a synagogue setting, while a Christian child may be required to pass a catechetical exam or be able to recite a creed, make a public confession or witness in an act of adult baptism. These kinds of tests have many parallels in traditional coming of age ceremonies where they take a variety of forms including periods of fasting, vision quests or being obliged to live outside the community and its normal standards. There is a wonderful account in *The Long Walk to Freedom*, the biography of Nelson Mandela, who with his peer cohort steal a pig and feast on it during their time outside of the community during their coming of age process.

We can see vestiges of the physical testing common to coming of age ceremonies in the hazing practices used in initiations to clubs, teams or fraternities. Belonging is not automatic in the ritual world and requires deliberate acts to mark passage and inclusion. Thus, a rite of passage provides both a strong sense of a larger community with traditions that transcend the present and, at the same time, gives the new adult a sense of achievement, having endured tests that also work to strengthen his or her sense of identity, achievement, industry and skill in affirming a new adult self.

Third, the process marks a clear border crossing. The child is declared a full member of the community, ready to take on adult life. It is not a half measure. The advantages of such a clear boundary between stages of life are many. The clarity built into a coming of age process makes the new status an emotional certainty as well as a witnessed public and social certainty. The former child knows what the expectations of the community are and they know that the child is now someone who can and will take up adult roles, tasks and responsibilities.

An example of the kind of certainty that occurs in a rite of passage is seen in Ann Cameron's (1981, in Mahdi et al., 1987) account of a Nootka girl in a coming of age passage who following a period of preparation is taken out in the ocean in a dugout canoe and must swim to shore following a "special chant" and "a special prayer".[2] The girl emerges from her ritual swim from offshore to the beach and describes her experience:

> The people would watch for you ...and when they finally saw you they'd start to sing a victory song about how a girl went for a swim and a woman came home and you'd make it to the beach ...And after that you were a woman and if you wanted to marry up with someone you could, and if you wanted to have children, you could, because you'd be able to take care of them the proper way (as cited in Sullwold, 1987, p. 115).

The assumption that the passage process has prepared this young woman for adult life is explicit in this account. One benefit of demarcating the end of a passage process is that it gives certainty to all involved and prevents the new adult from the mixed messages of being an adult yet still being treated and related to as a child. In some Indigenous communities, passage rites would recognize the change of status through a naming ceremony that would bestow a new name on the person to indicate their new responsibilities or new identity in the community. A similar practice has been used in Christian religious traditions where adult converts would receive a new Christian name when being received as full members of the community.[3] The important insight here is that it prevents an undermining of steps forward in a life journey. Having begun a new life one is provided with as many affirmations as possible to move on.

One of the difficulties of contemporary culture where such clear demarcations are lacking is the confusion that comes in a prolonged adolescence of mixed messages and muddled contexts where expectations shift from expectations to be and behave as an adult in one setting and in the next to being treated as a child. Perpetual adolescence is not a goal. There is concern that having left childhood and being between childhood and adulthood is a dangerous time spiritually. It is a time marked by uncertainty. It is vital to move through the transitional period to the next stage of life. Having shed the roles and mores of childhood the not yet adult is vulnerable to being shaped by social and spiritual influences. Rites of passage practices recognize that a shift in identity to a new status is happening and establishing that identity is a communal task. A new personal identity is being formed and such delicate human work requires support, affirmation and recognition. It also requires guides or elders who can offer protection, advice and education as needed in the process.

Victor Turner (1967, reprinted in Mahdi et al., 1987), drawing on Arnold van Gennep's earlier work, explores in detail the middle or liminal stage of the three-stage process of a rite of passage. The liminal period, the time between the leaving of one stage of life and entry into the new status and role is seen as one of vulnerability and fluidity. It is dangerous because the neophyte is malleable to being shaped, to being formed in terms of values and meaning. Turner notes that the learning or "arcane knowledge ...obtained in the liminal period is felt to change the inmost nature of the neophyte, impressing him [sic] as seal impresses wax, with the characteristics of his new state. It is not a mere acquisition of knowledge, but a change in being" (Mahdi et al., p. 11). Obviously, the nature and quality of the imprinting is socially and culturally critical and so the deliberate care is taken to manage passage processes. It is also spiritually significant as the shaping process gives form to the way a life is to be lived, establishing patterns, core beliefs and character.

The re-shaping and re-forming of a human being from one form, that of a child, to that of an adult that occurs during coming of age is both a personal and communal responsibility. It is recognized that as the physical body changes through puberty and sexual maturation, the inner person is shaped into a new person in the same time period. This is spiritual and even sacred work that requires care, education and nurture. It is not left to a child to accomplish this passage on his or her own: too much is at stake, both the success of the child in becoming an adult and the wellbeing of the community in birthing a new adult.

The wisdom of the rites of passage process is that in attending to communal needs the structure also attends to the developmental needs of the young person supporting the transition and providing guidance, encouragement and limit testing to ensure that appropriate values are imparted, a new and viable identity is formed, and a person has a recognized role and life direction in their community that is valued and respected.

Adolescent Experience: The Spiritual as Lived Experience

I want now to turn to adolescent experience in the contemporary context and see how the work of becoming adults is happening. My interest is to explore what in adolescent behaviour might indicate attempts to accomplish the tasks that are addressed in a coming of age rite of passage. The developmental tasks that were consciously or unconsciously embedded in rites of passage that formed an adult still need to be accomplished. Establishing one's cultural, sexual, vocational and personal identity can only be achieved in a social and cultural context. How then does contemporary society provide mechanisms to support passage to a new self? What in cultural processes address the inner or spiritual tasks that give a liveable form to a young man or woman so that they can take initiative, experience autonomy, enter relationships with trust and be willing to take up tasks to benefit their own context?

One of the anomalies in contemporary culture is the separation of physical maturation from a recognized beginning to adult life. Although we have experienced a gradual decline in the age of the onset of puberty, we have simultaneously delayed the markers of adult life. In Ann Cameron's account, the young Nootka women who has completed her rite of passage is ready to take on the tasks and roles of a adult woman in her culture. She is not asked to delay adult responsibility, relationships or sexuality for educational or financial reasons until a decade or more after becoming an adult physically. The idea of a prolonged adolescence is a recent cultural phenomena. In terms of rites of passage it means we have taken the liminal time, the dangerous middle period and stretched it out, leaving a large cohort of young people in a state of being neither children nor adults subject to a lengthy period of uncertainty. The uncertainty may take many external forms but the inner spiritual formational process is, for me, a central concern. To accept that rites of passage contain some developmental wisdom means accepting that we may be creating an extended period of spiritual vulnerability for our own children by leaving them in a period of spiritual malleability through delayed maturity, that has no evident conclusion or settling of identity. This does not imply that identity is suddenly frozen or fixed forever. New transitions/passages will occur. Becoming a parent, for instance, is another identity and form transition.

If the border between child and adult life has lost definition, thinned out over years, there will clearly be conflict and confusion about what is adult, when it should occur and who has responsibility for it. One of my concerns is recognizing how much earlier than expected the becoming adult process may be happening. To return to the examples provided by religious communities, their initiation ceremonies have traditionally happened between the ages of 12 and 15 years. This young adolescent period was recognized as a critical spiritual time for the inner formational process that would create the adult value shape for the rest of life.

Younger adolescents are still engaged in the inner and personal work of coming of age regardless of their cultural context. If they are entering physical puberty at earlier ages it may be that for some of them other developmental tasks are also beginning earlier. They may be leaving childhood and entering the vulnerable liminal stage sooner than is recognized. In conjunction with their emotional and cognitive development, young adolescent behaviour contains markers that have spiritual significance and indicate attempts to accomplish passage.

The Markers of Passage

The sense of wonderso often celebrated as a marker of spirituality (Hart, 2003) may take a different turn in the early adolescent years. As cognitive skills develop wonder can turn into wondering expressed as questioning and doubts. The beliefs of childhood learned at home begin to be doubted and set aside. Young adolescents go on a search for new beliefs, interpretations of life, meaning and perspectives to address the questions arising for them from the ideas they are experiencing with their new cognitive abilities. Their peer group becomes an important source of information, ideas and models to follow and imitate. Popular culture, through a wide range of media, offers many options and opportunities. In a rite of passage the cohort/peer group would be deliberately assembled and provided with forms and structures, mentors and elders to guide the questioning and provide direction amidst the uncertainty of leaving the simplicity and certainty of childhood ideas and beliefs. The business of acquiring adult beliefs and values was not seen as individual work, but as a communal process that had communal significance. There are clearly trade-offs between the differing approaches. A rite of passage insures that traditional values are more likely to be imparted and a way of life preserved while an individual process may lead to more independence and innovative thinking. Over time, however, there is some danger that communal values would be compromised as they would not be shared in common or deliberately imprinted in successive new generations.

Young adolescents, who are experiencing a combination of new cognitive abilities, first time social and emotional experiences and spiritual sensitivity, can become highly critical of their familial contexts because their capacities may provide them with incisive insights about the foibles, gaps and contradictions of their home context and its practices. The acuity of their perception, which is part of normal developmental processes, was integrated and focused through the visionary processes of a supervised rite of passage. Vision quests, extended fasts, deliberate periods of isolation, solo challenges and even the use of biochemical stimulants to encourage visionary experiences are part of coming of age practices that are directed by experienced mentors who not only prepare the participants but act as guides and can lead youth to insights for their own lives and for the community. An attraction to stimulants and substances that alter or extend perception has become a danger for adolescents in contemporary culture. It is hard for us now severed from spiritual history and traditions to acknowledge that mystical experiences may be an important part of the developmental and formational process. We know that those experiences can be dangerous and our urge is to prevent them rather than providing a communally sanctioned and directed process. It is also difficult for us to see in the midst of cultural concern about substance use and abuse that adolescents may be seeking something that has been occluded from their life processes. Their self-directed attempts for visionary experience may have some inner necessity for them. The risks entailed are a complex cultural issue as well as a spiritual danger.

Berger (1988) describes the tension of industry versus inferiority that Erikson has identified as a developmental task of late childhood and early adolescence, as learning to be productive and competent. The task of having a felt sense of accomplishment as well as a sense of purpose is built into the tests of rites of passage as I mentioned above. To succeed in the tests of a cultural ceremony comes with acknowledgement, celebration and a change of status. Through a rite of passage a young person has a clear sense of their role and task in culture. Their specific talents may be recognized and affirmed. One of the struggles for contemporary adolescents is coming to a sense of purposeful living in a context of a culture that may delay for years the taking up of a life purpose or vocation. The delay is not based on the needs or processes of human development but rather on economic and cultural needs to delay maturation. Media culture, occasionally, celebrates what are considered to be exceptional young adolescents who catch a glimpse of a challenge or need in society and overcome astonishing barriers to follow a sense of vocation by raising funds for charity, volunteering or performing a public service. There are two Canadian examples: visit Ryan's Well Foundation at www.ryanswell.ca for an example of a young person who found a focus of purpose early and had support to stay with his vision. Similarly Craig Kielburger's *Free the Children* begun when he was 12 years old in response to a story about child labour. In 2006, Keilburger won the World Children's Prize for the Rights of the Child, also known as the Children's Nobel Prize.

A desire for purpose and the meaning it gives remain critical for development and their deferral has spiritual developmental implications. A life without purpose is a life in spiritual danger even without the recognition that purpose matters early in the journey of maturation. To defer establishing a sense of meaning and value until later in life risks leaving adolescents in the dangers of the liminal state with no sense of direction or reason to live. Feeling good about one's self needs to be rooted in mattering for the community. This is difficult to accomplish on one's own and so the peer culture and its acknowledgements become the site for meaning making rather than the whole of society. Purposelessness becomes a danger. The developmental task of industry versus inferiority has become a primarily personal task addressed as an issue of self-esteem with an emphasis on overcoming inferiority. However, feeling good about one's self is difficult without an experience of one's life making a difference in and to a context or without tasks that matter to one's community. This is the challenge of vocation: a spiritual task of meaning and purpose whose lack does produce inferiority, purposelessness and their emotional, social, psychological and spiritual difficulties.

In the movement from childhood to adulthood there is loss. Childhood and its innocence are being left behind. So are its developmental accomplishments of trust, autonomy and initiative. There is a necessary recapitulation of these developmental tasks that must accompany the move through liminal space into the first stages of adult life and the formation of new adult identity. A broad array of new choices, feelings, ideas and decisions present themselves and a new orientation to them must be established. Facing them requires inner work, the development of personal strength rooted in a sense of personal wellbeing and integrity. Coming of age is hard work.

I see intense adolescent insights and ability to doubt and question as expressions of developing spirituality. Catching a personal vision of life is a spiritual task that integrates new cognitive and emotional capacities into a coherent form. Seeing into and seeing through can also be a visionary seeing beyond that is part of the spiritual astuteness evident in young adolescents. These gifts of insight may not be valued as they may be expressed as disdain, criticism, resistance to norms or disappointment with adult life and roles. Carol Gilligan's (2002) *The Birth of Pleasure* explores some of the struggle adolescent girls have in becoming women when they see their primary role models as having compromised themselves in order to take up societal tasks, roles and relationships. The losses they see in the adult women in their lives can create a loss of self and they may need female mentors who can help them negotiate the difficult passage into adult life that does not require them to abandon themselves to succeed. Gilligan (1982) also speaks to girls' work of coming to a different voice as adolescent developmental work. A rite of passage aims to provide a sustainable basis for adult identity that incorporates the insight, sense of purpose and nascent identity taking shape in the transition from child to adult.

Voice—coming to voice, owning voice and giving voice are part of the developmental work during coming of age. Speaking of oneself and for oneself is necessary if one is to establish adult autonomy, identity, claim initiative and move into intimacy. A child lives in a world of external adult authorities such as parents, grandparents and teachers. Children are imitators and learn through modelling and copying. They acquire language and the mores and concepts that accompany their mother and father tongues. The beliefs and ways of thinking that are part of having acquired a language come under review at adolescence. In the early stages of becoming adult there is a necessary movement from a reliance on the external (usually adult) authorities of childhood to an internal authority that is centred in one's own identity. This requires that adolescents become able to represent themselves and own their personal beliefs and values. Accepting and parroting the authority of others is no longer sufficient or sustaining. The risk of speaking for oneself is the work of coming to voice. Inferiority, shame, doubt and guilt can lead to silence and reticence. Encouragement and support are required to nurture the delicate formation of voice. First tries may be clumsy and awkward. It may be necessary to challenge and test the ideas of new adults so that they can hone their skills of articulation, thinking and expression. The values taking shape must be good for the life of the community and be forged in dialogue with others.

The religious ceremonies that require public voicing of adult beliefs are a ceremonial recognition of the key role of voice in marking adult status and capacity. A congruency between the inner work of coming to one's voice and self and the external voicing of meaning, insight and purpose in a communal context is necessary for adulthood. In recapitulating earlier developmental work a young adult must shape personal and moral values of their own and make choices in a newly developing voice. She/he needs to claim beliefs based on and sustained by inner authority to underpin their stances, limits, questions, concerns and doubts.

Voice may take a variety of forms. I use the term with a double sense of both speaking/representing oneself and a more metaphoric sense of expressing the self through forms such as music, art, sport, politics, religion or social concerns. (See Kathleen Philips, 2007, for an example of visual art as coming to voice.)

I have now arrived at one of the key accomplishments of rites of passage: their ability to impart a sense of belonging. All of the tasks that we identify as developmental work are accomplished in the context of other people and sustained by families, peers and communities. We tend to see them as personal and individual work which is only partially true. During the uncertainty of coming of age and the liminal, in between time, belonging and having a felt sense of belonging are critically necessary. In order to emerge from the liminal stage and enter the third phase of the passage process it is vital to be embraced by and welcomed into a community. There must be a community that welcomes the person who is becoming an adult to create home and belonging. This person is not the same as the child who once lived there but someone new and he or she needs to be embraced as new to affirm acceptance and establish belonging.

This is not a slight matter as the new-born adult, not unlike a new-born child, requires a tangible inclusion that gives a felt sense of belonging. I use the somewhat awkward phrase "being belonged" to underline how important it is for the belonging to be known and felt by a young adult. A new baby needs to be held as being held provides, among other things, a sense of security. Being held by a community is also necessary for a new adult. Rites of passage with ritual and ceremonial actions, elders and guides and the formation of cohorts and peer processes, insure belonging and support throughout entry into adult life. They have an experiential wisdom that accepts that being a new adult is an equivalent shift as that from inside the womb to life in the world. Coming of age, a child leaves the womb of the family and the familiar world of childhood to being in the much larger and unknown adult world. It is very difficult to accomplish on one's own and being left on one's own is spiritually unsafe.

I think in communities where rites of passage have faded in importance it is in part because the community has gradually lost its willingness to grant full adult status through a rite of passage. One of my concerns is that the compounding dangers that arise in an unsuccessful coming of age will almost guarantee that the capacity to function as useful or successful adults in a culture and for that culture will be jeopardized. Lives will be marked by the collapse of developmental achievements that Erikson saw as progressing throughout the life journey. Mistrust of others, shame and self-doubt, inferiority, a sense of failure and guilt and role confusion are not a good foundation for adult life and can lead to disengagement, despair, depression and acting out behaviours. We criminalize some of these behaviours, diagnose others while ignoring the underlying spiritual vacuum and psychoemotional traumas that shape them. Aberrant behaviours may be attempts to establish identity or belonging, or create an acceptable sense of place or achievement.

In some coming of age practices living outside the community and its norms is a strategy used to offer an experience of breaking the rules in order to understand the value of living within them. A controlled marginal experience provides a perspective on community life that makes inclusion attractive. It insures that being welcomed into the community mattered emotionally, psychologically and spiritually. Being forced to temporarily live apart from family and community is not a form of abandonment but rather is a process that is structured and monitored as a learning time. It provides a time apart to focus on establishing an adult identity, honing a vision for life with a sense of purpose and nurturing the formation of an inner moral and spiritual authority. Structured rites of passage are able to use the unsettling energy and attitudinal shifts of the developmental process to shape adults who can succeed in their adult lives. The community provides mentors to help the neophytes focus their insight and support the identities coming to be in their passage into adulthood. A time and space for reflecting on life, meaning, purpose and identity are repeated in the practices of solitude, retreat and meditation that are common across religious and spiritual traditions.

If a culture does not attend to inner spiritual development at coming of age, it will have to deal with the chaos and confusion that the absence produces. I turn again to the trajectory of development that Erikson suggests. If adolescence is marked by identity struggles to clarify vocation, sexual and cultural identity and roles, then the work ahead in adult life is also at stake. Adult intimacy requires both identity and inner authority to establish and sustain relationships. The formational work that takes place in coming of age, by providing the inner shape where the spiritual qualities of voice and vision, the capacity to wonder and liveable values are nested, make intimacy possible.

Similarly, generativity is based on having a sense of vocational purpose and life goals that give meaning to one's work and service in a community. Being ready to take on family life and social responsibilities requires confidence, initiative and autonomy. The recapitulation of these developmental tasks during coming of age prepares the way for and prefigures adult development. Integrity grows out of having the capacity for reflection and reconsideration but it also requires purpose, belonging and a vocational direction. The journey towards maturity that assesses life as meaningful and of worth depends on having lived an engaged and successful life along the way. As I have pointed out above, it is not something one does alone but with others and for others in a community. The village needed to raise a child is required over and over in the developmental journey, especially at points of passage.

But why am I claiming that the developmental tasks and transitional processes based in coming of age rites of passage are spiritual? What makes then spiritual? The wisdom that underlies a rite of passage is that it addresses the whole person through actions that are both functional and symbolic. In doing so it provides a process of integration that addresses the whole person in a communal context. There is a concern for relationships and connections to the self, beyond the self to others, to the presence of mystery in life and to the living context of those in passage. Attention is being paid to the inner work and the malleable state of meaning, values and purpose at points of passage while not ignoring the practical implications of coming of age. By invoking mystery and recognizing that ceremonial practices impart and affirm meaning, a coming of age rite of passage connects neophytes to their community and to their own life journey. The experiential nature of the activities ground each member of the community in a common orientation. At the heart of the process are a respect for relationships, context and an assumption of connection and wholeness both personally and communally. These spiritual qualities are not in isolation but are part of a matrix of developmental processes that include social, emotional, psychological, physical and cognitive needs. The spiritual serves an integrative role as the site of shape taking where values such as inclusion, respect, responsibility and integrity can evolve.

Although there may be traces of this wisdom in some cultural ceremonies like graduations and various membership practices it appears that we are not collectively addressing the needs of younger adolescents to be embraced by a deliberate process that would allow them to address the developmental challenges of coming of age in ways that would affirm them, give them a sense of belonging and set in motion values that would serve them and their home cultures. To ignore spiritual development as an important piece of maturation from the beginning of the process is to leave far too many young people in danger of missing key aspects of human development that they need to succeed.

Notes

1. There is a double meaning for me in informed: the idea of having information or knowledge but also in-formed or inwardly formed, that is, having taken on a integrated internal form that is viable and useable.
2. This ceremony is akin to a baptismal rite with the risk of a swim in open ocean waters as a final test part of the ceremony. Prayers and songs, special garments, immersion and re-birth are all included.
3. A practice seen in *The Acts of the Apostles* when Saul who has been persecuting the early church converts to become a disciple of the Christian way and changes his name to Paul.

References

Blos, P. (1979). *The adolescent passage: Developmental issues*. New York: International Universities Press Inc.
Berger, K. S. (1988). *The developing person through the life span*. New York: Worth Publishers.
Coles, R. (1990). The spritual life of children. Boston: Houghton Mifflin.
Eliade, M. (1958). *Rites and symbols of initiation* (W.R. Trask, Trans.). New York: Harper & Row.
Encarta® World English Dictionary. (1999). Microsoft Corporation. Developed for Microsoft by Bloomsbury Publishing Plc.
Gilligan, C. (1982). *In a different voice*. Cambridge, MA: Harvard University Press.
Gilligan, C. (2002). *The birth of pleasure*. New York: Alfred A. Knopf.
Gutterridge, D. (Ed.). (1979). *Rites of passage*. Toronto: McClelland and Stewart.
Hart, T. (2003). *The secret spiritual world of children*. Maui: Inner Ocean Press.
Hoffman, E. (1992). *Visions of innocence: Spiritual and inspirational experiences of childhood*. Boston: Shambhala.
Mahdi, L. C., Foster, S., & Little, M. (Eds.). (1987). *Betwixt & between: Patterns of masculina and feminine initiation*. Las Salle, IL: Open Court.
Mandela, N. (1994). *Long walk to freedom: The autobiography of Nelson Mandela*. Boston: Little Brown.
Markstrom, C. A., Berman, R., Sabino, V. & Turner, B. (1998). The ego virtue of fidelity as a psychosocial rite of passage in the transition from adolescence to adulthood. *Child and Youth Care Forum, 27*(5), 337–354.
Maslow, A. (1970). *Religion, values, and peak-experiences*. New York: Viking.
McPhilips, K. (2007). Shifting shelves: The struggle for identity and spirituality in the work of three young women artists. *International Journal of Children's Spirituality, 12*(3), 233–248.
Raphael, R. (1988). *The men from the boys: Rites of passage in male America*. Lincoln & London: University of Nebraska Press.
Robinson, E. (1983). *The original vision*. New York: The Seabury Press.
Sullwold, E. (1987). The ritual maker within at adolescence. In L. Mahdi, S. Foster, & M. Little (Eds.), *Betwixt & between: Patterns of masculine and feminine initiation*. La Salle, IL: Open Court.
Scott, D.G. (2004). Retrospective spiritual narratives: Exploring recalled childhood and adolescent spiritual experiences. *International Journal of Children's Spirituality, 9*(1), 67–80.

Chapter 25
Youthful Peak Experiences in Cross-Cultural Perspective: Implications for Educators and Counselors

Edward Hoffman and Fernando A. Ortiz

Abstract Since Abraham Maslow's death in 1970, his concept of peak experience has enlarged our understanding of human spirituality. It has also influenced a host of fields ranging from personality theory to education, health care, organizational psychology, and counseling. Though Maslow contended that children and teens undergo peak experiences, he never explored this topic systematically.

In this chapter, the authors advance a new theoretical model related to youthful peak-experience. This model has specific ramifications for both education and counseling. In presenting this perspective, they draw heavily upon cross-cultural studies conducted by international collaborators in Asia, South America, and North America.

Introduction

Educators and allied professionals today are increasingly recognizing the importance of spirituality in nurturing children's full development. Though such founders of modern psychology as William James had a strong interest in transcendent aspects of human experience, this view receded decisively with the rise of Freudian thought. In contrast, Freud's two major associates—Alfred Adler and Carl Jung—both regarded spiritual development as basic for inner health and societal wellbeing. Though promulgating very different psychological systems, Adler and Jung each offered compelling ideas for raising and educating children with greater spiritual awareness. However, these ideas had little impact on mainstream approaches for many decades.

It was not until Abraham Maslow articulated a new, inspiring vision of human potential based on his concept of self-actualization that the intellectual tide began to shift in the 1960s. Especially among educators and counselors interested in fostering creativity, Maslow's concept of *peak experiences*—moments of intense joy,

---

E. Hoffman (✉)
Department of Psychology, Yeshiva University, 500 W. 185th Street, New York, NY 10033

fulfillment, and meaning—had strong resonance. For the existence of peaks seemed to bridge the seeming gap between the spiritual and mundane, religious and secular, dimensions of human existence.

Unfortunately, Maslow died in 1970 before embarking on organized research on peak experiences and no one of comparable intellectual stature and influence came to sustain systematically this body of inquiry. As the *zeitgeist* shifted, education involving "new frontiers" of growth and learning was no longer regarded with excitement but with suspicion. New names, such as "transpersonal education" and "confluent education" occasionally arose, but the field remained sidetracked. Nevertheless, professional inquiry into early peaks never disappeared completely, and in recent years, it has regained attention with the rapid growth of the positive psychology movement and strength-based counseling.

In this chapter, our aim is threefold: (1) to trace the evolution of this concept in modern psychology; (2) to review relevant empirical research; and (3) to highlight its importance for all those professionally interested in fostering greater spiritual development in today's youth.

Modern Psychology and Youthful Spirituality

The father of modern personality theory, Sigmund Freud (1856–1939), was highly antagonistic toward the entire subject of spirituality. As a proud rationalist, Freud regarded childhood as a time in which our lowest, most animalistic impulses are strongest. For Freud, the infant and toddler are nearly all "id"—that is, seething with instinctual drives for self-gratification. He saw the preschool years as dominated by incestuous longings that ultimately require strict inner suppression. It is hard to imagine a more negative depiction of childhood.

Though Freud's former protégés, Alfred Adler and Carl Jung, both valued religious sentiment, neither said much about childhood spirituality. Even William James, who, as founder of American psychology possessed a keen interest in religious experience, never really turned his attention toward the early years. This widespread lack of professional interest persisted for over 50 years, until in the 1960s, there arose a glimmer of professional attention to this evocative topic generated by Abraham Maslow (1908–1970), who had helped foster the new movements of humanistic and then transpersonal psychology.

In the mid-1940s, Maslow was developing his theoretical approach to studying emotionally healthy people—those whom he called "self-actualizing." Much to Maslow's initial surprise, he found that such persons reported having transcendental moments of joy in their day-to-day lives. These moments often possessed mystical qualities, as individuals described them in phrases similar to that of history's great saints and sages.

This finding was both unexpected and compelling but committed to scientific method, Maslow persisted in careful investigation. Finally, in 1956, he felt ready to share his findings with colleagues. Fearful of rejection of his unorthodox paper, he did not submit it for formal publication but read it aloud at the American Psychological Association's annual convention that year. Titling his address, "Cognition of Being in the Peak Experiences," Maslow (1959) began by asserting that

> Self-actualizing people, those who have come to a high level of maturation, health, and self-fulfillment, have so much to teach us that sometimes they seem almost like a different breed of human beings. But because it is so new, the exploration of the highest reaches of human nature and of its ultimate possibilities ... is a difficult and tortuous task (p. 43).

Maslow went on to describe nearly 20 common features of the peak experience, which he linked to superb mental health. Based on phenomenological reports, these features included great happiness, feelings of wonder and awe, temporary disorientation with respect to time and space, and a complete though momentary loss of fear and defense before the grandeur of the cosmos. Typically, no one peak experience described by respondents had all the features.

To what extent do such peaks reflect genuine perceptions of the world, and not merely the regressive fantasies that Sigmund Freud and his supporters had pronounced them to be? Maslow (1959) answered this question by asserting

> If self-actualizing people can and do perceive reality more efficiently, fully, and with less motivational contamination than others do, then we may possibly use them as biological assays. Through their greater sensitivity and perception, we may get a better report of what reality is like ... just as canaries can be used to detect gas in mines before less sensitive creatures can (p. 64).

Finally, and perhaps constituting the most important aspect of his presentation, Maslow argued that peak experiences often leave profound and transformative effects in their wake, "Generally, the person is more apt to feel that life...is worthwhile, even if it is usually drab, pedestrian, painful, or ungratifying, since beauty, truth, and meaningfulness have been demonstrated...to exist" (p. 65).

Such conversion experiences, Maslow (1959) declared, "are of course plentifully recorded in human history but so far as I know have never received the attention of psychologists or psychiatrists" (p. 66). He called for further study into this highly intriguing but little understood phenomenon of healthy emotional functioning.

During the tumultuous years of the 1960s, Maslow devoted considerable attention to the topic of peak experience. Relying on the phenomenological reports of several hundred college students and colleagues, he became convinced of two key findings. First, that ordinary people may undergo genuine peaks in seemingly commonplace circumstances; while waiting for a bus on a sunlit street or preparing dinner for one's family. Maslow found it astounding that some of his own students unknowingly described their peak experiences in language of rapture similar to those of history's revered spiritual teachers. The implication was clear: We need not be great religious mystics or even practitioners to undergo an unforgettable epiphany in daily living.

Nor, as Maslow (1970) concluded, is it necessary to meditate in a Tibetan monastery or travel exotically to gain such a wondrous encounter. As he poetically remarked in *Religions, Values, and Peak-Experiences*, "The great lesson from the true mystics ... (is that) the sacred is in the ordinary, that it is to be found in one's daily life, in one's neighbors, friends, and family, in one's backyard" (p. x).

Maslow became sure that the more emotionally healthy we are, the greater the likelihood of a peak experience and also the more frequent such episodes in the stream of day-to-day events. For example, in exploratory findings relevant to organizational psychology, Maslow found that highly creative people appeared to undergo more frequent peaks—that is, moments of joy and fulfillment—than their less innovative co-workers.

The birth of Maslow's first grandchild in 1968 greatly awakened his interest in early development. He became convinced that even young children have the capacity for epiphanies and numinous moments, but lack the verbal means to articulate these. Maslow increasingly argued (Maslow 1968a/1971, 1968b/1971) that contemporary education vitally needed to incorporate peak experiences into both its philosophy and teaching methods—related to the goal of helping students to self-actualize. He hoped to begin systematic research on childhood peaks once his serious heart condition improved but died in 1970 before starting systematic exploration.

Exploring the Peaks of Childhood

More than a decade elapsed after Maslow's death before the emergence of a published study concerning childhood peak experience. The contributions of Robinson (1983) and Armstrong (1984) were largely theoretical and conceptual. Both argued that children are indeed capable of numinous and ecstatic experiences, though their weak language skills may hamper research into such phenomena. Likewise, both investigators noted that religious history presents many examples of childhood epiphanies associated with celebrated mystics and visionaries. Not surprisingly, both called for expanded research into this relatively unexplored realm of youthful experience.

Luber (1986) conducted a study of peak experiences among 144 children and adolescents to discover: (a) what types of questioning elicit accounts of true peak experiences, (b) what can be rated as true peak experiences for children and adolescents, (c) how they describe their true peak experiences, and (d) what are the characteristics of true peaks. A true peak experience was defined as one that strictly follows Maslow's criteria for a peak experience.

These experiences were scored into five categories: (1) happiest, or feeling pleasure or gladness, (2) proudest, or having a strong sense of satisfaction in a person or thing, (3) plateau, based on Maslow's definition as "serene and calm ... response to the miraculous, the awesome, the sacralized and the Unitive", (4) pre-peak, or feelings not quite transcendent, but more than merely happy or proud; that is, intense feelings in which youngsters had difficulty containing their excitement, and, this was usually the precursor to a (5) transcendent, peak experience of intense joy.

The results showed that youngsters from 9 to 16 years recounted few true peak experiences. The "triggers" included achievement, being with family, traveling, helping another, being with animals or pets, feeling more mature, socializing with others, and being with nature. Did peak experiences lead to positive personal change? Definitely so, for participants reported such benefits as gaining a greater appreciation of people, places, and/or living things after their experience, as well as enhanced self-esteem, greater happiness, knowledge, eagerness to learn, physical energy, and pleasant memories.

Coles (1990) and his associates interviewed approximately 500 children aged 6 through 13 in the United States, Central and South America, Europe, the Middle East, and Africa. The goal was to learn "that exquisitely private sense of things that nurtures their spirituality" (pp. 36–37). Using a phenomenological approach, Coles (1990) found that dreams, prayer, and especially intellectual musing in response to formal religious lessons comprised sources of spiritual nurturance identified by his youthful respondents. Coles (1990) made no attempt to categorize or provide a typology of childhood spiritual experiences.

Tamminen (1994) investigated religious experiences among nearly 3,000 Finnish children and adolescents from two viewpoints: reported experiences of God's closeness and guidance. Almost 95% of respondents belonged to the Lutheran Church and had been involved in religious education. Except for first graders, who were interviewed directly, participants responded mainly to written materials provided by outside researchers in classroom settings. Seven categories were established concerning the reported experience of God's presence: (1) emergencies, involving a crisis, personal illness or another's illness, sadness or bereavement; (2) loneliness or fear; (3) devotional and Church situations including prayer and meditation ; (4) school and religious education including school curriculum and class prayer; (5) joy and happiness; (6) moral action; and (7) nature and the outdoors.

Intriguingly, the category of emergencies—particularly involving illness or bereavement—was by far the greatest "trigger" for the reported experience of God's presence, followed, respectively, by the categories of loneliness and fear and devotional and Church situations; the latter's subcategories most frequently encompassed prayer and meditation. Relatively, few participants linked an experience of God's presence to moments of joy and happiness or moral action, and even fewer to nature and outdoors encounters. Tamminen (1994) found this latter finding "surprising (but it is possible that many more pupils experienced God's presence in nature than reported it; such situations may not have been felt strongly enough to be immediately recalled in the study" (p. 74). Though Tamminen (1994) did not develop this point, it is eminently possible that her participants' strong linkage of numinous experience with acute emotional distress rather than joy mirrored the content of their Lutheran training.

Tamminen (1994) also found significant gender differences. Girls, in almost all grades, reported experiences of God's nearness and guidance more often than did boys. Both in the quantity and quality of religious experience, girls were religiously more committed. Interestingly, gender differences were more striking with regard to actual religious experiences than to beliefs.

Hoffman (1992, 1998) obtained more than 250 retrospective reports of adult men and women who responded to an "authors' query" placed in dozens of newspapers and magazines throughout North America and western Europe including Britain, Denmark, and Germany. Respondents ranged in age from 16 years to over 80 years.

More than two-thirds were women. The majority of the respondents was in their twenties and thirties, and had at least some college education.

Based on their reports, which supported Maslow's view that childhood peaks exist and can be studied empirically, Hoffman (1992, 1998) established a typology of eight more or less distinct categories of youthful epiphanies:

1) Uplifting experiences involving nature. These could be identified as relating either to nature's scenic grandeur or to its "backyard" intimacy.
2) Near-death or health-crisis episodes.
3) Peak moments during intense and personalized prayer.
4) Exalted perceptions in formal religious settings.
5) Spontaneous moments of bliss or ecstasy triggered by esthetic delight.
6) Profound musings about self-identity, life and death, and related topics.
7) Uncanny perceptions such as involving vision or bodily kinesthetics.
8) Unforgettable dreams.

Scott (2004) studied childhood peaks as reported, retrospectively, by a sample of 22 adults, the majority of whom were Canadian women. Like those in Hoffman's study (1992, 1998), Scott's sample comprised volunteers responding to a researcher's call for information. Their retrospective reports frequently described childhood peaks of great joy, clarity, unity with the world around them, and contact with "something beyond the self that has acted on/in their lives" (p. 15).

In two separate studies conducted in Japan, Hoffman (2003) and Hoffman and Muramoto (2007) explored youthful peak experiences among non-Westerners. Hoffman (2003) obtained 84 retrospective reports from 65 undergraduates at Bukkyo University of a peak occurring before the age of 14. Participants were predominantly women majoring in education. The results suggested that Maslow's concept of childhood peak experience had cross-cultural validity and resonance. Also, similar to their Western counterparts in Hoffman's prior (1992, 1998) study, Japanese participants often recalled childhood peaks involving nature, and to a lesser extent, esthetic delight. But three new categories also emerged pertaining to (1) skill mastery, such as learning to ride a bicycle for the first time; (2) external achievement, such as winning a scholastic competition; and (3) interpersonal joy, such as feeling intense filial affection or group camaraderie.

Significantly, too, retrospective Japanese youthful peaks in general involved classmates, friends, parents, and siblings (example: "When our volleyball team won the tournament" or "When my friend and I sang a duet") to a strikingly greater extent than did North American childhood peaks—which tended to be individualistic.

Hoffman and Muramoto (2007) obtained 56 retrospective reports from 51 students and faculty at Ritsumeikan University. Participants were predominantly graduate women majoring in human services. Similar to their Bukkyo University counterparts, they frequently reported retrospective peaks involving interpersonal joy—which indeed constituted their *single most mentioned category*.

In seeking to explain this compelling finding, Hoffman and Muramoto (2007) discussed the well-known role of social harmony and cohesiveness in Japan culture and personality development. They also noted an important possible link between vocational interest and youthful peak experience, in that participants were overwhelmingly adults (average age of 33) training for a human services career—which presumably attracts persons who are most fulfilled vocationally by interpersonal relations.

Cross-Cultural Research in Progress

Beginning in 2005, Hoffman initiated several collaborative cross-cultural studies of youthful peak experiences. These encompassed retrospective reports by college students in Canada, Hong Kong, Mexico, Norway, and Turkey. In each study, the brief questionnaire developed by Hoffman (2003) was administered. For the Mexican, Norwegian, Hong Kong, and Turkish samples, the questionnaire was first translated into the dominant national language and then back translated independently to ensure accuracy before administration to students. Data collection has now been completed in three countries: Canada, Mexico, and Norway, but results have not yet been published. Data collection is currently ongoing in Hong Kong and Turkey. In addition, data collection involving retrospective youthful peak experiences among Singapore adults was initiated and recently completed. Smaller, pilot inquiries were also undertaken among college students in Venezuela and adults in China.

To our knowledge, these studies collectively represent the most significant cross-cultural investigation of youthful peak experiences ever conducted. For the Hong Kong, Mexican, and Turkish samples, they also represent the first empirical assessments of peak experiences at any age ever undertaken in their particular countries. Because these various investigations yet remain unpublished, we are presenting them in summary form. While conceptually intriguing, the findings are likewise offered tentatively.

Canada

Hoffman and Scott (2008) explored retrospective peak reported by 39 students at a large Northwestern Canadian University. In the fall of 2005, Scott visited two graduate courses in the Faculty of Education and four undergraduate courses in the School of Child & Youth Care, and briefly explained the focus of the study. In only one undergraduate course did the faculty member allow class time for students to respond to the questionnaire. For the other five courses, students completed the questionnaire after class. In all cases participation in the study was voluntary.

Approximately 150 students heard Scott's presentations. The 39 completed questionnaires was a return rate of 26%. In general terms, the gender distribution of the participants reflected that of the six classes, in which the vast majority of students were women. All of the responses were found to be relevant and usable. Because one participant reported two separate youthful peak experiences, the total number of scorable responses was 40. Ninety-seven percent of participants who identified their

Table 25.1 Types of childhood peak experience

Category of peak	Example
Interpersonal joy	Singing with my family during Christmas time
Philosophical musing	Though my relative died, I knew a connection would still continue
Nature encounter	Exploring the forest near my neighborhood
Skill mastery	Making a castle out of wooden blocks in kindergarten
Materialism	Receiving pink pants for my birthday
Esthetic bliss	Performing a musical show in my backyard
External achievement	Winning the school district's basketball Championship
Uncanny perception	Seeing a UFO

gender were women. Thirty-eight participants reported their ages, which ranged from 20 through 52 years old, with a mean age of 28.3 years. Thirty-eight identified their ethnicity by country of birth: 31 were Canadian, two were First Nations, and there was one each from diverse countries internationally. Several participants indicated Métis heritage; that is, mixed-race European and First Nations.

Table 25.1 presents the eight categories of youthful peak experience reported by participants in this sample, and provides an example drawn from their responses. Table 25.2 specifies the frequencies for the varying types of childhood peak experience that participants described.

As indicated, interpersonal joy accounted for more than 50% of all responses. Ranked in order of frequency, the next three comprised—10% each—philosophical musing, nature encounter, and skill mastery. Relatively few responses involved peaks related to esthetic bliss, external achievement, or uncanny perception. No responses involved the previously established categories of exalted perceptions in formal religious settings, personalized prayer, near-death experiences, recovery from health crisis or accident, or unforgettable dream.

It should be noted that Hoffman and Scott (2008) established an additional category of youthful peak experience, which they termed materialism: involving feelings of great happiness from receiving a material gift, such as for one's birthday or a holiday. Based on participants' reports, the authors suggested that typically the

Table 25.2 Reported frequencies of peak experience ($N = 40$)

Category of peak experience	Number	Percentage (%)
Interpersonal joy	20	50.0
Philosophical musing	4	10.0
Nature encounter	4	10.0
Skill mastery	4	10.0
Materialism	3	7.5
Esthetic bliss	2	5.0
External achievement	2	5.0
Uncanny perception	1	2.5

joy stemmed not only from acquiring a desirable material object, but from what it represented: interest and caring from a family member or other adult important to the child.

Mexico

A total of 99 students at the Centro de Enseñanza Técnica y Superior (CETYS) located in Tijuana, Mexico, provided complete data. Data were collected by the second author of this chapter and by Dr. Miguel Guzmán, faculty psychologist at CETYS. Undergraduate students from all levels (i.e., freshman, sophomore, junior, senior) and a variety of major fields of study (58 psychology, 15 accounting, 13 business administration, 5 architecture, 4 education, 2 engineering, 1 dentistry, and 1 computer science) were sampled. The sample was ethnically homogenous, predominantly from middle-class Catholic families, and everyone reported having been born in Mexico. The sample encompassed a relatively balanced gender ratio (58 women, 41 men). The mean age for females was 20.8 years (range 16–26) and for males 18.8 years (range 16–29).

Participants were recruited from five introductory psychology sections, each comprising approximately 20 students, producing almost perfect compliance. Participants were given the entire class time—about 50 min—to complete the questionnaire developed by Hoffman (2003) in Spanish translation. The narratives were subsequently translated into English by Ortiz

The two authors coded the responses independently using system developed by Hoffman and Scott (2008) and achieved a high level of inter-coder agreement (100%) across all of the peak experience coding categories. Minor coding disagreements (fewer than five protocols) were attributed to ambiguous descriptions provided by participants and were resolved by examining the definitions of the categories. Based on participants' responses, we also established a new category of youthful peak experience: developmental landmark. These encompassed moments of joy from attaining a new stage of personal growth and identity.

Table 25.3 presents the varying types of childhood peak experiences found in this Mexican sample and provides an example of each.

Table 25.4 shows the raw proportions of each peak experience category in the Mexican sample. Clearly, interpersonal joy was named most frequently in this sample as a source of youthful peak experience, nearly four times more prevalent than the second highest frequency, involving external achievement. Relatively small, similar percentages concerned peaks of esthetics, materialism, and skill mastery. Peak experiences involving nature accounted for only 4.8% of the overall reports and one participant identified a peak relating to recovery from a motorcycle accident. No responses involved the five previously established categories of philosophical musing, exalted perceptions in formal religious setting, personalized prayer, near-death experience, or unforgettable dream.

Gender differences were noteworthy in several respects. Females reported peaks of interpersonal joy (56%) and esthetic bliss (13%) more often than did males

Table 25.3 Types of Mexican peak experience

Category of peak	Example
Interpersonal joy	Celebrating Christmas at home with family and many relatives
External achievement	Graduation from elementary school and getting awards
Developmental landmark	Traveling abroad for the first time
Nature encounter	Visiting the foothills of the volcano Popocatepetl
Esthetic bliss	Developing a passion for dancing
Skill mastery	Learning to ride a bicycle without training wheels
Materialism	Getting a coveted toy motorcycle for my birthday
Recovery from health crisis or accident	Falling off a motorcycle without suffering major injury

(42 and 5%, respectively), who were much more likely to report a developmental landmark (15% compared to 1%) as a peak experience.

Norway

Dr. Valentina Iversen of the Norwegian University of Science and Technology directed the study in Norway. An associate professor in the Department of Neuroscience, she visited seven undergraduate classes at a teacher's college and five undergraduate classes at a college for health and social workers. After explaining the purpose of the study, she distributed Hoffman's (2003) questionnaire translated into Norwegian. Participation was voluntary, and approximately 30 min was allocated for completion. A total of 360 students received the questionnaire and 310 were completed, for a response rate of 86.3%. One completed questionnaire was not usable, yielding a number of 309 for data analysis.

The sample was highly homogeneous: 95% of the participants were born in Norway as were their fathers, whereas 94% of the mothers were Norwegian by birth. The sample's mean age was 23.6 years (range 19–45 years). They encompassed

Table 25.4 Reported frequencies of peak experience ($N = 124$)

Category of peak experience	Number	Percentage (%)
Interpersonal joy	61	49.2
External achievement	16	13.0
Esthetics	11	8.9
Developmental landmark	10	8.1
Materialism	10	8.1
Skill mastery	9	7.3
Nature	6	4.85
Recovery from illness or accident	1	0.9

Table 25.5 Types of Norwegian peak experience

Category of peak	Example
Interpersonal joy	Becoming an older sister again
Developmental landmark	Far traveling alone for the first time
Nature encounter	When I got a parakeet, my first pet
External achievement	Winning a skiing competition
Materialism	Getting a new bike for my birthday
Skill mastery	Climbing a tall chestnut tree
Esthetic bliss	Writing a poem during my parents' divorce
Near-death experience	Surviving a storm in a small boat off Greenland
Recovery from health crisis or accident	Recovering from appendicitis surgery

257 females and 52 males. In terms of college majors, 47.6% were in education, 25.6% in nursing, 15.2% in social work, and 11.7% in physical therapy. At both colleges, the overwhelming majority of students came from middle-class, Christian backgrounds. Most lived in apartments near campus, with smaller percentages, respectively, living in student housing or with their parents.

The 309 reports encompassed nine categories, but over 93% involved just five categories: interpersonal joy, developmental landmark, nature, external achievement, materialism, and skill mastery. There was not a single report involving any of these five categories: unforgettable dream, uncanny perception, philosophical musing, personalized prayer, or exalted perception in a religious setting.

As Table 25.6 indicates, interpersonal joy accounted for 45% of the reported peaks and represented the most prevalent category. This result parallels the result among both Canadian and Mexican samples, which likewise involved students predominantly planning careers in the human services or health-care fields. The relatively high percentage of Norwegian students identifying a developmental landmark as their peak may reflect unique facets of Norwegian culture related to the individuation process; for example, many Norwegians in their late teens move away from their parents and travel abroad without them as a way to develop their independence. As expected, peaks involving either nature or external achievement peaks were relatively high, too. Perhaps reflecting the participants' college majors—which did

Table 25.6 Reported frequencies of peak experience ($N = 309$)

Category of peak experience	Number	Percentage (%)
Interpersonal joy	139	45.0
Developmental landmark	48	15.5
Nature encounter	43	13.9
External achievement	39	12.6
Materialism	21	6.8
Skill mastery	9	2.9
Esthetic bliss	5	1.6
Recovery from health crisis or accident	4	1.3
Near-death experience	1	0.3

not include such fields as music, art, film, creative writing, and theater arts—peak experiences involving esthetics were infrequent.

Among the four college majors, there was very little variation with regard to the frequency of specific peaks reported. This may be due to the fact all the majors involved care giving either educationally, emotionally, or bodily—as opposed to, say, engineering, architecture, or accounting. Interestingly, the females reported that their youthful peak experience exerted a greater life impact than did the males. For example, whereas 9.8% of the males reported that their youthful peak experience affected their life "not at all," only 1 of the 257 female participants reported so. And while 53.8% of the females indicated that their youthful peak experience had impacted their lives "intensely" or "very intensely," this was true for only 37.2% of the males.

Singapore

Philip Ang, a senior counselor with the Tampines Family Service Center in Singapore, directed an exploratory study in his country. He obtained a convenience sample of 40 adults, all but one of whom was born in Singapore. Because English is taught to virtually all students in Singapore schools, Hoffman's (2003) questionnaire did not require translation.

The sample comprised 20 males and 20 females. The mean age of the males was 32.1 years and ranged from 22 to 67 years. The mean age of the females was 34.2 years and ranged from 24 to 63 years. The majority of respondents were employed in human services such as counseling and social work, but numerous other occupations from accounting and engineering to information technology and interior design were represented.

As Table 25.8 indicates, the categories of interpersonal joy and external achievement were tied for the most frequent type of youthful peak at 30% each. Peaks

Table 25.7 Types of Singapore peak experience

Category of peak	Example
Interpersonal joy	Receiving encouragement from my teacher
Nature encounter	Enjoying the sunshine as I sat at a windowsill
Esthetic bliss	Starting to draw pictures when I was 11
External achievement	When I was appointed student counselor in school
Skill mastery	Becoming successful in long-distance running
Materialism	Receiving a tailor-made dress for my birthday
Developmental landmark	When I became an apprentice at age 13
Personalized prayer	Saying the "Sinner's Prayer" at Christian camp
Exalted perception in religious setting	When I was baptized at the age of 8
Recovery from health crisis or accident	Recovering from dental surgery

Table 25.8 Reported frequencies of peak experience ($N = 40$)

Category of peak experience	Number	Percentage (%)
Interpersonal joy	12	30.0
External achievement	12	30.0
Materialism	5	12.5
Esthetic bliss	2	5.0
Developmental landmark	2	5.0
Personalized prayer	2	5.0
Exalted perception in religious setting	2	5.0
Nature encounter	1	2.5
Skill mastery	1	2.5
Recovery from health crisis or accident	1	2.5

involving materialism were also fairly prevalent at 12.5% and were typically associated with being the recipient of adult affection and kindness. All other named categories of childhood peak generated small percentages: these involved moments of esthetic delight, developmental landmarks, personalized prayer, exalted perceptions in religious settings, nature encounters, skill mastery, and recovery from health crisis or accident. None of the sample reported a peak involving the categories of philosophical musing, near-death experience, uncanny perception, or unforgettable dream. Interestingly, the two categories of personalized prayer and exalted perception in religious setting accounted for 10% of youthful peak reports, whereas none were identified in our Canada, Mexican, and Norwegian samples.

Venezuela

In the Venezuelan study, we wished to extend our investigations of youthful peak experiences into other Latin-American countries to examine the cross-cultural configuration of early peaks in another collectivistic culture. Venezuela is similar to other Latin-American countries (Hofstede, 1980). Hofstede (2001) ranked 53 cultures along four value-based dimensions (power distance, individualism–collectivism, masculinity–femininity, uncertainty–avoidance) and found that Venezuela ranked 12 on collectivism, compared to other Latin countries (average of 21), indicating that this culture is strongly collectivistic with close long-term commitment to groups (family and extended relationships).

Other cross-cultural indexes, for example, social axioms (Bond et al. 2004) have also shown Venezuela to be comparable to other Latin-American countries. Assuming that culture impacts youthful peak experiences, we have expected to find similarities as well differences in peak experiences among Venezuelan youth.

Data collection is currently ongoing, conducted by Vanessa Dos Santos, our research assistant at Universidad Metropolitina in Caracas. Hoffman's (2003) questionnaire was used in Spanish translation. Based on a convenience sample comprising Venezuelan college students and employed professionals, 20 reports have been received to date via e-mail. Our preliminary results confirm the existence of comparable peak experiences that fit the 13-category typology. Content analysis of the experiences reveals a similar structure in range of emotions expressed (joy, bliss, happiness), specific values mentioned (familism, collectivism, personal growth), and meaningful vividness of the event. For example, a 19-year-old female majoring in psychology reported this experience of interpersonal joy:

> When I was about 7 years old, my parents had a fight and they were on the verge of getting divorced. It was the worst when they shared that with me—but after a few weeks of separation, they reconciled and we all went together on a trip for a week: the *whole family* together. Knowing that all of us were going to be together made me feel extremely happy. I still remember the trip as if it was yesterday and I still remember how I felt. It was one of the best weeks of my life.

And a 25-year-old male studying graphic design recounted this peak involving esthetics:

> When I was 13, my mother enrolled me in classes of graphic design with a well-known artist. I used to like painting but didn't have much experience. The classes made me decide my vocation and I consider it as having a very strong influence on my attitude toward life. I'm now studying graphic design at the university.

Discussion

In this chapter, our aim has been to review the historical development and significance of the concept of youthful peak experience, within humanistic and positive psychology, to describe recent cross-cultural empirical research and to discuss educational considerations of early peak experiences.

Contemporary theories and models of psychology are heavily loaded with medical and deficit-based constructs like trauma, symptoms, syndrome, pathology, dysfunction, disability, illness, diagnosis, treatment, doctor, patient, clinic, and clinician. In contrast to the pathology-oriented and medically oriented clinical psychology, Maslow and the humanistic movement in psychology introduced a paradigmatic shift with the introduction of peak experiences. He introduced the term "positive psychology" in his book *Motivation and Personality* (1954). We intend this chapter to advance Maslow's vision and the tenets of positive psychology with its more optimistic and appreciative perspective regarding human meaning, potential, motives, and capabilities (Duckworth, Steen, & Seligman, 2005).

Cross-Cultural Considerations

Distinct youth peak experiences were identified in all of the cultures so far studied and replicability of most of the Hoffman (1992, 1998) peak experience categories across cultures was good. These results indicate that peak experiences meaningfully cohere around 8–13 categories. The salience of some peak experiences should be noted. Interpersonal joy, for example, emerged as a meaningfully powerful experience in all cultures. Happiness gained from nature and esthetics were other salient constituents of early peaks. Experiences of intense surprise elicited by crisis (death, accidents) were also vividly recalled.

Theoretically, these results are consistent with empirical research on the universal structure of the affective domain (Izard, 1977; Plutchik, 1980). For example, Izard (1977) has shown the existence of 10 basic and universal emotions: interest, surprise, joy, distress, fear, shame, contempt, disgust, anger, and guilt. Proponents of the evolutionary biological perspective propose that these basic emotions have adaptive significance and will be universal across cultures. A careful content analysis of the obtained cross-cultural data clearly reveals the emergence, in different degrees of intensity and relevance, of these basic 10 emotions in recalled peak experiences.

These particularly universally salient peak experiences also have their own cultural "flavors and geographies." Exploring "the forest" near a neighborhood was identified as a meaningful nature encounter in Canada, winning a "skiing" competition as an unforgettable external achievement in Norway and hitting a *piñata* in Mexico as an interpersonally joyous experience, to name just a few. One could posit that the salience of these peak experiences may be related to what is culturally desirable and valued in these respective cultures.

Many of the Mexican respondents in this study, for example, reported interpersonal joy as involving togetherness with their family (often extended family) or with someone special to them. They reported feelings of interconnectedness as in the words of one female participant:

> My parents celebrated my birthday when I was 8. We had a party at the garden with my grandparents, with *piñatas* and many other people, with games, and seeing all of my family together made me very happy and cheerful. This experience of being with my family has impacted me and motivated me to continue fighting for family unity.

From such narratives, it is clear that many Mexican youth felt that being with family, friends, and acquaintances gave them a sense of purpose and positive feeling. Mexican students recounted a variety of ways in which such interpersonally joyous experiences affected their lives. Many believed that their peak experience instilled ideals, an appreciation for others, love and care for family, and fostered enduring friendships.

This is consistent with the view that Latinos, particularly Mexican and Mexican-Americans, define themselves primarily through relational, interpersonal, collectivistic, sociocentric, and interdependent self-construals, in contrast to more individualistic or idiocentric conceptions of self found in other cultures (Hofstede, 1980, 2001). Diaz-Loving and Draguns (1999) have also noted the strong affective and joyous bonds within Mexican family; the affective foundation underlying long-term commitment and reciprocal obligations with friends (see also Diaz-Guerrero & Szalay, 1991).

Analysis of interpersonal peak experience and its frequent reference to the collective and family may also be understood from the perspective of *familismo*, which refers to the cohesiveness, mutual loyalty, and reciprocity found in immediate and extended Latino families (Carlo, Koller, Raffaelli, & de Guzman, 2007). "La familia viene primero" (family comes first) is a joyous shared sentiment and appropriately describes the content of this interpersonal joy peak experience. Consistent with *familismo*, *personalismo* is another highly valued cultural dimension and it refers to the preference to establish joyous, warm, and friendly interpersonal relationships (Diaz-Guerrero, 1987, 1993).

Several Mexican youth noted that an external achievement was tremendously impactful for them; examples included earning an academic acknowledgment or being recognized for a certain skill. A male participant reported

> Graduating from elementary school and earning achievement awards for which I put a lot of effort for a long time gave me a profound sense of pride. I also made my parents feel very proud and got acknowledged by my peers. It taught me to fight for my ideals to accept the way I am and to appreciate my parents as part of my life.

External achievements had a strong effect on these youths' psyches and it provided them with an enduring, high sense of internal locus of control, optimism, perseverance, discipline, and motivation. Some of the external achievement peaks also had an interpersonal content. Accomplishments occurred in the context of family, friends, and acquaintances, often in a spirit of cooperation and camaraderie (Kagan, Zahn, & Gealy, 1977; Okagaki, Frensch, & Dodson, 1996; Stevenson, Chen, & Uttal, 1990). In their study on achievement, Diaz-Loving, Andrade Palos and La Rosa (1989) concluded that in addition to the conceptual definition of achievement as comprising mastery, work, and competition, usually found in individualistic cultures, the Mexican operationalization of this experience—especially among children—comprises cooperation, abnegation and affiliative obedience.

Several students reported reaching defining and significant events in their lives. In addition to the commonly shared rites of passage found in other cultures (birth, ceremonies making the transition from puberty into adulthood), these students reported other important benchmarks. A male student recalled

> The day I turned 13 was a great experience in my life because I felt like I was becoming an adolescent and I felt like the oldest among my cousins, and this was a cool experience.

All of these developmental landmarks indicate transitions from one horizon to another and herald opportunities for personal growth and new responsibilities. For instance, one student reported that, "I realized that I was going to have new obligations and rules. Also, I learned that I was entering a new level of education and a new school with new friends." Consistent with culturally common developmental transitions (e.g., from boyhood to adolescence, Lara-Tapia & Gómez-Alegría, 1991), a content analysis of the responses reveals that several of the developmental marks among these Mexican male respondents have a tone of "machismo," with males boasting of minor conquests of the opposite sex, learning to drink alcohol, drive a car, and feeling emancipated to go to bars for the first time.

Japanese findings (Hoffman, 2003; Hoffman & Muramoto, 2007) on the salience of interpersonal joy and relatedness, social harmony and cohesiveness, and the collectivistic content of peaks involving classmates, friends, parents, and siblings can also be understood from the perspective of culturally relevant values and constructs. Most likely these intense interpersonal experiences among Japanese youth can be best understood from the perspective of the widely researched Japanese cultural concept of *amae* (Okonogi, 1992; Vereijken, Riksen-Walraven, & van Lieshout, 1997).

While there is no direct translation of *amae* into English, it has been described as "the strong desire to maintain lasting social bonds with peers and significant others" (Onuoha & Munakata, 2005, p. 397), and a "desire for physical and emotional closeness..." (Behrens, 2004, p. 11). To better understand the interpersonal dynamics of Japanese youths' peak experiences in the context of *amae*, this behavioral description by Niiya, Ellsworth, & Yamaguchi (2006) appears useful:

> *Amae* is best understood by Westerners in the mother–child relationship. A 6-year-old child climbing on the knees of her mother and asking her to read a storybook while the mother is working on the computer would be a typical example of *amae*. The child experiences a sweet sensation of being taken care of, while the mother feels needed and trusted. Although the prototype of *amae* occurs in the mother–child relationship, in Japan *amae* also commonly occurs between adults (e.g., in friendships, romantic relationships) (p. 279).

Doi (1973) called *amae* "a key concept for the understanding not only of the psychological makeup of the individual Japanese but of the structure of Japanese society as a whole" (p. 28).

Educational Implications

Recently, several authors have advanced the position that educational processes should be based on a holistic (Schlarb, 2007; Taggart, 2001) and culturally sensitive approach (Garcia, Skutnabb-Kangas, & Torres-Guzman, 2006). Such an outlook parallels today's growing emphasis on strength-based counseling (Seligman et al., 2005; Smith, 2006a, 2006b) in place of focusing on client weaknesses, flaws, and pathology. According to the holistic perspective, all children develop emotionally, socially, morally, and spiritually, as well as cognitively and physically (McLaughlin, 1996; Miller, 1991; SCAA, 1995). As Kirk (2000) suggested, the holistic approach acknowledges and fosters such culturally undervalued ways of knowing as imagination and intuition—sources of innovation and creativity. Lealman (1991) advocated the need to integrate the spiritual dimension in the classroom as a means of preventing emotional and social problems among adolescents. Lawson (1996) asserted that the development of the spiritual dimension nurtures a sense of connectedness with self and with others, and a sense of interdependence and social responsibility needed in our competitive and fragmented society.

We believe that peak experiences can be creatively and effectively promoted and utilized in a comprehensive and interculturally rich curriculum (Munkachy, 1974). We concur with Dunlap's (2002, p. 185) criticism of schools for not validating and using peak experiences; she has called on teachers "to acknowledge personal growth rather than focusing on achievement." In their educational approach of multiliteracies pedagogy, Garcia et al. (2006, p. 64) have similarly called for the "power of technology to amplify and enhance the peak experience."

The recent scholarly discussion in England to promote children's moral and spiritual development provides a viable conceptual framework for the incorporation of peak experiences into educational curriculum (SCAA, 1995). Consider, for example, the following views regarding the aspects of spiritual development:

> A sense of awe, wonder and mystery—being inspired by the natural world, mystery or human achievement (SCAA, 1995, p. 9).
>
> Experiencing feelings of transcendence—feelings which may give rise to belief in the existence of a divine being or the belief that one's inner resources provide the ability to rise above everyday experiences. (SCAA, 1995, p. 9).
>
> Tuning ... the kind of awareness which arises in heightened aesthetic experience, for example, when listening to music ... Apparently more ordinary events in a child's life could promote a similar sense of unity, for example through an intense sense of belonging, experienced at a family celebration (Nye & Hay, 1996, p. 148).
>
> Educationalists think they understand what is implied by the development of the intellect because cognitive concerns have controlled the curriculum for so long (Nye & Hay, 1996, p. 144)

These quotations highlight a significant emerging challenge to traditional pedagogy and child psychology. Certainly, an overemphasis on cognitively focused education and the mere acquisition of conceptual knowledge disregards children's moral and spiritual development. The humanistic perspective eloquently argued by Maslow (1968a, 1968b) suggests that virtually all children have the capacity for peak experiences and these can be constructively and suitably integrated in educational experiences.

Some Thoughts on Future Research

Space does not allow an extensive discussion of future research possibilities. A possible limitation of the studies reviewed in this chapter is the overreliance on phenomenological methods of uncertain objectivity, reliability, and validity. Relying heavily on the subjective impressions and free recollections of respondents may also limit cross-cultural comparisons. We believe that future research can benefit from a blend of qualitative and quantitative methodologies.

From a cross-cultural perspective on the structure and measurement of youthful peak experiences, perhaps the highest priority is to integrate the many categories that have been identified into a consensus taxonomy or typology and relate them to other spiritual dimensions, especially, spiritual categories found in children and adolescents in cross-cultural samples. Similarly, youthful peak experiences could be systematically related to well-established developmental models (Erikson, Piaget), personality dimensions, and measures of values (Schwartz Values Inventory).

A logical extension of the current cross-cultural investigations with convenient samples would be to conduct further research with purposive sampling strategies, for example, by purposefully comparing cultures on specific cultural dimensions (collectivism, individualism, and social axioms). Self-ratings on large and representative samples can be factor analyzed to derive an arguably comprehensive set of cultures and their youthful peak-experience taxonomies. Additional priorities for research include: (a) structural replication of early peak-experience categories assessed by valid and reliable instruments; (b) further elaboration of the nomological networks (e.g., behavioral correlates) of early peak experiences; (c) systematic comparisons of the youthful peak experiences identified using alternative methodological methods; and (d) intracultural studies, which address both the diversity and change of these experiences within given cultures.

Evolutionary theorists view certain universal human experiences as having evolved to solve adaptive problems of group living. The study of peak experiences from an evolutionary and psychological perspective seems a fertile area of research. For example, one could posit that, given our preliminary evidence suggesting the existence of universal and cross-cultural peak-experience categories, interpersonal joy may be related to the adaptive development of a "motivational system," which gets triggered by specific types of stimulation (e.g., the smell of a flower, the happiness of a child in close, intimate contact with its mother). Thus, future research can explore (a) the underlying psychological and motivational mechanisms of universal peak experiences and (b) the heritability evidence of characteriological and maturational trends of early peaks.

References

Armstrong, T. (1984). Transpersonal experiences in childhood. *Journal of Transpersonal Psychology, 16*(2), 207–230.
Behrens, K. Y. (2004). A multifaceted view of the concept of amae: Reconsidering the indigenous Japanese concept of relatedness. *Human Development, 47*, 1–27.
Bond, M. Leung, K., Au, A., Tong, K-T., Carrasquel, S.R., Murakami, S. et al. (2004). Culture-level dimensions of social axioms and their correlates across 41 cultures. *Journal of Cross-Cultural Psychology, 35*, 548–570.
Carlo, G., Koller, S., Raffaelli, M., & de Guzman, M. R. T. (2007). Culture-related strengths among Latin American families: A case study of Brazil. *Marriage & Family Review, 41*(3–4), 335–360.
Coles, R. (1990). *The spiritual life of children*. Boston: Houghton Mifflin.
Diaz-Guerrero, R. (1987). Historical sociocultural premises and ethnic socialization. In J. S. Phinney & M. J. Rotheram (Eds.), *Children's ethnic socialization: Pluralism and development* (pp. 239–250). Newbury Park, CA: Sage.
Diaz-Guerrero, R. (1993). Mexican ethnopsychology. In U. Kim & J. W. Berry (Eds.), *Indigenous psychologies: Research and experience in cultural context* (pp. 44–55). Newbury Park, CA: Sage.
Diaz-Guerrero, R., & Szalay, L. B. (1991). *Understanding Mexicans and Americans: Cultural perspectives in conflict*. New York: Plenum.
Diaz-Loving, R., Andrade Palos, P., & La Rosa, J. (1989) Orientación de logro: Desarrollo de una escala multidimensional (EOL) y su relación con aspectos sociales y de personalidad [Achievement orientation: The development of a multidimensional scale (EOL) and its relation to social and personality variables]. *Revista Mexicana de Psicología, 6*, 21–26.
Díaz-Loving, R., & Draguns, J. G. (1999). Culture, meaning, and personality in Mexico and in the United States. In Y.-T. Lee, C. R. McCauley, & J. G. Draguns (Eds.), *Personality and person perception across culture* (pp. 103–126). Mahwah, NJ: Lawrence Erlbaum.
Doi, T. (1973). *The anatomy of dependence*. Tokyo: Kodansha International.

Duckworth, A. L., Steen, T. A., & Seligman, M. E. P. (2005). Positive psychology in clinical practice. *Annual Review of Clinical Psychology, 1*, 629–651.

Dunlap, L. L. (2002). *What all children need: Theory and application*. Lanham, MD: University Press of America.

Garcia, O., Skutnabb-Kangas, T., & Torres-Guzman, E. M., (2006) *Imagining multilingual schools: Languages in education and globalization*. Clevedon: Multilingual Matters.

Hoffman, E. (1992). *Visions of innocence: Spiritual and inspirational experiences of childhood*. Boston: Shambhala.

Hoffman, E. (1998). Peak experiences in childhood: An exploratory study. *Journal of Humanistic Psychology, 38*(1), 109–120.

Hoffman, E. (2003). Peak-experiences in Japanese youth. *Japanese Journal of Humanistic Psychology, 21*(1), 112–121.

Hoffman, E., & Muramoto, S. (2007). Peak-experiences among Japanese Youth. *Journal of Humanistic Psychology, 47*(4), 524–540.

Hoffman, E., & Scott, D. G. (2008). *Youthful peak-experiences: Implications for spiritual counseling*. Unpublished manuscript. Department of Psychology, Yeshiva University, New York.

Hofstede, G. (1980). *Culture's consequences: International differences in work-related values*. Newbury Park, CA: Sage.

Hofstede, G. (2001). *Culture's consequences, comparing values, behaviors, institutions, and organizations across nations* (2nd ed.). Thousand Oaks: Sage Publications.

Izard, C. E. (1977). *Human emotions*. New York: Plenum.

Kagan, S., Zahn, G. L., & Gealy, J. (1977). Competition and school achievement among Anglo-American and Mexican-American children. *Journal of Educational Psychology, 69*, 432–441.

Kirk, R., III. (2000). Spirituality in education: A conceptual analysis (Unpublished doctoral dissertation, University of Connecticut). *Dissertation Abstract International, 61*(04), 1337.

Lara-Tapia, L., & Gómez-Alegría, P. (1991). Cambios socioculturales en respecto al machismo y la virginidad: Un estudio en relación al cambio social [Sociocultural changes regarding machismo and virginity: A study in relation to social change]. *Revista Mexicana de Psicología, 8*, 17–32.

Lawson, J. A. E. (1996). *An exploration of the relationship between children's spirituality and the curriculum*. Unpublished master's thesis, Simon Fraser University, British Columbia, Canada.

Lealman, B. (1991). Young people, spirituality and the future. *Religious Education, 86*, 265–275.

Luber, M. (1986). *Peak experiences: An exploratory study of positive experiences recounted by children and adolescents*. Unpublished doctoral dissertation, Bryn Mawr College, Bryn Mawr, PA.

Maslow, A. (1959). Cognition of being in the peak experiences. *Journal of Genetic Psychology, 94*, 43–66.

Maslow, A. (1968a/1971). Goals and implications of humanistic education. *Farther Reaches of Human Nature*. New York: Viking Press.

Maslow, A. (1968b/1971) Education and peak-experiences. *Farther Reaches of Human Nature*. New York: Viking Press.

Maslow, A. (1970). *Religion, values, and peak-experiences*. New York: Viking.

McLaughlin, T. (1996). Education of the whole child? In R. Best (Ed.), *Education, Spirituality and the Whole Child* (pp. 9–19). London: Cassell.

Miller, R. (1991). Holism and meaning: Foundations for a coherent holistic theory. *Holistic Education Review, 4*, 23–32.

Munkachy, L. D. (1974). *Peak experiences and self-actualization in traditional and alternative styles of education: An exploratory survey*. Unpublished doctoral dissertation, Michigan, University of Michigan.

Niiya, Y., Ellsworth, P. C., & Yamaguchi, S. (2006). Amae in Japan and the United States: An exploration of a "culturally unique" emotion. *Emotion, 6*, 279–295.

Nye, R., & Hay, D. (1996). Identifying children's spirituality: How do you start without a starting point? *British Journal of Religious Education, 18*, 144–154.

Okagaki, L., Frensch, P. A., & Dodson, N. E. (1996). Mexican American children's perceptions of self and school achievement. *Hispanic Journal of Behavioral Sciences, 18*, 469–474.

Okonogi, K. (1992). Amae as seen in diverse interpersonal interactions. *Infant Mental Health Journal, 13*, 18–25.

Onuoha, F. N., & Munakata, T. (2005). Implications of amae for HIV risk in Japanese young adults. *Adolescence, 40*, 397–402.

Plutchik, R. (1980). *Emotion: A psychoevolutionary approach*. New York: Harper & Row.

Robinson, E. (1983). *The original vision: A study of the religious experiences of childhood*. New York: Seabury.

SCAA. (1995). *Spiritual and moral development: A discussion paper*. London: SCAA Publications.

Schlarb, C. W. (2007). The developmental impact of not integrating childhood peak experiences. *International Journal of Children's Spirituality, 11(3)*, 249–262.

Scott, D. G. (2004). Retrospective spiritual narratives: Exploring recalled childhood and adolescent spiritual experiences. *International Journal of Children's Spirituality, 9(1)*, 47–65.

Seligman, M. E. P., Steen, T., Park, N. & Peterson, C. (2005). Positive psychology progress: Empirical validation of interventions. *American Psychologist, 60(5)*, 410–421.

Smith, E. J. (2006a). The strength-based counseling model. *The Counseling Psychologist, 34(1)*, 13–79.

Smith, E. J. (2006b). The strength-based counseling model: A paradigm shift in counseling. *The Counseling Psychologist, 34(1)*, 134–144.

Stevenson, H. W., Chen, C., & Uttal, D. H. (1990). Beliefs and achievement: A study of black, white, and Hispanic children. *Child Development, 61*, 508–523.

Taggart, G. (2001). Nurturing spirituality: A rationale for holistic education. *International Journal of Children's Spirituality, 6*, 325–339.

Tamminen, K. (1994). Religious experiences in childhood and adolescence: A viewpoint of religious development between the ages of 7 and 20. *The International Journal for the Psychology of Religion, 42(2)*, 61–85.

Vereijken, C. M. J. L., Riksen-Walraven, J. M., & van Lieshout, C. F. M. (1997). Mother-infant relationships in Japan: Attachment, dependency, and amae. *Journal of Cross-Cultural Psychology, 28*, 442–462.

Chapter 26
Peak Experiences Explored Through Literature

Ann M. Trousdale

Abstract A sense of connection with the natural world is an often-noted aspect of children's spirituality (Nye, 1998; Hart, 2003); it is in the natural world that many children report having "peak experiences" of peace, oneness, and timelessness (Schlarb, 2004). Yet encounter with the natural world is increasingly rare for many children today.

While direct, sustained experience with nature is most likely to provide such moments, literature offers a means by which children may find desire for such encounters quickened, or find confirmation for such instincts or experiences. This chapter discusses works of literature, ranging from picture books for young children to young adult novels which feature relationship with the natural world. Themes include a sense of awe and wonder at the natural world; the healing and restorative qualities of nature; a journey into the heart and rhythm of nature, including challenges of the untamed natural world; deeper understanding of oneself, of others and of the Divine through relationship with the natural world; and concern for the wellbeing of the earth and its inhabitants.

Introduction

Moments of awe and wonder, of connectedness with the natural world and of transcendence are often-noted aspects of children's spirituality. Craig Schlarb (2004) found that children's "peak experiences" frequently occur in natural surroundings, involving a sense of unity with the natural world, of timelessness, and a sense of peace. Similarly, one of the patterns that emerged in Tobin Hart's (2003) research into children's spirituality were experiences in the natural world involving "feelings of awe, connection, joy, insight, and deep sense of reverence and love," moments which may "open so far and deep that we find unity and ecstasy" (p. 48). In earlier research, Rebecca Nye (Hay with Nye, 1998) describes the core of children's

---

A.M. Trousdale (✉)
Department of Educational Theory, Policy and Practice, Peabody Hall, Louisiana State University, Baton Rouge, LA, USA
e-mail: atrous@lsu.edu

spirituality as "relational consciousness" (pp. 112–113). She noted four different types of "core categories" of such consciousness: child–God consciousness, child–people consciousness, child–self consciousness, and child–world consciousness (by which she means the natural world). Such research confirms Dwayne Huebner's earlier insights. In 1959, Huebner was writing of human beings' innate capacity for wonder, a capacity for marvel, a sense of mystery, of awe, of encountering the natural world in such a way that "the two of you are in relationship, participating in life together, journeying down through time, side by side, together, yet apart" (1959/1999, p. 5).

It is, of course, direct, sustained experience with nature that is most likely to provide such moments; but many children's lives today are disconnected from the natural world; they have little opportunity to experience such a transcending sense of awe and wonder, of connectedness with nature. This is the case with many inner-city children whose world is made mostly of concrete and brick, polluted with incessant noise and noxious air; but it is also the case with many children from suburban settings whose sense of connectedness lies primarily with electronic keyboards and remote control devices.

There is another way to experience this connectedness, or quicken a desire for closer connection, or perhaps to confirm experiences that the child has indeed known, and that is through the vicarious experience that literature provides. There are excellent literary works that evoke a sense of wonder, of awe, of transcendence, of the healing, and restorative powers of nature. The pull of the natural world can also derive from its wildness, its unpredictability, its other-than-human direction and purpose. The challenge of relinquishing an illusion of mastery, a willingness to enter the rhythm of untamed nature and to learn from it, can also prove to be an occasion for experiences of extraordinary beauty and unity. In this chapter, I provide an overview and discussion of a sampling of such books ranging from picture books for young children to novels appropriate for young adults.

Connection, Healing, and Restoration

Perhaps the first children's book in the Western European tradition that explores the healing and restorative qualities of nature is Frances Hodgson Burnett's *The secret garden* (1911). In this classic story, Mary Lennox, orphaned in faraway India, is sent to her widowed uncle's estate in Yorkshire. Mary—plain, sour, and self-centered—discovers in the house a crippled, sickly boy who is convinced he is soon to die. It is Colin, Mary's cousin. Querulous and self-pitying, the boy reminds Mary somewhat of herself.

On the grounds of the estate she meets Dickon, a charming and engaging boy whose older sister is a servant in the household. Dickon is joyfully at home on the moorlands; he fascinates Mary because he can communicate with animals.

One day Mary discovers a buried key that opens the door to a secret garden, abandoned for 10 years, ever since Colin's mother died of a fall there. Mary opens the door to discover a tangle of overgrown plants but on looking more closely she sees "sharp little pale green points" making their way out of the earth. "'It isn't quite a dead garden,' she cried out softly to herself. 'Even if the roses are dead, there are other things alive'" (p. 96). She takes a stick and begins to clear a way for the young shoots to grow. The garden is the first thing that has engaged her interest in all her young life, the first thing that has called her outside her self-preoccupation, to consider the welfare of any other living thing. In the garden Mary learns to care for something other than herself.

Mary and Dickon bring Colin, in his wheel chair, to the garden. It has a similarly transformative effect on Colin. He takes in the beauty and mystery of the place and is transformed before Mary and Dickon's eyes. "I shall get well! I shall get well!" he cries out. "Mary! Dickon! I shall get well! And I shall live forever and ever and ever!" (p. 255).

The children sense a "moreness" a presence of something "other" in the garden. Initially "magic" is the only word they know to describe it. As Colin says, "Even if it isn't real Magic, we can pretend it is. *Something* is there–*something*!" (282).

One day Colin looks at his hand holding the trowel, stands up, and realizes he is well. He wants to shout out "something thankful, joyful." At Colin's urge Dickon sings the Doxology, beginning "Praise God from whom all blessings flow." Colin finds that the song of praise to God expresses "just what I mean when I want to shout out that I am thankful to the Magic ... Perhaps they are both the same thing. How can we know the exact names of everything? Sing it again, Dickon. Let us try, Mary. I want to sing it too. It's my song. How does it begin? 'Praise God from whom all blessings flow'?" (p. 329).

The secret garden reflects the highly structured British class system of the early twentieth century and does not challenge the implicit social and economic inequity. But it presents the healing and restorative qualities of nature as equally present despite boundaries of class, of culture, of gender, and of time and space. The children's peak experiences in this book include their being caught up in the mystery of life, the wonder of communicating with animals, an impulse to care for something other than oneself, and a transcending sense of gratitude and joy in living.

Molly Bang also explores the restorative qualities of nature in *When Sophie gets angry–really, really angry* (1999). In this picture book for younger children, Sophie becomes angry when she must relinquish a toy she has been playing with to her sister. Her anger mounts to an uncontrollable rage and she runs and runs to a special tree. She climbs it and there "[s]he feels the breeze blow her hair. She watches the water and the waves" until "the wide world comforts her." Her equanimity restored, she climbs down the tree and returns home, where her family is waiting for her and "everything's back together again" (pages not numbered). Here the peak experience is not one of a heightened sense of ecstasy or discovery but rather one of peace, of unity, a gaining of perspective.

Communion with the natural world may inspire a deeper understanding of one's place in the wider universe, but it can also provide opportunity for communal bonding with other human beings. In Paul Fleischman's *Seedfolks* (1997) a group of lonely, alienated city dwellers find delight, meaning, and purpose for their lives as well as community with others through a garden that they develop on a blighted urban lot. The story is told through the perspectives of some 13 residents of the neighborhood.

Kim is a young Chinese immigrant who never knew her father, a farmer, who died before she was born. She knows that her father's spirit hovers overhead, but how is he to recognize her? She takes some dried beans, clears a small area in the lot, buries and waters them. "He would watch my beans break ground and spread, and would notice with pleasure their pods growing plump. He would see my patience and my hard work. I would show him that I could raise plants, as he had. I would show him that I was his daughter" (p. 3).

Gradually other residents in the neighborhood clear spaces for gardens: Tio Juan, an elderly Guatemalan immigrant, also a farmer, who seemed to have no knowledge or expertise that was useful in this American city; Sae Young, a Korean immigrant who had isolated herself in her apartment after being robbed and beaten; Mr. Myles, a stroke victim whose interest in the world has all but left him; Maricela, a pregnant 16-year-old Mexican immigrant, and all the others find new meaning for their lives through the garden. And they discover community.

They begin by working alone in their little staked-out plots, initially avoiding contact but gradually beginning to speak to one another or help one another out, until one day a rain shower drives them all under the shelter of a store overhang. As Nora, who cares for Mr. Myles, says,

> Then our solitary status ended ... The small dry space forced us together. In fifteen minutes we'd met them all and soon knew the whole band of regulars.
> Most were old. Many grew plants from their native lands ... Yet we were all subject to the same weather and pests, the same neighborhood, and the same parental emotions toward our plants. If we happened to miss two or three days, people stopped by on our return to ask about Mr. Myles' health. We, like our seeds, were now planted in the garden (pp. 49–50).

Amir, an Indian immigrant, reports that one day he and two other men working in the garden heard a woman screaming down the block. A man with a knife had taken her purse. Amir and the two other men ran after him and caught him. Royce, one of the gardeners, held the thief to a wall with his pitchfork until the police arrived. Amir reflects, "Not one of us had ever chased a criminal before. And most likely we wouldn't have except near the garden. There, you felt part of a community" (p. 60).

The peak experiences in this book tend to be gradual, cumulative. As Sae Young, an isolated widowed, childless Korean immigrant notes,

> Very hot and humid in July. Most people come early in evening, after work, when air is cool. People watering and pulling weeds. Even if don't talk to anyone, sound of people working together almost like conversation, all around. People visit friends. I listen to voices. Feel very safe. Then man walk over and ask about peppers. I grow hot peppers, like in Korea. First time that someone talk to me. I was so glad, have trouble talking (p. 38).

Later, seeing that people are having trouble getting water from the communal rain barrel into their individual containers, Sae quick go to store. Buy three funnels to make much easier filling containers. I put one by each garbage can. That day I see man use my funnel. Then woman. Then many people. Feel very glad inside. Feel part of garden. Almost like family (p. 39).

Owl moon (Yolen, 1987), a picture book for young children, portrays a sense of wonder and connection with nature afforded by both beauty and potential danger of the natural world. Late one snowy, moonlit winter night a young girl goes into the woods with her father hoping to spot an owl. It is both the fauna and the flora of the forest that are to captivate the child, even in the presence of fear:

We went into the woods.
The shadows
were the blackest things
I had ever seen.
They stained the white snow.
My mouth felt furry,
for the scarf over it
was wet and warm.
I didn't ask
what kinds of things
hide behind black trees
in the middle of the night.
When you go owling
you have to be brave.
        (pages not numbered)

John Schoenherr's illustrations contribute to the child's growing sense of awe as the story proceeds. The father calls for an owl several times, "Whoo-Whoo-who-who-who-who-whooooooo," and finally as they reach a meadow an echo comes back. The father and the owl continue to call back and forth and then suddenly an owl lifts off a tree branch, comes straight toward the child and her father, and lands on a branch just above them. Again, Schoenherr captures the transcendence of the moment, expressed through Yolen's poetic language:

For one minute,
three minutes,
maybe even a hundred minutes,
We stared at one another
        (pages not numbered)

The moment holds,

Then the owl
pumped its great wings
and lifted off the branch
like a shadow
without sound
It flew back into the forest.
        (pages not numbered)

The child has been so taken up by the experience that she is silent on the way home:

When you go owling
you don't need words
or warm
or anything but hope.
    (pages not numbered)

According to Huebner (1959/1999), one of the factors in our suppression or underdevelopment of the capacity for oneness with the natural world is the tendency to make of everything an object rather than a subject with which we communicate: "an over-emphasis on experience, with a resulting I-It attitude, to the neglect of relationship and the corresponding I-Thou attitude" (p. 5). The potential for an I–Thou relationship is explored in Byrd Baylor and Peter Parnall's *The other way to listen* (1978). In this picture book, an elder teaches a child to listen for the wisdom of the natural world—to hear the corn singing, wildflower seeds bursting open, a rock murmuring good things to a lizard—to "everything being right" (pages not numbered). The elder instructs the child that one must get to know one thing as well as one can, starting with something small; to respect whatever one is with, and not be afraid to learn even from bugs or sand. This takes a very long time, but finally one morning the child goes out to sing, "Hello, hello, hello" to the hills and hears the hills singing in response. *The other way to listen* suggests that a child may discover not only a connection, but a reciprocity with the natural world, a sense that the world itself is "waiting with eager longing for the revealing of the children of God," as St. Paul wrote in Romans 8:19. Peak experiences with nature may take time, and patience, and a cultivation of openness and receptivity.

The capacity of the natural world to speak or find expression is captured in Herman Hesse's *Siddhartha* (1922). The novel originally attracted an adult audience, but in recent years it has been recognized as appropriate for a young adult audience as well. The story is set in India. After years of physical and spiritual wanderings that do not lead to happiness, Siddhartha comes to live beside a river and finds there the sense of completion he has been seeking. Speaking in many voices, the river mediates to Siddhartha the sacred oneness of life. At times laughing and at other times lamenting with a sorrowful voice, the river passes through the seasons of the year and of the heart. It is in reflecting on the cycles of the water, from vapor to rain to source to brook to river, that Siddhartha comes to terms with his own life cycles and finds completion in his own sacred journey toward the divine.

In Gary Paulsen's Young Adult novel *The island* (1988), teenager Wil Neuton discovers a profound sense of identity with the natural world when he goes to live alone on an island in a lake in Northern Wisconsin. Wil begins to draw what he sees, to write about it, to dance with the heron, to swim with the fish, and to meditate. Reflecting on this process, Wil explains, "I could see the heron in all the things the heron was, without seeing the heron at all, and it changed me, made me look at all things that way, made me see in a new way and, finally, made me look at myself in that new way" (pp. 52–53). Susan, a girl who lives nearby, understands what Wil is about on the island and helps him manage his life there. She comes to the island one day and, so much are these young people caught in the innocence and purity of the place, that they swim nude, with no sense of shame or sexual interest in one another. When his family urge him to leave the island he responds, "...I know that if I leave here, if I go back without learning more, I will somehow lose what I am, and I don't want to do that. I don't ever want to do that" (p. 116).

In revealing this deeply sensitive potential in Wil, Paulsen cuts across male stereotypes, for Wil is not a bookworm, an intellectual, or an effete: he is a tall, muscular, athletic kid—one who draws, journals, dances, and communes with nature. In *The island* Paulsen presents an almost idyllic view of nature; violence and destructiveness come to the island only at the end of the book in the arrival of the school bully who is jealous of Wil and Susan's friendship. In *Hatchet* (1987) and its sequels, Paulsen explores more fully the challenges of survival in the untamed natural world.

Challenges: The Untamed Natural World

In the initial book, 13-year-old Brian Robeson, a boy who lives in a city, is on his way to visit his father in Canada. The pilot of the small plane in which he is flying suffers a heart attack and the plane crashes in a lake, leaving Brian on his own to survive in the wilderness with only a hatchet and the clothes he is wearing. Brian quickly learns to observe the natural world carefully in order to make a shelter, find food, and keep himself safe from potentially destructive natural elements. In his 54 days in the wilderness, Brian encounters danger from bears, moose, a porcupine, wolves, smothering hoards of mosquitoes, thunderstorms, and, finally, a tornado that destroys his shelter. But even in the midst of the most difficult challenges, Brian experiences moments of transcendence, of unity, of ecstasy at the beauty of the world and its creatures. In one episode, he has just escaped stepping between a mother bear and her cub (and almost certain death) when he looks up and sees a wolf on a nearby hill.

> "The wolf claimed all that was below him as his own, took Brian as his own. Brian looked back and for a moment felt afraid because the wolf was so ... so right. He knew Brian, knew him and owned him and chose not to do anything to him. But the fear moved then, moved away, and Brian knew the wolf for what it was–another part of the woods, another part of it all. Brian relaxed the tension on the spear in his hand, settled the bow in his other hand from where it had started to come up. He knew the wolf now, as the wolf knew him, and he nodded to it, nodded and smiled" (pp. 114–115).

In another episode as Brian struggles to come to terms with the destruction wrought by the tornado, he has a profound experience of the beauty of the natural world. He looks over at the lake and sees "[t]here was great beauty here–almost unbelievable beauty. The sun exploded the sky, just blew it up with the setting color, and that color came down into the water of the lake, lit the trees. Amazing beauty and he wished he could share it with somebody and say, "Look there, and over there, and see that ..." (p. 158).

The tornado that destroys his shelter also stirs up the lake to reveal the tail of the plane, where Brian finds the plane's survival pack intact. He brings the pack back to his shelter and inadvertently turns on the emergency transmitter, thinking it is a radio. Its signal brings about his ultimate rescue.

Brian's time in the wilderness has a life-changing effect. He has to let go of the person he was and become a new person. One day, when a plane flies over and does not spot him, Brian goes into a deep depression and tries to end his life by cutting himself with the hatchet. The next morning he awakens, sees the blood and "hated what he had done to himself." He has a kind of rebirth. He realizes that he is not the same that "the disappointment cut him down and made him new. He was not the same and would never be again like he had been" (pp. 116–117).

Paulsen received thousands of letters from readers asking about Brian's subsequent life. Three sequels followed, *The river* (1991), *Brian's winter* (1996), and *Brian's return* (1999).

Brian's winter offers an alternate ending to *Hatchet*. Paulsen says that he wrote *Brian's winter* in response to readers wanting to know what would have happened to Brian had he not been rescued when he was and had to survive a winter. The resulting book is a sheer survival story, punctuated by few moments of ecstasy or awe. There is one episode, however, in which Paulsen works to counteract any sentimentalized notion of nature, when Brian witnesses a pack of wolves bringing down a moose. Brian sees the moose's attempts to fight off the wolves, which attack the animal from the side, aiming at the bull's back legs and rear end. They pull at the hamstrings and cut the back legs until the moose is not able to stand. As he caves in the wolves began tearing at his rear end, eating him while he still lives, trying to pull himself away with his front legs. That night, sitting by his fire, Brian wonders

> How it could be so horrible–how nature could let an animal suffer the way the moose had suffered.
>
> The wolves were just being natural and he understood the need to kill–he himself would die if he did not kill.
>
> But so slowly ... (p. 122).

As winter is coming to an end, Brian finds a Cree trapping family, the Smallhorns, and is taken back to civilization in the plane that periodically brings them supplies.

In *The river* (1991) and *Brian's return* (1999) it is clear that Brian's experience has changed him in a radical way; the pull of the wilderness is strong, and Brian finds he has little tolerance for an urban life filled with the noise of car horns, sirens, television, and talking, with shopping malls and bicycles and video games. He tries to fit into urban teenage life, but feels more and more disengaged and distant– different.

Brian has gained notoriety, but people do not understand what he had experienced; news articles about him declare, "Boy conquers savage wilderness" or "Learns to beat nature" (*Brian's return*, p. 4.) Indeed, even the flyleaf of *The river* says that in the book Paulsen describes "the horrifying adventure that pits a boy against nature for the second time in his life."

"It wasn't that way", muses Brian in *Brian's return*. "Had never been that way. Brian hadn't conquered anything. Nature had whipped him, not the other way around; had beaten him down and pounded the stupidity out of his brain until he had been forced to bend, forced to give, forced to learn to survive. He had learned the most important fact of all, and that one that is so hard for many to understand or believe: Man proposes, nature disposes. He hadn't conquered nature at all–he had become part of it. And it had become part of him, maybe *all* of him" (p. 4).

In *The river* he returns to the wilderness with a government psychologist who wants to study the survival techniques that Brian learned. The psychologist is hit by lightning and goes into a coma; and it is up to Brian to rescue them both. Brian's subsequent focus is on getting the man back to civilization for medical treatment. It is in the final book of the series, *Brian's return* (1999) that relationship with the natural world is most fully explored.

In this story, Brian, back at home with his mother in the city, reacts to a bully's attack by reverting to pure animal instinct. He has to be pulled off the boy, whom he is beating senseless, and is referred to a counselor. The counselor understands Brian's crisis and advises him that he must return to the woods for his "mental health," to find what he "left there" (p. 33). Once he is in the wilderness again, he is immediately "taken by a peace he had not known for a long time" (p. 1). In relinquishing himself to the natural world, in committing himself to his oneness with it, Brian experiences one "peak experience" after another.

Brian's experience resonates with but goes a step further than the journey Huebner (1959/1999) describes, in which the human being and the natural world "are in relationship, participating in life together, journeying down through time, side by side, together, yet apart (p. 5). Brian's journey is into the heart and rhythm of the natural world, a relationship of union, not "apartness." In this book, Brian has been careful not to take too much equipment with him, lest he "lose what he had found, the beauty, the connection with the wild that had come into him" (p. 54). He finds that "no matter what he *thought* would happen, nature would do what it wanted to do. He had to be part of it, part of what it was really like, not what he or some other person thought it should be like" (p. 83).

As with many of these books, connection with the natural world involves other kinds of connection as well. In Bryan's experience in the wilderness, all four types of children's relational consciousness found by Nye (Hay with Nye, 1998) are manifest in varying degrees: child–God consciousness, child–people consciousness, child–world consciousness, and child–self consciousness.

Brian's time in the wilderness seems to open him to a sense of a divine presence beyond the material world. In *The river* (1991) it reveals itself through his spontaneous uttering of prayers of gratitude and prayers for deliverance. In *Brian's return* (1999) this sense is articulated more distinctly. Early in the story, when the counselor asks Brian to describe to him "one thing" about being in the woods, Brian chooses one particularly dramatic sunset. "It made him believe, made him *know*, that there was something bigger than he was, something bigger than everybody, bigger than all" (p. 20).

In *Hatchet*, Brian had experienced a moment of mutual recognition with a wolf; now he enters more deeply into a relationship of oneness. One night he is awakened and goes out into the lake in his canoe. He hears a loon call, and then, very close, a wolf howls, "[l]ong, sweet, and sad and happy and frightening and joyful all at once, a keening howl that started high and dropped low and ended almost hoarse." Brian answers the howl, waits, and the wolf answers. They go back and forth three more times, Brian matching and harmonizing with the wolf's call, until "they sang together that way, four more songs, a duet, boy and wolf in the moonlight, singing to beauty until at last the wolf grew tired of it and quieted." Brian returns to his campsite but does not sleep, thinking of the experience of oneness with the wolf, "Brian and the wolf mixed, Brian-wolf, wolf-Brian" (pp. 87–88).

On another occasion Brian is able to communicate his lack of fear and his "evenness" with a bear who had been toying with him as a cat plays with a mouse prior to the kill. Brian reaches his powerful hunter's bow and arrows, holds the bow ready, capable of killing the bear, looks the bear in the eye and speaks to it, "Go away. Go away now." He knows he could release the arrow and kill the bear, but has no need to kill the bear. The animal "hovered for a time," comes to a decision, turns and ambles away (pp. 103–106).

A visit from Billy, a man of the woods, introduces Brian to a spirituality that is reminiscent of Native American sensibilities. Billy too lives in the woods "the old way," without modern weapons, and is closely attuned to the sounds and scents of the life around him. He and Brian understand one another with few words. Billy speaks to Brian of the kind of hunting that gives animals time to prepare to enter "the next world"; of what is "good medicine" and "bad medicine." He introduces Brian to the idea that he has a "medicine animal": the mysterious deer whom Brian has just encountered, which will give him direction. Brian now realizes that, in his confrontation with the bear, it had been "good medicine" he has instinctively waved down from the sky that had protected him.

At the end of the novel, Brian comes to terms with himself and what his experience with nature has meant to his life. He recognizes in Billy what he will likely become: "an old man who looked carved in wood, moving through and with the forest, being of and with the woods, and he decided that it wouldn't be so bad a thing to be" (p. 109). Instead of joining the Smallhorns, which has been his plan, Brian decides to spend more time alone in the wilderness, following his medicine, finding the life that waits for him.

Jean Craighead George's *Julie of the wolves* (1972) is another story of a teenager's survival in the natural world set in the Arctic regions of Alaska. In this novel, deep connection with nature results in a heightened respect for the ecological balance of nature, and the threat that civilization poses to creatures of the wild. Thirteen-year-old Julie's adventure begins when she runs away from an undesirable arranged marriage, planning to make her way to San Francisco, where her pen pal Amy lives, but she soon finds herself lost, hungry, and in danger of dying on the snow-covered tundra of the North Slope. Julie's Eskimo name is Miyax, and that is the name by which she is called during most of the novel.

Miyax's survival depends upon her being accepted and protected by a wolf pack she encounters; and her early "peak experiences" derive from learning to communicate with them. By observing the wolves closely, she learns what certain gestures and sounds mean. She begins to imitate the wolves' signals and when the wolves respond to her, she "clapped her hands and settled down to watch this language of jumps and tumbles, elated that she was at last breaking the wolf code" (p. 23). Later, she succeeds in signaling her good will to the leader of the pack, and when he releases the odor from the glad on the top of his tail, she is "drenched lightly in wolf scent. Miyax was one of the pack" (p. 25).

Julie's growing sense of connectedness with the wolves and the environment and peak moments of joy or wonder come through varied experiences: being given food by the wolves, marveling at the wolves' skill or strength in hunting, finding natural fuel, and witnessing the beauty of the tundra. One evening she thinks of reaching Amy's white house in San Francisco, but the vision she has concocted

> vanished abruptly; for the tundra was even more beautiful–a glistening gold, and its shadows were purple and blue. Lemon-yellow clouds sailed a green sky and every wind-tossed sedge was a silver thread. "Oh," she whispered in awe, and stopped where she was to view the painted earth (p. 123).

The safety and security of an imagined life in San Francisco draw Julie during the first part of her journey, but eventually she comes to see the darker sides of Western European civilization: the wanton killing of the wild animals she has come to love and respect, the vanity and indifference of Western European consumerism, the distancing of oneself from the rhythms of the natural world, the indifference to its welfare.

She comes to see Amaroq, the magnificent leader of the wolf pack, as a surrogate father. A crisis occurs for her when Amaroq is shot and killed by hunters in a plane. Julie witnesses the killing and looks up into the belly of the plane, where she sees "great cities, bridges, radios, school books...long highways, TV sets, telephones, and electric lights. Black exhaust enveloped her, and civilization became this monster that snarled across the sky" (p. 141). Seeing Amaroq lying dead in the snow, the men in the cockpit laugh, the plane climbs, banks, and flies away. Julie realizes that the hunters are not going to collect Amaroq's body; they had killed the wolf heedlessly, not even to collect a bounty.

In her grief, Julie kneels at Amaroq's body, removes a carving she has made from her pocket, and holds it over the wolf's body, asking his spirit to enter the totem so that he might be with her forever. She holds the carving until "the pain in her breast grew lighter and she knew the wolf was with her" (p. 147).

When she reaches the village of Kongik, Julie finds her long-lost father, Kapugen, whom she thought was dead. Kapugen has married a Caucasian woman and is accommodating his life to Western civilization. Indeed, he had been the pilot of the plane carrying the hunter who had shot Amaroq. Appalled, Julie leaves the village, intending to return to the wild, to "live with the rhythm of the beasts and the land" as her ancestors have done (p. 169). However, that night Julie realizes that "the hour of the wolf and the Eskimo is over," and returns to her father's house (p. 169–170).

In the sequel, *Julie* (1994), there are fewer peak experiences portrayed, but other spiritual aspects of Julie's story are expanded. The conflicts in this novel are twofold: Julie struggles to adjust to a westernized life with her father and his wife, Ellen, all the while working to protect her wolves. The pack has followed her and are in danger of being hunted and killed by the villagers.

Julie's arrival seems to act as a corrective to Kapugen's accommodation to Western ways; he begins to remember Eskimo beliefs and traditions and to honor them. He has abandoned the Eskimo understanding of the interdependence of all things and has adopted the "Minnesota law" of his wife's people, which will justify the killing Julie's wolves to protect the village's herd of musk oxen. The oxen, which had once been plentiful, had been hunted to near extinction when guns were brought to Alaska by white people. This herd, a remnant of a once-bountiful species, is the foundation of an "industry" Kapugen has begun to develop in the village.

As Kapugen recovers his Eskimo sensibilities, he discovers that he has been the one responsible for Julie's beloved wolf's death. He asks Julie's forgiveness and names his first child Amaroq, explaining that "[i]t is customary among the Eskimo to give the name of deceased spirit to a baby. Then the baby becomes that one ... Like the wolf, he will be integrated into the universe" (p. 167).

In another powerful scene, her father, hunting walrus with other hunters, performs the Eskimo ceremony of respect for an animal one has killed. After a silence, Kapugen slits open the walrus' belly, reaches in, takes the heart and carries it to the edge of the sea. "Great Aiviq," he says, "I have borrowed your body. My flesh will be your flesh." He throws the heart into the sea. "I return your spirit to the sea. I give you birth again" (p. 201). This scene is a far cry from his careless shared laughter at the death of Amaroq.

Julie tries to explain to Ellen the Eskimo understanding of the cycles of life, of the Eskimos' relationship to all the animals, and the ecological function of the wolves in nature. Ellen maintains her adherence to the need for the "Minnesota law." Finally, when Julie sees that this approach is not working, she says, "I will stop lecturing and tell you a story" (p. 215). She tells her the story of her experience with the wolves and how the wolves had saved her life. When Julie finishes, Ellen says, "I understand. I was wrong. Please go tell Kapugen I am wrong: The Minnesota law does not work here" (p. 218). But Kapugen has already set the oxen free to live as their ancestors had lived, in natural relationship with the wolves and other animals of the tundra. As the novel ends, a rather tenuous balance between Western and Eskimo ways have been reached.

George makes a subtle but significant point in Julie and Ellen's conversation: all the lecturing Julie could do could not change Ellen's mind; it took a story to do that, to break through the layers of "education" and conditioning that Western European civilization had created. Stories have a capacity to reach children—and adults—on imaginative and affective levels that other kinds of discourse may not.

M. M. Bakhtin (1981) would call the kind of "lecturing" Julie was doing "authoritative" discourse. According to Bakhtin's definition, authoritative discourse is a type of discourse that strives to determine behavior or "ideological interrelations with the world" (p. 342). Authoritative discourse is characterized by distance from oneself, a lack of dialogic possibilities, a lack of play, of "spontaneously creative stylizing variants"; discourse that is static with its own single calcified meaning (pp. 342–343). A second type of discourse is one which Bakhtin describes as having interior persuasiveness. This type of discourse does not necessarily appeal to any external authority but is flexible, with malleable borders. It is contextualized and can be related to one's own life. This type of discourse offers further creative interaction; it is open, unfinished, and capable of further representation. Harold Rosen (1986) describes narrative discourse as having this interior persuasiveness. Julie's narrative discourse has carried an inner persuasiveness that has transformed Ellen's understanding.

A Relationship of Care

The objectification of the natural world has been attributed to many cultural factors: capitalism (Tambiah, 1990); modern science and its resultant mechanistic worldview Toolan, 2001); dualism (Sterling, 2001); industrialism (Worster, 1993); a patriarchal worldview (Diamond & Orenstein, 1990); anthropomorphism (Bowers, 1993). However manifold its causes, a distancing from the natural world and a disruption of a sense of oneness and interdependence with nature not only militate against an important aspect of children's spiritual nature, they lie at the heart of the present ecological crisis (DeMoor, 2004). A capacity for oneness with the universe and a sensitivity to the reciprocity inherent in such a relationship, on the other hand, are foundations for care for the environment and concern for the exploitation of the natural world. Several children's books address such ecological concerns, expressing what might be otherwise framed as authoritative discourse (having a rather clear underlying ideological agenda) but here cast in a narrative frame.

Lynne Cherry sets *The great Kapok tree* (1990) in the Amazon rain forest. In this picture book for young children a man comes into the forest with another man, who directs him to cut down a large Kapok tree and leaves. After a few blows with his ax, the man grows tired, sits down, and falls asleep. The animals who live in the Kapok tree approach him and begin to speak to him not just about the tree as their home but of the interdependence of all of nature. As the bee says, "Senhor, my hive is in this Kapok tree, and I fly from tree to tree and flower to flower collecting pollen. In this way I pollinate the tree and flowers throughout the rain forest. You see, all living things depend on one another" (pages not numbered). The monkeys speak next. They tell the man, "Senhor, we have seen the ways of man. You chop down one tree, then come back for another and another. The roots of these great trees will wither and die, and there will be nothing left to hold the earth in place. When the heavy rains come, the soil will be washed away and the forest will become a desert." In like manner other creatures who live in the tree or depend upon it speak to the man: a boa constrictor, a tree frog, a jaguar, tree porcupines, anteaters, and a three-toed sloth.

Finally a native child murmurs in his ear, "Senhor, when you awake, please look upon us with new eyes." The man awakens. His peak experience, which comes as something of an epiphany, lies in his seeing the world around him anew. He picks up his ax, drops it, and walks out of the forest.

The great Kapok tree illustrates for the young child the interdependence of all living things. A sense of reciprocity between humans and the natural world is subtly enhanced by the fact that in this book nature becomes the teacher of the human being. Cherry's approach is to arouse empathy in the young reader for the endangered animals who depend on the Kapok tree and a balanced ecology for their lives. However, the economic interests that promote the destruction of the rain forest are not directly addressed or critiqued.

In contrast, Dr. Seuss is unsparing in his depiction of the unrestrained greed that drives such exploitation in *The Lorax* (1971). Here children see an idyllic, peaceful, ecologically balanced world turned into a barren, toxic wasteland when the Once-ler arrives and proceeds to cut down the Truffula trees and destroy their entire habitat in order to make a fortune manufacturing Thneeds, objects no one really wants or needs. Throughout the story the Lorax pleads with the Once-ler on behalf of the trees and the animals who depend on the environment to live. The Once-ler is immutable—and self-justifying:

I meant no harm. I most truly did not.
But I had to grow bigger. So bigger I got.
I biggered my factory. I biggered my roads.
I biggered my wagons. I biggered the loads
of the Thneeds I shipped out. I was shipping them forth
to the South! To the East! To the West! To the North!
I went right on biggering...selling more Thneeds.
And I biggered my money, which everyone needs.

Finally, when the land is uninhabitable and the factories and workers leave, the Lorax himself departs, uttering one word, "Unless." The Once-ler remains, living alone, finally worrying over what he has done. At last a child appears. The Once-ler remembers the Lorax's last word, "Unless." Finally he understands. He says to the child,

UNLESS someone like you
cares a whole awful lot,
nothing is going to get better.
It's not.

He has one last Truffula seed left and he throws it to the child, calling out.

It's a Truffula Seed.
It's the last one of all!

You're in charge of the last of the Truffula Seeds.
And Truffula Trees are what everyone needs.
Plant a new Truffula. Treat it with care.
Give it clean water. And feed it fresh air.
Grow a forest. Protect it from axes that hack.
Then the Lorax
and all of his friends
may come back. (pages not numbered)

Will the child decide to take the seed, take care of the earth, restore balance, harmony—and life itself? The story closes without such an ending; Dr. Seuss leaves it up to the child reader to have the epiphany or not.

Concluding Thoughts

The books included in this sample feature people of different times, different cultures, and different social situations finding awe, wonder, comfort, peace, healing, challenge, wisdom, restoration, unity, and transcendence through communion with the natural world. They portray this aspect of children's relational consciousness not in terms of authoritative discourse but through narrative discourse, discourse with an interior persuasiveness. The beckoning to cultivate and value relationship with the natural world comes through invitation to the child's imagination, the child's compassion, and the child's instinct toward adventure. In many of these stories, relationship with the natural world leads to deeper and more satisfying relationship with other people, with oneself, and with the divine, supporting the whole of the child's spiritual life.

As cultural historian and theologian Thomas Berry (1997) has written,

The child awakens to a universe,
the mind of the child to a world of wonder,
imagination to the world of beauty,
emotions to a world of intimacy.
It takes a universe to make a child
both in outer form and inner spirit.
It takes a universe to educate a child,
a universe to fulfill a child.[1]

Note

1. I am grateful to Emily A. DeMoor for sharing this poem.

References

Bakhtin, M. M. (1981). *The dialogic imagination* (C. Emerson & M. Holquist, Trans.). Austin, TX: University of Texas Press.
Bang, M. (1999). *When Sophie gets angry–really, really angry*. New York: Scholastic.

Baylor, B., & Parnall, P. (1978). *The other way to listen.* New York: Aladdin Paperbacks.
Berry, T. (1997). It takes a universe. Unpublished poem.
Bowers, C. A. (1993). *Education, cultural myths, and the ecological crisis: Toward deep changes* (1st ed.). New York: State University of New York Press.
Burnett, F. H. (1911). *The secret garden.* Tasha Tudor, Illus. New York: HarperCollins.
Cherry, L. (1990). *The great Kapok tree: A tale of the Amazon rain forest.* San Diego: Harcourt Brace Jovanovich.
DeMoor, E. A. (2004) *Soils of regeneration: Exploring conceptualizations of the natural world as a context for an ecologically sensitive curriculum.* Unpublished doctoral dissertation, Louisiana State University.
Diamond, I., & Orenstein, G. F. (Eds.). (1990). *Reweaving the world, the emergence of ecofeminism.* San Francisco: Sierra Book Clubs.
Fleischman, P. (1997). *Seedfolks.* New York: Harper Trophy.
George, J. C. (1972). *Julie of the wolves.* New York: Harper & Row.
George, J. C. (1994). *Julie.* New York: HarperCollins.
Hart, T. (2003). *The secret spiritual world of children.* Makawao, HI: Inner Ocean.
Hay, D. with Nye, R. (1998). *The spirit of the child.* London: Fount.
Hesse, H. (1922/1999). *Siddhartha.* New York: Penguin.
Huebner, D. E. (1959/1999). The capacity for wonder and education. In V. Hillis (Ed.), *The lure of the transcendent: Collected essays by Dwayne E. Huebner.* Mahwah, NJ: Lawrence Erlbaum Associates, pp. 1–9.
Paulsen, G. (1987). *Hatchet.* New York: Aladdin Paperbacks.
Paulsen, G. (1988). *The island.* New York: Bantam Doubleday Dell.
Paulsen, G. (1991). *The river.* New York: Delacorte Press.
Paulsen, G. (1996). *Brian's winter.* New York: Delacorte Press.
Paulsen, G. (1999). *Brian's return.* New York: Delacorte Press.
Rosen, H. (1986). The importance of story. *Language Arts, 63*(3), 226–237.
Schlarb, C. (2004). Consequences of not assimilating childhood peak experiences. 2nd North American Conference on Children's Spirituality, Pacific Grove, CA, October 7–10.
Seuss, Dr. (Theodor Geisel). (1971). *The Lorax.* New York: Random House.
Sterling, S. (2001). *Sustainable education: Re-visioning learning and change* (Vol. 6). Bristol: Green Books.
Tambiah, S. J. (1990). *Magic, science, religion, and the scope of rationality* (1st ed.). New York: Cambridge University Press.
Toolan, D. (2001). *At home in the cosmos.* Maryknoll, NY: Orbis Books.
Worster, D. (1993). *The wealth of nature: Environmental history and the ecological imagination.* New York: Oxford University Press.
Yolen, J. (1987). *Owl moon.* John Schoenherr, Illus. New York: Philomel.

Chapter 27
Developing Spiritual Identity: Retrospective Accounts From Muslim, Jewish, and Christian Exemplars

Kevin S. Reimer, Alvin C. Dueck, Lauren V. Adelchanow, and Joseph D. Muto

Abstract This chapter considers developing spiritual identity in a sample of 45 Muslim, Jewish, and Christian individuals nominated by religious tradition for outstanding maturity. We suggest that developing spiritual identity is amenable to naturalistic study through a heuristic known as psychological realism. Study findings are presented from qualitative coding of retrospective exemplar interviews on identity precepts of *redemption*, *agency*, and *communion*. These findings are supplemented with grounded theory analysis to specify themes related to developmental process in spiritual identity. From this work, we propose that spiritual identity is developmentally understood as commitment consistent with a sense of self to interpersonal behaviors of transcendent, goal-corrected character emphasizing purpose, generativity, and social responsibility.

Introduction

Sayid (pseudonym) is a 32-year-old Sunni Muslim from the San Fernando Valley region of Los Angeles, a neighborhood rich with ethnic and socioeconomic diversity. Sayid came to the United States about 10 years ago to pursue graduate studies in his field of civil engineering. A native of south-central Turkey, Sayid is single and deeply committed to local humanitarian concerns. He became involved in the research project as a nominated exemplar—identified by area Muslims on their own criteria for persons demonstrating exceptional spiritual maturity. The weight of spiritual experience in Sayid's narrative is unmistakable:

> The most important thing is that I'm not alone. I don't feel alone. I know Allah and I know that the world and universe were not created by themselves—there is someone else. Allah is great in the universe. Allah created me and all human beings—people who can do things

K.S. Reimer (✉)
Department of Graduate Psychology, School of Behavioral & Applied Sciences, Azusa Pacific University, Azusa, CA, USA
email: kreimer@apu.edu

and learn. This vision is the most important thing to me, realizing that I am not alone in the world and I have been given meaning in this life. There is a reason that I am in this world. There is a reason that I am living this life. The reason is that I can learn from Allah to be a respectful human being, trying to follow him and become better educated in Islam. Islam is my preparation for the next life. The next life will not have any end, so this is very important to me.

Sayid's reflection presents a challenge for researchers interested to explore developmental processes associated with spirituality in general, and spiritual identity in particular. The recent bifurcation of religion and spirituality in social science reflects earnest effort to clarify potentially blurred elements of human experience (MacDonald, 2000; Roehlkepartain, Benson, King, & Wagener, 2005; Zinnbauer et al., 1997; Zinnbauer, Pargament, & Scott, 1999). Wishing to move beyond the scientific study of religion as a structured and institutionalized entity, spirituality offers an individual account of transcendent experience reflecting traits of awe and gratitude. In this sense, spirituality might be understood as "a search for the sacred, a process through which people seek to discourse, to hold on to and, when necessary, transform whatever they hold sacred in their lives" (Hill & Pargament, 2003). Sayid's narrative embraces sacred elements, expounding on spiritual experience through divine presence that offers security and hope. The depth of his reflection suggests that these ideas are firmly embedded in developmental process rather than the result of recent awakening. Yet Sayid seamlessly weaves spirituality into the regimented discipline of his religious practice as a Muslim. Full appreciation of Sayid's spiritual experience requires, at the very least, a basic role for religion as contextual influence. His example would seem to support criticism that attempts to separate religion from spirituality reflect the convenience of Western (particularly North American) interests to the exclusion of non-Western experience (Stifoss-Hanssen, 1999).

Keeping definitional concerns of spirituality squarely in view, this chapter outlines findings from a recent project to understand spiritual identity and its development. Psychological research on spiritual identity is sparse and skewed toward Christian perspectives (Kiesling, Sorell, Montgomery, & Colwell, 2006; Templeton & Eccles, 2005). Specifying the relationship between spirituality and religious practice will require study considering the experiences of non-Western individuals. Accordingly, this study took a naturalistic approach to spiritual identity through comparative study of nominated exemplars from Muslim, Jewish, and Christian contexts. The main goal was to construct a broad understanding of spiritual identity based on the experiences of individuals nominated for outstanding spiritual maturity on criteria established by these same religions. This objective reflected an interest to constrain normative theorizing about the nature of spiritual identity with the actual experiences of people widely recognized as spiritually exceptional, a principle known as *psychological realism* (Flanagan, 1991; Walker & Frimer, 2007; Walker & Pitts, 1998).

The chapter is organized into three sections serving the central study aim. The first section presents a rationale for naturalistic study of spiritual identity in exemplars along with a conceptual overview of identity in the developmental work of McAdams (Erikson, 1968; McAdams, 1997, 2006). The second section offers findings from qualitative coding of exemplar spiritual experience on McAdams' identity precepts of *redemption*, *agency*, and *communion*. The third section presents a grounded theory strategy designed to unearth themes related to the development of spiritual identity. Outcomes from two methodological moves are integrated toward a core definition of spiritual identity balancing theoretical assumptions with naturalistic observation.

Naturalistic Study of Spiritual Identity

How might we approach the psychological study of developing spiritual identity? The notion of spiritual identity moves the self to center stage. Self psychology is endowed with an illustrious legacy evoking the influential writings of Sigmund Freud. More recent theory maintains that the self is formed on the basis of social reciprocity across a range of developmental variations in time, place, and role (Balswick, King, & Reimer, 2005; Damon & Hart, 1988; Harter, 1999). Core self-understanding or *identity* is constructed through cumulative experiences in relationships. Through childhood this knowledge remains concrete and relatively unsophisticated. Grade school children make straightforward assessments based on immediate, real-world contingencies such as "I am a fast runner" or "I am friendly to new kids in class." Concrete self-understanding becomes conceptually richer through adolescence with the onset of abstract thinking. Assessments might grow to include reflections such as "I am a generous person" or "I am able to help others see the glass half full." The developmental challenge for adolescent identity is for youth to maintain a stable sense of self through a variety of social contexts and requirements (Arnett, 2006; Balswick et al., 2005; Damon & Hart, 1988; Erikson, 1968). Parents of adolescents commonly recognize the challenge through rapid shifts in youth attitudes, affect, and language across contexts such as athletic teams, peers, religious groups, or classroom environment.

Consolidation of identity in adolescence and early adulthood is marked by the capacity for individuals to maintain a core self in spite of situational pressures. Young adults eventually construct an episodic understanding of the self-in-relationships that may include authority figures, romantic attachments, peers, and the divine. Identity reflects a variety of trait and goal-oriented features of self which are experienced between different social contexts and woven into a coherent account. Traits and goals become familiar to an extent that the individual is afforded a framework for constructing an identity narrative; stories which document abstract and concrete aspects of self-understanding (McAdams, 2006; McAdams & Pals, 2006). Identity may be conceptualized as a general developmental achievement, or related to particular aspects of behavior which necessarily reference the self. By way of example, *moral identity* emphasizes a suite of ethical and caring behavior associated with the developing self-in-relationship (Aquino & Reed, 2002; Balswick et al., 2005; Hardy & Carlo, 2005; Reimer & Wade-Stein, 2004; Walker & Frimer,

2007). *Spiritual identity* is a newcomer to research in developmental psychology, with contemporary studies limited to predominantly Protestant Christian samples (Kiesling et al., 2006; Templeton & Eccles, 2005).

Current efforts to pin down a definition of spiritual identity reflect difficulties with parsing individual aspects of identity from social contexts fundamental to the development of self-understanding. Templeton and Eccles (2005) argue that religious identity reflects a *collective* dimension of accepted beliefs shared with others through a particular community. Spiritual identity is defined in terms of *personal* experiences noted in beliefs, values, and behaviors related to the divine. This is similar to a proposal from Kiesling et al. (2006), who conceptualize spiritual identity as "a persistent sense of self that addresses ultimate questions about the nature, purpose, and meaning of life, resulting in behaviors that are consonant with the individual's core values." Both definitions place a premium on individual values in the construction of a spiritual self. Assuming these values to have transcendent qualities (in the sense of being related to ultimate concerns), the developmental character of a highly individualized spiritual identity becomes a tougher sell. Over time, spiritual experience is likely to incorporate categories of transcendent value reflecting a spectrum of relational influences. Parent, peer, and romantic relationships are laden with the freight of values and expectations for conduct which end up in the episodic register of narrative identity. Religious influence may implicitly permeate these relationships, even if removed by degree or generation from formal practice. The identification of spiritual identity with personal values cleanly separable from collective influences may prove difficult in real-world experience.

Challenges with the definitional issue reflect the highly diffuse and abstract nature of spiritual experience. Rather than expend further effort toward a definitive theoretical understanding of spiritual identity, an alternative strategy might utilize a "bottom-up" approach found in parallel research involving behavioral abstractions such as morality (Flanagan, 1991). Because researcher notions of self-referencing spirituality may differ markedly from the experiences of real people, it may be appropriate to begin with everyday conceptions in the interest of definitions that are *psychologically realistic*. Flanagan's proposal is increasingly common in the literature on moral identity development, with study focused on everyday conceptions of ethical maturity in prototype theory and descriptive research on exemplars recognized for exceptional acts of justice, bravery, and caring (Colby & Damon, 1992; Hardy & Carlo, 2005; Hart & Fegley, 1995; Matsuba & Walker, 2004; Narvaez, Lapsley, Hagele, & Lasky, 2007; Reimer & Wade-Stein, 2004; Walker & Frimer, 2007; Walker & Reimer, 2005). In step with this trend, this study adopted the principle of psychological realism into research design with emphasis upon retrospective accounts of spiritual maturity in the experiences of exemplary individuals nominated from Muslim, Jewish, and Christian backgrounds. The project was premised on the identity theory of McAdams with the anticipation that ultimate definitions of spiritual identity would be shaped by real-world experiences of exemplars from different contexts of influence.

What features of identity theory are relevant to comparative religious study of spiritual maturity in nominated exemplars? The work of Dan McAdams at

Northwestern University offers a contemporary account of identity development in social context (McAdams, 1997, 2006; McAdams, Anyidoho, Brown, Huang, Kaplan, & Machado, 2004; McAdams, Diamond, de St. Aubin, & Mansfield, 1997; McAdams & Pals, 2006; McAdams, Reynolds, Lewis, Patten, & Bowman, 2001). McAdams argues that a developmental objective of identity is the establishment of personal legacy framed through contributions to others. This notion of *generativity* might be practically understood through childbirth; a situation where suffering yields a positive outcome in a newborn child along with deepened purpose in the parental vocation. People with generative identities might mentor youth, publish a book, or volunteer with the homeless. Identity maturity is characterized by an episodic understanding of self as an agent of change and goodness across varied social contexts. In the interest of outlining a framework capable of describing generative identity through assessment, McAdams designed the *life narrative interview*, a set of semi-structured questions dealing with developmental history, critical events, life challenges, significant people, potential future, moral conflict, personal ideology, and overall life theme (McAdams, 1997, 2006; Walker & Frimer, 2007).

Life narrative interviews conducted with hundreds of individuals yielded three precepts of mature identity (McAdams, 1997, 2006). The first precept, *redemption*, characterizes life narratives where participants recount the transformation of negative circumstances into something positive. The individual is directly involved in the transformative process, particularly through personal risk in the interest of making the most from situational difficulties. The second precept, *agency*, reflects aspects of power, autonomy, mastery, and achievement. Agency might reflect underlying traits and goals related to accomplishment. This could be aimed at vocation but also include relational and principled actions given to the promotion of human flourishing. The third precept, *communion*, describes identity process given to the formation of community and other relational networks. Communion is most clearly evident through narrative affirming warmth, compassion, and intimacy. Together, these precepts anticipate an understanding of spiritual identity as a personally significant cache of experiences in memory, framed within relational and social contexts that make those experiences meaningful.

This study explored retrospective accounts of narrative spiritual identity in exemplars nominated for exceptional maturity from Muslim, Jewish, and Christian contexts. The main assessment instrument was a version of the life narrative interview. Responses to the interview were content analyzed at two levels. First, McAdams' (1997, 1998) life narrative interview coding scheme was applied to narrative content on precepts of *redemption*, *agency*, and *communion*. The first level of analysis was designed to consider comparative elements of narrative identity in spiritual experience between religious contexts. Second, the same interview responses were independently coded using the grounded theory approach to qualitative study (Strauss & Corbin, 1990). This analysis offered an opportunity to discern developmental features of spiritual identity and experience that might not be immediately visible through the three precepts of identity outlined in McAdams (1997, 1998). Findings from both analyses were then used to offer definitional insights for spiritual identity in developmental context.

To construct an account of spiritual identity consistent with a principle of psychological realism, three focus groups were convened from Muslim, Jewish, and Christian religions, respectively. Focus groups were comprised of 6–12 leaders and clergy from each religion in the greater Los Angeles area. Leaders were invited from religious groups that were numerically well represented in the region, including Sunni Muslim, Reform Jewish, and Presbyterian Christian religions. Focus groups were conducted in English, asking individuals to identify nomination criteria that reflected spiritual maturity. Focus groups subsequently prioritized criteria, with similar descriptors collapsed into general statements. The resulting list of spiritual nomination criteria included (a) learning and being in continual process, (b) sense of (and acting on) responsibility for one's fellows, (c) sense of one's own faith that informs daily life, (d) God-consciousness, (e) believes in Qur'an/Torah/Bible as word of God and follows it in daily life, (f) lives life intentionally, (g) practices faith (e.g., prayer, fasting, observances, charity, declaration of faith, pilgrimage), (h) promotes peace among all peoples, (i) is actively engaged with God and others, (j) lives a joyful, balanced, and humble life, and (k) is interested in helping others grow spiritually in a quietly contagious manner.

Nomination criteria were provided to Muslim, Jewish, and Christian leaders that participated in the focus groups. Leaders were asked to nominate individuals from within their respective religion that demonstrated strong evidence of nomination criteria for spiritual maturity. Nominated exemplars included several religious leaders but mainly consisted of everyday individuals from area mosques, synagogues, and parishes. Nominated exemplars were contacted and invited to participate in the study. Interested exemplars were mailed consent forms and scheduled for a face-to-face interview. Participants were provided with a $50 honorarium as a token of appreciation for study involvement.

Of 36 exemplars nominated from Reform Jewish leaders and clergy, 15 participated. This sample group averaged 45.0 years of age (SD = 11.2, range = 25–66). The sample self-identified as ethnically Jewish (82.4%), European (11.8%), or Latino/a (5.9%). Level of education included high school completion (5.0%), bachelor's degree (30.0%), master's degree (55.0%), and doctoral degree (10.0%). Out of 27 nominations from Sunni Muslim leaders and clergy, 15 participated. The Muslim sample averaged 34.5 years of age (SD = 11.4, range = 23–79). This sample self-identified as ethnically European (70.6%) or Turkish (29.4%). Level of education included high school completion (5.0%), bachelor's degree (35.0%), master's degree (35.0%), and doctoral degree (25.0%). Of 32 nominations from Presbyterian Christian leaders and clergy, 15 participated. The Christian sample averaged 56.9 years of age (SD = 11.3, range = 33–72). This sample self-identified as ethnically European (80.0%), Latino/a (15.0%), or American Indian (5.0%). Level of education included high school completion (15.0%), trade school or associate's degree (5.0%), bachelor's degree (10.0%), master's degree (50.0%), and doctoral degree (20.0%). Overall, nominated exemplars were well-educated individuals engaged in professional vocations. All exemplars were fluent in the English language.

Life Narrative Coding

The first qualitative review of narrative identity data made use of McAdams' (1997, 1998) coding scheme focused on redemption, agency, and communion. Understood in terms of participant self-understanding through the redirection of difficult situations toward positive outcomes, *redemption* is thematically decomposed into five elements including (a) sacrifice, (b) recovery, (c) growth, (d) learning, and (e) improvement. For this study, a team of three qualitative raters were trained to evaluate exemplar responses using the McAdams (1997, 1998) coding scheme. The McAdams coding manual emphasizes conservative identification of elements on the basis of presence "1" or absence "0." The first three elements of redemption (e.g., sacrifice, recovery, and growth) were not substantively present in exemplar narratives across all three religious contexts. However, the last two redemption elements (e.g., learning and improvement) were substantially represented in participant narrative. *Learning*, or the notion that participants gain wisdom from a negative event, is concerned with instrumental rather than psychological benefit. As an example, "father is dying" might be associated with a redemptive learning outcome in "father gives sage words of advice." Interrater agreement for this element was 93%. *Improvement* relates to the transformation of a bad situation associated with negative emotions to one that is positive in outcome and affective quality. As an example, "terrified of public speaking" might change into an outcome where the participant "improves and becomes an effective speaker." Interrater agreement for this element was 82%.

The redemption/learning element was most strongly affiliated with Christian exemplars (5) with somewhat fewer codes noted for Muslim exemplars (3) and Jewish exemplars (2). This pattern was exactly replicated for the redemption/improvement element, with 5 coded occurrences for Christians as opposed to 3 for Muslims and 2 for Jews. The McAdams coding regimen calls for restraint in making positive code identifications. As a result, these scores suggest that redemptive narrative is well represented in the Christian exemplar group. Within the confines of the coding scheme, notation of a category across one-third of a study sample is considered robust (McAdams, 1998). The prominence of redemption/learning and redemption/improvement in the Christian exemplar sample may reflect developmental and situational processes associated with spiritual identity. Relative to Muslim and Jewish exemplars, Christians report more stories of redemptive significance which reference the self. Redemption is deeply embedded in participant developmental histories, with accounts commonly focused on adolescence and early adulthood. McAdams (2006) suggests that redemption is a prominent feature of identity in the American cultural context, reflecting Judeo-Christian belief systems. This interpretation may require qualification given study findings that, as with Christian exemplars, Jewish exemplars were typically born and raised in the United States. Yet this group did not evince nearly as many redemption codes in identity narratives.

The difference on redemption observed between Christian exemplars with Muslim and Jewish exemplars may reflect particular influences related to religious context. It is possible that Christian exemplars construct spiritual identity from a vantage analogous to a religious vision of redemption through belief in a messianic divinity (e.g., Jesus Christ). The Christian commitment to redemption through motifs of death and resurrection may provide a frame for identity process which prioritizes personal growth resulting from negative events (learning) with sometimes triumphal accounts of how these events form the basis for positive outcomes (improvement). Yet this basis for spiritual identity process could be overstated given that redemption/learning and redemption/improvement elements are moderately present in Muslim and Jewish exemplar narratives. A measured interpretation concludes that redemption is a noteworthy feature of exemplar spiritual identity, with potentially interesting valuations related to the priorities of particular religious contexts.

As with redemption, the *agency* aspect of power and achievement in narrative identity is supported by smaller elements of focused attention (McAdams, 1997). *Self-mastery* pertains to individual efforts to achieve physical, mental, emotional, or moral strength toward a measurable impact on other people. An example might include the recovering alcoholic's concerted effort to stay sober as a positive influence on his growing children. Interrater agreement for this element was 82%. *Status/victory* invokes work to achieve high status or position resulting in prestige. An example of this element might be a businesswoman's 15-year journey to rise through the ranks of her company to achieve a top management position. Interrater agreement for *status/victory* was 98%. *Achievement/responsibility* suggests self-sufficiency, freedom, and self-control. An example might consist of a college undergraduate's growing efficacy through successful management of a personal budget. Interrater agreement for *achievement/responsibility* was 87%. Finally, *empowerment* captured the notion of accomplishing goals affiliated with standards of excellence in efficiency, productivity, and effectiveness. An example might include the success of a middle-school math teacher through improved student achievement on standardized tests. Interrater agreement for *empowerment* was 89%.

The *self-mastery* element of agency was evenly distributed between spiritual exemplars from different religious contexts. Muslim exemplars were coded for 3 instances of this element, with 2 noted for Jewish exemplars and 3 for Christian exemplars. The *empowerment* element was similarly spread across groups, with 3 coded instances in Muslim exemplar narratives, 1 for Jewish exemplars, and 3 for Christian exemplars. Distribution of these elements in narrative suggests a moderately important place for self-mastery and empowerment in spiritual identity. To an extent, this finding may be an artifact of the nomination criteria for spiritual maturity derived from Muslim, Jewish, and Christian focus groups. Based on the criteria, spiritual exemplars are expected to demonstrate other-oriented maturity which includes personal discipline upholding excellence in attitude and behavior. Nomination criteria loosely reflect an aspect of spiritual leadership in exemplarity which seems well-served by the self-mastery and empowerment elements.

Some disparities were observed in coded outcomes on *status/victory* by religious context. Muslim exemplars scored highest on this agentic element (4), followed by Christian exemplars (2), and Jewish exemplars (0). This came as a surprise given that educational and vocational achievement between exemplar groups was roughly equivalent. While the element of status/victory is presumably available to all study participants by way of personal achievement, Muslim spiritual exemplars made more powerfully self-referential claims on this dimension than Christian and Jewish exemplars. The disparity became wider for the *achievement/responsibility* element, with coded notation for half the Muslim sample (8) as opposed to Jewish (2) and Christian (2) samples. It could be argued that highly agentic identity is reflected in the spiritual experience of Muslims who recently emigrated and quickly mastered vocational challenges in a foreign setting. But it seems equally plausible that these findings are attributed to the religious context of the Muslim sample. Spiritual identity for this group is potentially associated with values enjoining hard work with personal responsibility. *Status/victory* and *achievement/responsibility* elements were reflected in the developmental histories of Muslim exemplars, implying deep roots for identity processes that long preceded relocation to North America.

The final evaluated identity precept was *communion*. Four elements of communion were considered for exemplar participants. *Love/friendship* pertains to positive emotions experienced in the context of close, interpersonal relationship. An example of this element might be recounted through a mail carrier's friendship with an elderly resident known over years of brief, daily encounter. Interrater agreement for this element was 89%. *Dialogue/sharing* references intimacy through good conversation and mutuality including non-verbal cues. An example of this element might be a "breakthrough" conversation between a mother and her mildly estranged 15-year-old daughter. Interrater agreement for this element was 91%. *Care/support* describes how an individual cares for another or is cared for by another. An example might include a middle-aged woman's commitment to care for her Alzheimer's ravaged father. Interrater agreement for this element was 89%. *Unity/togetherness* is affiliated with a personal sense of harmony or synchronicity with other individuals, groups, or even the world at large. An example of this element might be captured by a former executive's move to non-profit work with the urban poor. Interrater agreement for this element was 91%.

Trends for the communion aspect in exemplar narrative identity were readily noted by religious context. The most pervasive incorporation of communion elements was observed in the narrative identities of Jewish exemplars. Overall, these exemplars evinced moderate to strong references to communal elements in spiritual identity. Jewish exemplars were coded for *love/friendship* (3), *dialogue/sharing* (2), *care/support* (3), and *unity/togetherness* (5). These findings were aligned with qualitative notation that Jewish exemplars identified strongly with family and community. Exemplar spiritual identity routinely referenced ethnic and cultural aspects of Jewishness. Experiences of the divine were framed on relational understanding, reflecting spiritual encounter that was collectively shared. This should not diminish the importance of individual spiritual experience for Jewish exemplars. Nevertheless, these exemplars seem to construct spiritual self-understanding in a way that prioritizes collective values and relational commitments.

Reviewing findings from other religious groups, Muslim exemplars scored high on two of the four elements from the communion motif. Muslim exemplars coded on *caring/help* (6) and *unity/togetherness* (4). Christian exemplars did not code strongly on communion, with the exception of *love/friendship* (4). Findings from the communion aspect raise noteworthy implications regarding summary understanding of spiritual identity. Of the three religious contexts considered through the study, Christian exemplars were least oriented toward the communion aspect in McAdams' (1997, 1998) scheme. This aligned Christian exemplar self-understanding with spiritual identity definitions emphasizing personal or individual values—an unsurprising outcome given that these definitions were premised upon studies of mostly Christian individuals (Kiesling et al., 2006; Templeton & Eccles, 2005). The prominence of communion in Jewish and Muslim exemplar self-understanding, however, underlines a broader notion of values orientation in spiritual identity. For these exemplars, spiritual experience is interpersonally situated. The divine is known in part on the basis of shared experiences with other Jews and Muslims. In addition, personally significant spiritual experiences precipitate other-oriented behaviors in caring and/or intimacy. The inclusion of non-Western exemplar perspectives in this study suggests that spiritual identity is "collective" as much as "personal," directly reflecting values originating in social and religious contexts.

Grounded Theory Coding

As a complement to the McAdams (1997, 1998) scheme, exemplar response data were analyzed in a second methodological move using grounded theory. Grounded theory is a systematic approach to qualitative data reliant upon first-level coding of *conditions*, *interactions*, *strategies*, and *consequences* (Strauss, 1987; Strauss & Corbin, 1990). First-level codes are applied to identity narrative through a process known as *constant comparison* whereby each code is referenced against all other codes by transcript. This process is continued until reaching a point of *theoretical saturation* or the cessation of new first-level code categories. The resulting list of first-level codes is subsequently applied to remaining interview transcripts. First-level codes are conceptually assessed for overlap and subsequently collapsed into higher-order categories known as *axial codes*. Axial codes are subjected to a similar process of recombination, resulting in themes. For this study, interview data were subjected to grounded theory coding by a single rater to evaluate aspects of spiritual identity potentially residing outside redemption, agency, and communion from the first methodological move.

Grounded theory analysis yielded five themes covering developmental aspects of spiritual identity across Muslim, Jewish, and Christian exemplar data. In order of prominence across the entire data set, themes included (a) *relational consciousness*, (b) *vocational identity*, (c) *stewardship*, (d) *tradition*, and (e) *divine as omnipotent*. We have outlined each theme in detail, offering a definition and brief comment on origins through the coding process. Exemplar quotations provide theme illustration, with summary comment on religious differences and developmental implications toward an improved understanding of spiritual identity. For reasons of space, we are unable to include quotations from all three religious contexts on a given theme.

Theme 1: Relational Consciousness

Spiritual identity narratives revealed a core developmental theme familiar to researchers involved with children's spirituality (Hay & Nye, 1998; Nye & Hay, 1996; Reimer & Furrow, 2001). *Relational consciousness* was defined in this setting as an interrelation of individual, interpersonal, community, and divine relationship that constitute a harmonious whole; particularly through devotion to the divine. The relational consciousness theme was constructed from lower-level codes emphasizing community, relationship, family, group membership, connection, and spiritual communication. In the reflection of a 42-year-old Jewish exemplar:

> It means that I have community. It means that I'm never alone in the world—that not only do I have a system of beliefs; I have a group of people who are committed to me and responsible to me as I am to them. It means I have an obligation to change the world for the better. It also means that I have a relationship with God that is unique. Family! I think for me the focus includes the family unit; the family within the community. For me, I have a looser definition of family ... for those who are not just my immediate family but those people I'm connected to not only as friends but through the synagogue. You know, this is my extended family. The development of that unit through religious life is something that I think is above and beyond any other part of my spiritual connection.

A 56-year-old Christian exemplar kept her account of relational consciousness succinct:

> I think probably establishing a relationship with God comes first. Everything else flows from that. It's all about establishing and maintaining a relationship with God in daily life.

In the former instance, the relational consciousness theme captured broadly communitarian experiences of spiritual identity reminiscent of communion aspect coding on Jewish exemplars (McAdams, 1997). The relational consciousness theme was also present through Muslim exemplar narratives, although it may be slightly less central to Muslim experience. Consistent with other developmental research, relational consciousness was recounted by exemplars as a significant aspect of spiritual awakening in childhood. These early accounts tended to be somewhat self-centered, characterized by experiences of awe or gratitude that were personalized or involved a few close confidants. With time and development relational consciousness grew to emphasize unity and oneness with the divine, often referencing group membership and solidarity. For those who did not have a strongly religious upbringing, relational consciousness seemed to debut shortly after resolution of core belief systems in early adolescence.

Theme 2: Vocational Identity

Exemplars take their vocations seriously, closely integrating their work with spiritual experience and understanding. We attempted to capture the issue as a function of *vocational identity* or a spiritual calling to divine service that consolidates personal efficacy, purpose, and generativity. Underlying code categories for this theme included obligation, acceptance of life circumstances, sense of being chosen, guidance, responsibility, and calling. Vocational identity was a touchstone for deeper existential reflection in the narrative of a 35-year-old Muslim woman:

> Why are we here? Why am I the person I am right now? Why am I not somebody different? What is my purpose? Where is the purpose of all things that are created? I find prospective answers to those questions in my spirituality. I think that is the most important part; it really explains why you are created, what your life should be like. What kind of life you should live—what you are supposed to do.

For a 40-year-old Christian exemplar involved in community service, the issues are similar even if the language is different:

> For me, service is a fulfillment of a calling. I can expand on that, but it's like breathing for me because I grew up in the church and that was an expectation for me as a child. I became a Christian at ten and the calling grew from my personal faith journey. It was there in college and still later again—a response to God's grace. Will I accept the calling? To be a Christian means to surrender to God's call in your life, to be God's child and to serve God, however that works out in your life.

Most exemplars reported a deep sense of fulfillment in their present vocations, resolution we would attribute to the consolidation of vocational identity. Vocation became a tangible, visible extension of spiritual commitment and experience. The vocational identity theme was evenly distributed throughout narrative responses from all three religious contexts. Interestingly, the theme did not show up in developmental accounts of early childhood. Vocational identity seems relegated to processes associated with late adolescence and early adulthood. This makes good psychological sense in that vocational concerns tend to be abstract and require sophisticated reflection prior to enaction through behavior. We note that exemplars as a group are unusually invested in vocational projects designed to "make a difference" or otherwise help others flourish.

Theme 3: Stewardship

The remarkable maturity of exemplars interviewed for the study was evident in a deep sense of spiritual responsibility and obligation. We labeled this intuition as *stewardship*—not just in a financial understanding, but where the individual realizes that he/she must consistently live in a manner that attends to the concerns of the divine, the community, other individuals, and the environment. Stewardship was derived from core notions of submission, respect, discipline, love, compassion, grace, honesty, and peacefulness. In the reflection of a 30-year-old Muslim exemplar:

> Well, the words "Islam" and "Muslim" come from the same root. The root of the word means *submission*. You submit to God without questioning what he is asking from you. You just do it, whether it's the daily prayers or wearing the scarf or fasting or giving to charities or visiting Mecca. I am doing it because God wants me to do it. The other meaning of "Muslim" is peace. Peace between people and in the universe; not cutting the tree or destroying the little animal because we believe that every created being has a way of saying

Allah's name. The cat is saying "meow," but actually is saying one of the names of Allah the most compassionate. You try to understand the relationship between the creatures and see the value of each thing in the universe.

Stewardship took a different turn in the account of a 41-year-old Jewish exemplar:

> I think there is a saying which Rabbi Hillel made. "If I am for myself only, then what am I? If I'm not for myself, who will be?" Take care of yourself so that you can treat others with honesty, kindness, and compassion.

The stewardship theme was present for exemplars from all three religious contexts, although it was particularly pronounced in Muslim experience. As with the vocational identity theme, stewardship was not developmentally evident until late adolescence when exemplars began to fully differentiate themselves at a spiritual level from parents. Many exemplars made comments to the effect that, when acting responsibly on behalf of others, they were serving as stewards for the divine and the creation. Stewardship grew to become a lifetime mission for exemplars, defining their ongoing behavior and self-understanding on the basis of keeping in step with the divine.

Theme 4: Tradition

The spiritual identity of nominated exemplars was characterized by commitment to religious tradition. The *tradition* theme was variously understood as *hadith* (Muslim), *Torah* (Jewish), or *scripture* (Christian); knowledge handed down through oral or written sources that helped to maintain culture, promote religious practice, and build community. Underlying code categories for this theme included study, worship, ritual, shared language, values, and culture. The tradition theme was present in Christian and Muslim exemplars, with overwhelming prominence in Jewish exemplar narratives. In the reflections of a 36-year-old Jewish exemplar:

> The first thing that I think about is my Jewish identity ... a certain responsibility to history. This is not really a documentary history like the Roman Empire or something, but the idea that I am receiver of ancient tradition passed down from generation to generation. I'm duty bound to honor that tradition and sometimes there are specific ways that I'm duty bound to act and within that way of life comes an opportunity to express my own individuality.

Tradition was similarly evident in the account of a 47-year-old Jewish exemplar involved with the Simon Wiesenthal Center:

> It's important for me to be engaged in healing the world and the community—engaged in that tradition, carrying on the tradition, passing on the tradition to my children in a real and meaningful way so that they grasp it.

Tradition was developmentally rich and pervasive. Jewish exemplars recounted moments of instruction from parents on matters of observance, holidays, and kosher laws at very young ages. Interestingly, most of the Jewish exemplars in this study did not keep kosher at the time of interview. The accoutrements of tradition offered a kind of scaffolding for spiritual identity, with developmental rites of passage that deepen unexpected experiences of the divine. Jewish exemplars related nearly every aspect of personal spiritual experience back to the tradition of their heritage. The tradition theme clearly converged with Jewish prioritization of communion in the McAdams coding section of the study.

Theme 5: Divine as Omnipotent

All exemplar participants noted the power of spiritual experience in general and the divine in particular. The *divine as omnipotent* theme was constituted from belief that the deity possesses ultimate power over the universe and its inhabitants. Far from a cosmic Santa Claus, the divine as omnipotent offers insight on practice of forgiveness, healing, and protection. This theme was often referenced through spiritual understanding of divine presence. Divine as omnipotent was particularly prevalent in Christian exemplar narratives. A 46-year-old Christian exemplar noted:

> I have a better relationship with God now because I feel that God doesn't have to do things the way I want. But I feel that God is at work whether I understand or not what's happening. I don't expect really, I don't expect a lot from God. I think God has given me so much that he doesn't have to do what I think he should.

The divine as omnipotent took a slightly different cast in the account of a 33-year-old Muslim exemplar:

> I think one thing that is most important is that you have to be aware that you are always being watched and kind of behave accordingly. Allah is always watching—if I say something wrong then he knows about it. I think that this forces you to live a more organized life. It's all about the love of God and fear of God. The balance of those two things plus being watched by Allah. You can always maintain that balance. You have to fear God but at the same time you have to know that he loves us and we love him.

The divine as omnipotent theme was found in every section of the interview, often in conjunction with good or bad circumstances. In the main, life's greatest uncertainties seemed associated with a strong spiritual sense of divine omnipotence and agency. Developmentally, this theme was particularly noteworthy in transitional life stages, when exemplars felt they had done something wrong, or while enduring a difficult time. Spiritual identity at this level is reliant upon an ongoing sense of divine foreknowledge and wisdom regarding human affairs. Prayer might be important, not to influence the divine but rather to more fully recognize and affirm divine prerogatives. An outsider might consider this fatalistic, but exemplars routinely reported liberation when basking in the knowledge that the divine was effectively "in charge."

Spiritual Identity Revisited

How might spiritual identity be theoretically constrained given outcomes from naturalistic study of nominated exemplars from Muslim, Jewish, and Christian contexts? Spiritual experience is ubiquitous across cultures and peoples. The propensity for people to use relational language to describe that experience suggests a complex interchange between self and social context in the development of spiritual identity. While exemplars often describe spiritual identity process with language that references the divine as a social "other," we quickly note that their understanding of spirituality also lives beyond what is immediately tangible and visible. Exemplar knowledge of the divine features aspects of self-understanding that incorporate values learned from various social networks along with teachings, holy writings, observances, and pilgrimages. Findings from this study suggest that exemplars incorporate these values into a relational partnership with the divine that powerfully shapes spiritual experiences relevant to self-understanding in identity. The origins of this partnership may be found in earlier (developmental) accounts of human others in social situations, growing to embrace the divine on spiritual terms.

This is reminiscent of a proposal from the great attachment theorist, John Bowlby, who argued that secure children developmentally alter their perceptions of caregivers with a growing appreciation of what things must be like for the parent. On the basis of newly acquired capacity for perspective taking (e.g., theory of mind), children and parents are able to construct shared identities reflecting deeper security in reciprocity and mutual negotiation (Bowlby, 1969). He defined this process in terms of a *goal-corrected partnership*. The prominence of themes like relational consciousness may reflect capacities for perspective taking on the part of exemplars who find security in a spiritual "other" such as the divine. Even if the divine transcends physicality, individuals may through prayer and ritual construct spiritual identity in a goal-corrected sense; a partnership reflecting dynamic give-and-take. Indeed, exemplars from all three religious contexts spoke extensively about their perceptions of the divine's current expectations for behavior, relationships, and vocation. Manifestations of organized religion (e.g., worship, prayer, ritual, observances, and pilgrimage) may further support the development of such a goal-corrected spiritual identity.

In fidelity to the principle of psychological realism central to the study, we offer a definition of spiritual identity on the basis of naturalistic investigation of nominated exemplar experience. Thus, spiritual identity is *commitment consistent with a sense of self to interpersonal behaviors of transcendent, goal-corrected character emphasizing purpose, generativity, and social responsibility*. This definition recognizes the developmental role of human and spiritual "others" in the formation of episodic self-understanding narrative, prioritizing values shared along personal–collective axes of influence. Underlying features of the definition break with the developmental literature to the extent that personal spiritual experience is reframed by contextual influences and shared understanding (Kiesling et al., 2006; Templeton & Eccles, 2005). The definition retains a distinction between religious and spiritual experience—recalling the uniquely sacred dimensions of spirituality which are not religious, yet reflect religious influences (Hill & Pargament, 2003). Returning to the case study at the beginning of the chapter, Sayid's spiritual identity is richly imbued with the presence of the divine. The depth of this goal-corrected experience is the "glue" which keeps Sayid enjoined with the ritual and practice of Islam.

Acknowledgments This project was made possible by a generous grant from the Metanexus Institute/John Templeton Foundation to the first two authors. The first author gratefully acknowledges the Beverly Hardcastle Stanford fellowship in ethics and values at Azusa Pacific University which created release time to write the manuscript. We acknowledge the dedicated efforts of our research assistants, including Anthony Ferreras, Brianne DeWitt Goudelock, Deb Kessel, Alexandra Linscott, Josh Morgan, Hana Shin, Tracy Sidesinger, Sherry Steenwyk, and Robert Strong.

References

Aquino, K., & Reed, A., II. (2002). The self-importance of moral identity. *Journal of Personality and Social Psychology, 83*, 1423–1440.
Arnett, J. (2006). *Emerging adulthood: The winding road from late teens through the twenties.* New York: Oxford.
Balswick, J., King, P., & Reimer, K. (2005). *The reciprocating self.* Downer's Grove, IL: InterVarsity.
Bowlby, J. (1969). *Attachment and loss: Vol. 1. Attachment.* New York: Basic.
Colby, A., & Damon, W. (1992). *Some do care: Contemporary lives of moral commitment.* New York: Free Press.
Damon, W., & Hart, D. (1988). *Self-understanding in childhood and adolescence.* New York: Cambridge University Press.
Erikson, E. (1968). *Identity: Youth and crisis.* New York: Norton.
Flanagan, O. (1991). *Varieties of moral personality: Ethics and psychological realism.* Cambridge, MA: Harvard University Press.
Hardy, S., & Carlo, G. (2005). Identity as a source of moral motivation. *Human Development, 48*, 232–256.
Hart, D., & Fegley, S. (1995). Prosocial behavior and caring in adolescence: Relations to self-understanding and social judgment. *Child Development, 66*, 1346–1359.
Harter, S. (1999). *The construction of the self: A developmental perspective.* New York: Guilford.
Hay, D., & Nye, R. (1998). *The spirit of the child.* London: Fount.
Hill, P., & Pargament, K. (2003). Advances in the conceptualization and measurement of religion and spirituality: Implications for physical and mental health research. *American Psychologist, 58*, 64–74.
Kiesling, C., Sorell, G., Montgomery, M., & Colwell, R. (2006). Identity and spirituality: A psychosocial exploration of the sense of spiritual self. *Developmental Psychology, 42*, 1269–1277.
MacDonald, D. (2000). Spirituality: Description, measurement, and relation to the five factor model of personality. *Journal of Personality, 68*, 157–197.
Matsuba, M., & Walker, L. J. (2004). Extraordinary moral commitment: Young adults working for social organizations. *Journal of Personality, 72*, 413–436.
McAdams, D. (1997). *The stories we live by: Personal myths and the making of the self.* New York: Guilford.
McAdams, D. (1998). *Contamination sequence coding guidelines.* Unpublished manuscript, Northwestern University, Evanston, IL.
McAdams, D. (2006). *The redemptive self: Stories Americans live by.* New York: Oxford.

McAdams, D., Anyidoho, N., Brown, C., Huang, Y., Kaplan, B., & Machado, M. (2004). Traits and stories: Links between dispositional and narrative features of personality. *Journal of Personality, 72*, 761–784.

McAdams, D., Diamond, A., de St. Aubin, E., & Mansfield, E. (1997). Stories of commitment: The psychosocial construction of generative lives. *Journal of Personality and Social Psychology, 72*, 678–694.

McAdams, D., & Pals, J. (2006). A new big five: Fundamental principles for an integrative science of personality. *American Psychologist, 61*, 204–217.

McAdams, D., Reynolds, J., Lewis, M., Patten, A., & Bowman, P. (2001). When bad things turn good and good things turn bad: Sequences of redemption and contamination in life narrative and their relation to psychosocial adaptation in midlife adults and in students. *Personality and Social Psychology Bulletin, 27*, 474–485.

Narvaez, D., Lapsley, D., Hagele, S. & Lasky, B. (2007). Moral chronicity and social information processing: Tests of a social cognitive approach to the moral personality. *Journal of Research in Personality, 40*, 966–985.

Nye, R., & Hay, D. (1996). Identifying children's spirituality: How do you start without a starting point? *British Journal of Religious Education, 18*, 145–154.

Reimer, K., & Furrow, J. (2001). A qualitative exploration of relational consciousness in Christian children. *International Journal of Children's Spirituality, 6*, 7–24.

Reimer, K., & Wade-Stein, D. (2004). Moral identity in adolescence: Self and other in semantic space. *Identity, 4*, 229–249.

Roehlkepartain, E., Benson, P., King, P., & Wagener, L. (2005). Spiritual development in childhood and adolescence: Moving to the scientific mainstream. In E. Roehlkepartain, P. King, L. Wagener, & P. Benson (Eds.), *The handbook of spiritual development in childhood and adolescence* (pp. 1–16). Newbury Park, CA: Sage.

Stifoss-Hanssen, H. (1999). Religion and spirituality: What a European ear hears. *International Journal for the Psychology of Religion, 9*, 25–33.

Strauss, A. (1987). *Qualitative analysis for social scientists*. New York: Cambridge.

Strauss, A., & Corbin, J. (1990). *Basics of qualitative research: Grounded theory procedures and techniques*. Newbury Park, CA: Sage.

Templeton, J., & Eccles, J. (2005). The relation between spiritual development and identity processes. In E. Roehlkepartain, P. King, L. Wagener, & P. Benson (Eds.), *The handbook of spiritual development in childhood and adolescence* (pp. 252–265). Newbury Park, CA: Sage.

Walker, L. J., & Frimer, J. (2007). Moral personality of brave and caring exemplars. *Journal of Personality and Social Psychology, 93*, 845–860.

Walker, L. J., & Pitts, R. C. (1998). Naturalistic conceptions of moral maturity. *Developmental Psychology, 34*, 403–419.

Walker, L. J., & Reimer, K. (2005). The relationship between moral and spiritual development. In E. Roehlkepartain, P. King, L. Wagener, & P. Benson (Eds.), *The handbook of spiritual development in childhood and adolescence* (pp. 265–301). Newbury Park, CA: Sage.

Zinnbauer, B., Pargament, K., Cole, B., Rye, M., Butter, E., & Belavich, T. (1997). Religion and spirituality: Unfuzzying the fuzzy. *Journal for the Scientific Study of Religion, 36*, 549–564.

Zinnbauer, B., Pargament, K., & Scott, A. (1999). The emerging meanings of religiousness and spirituality: Problems and prospects. *Journal of Personality, 67*, 889–919.